DATA THEORY

DATA THEORY

Peter C. Jones

Amplex Systems
Malden, Massachusetts

Paul E. Jones, Jr.

Arthur D. Little, Inc.
Cambridge, Massachusetts

PRENTICE HALL, Englewood Cliffs, New Jersey 07632

Library of Congress Cataloging-in-Publication Data
JONES, PETER C. (Peter Cunningham)
Data theory / Peter C. Jones, Paul E. Jones, Jr.
p. cm.
Includes bibliographical references.
Includes index.
ISBN 0-13-199704-1
1. Data base management. I. Jones, Paul E. II. Title.
QA76.9.D3J665 1991 90-35999
005.74—dc20 CIP

Editorial/production supervision
and interior design: *Jean Lapidus*
Cover design: *Joseph Di Domenico*
Manufacturing buyer: *Kelly Behr and Susan Brunke*

Published by Prentice-Hall, Inc.
A Simon & Schuster Company
Englewood Cliffs, New Jersey 07632

This book can be made available to businesses and organizations at a special discount when ordered in large quantities. For more information contact:

Prentice-Hall, Inc.
Special Sales and Markets
College Division
Englewood Cliffs, N.J. 07632

ISBN 0-13-199704-1
90000>
9 780131 997042

Printed in the United States of America

10 9 8 7 6 5 4 3 2 1

ISBN 0-13-199704-1

PRENTICE-HALL INTERNATIONAL (UK) LISTED, *LONDON*
PRENTICE-HALL OF AUSTRALIA PTY. LIMITED, *SYDNEY*
PRENTICE-HALL CANADA INC., *TORONTO*
PRENTICE-HALL HISPANOAMERICANA, S.A., *MEXICO*
PRENTICE-HALL OF INDIA PRIVATE LIMITED, *NEW DELHI*
PRENTICE-HALL OF JAPAN, INC. *TOKYO*
SIMON & SCHUSTER ASIA PTE. LTD., *SINGAPORE*
EDITORA PRENTICE-HALL DO BRASIL, LTDA., *RIO DE JANEIRO*

Contents

Preface

The book examines the fundamental nature of data, and presents new techniques for designing data bases, including many new data structures that are not recognized by current data models. All data structures in common use, whether relational, hierarchical, network, object-oriented, or otherwise, are unified under a single theoretical framework. A new graphic notation for data base design is presented that exploits this framework. The notation and techniques developed in this book may be applied where current theories fail, such as in the design of interdependencies among two or more relations, and the design of ternary relations with null values.

Since the approach is implementation independent, it may be applied equally well to relational and nonrelational systems, to object-oriented environments, and to data intensive areas of artificial intelligence such as knowledge engineering. We show how the subclass structures of object-oriented systems can be extended into more general subrelation structures, and how these structures interact with relational operations such as joins. By viewing the contents of data bases as propositions, we link the field of artificial intelligence with data bases. In particular, we show how the logical operation of "or" can be incorporated into data bases, allowing data bases to specify alternatives freely rather than solely expressing facts.

Most current theories of data are based on the symbolic logic of mathematics. We argue, however, that symbolic logic is too limited to be used as the foundation for data theory. A fundamental difficulty with applying symbolic logic to data is exposed by attempting to define a data base relation as a "time-varying set." There is no such thing as a time-varying set in symbolic logic or in mathematics—the idea violates the basic rule that a set is defined by its members. If the members of a set change, it must become a different set. Attempting to define a data base constraint, such as a functional dependency, using symbolic logic fails in a similar way. We develop data theory without using sets, and we concentrate on how a data base relation is defined, rather than on its population. We show that even such basic ideas as "if-then," "or," and "not" must be treated differently in data than in the abstract environment described by symbolic logic.

We develop a new system of logic, which we call *data logic,* specifically for describing data. Data logic ties many aspects of data into a unified framework, using the logical device of a *positive embracing*. Specifically, positive embracings incorporate functional dependencies, foreign key constraints, subtypes, generalized functional dependencies, tableau dependencies, Horn clauses, and more. Data logic also allows many other forms of positive embracings that are not handled by today's data models. In particular, positive embracings allow the logical operations of ''and'' and ''or'' to be incorporated into data structures to a far greater extent than is possible today. We show how positive embracings can be put to work on practical design problems, through illustrations and through extensive imaginary case studies on special topics.

Using data logic, we propose changes to the foundations of mathematics. We show how restrictions on the use of ''not'' in the syntax of propositions render data logic consistent. We show how the same method resolves many of the classical paradoxes, including Russell's paradox. This means that the awkward theory of logical types can be dispensed with. We introduce new definitions of the natural numbers, apply them to the construction of the real numbers, and sketch new foundations for differential calculus.

We introduce a new data design notation, called *extended associative notation,* which exploits the new capabilities of data logic. It is an extension of the Associative Data Model notation, which the authors and their colleagues have used for over 20 years in practical design projects. Extended associative notation is particularly geared to the data structures similar to ternary relations, which we call *trio complexes*. Trio complexes differ from ternary relations by allowing null values freely in all positions. We show how positive embracings may be used to describe data structures that include null values. We demonstrate in an extensive case study how extended associative notation may be used to model all forms of trio complexes.

The field of data science is very broad, and there are many subjects that this book does not cover. We do not discuss physical data base design, indexing schemes, performance measurement, device assignment, or other similar problems of implementing data bases on computers. We do not survey existing data models. Most of the techniques that we introduce are not supported by today's software and would require special programming. Our focus is on how data behaves, and how to introduce new techniques for describing data more thoroughly.

We find often that common words for describing data are too imprecise to be reliable in a study of data theory. We therefore propose a far greater variety of new terms than do most books on data. We have included a glossary at the end of the book for quick reference, which contains definitions of all the new terms and special symbols that we introduce.

The text is organized into three parts: Foundational Data Theory, Theory of Data Bases, and Data Structures. Each part builds on the results from the parts before. In Part 1, Foundational Data Theory, we discuss basic issues in the philosophy of thought, we develop definitions of basic terms (such as ''data''), we develop data logic, and we discuss the implications for advanced problems in philosophy. We assume that a reader of this part is familiar with symbolic logic, and has had some exposure to the issues involved in the philosophy of thought. We rarely mention computers in Part 1, because we are more concerned with the foundational disciplines of philosophy, linguistics, and logic.

Part 2, Theory of Data Bases, applies the theory developed in Foundational Data Theory to the problems of data bases. Our major focuses are the rigorous specification of user data requirements and the design of new logical capabilities for data base management systems. We develop logical formulations of common data base constraints (such as *mandatory* and *to one*), we discuss how data logic predicts new types of constraints and new types of populations not recognized by today's data models, and we introduce a graphic notation for communicating these new data structures. Although we assume that a reader of this part is familiar with computerized data bases, we have addressed this part to people in the full range of computer-related specialties, from business analysts to technical experts.

Part 3, Data Structures, is concerned with particular problems in the logical design of data bases. This part is geared to data designers. We develop analytical techniques that can be used to describe the interaction of multiple constraints on multiple relations, we discuss new varieties of constraints, particularly constraints in which the populations of two or more binary relations are interrelated, and we show how data logic permits design of ternary relations with null values in all positions (including the key). We assume that a reader of this part has a thorough understanding of data base design.

The order of the chapters is dictated by the needs of proof, each chapter building upon the chapters that have come before. We find, for example, that the rigorous description of trio complexes requires material from all the preceding chapters. Readers who skip sections may therefore be unable to follow the proofs, but we hope will be able to understand the flow of the narrative with aid from the glossary.

Our thanks to Janet Jones and David Jones for their tireless support. Thanks to Patty Mallahan, who diligently typed the manuscript. Thanks also to Paul Becker, Monte Davidoff, Carol Donnelly, Mary Edwards, Steve Howell, Jean Lapidus, Tamara McCracken, and Mary Perullo.

Peter C. Jones

Paul E. Jones, Jr.

PART 1
Foundational Data Theory

INTRODUCTION TO PART 1

In the first part of this book, we discuss the nature of data, and we develop methods for deriving results about data. To understand data fully, we take a broader view of data than most works on computerized data management. For example, a record in an audit trail is data just as much as a record in a file, and a hand-written record is data just as much as a record on a disk. Data can be words, data can be pictures, and data can be magnetic disturbances. There was data long before there were computers, and the data of the future may appear very different from the data bases of today. To understand data, we must look beyond its physical form to what data represents.

Data is ultimately a means of expressing human thought. We explore precisely how data relates to thought in Chapter 1, Representation of Opinion. We discuss varieties of thoughts, how thoughts are intercombined to form assertions, and limitations on our ability to comprehend thought. A subsidiary topic of the same chapter, one of considerable importance to computer systems, is the rigorous description of methods for managing physical symbols. Data is, after all, a physical thing: it is marks of ink, or magnetic disturbances, or exposed photographic film. By studying symbols and ideas together, we are able to draw conclusions about both the physical appearance and the mental interpretation of data.

No specific background material is required for Chapter 1. However, we treat the study of data as a topic with a long history, dating back to the ancient Greeks, and some acquaintance with philosophical works on the nature of thought would be helpful. Aristotle, *Categories* (350B.C.a) and Locke, *An Essay Concerning Human Understanding* (1690) are recommended. We also refer to contemporary works on computerized data management as a guide to the technical reader. Kent, *Data and Reality* (1978) is recommended.

In Chapter 2, Principles of Data Logic, we develop a new method we call *data logic* for manipulating data to reach conclusions. Data logic is a modal logic, that is, it contains an operation similar to "must" in natural language. This operation enables data logic to distinguish between a data base schema and a data base population. Data logic also makes distinctions about negation not made by symbolic logic. For example, the two classes "a car" and "not a car" are treated differently in data logic.

We assume in Chapter 2 that the reader is familiar with symbolic logic. Many introductory texts on symbolic logic are available. Hilbert and Ackermann, *Principles of Mathematical Logic* (1938) is recommended. Some acquaintance with works on the foundations of logic would be helpful. Frege, *Begriffschrift* (1879), and Quine, *From a Logical Point of View* (1980) are recommended. We criticize logic at its most basic assumptions, so readers who are intimately familiar with symbolic logic should be on guard: many common patterns of deduction in symbolic logic are invalid in data logic.

Chapter 3, Advanced Data Logic, examines advanced problems in philosophy, such as the axiomatization of logic, the nature of paradox, the logical foundations of mathematics, and logical completeness. Chapter 3 is geared to readers who are already familiar with these topics. Data logic departs significantly from symbolic logic in each of the areas covered. Readers whose interests do not include these topics may skip Advanced Data Logic and proceed directly to Part 2.

1

Representation of Opinion

1.1 INTRODUCTION

In Section 1.2, Physical Detection of Symbols, we study the symbols that can be used to express data. Although our primary interest in this book will be the representation of ideas, we begin with symbols because symbols are tangible, and are therefore more accessible to analysis than ideas. We will later be able to apply conclusions about symbols to ideas by analogy. We conclude that the basic mechanism for managing symbols is a *detector*, which is a process that defines when two physical things are the same symbol.

In Section 1.3, Mental Images, we apply the study of symbols to the study of ideas. We reason that the underlying mechanisms of thought are similar to the ways people detect symbols. We are able, in this way, to describe basic characteristics of how ideas are interrelated. In particular, we reason that detectors have an analog in *recognizers*, which are conceptual processes that define individual ideas.

In Section 1.4, Physical Classification of Things, we discuss processes that may accept different symbols (recall that a detector accepts only those things that are the same symbol). We call a general acceptance process a *binding site*. For example, the process that accepts all six-letter character strings is a binding site. We discuss how binding sites may obey rules of construction that affect what things they accept. In particular, we say that a binding site *A* *embraces* a binding site *B* if any thing accepted by *B* must also be accepted by *A*.

In Section 1.5, Mental Classes, we present a systematic definition of a *class* by drawing an analogy with binding sites. For example, the class of cars is defined to be a conceptual mechanism that accepts those mental images that qualify as images of cars. By defining a class as a conceptual mechanism, we are able to consider as cars such ideas as cars of the past known only by photographs, future models that have not started production, and so on. We could not be so inclusive if we required a car to pass a physical test. We also define an *embracing of classes*, which will be the foundational tool for describing data structures.

We show that a class is different from a set. Specifically, a set is defined by its members: different members form a different set. A class is not defined by its members: its members (which we call *instances* to avoid confusion) can change without affecting the class. Indeed, two classes may both have no instances yet still be different. It is these properties of classes that make classes, rather than sets, the proper fundamental concepts for studying data.

Many of the characteristics of classes apply also to recognizers. For example, recognizers may be embraced just as classes may. We explore the interrelationships between classes and recognizers in Section 1.6, Plans. We discuss how all classes and recognizers may be formed from *plans*. Recalling that a class is a conceptual process, the plan of a class is analogous to a list of instructions that define the process.

In Section 1.7, Physical Transformation of Symbols, we consider processes that may operate on many things simultaneously. We call such a process an *engine*. We consider one engine in detail, the engine that permits symbols to be combined with other symbols to form sequences.

In Section 1.8, Mental Associations, we define an *association* to be the analog of an engine in ideas. An association differs from an engine in that an association is a conceptual process, while an engine is a physical process, and an association operates on ideas, while an engine operates on tangible things. The analogy between associations and engines is therefore similar to the analogy between classes and binding sites. Indeed, we find that a class is a special case of an association, and a binding site is a special case of an engine.

Associations are to relations as classes are to sets: the members of an association may change without the association changing, while the members of a relation can not. We use the term "relation" in its precise mathematical meaning (Zuckerman 1974), where it is defined as a set. The definition of a relation as a "time-varying set," which is seen in works on data, is contradictory, and is unsuitable for foundational work. Thus we find that associations, not relations, are the fundamental components of data design.

In Section 1.9, Identity of Mental Images, we show that the definition of "same" may differ from class to class. For example, we often find in data design that two things can be the "same part" yet different "purchasing items" (suppose, for example, that the part may be supplied by two different vendors at different prices). We investigate counting instances of a class, and the ancient philosophical problem of the one and the many.

In Section 1.10, Propositions, we discuss how a proposition q is associated with a recognizer that accepts ideas evoked by q: the proposition « the sky is blue » is associated with a recognizer that accepts mental pictures of a blue sky. We also discuss formation of simple propositions, such as « Fred is a farmer » from a class, « Farmer », and a recognizer « Fred ».

In Section 1.11, Conversion Between Symbols and Ideas, we study how symbols may be used to represent ideas. For example, we can represent the idea « the basket contains five apples » (ideas are always written inside angle quotes «   ») by a drawing of a basket containing five apples, by the writing "the basket contains five apples", or by placing the binary impulses "101" in an electronic memory location associated with apples in a basket. In each case the idea is the same, only the symbols are different. We call a process that converts symbols to ideas an *interpreting agent*, and discuss the effects of different interpreting agents on understanding.

In Section 1.12, Data, we define a *piece of data* to be a symbol that represents a proposition (via an interpreting agent). We discuss how data has the further characteristic that it is *claimed*. That is, a symbol is not data unless there is some observable action that allows the symbol to be interpreted as being affirmed.

1.2 PHYSICAL DETECTION OF SYMBOLS

Tools for Representation (Symbols) Are Needed

A physical object that can be used to express data will be called a *symbol*. In computerized data bases, numbers and letters are typically used as symbols, such as when an employee is identified as "employee number 4103", or a car is identified as "license ARN–619". When data is expressed without a computer, other symbols are used: marks of ink (as on a printed report), sounds (such as the sound of a bell on a television game show that indicates the contestant has won a prize), drawings (such as a blueprint of a building), and so on. Inside a computer, a variety of forms of electromagnetic disturbances are used to retain data. In this section, we investigate what objects can and what objects can not be used as symbols.

We will call a tangible object, animate or inanimate, a *thing*. Tangible objects are constantly changing: paper swells and cracks, ink runs, electromagnetic disturbances decay, and so on. We can not say precisely that a thing remains physically the same for even brief periods of time. A symbol, in contrast, must have a certain degree of permanence to be useful. If we write the symbol "ARN–619" on a piece of paper as part of a list of license plate numbers, for example, we would like some assurance that what we wrote will still appear as "ARN–619" when we look again at the piece of paper some time in the future, even though the ink's color may have changed, and the paper changed its shape.

To understand how a symbol behaves in time, we imagine a *detection process* that decides whether or not a thing qualifies as the symbol it detects. If a thing qualifies, the detection process *accepts* the thing. A detection process may be executed many times, allowing the same symbol to be identified over a period of time. Two things may then be defined to be the same symbol when they are both accepted by the same detection process. We will call a detection process, more briefly, a *detector*. If a detector for some symbol accepts a thing, we say that the thing is a *manifestation* of the detector.

For example, a detector for determining when a piece of metal type is considered the letter "A" could be a plastic mold that shows the outline of the shape "A" in reverse. Any number of shapes could be tested, and those that fit the mold snugly would be considered manifestations of the letter "A". The softness of the plastic would make it insensitive to small aberrations such as burrs on the surface of the metal. As long as the aberrations were not significant enough to require forcing the metal into the mold, the piece of type would be accepted.

Since a symbol is defined by a detection process, a thing will be several symbols simultaneously if the thing is detected by several different detectors. Thus, the mark "x" can be considered a letter x, or a multiplication sign, or the signature of an illiterate person. A particular mark "x" is a thing, while the processes that define the letter x, the notation for multiplication, and so on, are detectors. Each characterizes the mark "x" as a different symbol by accepting it.

We may also conclude that a thing will not be a symbol if there is no detector that detects the thing. For example, pulses of ultraviolet light existed before their discovery by mankind, and were therefore things, but they were not symbols because they were undetectable.

Detectors Operate According to a Describable Pattern

To determine whether or not a given thing qualifies as a candidate symbol, a detector must *examine* the thing, inspecting it for whatever characteristics it uses to make a determination. Consider, for example, a bill changer that inspects selected features of a paper-like thing inserted into it before giving change. This inspection is an examination by the bill changer, which is a detector (the bill changer detects a bill if it returns change).

As a physical process, a detector can not freely examine a thing located too far away or located in the past or future. To be examined, the thing must be brought into proximity of the detector in space and time, and it often must be prepared in some way. Thus, a bill must be physically inserted into the bill changer, and must be flattened first. A bill changer can not examine a bill inside the wallet of a man across the room. Before a thing can be examined by a detector, then, the thing must be *presented* to the detector.

Since what we can present to a detector limits what the detector can examine, we would like to have as few constraints as possible on the things that we can present to a detector. Consider, for example, a bill that is too big to fit into the slot provided by a bill changer. An attempt to fit the bill into the slot is a presentation of a thing, the bill, to a detector, the bill changer. However, the bill changer does not *examine* the bill if the bill is never inserted into the machine. Therefore, a presentation of a thing might not be followed by an examination of the thing.

An examination may result in the detector *accepting* or *rejecting* the thing (the bill changer either accepts the bill and returns change or rejects the bill by returning it). The verdict of acceptance or rejection will be called the *outcome*. A detector *detects* a thing if it accepts the thing.

An ambivalent detector that both accepts and rejects a thing is not useful for determining whether or not the thing qualifies as the candidate symbol. Similarly, an indecisive detector that neither accepts nor rejects a thing that it examines is not useful. We therefore require that a detector render exactly one outcome (acceptance or rejection) for any thing it examines.

The entire sequence of events from presentation, through examination and the rendering of an outcome, must be defined as a unit to link the outcome with the thing that is presented. The entire unit is called a *performance*. Because a detector is a physical process, a detector may only participate in a finite number of performances in any bounded period of time.

We will generally call a process that examines a thing, accepting or rejecting it, a *binding site*. We use the word "site" to emphasize that we view each process as a unit with a circumscribed function. The analogy is to a reaction site in Chemistry, a place where reactions occur when the proper substrate is provided. A detector is a special type of binding site, one that satisfies some additional criteria to be described later in this section. An action of operating a binding site is called a *performance*. We may summarize the properties of a performance as follows:

(i) A performance includes a presentation.

(ii) The collection of stuff presented to the binding site is viewed as a unit, called a *thing*.

(iii) A performance may include an examination of the thing that is presented. A performance may also include no examination.

(iv) If there is no examination, the performance is complete.

(v) If the thing is examined, exactly one outcome is rendered for the performance, either acceptance or rejection.

Detectors Exhibit Repeatable Behavior

For a detector to be useful, we must be confident that the same detector used on the same thing at different times or under different circumstances will give the same outcome each time. We are speaking informally here, since we have no definition of "same thing" apart from that given by detectors. We will call a binding site whose behavior may be reasonably expected to remain unchanged under normal operating conditions and for a suitably long period of time a *permanent* binding site. A detector that detects a suitably high signal voltage along a given wire, for example, is permanent, because we can imagine building a reliable device that performs this function repeatedly. On the other hand, a roulette wheel, which detects whatever number slot the ball rolls into, is not permanent, because the number the roulette wheel detects changes with circumstance. A detector must be a permanent binding site.

Replicas of Symbols Are Needed

Symbols serve not only as means to represent thoughts, but also as objects that may be intercombined to reach new conclusions. The symbol "x" within the expression "$x = 0$" has this combinatorial quality, since we want to be able to use "x" in other expressions, such as "$x + y = y$" and "$zx = x$". Of course, we want to reuse the symbol without being concerned about whether or not it is possible to construct physical objects, here the different marks of ink, each time the letter x is used. Not all permanent binding sites permit such reuse of a symbol. For example, a binding site that accepts a solar eclipse is permanent. We can have confidence that the next time a solar eclipse occurs, the binding site will detect it as such. But the difficulty of producing a solar eclipse at will makes it impractical to use a solar eclipse as a symbol.

When it is possible to construct or obtain a sufficiently large number of things that will be accepted by a binding site under any reasonable circumstances, we say that the binding site is *formative*. The binding sites that detect letters of the alphabet are formative, for we may readily create a new manifestation of a letter by drawing one or typing one on a typewriter or computer terminal. The binding site that detects a certain voltage along a signal line in a computer as a "1" is also formative, for we can create such a voltage at will from an electrical source.

Formativeness is an informal concept, because it relies upon an undefined method of obtaining things, and is imprecise about how long it takes to form an acceptable thing, what environmental conditions are required, and so on. Nevertheless, it serves to clarify definitions and to exclude certain evanescences from consideration as symbols. For example, from the two requirements of permanence and formativeness, we may conclude that an event is not a symbol. An event, once it has occurred, can not be repeated. Therefore, if a permanent binding site were constructed to detect an event, it could only accept the event (a thing) while it was occurring. Before the event occurred, and after it had occurred, there would be no thing that the binding site could accept, so the binding site would not be formative.

It is different with a binding site that accepts not a particular event, but a type of activity. For example, consider a binding site that accepts the action of pushing a lever. The action is repeatable, and so the binding site is formative. If the binding site were only to accept the pushing of the lever on a certain date, it would not be formative (as long as the time that we were interested in the outcome of performances lasted beyond that day).

It Is Possible to Predict the Behavior of Detectors

So far, we have been insisting that a thing be accepted by a detector in order to be considered a symbol. Actual acceptance requires that a performance occur. Of course, it would be impractical to require that a thing be presented to a detector each time it is used. In practice, one can predict that a thing will be accepted without a performance, reasoning that a thing if undisturbed will not change significantly, or that a thing must be accepted by a detector if it possesses all the characteristics that determine the outcome. We say therefore that it suffices that it be *predicted* that a thing will be accepted by a detector and that an actual performance is unnecessary. We do not mean to imply that the criteria for determining the outcome of a performance may be relaxed or defined vaguely. Quite the contrary, it is essential that detectors be defined with precision if they are to be useful. However, we may reason about the operation of detectors, and avoid the need for performances, by accepting the principle that detectors operate within rigorous physical laws that can be exploited.

We may therefore define the terms *symbol*, *same symbol*, and *detector* as follows:

> A *symbol* is a thing that is predicted to be accepted by a detector.
> Two things are the *same symbol* if they are each predicted to be accepted by the same detector.
> A *detector* is a permanent and formative binding site.

Notation for Symbols

We will write a symbol by writing a sample thing surrounded by quotes. Thus "x" indicates the symbol, the letter x. There is some ambiguity in this notation, since it does not make clear whether the symbol referred to is the letter x, the letter x in the particular font used in this printing, the particular molecules of ink surrounded by quotes, etc. We will mean the letter x when we write "x", the numeral two when we write "2", and so on.

Properties of Detectors Are Formalized by Postulates

When we assume the ability to form a process that operates on physical things, we will identify that assumption as a *postulate*. Here we follow Euclid's approach to postulates (Euclid 300B.C.). For example, Euclid's first postulate is translated precisely as follows: "Let the following be postulated: to draw a straight line from any point to any point." This is not the same statement as "there is a straight line between every two points," which is found in modern textbooks. Euclid is concerned with the processes needed for geometry— in this case, he identifies the need for a process that forms a straight line. He does not assume that all straight lines are available ready-formed. Similarly, we will state postulates as assumptions about the ability to perform processes, such as the ability to create a detector. We do not assume that all detectors are available ready-formed.

We have made three assumptions that require formalization as postulates:

(P1) It is possible to form an arbitrarily large number of detectors.

(P2) Any detector is a binding site.

(P3) In any performance of a binding site, an examination results in exactly one outcome, either acceptance or rejection.

The postulate (P1) assumes an ability to form an arbitrarily large number of detectors, so that our ability to express data will never be limited by having exhausted the available symbols. Since detectors are physical processes, it requires some amount of time to form a detector. It would therefore be improper to assume an infinite number of detectors, since an infinite number could not be formed in a bounded period of time. For example, since we can create an arbitrarily large number of numerals by stringing digits together (1, 12, 128, etc.), numerals are good candidate symbols for expressing data (as the vast variety of "official identification numbers" attests). At the same time, we can never form an infinite number of numerals.

Sets of Physical Objects Should Not Be Used Rhetorically

Sets are often used improperly to establish a topic for discussion, where it is simpler and more accurate to define the topic directly. For example, one may find the statement "let c be a member of the set of all carbon atoms" as a lengthy way of saying "let c be a carbon atom." These two statements have become almost interchangeable in scientific writing, yet they have fundamentally different meanings.

The first statement, "let *c* be a member of the set of all carbon atoms," presumes that it is possible to form "the set of all carbon atoms." It is manifestly impossible to form such a set physically, for there is no way to identify all the carbon atoms in the universe. Further, it is impossible to imagine all the members of such a large set without an extreme degree of approximation or metaphorical thinking. Introducing this sort of fuzziness at the beginning of an investigation places the investigation immediately on very uncertain ground.

Further, sets are not clearly defined unless they specify how their members are to be detected. For example, the phrase "the set of all physical objects" does not explain whether the mark "x" is to be considered two objects if viewed as both a letter x and a signature, if it is to be viewed as the same object after being obscured with correction fluid, and so on. The statement "let *j* be a physical object," in contrast, merely evokes some detector that recognizes *j*. When we speak of *j* as a member of the set of all physical objects, we imply that we can determine how all the detectors that might recognize a manifestation of *j* behave, a much more difficult task.

A primary weakness in the use of such extremely broad sets is that they accumulate all the uncertainties of the procedures used to form them. If it is uncertain whether or not any one thing is a member of a set, then the validity of the entire set is in question. For example, we might debate whether or not a vacuum is a physical object. This debate immediately implies a question about what the set of physical objects is: whether or not it contains a vacuum. Knowledge is usually gained by building on what is certain, and treating the uncertainties as exceptions. This use of sets acts in the opposite way, raising all the uncertainties at the outset.

Instead of preceding an investigation with the statement "let *s* be a member of the set of all symbols," one should write "let *s* be a symbol." Whereas the former statement presupposes an ability to identify all symbols, the latter does not. It merely supposes that some symbol *s* has been selected for study. This method of reasoning avoids the physical impossibility of forming the set of all symbols, and allows us to separate out things whose status as symbols is uncertain, while retaining the ability to reason about things that clearly are symbols.

For example, if we admit that there can be a difference of opinion about whether or not a vacuum is a symbol, then there is a difference of opinion about whether or not the results in this book apply to a vacuum. The substitution of a vacuum for "*s*" in "let *s* be a symbol" is therefore suspect. However, this uncertainty does not lead us to question that the numeral "6" is a symbol, so the substitution of "6" for "*s*" in "let *s* be a symbol" can proceed unhindered. It remains uncertain whether "the set of all symbols" has any existence at all, but this does not prevent us from studying the characteristics of those symbols that we have at hand.

Conclusion

We have established that symbols are defined by the processes that detect them. Without a detection process, a thing can not be detected for more than an instant. Such things are therefore useless for recording data. A process that detects things, called a *detector*, is a special case of a more general type of process called a *binding site*. Binding sites follow a standard pattern, consisting of a presentation, possibly an examination, and if so, an outcome, either acceptance or rejection.

We have seen that while the possible varieties of symbols are extensive, they are not limitless. There are certain restrictions that symbols must obey to be useful. In particular, a detector used to define a symbol must be permanent (its behavior should remain unchanged under normal operating conditions) and formative (it should be possible to form replicas of symbols with ease).

In data processing, detectors are usually preestablished by the computer hardware. In some applications such as image processing and analog-to-digital conversion, considerable attention may be devoted to determining precisely what things will be detected and under what circumstances two things will be treated as the same symbol.

1.3 MENTAL IMAGES

A Symbol Represents an Idea, Not a Thing

Data often appears to be concerned primarily with concrete objects, such as parts, machines, buildings, and the like. Actually, data is concerned perhaps more often with concepts that are not so concrete: accounts, projects, organizations, and so on. It is even possible to design a data base about fictitious concepts: a medical history data base for unicorns, for example. Further, supposedly concrete things like parts are often subject to differences of opinion that affect how they behave as data: is the thing x, made to the same specifications as the thing y, but made of a different material, the same part? Does the thing x remain the same part over time, even after it has fallen out of tolerance because of wear? Every data designer is aware of the need to ask questions of this kind when undertaking a data design.

None of these questions can be answered solely by inspecting physical objects. Measuring a physical part, for example, does not indicate what variations in dimensions are allowed in the part's specification. Even inspecting all available physical parts does not suffice, for it is possible, even likely, that the available physical parts have not exhausted all the differences allowed in the specification. Thus, the characteristics recorded in a data base, in this case characteristics of a part, are not characteristics of a physical object, but characteristics of how a physical object is perceived. That is, the symbols used in data do not represent things. They represent ideas. This characteristic of symbols was first recognized by Hobbes over three centuries ago, but still causes confusion today (Hobbes 1655).

When physical characteristics and mental ideas conflict, the mental idea takes precedence. Consider, for example, a clay pot found in an archaeological dig. Imagine that the pot was actually fashioned 5000 years ago, but because of incomplete evidence the archaeologist concludes that it was fashioned 4900 years ago. An archaeological data base will record the concept of the archaeologist, namely, that his or her conception of the object is associated with an age of 4900 years. This date bears no association with the actual object, the clay pot, and indeed contradicts its physical characteristics.

The conclusion that symbols represent ideas and not things has practical consequences. In particular, it demonstrates that data designs can not be deduced by an impartial examination of the physical world, nor can they be validated by a purely experimental procedure. Data designs reflect a conception of the world, not the world itself. The conception may intentionally be in conflict with the physical world. For example, a company may wish to institute a policy whereby every supplier is associated with one billing office that processes payments. Suppose that this policy is not followed today, but that it is the express intention of management to enforce it in the future. The data design may then specify that every supplier is associated with one billing office, reflecting management's intention, and not the current state of affairs. Further discussion of the need to plan for the future (which is inherently unmeasurable, and can only be imagined) in data base design may be found in (Martin 1976) and (Jones and Curtice 1988).

Notation for Ideas

Since we can not exhibit an idea directly, we will depict an idea suggestively through language. To make it clear when we are speaking of words as symbols and when we are speaking of words as ideas we will use quotation marks (" ") to indicate symbols and angle quotes (« ») to indicate ideas. Thus the symbol "house", that is, the string of letters "h" followed by "o", "u", "s", and "e" is distinguished from a mental image of a house, which we will denote « house ». That is, we would write:

"house" is a five-letter word

Mary's « house » is white

Notice that in ordinary discourse, a word refers to an idea, not a symbol. Thus, omitting the angle quotes in the second example does not change its ordinary meaning.

Language Shows That Ideas Take Many Forms

Logic and data bases both distinguish ideas that are classifying, such as « person » and « customer », from ideas that are complete in themselves, such as « Fred Philbin » and « Rex's drug store ». The difference between the two kinds of ideas may be seen by how they are combined in language: "Fred Philbin is a person" and "Rex's drug store is a customer" are both well-formed sentences. In contrast, "person is a Fred Philbin" and "customer is a Rex's drug store" are nonsense.

Although language shows this distinction clearly with ordinary words, reasoning through language becomes circular when new words are created to describe unfamiliar terms. To say that a thought is only well-formed if its expression in language is syntactically correct presupposes that the new words are assigned the correct part of speech. The correct part of speech, in turn, is defined by whether or not the new words combine with other words to form syntactically correct sentences. We must therefore explore more carefully to discern the distinguishing features of the different types of ideas.

We will call a classifying idea such as « person » or « customer » a *class*. We will postpone considering classes to Section 1.5. We call an idea such as « Fred Philbin » or « Rex's drug store » an *image*. Studying images will be the main topic of the remainder of this section.

An Image Is Defined by a Conceptual Recognizing Mechanism

When we try to contemplate a chosen image, we face a difficulty similar to that which we faced in defining a symbol, namely, that the same image may take many forms. Consider, for example, a large customer « United Motors ». Clearly, the legal identity of United Motors may change as it acquires and divests itself of businesses, or is itself acquired. Salesmen may want to define different divisions of United Motors to be different customers for the purposes of establishing territorial control. Distributors may want to define different receiving locations of United Motors to be different customers to improve resupply procedures. In such situations, which are common in data base design, it requires an act of will to decide what does, and what does not, constitute the same image, in this case the customer « United Motors ».

We define an image in a fashion that is directly analogous to the method we used to define a symbol. We will call a particular thought an *impression*, the analog of a *thing*. We do not refer only to sense-impressions, but to any thought that is presented for contemplation. Thus, the sensation felt from stepping on a sharp stone is an impression, but so also is a recollection of a past event, or an imaginary conception of a unicorn crossing a road.

An impression, like a thing, has no inherent permanence. After we step on the stone, it requires an act of imagination to recall the event. Each recollection is a different impression. To say that two impressions are the *same image*, we must employ some technique analogous to a detector.

A detector, we recall, is a process that determines when two things are the same symbol. We can not assume that the means of determining when two impressions are the same image is a *process*, since it occurs unobservably in the mind. We will therefore use a different term, *conceptual mechanism*, for this assumed mental faculty. We may perceive the workings of a conceptual mechanism in our ability to recollect thoughts, yet its essential nature remains mysterious.

We call a conceptual mechanism that establishes an image a *recognizer*. A recognizer is *performed* in a fashion that is analogous to the way a binding site is performed. That is,

- **(i)** A performance is an occasion of exercising a recognizer (in particular, a performance occurs within an interval of time, the duration of the interval being related to the speed of thought).
- **(ii)** A performance includes a presentation.
- **(iii)** The thought presented to the recognizer is viewed as a unit, called an *impression*.
- **(iv)** A performance may include an examination of the impression that is presented.
- **(v)** If there is no examination, the performance is complete.
- **(vi)** If the impression is examined, exactly one outcome is rendered for the performance, whether acceptance or rejection. (Actually true only for *constructive* recognizers, other varieties will be discussed in the development of logic).

Two impressions are the *same image* if they are accepted by the same recognizer. For example, suppose that United Motors sold heavy-duty trucks at one time, but does not sell them now. We could then imagine two impressions: « United Motors selling heavy-duty trucks » and « United Motors not selling heavy-duty trucks ». Most applications would probably consider these two impressions to be the same company. The recognizer for « United Motors » would then accept both impressions.

If the data base is being designed for a trucking supply company, however, the purchasing behavior before and after the switch away from heavy-duty trucks might be so significant that the data base would want to identify the two incarnations of the company differently. There would then be two recognizers, « United Motors_1 » that accepted « United Motors selling heavy-duty trucks », and « United Motors_2 » that accepted « United Motors not selling heavy-duty trucks ». Notice that these two recognizers do not accept only one impression each: United Motors may have gone in and out of the motorcycle business while it was selling heavy-duty trucks, but this may have had no impact on the trucking supply company. Then « United Motors_1 » would accept both the impressions « United Motors selling heavy-duty trucks and motorcycles » and « United Motors selling heavy-duty trucks and not selling motorcycles ».

Just as a symbol may be pictured as a thing bound to a detector, so an image may be pictured as an impression *compounded with* a recognizer. When an impression is accepted by a recognizer, we say that the resulting image is a *manifestation* of the recognizer. Figure 1.1 shows the close analogy between physical detection of things and mental recognition of impressions.

Recognizers Have Different Characteristics from Detectors

The analogy between detectors and recognizers is not perfect. In particular, there are no analogous requirements to permanence, formativeness, and prediction in the definition of a recognizer. Thus, the acceptance behavior of a detector does not change, because a detector is assumed to be permanent. Yet the acceptance behavior of a recognizer can change. For example, consider the recognizer « yesterday », which accepts different concepts of time each day. These changeable recognizers are no less important to data than recognizers that may be considered permanent.

A formative binding site is one for which there is always a ready manifestation. A recognizer can be viewed as having a ready manifestation if it is possible to imagine an impression that the recognizer would accept. We will find it useful, however, to allow for recognizers that have no manifestation.

Prediction was introduced into the definition of a symbol to avoid performing a detection process each time a thing is used as a manifestation of a detector. In thought, we are not limited by the practicality of executing a recognizer. Moreover, as we will see, impressions, unlike things, have a most precarious existence if separated from recognizers. We therefore require acceptance, not merely predicted acceptance, in the definition of an image.

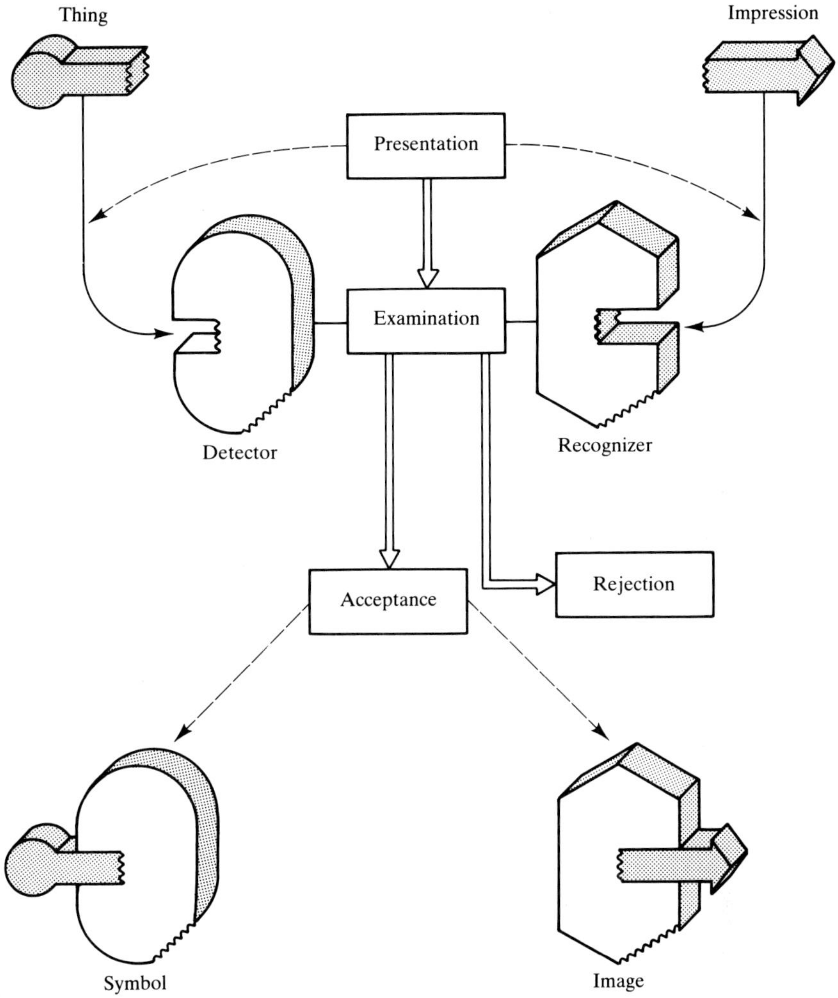

Figure 1.1 The analogy between symbols and images.

A Symbol Represents a Recognizer

Data is primarily concerned with recognizers rather than images. Thus, when we consider the concept « Fred Smith », we are not concerned with a particular impression of Fred Smith (such as how we saw him when we passed him in the street yesterday), but with the more general mechanism, or recognizer, that allows us to view all impressions of Fred Smith as one concept. Thus, the symbol ''Fred Smith'' represents a recognizer (rather than an impression or an image). When we imagine « Fred Smith », we imagine an impression, a mental picture, that satisfies the criteria of the recognizer. That is, we imagine an image.

Impressions Can Not Be Isolated Using Recognizers

We consider next to what extent it is possible to describe an impression. In particular, we ask whether or not we can form a recognizer that accepts only one impression, rather than accepting many impressions that are viewed as the same image. For example, consider the recognizer

« the Washington Monument »

This recognizer accepts many different ideas, which we might describe as:

« the Washington Monument on a clear day »

« the Washington Monument in September »

However, these ideas are not impressions, but other recognizers. Thus, we may imagine many impressions of the Washington Monument on a clear day, or the Washington Monument in September. We might combine the two recognizers to reach one that is more specific:

« the Washington Monument on a clear day in September »

Yet we may still imagine many impressions of the Washington Monument on a clear day in September. Indeed, we may continue this process indefinitely, creating ever finer recognizers but *never reaching an impression*.

We believe that the pattern illustrated is a fundamental characteristic of thought. There are two principles involved: The *indefinite refinement principle* states that for any given recognizer d, we may form a recognizer that is finer than d, as « the Washington Monument on a clear day » is a finer recognizer than « the Washington Monument ». The precise meaning of "finer" will be discussed in Section 1.5. The other principle, the *uncertainty principle of impressions*, states that no recognizer may be made so fine that it accepts exactly one impression. That is:

Any recognizer that accepts an impression may accept many impressions.

Consequences for the Philosophy of Thought

Because of the uncertainty principle, we can never form a deduction about an impression. Thus, the statement "if the impression ι has the characteristic b then ι has the characteristic c" is malformed, for we can never be certain that it is ι that has the characteristic c, and not some other impression κ that happens to be the same image as ι. This suggests that recognizers, not impressions, are the basic constituents of thought, because thought requires the ability to contemplate the same idea in many different contexts, and only recognizers are able to identify different impressions as the same idea. Here we differ from Hume, who argued that impressions have primacy (Hume 1739).

The uncertainty principle suggests further that the mental faculty of memory retains recognizers, because the act of recalling a past experience involves forming an impression in the present that is similar to an impression of the past. A recognizer is required to determine that the two impressions, the one in the present and the one in the past, are similar.

Since recognizers can be refined indefinitely, we must reject philosophies that treat thought as the accumulation of indivisible units. In particular, we must reject Leibniz's view that all ideas can be defined systematically from other, more fundamental, ideas, with the exception of certain "primitive concepts" that are not decomposable further (Leibniz 1683). Hume adopts the similar view that "complex ideas" are resolved into combinations of "simple ideas"; Wittgenstein recasts Leibniz's views in modern terms, saying that "facts" may be decomposed into "independent atomic facts" (Hume 1739, Wittgenstein 1921).

By the indefinite refinement principle, we can always form a refinement of any candidate "primitive concept," so that Leibniz's method of analysis will produce only an ever-growing proliferation of more and more specific ideas. It will be more fruitful, we feel, to try to establish a specification language for how recognizers are formed in thought. For example, one might try to write a computer program to recognize an apple as a model of the recognizer for an « apple ». The individual "words" of this language could then be considered to be primitive elements of thought, but these "words" would combine not as atoms combine to form molecules (to use Wittgenstein's metaphor), but as statements combine in a computer program. The order of processing the "words," for example, could be significant. We will return to this topic in Section 1.6.

Conclusion

Symbols represent ideas, not things. In particular, a symbol may represent a *recognizer*, which is a conceptual mechanism that determines when two impressions are to be considered to be the same concept, or *image*. Recognizers are performed as detectors are: a recognizer may accept, reject, or not examine an impression in the course of a performance. Impressions, the analog of things, are inherently unisolable, and are generally beyond the realm of analysis.

1.4 PHYSICAL CLASSIFICATION OF THINGS

A Binding Site May Accept Things That Are Different Symbols

We defined "same symbol" in Section 1.2 by saying that two things are the same symbol if each is predicted to be accepted by the same detector. While this treatment of two things as the same symbol applies to detectors, it is not inherent in a binding site. It is a choice we make in interpreting the outcome of a performance. Given a performance in which a binding site B accepts a thing t, and a performance in which B accepts a thing u, we may view t and u as different symbols provided we have detectors T and U such that T accepts t but does not accept u, and U accepts u but does not accept t. Thus a binding site may accept things that are different symbols.

A common example of a binding site that accepts things that are different symbols is a memory location in a computer. Many binary numbers, encoded as a sequence of electrical pulses, may be accepted by (may be stored in) the memory location. Each such sequence of electrical pulses is a thing. Each binary number is a symbol, and the process by which a sequence of electrical pulses is translated into a binary number is a detector. Many symbols (binary numbers) may therefore be accepted by the binding site (the memory location).

As a rule, any device that accepts physical input is a binding site. A typewriter is a binding site, the things it accepts being strokes upon the keys. A tape recorder is a binding site, the things it accepts being sounds. A computer routine while being run is several binding sites, one for each variable that it takes as input.

Any device that yields physical output may also be viewed as a binding site. Consider, for example, a device that receives two numbers and outputs their sum. The two numbers are initially input as things that are detected by detectors to be numbers. The device then adds the two numbers and determines that a thing should be output that is a manifestation of the detector that detects the sum. In the process of finding or constructing such a thing, the output mechanism acts as a binding site. It will accept (present as output) only those things that would be accepted by the detector that detects the sum.

Notice that the acceptance behavior of a binding site may change with changing circumstance. A memory location, when protected, will not accept any number for storage; when unprotected, it will. The output binding site of the adding device changes with every new sum, its acceptance behavior being dependent entirely on the things that are input. Many useful binding sites are therefore not permanent.

The Things Accepted by a Binding Site Are Occupants

We consider how to describe more precisely the acceptance behavior of a binding site. We recall that the identity of a thing is determined by detectors: if we are to make a permanent record that a binding site accepts a thing, then, we must retain a detector that accepts the thing.

If a thing t is accepted by a binding site B, and t is a manifestation of a detector T, then we say that the detector T is an *occupant* of B. For example, consider a binding site L that accepts printed Roman letters. L accepts the ink mark:

q

This ink mark is also accepted by the detector Q that accepts manifestations of the letter q. Therefore, Q is an occupant of L.

If a detector T is an occupant of a binding site B, then there is at least one thing that is accepted by both T and B. The detector T may also accept things that are not accepted by B. For example, imagine that the detector Q detects the letter q printed in any color, while the binding site L only accepts marks that are black. A letter q printed in black would then be accepted by both Q and L, but a letter q printed in red would only be accepted by Q. Nevertheless, Q remains an occupant of L because both Q and L accept a black letter q.

A Binding Site Is Not a Set

A binding site is not the same as the set of all its occupants. The habit of equating these two different objects grew from the use in mathematics of abstract and unchanging items, such as lines or numbers. There is little difference in mathematics between the set of all lines in a plane and a process that recognizes a line in the plane, or between the set of prime numbers and a process that recognizes a prime number.

Things, however, are different from mathematical concepts. The collection of things within our experience is constantly changing, and is never known to its finest detail. Consider a binding site that accepts any sheep. We could never physically enumerate every sheep in the world, every thing that is accepted by the binding site. Nor can we even predict what the population of sheep will be in the future, since new sheep will be born, and old ones will die. Such fantasies as a set of all things that are accepted by a binding site are shown to be preposterous when one considers physically constructing them. Moreover, they are unnecessary to reasoning, for we can acknowledge that sheep give wool without ever contemplating collecting together all sheep, or all tufts of wool.

Treating a binding site as a set also yields incorrect conclusions. If a binding site were a set, then two binding sites with the same occupants would be the same binding site. In particular, two binding sites that each had no occupants would be the same. Imagine a binding site that accepts green sheep, and another that accepts purple rabbits. Under ordinary circumstances, neither binding site will accept any thing, there being no things that meet their requirements. They will therefore both have no occupants, yet they are still different binding sites. Their difference may be shown by dyeing a sheep green and a rabbit purple and presenting the two animals to the binding sites. Claiming, as set theory would have us do, that the two binding sites were the same but became different once the dyeing was accomplished, is clearly a misunderstanding of what is the same (the binding sites) and what is different (the things that are available).

Embracings Interrelate Binding Sites

It frequently happens that acceptance by one binding site implies acceptance by another. Consider, for example, a binding site *TR* that accepts text written in the Times-Roman font, and a binding site *F* that accepts text written in a variety of fonts, including Times-Roman. It follows that any thing (any block of text) that is accepted by *TR* would be accepted by *F*.

These two binding sites bear a relationship of *embracing* with each other. A binding site *C* is said to *embrace* a binding site *B* if any thing that is accepted by *B* must be accepted by *C*. If *C* embraces *B* and *B* embraces *C*, we say that *B* and *C* are *equivalent*. In the example, the binding site *F* embraces the binding site *TR*.

Notice that we were able to define embracing without referring to a set of all symbols accepted by a binding site. It is true that if *S* is a set of occupants of *B*, and *C* embraces *B*, then each member of *S* must be accepted by *C*. However, inclusion of sets of occupants does not, in reverse, imply an embracing. For example, imagine that the only text that has been presented to *F* above has been in the Times-Roman font. The set of symbols that have been accepted by *F* is then the same as the set of symbols that have been accepted by *TR*. Yet we may not conclude that *F* is equivalent to *TR*, as is shown by presenting text to *TR* that is not in the Times-Roman font. An embracing is a statement about the *structure* or *capacity* of a binding site, not about its occupants.

Indeed, we may conclude that one binding site embraces another without considering any occupants of either binding site. For example, consider the two molds made of packed sand illustrated in Figure 1.2. Each mold is said to *accept* a thing if the thing fits within the mold: the thing need not fit snugly, but it must fit inside. By measuring the dimensions of each mold, we may conclude that the mold *C* embraces the mold *B*, without ever actually testing that any thing fits in either mold.

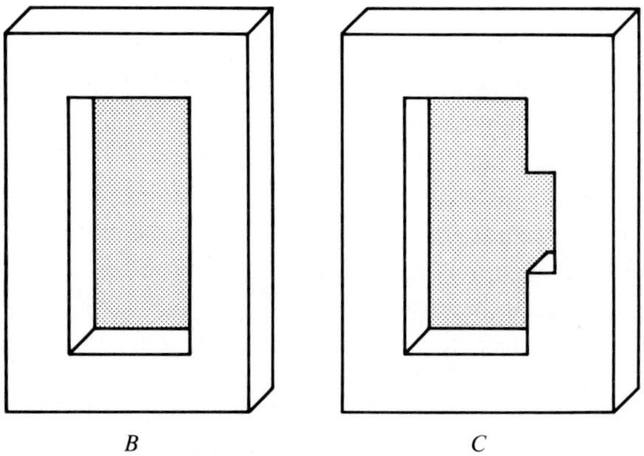

Figure 1.2 The binding site *C* embraces the binding site *B*.

Indistinguishability Is Defined by Binding Sites

We consider next how to define when two things are ''identical.'' To conclude that two things are identical, we must examine both things. For example, we could examine both things by equivalent detectors. We could then conclude that the two things were the same symbol if both were accepted. Yet we can not therefore conclude that the two things are identical, for there may be other detectors that accept one thing and reject the other. For example, a letter q in black and a letter q in red would both be accepted by a detector that accepts a letter q, but only one would be accepted by a detector that accepts a red thing.

For two things to be identical, they must show equal patterns of (predicted) examination, acceptance, and rejection for all binding sites. If it were otherwise, we could identify a difference between the two things. More significantly, there can be no other definition of identity besides equal patterns over all binding sites, since any definition of identity must involve examination, and any examination may be viewed as a binding site.

The definition of identity is therefore dependent upon the available binding sites. Since binding sites are physical processes, we can not assume that all possible binding sites are available pre-formed. On the contrary, it is much more likely that there are many potential binding sites that we have not formed, such as those that detect unknown subatomic particles or unknown chemicals inside a cell. Each new binding site changes the definition of identity. It follows directly that two things may be physically different, but identical, simply because we have no available binding site that can differentiate between them.

Consider further a thing that is examined by no binding site. Recall that, though we permitted any thing to be presented to a binding site, we did not require that every thing that is presented must be examined. If a thing is examined by no binding site, it is impossible to demonstrate that it is identical to any other thing. In particular, we can not demonstrate that it is identical to itself.

We can go further. Since the only definition of identity requires examination by a binding site, and since the thing is examined by no binding site, the thing is not identical with itself. Not only does the definition of identity change with changing binding sites, but so does the collection of things that are identical to themselves, which might not be all things. Identity is therefore not innate in things as was argued by Leibniz (1686), but is a consequence of the methods we use to examine things.

The term "identity" can be applied to both things and ideas. To keep terms clear, we will say that two things are *indistinguishable* if they show the same patterns of examination, acceptance, and rejection for all available binding sites. That is, two things are indistinguishable if they are identical according to this discussion.

Conclusion

Many common methods for the input, output, and storage of symbols may be treated as binding sites. We have seen that binding sites are different from sets, an observation that will lead us to construct a new theory of classification, departing from symbolic logic. In a further departure, we have concluded that identity is not a fundamental characteristic of things, but is derived from performances of binding sites.

We have defined an embracing of binding sites, which is analogous to inclusion of sets. A binding site C embraces a binding site B if B and C are formed so that any thing that B accepts must be accepted by C. The set of things accepted by B might be included in the set of things accepted by C, yet C would not embrace B, if B were capable of accepting things that C did not.

1.5 MENTAL CLASSES

Classes Are Defined by Analogy with Binding Sites

We seek to define the concept of a *class*, which, speaking loosely, is an idea used to characterize ideas. A class may be defined by analogy with a binding site: as a conceptual mechanism that, upon examining an idea, either accepts the idea or rejects it. This definition leaves, however, three types of ideas that a class could examine: impressions, images, and recognizers. We investigate next whether all these types of ideas are indeed examinable by classes.

A class is normally represented in language by a noun or noun phrase, such as

« Horse », « Banker », « Fire Engine », and so on. We will normally write classes with initial capital letters to distinguish them from recognizers, which are normally written in lower-case. A class may also be conveniently represented by replacing a word from a complete sentence with a *blank*, as in:

« _____ Is A Hatrack »

« _____ Fell Down The Stairs »

Here, we imagine that an idea is tested by inserting it into the blank, and asking whether the resulting sentence is believed. For example, if we believe that Fred fell down the stairs then we say that the class « _____ Fell Down The Stairs » accepts the idea « Fred ».

A class like « Horse » represented by a single word can also be represented by the phrase « _____ Is A Horse ». Only *countable* noun phrases, noun phrases that can be preceded by "a" or "an", should be used to represent a class. Mass nouns like "water" or "sand" should be avoided as class names, as should proper nouns like "Monica".

The class « _____ Fell Down The Stairs » does not accept the *recognizer* « Fred », but rather an *image* of « Fred ». It is not true that every impression of « Fred » fell down the stairs. For example, « Fred driving to work last Tuesday », « Fred watching TV last Sunday », and so on, did not fall down the stairs. It is rather a specific impression of Fred (possibly several impressions) that fell down the stairs. The other impressions cited bear no relationship to falling down the stairs beyond being other manifestations of the recognizer « Fred ».

The analogy with binding sites would lead one to expect a class to accept *impressions*, the analog of things, but classes actually accept *images*. An impression accepted by a class makes no progress to thought, since the impression, divorced from a recognizer, can not be recalled. Recollection requires a recognizer, which is provided in an image. A *class* is therefore a conceptual mechanism that is performed as follows:

(i) A performance includes a presentation of an image to the class.
(ii) A performance may include an examination of the image that is presented.
(iii) If there is no examination, the performance is complete.
(iv) If the image is examined, exactly one outcome is rendered for the performance, either acceptance or rejection (actually true only for *constructive* classes, other varieties will be discussed in the development of logic).

A class differs from a recognizer in two ways: a recognizer accepts *impressions*, while a class accepts *images*; and two impressions accepted by a recognizer are viewed as the same image, while a class may accept two different images.

Classes Are More Diverse than Predicates

When the subject of a simple sentence is removed, what remains is called grammatically a predicate. Writers on logic have often emphasized viewing a class as a "predicate" (Aristotle 350B.C.a, Quine 1960), however, classes need not be expressed as predicates. We may, for example, replace the verb of a sentence with a blank:

« Fred _____ The Stairs »

This expression represents a class that accepts images of actions, such as « fell down », « built », « will inspect », and so on. We could also replace a preposition with a blank:

« Fred Fell _____ The Stairs »

This expression represents a class that accepts such images as « down », « near », or « through ».

These examples show the dangers in defining fundamental concepts by how they are represented in language. Many useful ideas, such as abstract ideas in mathematics, are not clearly described by language, so some other means must be used to determine their properties. Moreover, common grammatical categories such as "predicate" or "noun" are exceedingly difficult to define precisely, even in natural language [see (Boas 1911) and (Sapir 1921) for some of the difficulties]. We have therefore defined a class not by its linguistic representation, but by how it is performed as a conceptual mechanism.

Classes May Examine Both Constituents of an Image

A class, we recall, examines images. An image may be viewed as a compound state of an impression together with a recognizer. The class may therefore examine the recognizer as well as the impression to determine whether or not the image will be accepted, as shown in Figure 1.3. If a class examines only the impression in an image, and disregards the recognizer, then we say that the class is *contentual*. A contentual class is illustrated in Figure 1.4.

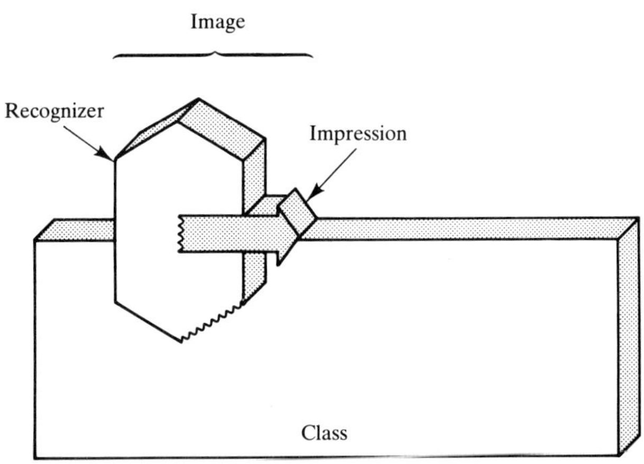

Figure 1.3 A class accepts an image.

The combination of a class with an image that it accepts is called an *assembly manifestation*. The word "manifestation" is used because we will define an *assembly* later as a conceptual mechanism (see Section 1.8). Thus, Figures 1.3 and 1.4 each illustrate an assembly manifestation. An assembly manifestation often suggests an image acting in a "role." For example, suppose that John is a painter. The class « Painter » then accepts an image « John ». The assembly manifestation of « Painter » with an image of « John » is « John as a painter », an image of John in the role of a painter.

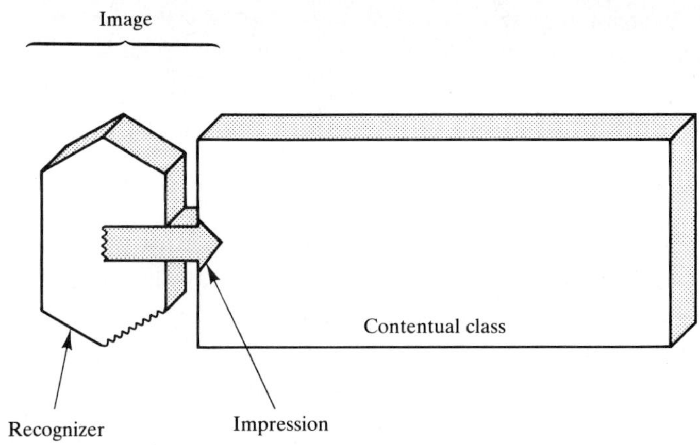

Figure 1.4 A contentual class examines only the impression portion of an image.

Recognizers Are Instances of Classes

Although a class accepts images, we can not represent an image directly because of the uncertainty principle of impressions. Instead, we represent the recognizer within the image. Specifically, we say that a recognizer « d » is an *instance* of a class « C » if there is predicted to be an impression ι such that the compound of « d » with ι would be accepted by « C ». An instance is the analog of an *occupant* of a binding site, or in mathematics, the analog of a *member* of a set. The concept of prediction is introduced into the definition of an instance to permit the application of logic. Figure 1.5 illustrates an instance.

Classes Are More Diverse than Sets

When we use the word *set*, we mean a collection that is defined by its *members*. Two collections with different members are different sets. We will use the word *set* in two meanings, as a collection of symbols, and as a collection of recognizers. We will discuss sets of symbols in Section 1.7.

Consider, for example, the class « Fire Hydrant ». To be specific, let us focus on the concept of a fire hydrant in the mind of some observer Frank. The class « Fire Hydrant » is then the conceptual mechanism that Frank uses to decide when an impression qualifies as a fire hydrant. The instances of « Fire Hydrant » are the recognizers of all fire hydrants, real or imagined, in Frank's mind. At any given time, there is a set of all the real and imaginary fire hydrants that Frank has perceived or thought of. This set of recognizers is called the *population* of the class « Fire Hydrant ». We will often designate a population using a caret: $\hat{B}$ for a population of a class B.

Suppose that Frank sees a fire hydrant he has never seen before. His conception of this new fire hydrant is a new instance of the class « Fire Hydrant ». It is still the same class, since Frank's conceptual mechanism for recognizing fire hydrants has not changed. There is, however, a different set of all fire hydrants, a new population, with one more member.

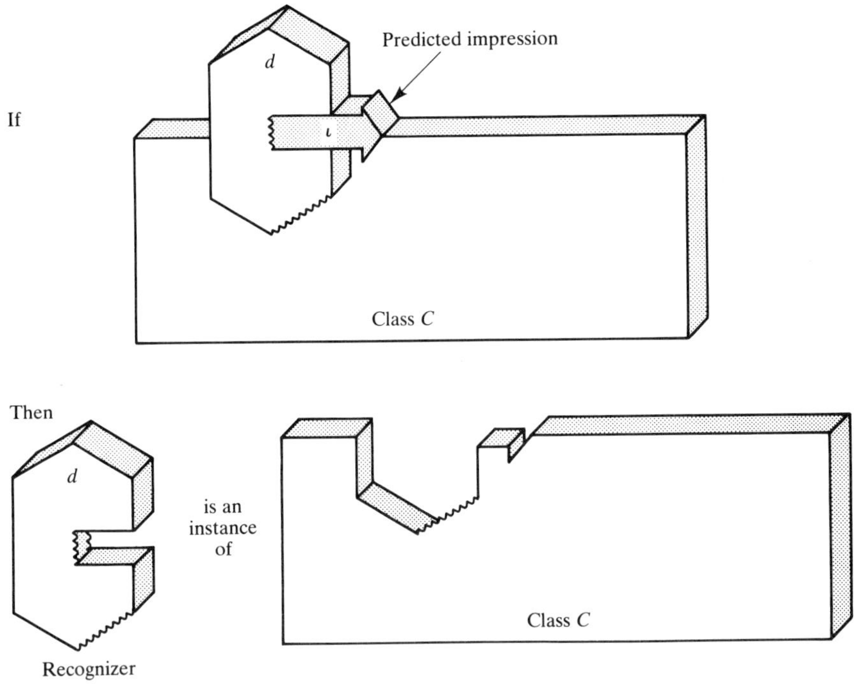

Figure 1.5 Recognizers are instances of classes.

A class may also change without its population changing. Fire hydrants in a given municipality are usually of fairly uniform appearance. However, turn of the century fire hydrants, which still survive in many cities, look quite different. Suppose that Frank reads a description of these old fire hydrants. Without ever seeing an old fire hydrant, Frank may alter his conceptual mechanism for recognizing a fire hydrant to fit the new information. The set of fire hydrants Frank has seen does not change. However, there is now a new class, « Fire Hydrant′ », with the same population as « Fire Hydrant », but with a different acceptance mechanism.

Instances May Be Predicted by Embracings

Just as with embracings of binding sites, we may be able to deduce that a class would accept an image given that another class accepts the image. We say that a class C *embraces* a class B if, for any image d that B accepts, it is predicted that C must accept d. We do not require that an image be examined by the class C, that is, we do not require an actual performance to occur. Embracings are a means of predicting acceptance, as they are with binding sites. The statement that C embraces B will be written

$$B \subseteq C$$

Notice that the word "must" is used in the definition of an embracing. This word indicates that an embracing is concerned with the mechanisms of the classes (how the classes are defined) and not with their populations (what the classes have accepted).

An Embracing Is Different from an Inclusion of Populations

An embracing of classes is the analog of an "is a" relationship in semantic data models (Tsichritzis and Lochovsky 1982) or an "inheritance" structure in object-oriented systems (Goldberg 1984). That is, the following are embracings:

« any car is also a vehicle » (« Vehicle » embraces « Car »)

« any branch manager is also an employee »

(« Employee » embraces « Branch Manager »)

If a class C embraces a class B, every instance of B is an instance of C. If the population of C includes the population of B, we say that *C appears to embrace B*. A class may appear to embrace another class, yet not embrace it. For example, imagine that the class « Car », the conceptual mechanism for defining a car, does not consider the presence or absence of safety belts in determining whether or not a given image is a car. It may be, however, that all cars that an observer has seen do have safety belts. The class of images with safety belts then appears to embrace the class of cars. Yet, the class « _____ has a safety belt » does not embrace the class « Car », because it is possible for a car not to have a safety belt.

Embracings Apply to Recognizers

We may imagine embracings of recognizers in the same way that we imagine embracings of classes. Thus, we may say that the recognizer « the Washington Monument » embraces the recognizer « the Washington Monument on a Spring day » just as we say that the class « Monument » embraces the class « Stone Monument ». Embracing of recognizers therefore describes the phenomenon of "finer" recognizers discussed in Section 1.3: A recognizer d is *finer* than a recognizer e if e embraces d.

Embracings of recognizers are not perfectly analogous to embracings of classes. Recognizers do not accept images, but impressions, and impressions are subject to uncertainty. We say that a recognizer e *embraces* a recognizer d if any impression that is accepted by d would have been accepted by e, had it been examined by e. The transitory nature of impressions makes it impossible to view this predicted acceptability by e as creating an image of e. To form an image requires an actual acceptance of an impression.

We write the statement that a recognizer e embraces a recognizer d as

$$d \subseteq e$$

The uncertainty principle of impressions makes it impossible to refute an embracing of recognizers by direct appeal to impressions. We can not, for example, exhibit an impression that is accepted by one recognizer but rejected by another, since we can not be certain that the impression that we accepted is the same as the impression that was rejected. We can, however, refute an embracing by appealing to logic, by showing, for example, that there is a recognizer c embraced in d but not in e. This would show that e does not embrace d.

Equivalence Is Defined by Embracings

If a class C embraces a class B, and B embraces C, then B and C are *equivalent*. Two equivalent classes must have the same instances. If the instances of one class change, the instances of an equivalent class change in parallel. Similarly, if a recognizer d embraces a recognizer e, and e embraces d, then d and e are *equivalent*. Two equivalent recognizers must accept the same impressions. We write the statement that the class B is equivalent to the class C as

$$B \equiv C$$

and the statement that the recognizer d is equivalent to the recognizer e as

$$d \equiv e$$

Contentual Classes Follow the Embracings of Their Instances

Suppose that C is a contentual class and that C accepts a manifestation i of a recognizer d. Let a recognizer e embrace d. Then e would accept the impression that is found in i. Since C examines only the impression in i, e is an instance of C. Therefore, we conclude:

> If C is a contentual class, d is an instance of C, and e embraces d, then e is an instance of C.

Conclusion

A *class* is a conceptual mechanism that examines images, accepting or rejecting them. A class is therefore analogous to a binding site, which is a physical process that examines symbols. This definition of a class does not appeal to linguistic concepts such as "nouns" or "predicates," and can therefore be applied where language is an uncertain guide.

An *instance* of a class is a recognizer for which there is a manifestation (an image) that the class accepts. A mathematical set is a class, but a class need not be a set. The members of a set can not change, but the instances of a class, in general, can change without the class changing.

An *embracing* of classes is a statement that any instance of one class must be an instance of another. Embracings may be applied to recognizers as well as to classes. The concepts of *class, instance,* and *embracing* will be particularly fundamental to the discussions that follow.

1.6 PLANS

A Class Is Formed According to a Plan

A class is similar to an executable computer program, one that accepts certain symbols as input while rejecting others. Thus, a class, like a computer program, may be performed repeatedly, and the images examined by a class are akin to the inputs of the program. The method by which an executable program acts on its inputs is defined by writing the program in a computer language. Each such written or *lexical* program is a collection of symbols that may be converted unambiguously to executable form by a compiler. In the same way, we may imagine that a class is defined by a *plan* which establishes what the class will accept and what it will reject. The class stands to its plan in the same way as an executable program stands to its lexical representation.

The behavior of plans must be deduced indirectly, because it is difficult to contemplate a plan in the same way that we can contemplate a recognizer or a class. Nevertheless, we will find many aspects of thought that are best explained by referring to plans. We will assume that a class is formed from a plan by a mental faculty that we call a *conceptual factory*. We imagine that all classes are formed from plans by the conceptual factory (so that no class arises without a plan). The class formed from a plan s will be called the *realization* of s, and will be written "Яs". Since we will often have a ready name for the class that is formed from a plan, we will also use a shorthand notation "λC" for a plan whose realization is the class C. We do not assume, however, that we may always form a plan from a class; that is, we do not assume that we can run the conceptual factory in reverse. The symbol "λ", therefore, does not represent an operation, but is only a conventional way of representing plans.

A Recognizer Is Formed According to a Plan

We assume that recognizers are formed by the conceptual factory just as classes are. That is, certain plans cause the conceptual factory to form recognizers rather than classes. The plan contains within itself the information that it is a plan for a recognizer rather than a class. For example, suppose that we are considering a particular matched pen and pencil set, and that we have imagined a recognizer b that recognizes the pen and a recognizer c that recognizes the pencil. We might then imagine a new recognizer d that recognizes either the pen or the pencil. We can think of d as « one of the members of the matched set ». If we see either the pen or the pencil from a distance, we may not be able to tell whether it is the pen or the pencil. We would say then that we see a manifestation of d, since we believe that it is one of the items in the matched set, but we would not see a manifestation of b or of c, because we do not know which member it is.

This new recognizer d is the *union* of the two recognizers b and c, and will be discussed further when we come to logic (Section 2.5). We notice here that the formation of d from b and c is a regular process that does not depend upon the individual characteristics of b and c: we can form the union of any two recognizers in the same way. That is, the plan of the recognizer d is formed from the two plans λb and λc by combining them in a standard way that indicates « union » to the conceptual factory.

The concept of a plan gives an approach to understanding the biological basis of thought. If we assume that a conceptual factory is genetically inherited in some way, then we can assume that all classes and recognizers are formed from plans in the developing mind. Plans may be intercombined to form new plans, as in the formation of a union recognizer. We may imagine, then, that a small number of *bootstrap plans* are inherited. Whatever innate classes and recognizers there may be are formed from the bootstrap plans by repeated operation of the conceptual factory.

A Class Has a Handle That Is a Recognizer

We will also find it valuable to assume that we may form a recognizer to stand for a class in formulas. We will assume that most classes C have a *handle*, which we write "νC", that is a recognizer. The handle provides a way to treat classes as instances of classes. For example, suppose we wanted to form the class P of classes that have at least one instance. We can not say precisely that a *class* C is an instance of P, because an instance must be a recognizer, not a class. We therefore say that the *handle* νC is an instance of P instead.

We will assume that all classes in ordinary applications such as data bases have handles. We will leave open the possibility, however, that there may be classes that have no handle. A class with no handle can not appear as an instance of any class.

A Recognizer May Be Converted to a Class by Granulation

A class is very similar to a recognizer: each is a conceptual mechanism that examines impressions. The primary difference is that a recognizer examines an impression directly, whereas a class examines an impression compounded with a recognizer (an image). We will see that it is possible to convert a class into a recognizer, and a recognizer into a class, by changing the method used for examination. In this way, we will be able to link the logic of classes with the logic of recognizers. This will give us new insight into the variety of phenomena presented by recognizers, and will clarify the nature of contentual classes.

Consider, for example, the recognizer « the Washington Monument », which accepts impressions of the Washington Monument. Call this recognizer w. Suppose that we were to establish new recognizers that recognize views of the Washington Monument, such as « the Washington Monument as seen from the North », « the Washington Monument as seen from above », and so on. We might then form the class W_1 of these views, and ask how this class is related to the recognizer w.

Alternatively, suppose that we were to establish new recognizers that recognize impressions of the Washington Monument set in time, such as « the Washington Monument in 1915 », « the Washington Monument in 1965 », and so on. Again, we might form the class W_2 of these new recognizers, and ask how this class is related to w.

In either W_1 or W_2, the conceptual mechanism for determining whether or not an *impression* is a manifestation of the Washington Monument does not change. That is, an impression ι is a manifestation of the Washington Monument if and only if ι is accepted by w. This same impression may also be accepted by one or more of the new recognizers. For example, an impression of the Washington Monument seen from the North in 1965 is accepted by both « the Washington Monument as seen from the North » and « the Washington Monument in 1965 ». The impression ι participates in two different images, because of the two different recognizers, but both images are images of the Washington Monument because, in both cases, the impression is accepted by the recognizer w.

Therefore, the class of *images* of the Washington Monument is just the class of recognizers that accept *impressions* of w. This class is contentual, because it considers only the impressions of the images that it accepts. The class of recognizers that accept impressions accepted by w is called the *granulation* of w and is written "Γw". Figure 1.6 illustrates the granulation.

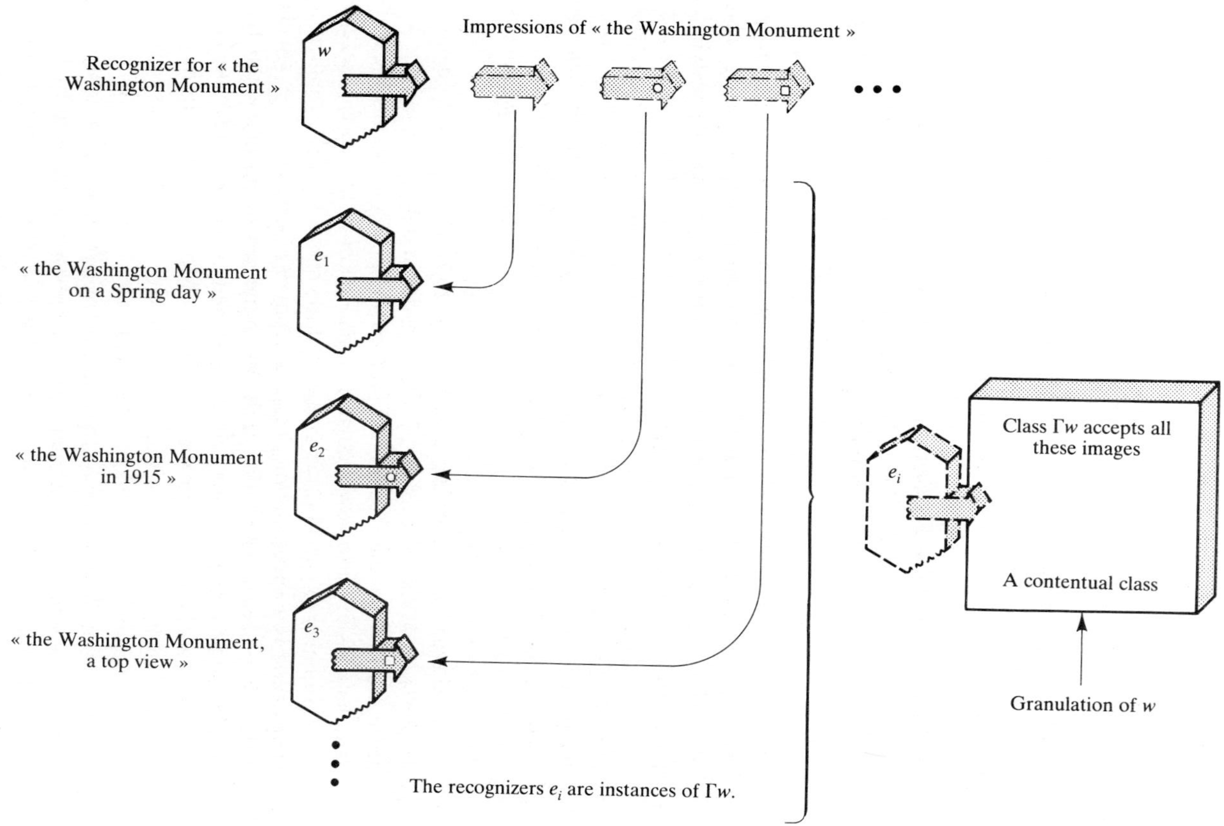

Figure 1.6 The granulation of a recognizer.

Both W_1 and W_2 are embraced in Γw. They are not equivalent to Γw because each restricts the kinds of recognizers that are accepted, one accepting only views, the other accepting only temporal constructions. The granulation accepts both kinds of recognizers, as well as any other means of organizing the impressions of w. Notice that Γw also accepts images whose recognizers accept impressions other than the Washington Monument. For example, the recognizer that accepts all impressions of stone monuments is an instance of Γw.

A Class May Be Converted to a Recognizer by Melding

Consider, conversely, a class such as the class of marbles. We seek to convert this class to a recognizer. To begin, we may imagine several impressions that are each a « marble » but are manifestations of different images. For example, they may be impressions of physically distinguishable marbles, with different colors and patterns. We may imagine recognizers that distinguish colors, patterns, and the like, so that each impression is accepted by a different recognizer, hence participates in a different image.

Now consider a conceptual mechanism that accepts any impression of any « marble » (that is, that accepts any impression ι that would be accepted by the class « Marble » if ι were compounded with some recognizer). This conceptual mechanism is a recognizer that will be called the *melding* of the class « Marble », and will be written "μ(Marble)". All impressions of marbles are treated by the melding as manifestations of a single image that we might write as « a marble ». Figure 1.7 illustrates the melding.

The melding of a class is the direct analog of Plato's forms. For example, the form « beauty » may be viewed as the melding of the class « _____ Is Beautiful » (Plato 380B.C.a). This connection is explored further in Section 1.9.

Melding and Granulation Are Not Perfect Inverses

Granulations and meldings interact with embracings to establish a logic of recognizers. We begin the study of this logic below; it will be developed further in Chapter 2.

Consider the melding of the granulation of a recognizer e, $\mu\Gamma e$. This is a recognizer that accepts any impression that is incorporated in an image accepted by Γe. The class Γe is contentual, and accepts any image that incorporates an impression accepted by e. The recognizer $\mu\Gamma e$ therefore accepts an impression if and only if the impression is accepted by e, so e and $\mu\Gamma e$ are equivalent:

$$\mu\Gamma e \equiv e$$

Now consider the granulation of the melding of a class B, $\Gamma\mu B$. This is a class that accepts any image that incorporates an impression accepted by μB. The recognizer μB accepts any impression incorporated in an image that is accepted by B. The class $\Gamma\mu B$ therefore accepts any image that incorporates an impression that is incorporated in an image accepted by B. The operation « $\Gamma\mu$ » thus introduces a new criterion not in the definition of B: " . . . incorporates an impression that is incorporated in an image." In general, this additional criterion makes $\Gamma\mu B$ different from B.

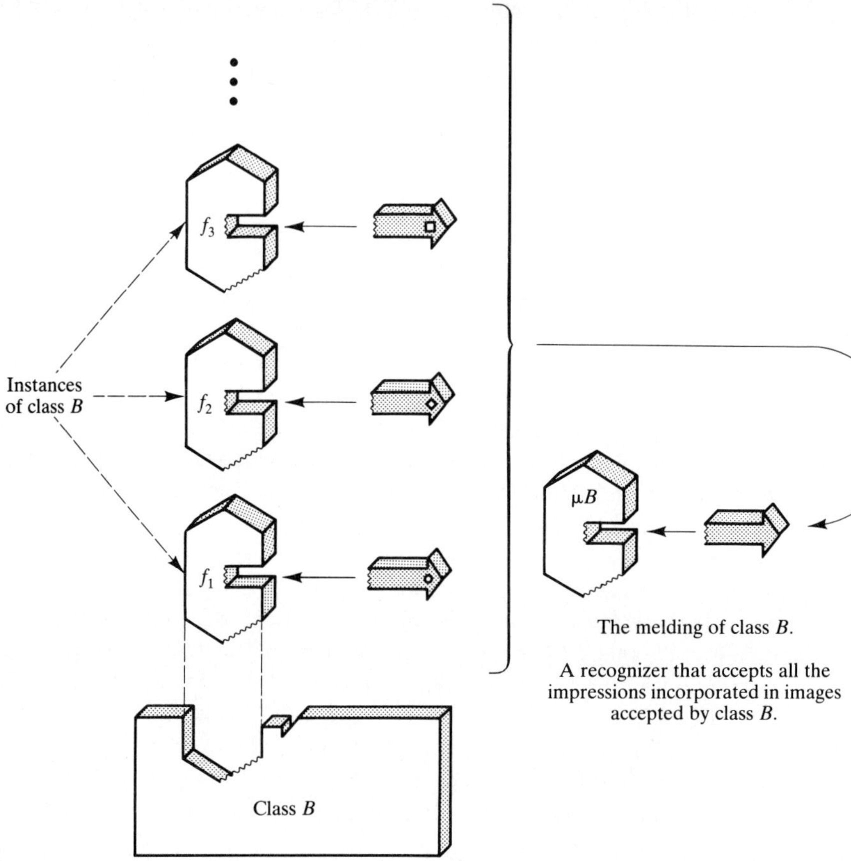

Figure 1.7 The melding of a class.

If an image i is accepted by B, then the impression incorporated in i is accepted by μB. Therefore, i is accepted by $\Gamma\mu B$. Thus, $\Gamma\mu B$ always embraces B:

$$B \subseteq \Gamma\mu B$$

The difference between the two classes arises if B is not contentual, that is, if B examines recognizers as well as impressions. When the melding of B is formed, any distinctions about recognizers are lost—μB, being a recognizer, examines only impressions. When μB is granulated, the result is a contentual class, which does not restrict images because of their recognizers. The class $\Gamma\mu B$ is therefore equivalent to B only if B is contentual:

$$\text{If } B \text{ is contentual, then } B \equiv \Gamma\mu B$$

Indeed, this formula may be used as a definition of the term *contentual*.

Embracings of Granulations and Meldings

If a class C embraces a class B, then any image accepted by B must be accepted by C. If an impression ι is accepted by the melding μB, then there must be some recognizer d such that d compounded with ι is accepted by B. Since C embraces B, the image of d compounded with ι must be accepted by C. Therefore, the impression ι must be accepted by the melding μC:

$$\text{If } B \subseteq C \text{ then } \mu B \subseteq \mu C$$

If a recognizer e embraces a recognizer d, then any impression accepted by d must be accepted by e. An image i is accepted by the granulation Γd if and only if the impression incorporated in i is accepted by d. This impression must be accepted by e because e embraces d. The image i must therefore be accepted by Γe:

$$\text{If } d \subseteq e \text{ then } \Gamma d \subseteq \Gamma e$$

In contrast, an embracing of the meldings of two classes does not generally imply an embracing of the two classes. The difficulty arises if either class is not contentual. All we may conclude from an embracing of meldings is that the two classes accept images that incorporate the same impressions. The two classes may, however, accept images that are manifestations of different recognizers, in which case there is no embracing. If the two classes are contentual, the difficulties are eliminated:

$$\text{If } B \text{ and } C \text{ are contentual and } \mu B \subseteq \mu C, \text{ then } B \subseteq C$$

Instancehood Is Comparable to Overlap of Recognizers

We say that two recognizers *overlap* if there is an impression that is predicted to be accepted by both recognizers. Suppose that the recognizer e is an instance of the class B. There is then an impression that is accepted both by e and, compounded with d to form an image, by B. This impression is therefore accepted both by e and by μB:

$$\text{If } e \text{ is an instance of } B, \text{ then } e \text{ and } \mu B \text{ overlap}$$

Suppose that the class B is contentual. If a recognizer e overlaps the melding of B, then there is an impression that is accepted by both e and μB. The image formed by e accepting this impression will then be accepted by B, so e is an instance of B:

$$\text{If } B \text{ is contentual and } e \text{ overlaps } \mu B, \text{ then } e \text{ is an instance of } B$$

In particular, the granulation of any recognizer is a contentual class. Therefore,

$$d \text{ and } e \text{ overlap if and only if } e \text{ is an instance of } \Gamma d$$

Conclusion

We have suggested that every class is formed in thought from a *plan*. A plan is akin to a blueprint for a conceptual mechanism; it is not the conceptual mechanism itself, just as a blueprint for a building is not the building. Yet the plan, like a blueprint, contains all the information necessary to form the class. A plan is transformed into a class by a mental faculty called the *conceptual factory*.

We have also assumed that most classes C are associated with a recognizer νC called the *handle* of the class. The handle is used in formulas that involve "sets of sets" in symbolic logic. Rather than saying that a set B is a member of a set C, we say that the handle νB of the class B is an instance of the class C. This additional apparatus enables us to maintain that all instances are recognizers.

Classes and recognizers may be interconverted in another way: for any recognizer *d*, there is a class called the *granulation* of *d* that accepts any image that incorporates an impression that would be accepted by *d* (recall that an image is a recognizer compounded with an impression). Conversely, for any class *C*, there is a recognizer called the *melding* of *C* that accepts any impression that is incorporated in an image accepted by *C*.

1.7 PHYSICAL TRANSFORMATION OF SYMBOLS

An Engine Is a Process That Operates on Things

We seek to extend the results about binding sites to more general processes that may accept many different symbols in a performance (a binding site may accept only one symbol during any performance). We call these more general processes *engines*. An engine has zero or more *input sites*, which are means of accepting things. An engine also has zero or more *output sites*, which are means of presenting things that may have been formed by the engine during the course of a performance. For example, a computer program executing on a computer is an engine: the storage locations or other data capturing devices by which symbols are presented to the program are input sites, and the storage locations or other data presentation devices by which the results of the program are preserved are the output sites. An assembly line is also an engine: the methods for receiving materials into the line are input sites, and the means of delivery of the assembled item from the line is an output site.

Input Sites and Output Sites Are Binding Sites

The input sites and output sites of an engine are binding sites. Thus, any collection of things presented to an input site will be accepted or rejected as a whole, and one performance of the engine can include at most one performance of each input site (that is, if two inputs are required, then two input sites must be used). An input site may reject a thing if it is not acceptable to the engine. For example, a computer program may contain certain preedits, such as requiring that one of the inputs be an integer. These preedits may be considered to be properties of the input site. Any symbol that is presented to the input site and is not an integer will be rejected. Similarly, an assembly line may require certain physical characteristics of each component. Any thing that is presented that does not meet these characteristics is rejected by the input site (each component of the assembly must therefore be examined by a different input site).

An output site is treated as a binding site as follows: we view the appearance of a thing *x* at the output site *Y* as *Y accepting x*. The output site *Y* is then a binding site that only accepts *x*. Notice that an output site is usually *not* a permanent binding site, because what it accepts usually depends upon what was accepted by the input sites during the performance.

This method of treating input and output sites as binding sites is most effective when we confine our attention to engines that operate on symbols (rather than things in general). We may then dispense with the distinction between input sites and output sites, as follows. Since each occupant of either an input site or an output site is a symbol, it is associated with a detector. Detectors are formative, so it is easy to create a thing that is the same symbol as each occupant. Imagine that an oversight process records every symbol input to and output from the engine during the performance. Once the performance is complete, this oversight process may form a single picture that shows all the symbols simultaneously, indicating what symbol was accepted or rejected by what site. This single picture of the operating of an engine is called the *symphonic view* of the performance, as if all the sites acted simultaneously. We could not construct a symphonic view if things were consumed during the course of a performance, as occurs in an assembly line, so it is the formative nature of detectors that permits this simplification.

We may use engines to define a physical set. Thus, we define a *set of detectors* to be an engine where each site acts independently as a detector, but where the engine only accepts during a performance if each site accepts some thing. A *set of symbols* is then the total collection of material accepted by a set of detectors. We will apply the same notation as modern set theory for describing sets: "$t \in S$" for "t is a member of S," "$S = T$" for "S equals T," and "$S \subset T$" for "T includes S."

Our interest in engines is somewhat limited, since we are concerned with the results of performances rather than the intricacies of constructing engines or the events that can occur during performances. Thus, we will limit ourselves to engines that operate on symbols, so we may adopt the symphonic view of performances. An engine may then be viewed as a collection of binding sites that act in concert, each binding site rendering an outcome simultaneously. Moreover, we are more concerned with acceptance of symbols than with rejection, so we may ignore the situations in which any of the binding sites reject during a performance. Thus, we define *acceptance* by an engine to be a performance in which all the binding sites that are presented a thing accept what is presented. If any of the binding sites reject, we say that the engine *rejects*. Notice that we do not require that every binding site be presented a thing in order for there to be a performance of the engine. There is a performance if a thing is presented to any of the binding sites.

Engines Are Related by Embracings

The number of binding sites of an engine will be called the *degree* of the engine. A binding site is an engine of degree one. Consider two engines R and S of the same degree. If we may predict that any acceptance of symbols by each binding site of R would imply a parallel acceptance of the same symbols by the binding sites of S, then we say that the engine S *embraces* the engine R. Notice that it is necessary to match the binding sites of R to the binding sites of S in order to specify an embracing. For example, suppose that R and S are both of degree two, that R contains the binding sites B_1 and B_2, and that S contains the binding sites C_1 and C_2. Matching B_1 to C_1 and B_2 to C_2, saying that S embraces R is saying that if B_1 accepts a thing t and B_2 accepts a thing u, then C_1 must accept t and C_2 must accept u. However, matching B_1 to C_2 and B_2 to C_1, saying that S embraces R is saying that if B_1 accepts t and B_2 accepts u, then C_2, not C_1, accepts t, and C_1, not C_2, accepts u.

Rather than describe a means of matching sites each time we declare an embracing, we will assume that each engine carries a standard order to its sites. Thus, the engine R with sites ordered "B_1 then B_2" is a different engine from the engine R ordered "B_2 then B_1." These two engines are called *permutations* of each other, since they differ only in how the sites are ordered. When we say that an engine S embraces an engine R, then, we mean that the first site of R is matched to the first site of S, the second site of R to the second site of S, and so on. So, two permutations of an engine normally do not embrace each other. When an engine S embraces an engine R and R embraces S, we say that R and S are *equivalent* engines.

Symbols May Be Arranged in Conglomerations

We can imagine an ordered pair (t, u) to be a physical conglomeration of a symbol t, a symbol u, and a *connector* that attaches t to u and distinguishes the first from the second element of the pair. We can construct a detector that recognizes the pair (t, u) by detecting the connector, detecting the first element of the pair using a detector equivalent to the detector that detects t, and detecting the second element of the pair using a detector equivalent to the detector that detects u.

We need not rest with connectors that can attach two symbols to each other. We can indeed imagine, for any positive integer n, a connector that can attach n symbols together, each symbol being identified as occupying a different *position*. Such a connector may be visualized as a golf ball with every dimple numbered, and every dimple capable of attaching to a symbol.

Any combination of a connector and attached symbols will be called a *conglomeration*. Each symbol bound to the connector will be called a *constituent*, or precisely, an *external constituent* of the conglomeration. A conglomeration is itself a symbol, since we can form a detector to detect a conglomeration in the same way that we formed a detector to detect a pair. We may form new conglomerations by connecting conglomerations together. When all connectors are removed from a conglomeration, each symbol that remains is called an *ultimate constituent* of the conglomeration.

We may write conglomerations using a similar notation to that used for mathematical sequences. Recalling the golf ball analogy, we may imagine without loss of generality that the various dimples are sequentially numbered. Writing down the connected symbols in the sequence of the dimples will therefore suffice to describe the conglomeration. Notice, however, that some dimples may be connected to no symbols. We may therefore have unoccupied positions in the sequences. Since the constituents of a conglomeration may themselves be conglomerations, we may have sequences within sequences as well. The following examples, therefore, are all valid, and different, conglomerations:

$$(x, y, z)$$
$$(y, x, z)$$
$$((x, y), z)$$
$$(x, (y, z))$$
$$(x, (y, \ , \ ), z)$$
$$((\ , \ ), (x), \ , y, (z))$$
$$(x, y, z, y)$$

A *sequence* is a conglomeration in which every position is occupied. Thus "(a, b, c)" is a sequence with constituents "a", "b", and "c", and "$((a), (b, c))$" is a sequence with constituents "(a)" and "(b, c)". The conglomeration "$(a, \ , b, c)$" is not a sequence because the second position is unoccupied.

Conglomerations are most valuable as a means of describing the outcome of a performance of an engine. The symphonic view, we recall, is formed by indicating which symbols are presented to which binding sites, and whether the symbols are accepted or rejected. Since we assume that the binding sites are ordered, we may represent a performance as a conglomeration by placing each symbol presented to each site in a position corresponding to the order position of the site. Since some of the sites may be presented with no symbols, there may be unoccupied positions in the conglomeration. Since we consider the engine to have rejected whenever any of the sites reject, a performance is completely described by giving such a conglomeration and indicating whether the conglomeration as a whole was accepted or rejected.

Conglomerations Are Formed by Connecting Engines

A conglomeration is formed from its constituents by a *connecting engine*, which accepts the constituents as inputs and produces the conglomeration as an output. Figure 1.8 illustrates a connecting engine.

The assumption that conglomerations may be formed is an assumption of an ability to perform a physical construction. As with any such construction that we assume, we state the assumptions in postulates:

(P4) It is possible to form a connecting engine that forms a conglomeration from any arbitrarily large collection of symbols.

(P5) Any conglomeration of symbols is a symbol.

(P6) Two conglomerations t and u are the same symbol if and only if the constituent of t in each position i is the same symbol as the constituent of u in the position i.

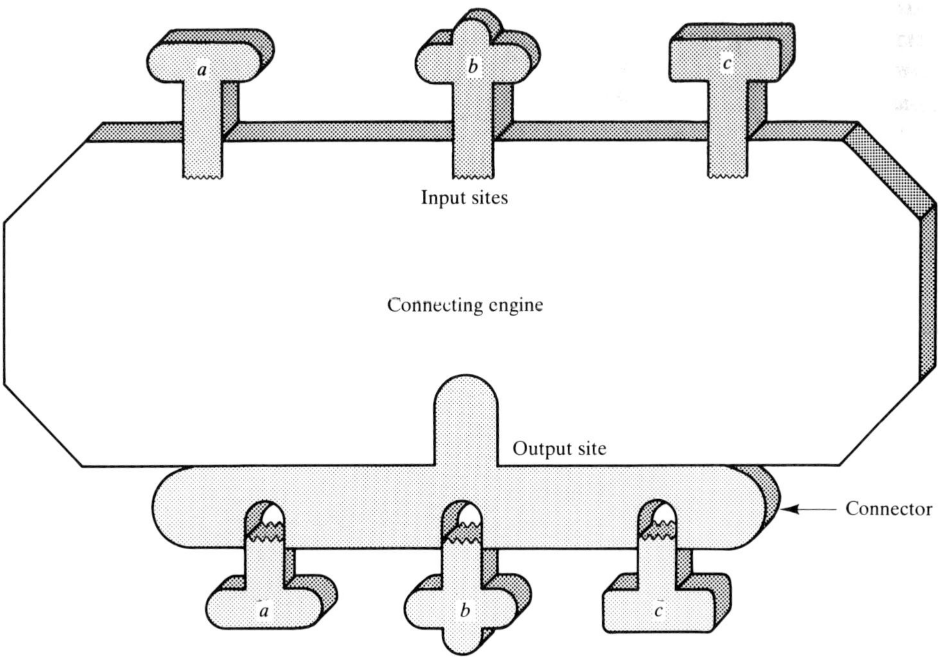

Figure 1.8 A connecting engine.

Constituents Are Determined by a Separating Engine

Given a conglomeration, we require an engine that strips away the connector and yields the external constituents. Such an engine is called a *separating engine*. It differs from a connecting engine only in that the conglomeration is accepted by the input site rather than the output site, and that the constituents are accepted by output sites rather than by input sites. In the symphonic view, a performance of a separating engine and a performance of a connecting engine look alike.

For conglomerations to be useful, the constituents separated from a conglomeration must be the same symbols in the same positions that were input to a connecting engine when the conglomeration was formed. Conversely, the conglomeration formed by separating a conglomeration into its constituents, then reconnecting them in the same positions, must be the same symbol as the initial conglomeration. That is, the separating engine and the connecting engine must be permutations of each other.

When an engine R has a permutation in which the input sites are changed to output sites, and the output sites to input sites, we say that R is *reversible*. We have therefore assumed another postulate:

(P7) Any connecting engine is reversible.

We use the phrase "*any* connecting engine" in this postulate because we mean it to be a criterion that any engine must satisfy in order to be considered to be a connecting engine. There are many possible varieties of connecting engines, and it is important for the postulates to be general enough to describe all of them.

Conclusion

An *engine* is a physical process that may accept many symbols in one performance. An engine can only accept some finite maximum number of symbols in any performance. This maximum number is the *degree* of the engine. A binding site is a special case of an engine, specifically, a binding site is an engine of degree one.

We assume that the *sites* where an engine may accept symbols are ordered in a sequence. Different orderings give different engines. An engine F embraces another engine E if any things accepted by E must be accepted by F if each thing is presented to the same sequence number site of F as it is presented to E.

Symbols may be combined to form new symbols called *conglomerations*. Examples of conglomerations include sequences, sequences of sequences, and the like. We have shown how conglomerations of symbols may be defined using engines, and have stated in postulates the requirements for forming such engines.

1.8 MENTAL ASSOCIATIONS

In this section, we generalize classes, which accept one image, to associations, which may accept many images. This generalization is often treated hastily in works on logic by forming a class of sequences. We will see that the additional concepts involved in forming associations merit greater attention.

A Correspondence Is Analogous to an Engine

A conceptual mechanism that determines when two images are associated must examine both images, and can be viewed as accepting both images if they are associated and rejecting both if they are not. Such a conceptual mechanism will be called a *correspondence*, and the two mechanisms that accommodate images will be called *positions*. The word ''position'' is also used in describing conglomerations, but the two meanings should not be confused because conglomerations are things, whereas correspondences are ideas.

A correspondence is often written as a transitive verb, such as « Purchases » or « Carries ». We will write correspondences with initial capital letters, as we write classes. The two images in this representation are the subject and object of the verb. Thus, an image « *b* » is associated with an image « *c* » by the correspondence « Carries » if « *b* carries *c* ». Notice that the position occupied by each image is significant—the idea « *b* carries *c* » is different from the idea « *c* carries *b* ». Intransitive verbs like « Snores » should not be used as correspondence names, because an intransitive verb defines a class: « _____ Snores », that is, « _____ Is A Snorer ».

A correspondence accepts exactly one image in each of the two positions. Thus, for example, a performance could test whether the image « Sally » carries the image « the yellow basket ». The image « Sally » alone, or the image « the yellow basket » alone, would not be accepted.

A correspondence is thus analogous to an engine of degree two, the two positions in which images are placed being analogous to the two binding sites of the engine. As with engines, we assume that the positions in a correspondence are given a fixed order. The two ideas « *b* carries *c* » and « *c* carries *b* » are distinguished by the symbols ''①'' and ''②'', called *position designators*. For example, we write

« ① Carries ② »

This correspondence accepts the image « Sally » in position ① together with « the yellow basket » in position ②, but does not accept « the yellow basket » in position ① together with « Sally » in position ②.

The correspondence

« ② Carries ① »

operates exactly oppositely, accepting images in position ① when they are accepted above in position ②, and images in position ② when they are accepted above in position ①.

The two correspondences « ① Carries ② » and « ② Carries ① » are called *converses*, and are in general different correspondences. The placement of ① and ② is referred to as the *orientation* of the correspondence. The converse correspondence « ② Carries ① » will often be written as

« ① Carries* ② »

The correspondence « Carries* » may also be written as the passive « Is Carried By ».

A Correspondence Is a Conceptual Mechanism

A *correspondence* is a conceptual mechanism that is performed as follows:

(i) A performance includes a presentation of an image to position ① and an image to position ② of the correspondence.

(ii) A performance may include an examination of the images that are presented.

(iii) If there is no examination, the performance is complete.

(iv) If the images are examined, exactly one outcome is rendered for the performance, acceptance if both positions accept or rejection if either position rejects (actually true only for constructive associations, other varieties will be discussed in the development of logic).

A Correspondence Attaches Recognizers

An acceptance by a correspondence is illustrated in Figure 1.9. When the first position of a correspondence G accepts a manifestation of a recognizer b, and the second position accepts a manifestation of a recognizer c, we say that G *attaches* b *to* c.

The combination of a correspondence G with two images accepted by G is called an *attachment manifestation*. Figure 1.9 illustrates an attachment manifestation. Consider a conceptual mechanism M that accepts any attachment manifestation that incorporates the correspondence G and the recognizers b and c, as shown in Figure 1.9. The ideas accepted by M differ only in the impressions that fill the slots of ι and κ in Figure 1.9, so M is akin to a recognizer, and an attachment manifestation is akin to an image that is a manifestation of

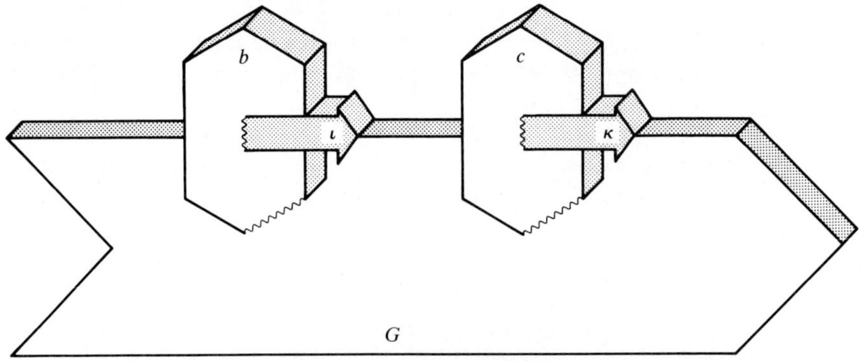

Figure 1.9 Correspondence G attaches the recognizer b to the recognizer c.

M. We will assume that *M* is a recognizer, and that an attachment manifestation is an image. This assumption is called the *assembly image principle*.

The recognizer *M* is called an *attachment*, and is written "$G(b, c)$". The recognizer *b* is called the *source* of the attachment, and the recognizer *c* is called the *destination* of the attachment. The correspondence *G* is said to *control* the attachment. An attachment is usually represented in language using an "-ing" form of a verb. For example, the conceptual mechanism that accepts any impression of « Sally carrying the yellow basket » is an attachment controlled by « Carries » of the recognizer « Sally » with the recognizer « the yellow basket ». An attachment is often represented in computerized data bases by a record or "tuple" that contains two fields. Thus, the attachment « Carries (Sally, the yellow basket) » might be represented by a record "(Sally, the yellow basket)" in the "Carries" file.

We assume that any correspondence *G* has a *plan* λG from which it is formed by realization. We also assume that any correspondence *G* has a *handle* νG, which is a recognizer. Since a correspondence attaches two images, and each image contains an impression, a correspondence may examine two impressions. Since a melding only examines one impression, each position of a correspondence has a melding.

Correspondences Are More Diverse than Transitive Verbs

A correspondence may be formed by replacing any two phrases in a sentence by the position designators ① and ②, not solely by replacing the subject and object. For example, we have the correspondence

« Sally ① the yellow ② »

which accepts « carries » (precisely, the handle of the correspondence « Carries ») in position ① and « basket » in position ②.

Although the correspondences in data base design may usually be expressed by replacing parts of complete sentences with position designators, other forms of correspondences are possible. For example, consider the following correspondence that accepts any images such that the resulting phrase is a valid verb phrase according to English syntax:

« ① Lucy for ② »

The images « asks » and « peanuts » would be accepted by this correspondence, because the phrase « asks Lucy for peanuts » is a valid verb phrase, even though it is not a complete sentence. The images « inquires » and « peanuts » would not be accepted, however, because « inquires Lucy for peanuts » is not a valid verb phrase. We may apply correspondences in this way to study the different characteristics of similar words such as « asks » and « inquires », as recognized by Chomsky (1965).

A Correspondence Is Not a Set

A correspondence is the analog of a binary relation in symbolic logic or in the relational data model. In symbolic logic, a binary relation is defined as a set of pairs, each pair being the analog of an attachment (Whitehead and Russell 1927, Zuckerman 1974). Leaving aside the question of whether an attachment is properly viewed as a pair, it is nonetheless clear that a correspondence may be different from the set of its attachments. Each new conception of an act of carrying will change the set of attachments of « Carries », for example, without changing the correspondence (that is, the mechanism that establishes what qualifies as carrying). The mathematical definition of a relation is therefore inadequate for an accurate characterization of data, since it does not distinguish between a correspondence and a set.

Correspondences May Be Interrelated by Embracings

Given two correspondences F and G, it may be possible to predict attachments of G from attachments of F. We say that a correspondence G *embraces* a correspondence F if, for any images i and j such that F accepts i in position ① and j in position ②, it is predicted that G must accept i in position ① and j in position ②. Notice that an embracing preserves orientation — the correspondence « ① Transports ② » embraces the correspondence « ① Carries ② », but not the correspondence « ② Carries ① ». We write the statement that G embraces F as

$$F \subseteq G$$

If a correspondence G embraces a correspondence F, and F embraces G, we say that F and G are *equivalent*, and write

$$F \equiv G$$

Correspondences May Be Generalized to Associations

A correspondence is a conceptual mechanism with two positions, a class is a conceptual mechanism with one. We may generalize correspondences to conceptual mechanisms with many positions, which are called *associations*. The number of *positions* of an association is called the *degree* of the association. A class is an association of degree one, and a correspondence is an association of degree two.

An *association of degree r* is a conceptual mechanism that is performed as follows:

- **(i)** A performance includes a presentation of images to each of the positions ① to r of the association.
- **(ii)** A performance may include an examination of the images that are presented.
- **(iii)** If there is no examination, the performance is complete.
- **(iv)** If the images are examined, exactly one outcome is rendered for the performance, acceptance if all the positions accept or rejection if any position rejects (actually true only for constructive associations, other varieties will be discussed in the development of logic).

An association of degree three will be called a *trio*, and an association of degree four will be called a *quartet*.

Associations are often represented by replacing r phrases in a complete sentence by position designators, as in the association of degree four:

« ① gives ② a ③ of mashed ④ »

This association accepts the images « Joan » in position ①, « Frank » in position ②, « third helping » in position ③, and « potatoes » in position ④.

The combination of an association R of degree r with r images that R accepts is called an *assembly manifestation*. The conceptual mechanism that accepts an assembly manifestation is called an *assembly*, and is assumed to be a recognizer. This is the general form of the assembly image principle, which applies to associations of all degrees. The association R is said to *control* its assemblies. An attachment is an assembly controlled by a correspondence. Notice that since every position in an assembly is filled, an assembly is an association of degree zero. Figure 1.10 illustrates an assembly.

An association has an orientation that is represented by the sequence of position designators. Changing the order results in a new association called a *permutation*. The only permutation of a correspondence is its converse. Associations of higher degree have more complicated permutations.

An association, like a correspondence, is generally not a set. An association S *embraces* an association R of the same degree r if for any images $x_1, \ldots, x_r$ such that R accepts x_1 in position ①, . . . , x_r in position r, it is predicted that S would accept x_1 in position ①, . . . , x_r in position r. An embracing thus preserves the orientation of the associations. If S embraces R, we write $R \subseteq S$. If $R \subseteq S$ and $S \subseteq R$, we say that R and S are *equivalent*, and write $R \equiv S$.

We assume that any association R has a plan λR from which it is formed by realization. We will generally assume that any association R has a handle, νR, which is a recognizer, although we will allow an association to have no handle. Each position of an association has a melding.

The Concentration of an Association Is the Class of Its Assemblies

We consider next how to form the analog of the "set of sequences" or "set of tuples" used to define a relation in symbolic logic. It is tempting to reason directly by analogy with conglomeration of symbols, and to define an "ordered pair of images" such as « Sally-shoes » that could be viewed as an instance of a class of « purchases » (that is, Sally purchases shoes).

However, there is no evidence that such constructions are present in thought. Indeed, the evidence from language is that such constructions are not imagined, because nominal compounds like « Sally-shoes » or « Gary-pants » are not syntactically valid. To be English phrases, a verb must be supplied that relates the two nouns: « Sally purchases shoes » differs from « Sally sells shoes » or « Sally makes shoes ».

An assembly manifestation formed from images is therefore the analog in ideas of a conglomeration formed from symbols. Whereas there is only one conglomeration (x, y, z) that is formed from three symbols "x", "y", and "z", there are many possible assembly manifestations that may be formed from three images « a », « b », and « c », depending

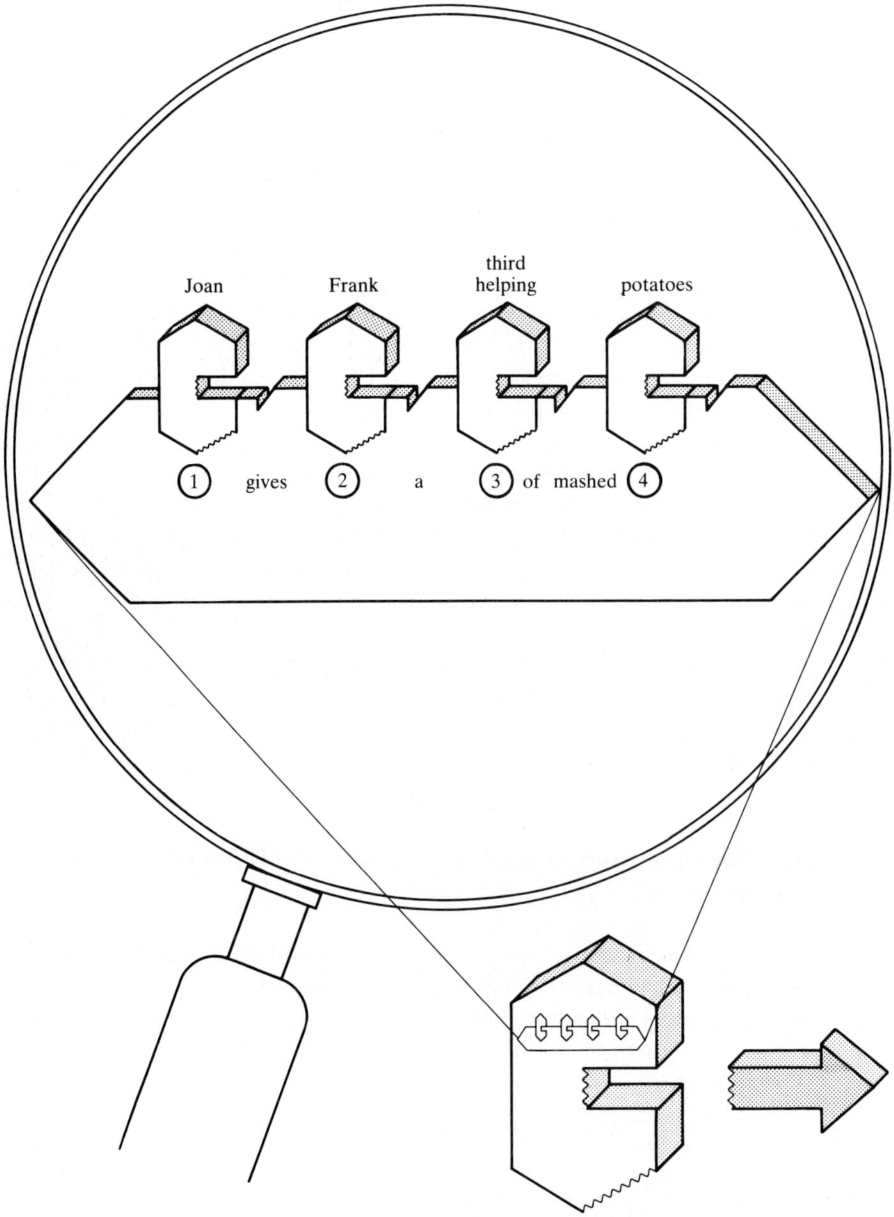

An assembly. This recognizer accepts impressions of « Joan giving Frank a third helping of mashed potatoes »

Figure 1.10 An assembly.

on the association the three are viewed as participating in. Figure 1.11 illustrates this contrast.

The analog to a set of tuples of a relation R is the class of assemblies controlled by an association R. This class is called the *concentration* of R, and is written "C^1R". The concentration of R differs from the set of tuples of symbolic logic in that the instances of the concentration incorporate R, whereas tuples of a relation do not incorporate the relation. Thus, the instances of C^1G are assemblies of the form $G(b, c)$, not pairs of the form (b, c) as in symbolic logic.

Concentrations are defined so that if two associations are embraced, then their concentrations are embraced. For example, if « Transports » embraces « Carries » then any assembly manifestation of an image i carrying an image j is also considered to be an image of i transporting j. Writing formally, if R accepts manifestations of the recognizers $b_1, \ldots, b_r$ and $R \subseteq S$ then $R(b_1, \ldots, b_r)$ is an instance of C^1S as well as an instance of C^1R.

Relationship of Positions to Plans

It is reasonable to assume that the conceptual mechanism that places images in positions is carried on entirely through plans. That is, there is a conceptual mechanism that takes the plan of « ① Carries ② », the plan of « Sally », and the plan of « the yellow basket », and

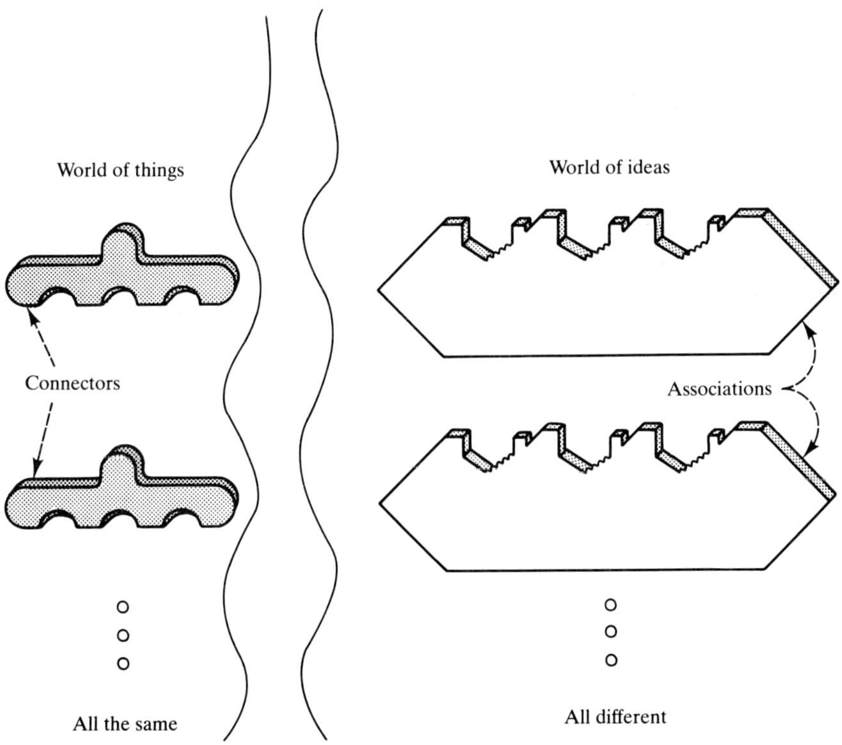

Figure 1.11 The distinction between connectors and associations.

forms the *plan* of « Sally carries the yellow basket ». A position, then, is part of a plan, that part which the conceptual factory replaces with other plans. A position designator therefore represents a portion of the plan of an association. To maintain the contrast between a « position » as a portion of an association and a « position » as a portion of a plan of an association, we will refer to the portion of a plan more specifically as a *programmatic position.*

Conclusion

An *association* is a conceptual mechanism that can accept many images in one performance. An association is therefore akin to an engine, except that an engine is a physical process that operates on things, and an association is a conceptual mechanism that operates on ideas. An association can only accept a finite maximum number of images in any performance. This maximum number is the *degree* of the association. A class is a special case of an association, specifically, a class is an association of degree one. Associations are different from relations, just as classes are different from sets. That is, the population of an association can change without the association changing, whereas the population of a mathematical relation can not change.

We assume that the positions where an association may accept images are ordered in a sequence. Different orderings give different associations, called *permutations*. An association S embraces another association R if any images accepted by R must be accepted by S when each image is presented to the same sequence number position of S as it is presented to R. Embracings of associations, especially of correspondences (associations of degree two), will be used extensively.

Any association R has a corresponding class called the *concentration* of R. The instances of the concentration of R are assemblies of R with r recognizers, where r is the degree of R. The concentration of R is analogous to the set of tuples of R in symbolic logic. However, the members of the set of tuples are of the form $(x_1, \ldots, x_r)$, while the instances of the concentration of R are of the form $R(x_1, \ldots, x_r)$. We have argued that the formal construction "$(x_1, \ldots, x_r)$" has no interpretation in thought, and so should not be used.

1.9 IDENTITY OF MENTAL IMAGES

Sameness Can Differ from Class to Class

We consider next what is meant by saying that two images are the *same*. The word "same" is usually employed in English in combination with some class, as in "same customer," "same car," and so forth. It is quite possible to imagine two classes B and C such that two images are the « same B » but not the « same C ». For example, we may define a « registered object » to be a car as it is registered with a Department of Motor Vehicles. Two « registered objects » are different if they have different license plate numbers. We may define a « motorized vehicle » to be a car viewed as a superstructure surrounding a motor. Two « motorized vehicles » are different if they contain different motors.

Imagine a car that is reregistered without changing its motor. The resulting car, a new image, is a different « registered object » but is the same « motorized vehicle ». Imagine, alternatively, a car whose motor is changed without being reregistered. The resulting car, a new image, is the same « registered object » but is a different « motorized vehicle ».

Identity Is a Correspondence

The idea « ① is the same car as ② » is a correspondence, since it is a conceptual mechanism that accepts two images. Correspondences that establish sameness or *identity* of images will be called *identity correspondences*. Identity correspondences have several characteristics that set them apart from other correspondences. First, they are *symmetric*: if an image x is the same car as an image y, then y is the same car as x. Second, they are *transitive*: if an image x is the same car as an image y, and y is the same car as an image z, then x is the same car as z.

Identity correspondences are ordinarily not contentual in either position. Imagine that « Mary's red car » is a particular car, the same car as « the car with license number M7184 ». Now the recognizer « Mary's possession » embraces the recognizer « Mary's red car », since any impression of « Mary's red car » is an impression of « Mary's possession ». If the correspondence « Same Car » were contentual in either position, then « Mary's possession » would be the same car as « the car with license number M7184 ». Yet this is absurd, since Mary may own many possessions besides her red car, and may indeed own more than one car. Thus, « Same Car » must examine not only the impression in an image, but the recognizer as well.

Classes May Be Defined via Identity Correspondences

As we have seen, the image « Mary's possession » is not identical to any image of a car, since it embraces images other than cars. In general, no image j will be the « same car » as a car unless j is itself a car. Conversely, any image of a car will be the same car as itself. We may therefore define the class « Car » by means of the identity correspondence « Same Car » as follows:

$$x \text{ is a } \textit{car} \text{ if and only if } x \text{ is the } \textit{same car} \text{ as } x$$

Identity Is Required for Counting

Imagine that we were to ask how many cars were in the population of the class « Car ». Without a definition of « Same Car », we can not give an unambiguous answer. Are two images that differ only in their registration to be viewed as two cars or one? Are two images that differ only in their motor to be viewed as two cars or one? Counting is therefore always in reference to an identity correspondence. Counting is so critical to data applications that we will generally assume that each class B is associated with an identity correspondence written "ΔB". A recognizer x is an instance of B if and only if ΔB attaches x to x.

Multiple identity correspondences for the same class are sometimes needed in artificial intelligence applications. For example, the LISP programming language includes four progressively less restrictive tests for equality (EQ, EQL, EQUAL, and EQUALP). If two different variables A and B are both set to the same value, then A and B are EQUAL, but they are not EQL because they are different variables (Charniak, Riesbeck, McDermott, and Meehan 1987). Multiple identity correspondences are permitted in data theory; however, one must use extra care to identify which identity correspondence is meant whenever one is used. We will normally assume that every class is associated with exactly one identity correspondence.

The One and the Many

The ancient problem of the one and the many, simply stated, concerns how it is possible to say that there is one form, such as « beauty », while there are many items that partake of the form, many beautiful ideas (Plato 380B.C.b). We use the word "idea" here to include things as they are perceived, since we have not established whether these perceptions should be considered to be impressions, images, or recognizers. We discussed in Section 1.6 how the form « beauty » may be viewed as the melding of the class « _____ Is Beautiful ». The form « beauty » is therefore a recognizer, and all impressions accepted by « beauty » are the same image with respect to this recognizer. This establishes the "one" side of the problem.

An image partakes of beauty if it is accepted by the class « _____ Is Beautiful ». We may define the class « _____ Is Beautiful » to be the granulation of the recognizer « beauty ». The class « _____ Is Beautiful » is then contentual. An image partakes of beauty, that is, an image is accepted by « _____ Is Beautiful » so defined, if and only if its recognizer overlaps the recognizer « beauty ». We may therefore see an image « partaking of » a form quite directly as two recognizers sharing an impression in common. Notice, however, that only contentual classes may be defined from forms.

There may be many beautiful ideas because there are many potential identity correspondences for the class « _____ Is Beautiful ». That is, the form « beauty » does not establish any definition of « Same Beautiful Idea » other than the trivial definition by which all recognizers that overlap with « beauty » are considered to be the same. Any other definition of « Same Beautiful Idea » [that is, any other definition of $\Delta\Gamma$(beauty)] is valid, so long as what is beautiful is not changed (that is, so long as any recognizer that overlaps with « beauty » is considered to be the same beautiful idea as itself). The definition of what is one instance and what is many, in short, is not determined by the form, but is an entirely independent judgment.

Conclusion

The correspondence « ① Is The Same *B* As ② » is called an *identity correspondence*, and is written "ΔB". We have shown that the definition of « ① Is The Same *B* As ② » is not determined by the definition of « _____ Is A *B* ». Data definitions in practical data base designs, therefore, should specify when two images are the *same* instance of a class, rather than only specifying when an image is *an* instance of the class.

1.10 PROPOSITIONS

Problems in Defining a Proposition

A proposition is, loosely, an idea that can be believed, such as « shipment 5 was loaded on truck 6 », « the sky is blue », or « the world is flat ». Notice that an idea need not be in accordance with reality to be a proposition, as the last example shows. If we can imagine a situation in which the world is flat, then « the world is flat » is a proposition.

This characterization of a proposition, however, does not fully describe the place of propositions in thought. Thus, if the test of whether or not an idea is a proposition is whether or not the proposition can be believed, then one would expect that we would doubt whether ideas that are improbable or difficult to comprehend are propositions. For example, we would expect that an idea such as « air is heavier than steel » would provoke doubt about whether it is a proposition or not. Yet, whatever difficulty we might have imagining this idea, we do not doubt that it is a proposition. At the same time, we have confidence that ideas such as « sand » or « to laugh » are not propositions, even though sand and laughter are easy to imagine.

The solution to this difficulty is to recognize that whether or not an idea is a proposition is a characteristic of how the idea is *formed*. Thus, any idea of the form « an A is a B » is a proposition, so long as A and B are classes. Since ideas are formed from plans, we would therefore expect that plans and propositions are closely related. Before we can explore this relationship further, we must examine more closely how propositions are used.

Propositions Evoke Impressions

A proposition is closely associated with those situations that the proposition *evokes*. For example, the proposition « Sally is carrying the yellow basket » evokes ideas, mental pictures, of Sally carrying the yellow basket—perhaps a picture of her carrying it along the beach, over a bridge, and so on. These mental pictures are impressions. The question of whether or not they are evoked by the proposition is not affected by how the ideas are recognized.

For example, recall the matched pen and pencil set from Section 1.6. Consider the recognizer b that accepts only impressions of the pen, and the recognizer d that accepts impressions of either the pen or the pencil. The proposition « the pen is empty » will therefore evoke some manifestations of b, but only those in which the impression is of an empty pen. Since b is embraced by d, any manifestation of b has a corresponding manifestation of d, in which the impression of the empty pen is considered to be a manifestation of « either the pen or the pencil ». This manifestation of d is also evoked by « the pen is empty », showing that the proposition is not affected by which recognizer accepts an impression.

A Proposition Is a Plan

The idea « what the proposition q evokes » is therefore a recognizer, because it accepts impressions. A recognizer of this form is called a *topic recognizer*. The topic recognizer is not the same as the proposition q, for the idea « the pen is empty » is a different idea from the recognizer « an impression evoked by « the pen is empty » », that is, « an empty pen ». We suggest that a proposition q is the *plan* for the topic recognizer « what the proposition q evokes ». The topic recognizer is therefore the realization $Яq$ of q.

Defining a proposition to be a plan explains why whether or not an idea is a proposition is a characteristic of how the idea is formed. Specifically, a proposition such as « Joe is a banker » is formed by combining the *plans* of « Joe » and « banker » in a standard way. The realizations of the constituents of the proposition, the recognizer « Joe » and the class « banker », are not considered in forming the proposition. That is, the following is a fundamental rule of thought, called the *instantiation law*:

> For any recognizer d and any class B, the idea « d is an instance of B » is a proposition.

Not All Recognizers Are Topic Recognizers

Topic recognizers have a *panoramic* quality in how they accept impressions. For example, the topic recognizer of « the sky is blue » accepts impressions of a blue sky, but it also accepts complex impressions that incorporate a blue sky with other ideas, such as an impression of a county fair, complete with people, amusements, and farm animals, beneath a blue sky. A complex impression of this kind is called a *scene*. In general, any scene accepted by a topic recognizer can be broadened to incorporate further impressions (such as by adding impressions of food vendors to the impression of the county fair), and the resulting broader scene will also be accepted by the topic recognizer.

In contrast, the recognizer « a blue sky » accepts only *cropped* versions of the scene, that is, it accepts only impressions of a blue sky. The scene of the county fair, for example, is not a manifestation of a blue sky. Most recognizers that we will consider have some such cropping effect. Topic recognizers are examples of recognizers that do not.

Notation for Propositions

The proposition « d is an instance of B » is written "B:(d)". It is called a *simple proposition* because it does not contain any of the logical operations such as *and* or *or* to be introduced later. The associations and recognizers used in forming a proposition are called the *constituents* of the proposition. Thus, « d » and « B » are the constituents of the proposition « B:(d) ».

The idea that a correspondence G attaches a recognizer b to a recognizer c is also a simple proposition, written "G:(b, c)" or "(b)G:(c)". Acceptances by associations of higher degree are represented by expressions with successively more positions, such as "T:(a, b, c)" or "(a)T:(b)U(c)". Both of these expressions represent acceptances by trios. Propositions are usually expressed in language as complete sentences, such as:

> "(Joe) is a banker", or equivalently, "Banker: (Joe)"
>
> "(Sally) carries (the yellow basket)", or equivalently,
> "Carries: (Sally, the yellow basket)"

Assemblies Are Topic Recognizers of Simple Propositions

The topic recognizer of the simple proposition « John is a painter » accepts impressions in which John acts as a painter. It therefore serves as a recognizer for the assembly of « John » and the class « Painter » (see Section 1.5). The manifestations of this recognizer are images of John acting in the role of a painter. A simple proposition is therefore the plan of an assembly. Specifically, the proposition $B:(d)$ is the plan of the assembly $B(d)$. More generally, the proposition $R:(b_1, \ldots, b_r)$ is the plan of the assembly $R(b_1, \ldots, b_r)$.

Conclusion

A proposition *evokes* an impression. For example, the proposition « the sky is blue » evokes an impression of a blue sky. The recognizer that accepts the impressions that a proposition p evokes is called the *topic recognizer* of p, and is written Яp. We have argued that a proposition is a plan, and that the topic recognizer of a proposition is its realization.

Propositions arise in data bases as statements that a recognizer is an instance of a class. For example, the idea « Janice is a piano tuner » is a proposition. This proposition is written "Piano Tuner: (Janice)". It is often implemented in a data base by putting the symbol "Janice" in the "Piano Tuner" file.

1.11 CONVERSION BETWEEN SYMBOLS AND IDEAS

Representation Is Described by Interpreting Agents

In this section, we look more closely at how symbols are used to stand for or to *represent* ideas. When an observer contemplates a physical symbol such as "horse", he or she must first perceive the symbol, that is, must first form some picture in his or her mind of the string of letters "horse". This perceived impression is then associated with the idea of a horse, which we write « horse ». We will call the entire collection of faculties that permit a person to perceive a physical object and to associate it with an idea an *interpreting agent*. We will describe an interpreting agent as a process with an input site that accepts things and an output site that accepts ideas. In the example, the input site accepts the physical symbol "horse" while the output site accepts the idea « horse », within a single performance of the interpreting agent. For a more thorough discussion of how symbols and ideas are associated in language, see (Frege 1892), (de Saussure 1915), and (Lyons 1977).

We will ordinarily consider an interpreting agent to be reversible. That is, we will suppose that we may view the site that accepts ideas as the input site and the site that accepts symbols as the output site. Such a mechanism will be called a *tagging agent*. If a symbol "s" is accepted by the output site of a tagging agent and an idea « j » is accepted by the input site, we say that the symbol "s" is a *tag* of the idea « j ». In the example, "horse" is a tag of « horse ».

It is difficult to imagine how the output site of an interpreting agent could accept all the kinds of ideas that we have discussed. For example, it would appear that a site that accepted a correspondence would need to be formed quite differently from a site that accepted a recognizer. If there were different output sites in an interpreting agent for different kinds of ideas, then we would expect to see symbolic signals in language that distinguish different parts of speech, as a clue to which output site should be consulted for the meaning of a word. In English, at least, we do not find these signals. Unless one knows the meaninig of an English word, or encounters it in context, there is no general way to determine its part of speech. Indeed, it is common for the same spoken word to represent ideas of many different kinds, such as the word ''rock'', which can be a mass noun, a countable noun, a verb, or a person's name.

It seems more likely that an interpreting agent has one output site that is able to handle all kinds of ideas. This can be explained if the output site accepts *plans* of ideas rather than the ideas we normally think of as the interpretations of symbols. That is, the interpreting agent converts the symbol ''horse'' into the *plan* of the idea « horse ». If we then want to imagine a horse, the realization of the plan is recalled from memory as a separate step.

A Symbol Can Have More than One, or No, Interpretant

A symbol may represent more than one idea. For example, the English word ''bank'' represents all of the following ideas:

« financial institution »
« the edge of a river »
« to cover a fire »
« to rotate an airplane »

Each idea represented by a symbol is called an *interpretant* of the symbol. The set of ideas assigned to a symbol by an interpreting agent (in some identified set of performances) is called the *interpretation* of the symbol.

When an interpretation contains more than one idea, the member ideas are connected by « or », where « or » means that at least one of the ideas is intended. For example, consider the word ''bank'' in the expression ''Joe went to the bank.'' The last two interpretants of « bank » may be eliminated because they do not fit the given context. But both of the first two interpretants remain possible since « Joe went to the financial institution » and « Joe went to the edge of a river » are both possible. The interpretation of the sentence is therefore

« Joe went to the financial institution or Joe went to the edge of a river »

Just as a symbol may represent more than one idea, so a symbol may represent no idea. For example, an interpreting agent that only is capable of interpreting English phrases will assign no interpretation to the French sentence ''*la porte est ouverte*.'' A symbol that has no interpretation will be called *vacant*.

Conversely, an idea may have many tags. For example, a typical person may be identified simultaneously by many tags: Social Security number, driver's license number, employee number, and so on. Such multiple tagging schemes have often been avoided in data designs. We discuss how they may be managed effectively using identity correspondences in Section 4.7.

A Symbol's Interpretation May Change

We may imagine a symbol that represents one interpretant at one time and two interpretants at a different time. This can happen readily in a paper record-keeping system. Imagine that a tax filing (i.e., a submitted return) is identified by a unique number on the filing, so that there is exactly one number per filed return. Make a photocopy of one tax return, and its number simultaneously identifies two physical returns. Between the time when the original was completed and the time when the photocopy was made (and its existence communicated to the interpreting agent) the number of interpretants assigned to the filing's identification number increased by one.

Different interpreting agents can give different interpretations to the same symbols. It is common, during the course of deciding on a data base design, to change the interpretation of a symbol several times—viewing the interpretation of ''part'' as now containing, now excluding, purchased items, for example. Each such change should be viewed as the substitution of a new interpreting agent: the symbol, ''part'', does not change.

Conclusion

We have shown how representation may be viewed as the application of an *interpreting agent*. An interpreting agent is a conceptual mechanism that converts a symbol into the ideas that it represents. The reverse of an interpreting agent, a *tagging agent*, is a conceptual mechanism that converts an idea into the symbol or symbols that represent it.

1.12 DATA

Varieties of Ideas Will Be Indicated by Symbol Formats

Before concluding this chapter, we take this opportunity to inventory the terms and symbols that we use to describe data. We will generally differentiate the kinds of ideas represented by the types of symbols we use. A recognizer will be represented by a lower case letter, such as ''b'' or ''c'', sometimes subscripted such as ''b_2''. A symbol that represents a recognizer will be called an *individual*.

A class will be represented by an upper case letter, usually ''A'', ''B'', or ''C'', or by an English nominal phrase written with initial capital letters. A symbol that represents a class will be called a *class tag*. We write the proposition that an image « b » is an instance of a class « B » as the conglomeration ''B:(b)''. We will often write the instances of a class using the lower case of the letter that represents the class, using subscripts to distinguish the individuals, as in ''B:(b_1)'', ''B:(b_2)'', etc.

An association will also be represented by an upper case letter, or by an English phrase containing a verb, written with initial capital letters. We will typically use ''F'',

“*G*”, and “*H*” for correspondences, “*Q*”, “*R*”, “*S*”, and “*T*” for associations of higher degree. We call a symbol that represents an association an *association tag*, or, more specifically, a *class tag, correspondence tag, trio tag,* and so forth. A proposition will either be written as a conglomeration, such as “(*b*)*G*:(*c*)”, or, if its constituents are not specified, as a lower case letter, usually “*p*”, “*q*”, or “*r*”.

We will use association tags so that each tag has a fixed *degree*. This degree is shown by the number of places following the tag, separated by commas. Thus, the expression “*T*(, ,)” shows that “*T*” has degree three, and therefore the symbol “*T*” represents an association of degree three. Each of the three spaces in “*T*(, ,)” will be called a *position*. Thus, in “*T*:(*a*, *b*, *c*)”, “*a*” occupies position ①, “*b*” occupies position ②, and “*c*” occupies position ③.

We will often have occasion to use ordinary words such as “customer” or “part” when illustrating data bases. When we use words in their ordinary meaning, as we have been doing up to now, we write the words in plain text. When we use ordinary words to illustrate a data base example, and therefore assign them a specific meaning that may differ from the general one, we will write the words in italics: *Customer*, *Part*.

We note that the decisions about which symbols to use for representation are purely arbitrary. For example, we might represent the proposition « *United Industries purchases wheat* » by the proposition tag “*Purchases*: (*United Industries*, *wheat*)”. We could just as easily have used a corporation identification number such as “7” to represent « *United Industries* » and a commodity identification number such as “09-21-43” to represent « *wheat* ». If so, the proposition tag would be “*Purchases*: (7, 09-21-43)”. Or, we could use icons as tags, as shown in Figure 1.12. All these tags are acceptable to the theory.

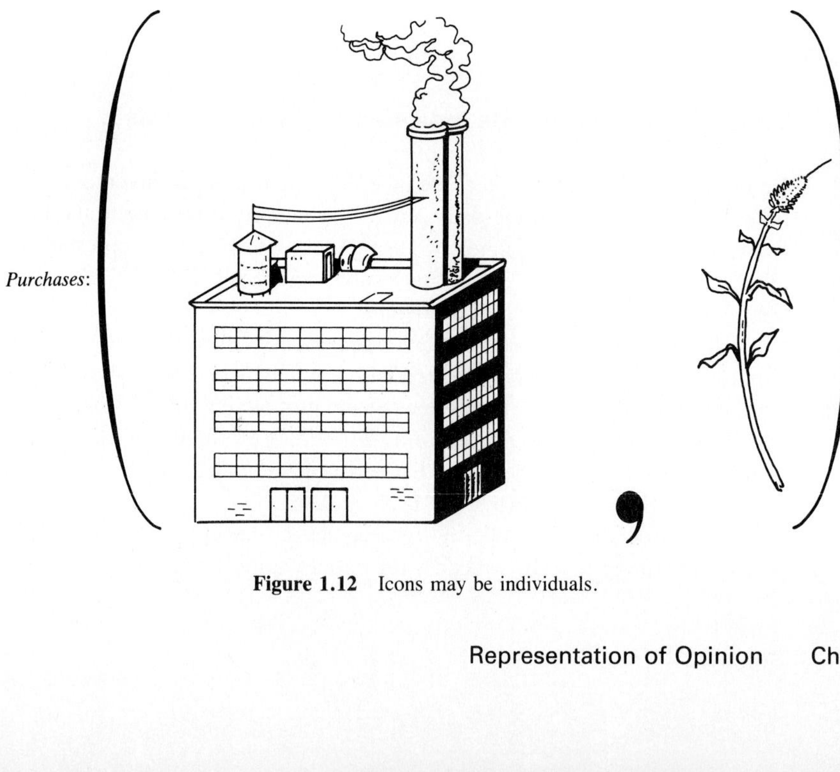

Figure 1.12 Icons may be individuals.

The Phrase "Piece of Data" Will Be Preferred to the Word "Datum"

"Data" is a general term that characterizes collections of *pieces of data*. We prefer the phrase "a piece of data" to the word "datum" which is seen occasionally. "Datum" is a Latin word for which, in Latin, "data" is the plural. In English, however, "data" is a singular mass noun, like "spaghetti," "graffiti," and other nouns that are plural in the originating language. The word "data" is comparable to the word "information," which is used in the plural in Italian (*informazioni*) and other Romance languages, but is singular in English. If "data" were the plural of "datum" in English, then we should be able to count "one datum," "two data," "three data," and so on, but these expressions are not part of the language. Instead, as we say "one grain of sand," "two grains of sand," or "one piece of evidence," "two pieces of evidence," we should say "one piece of data," "two pieces of data." Similarly, as we say "the sand is white," or "water is wet," we should treat "data" as singular, as in "the data is conclusive," or "data about charcoal is kept under *C*."

We will also consistently write "data base" instead of the one word "database." New words are rarely formed in modern English by pasting two nouns together. Thus, in words like "skyscraper" and "screwdriver," one of the compound elements is clearly derived from a verb. English has no other noun-noun strings with "data" as the first noun or "base" as the second; compare, for example, the phrases "data requirements," "data flow," "data model," "rate base," and "army base."

A Piece of Data Is a Proposition Tag

A simple example of a piece of data is a record in a file, or, in the relational data model, a tuple in a relation. The name of the file, or the name of the relation, is an association tag. For example, if

(Joe Peavey, rakes, Oshkosh)

is a tuple in the relation *Sells In*, we interpret the tuple as claiming that « Joe Peavey sells rakes in Oshkosh ». A tuple in a relation therefore represents a proposition, in this case, the proposition

(Joe Peavey) sells (rakes) in (Oshkosh)

A piece of data is therefore a symbol that represents a proposition, a proposition tag. However, not all proposition tags qualify as pieces of data. To be a piece of data, there must be some physical characteristic of the proposition tag that allows us to conclude that the proposition represented by the tag is believed. For example, if an official weather report states that the temperature in Cleveland, Ohio is 57°, then we are justified in treating the symbol "Temperature: (Cleveland, 57)" as a piece of data. Its presence (or the presence of a symbol materially like it) on a weather report gives it credence. On the other hand, the same statement, "the temperature in Cleveland, Ohio is 57°," in the midst of a novel, is not data, because it is not claimed that the statement is believed.

Placing a proposition tag in a data base population is one way to indicate that the proposition represented by the tag is believed. Therefore, all proposition tags resident in a data base population are pieces of data. When a proposition tag "p" is resident in a data base population, we will say that "p" is *claimed*, and we will call "p" a *claim*. We will also say that the proposition « p » that "p" represents is claimed. If "p" represents two propositions « p_1 » and « p_2 », then the proposition « p_1 or p_2 » is claimed (see Section 2.9).

We will say that a proposition tag is *affirmed* if the proposition tag can be deduced logically from claims. The term *claim* will be reserved for proposition tags that are physically resident in a data base population. We write the statement that p is affirmed as "$\vdash p$". We will also say that a *proposition* is affirmed if a tag of the proposition may be deduced logically from claims.

We will be primarily concerned with describing which propositions are affirmed, rather than only which propositions are claimed. For example, we will say that an individual "b" is an *instance* of a class tag "B" if "B:(b)" is affirmed. Thus, logical consequences of the contents of a data base are treated as part of the data base, whether or not they are physically resident.

We will avoid the terms "true" and "false" when speaking about propositions, because our concern is with the consequences of claims, not with whether or not the claims are "true." In common speech, a "true" statement is a statement that reflects reality. Propositions may be affirmed that are not true in this sense, such as when inaccurate or out-of-date data is retained in a data base, or when the data base contains fictitious claims, such as "Harry the unicorn likes carrots."

A practical data base must have policies about the degree of assurance needed before a proposition tag may be entered into the data base. These policies typically differ according to the use of the data: corporate financial figures, for example, may require elaborate backup and authorizations before being entered, while day-to-day project schedules may be under the free control of the responsible line manager. In general, we feel that data bases today are too limited to facts. A data base can and should retain opinions, study results, recommendations, predictions, policies, regulations, and other data that represents the ideas of an organization. A data base should be a medium of communication, not merely an authority.

A Data Base Is a Binding Site

In data processing, the population of a data base consists of symbols resident on certain physical storage devices under the control of a data base management system. The data base management system and associated hardware and software constitute a binding site: they determine whether or not a given symbol is a member of the data base population.

Since a data base is a binding site, its population can change while the data base remains the same. For example, consider a data base that retains a list of customers' names and addresses—call it the "customer mailing list" data base. The population of this data base, the actual customers and their addresses, changes frequently, yet it remains the "customer mailing list" data base. We will discuss the structure of data bases more fully, especially the relationship of a data base to its data base design, in Section 4.2.

Data Is Defined Semantically, but Acts Syntactically

A data base binding site establishes a practical definition of a claim. That is, any symbol that the data base binding site accepts is considered by the data base and all programs that use the data base to be a claim. This definition supersedes, in practice, the definition of a claim as a proposition tag. Since a computer has no access to the interpretation of a symbol, a computer can not determine whether or not a symbol does in fact represent a proposition.

A data base binding site recognizes proposition tags by their syntax. For example, the binding site might accept any symbol of the form "x:(y)" as a valid proposition tag because it fits the syntax of an individual y as an instance of the class x. The data base binding site may make additional checks, but in each case, the data base binding site decides to accept or to reject a symbol entirely on its appearance, not on its interpretation.

There are, then, two definitions of a claim. One is that a claim is a *proposition tag* that is an occupant of the data base binding site. This is called the *semantic definition* of a claim, because it relies on how a claim is interpreted (namely, that it is interpreted as a proposition). However, the engines that manage data act as if a claim is any *thing* that is an occupant of the data base binding site. This is called the *syntactic definition* of a claim, because it contains no reference to how a claim is interpreted. Tags in general will have both a semantic and a syntactic definition.

We will devote much of Chapters 2 and 3 to defining a syntax for proposition tags that is sufficiently diverse to meet the needs of complex data base populations. For now, we state the assumption that there can be a binding site that accepts proposition tags as a postulate:

(P8) It is possible to form a binding site that accepts proposition tags.

This postulate enables there to be data bases. The postulate (P8) does not assert that a binding site may be formed that enforces the syntactic rules of proposition tags, since these rules have not yet been presented. The postulate (P8) asserts only that one may form a binding site that accepts unstructured symbols, which we choose to call proposition tags.

Conclusion

A data base is a binding site whose occupants are proposition tags. The set of occupants of a data base at any time is called the *population* of the data base. Since a data base is not a set, the population of a data base may change while the data base remains the same.

Data is a general term for collections of pieces of data. A *piece of data* is a proposition tag that is a member of a data base population.

1.13 CONCLUSION

Proper appreciation of data requires an understanding of human thought. Data is, superficially, symbols, physical things. Yet the way data behaves is determined by how these symbols are interpreted. We have shown that the symbols used for data represent a wide variety of ideas: recognizers, classes, correspondences, propositions, and so on. Understanding how these ideas combine in thought is the key to understanding data. Our final definition of a piece of data, a symbol that represents a proposition and that is claimed, incorporates results from all these lines of investigation.

We have seen that a class must be distinguished from its population. A population is a set: any change in its members is a new population. But the same class may have many different populations, just as the population of the class of living people changes each time a person is born or dies.

We have seen how ideas may be related by *embracings*. For example, a class C is said to *embrace* a class B if any image accepted by B must also be accepted by C. Just as a class is different from a set, so an embracing is different from an inclusion of sets. The class C only embraces the class B if B and C are defined so that any image accepted by B must be accepted by C. Merely noting that all images that have ever been accepted by B have also been accepted by C does not establish an embracing, since this could be merely a coincidence.

The primary contribution of this chapter to later chapters will be its clarification of the different varieties of ideas, principally recognizers, associations, propositions, and embracings. To the extent that our discussion has encompassed all forms of ideas—opinions, conceptions of things, deductions, visions, flights of fancy—the theory may be applied far more broadly than other theories that concentrate on data's physical form.

2

Principles of Data Logic

2.1 INTRODUCTION

Logic is the study of how propositions may be deduced reliably from other propositions. Since a piece of data represents a proposition, logic determines how to form conclusions from pieces of data. In addition, data base constraints, such as "a safety deposit box is located in at most one bank," are themselves propositions. Thus, logic determines how to apply data base constraints to members of a data base population (for example, what to do when a user attempts to add a record of a new safety deposit box). Logic is therefore central to the study of data.

Around the turn of the twentieth century, the word "logic" was adopted by researchers in the foundations of mathematics, who restricted the meaning of "logic" to manipulation of symbols without concern for their interpretations. Unfortunately for the study of data, it is this formulation of *symbolic* logic that is normally taught today. We will assume that the reader is familiar with the basic principles of symbolic logic. Any introductory text would suffice; (Hilbert and Ackermann 1938) is recommended.

In this chapter, we develop a new system of logic, based on the nature of data. We call this system *data logic*. This chapter is concerned entirely with describing data logic and giving rudimentary examples of its behavior. Applications of data logic to problems of philosophy and mathematics are discussed in Chapter 3, and applications of data logic to data bases are discussed in Chapter 4. All results in later chapters are proved using data logic.

All expressions of symbolic logic are expressions of data logic, but there are expressions of data logic that can not be formed from symbolic logic, and there are formulas of symbolic logic that behave differently in data logic. When considering data, we must allow for expressions and means of reasoning that do not arise in mathematics.

For example, we have already discussed the difference between a class and a set, and more generally, the difference between an association and a relation. These differences are not recognized by symbolic logic—there is no place in symbolic logic for an association whose population can change. These limitations may be appreciated by recalling that symbolic logic was developed for mathematics, particularly to define numbers, points, lines, and the like, which are idealizations that do not change with changing circumstance. In data bases, however, the population of a class changes frequently, and must not be confused with the class itself.

By a similar omission, symbolic logic makes no distinction between logical implication and coincidences obeyed by the population. Again, this is because symbolic logic works with an essentially static world: if the population never changes, and if there are no tags that violate a proposed rule, then we can conclude that the rule will hold forever. In data, of course, this manner of deduction is erroneous. For example, a schema could contain no rule that forces each instance of a class A to relate to some instance of a class B, yet we may observe that all instances of A, present and past, do indeed relate to an instance of B. It does not follow that A is in *mandatory* association with B, for the next time the data base is updated, we may find an instance of A associated with no instance of B. Indeed, it does not follow that A was in *mandatory* association with B at any time in the past. Symbolic logic can not adequately represent such contrasts as these.

Symbolic logic is particularly deficient in its treatment of negation. In symbolic logic, every proposition must either be affirmed or denied. Data is not so clearly cut. A typical personnel data base, for example, will make no claim about the number of planets in the solar system: it neither affirms nor denies that there are nine planets. In symbolic logic, it is impossible for a proposition to be neither affirmed nor denied. This limitation of symbolic logic leads to the "closed world assumption," by which any proposition not known to be true is assumed to be false. A person not listed in the data base as innocent is assumed to be guilty. Clearly, such reasoning is inadequate for practical situations.

We will develop data logic gradually, pausing on each new concept before continuing. Generally speaking, the operations of data logic may be applied in a parallel way to recognizers, classes, and associations of higher degree. For example, it is easy to see how « and » behaves in all three cases, once it is explained how « and » behaves for any one of the three. We will usually introduce new terms as operations on classes, since classes are the variety that we find is closest to ordinary experience. We will then generalize the operations to recognizers and associations after most of the basic concepts have been introduced. Readers who prefer a development from first principles may refer to the complete set of postulates, definitions, and axioms at the beginning of Chapter 3.

In Section 2.2, Inexhaustibility and Negation, we show that there are two fundamentally different varieties of classes, which we call *constructive* and *omissive*. The two varieties, constructive and omissive, are called *performance types*. Every constructive class has an omissive counterpart called its *complement*, just as every omissive class has a constructive counterpart. Every class is either constructive or omissive, and no class is both. We will argue that the failure of symbolic logic to distinguish between constructive and omissive is the primary reason for the presence of logical paradoxes in symbolic logic (paradoxes are explored fully in Chapter 3, once the development of data logic is complete).

In Section 2.3, Basic Logic of Embracings, we discuss the basic logical rules obeyed by embracings, which are similar to the logical rules obeyed by inclusion in symbolic logic. We discuss the *unpopulable class*, which is analogous to the empty set in symbolic logic, and the *universal class*, which is analogous to the complement of the empty set.

In Section 2.4, Intersection and Union, we describe the basic logical properties of intersection and union of classes, which are analogous to intersection and union of sets in symbolic logic. We show, however, that the images *rejected* by intersections and unions of classes behave somewhat differently than would be predicted by symbolic logic.

In Section 2.5, Recognizers, we generalize the results achieved so far to recognizers. Thus, we show that recognizers may be complemented, intersected, and united just as classes may. There is no counterpart in symbolic logic to the logic of recognizers.

In Section 2.6, Propositions, we discuss how a recognizer d may be combined with a class C to form a proposition we might loosely write as « d is a C ». We find that there are two different ways of forming such a proposition, which we write as « d is an *instance* of C » and « d is a *conformer* of C ». These two forms are interchanged by negation. Symbolic logic does not recognize the distinction between instances and conformers.

In symbolic logic, a single contradiction causes *all* propositions to become contradictory. This overreaction often makes automatic reasoning about practical problems impossible, because practical situations frequently contain some contradictory elements. We show in Section 2.7, Management of Contradictions, how contradictions may be isolated in data logic, allowing reasoning about unrelated topics to continue.

In Section 2.8, Performance Type Integrity, we apply our study of constructive and omissive classes to embracings, and show that certain forms of embracings are prohibited. This prohibition has no counterpart in symbolic logic, and is a major departure of data logic. Performance type integrity is the primary means for avoiding logical paradoxes.

In Section 2.9, Propositional Logic, we show how logical implication may be defined as an embracing. We apply the logic of intersection, union, and complement to develop the logic of « and », « or », and « not ». We define a performance type integrity law for propositions, and show how this law avoids the liar paradox.

In Section 2.10, Quantification, we describe the logic of constructions such as « for some » and « for all », which are known as *quantifiers* in symbolic logic. There are many more kinds of quantification in data logic than there are in symbolic logic. Because data logic avoids Russell's paradox, data logic is able to permit unrestrained quantification over associations. In contrast, relational algebra, which is based on symbolic logic, prohibits any quantification over relations. We also discuss quantification over impressions, which has no counterpart in symbolic logic.

In Section 2.11, Associations, we show how associations may be complemented, intersected, and united, and we discuss operations such as permutations that only apply to associations of degree two and higher.

In Section 2.12, Proposal Methods, we discuss how the distinction between instances and conformers is generalized to associations of arbitrary degree. We show how the performance type of a simple proposition may be computed from the performance types of its constituents, whatever the degree of the constituent association might be.

In Section 2.13, Inclusion and Deduction, we explore the difference between an *inclusion* of classes, which may be caused by a temporary circumstance, and an embracing of classes, which is a characteristic of the way the classes are formed. For example, since we have never retrieved a rock from Pluto, we could say that the class « _____ Is A Rock From Pluto » is empty. This class is *included* in every other class, just as the empty set is included in every set in symbolic logic. However, the class « _____ Is A Rock From Pluto » is not *embraced* in the class « _____ Is A Can Opener », because it is not the case that any rock from Pluto, should we find one, must be a can opener.

In Section 2.14, Modal Operators, we study *definitive* propositions, which describe characteristics of how ideas are formed, rather than characteristics of particular populations. For example, we show that an embracing may be viewed as a definitive inclusion: two classes that embrace each other must include each other by virtue of the way that they are formed. Other propositions besides inclusions also have definitive counterparts. In data base applications, statements of a schema are definitive, while statements of a population are not definitive, but *incidental*. By making this distinction, we may properly distinguish between a data base constraint and a coincidence of the population. Definitiveness resembles what writers on modal logic call "necessity."

In Section 2.15, Modal Logic, we develop the logic of « and », « or », and « not » for definitive propositions. We also discuss the logic of *possible* propositions, which are negations of definitive propositions. We include a brief discussion of how data logic avoids the criticisms Quine has offered against other systems of modal logic.

2.2 INEXHAUSTIBILITY AND NEGATION

A Binding Site Can Not Examine All Things

A binding site, we recall, is a process that, when presented with a thing, may examine it, and if it does so, either accepts the thing or rejects it. A binding site is physical — we should be able to imagine constructing it. Consider the process that a binding site uses to *examine* a thing. Any physical examination process has limitations. For example, a binding site designed to accept certain electrical signals will ordinarily not even detect an audio signal, so it can not reject an audio signal. Similarly, a highly sensitive optical device will have some very high or very low electromagnetic frequencies that it can not detect, and it can not in any case detect sounds. We can never construct a physical examination process that can examine every thing. It follows, then, that we can never form a binding site that will examine every thing.

Rejection by a Class Is Equivalent to Acceptance by an Opposite

The analog of a binding site in ideas is a *constructive* class (the definition of a *class* in the prior chapter is the definition of a constructive class). When an image is examined by a constructive class, the image is either accepted or rejected, never both (we are assuming that the class is sheath–free, see Section 2.7). Thus, in order to examine an image, a class must be capable of making a judgment with certainty—either acceptance or rejection. An image that the class is incapable of judging is not examined.

Rejecting an image is just as decisive an action as accepting an image. In English, the statement that an image is rejected is often represented by an adjective that contains one of the prefixes "un-" or "in-." For example, an image accepted by the class « _____ is tidy » is called *tidy*, while one that is rejected is called *untidy*. Adjectives such as "untidy" will be called *opposites* of the adjectives such as "tidy" from which they are formed. Other words do not have opposites formed with "un-" or "in-," such as the opposites "beautiful" and "ugly," or "hot" and "cold."

We define the *opposite* of a class C to be the class "$°C$" such that:

(i) $°C$ accepts an image i if and only if C rejects i

(ii) $°C$ rejects an image i if and only if C accepts i

Since the images that are examined by a class are those that are either accepted or rejected, a class and its opposite examine the same images. The opposite of a class is illustrated in Figure 2.1, which resembles a Venn diagram. The large rectangle represents the universe of all images, and each circle surrounds a collection of images acted on by C.

Recall that two classes are equivalent if they must accept the same images. Two equivalent classes may, however, reject different images. Two equivalent classes may therefore have different opposites, just as « cold » may be viewed as having the opposite « hot » or the opposite « warm ».

A Constructive Class Can Not Examine All Images

Consider then the class of all images that are accepted by either a class C or its opposite, that is, the class of all images examined by C. This class will be called the *jurisdiction* of C. Examples of jurisdictions are « _____ is tidy or untidy », « _____ is beautiful or ugly », and « _____ is hot or cold ». Each of these classes excludes some images: the tolling of a bell is neither tidy nor untidy, most photographs are neither beautiful nor ugly, and a steel bar hot on one end but cold on the other is neither hot nor cold. The behavior of ordinary words is often a powerful indicator of characteristics of thought. Thus, it is a potent observation that for any opposite pair of classes represented by ordinary words, like "hot" and "cold," it is a simple matter to conceive of an image that is accepted by neither class.

We believe that this inability to form completely exhaustive opposites is characteristic of constructive conceptual mechanisms in general. Just as a binding site can not examine all things, so a constructive class can not examine all images. We call this result the *inexhaustibility principle of (constructive) classes*. Inexhaustibility will be seen to apply to associations and recognizers as well as to classes.

> For any constructive class C, it must be possible to imagine an image i such that C would not examine i if it were presented.

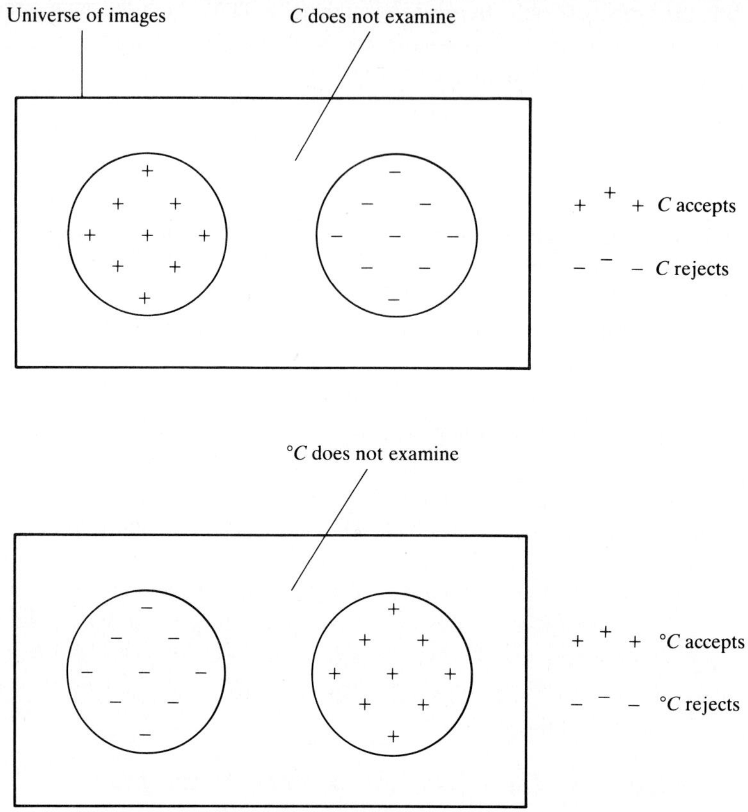

Figure 2.1 The opposite of a class.

The phrase "must be possible to imagine" means that it is impossible to construct C in such a way as to prevent imagining some image i with the given characteristics. The inexhaustibility principle therefore establishes a limitation on thought.

The Complement of a Constructive Class Is an Omissive Class

A class is a conceptual mechanism that accepts or rejects any image that it examines. Consider next a conceptual mechanism that accepts any image that a given constructive class C does not accept, and rejects any image that the class C does not reject. This conceptual mechanism will be called the *complement* of the class C and will be written "$\overline{C}$". It is an example of an *omissive class*. Figure 2.2 illustrates the complement of a class.

The complement is represented in English by the word "not." Thus, the complement of « _____ Is Tidy » is « _____ Is Not Tidy », the complement of « _____ Is A Car » is « _____ Is Not A Car », and so on. Notice that the complement $\overline{C}$ embraces the opposite °C, but that $\overline{C}$ may accept other images that °C does not accept. Symbolic logic makes no distinction between the complement and the opposite of a class.

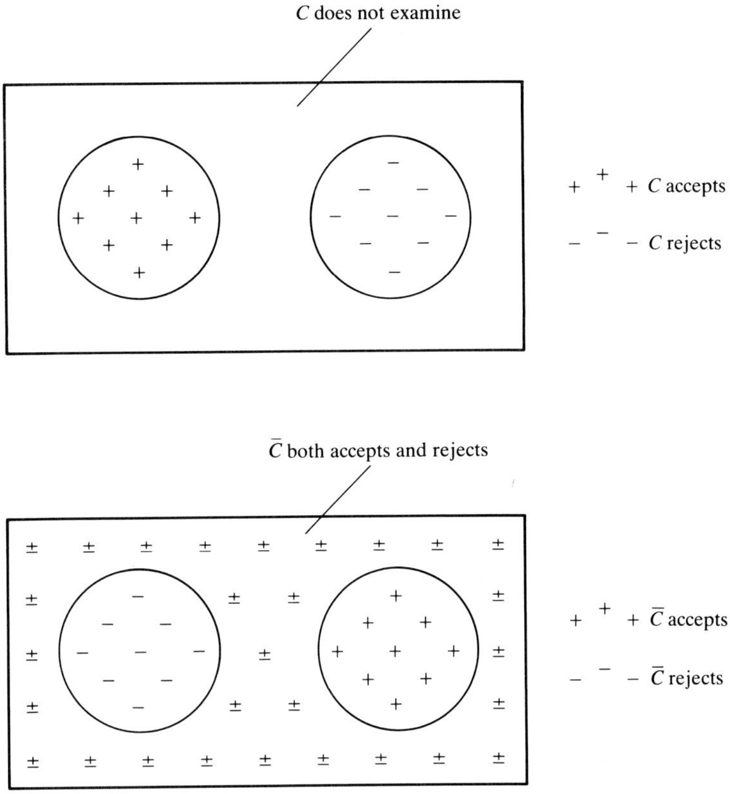

Figure 2.2 The complement of a class.

Since the omissive class $\overline{C}$ accepts any image that C does not accept, $\overline{C}$ accepts any image that C does not examine. Because images may be accepted by $\overline{C}$ without ever being examined by C, it is not proper to say that an omissive class *examines* an image. Acceptance by an omissive class is usually a consequence of deduction rather than active perusal of the image. A performance of $\overline{C}$ may thus be viewed as a performance of C together with an additional mechanism that complements the results, as follows:

(i) A performance of $\overline{C}$ includes a presentation of an image to C.

(ii) The image may be examined by C. If it is not examined, the image is accepted by $\overline{C}$.

(iii) If the image is accepted by C, it is rejected by $\overline{C}$. If the image is rejected by C, it is accepted by $\overline{C}$.

Thus, an image that is not examined by C is accepted by $\overline{C}$ by decree, rather than by contemplation of the image itself.

The distinction between constructive and omissive classes is similar to that made by Aristotle between "nouns" (constructive classes) and "indefinite nouns" (omissive classes) (Aristotle 350B.C.b). Aristotle also discussed the difference between an opposite and a complement in (350B.C.c, pp. 394–405). Data logic goes beyond Aristotle by defining these distinctions through how conceptual mechanisms behave rather than through language. Thus, the distinction between constructive and omissive may be applied where language is an uncertain guide, as it is when discussing abstract concepts.

Omissive Classes Exhibit Ambivalence

Since the constructive class C does not both accept and reject any image, its complement $\overline{C}$ either accepts or rejects each image (we are assuming that $\overline{C}$ is sheath-free, see Section 2.7). The jurisdiction of an omissive class must therefore accept all images, whereas the jurisdiction of a constructive class must omit some images by the inexhaustibility principle.

By the inexhaustibility principle, the constructive class C must fail to examine some image i, that is, it must neither accept nor reject i. The complement $\overline{C}$ must therefore both accept i (because C does not accept it) and reject i (because C does not reject it). We call this result the *ambivalence principle of (omissive) classes*:

For any omissive class D, it must be possible to imagine an image i such that D would both accept and reject i if it were presented.

This is not a new principle, but a derivation from the inexhaustibility principle of constructive classes stated earlier.

If an omissive class D both accepts and rejects an image i, then D is said to be *ambivalent* about i. The class of images that D is ambivalent about is called the *ambivalence* of D. As can be seen by inspecting Figure 2.2, the ambivalence of $\overline{C}$ is the complement of the jurisdiction of C.

A class is said to be *populable* if it is possible for there to be an image that the class accepts. Otherwise, the class is said to be *unpopulable*. The inexhaustibility principle states that the ambivalence of an omissive class is populable. The ambivalence of a constructive class, however, is unpopulable by the definition of *constructive*. The difference between the opposite and the complement of a constructive class C is reflected in their ambivalences: the complement $\overline{C}$ has a populable ambivalence and is omissive, whereas the opposite $°C$ has an unpopulable ambivalence and is constructive.

Classes Are Characterized by Performance Type

The choice of « constructive » or « omissive » is called the *performance type* of a class. Every class in data logic is either constructive or omissive, and no class is both. The two performance types « constructive » and « omissive » are said to be *complementary* to each other. The performance type of a class may be determined by examining its jurisdiction and ambivalence. That is,

(i) A *constructive* class never both accepts and rejects an image in the same performance (its ambivalence is unpopulable). However, by inexhaustibility, a constructive class must be able to not examine some image (its jurisdiction is *limited*).

(ii) An *omissive* class must accept or reject any image that it is presented with (its jurisdiction is universal). However, by inexhaustibility, an omissive class must be able to both accept and reject some image (its ambivalence is populable).

These criteria define *constructive* and *omissive* without recourse to complements.

The Complement of an Omissive Class

The concepts of complement and opposite apply to omissive as well as to constructive classes. They are defined as follows:

(i) The complement $\overline{E}$ of a class E accepts what E does not accept and rejects what E does not reject.

(ii) The opposite $°E$ of a class E accepts what E rejects and rejects what E accepts.

By definition then, the complement of the complement of any class E is equivalent to E.

The complement $\overline{D}$ of an omissive class D both accepts and rejects an image i if and only if D neither accepts nor rejects i. Since D is omissive, D must either accept or reject any image. Therefore $\overline{D}$ does not both accept and reject any image, so $\overline{D}$ is constructive.

The opposite of an omissive class D both accepts and rejects an image i if and only if D both rejects and accepts i. Thus, $°D$ is ambivalent about the same images as D, so $°D$ is omissive. Notice that the opposite of an omissive class, $°D$, embraces the complement, $\overline{D}$.

The opposite of the complement of a class is equivalent to the complement of its opposite, as shown in Figure 2.3.

Conclusion

We have distinguished two *performance types* of classes, *constructive* and *omissive*. Every class in data logic is either constructive or omissive, and no class is both. The performance type of a class may be determined by describing how it examines images: a constructive class does not examine some images (this is the *inexhaustibility principle*), while an omissive class examines all images, but accepts and rejects some images simultaneously. The distinction between constructive and omissive is one of the primary departures from symbolic logic, which recognizes no such distinction.

The classes that were discussed in Chapter 1 were all constructive. Omissive classes are formed from constructive classes by applying a process of complementation. That is, we may imagine testing whether or not an omissive class D accepts an image i by testing whether or not its complement $\overline{D}$, which is constructive, accepts i. D will then accept i if $\overline{D}$ does not accept i. Data base design has traditionally been concerned only with constructive classes. Most ordinary nouns and adjectives represent constructive classes. However, omissive classes occur frequently in mathematics and in formal logic. Maintaining the distinction between performance types permits data logic to avoid such anomalies as Russell's paradox that hamper other logical systems.

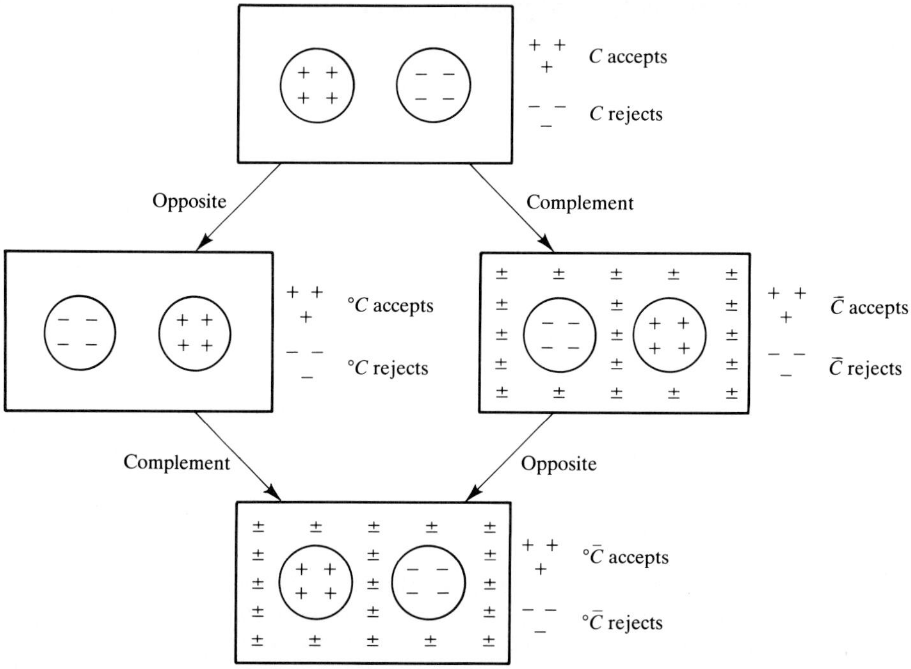

Figure 2.3 The opposite of the complement is equivalent to the complement of the opposite.

2.3 BASIC LOGIC OF EMBRACINGS

An Embracing Implies Its Contrapositive

Suppose B and C are two classes and C embraces B. Then any image accepted by B must be accepted by C. Now suppose that an image i is not accepted by C. If i were accepted by B, we would have to conclude that i was accepted by C by the embracing, which would contradict the assumption. Therefore i is not accepted by B. The image i is not accepted by C if and only if it is accepted by its complement $\overline{C}$, and, similarly, i is not accepted by B if and only if it is accepted by B's complement $\overline{B}$. Therefore, we have the law of logic:

$$\text{If } B \subseteq C \text{ then } \overline{C} \subseteq \overline{B} \tag{1}$$

The embracing $\overline{C} \subseteq \overline{B}$ is called the *contrapositive* of the embracing $B \subseteq C$, as in symbolic logic. The rule (1) is called the *contrapositive law*. We will formalize the contrapositive law later as an axiom, once we have completed introducing the laws of data logic.

A Class Is Equivalent to Its Double Complement

A class C accepts an image i if and only if the complement $\overline{C}$ does not accept i. The complement of $\overline{C}$, $\overline{\overline{C}}$, accepts i if and only if $\overline{C}$ does not accept i. Therefore, $\overline{\overline{C}}$ accepts an image if and only if C accepts the image, so the two classes are equivalent:

$$C \equiv \overline{\overline{C}}$$

Embracings Are Transitive

Suppose C embraces B and D embraces C. If B accepts an image i, then C must accept i since $B \subseteq C$. Since moreover $C \subseteq D$, D must accept i. Therefore D embraces B:

$$\text{If } B \subseteq C \text{ and } C \subseteq D, \text{ then } B \subseteq D$$

The three laws just introduced should be familiar to readers acquainted with logic.

An Unpopulable Class Must Accept No Image

In the last section, we defined an *unpopulable* class to be a class that must accept no image, that is, a class such that any image that is presented must either be rejected or not examined. The symbol "$\varnothing$" will often be used to represent an unpopulable class. An unpopulable class can not both accept and reject an image, since it never accepts an image. Therefore, an unpopulable class is constructive.

By the inexhaustibility principle, an unpopulable class, being constructive, must fail to examine some image. Since any image that is examined is rejected, even an unpopulable class must fail to reject some image. There may therefore be many unpopulable classes, each rejecting different images. Since equivalence is based entirely on acceptance, however, all unpopulable classes are equivalent. We will therefore refer to *the* unpopulable class. Any class embraces the unpopulable class:

$$\varnothing \subseteq B$$

The Universal Class Must Accept Any Image

A class that accepts any image that is presented to it is called a *universal class* and is often written "$\Box$". Since a universal class accepts any image, its jurisdiction is universal, so it is omissive.

By the ambivalence principle, a universal class, being omissive, must both accept and reject some image. Different universal classes may reject different images, but since equivalence is based entirely on acceptance, all universal classes are equivalent. Any class is embraced by the universal class:

$$B \subseteq \Box$$

Conclusion

Embracings obey a *contrapositive law*: if a class C embraces a class B then the complement $\overline{B}$ embraces the complement $\overline{C}$. Embracings are transitive: if D embraces C and C embraces B then D embraces B. Both these properties will be used extensively in proofs.

2.4 INTERSECTION AND UNION

The Intersection of Two Classes Accepts What Both Classes Accept

We define the *intersection* of two classes B and C, written "$B \cap C$", to be the class that accepts an image i if and only if B accepts i and C accepts i. Notice that this definition refers to the *images* accepted by B and by C, not to the *recognizers* that are instances of B and of C. If a recognizer d is an instance of $B \cap C$, then $B \cap C$ accepts some manifestation i of d. Therefore B accepts i, so d is an instance of B, and C accepts i, so d is an instance of C:

$$\text{If } B \cap C{:}(d) \text{ then } B{:}(d) \text{ and } C{:}(d)$$

Conversely, however, if d is an instance of B and d is an instance of C, then B and C might accept only different manifestations of d. That is, d need not be an instance of $B \cap C$.

For example, let B be the class « _____ Is Red » and let C be the class « _____ Is Green ». Imagine that some table is painted red, and is then repainted green. Let d be a recognizer for the table, and suppose that d is insensitive to color. The recognizer d then accepts two impressions of the table, one with the table painted red, and the other with the table painted green. Let r indicate the image of the red table, and let g indicate the image of the green table. Then B accepts r but not g and C accepts g but not r. Since B and C do not accept the same image, d is not an instance of the intersection $B \cap C$.

Intersection obeys the following rules:

$$B \cap C \subseteq B$$

$$B \cap C \subseteq C$$

$$B \cap C \equiv C \cap B$$

$$B \cap B \equiv B$$

$$B \cap (C \cap D) \equiv (B \cap C) \cap D$$

$$\text{If } B \subseteq C \text{ then } (B \cap D) \subseteq (C \cap D)$$

$$\text{If } B \subseteq C \text{ and } B \subseteq D, \text{ then } B \subseteq (C \cap D)$$

The Union of Two Classes Accepts What Either Class Accepts

We define the *union* of two classes B and C, written "$B \cup C$", to be the class that accepts an image i if and only if B accepts i or C accepts i. That is, $B \cup C$ accepts i if there is a performance in which B accepts i or if there is a performance in which C accepts i.

If a recognizer d is an instance of $B \cup C$ then some manifestation i of d is accepted by B or by C, so d is an instance of B or d is an instance of C. If d is an instance of B then some manifestation i of d is accepted by B, so i is accepted by $B \cup C$, and d is an instance of $B \cup C$. Similarly, if d is an instance of C then d is an instance of $B \cup C$. Thus, unlike intersection, there is no difference between the statements "$B{:}(d)$ or $C{:}(d)$" and "$B \cup C{:}(d)$":

$$B \cup C{:}(d) \text{ if and only if } B{:}(d) \text{ or } C{:}(d)$$

Union obeys the following rules:

$$B \subseteq B \cup C$$
$$C \subseteq B \cup C$$
$$B \cup C \equiv C \cup B$$
$$B \cup B \equiv B$$
$$B \cup (C \cup D) \equiv (B \cup C) \cup D$$
$$\text{If } B \subseteq C \text{ then } (B \cup D) \subseteq (C \cup D)$$
$$\text{If } B \subseteq D \text{ and } C \subseteq D, \text{ then } (B \cup C) \subseteq D$$

The Complement of an Intersection Is a Union

The complement of the class $B \cap C$ accepts what $B \cap C$ does not accept. That is, $\overline{B \cap C}$ accepts an image i if and only if B does not accept i or C does not accept i. Therefore,

$$\overline{B \cap C} \equiv \overline{B} \cup \overline{C}$$

Similarly, the complement of the class $B \cup C$ accepts what $B \cup C$ does not accept. That is, $\overline{B \cup C}$ accepts an image i if and only if B does not accept i and C does not accept i. Thus:

$$\overline{B \cup C} \equiv \overline{B} \cap \overline{C}$$

Intersection Distributes with Union

The operations of intersection and union are distributive as in set theory:

$$B \cap (C \cup D) \equiv (B \cap C) \cup (B \cap D)$$
$$B \cup (C \cap D) \equiv (B \cup C) \cap (B \cup D)$$

The Performance Type of an Intersection Is Determined from Its Constituents

We consider next how to determine the performance type of the intersection $B \cap C$. To do so, we must derive an opposite for $B \cap C$. As with any class, many opposites are possible. However, since $B \cap C$ is derived from the classes B and C, we may derive an opposite for $B \cap C$ from the opposites of B and C, and determine the performance type thereby.

Ideally, the performance type of the intersection of two classes should be determinable from the performance types of the classes themselves. The unpopulable class and the universal class therefore show what the performance types should be:

$\varnothing \cap \varnothing \equiv \varnothing$	[constructive]	$\cap$	[constructive]	$\equiv$	[constructive]
$\varnothing \cap \square \equiv \varnothing$	[constructive]	$\cap$	[omissive]	$\equiv$	[constructive]
$\square \cap \square \equiv \square$	[omissive]	$\cap$	[omissive]	$\equiv$	[omissive]

Suppose that B and C have the same performance type. A logical choice for $°(B \cap C)$ would then be $°B \cup °C$. This choice is easily verified by considering $B \cap B$. The class $°(B \cap B)$ must be just $°B$, which is the same as the predicted result $°B \cup °B$.

Now suppose that B and C have different performance types. As a test case, let B be constructive and let C be $\overline{B}$, and therefore omissive. If we preserve the definition of $°(B \cap C)$ as a union of two classes, one derived from B and the other from C, there are four potential choices:

$$°B \cup °C \equiv °B \cup °\overline{B} \equiv \Box$$
$$°B \cup \overline{C} \equiv °B \cup B$$
$$\overline{B} \cup °C \equiv \overline{B} \cup °\overline{B} \equiv \Box$$
$$\overline{B} \cup \overline{C} \equiv \overline{B} \cup B \equiv \Box$$

(We are assuming that B and $°B$ are sheath–free to simplify the presentation, see Section 2.7).

If B and C have different performance types, then their intersection $B \cap C$ is constructive (by virtue of $\varnothing \cap \Box \equiv \varnothing$). The opposite $°(B \cap C)$ is therefore also constructive, so by the inexhaustibility principle, $°(B \cap C)$ can not be universal. Therefore the only possible choice is the second one, $°B \cup \overline{C}$, the union of the opposite of the constructive class with the complement of the omissive class.

The intersection of a constructive class with an omissive class is often used in forming a *relative complement*. That is, imagine two constructive classes B and C with $B \subseteq C$. The *relative complement* of B in C is then the class $C \cap \overline{B}$. It accepts any image that C accepts and B does not accept. It rejects any image that C rejects or B *accepts*.

The Performance Type of a Union Is Determined from Its Constituents

We may derive $°(B \cup C)$ in the same way as we derived $°(B \cap C)$. The performance type of $B \cup C$ is given by examining $\varnothing$ and $\Box$:

$\varnothing \cup \varnothing \equiv \varnothing$	[constructive] ∪ [constructive] ≡ [constructive]
$\varnothing \cup \Box \equiv \Box$	[constructive] ∪ [omissive] ≡ [omissive]
$\Box \cup \Box \equiv \Box$	[omissive] ∪ [omissive] ≡ [omissive]

If B and C have the same performance type, then $°(B \cup C)$ is reasonably taken to be $°B \cap °C$. If B and C have different performance types, then as before, suppose B is constructive and C is $\overline{B}$. We then have the choices:

$$°B \cap °C \equiv °B \cap °\overline{B} \equiv \varnothing$$
$$°B \cap \overline{C} \equiv °B \cap B \equiv \varnothing$$
$$\overline{B} \cap °C \equiv \overline{B} \cap °\overline{B}$$
$$\overline{B} \cap \overline{C} \equiv \overline{B} \cap B \equiv \varnothing$$

Since $B \cup C$ is omissive if B and C have different performance types, the class $°(B \cup C)$ must be populable. Thus, only the third choice, $\overline{B} \cap °C$, is possible.

We may summarize these results by the following table:

Type of B	Type of C	$°(B \cap C)$	$°(B \cup C)$
constructive	constructive	$°B \cup °C$	$°B \cap °C$
constructive	omissive	$°B \cup \overline{C}$	$\overline{B} \cap °C$
omissive	constructive	$\overline{B} \cup °C$	$°B \cap \overline{C}$
omissive	omissive	$°B \cup °C$	$°B \cap °C$

Conclusion

We have introduced the operations of *intersection* and *union* of classes, which are akin to intersection and union of sets in symbolic logic. The performance type of an intersection or union is determined from the performance types of its constituents. If two classes have the same performance type, their intersection and their union have the same performance type as the classes. If two classes have different performance types, their intersection is constructive and their union is omissive.

2.5 RECOGNIZERS

Recognizers May Be Constructive or Omissive

Recognizers may be complemented just as associations may be. For example, the complement of a recognizer for a chosen hammer, « this hammer », may be thought of as the recognizer « any impression other than this hammer ». The recognizer « any impression other than this hammer », or simply, « not this hammer », is *ambivalent* about an impression if it is uncertain whether or not the impression is a manifestation of « this hammer ».

Imagine, for example, the hammer melting in a furnace together with some scrap. There is no clear point at which the lump of metal ceases to be « this hammer ». Where there is indecision, the complement « not this hammer » is ambivalent. The recognizer « not this hammer » is therefore omissive (because its ambivalence is populable).

An *omissive recognizer* is a conceptual mechanism that is performed as follows:

(i) A performance includes a presentation of an impression to the recognizer.

(ii) The recognizer accepts or rejects the impression. The recognizer may both accept and reject the impression in the same performance.

The *complement* of a constructive recognizer d is the omissive recognizer $\overline{d}$ that accepts any impression that d does not accept, and rejects any impression that d does not reject. The *complement* of an omissive recognizer e is the constructive recognizer $\overline{e}$ that accepts any impression that e does not accept, and rejects any impression that e does not reject. The *opposite* of a recognizer d is the recognizer $°d$ that accepts what d rejects and rejects what d accepts. The opposite of d has the same performance type as d.

Inexhaustibility of Recognizers

Inexhaustibility applies to recognizers as well as to classes. For example, consider a toaster that is gradually disassembled and reassembled with entirely new parts, so that none of the original parts remain. At some point, we have formed a new « toaster », but an ordinary appliance user may not be able to define the precise stage of repair when his conception of the original toaster, « toaster x », changed to a conception of a new toaster. Consider, then the recognizer that recognizes « toaster x ». This recognizer rejects an impression when the impression is certainly not « toaster x ». The impressions of intermediate stages of repair of the toaster are not certainly not « toaster x », and so they are not rejected. Nor are they accepted, for they are not certainly impressions of « toaster x ». Thus, there are impressions that are neither accepted nor rejected by the recognizer.

The *inexhaustibility principle of recognizers* is then:

> For any constructive recognizer d, it must be possible to imagine an impression that d would neither accept nor reject if it were presented.

and the *ambivalence principle of recognizers* is:

> For any omissive recognizer d, it must be possible to imagine an impression that d would both accept and reject if it were presented.

Intersection and Union

The *intersection* of two recognizers d and e, written "$d \cap e$", accepts any impression that both d and e accept. The *union* of d and e, written "$d \cup e$", accepts any impression that d accepts or that e accepts. Intersection and union of recognizers obey similar laws to intersection and union of classes:

$$d \cap e \subseteq d$$

$$d \cap e \subseteq e$$

$$d \cap e \equiv e \cap d$$

$$d \cap d \equiv d$$

$$d \cap (e \cap f) \equiv (d \cap e) \cap f$$

$$\text{If } d \subseteq e \text{ then } (d \cap f) \subseteq (e \cap f)$$

$$\text{If } d \subseteq e \text{ and } d \subseteq f \text{ then } d \subseteq (e \cap f)$$

The complement of an intersection is a union, and vice versa:

$$\overline{d \cap e} \equiv \bar{d} \cup \bar{e}$$

$$\overline{d \cup e} \equiv \bar{d} \cap \bar{e}$$

The logic of union is obtained by applying these formulas to the logic of intersection described above.

Unpopulable and Universal Recognizers

A recognizer that must accept no impression is called *unpopulable*. An unpopulable recognizer may be written $\mu\varnothing$, since it is the melding of an unpopulable class. A recognizer that must accept any impression that is presented to it is called *universal*, and is written $\mu\Box$. Any recognizer embraces $\mu\varnothing$ and is embraced by $\mu\Box$.

Logic of Melding

An impression accepted as part of an image by $B \cap C$ will be accepted as that image by both B and C, so

$$\mu(B \cap C) \subseteq \mu B \cap \mu C$$

Consider, however, two classes that accept the same impression ι, but only when compounded with different recognizers, that is, when appearing as different images. The impression ι will then be accepted by both meldings, which are blind to recognizers, but it will not be part of an image that is accepted by both classes, so it will not be accepted by the melding $\mu(B \cap C)$. Thus, $\mu(B \cap C)$ need not embrace $\mu B \cap \mu C$. If one of the classes, say B, is contentual, then any impression accepted by μB and μC must be accepted as some image i by C, and B must accept i. The impression must therefore be accepted by $\mu(B \cap C)$:

$$\text{If } B \text{ is contentual or } C \text{ is contentual, then } \mu B \cap \mu C \subseteq \mu(B \cap C)$$

Similarly, if an impression is accepted as part of an image by B or by C, then that image is accepted by $B \cup C$, so

$$\mu B \cup \mu C \subseteq \mu(B \cup C)$$

Unlike intersection, however, if an impression is accepted as part of an image by $B \cup C$, then that image is accepted by B or by C, regardless of whether or not B or C is contentual. Thus,

$$\mu(B \cup C) \subseteq \mu B \cup \mu C$$

Varieties of Expressions That Use Recognizers

The operations of complement, granulation, melding, and realization can be combined to create a wide variety of distinct ideas. Consider, for example, the class « _____ Is A Marble », which we will write symbolically as ''M''. This class is assumed to have a handle, written νM. We have then the following different ideas:

« _____ Is A Marble »	M
« a marble »	μM
« the class of marbles »	νM

Applying complementation, we may form the further ideas:

« _____ Is Not A Marble »	$\overline{M}$
« something that is not a marble »	$\mu\overline{M}$
« the class of things that aren't marbles »	$\nu(\overline{M})$
« something that is not the class of marbles »	$\overline{\nu M}$
« _____ Is Not The Class Of Marbles »	$\Gamma(\overline{\nu M})$

Using data logic, each of these ideas may be recognized as distinct and may be subjected to rigorous study.

Conclusion

Recognizers obey a logic that is similar to the logic of classes. That is, recognizers may be intersected, united, complemented, and embraced just as classes may be. Recognizers, like classes, are always either constructive or omissive, never both. The logic of recognizers and the logic of classes are related by the operations of granulation and melding. The logic of recognizers has no counterpart in symbolic logic.

2.6 PROPOSITIONS

The Performance Type of a Simple Proposition

We will find it valuable to assume that a proposition has a performance type, just as classes and recognizers have performance types. The performance type of a proposition $C{:}(d)$ may be studied by imagining that C is contentual. The calculation of performance types will apply to all classes, however, not only to contentual classes.

If C is contentual, the proposition $C{:}(d)$ is a statement that μC and d overlap, that is, that there is some impression that is accepted simultaneously by d and (compounded in an image to d) by C. It is therefore a statement about the intersection of d with the melding of C, so its performance type follows the pattern of intersections:

C	d	$C{:}(d)$
constructive	constructive	constructive
constructive	omissive	constructive
omissive	constructive	constructive
omissive	omissive	omissive

That is, $C{:}(d)$ is constructive if d is constructive, and $C{:}(d)$ has the same performance type as C if d is omissive.

To illustrate the various forms of $C{:}(d)$, imagine the constructive recognizer « this table », written "t", and the constructive class « _____ Is Red », written "R". We have then:

R:(t) « some impression of this table is red »

R:($\bar{t}$) « something other than this table is red »

$\overline{R}$:(t) « some impression of this table is not red »

$\overline{R}$:($\bar{t}$) « something other than this table is not red »

The form we will use most frequently is where both items are constructive, R:(t). Notice in particular that R:(t) and $\overline{R}$:(t) may be affirmed simultaneously: they merely claim that « this table » has been imagined red at one time and not red at another. The identity of the table might, for example, be determined by its structural members, so it remains the same table when it is repainted.

The Negation of a Simple Proposition

The *negation* of a proposition q, written "$\tilde{}q$", evokes the impressions that q does not evoke, and does not evoke the impressions that q evokes (see Section 1.10 for a discussion of how a proposition evokes impressions). We will study negation more closely by examining the negation of the simple proposition C:(d).

The proposition C:(d) states that some impression is accepted by d and (as an image) is accepted by C. The *negation* of C:(d), written "$\tilde{}$(C:(d))" or simply "$\tilde{}C$:(d)", states therefore that each impression is either not accepted by d or is not accepted (as an image) by C. Notice that two new ideas are introduced in the negation of C:(d)—« each impression » rather than « some impression » and two clauses joined by « or ».

The phrase « each impression » used above means each impression that has been imagined when the proposition is conceived. It does not preclude some impression being imagined later that invalidates the proposition. For example, suppose that Jean has never been a lawyer. The proposition $\overline{Lawyer}$:($Jean$) states that Jean has at one time not been a lawyer. The embracing $Jean \subseteq \mu(\overline{Lawyer})$ states that Jean by definition can not be a lawyer, which is not the case. The correct proposition is $\tilde{}Lawyer$:($Jean$), which states that each image of « Jean » so far is not a lawyer.

Conformers

The proposition « each impression either is not accepted by d or is accepted as an image of d by C » is written "C:[d]". A recognizer d that satisfies C:[d] will be called a *conformer* of C. If C is contentual, C:[d] may be viewed as stating that d is included in the melding of C, μC, as shown in Figure 2.4 (we are assuming that C is sheath-free, see Section 2.7). The proposition C:[d] is considered to be a *simple proposition*, as is C:(d).

If C is contentual and sheath–free, the statement that d is not an instance of C may be viewed as stating that μC and d do not overlap. The recognizer d is then a conformer of $\overline{C}$, as shown in Figure 2.5, because d is included in $\overline{\mu C} \equiv \mu\overline{C}$.

The same reasoning holds for classes that are not contentual. That is, for any class C and any recognizer d,

$$\tilde{}C:(d) \text{ if and only if } \overline{C}:[d]$$

The term *conformer* is motivated by the following reasoning. The proposition that a recognizer d is a conformer of a class C is a statement about *all* the manifestations of d.

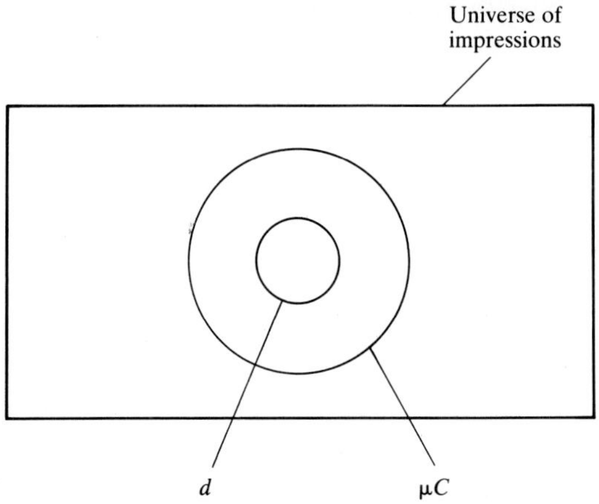

Figure 2.4 The recognizer *d* is a conformer of the class *C*.

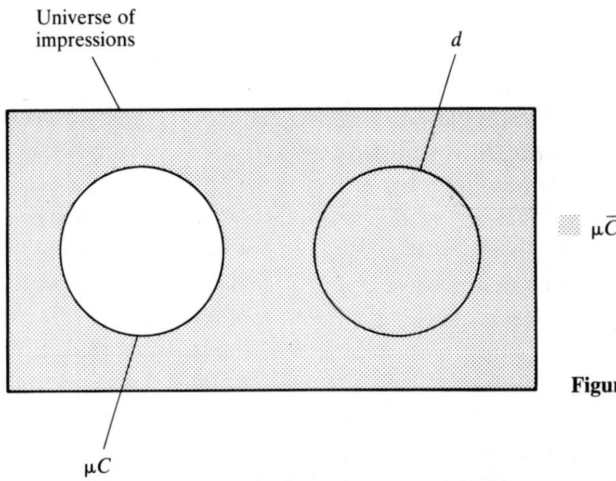

Figure 2.5 *d* is not an instance of *C*.

Unless *d* has few manifestations, it would be impractical for *C* to examine all the manifestations of *d* systematically. It is likely, therefore, that the impressions compounded with *d* are disregarded by *C*, so that *C* considers only the recognizer *d* when examining an image of the form $d.\iota$. If we imagine that a recognizer specifies the form of an image, then the examination of *d* is a test of whether or not *d conforms* to the standards of *C*.

This reasoning is illustrated further in Figure 2.6. A class that always disregards the impression portion of an image will be called a *literal class*. A *contentual* class, in contrast, examines only the impression portion of an image. Literal classes are often found in mathematics and other formal systems. Any instance of a literal class is a conformer of the class. Note, however, that a class that is not literal may also have conformers.

Extending our example, we may illustrate the various forms of C:[d] as follows:

R:[t]	« this table is always red »
R:[$\bar{t}$]	« everything but this table is red »
$\bar{R}$:[t]	« this table is never red »
$\bar{R}$:[$\bar{t}$]	« everything but this table is not red »

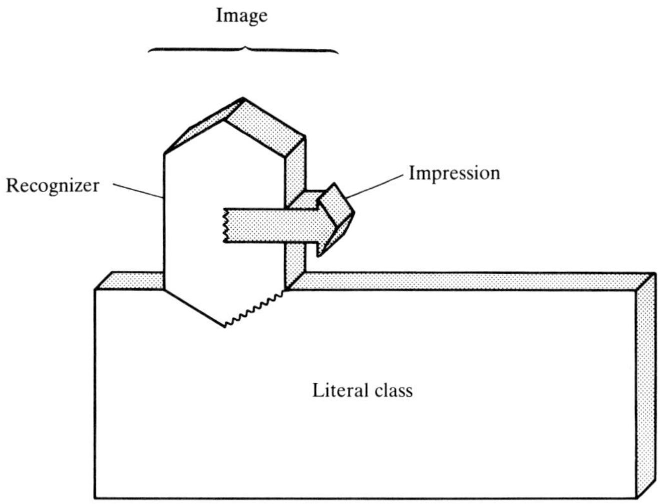

Figure 2.6 A literal class examines only the recognizer portion of an image.

The words "always" and "never" in this example are illustrative only—there is no implied sense of time in a conformer. The proposition C:[d] refers to all impressions of d, over whatever time, space, or other parameters are relevant to « d ».

Unless otherwise stated, we will consider instances of a constructive class and conformers of an omissive class. These are the most important forms for data base applications, although the other forms do arise in theoretical work. For example, while no recognizer is an instance of the constructive class $\varnothing$, any recognizer is a conformer of the omissive class $\square$.

Negation Interchanges Performance Types

Negation converts a constructive to an omissive proposition and vice versa. Thus, the performance types of conformer propositions are given by the table:

C	d	C:[d]
constructive	constructive	omissive
constructive	omissive	constructive
omissive	constructive	omissive
omissive	omissive	omissive

That is, C:[d] is omissive if d is constructive, and has the same performance type as C if d is omissive.

The pattern of performance types is that of a union. Thus, if $\overline{C}$ is contentual, then $\overline{C}$:(d) is a statement that some impression is accepted by $\mu\overline{C} \cap d$. The negation C:[d] is then a statement that each impression is accepted by $\mu C \cup \overline{d}$. The asymmetric result that C:[d] is constructive only when d is omissive arises from the presence of the complement $\overline{d}$ in the expression that defines C:[d].

The Topic Recognizer of an Omissive Proposition

We will say that an impression *supports* a proposition if the impression illustrates the contention made by the proposition. For example, an impression of a blue sky supports the proposition « the sky is blue ».

If a proposition q is constructive, then its topic recognizer $Яq$ accepts impressions that support q and rejects impressions that support $\tilde{}q$. For example, consider the constructive proposition « there is life on Mars ». The topic recognizer of this proposition accepts impressions of curious creatures cavorting on Mars. It rejects impressions of Mars as a barren wasteland. It neither accepts nor rejects impressions that have no relevance to the question of there being life on Mars, such as an impression of a teacup.

The topic recognizer of an omissive proposition p behaves somewhat differently. It accepts any impression that does not support $\tilde{}p$, and rejects any impression that does not support p. Thus, the topic recognizer of « there is not life on Mars » both accepts and rejects an impression of a teacup, because the impression neither supports the proposition nor its negation.

The proposition that only accepts impressions that support there being no life on Mars is not the negation but the *opposite* of « there is life on Mars ». The topic recognizer of the opposite $°q$ of a constructive proposition q accepts impressions that support $\tilde{}q$ and rejects impressions that support q.

Thus, topic recognizers are defined so that the following formulas are obeyed for any proposition s:

$$Я(\tilde{}s) \equiv \overline{Яs}$$

$$Я(°s) \equiv °(Яs)$$

A Proposition Has the Same Performance Type As Its Topic Recognizer

We may use these formulas to compute the performance type of a topic recognizer, considering simple propositions of the classes $\varnothing$ and $\square$. If d is a recognizer, then no impression may support the proposition $\varnothing$:(d). Thus, the topic recognizer $\varnothing(d)$ is unpopulable, so $\varnothing(d)$ is constructive. Since we would like the performance type of the proposition C:(d) to be determined by the performance types of C and d, if C is constructive, the performance type of $C(d)$ is the same as the performance type of $\varnothing(d)$. Therefore, $C(d)$ is constructive whenever C is constructive.

Conversely, no impression does not support the proposition $\square$:$[d]$. Thus, the topic recognizer $\square[d]$ is universal, so $\square[d]$ is omissive. Therefore, $C[d]$ is omissive whenever C is omissive.

Consider next the proposition that a recognizer d is a *conformer* of $\varnothing$, $\varnothing$:$[d]$. This proposition is read « each impression is not accepted by d or is accepted as an image of d by $\varnothing$ ». Since $\varnothing$ can not accept any image, the expression reduces to « each impression is not accepted by d », or « some impression is accepted by $\overline{d}$ ». The topic recognizer of the latter proposition has the same performance type as $\overline{d}$. Thus, $C[d]$ has the complementary performance type to d if C is constructive.

By the contrapositive law, then, $\square(d) \equiv \overline{\varnothing[d]}$ has the same performance type as d. Thus, $C(d)$ has the same performance type as d when C is omissive. These formulas may be compared with the tables given earlier for the performance types of C:(d) and C:$[d]$ to show that a proposition has the same performance type as its topic recognizer.

Conclusion

There are two ways that a recognizer d may be combined with a class C to form a proposition: one may propose that d is an *instance* of C, which is the normal method when C is constructive, or one may propose that d is a *conformer* of C, which is the normal method when C is omissive. Conformers arise most frequently in connection with negation of propositions: the negation of the proposition « d is an instance of C » is the proposition « d is a conformer of $\overline{C}$ ». Symbolic logic does not distinguish between instances and conformers.

We have shown that propositions have performance types, and that the performance type of a simple proposition may be determined from the performance types of its constituent elements (that is, from the performance type of the class and the performance type of the recognizer). We will show in Section 2.12 how the performance types of more complex propositions may also be determined from their constituents, so that all performance types may be computed once the performance types of the constituent associations and recognizers are known.

We can often determine whether we are dealing with instances or with conformers by examining performance types. For example, the proposition « d is an instance of C » is always constructive if d is constructive, but the proposition « d is a conformer of C » is always omissive if d is constructive. Instances are by far the dominant form in data base applications, while conformers are used heavily in formal systems such as mathematics and the axiomatization of logic.

2.7 MANAGEMENT OF CONTRADICTIONS

Contradictions Must Be Managed

Two classes are said to be *disjoint* if their intersection is unpopulable. Suppose that a class B and a class $\overline{C}$ are disjoint:

$$B \cap \overline{C} \subseteq \varnothing$$

Then no image may be accepted by B and not be accepted by C.

In symbolic logic, the two statements "$B \subseteq C$" and "$B \cap \overline{C} \subseteq \varnothing$" are equivalent. This leads to difficulties in managing contradictions. For suppose we have the contradiction that some d is both an instance and not an instance of a class B. In symbolic logic, for any classes B and C,

$$\varnothing \subseteq C$$

$$\varnothing \equiv B \cap \overline{B}$$

Therefore,

$$B \cap \overline{B} \subseteq C$$

Since d is an instance of $B \cap \overline{B}$, d must be an instance of C, according to symbolic logic. Therefore, because of a single contradiction, d becomes an instance of every class. This result makes it impossible to apply symbolic logic to contradictory data, because a single contradiction propagates uncontrollably throughout the population.

Contradiction Is Described by Sheaths

Ordinary reasoning reaches contradictions frequently, either from faulty reasoning or by deduction from contradictory premises. In many practical situations, it is valuable to retain a contradiction until the reason for the contradiction can be determined. Reasoning on other topics should be able to proceed unimpeded while the contradiction is studied. To manage data that contains contradictions, data logic allows there to be recognizers that are both instances of B and conformers of $\overline{B}$.

The class $B \cap \overline{B}$ is called the *sheath* of the class B. The sheath of a class B is also the sheath of its complement $\overline{B}$. Similarly, the recognizer $d \cap \overline{d}$ is called the *sheath* of the recognizer d.

If the sheath of B is unpopulable, then $B \cap \overline{B} \equiv \varnothing$, and $B \cup \overline{B} \equiv \square$. We say in this case that B is *sheath-free*. However, if the sheath of B is populable, then $B \cup \overline{B}$ is not equivalent to $\square$. There may then be images that B neither accepts nor does not accept. A recognizer d is *sheath-free* if the sheath of d must accept no impression.

In our discussions of the laws of data logic, we will often consider classes to be sheath-free to simplify the presentation. However, the laws of data logic apply to classes with populable sheaths as well as to sheath-free classes.

Performance Types and Sheaths

Since a sheath is an intersection of a constructive with an omissive class, a sheath is constructive. If B is constructive, we have:

$$°(B \cap \overline{B}) \equiv °B \cup B \supseteq B \cap \overline{B}$$

Thus, a sheath rejects all the images that it accepts, although a sheath-free constructive class can not both accept and reject any image.

We must therefore modify the definitions of constructive and omissive to accommodate classes with populable sheaths. In a constructive class, any image that is both accepted and rejected must be an instance of the sheath of the class. When the sheath is unpopulable, this definition reduces to that given in Section 2.2. Similarly, for an omissive class, any image that is neither accepted nor rejected must be an instance of the sheath of the class.

Logical Reasoning Using Sheaths

Contradictory reasoning presents many unusual phenomena. For example, a sheath is actually embraced in its complement:

$$B \cap \overline{B} \subseteq B \cup \overline{B} \equiv \overline{B \cap \overline{B}}$$

Every instance of a sheath is therefore also not an instance of the sheath.

Despite such bizarre properties, sheaths may be manipulated with the same rigor as other classes. For example, the sheath of an intersection $B \cap C$ may be computed as follows:

$$\begin{aligned}(B \cap C) \cap \overline{B \cap C} &\equiv B \cap C \cap (\overline{B} \cup \overline{C}) \\ &\equiv (B \cap \overline{B} \cap C) \cup (B \cap C \cap \overline{C}) \\ &\equiv (C \cap \text{sheath } B) \cup (B \cap \text{sheath } C)\end{aligned}$$

Contradictions are therefore a special variety of propositions that are subject to the same laws as all other propositions. Logic can function in the presence of contradictions, so avoiding contradictions is not a prerequisite to reasoning as was argued by Hilbert (Hilbert and Ackermann 1938).

Disjointness versus Embracing

The difference between $B \subseteq C$ and $B \cap \overline{C} \subseteq \varnothing$ is explained by sheaths. Thus, by intersecting both sides of the embracing with $\overline{C}$, we obtain:

$$\text{If } B \subseteq C \text{ then } B \cap \overline{C} \subseteq C \cap \overline{C}$$

That is, if C embraces B, then $B \cap \overline{C}$ is only unpopulable if C is sheath-free. More generally, $B \cap \overline{C}$ is embraced in the sheath of C. Notice that $B \cap \overline{C}$ is also embraced in the sheath of B:

$$\text{If } B \subseteq C \text{ then } \overline{C} \subseteq \overline{B}$$

$$\text{If } \overline{C} \subseteq \overline{B} \text{ then } B \cap \overline{C} \subseteq B \cap \overline{B}$$

Suppose, conversely, that B and $\overline{C}$ are disjoint. We may conclude, then:

$$\text{If } B \cap \overline{C} \subseteq \varnothing \text{ then } (B \cap \overline{C}) \cup (B \cap C) \subseteq \varnothing \cup (B \cap C) \subseteq C$$

Therefore,

$$\text{If } B \cap \overline{C} \subseteq \varnothing \text{ then } B \cap (C \cup \overline{C}) \subseteq C$$

If C is sheath-free, then $C \cup \overline{C}$ is universal, and $B \subseteq C$.

By the contrapositive law, if $B \cap \overline{C} \subseteq \varnothing$ then $\square \subseteq \overline{B} \cup C$. Intersecting both sides of the latter formula with B gives:

$$\text{If } B \cap \overline{C} \subseteq \varnothing \text{ then } B \subseteq (B \cap \overline{B}) \cup (B \cap C) \subseteq (B \cap \overline{B}) \cup C$$

That is, if B and $\overline{C}$ are disjoint then B is embraced in the union of the sheath of B with C. If B is sheath–free, then C embraces B. More generally, if B and $\overline{C}$ are disjoint, then C embraces B if C embraces the sheath of B.

Sheaths Prevent Propagation of Contradictions

Sheaths prevent propagation of contradictions in the following way. Suppose that some recognizer d is found to be both an instance of B and a conformer of $\overline{B}$. If a class C bears no logical relationship to B, we can conclude nothing about how d relates to C. If C embraces B, then d is an instance of C. However, we can not conclude that d is also a conformer of $\overline{C}$. Conversely, if a class D is embraced by B, then we can conclude that d is a conformer of $\overline{D}$ (by the contrapositive $\overline{B} \subseteq \overline{D}$), but we can not conclude that d is an instance of D.

In a practical setting, we may want to consider any deductions from a contradiction to be suspect. We would then question, if d is both an instance of B and a conformer of $\overline{B}$, whether d is properly an instance of any class that embraces B or a conformer of any class that B embraces. However, there is no reason to question a proposition that d is an instance of some unrelated class E, or to question other instances of B or other conformers of $\overline{B}$. Thus, contradictions do not hinder reasoning about unrelated topics. Independent investigations can continue undisturbed while a contradiction is being resolved.

Conclusion

We have seen that the statement "C embraces B" is different from the statement "there must be no recognizer that is an instance of both B and $\overline{C}$." These two statements are considered to be the same in symbolic logic, which causes extreme consequences in managing contradictions. By distinguishing between the two statements, data logic is able to accommodate contradictions and to isolate them from unrelated propositions. This ability of data logic may assist automated reasoning, because it describes how a formal process can continue to operate even after it reaches a contradiction.

2.8 PERFORMANCE TYPE INTEGRITY

A Constructive Class May Not Embrace an Omissive Class

As previously noted, any class embraces the unpopulable class and is in turn embraced by the universal class. For a constructive class C then, we have the following embracings, with the performance types of each class noted to the side:

$\varnothing \subseteq C$	[constructive]	$\subseteq$	[constructive]
$\varnothing \subseteq \overline{C}$	[constructive]	$\subseteq$	[omissive]
$C \subseteq \square$	[constructive]	$\subseteq$	[omissive]
$\overline{C} \subseteq \square$	[omissive]	$\subseteq$	[omissive]

These embracings furnish examples of all possible pairs of performance types save one: the embracing of an omissive class in a constructive class.

If C is sheath-free, then one such embracing in particular would violate the inexhaustibility principle, namely:

$$\overline{C} \subseteq C$$

This embracing would force any image not accepted by C to be accepted by C, that is, it would force C to be universal. However, since C is constructive, C can not be universal by the inexhaustibility principle. Indeed, any embracing of the form $\overline{B} \subseteq C$ with B constructive leads to a violation of inexhaustibility, since $\overline{B} \subseteq C$ implies $\overline{B} \cap \overline{C} \subseteq \varnothing$ (because C has an unpopulable sheath) which implies by the contrapositive law that $\square \subseteq B \cup C$.

Notice that the similar embracing with performance types reversed does not cause difficulty:

$$C \subseteq \overline{C}$$

Here, any image accepted by C must not be accepted by C, so C is unpopulable. C may be unpopulable because C is constructive.

To preserve inexhaustibility, embracings of omissive classes in constructive classes are banned. We call this ban the *performance type integrity law*:

If $B \subseteq C$ and B is omissive, then C is omissive

or, equivalently:

If $B \subseteq C$ and C is constructive, then B is constructive

Although we have derived the performance type integrity law using classes with unpopulable sheaths, the law applies to classes with populable sheaths as well. The performance type integrity law has no counterpart in symbolic logic.

Performance type integrity also applies to recognizers:

If $d \subseteq e$ and d is omissive, then e is omissive

If $d \subseteq e$ and e is constructive, then d is constructive

Consequences of Performance Type Integrity

Performance type integrity prohibits defining a constructive class entirely by omissive classes. For example, the statement

Anything that is not a B is a C (1)

violates performance type integrity if both B and C are constructive. Since most ordinary nouns represent constructive classes, Formula (1) is not permitted in data logic when "*B*" and "*C*" are ordinary words (rather than phrases including the word "not" or specially defined terms).

We will see in Section 2.14 that it is helpful to consider Formula (1) to be a proposition even though it violates performance type integrity. This assumption will enable us to analyze such statements within the framework of logic. A proposition that violates performance type integrity is said to be *fat*. Although a fat proposition may be discussed, a fat proposition may not be affirmed.

The following statement is an example of a fat proposition formed from ordinary words:

If something has not been delivered, then it must be in transit. (2)

This statement is clearly false as it stands, for there are images that can neither be delivered nor be in transit, such as an organization or an account. The inexhaustibility principle states that there may always be such images, however we define « delivered » or « in transit », provided that both the classes « _____ Has Been Delivered » and « _____ Is In Transit » remain constructive (that is, provided that the classes are not defined as being *not* something constructive).

We might modify Formula (2) to read:

If a shipment has not been delivered, then it must be in transit. (3)

The premise of Formula (3) is that an image is an instance of an intersection of two classes: « _____ Has Not Been Delivered », an omissive class, and « _____ Is A Shipment », a constructive class. This intersection is constructive, because the intersection of any class with a constructive class is constructive. That is, Formula (3) is the embracing:

$$\text{Has Not Been Delivered} \cap \text{Is A Shipment} \subseteq \text{Is In Transit}$$

The left side of this embracing is a constructive class, so Formula (3) obeys performance type integrity. In Formula (3), a « shipment » is defined to be something that is either delivered or in transit. Anything that is neither, such as a bunch of goods that burned *en route*, is, according to Formula (3), not a shipment.

Performance type integrity applies to general terms of vague definition as well, as in the fat proposition:

Anything that is not real is fictional

If we accept that « Real » and « Fictional » are constructive, then this statement violates performance type integrity. By the inexhaustibility principle, it must be possible for there to be an image that is neither real nor fictional, since the union of « Real » and « Fictional » is a constructive class. An example of such an image might be a live performance of a play, or a natural number.

Conclusion

The *performance type integrity law* states that no constructive class may embrace any omissive class. This law is a consequence of the inexhaustibility principle introduced in Section 2.2. The performance type integrity law is not enforced in symbolic logic. We will argue that failure to observe this law causes many of the paradoxes of symbolic logic.

2.9 PROPOSITIONAL LOGIC

Implication Is Embracing of Topic Recognizers

We will say that a proposition p *implies* a proposition q if any impression evoked by p must also be evoked by q. An implication is therefore an embracing of the topic recognizer of p in the topic recognizer of q. We will write the proposition « p implies q » as "$p \Rightarrow q$". Formally, then,

$$(p \Rightarrow q) \text{ if and only if } (Яp \subseteq Яq)$$

The proposition p will be called the *premise* of the implication $p \Rightarrow q$, and the proposition q will be called the *conclusion*. We will write "$p \Leftrightarrow q$" when p implies q and q implies p. We say then that p and q are *interchangeable*.

In symbolic logic, the symbol "$\supset$" is often used for "$\Rightarrow$". This unfortunate symbol, which we do not use, is a corruption of the notation introduced by Peano, a capital C standing for *conseguenza* facing backwards (Peano 1889). The symbol "$\supset$" causes much confusion because it faces in the wrong direction. Thus, if a set T embraces a set S, then, for any x, if x is a member of S, then x is a member of T. In symbolic logic, one would write $(x \in S) \supset (x \in T)$, even though T has more members than S. The capital C facing in the correct direction was actually introduced first, but was curiously abandoned (Gergonne 1817).

An Omissive Proposition May Not Imply a Constructive Proposition

By performance type integrity, a constructive recognizer may not embrace an omissive recognizer. This law applies to topic recognizers, since they are recognizers. Since the performance type of a topic recognizer is the same as the performance type of its proposition, and since implication is embracing of topic recognizers, it follows that an omissive proposition may not imply a constructive proposition. That is, if p and q are constructive propositions, the statement $(\tilde{}p) \Rightarrow q$ is forbidden.

Basic Properties of Negation

The following properties of negation are identical to symbolic logic:

$$p \Leftrightarrow \tilde{}\tilde{}p$$

$$(p \Rightarrow q) \Rightarrow ((\tilde{}q) \Rightarrow \tilde{}p) \qquad (1)$$

The proposition $(\tilde{}q) \Rightarrow \tilde{}p$ is called the *contrapositive* of the proposition $p \Rightarrow q$. Formula (1) is called the *contrapositive law of propositions*.

Basic Properties of Conjunction (and)

The proposition « p and q » evokes those impressions that are evoked both by p and by q. We will write « p and q » as "p & q", and will call it the *conjunction* of p and q. The conjunction is defined by the formula

$$Я(p \,\&\, q) \equiv Яp \cap Яq$$

The logic of intersection leads therefore to the familiar properties of conjunction:

$$(p \,\&\, q) \Rightarrow p$$

$$(p \,\&\, q) \Leftrightarrow q \,\&\, p$$

$$(p \,\&\, p) \Leftrightarrow p$$

$$(p \,\&\, (q \,\&\, r)) \Leftrightarrow (p \,\&\, q) \,\&\, r$$

$$(p \Rightarrow q) \Rightarrow (p \mathbin{\&} r \Rightarrow q \mathbin{\&} r)$$

$$((p \Rightarrow q) \mathbin{\&} (p \Rightarrow r)) \Leftrightarrow (p \Rightarrow (q \mathbin{\&} r))$$

Basic Properties of Alternation (or)

The proposition « p or q » evokes those impressions that are evoked either by p or by q. We will write « p or q » as "$p \vee q$", and will call it the *alternation* of p and q. The alternation is defined by the formula

$$Я(p \vee q) \equiv Яp \cup Яq$$

The logic of union leads therefore to the familiar properties of alternation:

$$p \Rightarrow p \vee q$$

$$(p \vee q) \Rightarrow q \vee p$$

$$(p \vee p) \Leftrightarrow p$$

$$(p \vee (q \vee r)) \Leftrightarrow (p \vee q) \vee r$$

$$(p \Rightarrow q) \Rightarrow (p \vee r \Rightarrow q \vee r)$$

$$(p \Rightarrow r) \mathbin{\&} (q \Rightarrow r) \Rightarrow ((p \vee q) \Rightarrow r)$$

$$\tilde{}(p \mathbin{\&} q) \Leftrightarrow (\tilde{}p \vee \tilde{}q)$$

$$\tilde{}(p \vee q) \Leftrightarrow (\tilde{}p \mathbin{\&} \tilde{}q)$$

$$p \mathbin{\&} (q \vee r) \Leftrightarrow (p \mathbin{\&} q) \vee (p \mathbin{\&} r)$$

$$p \vee (q \mathbin{\&} r) \Leftrightarrow (p \vee q) \mathbin{\&} (p \vee r)$$

Notice that formulas of symbolic logic that rely on the equivalence of $\tilde{}p \vee q$ with $p \Rightarrow q$ are often not followed by data logic. For example, data logic admits only the single implication:

$$\begin{aligned} ((p \Rightarrow q) \vee (p \Rightarrow r)) &\Leftrightarrow ((Яp \subseteq Яq) \vee (Яp \subseteq Яr)) \\ &\Rightarrow (Яp \subseteq (Яq \cup Яr)) \\ &\Rightarrow (p \Rightarrow (q \vee r)) \end{aligned}$$

That is, if p implies q or p implies r, then p implies (q or r). However, p may imply (q or r) without p implying q or p implying r. For example, if the red queen is in play in a game of chess, then the red queen is on a white square or the red queen is on a black square. However, the red queen being in play does not imply that the red queen is on a white square, since it could be on a black square; nor does it imply that it is on a black square, for the same reason. Symbolic logic does not recognize this contrast.

Logic of Intersection and Union

In Section 2.4, we derived the formulas:

$$B \cap C{:}(d) \Rightarrow B{:}(d) \;\&\; C{:}(d)$$

$$B \cup C{:}(d) \Leftrightarrow B{:}(d) \vee C{:}(d)$$

Applying the contrapositive law yields similar formulas for conformers:

$$B{:}[d] \vee C{:}[d] \Rightarrow B \cup C{:}[d] \qquad (2)$$

$$B{:}[d] \;\&\; C{:}[d] \Leftrightarrow B \cap C{:}[d]$$

Recall that if B and d are sheath-free, $B{:}[d]$ can be thought of as saying that each manifestation of d is accepted by B, in contrast to $B{:}(d)$ which states only that some manifestation of d is accepted by B. The proposition $B \cup C{:}[d]$ therefore states that each manifestation of d is accepted by B or by C. This does not imply that each manifestation of d is accepted by B or that each manifestation of d is accepted by C, hence the single implication in Formula (2).

An Embracing of Classes Yields Implications

If a class C embraces a class B, then any recognizer d that is an instance of B is also an instance of C. Thus,

$$(B \subseteq C) \Rightarrow (B{:}(d) \Rightarrow C{:}(d))$$

We may apply the contrapositive of embracings and the contrapositive of propositions to yield:

$$(B \subseteq C) \Rightarrow (\overline{C} \subseteq \overline{B})$$

$$(\overline{C}{:}(d) \Rightarrow \overline{B}{:}(d)) \Rightarrow (B{:}[d] \Rightarrow C{:}[d])$$

Combining these three formulas, we achieve the following as well:

$$(B \subseteq C) \Rightarrow (B{:}[d] \Rightarrow C{:}[d])$$

That is, if C embraces B then any conformer of B is also a conformer of C.

Embracings and Implications Are Omissive

As discussed in Section 2.7, if B and C are both sheath-free, then an embracing is equivalent to a statement of disjointness:

$$(B \cap \overline{C} \subseteq \varnothing) \Leftrightarrow (B \subseteq C) \qquad (3)$$

The left side of the embracing, $(B \cap \overline{C} \subseteq \varnothing)$, states that for any recognizer x,

$$\tilde{}(B \cap \overline{C}){:}(x)$$

If B is constructive or C is omissive, this proposition is omissive. These are the same conditions for the embracing $B \subseteq C$ to obey performance type integrity. Thus, whenever the proposition $B \subseteq C$ obeys performance type integrity, the left side of Formula (3) is omissive. Applying performance type integrity to Formula (3), the right side, $B \subseteq C$, must also be omissive. Thus, any embracing that obeys performance type integrity is omissive. Since an implication is defined to be an embracing of topic recognizers, any implication that obeys performance type integrity is omissive as well.

Data Logic Avoids the Liar Paradox

The ancient paradox of the liar refers to a hypothetical person who claims that everything he says is a lie. He then claims to be lying, which implies he is telling the truth, which in turn implies he is lying. The liar paradox is an example of a contradiction that can be set up as a consequence of the basic apparatus of logic when that apparatus is ill-formed.

In data logic, the liar's initial statement that everything he says is a lie is the statement that for any proposition p,

$$p \Rightarrow \tilde{}p$$

(we may reflect the statement more precisely by adding consideration of the liar making a claim, but doing so does not enrich the argument). This implication is only well-formed when p is constructive, for if p is omissive then $\tilde{}p$ is constructive, and the implication is prohibited by performance type integrity. That is, the statement ''everything I say is a lie'' is inadmissible in data logic. The liar can only say ''every constructive proposition I claim is a lie''. The liar could then claim omissive propositions without contradiction. Since the proposition $p \Rightarrow \tilde{}p$ is omissive, it does not contradict itself, and there is no paradox.

Contradictions Are Described by Sheaths

A *contradiction* is a proposition of the form $p \mathbin{\&} \tilde{}p$. In general, the proposition $p \mathbin{\&} \tilde{}p$ will be called the *sheath* of the proposition p. Data logic allows propositions to have sheaths; that is, data logic allows contradictory propositions to be affirmed.

The topic recognizer of the sheath of a proposition p is equivalent to the sheath of the topic recognizer of p:

$$\begin{aligned} Я(\text{sheath } p) &\equiv Я(p \mathbin{\&} \tilde{}p) \\ &\equiv (Яp) \cap (Я\tilde{}p) \\ &\equiv (Яp) \cap (\overline{Яp}) \\ &\equiv \text{sheath } (Яp) \end{aligned}$$

A proposition p is said to be *sheath-free* if its topic recognizer $Яp$ is sheath-free. A sheath-free proposition can not be contradicted.

Since contradictions are permitted in data logic, proofs by contradiction or *reductio ad absurdum* in symbolic logic may lead to different results when formulated in data logic. Thus, if we have both $q \Rightarrow p$ and $q \Rightarrow \tilde{}p$, we can conclude that q implies the sheath of p. Unless p is sheath-free, this conclusion does not violate any premises. We can conclude by the contrapositive law that $\tilde{}p \Rightarrow \tilde{}q$ and $p \Rightarrow \tilde{}q$; thus $q \Rightarrow \tilde{}q$. Therefore, any proposition q that implies a contradiction is contradictory if it is affirmed. However, since q is allowed to be contradictory, this method of reasoning does not establish $\tilde{}q$ to the exclusion of q, as it would in symbolic logic.

Proofs by contradiction are often more concerned with the intricacies of contradictory statements than with pure deduction. They are therefore best avoided in ordinary reasoning.

Conclusion

The proposition « p implies q » is equivalent to the proposition « any impression that p evokes must also be evoked by q ». Logical implication is thus an embracing of the topic recognizer of one proposition in the topic recognizer of another.

The link between implications and embracings allows us to develop propositional logic by applying the results about embracings obtained earlier. Thus, conjoining propositions (combining propositions with « and ») leads to an intersection of their topic recognizers, and alternating propositions (combining propostions with « or ») leads to a union of their topic recognizers. The logic of intersection and union developed earlier therefore determines the logic of « and » and « or ».

We have shown that data logic avoids the liar paradox by performance type integrity. If a proposition p is omissive, then p can not imply $\tilde{}p$ because an omissive proposition may not imply a constructive proposition. If p is constructive, then $\tilde{}p$ can not imply p by the same reasoning. Thus, p and $\tilde{}p$ can never both imply each other.

2.10 QUANTIFICATION

Existential Quantification

The proposition « B accepts some image » will be written "$(\exists x)\ B{:}|x|$". The symbol "$(\exists x)$" is read « for some x », and is called an *existential quantifier*. The symbol "x" is called a *placetaker*, and stands for the programmatic position at which B examines images (see Section 1.8). The vertical bars in the expression "$B{:}|x|$" indicate that B accepts x as an image. Notice that we do not actually contemplate an image in « $(\exists x)\ B{:}|x|$ » (to do so would violate the uncertainty principle of impressions); we merely propose that B has rendered an acceptance during some performance. A class that has accepted some image is said to be *populated*.

If some recognizer d is an instance of B, then B accepts some manifestation of d. Thus,

$$B{:}(d) \Rightarrow (\exists x)\ B{:}|x|$$

Moreover, if $B{:}(d) \vee B{:}(e)$, then B accepts some manifestation of d or B accepts some manifestation of e, so B accepts some image:

$$B{:}(d) \vee B{:}(e) \Rightarrow (\exists x)\ B{:}|x|$$

In data logic, unlike symbolic logic, B may have a population that consists of an alternation $B{:}(d) \vee B{:}(e)$, without having either $B{:}(d)$ or $B{:}(e)$.

For example, suppose that Nate keeps two old screwdrivers handy for odd jobs. One day, Nate uses one of the screwdrivers to pry off the top of a can, but he soon forgets which screwdriver he used. If B represents « Nate Used _____ To Pry Open The Can », and d and e represent the two screwdrivers, then we can conclude only the alternation $B{:}(d) \vee B{:}(e)$.

We might question whether the statement $(\exists x)\ B{:}|x|$ is interchangeable with the alternation:

$$B{:}(d_1) \vee B{:}(d_2) \vee \ldots \vee B{:}(d_n) \tag{1}$$

where $d_1, \ldots, d_n$ are all the recognizers that have been imagined. Although Formula (1) clearly implies $(\exists x)\ B{:}|x|$, we will find it useful to be able to declare that $(\exists x)\ B{:}|x|$ without declaring Formula (1). For example, suppose that a number is picked in a state-sponsored lottery every day. We may conclude that some number was picked last Tuesday, even if we do not know the number, and so can not put the actual number in the data base. The difference between $(\exists x)\ B{:}|x|$ and Formula (1) is also exploited in the treatment of infinity (see Section 3.6).

Since a placetaker represents a position, a placetaker may stand for any idea that combines in a regular way with other ideas in an expression. In particular, a placetaker may stand for a recognizer, or for an association. Thus, we have:

$$B{:}(d) \Rightarrow (\exists x)\ B{:}(x)$$

$$B{:}(d) \Rightarrow (\exists x)\ x{:}(d)$$

Symbolic logic is prevented from employing placetakers this freely by Russell's paradox. Data logic avoids Russell's paradox by performance type integrity (see Section 3.5), so data logic can employ quantification without restriction, as quantification was originally envisioned by Frege (1879).

Logic of Existential Quantification

If B accepts some image x and C accepts the same image x, then $B \cap C$ accepts x. Conversely, if $B \cap C$ accepts y, then B accepts y and C accepts y:

$$((\exists x)\ B{:}|x|\ \&\ C{:}|x|) \Leftrightarrow (\exists y)\ B \cap C{:}|y|$$

The use of images rather than recognizers avoids the difference between conjunction and intersection seen with instances. Thus, with x and y standing for recognizers we have only

$$(\exists y)\ B \cap C{:}(y) \Rightarrow (\exists x)\ B{:}(x)\ \&\ C{:}(x)$$

When x stands for an image, we have

$$(\exists x)\ B{:}|x|\ \&\ C{:}|x| \Rightarrow (\exists y)\ B{:}|y|\ \&\ (\exists z)\ C{:}|z|$$

If B accepts some image x or C accepts some image y, then $B \cup C$ accepts some image (x or y). Conversely, if $B \cup C$ accepts some image, then B accepts some image or C accepts some image:

$$((\exists x)\ B{:}|x| \vee (\exists y)\ C{:}|y|) \Leftrightarrow (\exists z)\ B \cup C{:}|z|$$

Unlike the similar formula using conjunction, the two existential quantifiers on the left side may be replaced by one:

$$((\exists x)\ B{:}|x| \vee (\exists y)\ C{:}|y|) \Leftrightarrow (\exists z)\ B{:}|z| \vee C{:}|z|$$

If $B \subseteq C$, then if some image is accepted by B, then some image is accepted by C:

$$(B \subseteq C) \Rightarrow (((\exists x)\ B{:}|x|) \Rightarrow (\exists y)\ C{:}|y|)$$

Exhaustive Quantification

The negation of « $\overline{B}$ accepts some image » is « $\overline{B}$ accepts no image », or equivalently, « B accepts each image ». This proposition will be written "$(\forall x)\ B{:}|x|$". The symbol "$(\forall x)$" is read « for each x », and is called an *exhaustive quantifier*. The symbol "x" is called a *placetaker*, just as the symbol "x" in "$(\exists x)$". A class that accepts each image is said to be *exhaustive*.

The logic of exhaustive quantification may be determined by applying the contrapositive law to the logic of existential quantification. For example, we have

$$((\forall x)\ B{:}|x|) \Rightarrow B{:}[d]$$

That is, every recognizer is a conformer of an exhaustive class. We have further:

$$((\forall x)\ B{:}|x| \vee C{:}|y|) \Leftrightarrow (\forall y)\ B \cup C{:}|y|$$

$$((\forall x)\ B{:}|x| \vee (\forall y)\ C{:}|y|) \Rightarrow (\forall z)\ B{:}|z| \vee C{:}|z|$$

$$((\forall x)\ B{:}|x|\ \&\ C{:}|x|) \Leftrightarrow (\forall z)\ B \cap C{:}|z|$$

$$((\forall x)\ B{:}|x|\ \&\ (\forall y)\ C{:}|y|) \Leftrightarrow (\forall z)\ B{:}|z|\ \&\ C{:}|z|$$

$$(B \subseteq C) \Rightarrow (((\forall x)\ B{:}|x|) \Rightarrow (\forall y)\ C{:}|y|)$$

Quantifiers may also be rearranged in various ways in logical formulas. For example, if p and q do not contain "x" in their expression, and $\mathcal{F}{:}|x|$ is some logical formula that does contain "x", then:

$$(p \Rightarrow (\forall x)\ \mathcal{F}{:}|x|) \Leftrightarrow (\forall x)\ (p \Rightarrow \mathcal{F}{:}|x|)$$

$$(((\exists x)\ \mathcal{F}{:}|x|) \Rightarrow q) \Leftrightarrow (\forall x)\ (\mathcal{F}{:}|x| \Rightarrow q)$$

The rules for this sort of rearrangement are the same as the rules in symbolic logic.

Universal Quantification

Quantification over images is used to describe an embracing as follows. If a class C embraces a class B, then each image accepted by B is also accepted by C. Thus,

$$(B \subseteq C) \Rightarrow (\forall x)\ (B{:}|x| \Rightarrow C{:}|x|) \qquad (2)$$

The right side of Formula (2) proposes that each image that has been accepted by B has also been accepted by C. However, it remains possible that some image could be presented to B

that C would not accept. If C embraces B, then this possibility is forestalled. If C embraces B, then the plans of B and C are so formed that any image accepted by B must also be accepted by C. For example, if one of the conditions for an image being accepted by B is that the image must first be accepted by C, then C embraces B.

An embracing is an example of a proposition that is obeyed for *any* image, because an embracing $B \subseteq C$ is a characteristic of the plans of the classes B and C, and is therefore independent of what images are presented. We write the idea « for any x » as the *universal quantifier* "(Ax)". We have, therefore,

$$\boxed{(B \subseteq C) \Leftrightarrow (\mathrm{A}x)\ (B{:}|x| \Rightarrow C{:}|x|)} \tag{3}$$

This interchangeability will be used extensively in proofs to provide a means of translating results about embracings to results about propositions, and vice versa. It is essential that x stands for an image rather than a recognizer in Formula (3). Thus, we have only the single implication

$$(B \subseteq C) \Rightarrow (\mathrm{A}x)\ (B{:}(x) \Rightarrow C{:}(x))$$

For example, suppose the class D obeys the rule

$$(\mathrm{A}x)\ (D{:}(x) \Leftrightarrow B{:}(x)\ \&\ C{:}(x)) \tag{4}$$

We can not conclude from Formula (4) that D is equivalent to $B \cap C$, because B could accept only different manifestations of x from the manifestations accepted by C. Then D would accept x, but $B \cap C$ would not.

Quantification Over Impressions

We may also define quantification over impressions, that is, expressions that involve the ideas « for some impression » and « for each impression ». Although the uncertainty principle states that we may not represent one impression, we may propose characteristics of impressions in general. In particular, we may propose that there is some impression that is accepted by a recognizer without representing the impression itself. The proposition that there is some impression that is accepted by the recognizer d, that is, that d is *populated*, is written

$$(\exists \iota)\ d{:}\iota$$

We use small Greek letters such as ι to indicate impressions so that recognizers will not be confused with classes. We do not surround ι with brackets because there is no analog of the distinction between instances and conformers in impressions. The symbol "$(\exists \iota)$" is read « for some impression ι ». For the purposes of enforcing performance type integrity, the expression "$d{:}\iota$" has the same performance type as d. The proposition $(\exists \iota)\ d{:}\iota$ also has the same performance type as d.

Existential quantification of impressions is used to describe overlap of recognizers. Thus, two recognizers d and e overlap if

$$(\exists \iota)\ (d \cap e){:}\iota$$

One may also apply the exhaustive quantifier $(\forall \iota)$, « for each impression ι », as in

$$(\forall\iota)\ d{:}\iota$$

This proposition is read « the recognizer d accepts each impression ι ». The most common application of this expression is to state that no impression is accepted by a recognizer d, that is,

$$(\tilde{}(\exists\iota)\ d{:}\iota) \Leftrightarrow (\forall\kappa)\ \bar{d}{:}\kappa)$$

A recognizer d that satisfies this condition is said to be *empty*.

Logical Reasoning Using Impressions

If a recognizer e embraces a recognizer d, then e may be substituted for d in quantified expressions. That is, if $d \subseteq e$, then:

$$((\exists\iota)\ d{:}\iota) \Rightarrow (\exists\kappa)\ e{:}\kappa$$

$$((\forall\iota)\ d{:}\iota) \Rightarrow (\forall\kappa)\ e{:}\kappa$$

Intersection and union behave as with classes:

$$((\exists\iota)\ d{:}\iota\ \&\ e{:}\iota) \Leftrightarrow (\exists\kappa)\ (d \cap e){:}\kappa$$

$$((\exists\iota)\ d{:}\iota\ \&\ e{:}\iota) \Rightarrow (\exists\kappa)\ d{:}\kappa\ \&\ (\exists\lambda)\ e{:}\lambda$$

$$((\exists\iota)\ d{:}\iota \vee (\exists\kappa)\ e{:}\kappa) \Leftrightarrow (\exists\lambda)\ (d \cup e){:}\lambda$$

$$((\exists\iota)\ d{:}\iota \vee (\exists\kappa)\ e{:}\kappa) \Leftrightarrow (\exists\lambda)\ d{:}\lambda \vee e{:}\lambda$$

An embracing of recognizers is interchangeable with a universally quantified implication:

$$(d \subseteq e) \Leftrightarrow (\mathrm{A}\iota)\ (d{:}\iota \Rightarrow e{:}\iota)$$

A manifestation of a recognizer d may be written "$d.\iota$", where ι represents the impression accepted by d. Because of the uncertainty principle, this expression is only allowed if ι is quantified in some way. Thus, we have:

$$\boxed{B{:}(d) \Leftrightarrow (\exists\iota)\ B{:}|d.\iota|}$$

The performance type of $B{:}|d.\iota|$ is therefore the same as the performance type of the instantiation $B{:}(d)$ (constructive if either B or d is constructive, omissive if both B and d are omissive).

Applying the contrapositive law yields:

$$\boxed{B{:}[d] \Leftrightarrow (\forall\iota)\ B{:}|d.\iota| \vee \bar{d}{:}\iota} \qquad (5)$$

The alternation in Formula (5) arises because the proposition $B{:}|d.\iota|$ used in defining $B{:}(d)$ is a conjunction of d accepting ι and B accepting the image $d.\iota$. The negation of this conjunction is the alternation shown.

Simple propositions imply quantifications over impressions as follows:

$$B{:}(c) \Rightarrow ((\exists\iota)\ (\mu B \cap c){:}\iota) \Rightarrow (\exists\iota)\ c{:}\iota$$

Thus, if a recognizer is an instance of some class, then the recognizer is populated. By the contrapositive law,

$$((\forall\iota)\ \bar{c}{:}\iota) \Rightarrow ((\forall\iota)\ (\mu B \cap \bar{c}){:}\iota) \Rightarrow \tilde{}B{:}(c) \Rightarrow \bar{B}{:}[c]$$

Thus, an empty recognizer is an instance of no class, and a conformer of every class.

Quantification Over Impressions Describes Granulations

The granulation of a recognizer may be defined using quantification over impressions as follows:

$$(\mathrm{A}x)\ (\mathrm{A}\iota)\ \Gamma d{:}|x.\iota| \Leftrightarrow d{:}\iota$$

That is, the image $x.\iota$ is accepted by the granulation of d if and only if d accepts the impression ι.

This formulation may be used to prove the basic results about the logic of granulation. Thus, we have:

$$\begin{aligned}(d \subseteq e) &\Leftrightarrow (\mathrm{A}\iota)\ (d{:}\iota \Rightarrow e{:}\iota)\\ &\Leftrightarrow (\mathrm{A}\iota)\ (\mathrm{A}x)\ (\Gamma d{:}|x.\iota| \Rightarrow \Gamma e{:}|x.\iota|)\\ &\Leftrightarrow (\Gamma d \subseteq \Gamma e)\end{aligned}$$

The granulation of the complement of d is equivalent to the complement of the granulation of d:

$$\begin{aligned}(\mathrm{A}x)\ (\mathrm{A}\iota)\ \Gamma(\bar{d}){:}|x.\iota| &\Leftrightarrow \bar{d}{:}\iota\\ &\Leftrightarrow \tilde{}(d{:}\iota)\\ &\Leftrightarrow \tilde{}(\Gamma d{:}|x.\iota|)\\ &\Leftrightarrow \overline{\Gamma d}{:}|x.\iota|\end{aligned}$$

The granulation of the intersection of two recognizers is equivalent to the intersection of the granulations of the recognizers:

$$\begin{aligned}(\mathrm{A}x)\ (\mathrm{A}\iota)\ \Gamma(d \cap e){:}|x.\iota| &\Leftrightarrow (d \cap e){:}\iota\\ &\Leftrightarrow d{:}\iota\ \&\ e{:}\iota\\ &\Leftrightarrow \Gamma d{:}|x.\iota|\ \&\ \Gamma e{:}|x.\iota|\end{aligned}$$

We may define the melding by the formula

$$(\mathrm{A}\iota)\ \mu C{:}\iota \Leftrightarrow (\exists x)\ C{:}|x.\iota|$$

The melding of the granulation of a recognizer is equivalent to the recognizer:

$$\begin{aligned}(\mathrm{A}\iota)\ \mu\Gamma d{:}\iota &\Leftrightarrow (\exists x)\ \Gamma d{:}|x.\iota|\\ &\Leftrightarrow d{:}\iota\end{aligned}$$

Conclusion

We have discussed the operators « for some x » and « for each x », as they apply to propositions involving classes. Data logic allows the placetaker x to stand for an image, a recognizer, or a class (more generally, an association as well), which provides a greater diversity of quantified expressions than symbolic logic. The use of a placetaker to stand for an image is especially valuable, because it opens images to analysis, since direct study is prohibited by the uncertainty principle of impressions. In particular, we have determined an interchangeable formula for an embracing as a universally quantified implication:

$$(B \subseteq C) \Leftrightarrow (\mathrm{A}x)\ (B{:}|x| \Rightarrow C{:}|x|)$$

Data logic allows associations to be quantified as well as recognizers. That is, from a proposition $C{:}(d)$ we may conclude $(\exists x)\ x{:}(d)$ as well as $(\exists y)\ C{:}(y)$. Symbolic logic does not permit both forms of quantification without restraint. In particular, quantifying over associations, as in $(\exists x)\ x{:}(d)$, is prohibited in relational algebra. We will see that the greater flexibility of data logic allows us to reach conclusions that apply to any data structures, regardless of the particular associations that they contain.

Data logic also permits quantification over impressions. Quantification over impressions is most useful as a "transition state" between other propositions that do not involve impressions. Reasoning through an appeal to impressions is therefore another means of proof.

2.11 ASSOCIATIONS

Fundamental Logic of Associations

When an association S embraces an association R, we recall, any images accepted by R are accepted, in the same positions, by S. Thus, for two associations R and S of degree three (trios), the embracing $R \subseteq S$ may be written

$$(\mathrm{A}x)\ (\mathrm{A}y)\ (\mathrm{A}z)\ R{:}|x,\ y,\ z| \Rightarrow S{:}|x,\ y,\ z|$$

The notation "$R{:}|x, y, z|$" indicates that R accepts x in position one, y in position two, and z in position three. The symbols "x", "y", and "z" are placetakers that stand for images. Notice that the associations on either side of the embracing symbol "$\subseteq$" always have the same degree. This degree is called the *degree of the embracing*.

Two associations *of the same degree* may be intersected and united. Using trios again for illustration, we have:

$$(\mathrm{A}x)\ (\mathrm{A}y)\ (\mathrm{A}z)\ (R \cap S){:}|x,\ y,\ z| \Leftrightarrow R{:}|x,\ y,\ z|\ \&\ S{:}|x,\ y,\ z|$$

$$(\mathrm{A}x)\ (\mathrm{A}y)\ (\mathrm{A}z)\ (R \cup S){:}|x,\ y,\ z| \Leftrightarrow R{:}|x,\ y,\ z| \vee S{:}|x,\ y,\ z|$$

The *opposite* of an association R of degree r, written $^{\circ}R$, accepts the images x_1 in position ①, . . . , x_r in position r if R rejects x_1 in position ①, . . . , x_r in position r. The opposite $^{\circ}R$ rejects images if R accepts them, in the same way. The *complement* of R, written $\overline{R}$, accepts the images that R does not accept and rejects the images that R does not reject. We define both $^{\circ}R$ and $\overline{R}$ to have the same degree as R.

An association is *constructive* if it never accepts and rejects in the same performance, and *omissive* if it always accepts or rejects in any performance. That is, an *omissive association* of degree r is a conceptual mechanism that is performed as follows:

(i) A performance includes a presentation of images to each of the positions ① to r of the association.

(ii) The association accepts if some of the positions accept. The association rejects if each of the positions rejects. Some of the positions may accept and reject in the same performance.

Logic of Concentrations

The concentration of an association R is the class of assemblies controlled by R. For example, the concentration of a trio T is defined by the formula:

$$(\mathrm{A}x)\ (\mathrm{A}y)\ (\mathrm{A}z)\ \mathrm{C}^1T{:}|T|\,x,\ y,\ z|| \Leftrightarrow T{:}|x,\ y,\ z|$$

Here, the symbol "$T|x, y, z|$" represents an assembly manifestation formed by assembling T with the images x, y, and z. The assembly image principle states that any assembly manifestation is an image, so C^1T is a class (see Section 1.8).

An association R is embraced in an association S if and only if the concentration of R, C^1R, is embraced in the concentration of S:

$$R \subseteq S \text{ if and only if } \mathrm{C}^1R \subseteq \mathrm{C}^1S$$

Consequently, the concentration of the intersection of two associations is the intersection of the two concentrations, and the concentration of the union of two associations is the union of the two concentrations. The concentration of an association has the same performance type as the association itself.

Inexhaustibility and Ambivalence

Associations exhibit inexhaustibility as do classes. The appropriate principles may be derived by applying the inexhaustibility principles of classes to the concentrations of associations. Thus, we have the *inexhaustibility principle of associations*:

> For any constructive association R of degree r, it must be possible to imagine images $b_1, \ldots, b_r$ such that R would neither accept nor reject $b_1, \ldots, b_r$ if they were presented.

and the *ambivalence principle of associations*:

> For any omissive association R of degree r, it must be possible to imagine images $b_1, \ldots, b_r$ such that R would both accept and reject $b_1, \ldots, b_r$ if they were presented.

Unpopulable and Universal Associations

An *unpopulable association of degree r*, written "$\varnothing^r$", must accept no images. Thus, for any association R of degree r,

$$\varnothing^s \subseteq R \text{ if and only if } s = r$$

An unpopulable association of any degree is constructive. Notice that $\varnothing$ and $\varnothing^r$ $(r \neq 1)$ are different associations in data logic, because they have different degrees. $\varnothing$ and $\varnothing^r$ are the same set in symbolic logic.

The *universal association of degree r*, written "$\square^r$", must accept any r images that are presented to it. Therefore, for any association R of degree r,

$$R \subseteq \square^r$$

A universal association of any degree is omissive.

Performance Type Integrity

These principles lead to a performance type integrity law for associations, a generalization of the performance type integrity law for classes. Thus, if it were possible to declare that $\overline{R} \subseteq R$ for some constructive sheath-free association R, then R would embrace $R \cup \overline{R} \equiv \square^r$, violating the inexhaustibility principle. We conclude therefore, that for any associations R and S,

If $R \subseteq S$ and R is omissive, then S is omissive

Permutations of Associations

Any correspondence G has a *converse* G^* defined by the formula:

$$(\text{A}x)\ (\text{A}y)\ G^*{:}|x, y| \Leftrightarrow G{:}|y, x|$$

If G is an active transitive verb like « Purchases », G^* is the passive, « Is Purchased By ».

A converse is an example of a *permutation* of an association, which is a new association that differs only in the sequence of positions. A permutation is expressed by numbering the positions with consecutive positive integers, then writing the integers in the desired permuted order as superscripts after the symbol "π". For example, the trio $\pi^{231}T$ is defined by:

$$(\text{A}x)\ (\text{A}y)\ (\text{A}z)\ \pi^{231}T{:}|x, y, z| \Leftrightarrow T{:}|z, x, y|$$

The converse G^* may also be written as $\pi^{21}G$. Permutations maintain performance types unchanged.

Localization Forms Associations of Lower Degree

Given a correspondence G and a recognizer b, we may form the class of recognizers x such that G attaches b to x. This class is called a *localization* of G at b, and is written "$G(b, \ )$" or "$b.G$". For example, the class of images « owned » by « Harold » is the localization:

$$\textit{Owns}\ (\textit{Harold},\ ) \equiv (\textit{Harold})\ \textit{Owns}\ (\ ) \equiv \textit{Harold.Owns}$$

A recognizer may be substituted for an unfilled position in an association of any degree. The degree of the association is reduced by one for each such substitution. For example, the following is a correspondence:

$$R(\ , b, c, \ , b)$$

Cartesian Products

Given a class B and a class C, the correspondence "$B \times C$", called the *Cartesian product* of B with C, accepts two images i and j if B accepts i and C accepts j. That is, the attachments of $B \times C$ are analogous to pairs of instances of B with instances of C.

Since the Cartesian product is defined from two conditions connected by « and », its effect on performance types is parallel to the effect of an intersection. That is, $B \times C$ is omissive if both B and C are omissive, and it is constructive if either B or C is constructive.

One may form Cartesian products of associations of arbitrary degree. Thus, the Cartesian product of two associations R and S is the association $R \times S$ defined by

$$(R \times S){:}|x_1, \ldots, x_r, y_1, \ldots, y_s| \Leftrightarrow R{:}|x_1, \ldots, x_r| \ \&\ S{:}|y_1, \ldots, y_s|$$

where it is understood that the variables x_i and y_i are universally quantified. Although Cartesian products are central to geometry, their relevance to data has often been overestimated. A Cartesian product is rightly seen as one of the least interesting of associations, since it can be derived unambiguously from the associations from which it is formed. Cartesian products do arise frequently in theoretical work, however. For example, the universal associations are Cartesian products of the universal class, such as

$$\square^3 \equiv \square \times \square \times \square$$

Existential Quantification of Associations Yields Projections

Given a correspondence « ① G ② », we may form the class « for some x, ____ *Gs x* ». The suffix "*–s*" in "*Gs*" indicates that a verb G should be written in the third person singular. For example, if G is « *Repairs* », we form « for some x, ____ *Repairs x* », or more briefly, « ____ *Is A Repairer* ». This class is called the *projection of G onto the first position*, and is written "$\pi^1 G$". In symbolic logic, $\pi^1 G$ is written $\pi_2 G$, the "2" indicating the position that is projected out. Thus, we have the formula:

$$(\text{A}x)\ \pi^1 G{:}|x| \Leftrightarrow (\exists y)\ G{:}|x, y|$$

Existential quantification may be applied to associations of any degree. For example, $\pi^{13}T$ is a correspondence that assembles an image x with an image z if there is some y such that T assembles x to y to z. This correspondence is called the *projection onto positions* ① *and* ③ *of* T, and is defined by the formula:

$$\boxed{(\mathrm{A}x)\ (\mathrm{A}z)\ \pi^{13}T{:}|x,\ z| \Leftrightarrow (\exists y)\ T{:}|x,\ y,\ z|}$$

Projections obey the basic implication

$$(\mathrm{A}x_2)\ .\ .\ .\ (\mathrm{A}x_r)\ R{:}|t,\ x_2,\ .\ .\ .\ ,\ x_r| \Rightarrow (\exists x_1)\ R{:}|x_1,\ x_2,\ .\ .\ .\ ,\ x_r|$$

That is, if R assembles t with some images $x_2, \ldots, x_r$, then R assembles some image x_1 (namely t) to $x_2, \ldots, x_r$.

Projection of a class yields the assembly $(\exists x)\ B|x|$, which is the topic recognizer of the proposition that B is populated, $(\exists x)\ B{:}|x|$.

Conclusion

We have seen how the operations of data logic, such as intersection, union, complement, and embracing, extend naturally from classes to associations of higher degree. Associations of higher degree have additional properties: *concentration* forms a class from an association of any degree, *permutation* interchanges the positions of an association without affecting its degree, *localization* reduces an association's degree, and *Cartesian products* form associations of higher degree.

Data logic uses a different notation from symbolic logic for projection. Thus, we use the symbol π^1R to indicate the projection *onto* the first position of an association R (that is, the result of projecting *out* all positions except the first). Thus, π^1R is always a class, whatever the degree of R may be.

2.12 PROPOSAL METHODS

Propositions Exhibit Proposal Methods

A class B can form two different kinds of simple propositions with a recognizer d, namely the *instantiation* $B{:}(d)$ and the *conformalization* $B{:}[d]$. We say then that there are two potential *proposal methods* of a class: instantiation, indicated by ( ), and conformalization, indicated by [ ].

A correspondence has two potential proposal methods in each of its two positions. For example, let G be the Cartesian product of two classes, $B \times C$. Then we write:

$$(x)G{:}(y) \Leftrightarrow B{:}(x)\ \&\ C{:}(y)$$

$$(x)G{:}[y] \Leftrightarrow B{:}(x)\ \&\ C{:}[y]$$

$$[x]G{:}(y) \Leftrightarrow B{:}[x]\ \&\ C{:}(y)$$

$$[x]G{:}[y] \Leftrightarrow B{:}[x]\ \&\ C{:}[y]$$

The proposal methods shown around x and y are called *positional* proposal methods. Correspondences have an additional *quadratic* proposal method that applies to the combination of both positions. This additional proposal method may be appreciated by studying performance types. For example, consider the two formulas:

$$(x)G:[y] \Leftrightarrow B:(x) \ \& \ C:[y]$$

$$(x)H:[y] \Leftrightarrow B:(x) \lor C:[y]$$

If x and y are both constructive, then $B:(x)$ is constructive and $C:[y]$ is omissive. Therefore $(x)G:[y]$ is constructive while $(x)H:[y]$ is omissive. If we are to retain the ability to deduce the performance type of a proposition from the performance types of its constituents, we must distinguish G from H in some way. We do so by saying that the quadratic proposal method of G is instantiation, ( ), while the quadratic proposal method of H is conformalization, [ ]. We write the quadratic proposal method around the two positional proposal methods:

$$G:((x), [y])$$

$$H:[(x), [y]]$$

Negation changes each proposal method to the complementary proposal method. Thus, we write:

$$\overline{G}:[[x], (y)] \Leftrightarrow \overline{B}:[x] \lor \overline{C}:(y)$$

$$\overline{H}:([x], (y)) \Leftrightarrow \overline{B}:[x] \ \& \ \overline{C}:(y)$$

In data base applications, one is concerned almost exclusively with correspondences that are constructive and whose proposal methods are all instantiations. That is, we consider propositions of the form $G:((x), (y))$. This proposition will be written more simply as "$G:(x, y)$". Its negation, $\overline{G}:[[x], [y]]$, will be written "$\overline{G}:[x, y]$". However, the more complex proposal methods do arise in theoretical work, such as in the formation of logical axioms.

Computation of Proposal Methods

When a correspondence G is defined by a formula that uses placetakers, the performance type of G and the proposal methods may be computed by the following method. We consider the performance type of a simple proposition with x in the first position and with y in the second position:

- **(i)** The performance type of G is the performance type of the proposition when x and y are both omissive.
- **(ii)** The quadratic proposal method is instantiation, ( ), if the proposition is constructive when x and y are both constructive. The quadratic proposal method is conformalization, [ ], if the proposition is omissive when x and y are both constructive.
- **(iii)** The proposal method in the first position is instantiation, ( ), if the proposition is constructive when x is constructive and y is omissive. The proposal method in

the first position is conformalization, [ ], if the proposition is omissive when x is constructive and y is omissive.

(iv) The proposal method in the second position is instantiation, ( ), if the proposition is constructive when x is omissive and y is constructive. The proposal method in the second position is conformalization, [ ], if the proposition is omissive when x is omissive and y is constructive.

The performance type and proposal methods of a simple proposition may also be shown as a binary matrix. The performance type is shown in the upper left corner, using 1 for constructive and 0 for omissive. The proposal method of the first position is shown in the lower left, using 1 for instantiation and 0 for conformalization. The proposal method of the second position is shown in the upper right. The quadratic proposal method is shown in the lower right. Thus, if G is constructive, G:[[x], (y)] is written:

$$\begin{bmatrix} 1 & 1 \\ 0 & 0 \end{bmatrix}$$

This matrix is called the *method matrix* of the proposition. Often, the same proposal methods are used in all the simple propositions that a correspondence appears in. In this case, we say that the matrix is the *method matrix of the correspondence*.

Proposal Methods of Associations of High Degree

In generalizing from correspondences to trios, the 2×2 method matrix becomes a $2 \times 2 \times 2$ *method tensor*, there being three quadratic proposal methods and one *cubic* proposal method. This is too much information to write clearly on a single line, so a simple proposition of a trio T is normally written showing only the positional proposal methods and the cubic proposal method.

The cubic proposal method is written enclosing all three positions. Thus, ''T:([x], [y], (z))'' represents a simple proposition where the cubic proposal method is instantiation, the proposal methods in the first and second positions are both conformalization, and the proposal method in the third position is instantiation. The symbol ''T:(x, y, z)'' will be used as an abbreviation for ''T:((x), (y), (z)).'' Similarly, the symbol ''T:[x, y, z]'' will be used as an abbreviation for ''T:[[x], [y], [z]]''.

The method matrix of a simple proposition of an association R of degree r, using the placetakers x_1 in position ①, . . . , x_r in position r, is determined by the following rules:

(i) The performance type of R is the performance type of the proposition when $x_1, \ldots, x_r$ are all omissive.

(ii) Let S be a set of position designators. Then the proposal method of R relative to S is given by the performance type t of the proposition when, for all i in S, x_i is constructive, and for all j not in S, x_j is omissive. If t is constructive, the proposal method is instantiation; if t is omissive, the proposal method is conformalization.

Conclusion

We saw in Section 2.6 that there are two ways of combining a class and a recognizer to form a simple proposition, either as an instance or as a conformer. However, there are more generally $2^{(2^r - 1)}$ ways of combining an association of degree r with r recognizers to form a simple proposition. These additional methods arise because each position of an association can be combined either as an instance or as a conformer, and, moreover, the various positions can interact with each other. The additional complication is easily managed for associations of degree two (correspondences). However, trios and associations of higher degree may require use of a *method tensor* that keeps track of the method used. In data base applications, one method predominates over all others, namely, that in which all positions act in the same way—as instances when the correspondence is constructive, and as conformers when the correspondence is omissive.

2.13 INCLUSION AND DEDUCTION

Embracing Differs from Inclusion

If each image accepted by a class B is also accepted by a class C then we say that C *includes* B and write $B \underset{\cdot}{\subset} C$. C includes B if the populations of B and C are included as sets (using the terminology of set theory). An inclusion $B \underset{\cdot}{\subset} C$ does not imply the embracing $B \subseteq C$ because an inclusion describes a coincidence that depends upon a choice of images, while an embracing describes characteristics of the way the two classes are formed (that is, an embracing characterizes the plans of the two classes).

If a class C includes a class B, we say that B is *less extensive* than C, and that C is *more extensive* than B. If B includes C and C includes B, then we say that B and C are *equally extensive*, and write $B \underset{\cdot}{=} C$. Note that the contrast between the symbols "$\underset{\cdot}{\subset}$" and "$\subseteq$" is not the contrast between "proper" and ordinary inclusion used in set theory: we may have both $B \underset{\cdot}{\subset} C$ and $B \underset{\cdot}{=} C$ simultaneously.

For example, imagine a car dealership where it happens that every car on the lot is red. The class « _____ Is A Car » is therefore included in the class « _____ Is Red ». Although each car within the purview of discussion is red, it does not follow that a thing must be red in order to be a car. That is, it does not follow that « _____ Is A Car » is embraced in « _____ Is Red ».

In general, a proposition that characterizes populations will be called *incidental*, while a proposition that describes plans will be called *definitive*. Thus, an inclusion is incidental while an embracing is definitive.

Logic of Inclusions

If each image accepted by B is also accepted by C, and each image accepted by C is also accepted by D, then each image accepted by B is also accepted by D:

$$(B \underset{\cdot}{\subset} C) \ \& \ (C \underset{\cdot}{\subset} D) \Rightarrow (B \underset{\cdot}{\subset} D)$$

If each image accepted by B is also accepted by C, and each image accepted by B is also accepted by D, then each image accepted by B is also accepted by $C \cap D$. Conversely, if each image accepted by B is accepted by $C \cap D$, then each image accepted by B is accepted by C and each image accepted by B is accepted by D:

$$(B \subsetneq C) \ \& \ (B \subsetneq D) \Leftrightarrow (B \subsetneq C \cap D)$$

Similarly, if D includes B and D includes C, then any image accepted by B or by C is accepted by D. Conversely, if D includes $B \cup C$, then D includes B and D includes C:

$$(B \subsetneq D) \vee (C \subsetneq D) \Leftrightarrow (B \cup C \subsetneq D)$$

The inclusion $B \subsetneq C$ implies the *contrapositive* $\overline{C} \subsetneq \overline{B}$. To manage contradictions, the propositions $B \subsetneq C$ and $B \cap \overline{C} \subsetneq \varnothing$ are not generally interchangeable.

Although a constructive class can not embrace an omissive class by performance type integrity, a constructive class may include an omissive class. That is, each recognizer that is not an instance of some constructive class B may, incidentally, be an instance of some constructive class C. Performance type integrity states that one may not *require* all conformers of $\overline{B}$ to be instances of C, but there may still be coincidences in which C includes $\overline{B}$.

If the class D is constructive or the class E is omissive, then the inclusion $D \subsetneq E$ is said to *follow* performance type integrity, since the analogous embracing $D \subseteq E$ would obey performance type integrity. While an embracing must obey performance type integrity, inclusions are permitted that do not follow performance type integrity. An inclusion that follows performance type integrity is an omissive proposition; an inclusion that does not follow performance type integrity is a constructive proposition.

Implication Differs from Deduction

Given an incidental inclusion $B \subsetneq C$, we may reason that if x is an instance of B, then x is an instance of C. Yet we may not reason that the proposition $B{:}(x)$ *implies* the proposition $C{:}(x)$, because under a different choice of impressions, there might be some x that is an instance of B but not an instance of C. The statement "if $B{:}(x)$, then $C{:}(x)$" is therefore a new form of reasoning, which we will call *deduction*, and which we will write with a single shafted arrow " $\rightarrow$ " rather than the double shafted arrow " $\Rightarrow$ " used for implication. Thus, we write $B{:}(x) \rightarrow C{:}(x)$. If $C{:}(x)$ may be deduced from $B{:}(x)$ and $B{:}(x)$ may be deduced from $C{:}(x)$, then we write $B{:}(x) \leftrightarrow C{:}(x)$. Deduction is incidental, while implication is definitive.

The difference between implication and deduction is reflected in the topic recognizers of the propositions $B{:}(x)$ and $C{:}(x)$. If $C{:}(x)$ is deduced from $B{:}(x)$, then each impression evoked by $B{:}(x)$ is also evoked by $C{:}(x)$. Thus, the topic recognizer $C(x)$ includes the topic recognizer $B(x)$. In contrast, if $B{:}(x)$ implies $C{:}(x)$, then any impression evoked by $B{:}(x)$ must be evoked by $C{:}(x)$ by virtue of the way B and C are defined. Thus, the topic recognizer $C(x)$ embraces the topic recognizer $B(x)$.

The relationship between inclusion and deduction may be extended to arbitrary propositions, not just to the simple propositions $B{:}(x)$ and $C{:}(x)$. Deduction and implication therefore obey the following formulas:

$$(p \rightarrow q) \Leftrightarrow (Яp \subsetneq Яq)$$
$$(p \Rightarrow q) \Leftrightarrow (Яp \subseteq Яq)$$

Logic of Deduction

The inclusion $B \subsetneq C$ states that each image x that B accepts is also, incidentally, accepted by C. We may therefore write:

$$(B \subsetneq C) \Leftrightarrow (\forall x)\ B{:}|x| \rightarrow C{:}|x| \qquad (1)$$

Formula (1) is called the *image exhaustion principle*. Notice the similarity to the formula for an embracing derived in Section 2.10:

$$(B \subseteq C) \Leftrightarrow (\mathrm{A}x)\ B{:}|x| \Rightarrow C{:}|x|$$

Formula (1) is easily generalized to associations of any degree. For example, an inclusion of trios obeys the formula

$$(R \subsetneq S) \Leftrightarrow (\forall x)\ (\forall y)\ (\forall z)\ R{:}|x, y, z| \rightarrow S{:}|x, y, z|$$

If a class C includes a class B, then C may be substituted for B in existentially and exhaustively quantified expressions:

$$(B \subsetneq C) \Rightarrow (((\exists x)\ B{:}|x|) \rightarrow (\exists y)\ C{:}|y|)$$
$$(B \subsetneq C) \Rightarrow (((\forall x)\ B{:}|x|) \rightarrow (\forall y)\ C{:}|y|)$$

Similar expressions hold for inclusion of recognizers:

$$(d \subsetneq e) \Rightarrow (((\exists \iota)\ d{:}\iota) \rightarrow (\exists \kappa)\ e{:}\kappa)$$
$$(d \subsetneq e) \Rightarrow (((\forall \iota)\ d{:}\iota) \rightarrow (\forall \kappa)\ e{:}\kappa)$$

Notice that an inclusion implies deductions ($\rightarrow$), not implications ($\Rightarrow$).

Conjunctions and alternations behave according to the laws:

$$(p \rightarrow q)\ \&\ (p \rightarrow r) \Leftrightarrow (p \rightarrow (q\ \&\ r))$$
$$(p \rightarrow r)\ \&\ (q \rightarrow r) \Leftrightarrow ((p \vee q) \rightarrow r)$$

Deductions are transitive, like implications:

$$(p \rightarrow q)\ \&\ (q \rightarrow r) \Rightarrow (p \rightarrow r)$$

The proposition $p \rightarrow q$ is interchangeable with the *contrapositive* $\tilde{}q \rightarrow \tilde{}p$. To manage contradictions, the propositions $p \rightarrow q$ and $\tilde{}p \vee q$ are not generally interchangeable. The difference between these propositions will be discussed further in Section 2.15. A proposition $(p \rightarrow q)$ is said to *follow* performance type integrity if p is constructive or q is omissive. A deduction need not follow performance type integrity.

Conclusion

Two classes may be *included* without being *embraced*. A class C *includes* a class B if it happens that each instance of B is also an instance of C. However, a class C only *embraces* a class B if C must include B by virtue of the way B and C are formed from their plans.

In the same way, we may *deduce* a proposition q from a proposition p if it happens that each impression evoked by p is also evoked by q. For example, suppose that each time we have observed p, we have also observed q, but we have no explanation for why the two have always occurred together, and indeed we expect it to have been mere coincidence. In this case, from the statement that we have observed p on some occasion, we can conclude that we have observed q. However, if we observe p in the future, we have no reason to assume that we will also observe q. In this case, p does not *imply* q, but q is *deduced* from p.

A similar contrast is obeyed by quantification: it may be that *all* instances of a class B are also instances of a class C. This is exhaustive quantification, and it is a statement that B is *included* in C. However, if B is *embraced in* C, then B and C are so formed that *any* instance of B *must be* an instance of C.

2.14 MODAL OPERATORS

A Proposition Is Definitive if Its Topic Recognizer Is Universal

A proposition q is *definitive* if it characterizes the plans of its constituents, and is therefore independent of a choice of populations. We write the proposition that q is definitive as "$!q$". When q is expressed in language, we will often express "$!q$" by inserting the auxiliary verb "*must*". Thus "$!\overline{B}{:}[d]$" is read « it must be that d is not an instance of B » or « d must not be an instance of B ». The symbol "!" is called the *definitive operator*.

Definitiveness resembles what writers on modal logic call "necessity" (Aristotle 350B.C.b, Lewis 1918, Chellas 1980). We prefer to avoid this term because it suggests a proposition that may under no circumstances be denied. A definitive proposition holds by virtue of definition, but definitions may be changed. Thus, a definitive proposition need not be necessary in the sense used by these writers. Moreover, certain propositions such as the laws of Physics need not be definitive in data theory (we may consider imaginary impressions in which they operate differently), yet such propositions are sometimes considered to be necessary because they express what are believed to be unalterable properties of nature. Thus, a necessary proposition need not be definitive.

Definitiveness also does not rely on sets of "possible worlds." For example, Leibniz considered a proposition to be "necessary" if it were true in all possible worlds (Leibniz, 1714). However, we can not form a set of all possible worlds, any more than we can form a set of all possible sheep—there is no method that will be exhaustive. A proposition is definitive because it follows from the plans of its terms, not because of the possible worlds it describes.

Any universally quantified expression is definitive. That is, if a proposition holds for any x, then it holds definitively for any x:

$$((\mathrm{A}x)\ B{:}|\,x\,|) \Rightarrow\ !(\mathrm{A}x)\ B{:}|\,x\,|$$

Thus, embracings and implications are definitive. Most propositions that are expressed in language as definitions or as tautologies are definitive.

Recall that if a class C includes a class B, we say that C *appears* to embrace B. The term *appears* indicates that it is impossible to tell the difference between an embracing and an incidental inclusion by examining the instances of the classes alone. More generally, the proposition q may be expressed as "it appears that $!q$." For example, if there is an incidental deduction $p \rightarrow q$, then it appears that p implies q.

When the topic recognizer of a proposition q is unpopulable, we say that q is *undescriptive*. No impression may be evoked by an undescriptive proposition. A proposition q is undescriptive if and only if its negation $\tilde{}q$ is definitive. An undescriptive proposition is similar to a "necessarily false" proposition, while a definitive proposition is similar to a "necessarily true" proposition.

Definitive Propositions Must Be Omissive

If $!q$, then no impression may support the negation of q. That is, if q is definitive, then $\overline{\text{Я}\tilde{}q} \equiv \text{Я}q$ is universal. Conversely, if $\text{Я}q$ is universal, then any impression whatever must be evoked by q. The behavior of $\text{Я}q$ is therefore independent of a choice of impressions, so q is definitive. We have therefore derived the formula:

$$\boxed{(!q) \Leftrightarrow (\text{A}\iota)\ \text{Я}q{:}\iota}$$

Or, equivalently:

$$\boxed{(!q) \Leftrightarrow (\square \subseteq \text{Я}q)} \qquad (1)$$

Since only an omissive recognizer may be universal, q may only be definitive if $\text{Я}q$ is omissive. Since $\text{Я}q$ has the same performance type as q, we may conclude:

$$\boxed{\text{If } !q\text{, then } q \text{ is omissive}}$$

If q is omissive, then $!q$ is also omissive.

It is valuable to consider "$!q$" to be a proposition even if q is constructive. If q is constructive, then "$!q$" is undescriptive. Since an undescriptive proposition is constructive, $!q$ is constructive if q is constructive.

Sets Are Defined Using Definitiveness

Recall that a set of recognizers is a class defined by its members. That is, all members of a set are definitively members of the set. For example, the set $S \equiv \{a, b, c\}$ is defined by the formula

$$(\text{A}x)\ S{:}[x] \Leftrightarrow (x \equiv a) \vee (x \equiv b) \vee (x \equiv c) \qquad (2)$$

If a, b, or c may be constructive, x may be constructive. Since the right side of Formula (2) is omissive, $S{:}[x]$ must be omissive whatever the performance type of x. Therefore, a member of a set is a conformer, rather than an instance, of the set, and any set is omissive. Any set is also a literal class (see Section 2.6).

Two sets are *equal* if they have the same members, that is, if they include each other. We write "$S = T$" if S and T are equal. Since a set is defined by its members, if a set T includes a set S, then T embraces S. Since there are only a finite number of recognizers, all sets in data logic are finite. The properties of sets will be discussed further in Section 3.7.

Definitive Propositions Are Sheath-Free

Definitive propositions may not be contradicted in data logic as incidental propositions may. The topic recognizer of a definitive proposition q is universal, so, for any proposition p, $Яq$ embraces $Яp$, and therefore $p \Rightarrow q$. That is, any proposition implies a definitive proposition.

The contrapositive of $(p \Rightarrow q)$ is $(\tilde{}q \Rightarrow \tilde{}p)$. Thus, if q is definitive, $\tilde{}q$ implies every proposition. A contradiction of a *definitive* proposition therefore propagates uncontrollably, like a contradiction in symbolic logic. Any definitive proposition must therefore be sheath-free.

Elementary Logic of Definitiveness

The logic of definitiveness may be deduced from Formula (1). Thus,

$$!(p \ \& \ q) \Leftrightarrow (\Box \subseteq (Яp \cap Яq))$$

$$\Leftrightarrow ((\Box \subseteq p) \ \& \ (\Box \subseteq q))$$

$$\Leftrightarrow \ !p \ \& \ !q$$

$$!p \vee \ !q \Leftrightarrow (\Box \subseteq Яp) \vee (\Box \subseteq Яq)$$

$$\Rightarrow \Box \subseteq (Яp \cup Яq)$$

$$\Rightarrow \ !(p \vee q)$$

Notice that $(p \vee q)$ may be definitive without p being definitive or q being definitive. For example, a proposition q is sheath-free if and only if $(q \vee \tilde{}q)$ is definitive. The proposition $!(q \vee \tilde{}q)$ still permits q to be affirmed, $\tilde{}q$ to be affirmed, or neither q nor $\tilde{}q$ to be affirmed. It only prohibits q and $\tilde{}q$ from being affirmed simultaneously.

If q is definitive, then q:

$$(!q) \Rightarrow q$$

If $p \Rightarrow q$, then $(!p) \Rightarrow (!q)$. Thus, suppose $p \Rightarrow q$, so $Яp \subseteq Яq$. We have then:

$$(!p) \Leftrightarrow (\Box \subseteq Яp)$$

$$\Rightarrow (\Box \subseteq Яq)$$

$$\Rightarrow \ !q$$

Definitive propositions may only be deduced from a conjunction if all the conjoined propositions are definitive. Thus, consider the implication $(p \ \& \ q) \Rightarrow r$, which we write more simply as "$p \ \& \ q \Rightarrow r$". Since $!p$ implies p, and $!q$ implies q, we may conclude:

$$(!p) \ \& \ q \Rightarrow r$$

$$p \ \& \ (!q) \Rightarrow r$$

Notice that neither premise implies $!r$. Only the conjunction of both $!p$ and $!q$ implies $!r$:

$$(!p) \,\&\, (!q) \Rightarrow !r$$

Possibility Complements Definitiveness

If $\tilde{}q$ is not definitive, then we say that q is *possible*. That is, q is possible if $\tilde{}!\tilde{}q$. We will write the proposition that q is possible as "$;q$", read « it might be that q ». The symbol ";" is called the *possibility operator*. Both ";" and "!" are called *modal operators*. The proposition $;q$ has the same performance type as the proposition q.

If q is omissive, then we have already concluded that $\tilde{}q$ can not be definitive. Therefore q is possible:

$$\text{If } q \text{ is omissive, then } ;q \tag{3}$$

We will see in Chapter 4 that all data base constraints may be formulated as definitive, hence omissive, propositions. Formula (3) shows therefore that it is always possible for a data base to obey any proposed constraint.

Elementary Logic of Possibility

The logic of possibility may be determined by applying the contrapositive law to the logic of definitiveness:

$$;(p \vee q) \Leftrightarrow ;p \vee ;q$$

$$;(p \,\&\, q) \Rightarrow ;p \,\&\, ;q$$

Merely stating that p is possible and q is possible does not imply that p and q are possible simultaneously. Consider for example the propositions that an object is in Providence and that it is in San Diego. It might be in either place, but not in both places at once.

We have, further:

$$q \Rightarrow ;q \tag{4}$$

$$(p \Rightarrow q) \Rightarrow ((;p) \Rightarrow ;q)$$

Concatenation of Modal Operators

Modal operators may be concatenated to form new propositions. Consider, for example, the proposition $;;p$, « it is possible that p is possible ». By Formula (4), we have

$$(;p) \Rightarrow ;;p$$

We will assume further that if it is possible for p to be possible, then p is possible. That is, there is no progression of successively weaker degrees of possibility (; , ;; , ;;; , . . .):

$$(;;p) \Rightarrow ;p$$

By the contrapositive law, we have

$$(!p) \Leftrightarrow !!p$$

When working with concatenations of modal operators, it can be important to distinguish between the two propositions « suppose that p is definitive » and « if p is supposed, then p

is definitive ». The former proposition is written "$!p$", the latter proposition is written

$$p \Rightarrow !p$$

A proposition that satisfies this formula is said to be *inherently definitive*. An inherently definitive proposition need not be affirmed. For example, the proposition that a recognizer d is sheath-free, $(A\iota)\ (d \cup \bar{d}):\iota$, is inherently definitive, but it is only affirmed that this proposition is definitive if it is affirmed that d is sheath-free.

Concatenation of Possibility and Definitiveness

Modal operators may be concatenated further. Consider, for example, the proposition $!;p$, « it is definitive that p is possible ». This proposition is completely determined by the performance type of p. Thus, if p is constructive, then $;p$ is constructive, so $!;p$ is undescriptive. Conversely, if $!;p$ is undescriptive, then $!;p$ is constructive, so p is constructive. Therefore, $!;p$ is undescriptive if and only if p is constructive.

If p is omissive, then p must be possible, that is, $!;p$ is definitive. Conversely, if $!;p$ is definitive, then $;p$ is omissive, so p is omissive. Therefore, $!;p$ is definitive if and only if p is omissive.

Consider the similar proposition $;!p$. Using the interchangeability $;q \Leftrightarrow \tilde{}!\tilde{}q$, we find that $;!p \Leftrightarrow \tilde{}!\tilde{}!p \Leftrightarrow \tilde{}!;\tilde{}p$. Therefore,

$$\begin{aligned}
(p \text{ is constructive}) &\Leftrightarrow (\tilde{}p \text{ is omissive}) \\
&\Leftrightarrow (!;\tilde{}p \text{ is definitive}) \\
&\Leftrightarrow (\tilde{}!;\tilde{}p \text{ is undescriptive}) \\
&\Leftrightarrow (;!p \text{ is undescriptive}) \\
(p \text{ is omissive}) &\Leftrightarrow (\tilde{}p \text{ is constructive}) \\
&\Leftrightarrow (!;\tilde{}p \text{ is undescriptive}) \\
&\Leftrightarrow (\tilde{}!;\tilde{}p \text{ is definitive}) \\
&\Leftrightarrow (;!p \text{ is definitive})
\end{aligned}$$

Therefore, $;!p$ is determined by the performance type of p in exactly the same way as $!;p$. That is,

$$;!p \Leftrightarrow !;p$$

This rather dull looking statement has a remarkably provocative interpretation, which incorporates definitiveness, possibility, and by implication performance types into one expression:

« it is possible for p to be definitive if and only if it is definitive that p is possible »

Conclusion

A proposition whose topic recognizer is universal is called a *definitive* proposition. A definitive proposition must evoke every impression, therefore, a definitive proposition must always be affirmed, whatever impressions are chosen. An embracing is an example of a definitive proposition, because an embracing characterizes the plans of the associations that are embraced, and is therefore independent of a choice of impressions.

Since the topic recognizer of a definitive proposition is universal, a definitive proposition must be omissive because of the inexhaustibility principle of recognizers. Any proposition implied by a definitive proposition must also be omissive because of performance type integrity. These rules will be used often to determine performance types.

2.15 MODAL LOGIC

Interaction of Definitiveness with Exhaustive Quantification

If a class B must accept any image presented, then for each image x, B must accept x:

$$!(\forall x)\ B{:}|x| \Rightarrow (\forall x)\ !B{:}|x|$$

Conversely, however, if for each image x that has been presented, B must have accepted x, B might still be formed so that B would not accept some other image y. Thus, $(\forall x)\ !B{:}|x|$ does not imply $!(\forall x)\ B{:}|x|$.

When substituting into quantified expressions, one should note that the conjunction of a definitive proposition with an incidental proposition is incidental. For example, we have:

$$((\forall x)\ B{:}|x|\ \&\ B \underset{\cdot}{\subset} C) \Rightarrow (\forall x)\ C{:}|x|$$

$$((\mathrm{A}x)\ B{:}|x|\ \&\ B \underset{\cdot}{\subset} C) \Rightarrow (\forall x)\ C{:}|x|$$

$$((\forall x)\ B{:}|x|\ \&\ B \subseteq C) \Rightarrow (\forall x)\ C{:}|x|$$

$$((\mathrm{A}x)\ B{:}|x|\ \&\ B \subseteq C) \Rightarrow (\mathrm{A}x)\ C{:}|x|$$

An Embracing Is a Definitive Inclusion

A class C embraces a class B if C must include B, whatever images are presented to B or to C. Thus, an embracing is a definitive inclusion:

$$\boxed{(B \subseteq C) \Leftrightarrow\ !(B \underset{\cdot}{\subset} C)}$$

An implication is, similarly, a definitive deduction:

$$(p \Rightarrow q) \Leftrightarrow (\text{Я}p \subseteq \text{Я}q)$$

$$\Leftrightarrow\ !(\text{Я}p \underset{\cdot}{\subset} \text{Я}q)$$

$$\Leftrightarrow\ !(p \rightarrow q)$$

We may also reach these conclusions by manipulating quantifiers. Thus, the universal quantifier "(Ax)" may be defined by the formula:

$$\boxed{(\mathrm{A}x)\ B{:}|x| \Leftrightarrow\ !(\forall x)\ B{:}|x|}$$

That is, a universal quantifier is a definitive exhaustive quantifier. This formula may also be generalized to placetakers for recognizers, associations, or impressions:

$$(!(\forall x)\ B{:}[x]) \Leftrightarrow (\mathrm{A}x)\ B{:}[x]$$

$$(!(\forall y)\ y{:}[b]) \Leftrightarrow (\mathrm{A}y)\ y{:}[b]$$

$$!(\forall \iota)\ \text{Я}q{:}\iota \Leftrightarrow (\mathrm{A}\iota)\ \text{Я}q{:}\iota$$

Since $!B{:}|x|$ implies $B{:}|x|$, we have:

$$(!(\forall x)\ !B{:}|x|) \Rightarrow\ !(\forall x)\ B{:}|x|$$

Conversely, we have:

$$(!(\forall x)\ B{:}|x|) \Rightarrow\ !!(\forall x)\ B{:}|x|$$

Since $!(\forall x)\ B{:}|x|$ implies $(\forall x)\ !B{:}|x|$, we have:

$$(!!(\forall x)\ B{:}|x|) \Rightarrow\ !(\forall x)\ !B{:}|x|$$

Combining these two expressions yields:

$$(!(\forall x)\ B{:}|x|) \Rightarrow\ !(\forall x)\ !B{:}|x|$$

We have, then, the interchangeability:

$$((\mathrm{A}x)\ !B{:}|x|) \Leftrightarrow (!(\forall x)\ B{:}|x|) \Leftrightarrow (\mathrm{A}x)\ B{:}|x|$$

This line of reasoning did not depend on B being a class, so it applies to any universally quantified expression. In particular, we have the formula for an embracing:

$$\begin{aligned}(B \subseteq C) &\Leftrightarrow ((\mathrm{A}x)\ B{:}|x| \Rightarrow C{:}|x|)\\ &\Leftrightarrow ((\mathrm{A}x)\ !(B{:}|x| \rightarrow C{:}|x|))\\ &\Leftrightarrow ((\mathrm{A}x)\ B{:}|x| \rightarrow C{:}|x|)\\ &\Leftrightarrow (!(\forall x)\ B{:}|x| \rightarrow C{:}|x|)\\ &\Leftrightarrow\ !(B \underset{\cdot}{\subset} C)\end{aligned}$$

We can compare a definitive proposition $!p$ to the proposition p that results from removing the definitive operator "!". An impression is said to *appear* to be evoked by $!p$ when the impression is evoked by p. For example, if C includes B, then C *appears* to embrace B. The term *appears* is used because there is no way to distinguish an inclusion from an embracing by performances alone; we must appeal instead to their plans.

Interaction of Modal Operators with Existential Quantification

If for some image x, it must be that B accepts x, then B must accept some image:

$$((\exists x)\ !B{:}|x|) \Rightarrow\ !(\exists x)\ B{:}|x|$$

However, it may be that B must accept some image without there being an image that B accepts definitively. For example, if $!(\exists x)\ B{:}|x|$ we may have the incidental affirmation $B{:}(d)$. The proposition $!(\exists x)\ B{:}|x|$ merely states that there must be some image that B accepts. It does not require that there be an image that B accepts definitively.

We may obtain formulas for the interaction of possibility with existential quantification by applying the contrapositive law to the formulas obtained above for the interaction of definitiveness with universal quantification:

$$((\exists x)\ ;B{:}|x|) \Rightarrow\ ;(\exists x)\ B{:}|x|$$

$$(;(\exists x)\ ;B{:}|x|) \Leftrightarrow\ ;(\exists x)\ B{:}|x|$$

If it might be that some image would be accepted by B, it does not follow that there actually is an image that might be accepted by B. For example, we might admit that there is no law that prohibits the Loch Ness monster from existing, without actually conceiving of something that might be the Loch Ness monster. Thus, even though alternation distributes with possibility, existential quantification does not.

The expression ";$(\exists x)$" is also written "$(\mathrm{E}x)$". It is called a *potential quantifier* and is read « there *might* be an x ». The proposition $(\mathrm{E}x)\ B{:}|x|$, « B might accept some image », can be thought of as the statement « there is no characteristic of the plan of B that prevents B from accepting an image ». A placetaker in a potential quantifier may stand for other ideas besides a class. For example, the potential quantifier of impressions is written $(\mathrm{E}\iota)$, « there might be an impression ι », defined by:

$$({}^{\sim}(\mathrm{A}\iota)\ d{:}\iota) \Leftrightarrow (\mathrm{E}\kappa)\ \bar{d}{:}\kappa$$

Different Varieties of Quantification Describe Different Varieties of Classes

Recall that a class B is said to be *unpopulable* if there must be no image that B accepts. That is, B is unpopulable if

$$(\mathrm{A}x)\ {}^{\sim}(B{:}|x|)$$

In contrast, a class B is said to be *empty* if there is, incidentally, no image that B accepts. That is, B is empty if

$$(\forall x)\ {}^{\sim}(B{:}|x|)$$

A class may be empty and still be populable. For example, let B be the class of customers of a new firm that, as yet, has no customers. The class B is empty, but it is not unpopulable, because there is no prohibition in the definition of B that prevents it from having instances. A class is unpopulable if it is *embraced* in an unpopulable class, but it is empty if it is *included* in an unpopulable class.

A class B is said to be *populable* if there may be an image that B accepts. That is, B is populable if

$$(\mathrm{E}x)\ B{:}|x|$$

In contrast, a class B is said to be *populated* if there *is* an image that B accepts. That is, B is populated if

$$(\exists x)\ B{:}|x|$$

The same terms will also be applied to recognizers. Thus, a recognizer d is *unpopulable* if $(\mathrm{A}\iota)\ \bar{d}{:}\iota$, *empty* if $(\forall\iota)\ \bar{d}{:}\iota$, *populable* if $(\mathrm{E}\iota)\ d{:}\iota$, and *populated* if $(\exists\iota)\ d{:}\iota$.

A class B is said to be *universal* if any image must be accepted by B. A class is universal if and only if its complement is unpopulable. Thus, B is universal if

$$(\mathrm{A}x)\ B{:}|x|$$

In contrast, a class B is said to be *exhaustive* if *each* image is accepted by B. A class is exhaustive if and only if its complement is empty. Thus, B is exhaustive if:

$$(\forall x)\ B{:}|x|$$

A recognizer d is *universal* if $(\mathrm{A}\iota)\ d{:}\iota$, and *exhaustive* if $(\forall \iota)\ d{:}\iota$.

Intersection and Union

Definitive quantification interacts with intersection and union as follows:

$$\begin{aligned}(\mathrm{A}x)\ B \cap C{:}|x| &\Leftrightarrow\ !(\forall y)\ B \cap C{:}|y|\\ &\Leftrightarrow\ !(\forall y)\ B{:}|y|\ \&\ C{:}|y|\\ &\Leftrightarrow\ !((\forall y)\ B{:}|y|\ \&\ (\forall z)\ C{:}|z|)\\ &\Leftrightarrow (!(\forall y)\ B{:}|y|)\ \&\ (!(\forall z)\ C{:}|z|)\\ &\Leftrightarrow (\mathrm{A}y)\ B{:}|y|\ \&\ (\mathrm{A}z)\ C{:}|z|\\ (\mathrm{A}x)\ B \cup C{:}|x| &\Leftrightarrow\ !(\forall y)\ B \cup C{:}|y|\\ &\Leftrightarrow\ !(\forall y)\ B{:}|y| \vee C{:}|y|\\ &\Leftarrow\ !((\forall y)\ B{:}|y| \vee (\forall z)\ C{:}|z|)\\ &\Leftarrow (!(\forall y)\ B{:}|y|) \vee (!(\forall z)\ C{:}|z|)\\ &\Leftarrow (\mathrm{A}y)\ B{:}|y| \vee (\mathrm{A}z)\ C{:}|z|\end{aligned}$$

Applying the contrapositive law yields:

$$((\mathrm{E}x)\ B \cap C{:}|x|) \Rightarrow (\mathrm{E}y)\ B{:}|y|\ \&\ (\mathrm{E}z)\ C{:}|z|$$

$$((\mathrm{E}x)\ B \cup C{:}|x|) \Leftrightarrow (\mathrm{E}y)\ B{:}|y| \vee (\mathrm{E}z)\ C{:}|z|$$

Reasoning About Deduction

The power of logic is greatly increased by stating the principles of deduction within the logical system. In this way, data logic can describe its own operation. The primary rule of deduction is that a proposition p together with the proposition « if p then q » together imply q. This law is sometimes referred to by the enigmatic name *modus ponens*. We will call it the *direct deduction law*. In data logic it is

$$(p\ \&\ (p \rightarrow q)) \Rightarrow q$$

Since $(p \Rightarrow q)$ implies $(p \rightarrow q)$, we may also conclude that

$$(p\ \&\ (p \Rightarrow q)) \Rightarrow q$$

Certain definitive propositions are assumed as part of data logic. These propositions are called *axioms* and will be discussed in Section 3.4. A proposition p is said to be *proved* if p is implied by the conjunction of some or all of the axioms. A chain of implications that leads from the axioms to p is called a *proof* of p. Since each axiom is omissive, only omissive propositions may be proved, by performance type integrity. Since each axiom is definitive, all propositions that are proved are definitive.

Deduction versus Alternation

In symbolic logic, the two propositions $(\tilde{}p \lor q)$ and $(p \rightarrow q)$ are interchangeable. These propositions are, in general, different in data logic, but they are logically related. For example, we have directly

$$(p \rightarrow q) \;\&\; (\tilde{}p \lor p) \Rightarrow (\tilde{}p \lor q)$$

The proposition $\tilde{}p \lor p$ is definitive if p is sheath-free. Thus, if p is sheath-free, then $p \rightarrow q$ implies $\tilde{}p \lor q$.

Consider, conversely, the definitive proposition $!(\tilde{}p \lor q)$. This proposition is equivalent to

$$\square \subseteq \text{Я}\tilde{}p \cup \text{Я}q$$

Intersecting both sides of the embracing with $\text{Я}p$ yields

$$\begin{aligned} \text{Я}p &\subseteq (\text{Я}p \cap \text{Я}\tilde{}p) \cup (\text{Я}p \cap \text{Я}q) \\ &\subseteq (\text{Я}p \cap \text{Я}\tilde{}p) \cup \text{Я}q \end{aligned}$$

That is,

$$p \Rightarrow (p \;\&\; \tilde{}p) \lor q$$

So, if p is sheath-free, then $!(\tilde{}p \lor q)$ implies $p \Rightarrow q$.

Conclusions from Conjunctions

In symbolic logic, the statements "if p & q, then r" and "if p, then if q then r" are equivalent [see *3.3 in (Whitehead and Russell 1927)]. Since there are several formulations of "if-then" in data logic, some care is required in examining this rule. The most elementary formulation is with "if-then" taken to be incidental deduction:

$$(p \rightarrow (q \rightarrow r)) \Rightarrow ((p \;\&\; q) \rightarrow r) \qquad (1)$$

This formula may be proved as follows:

$$\begin{aligned} (p \rightarrow (q \rightarrow r)) &\Rightarrow ((p \;\&\; q) \rightarrow ((q \rightarrow r) \;\&\; q)) \\ &\Rightarrow ((p \;\&\; q) \rightarrow r) \end{aligned}$$

Applying the definitiveness operator to both sides of Formula (1) yields

$$(p \Rightarrow (q \rightarrow r)) \Rightarrow ((p \;\&\; q) \Rightarrow r)$$

In particular, since $(q \Rightarrow r)$ implies $(q \rightarrow r)$,

$$(p \Rightarrow (q \Rightarrow r)) \Rightarrow ((p \ \& \ q) \Rightarrow r)$$

Conversely, suppose that p is definitive. Then we have

$$\begin{aligned}(!p) &\Rightarrow (q \Rightarrow p) \\ &\Rightarrow (q \Rightarrow (p \ \& \ q))\end{aligned}$$

Therefore, since any proposition implies the implication $(!p) \Rightarrow (q \Rightarrow (p \ \& \ q))$,

$$\begin{aligned}((p \ \& \ q) \Rightarrow r) &\Rightarrow ((!p) \Rightarrow (q \Rightarrow (p \ \& \ q))) \\ &\Rightarrow ((!p) \Rightarrow (q \Rightarrow r))\end{aligned}$$

Quine's Criticisms of Modal Logic

Quine has offered many criticisms of earlier systems of modal logic. We will discuss some of these criticisms to show how data logic avoids the pitfalls of other modal systems. For example, in *From A Logical Point of View*, Quine cites the following faulty chain of reasoning that may be formed in some modal logics (Quine 1980, pp. 139–159):

> 9 is necessarily (definitively) greater than 7.
>
> The number of planets in the solar system = 9.
>
> Therefore the number of planets in the solar system is necessarily (definitively) greater than 7. (2)

Data logic shows why this pattern of reasoning is incorrect. The first two expressions may be written in data logic as follows:

$$!(9) \text{ Is Greater Than: } (7) \quad \text{(abbreviated } !q\text{)}$$

$$\text{number of planets} \doteqdot 9 \text{ (abbreviated } p\text{)}$$

The proposition q that 9 is greater than 7 is definitive because it follows from the definitions of the numbers 7 and 9. The proposition p that the number of planets equals 9 is incidental, not definitive, because the solar system could have a different number of planets. If a tenth planet were discovered tomorrow, for example, we would not say that we were living in a new solar system.

From the proposition $p \ \& \ !q$ we may conclude the incidental proposition $p \ \& \ q$, but not the definitive proposition $!(p \ \& \ q)$. Thus, the proper deduction is:

> The number of planets in the solar system is greater than 7.

Not the definitive proposition (2).

In *Word and Object*, Quine offers the following argument (Quine 1960, pp. 195–200). Suppose that two classes F and G each determine the recognizer x up to equivalence (in Quine's terms, up to "equality"). That is, suppose:

$$(\forall w) \ F{:}[w] \Leftrightarrow (w \equiv x)$$

$$(\forall w) \ G{:}[w] \Leftrightarrow (w \equiv x)$$

From these two propositions we may conclude:

$$(\forall w)\ F{:}[w] \Leftrightarrow G{:}[w]$$

Imagining that p is affirmed, and that x is equivalent to some recognizer y, Quine then cites the two propositions:

$$(\forall w)\ (p\ \&\ (w \equiv y)) \Leftrightarrow (w \equiv x) \tag{3}$$

$$(\forall w)\ (w \equiv y) \Leftrightarrow (w \equiv x) \tag{4}$$

Combining Formulas (3) and (4) yields

$$(\forall w)\ (p\ \&\ (w \equiv y)) \Leftrightarrow (w \equiv y)$$

and therefore,

$$p \Leftarrow (y \equiv y) \tag{5}$$

If this pattern of reasoning were allowed, then since $(y \equiv y)$ is definitive, any affirmed proposition p would be definitive. There would then be no difference between definitive propositions and affirmed propositions.

In data logic, Formula (3) is only valid if p is definitive. Otherwise we have only one direction of implication:

$$(\forall w)\ (p\ \&\ (w \equiv y)) \Rightarrow (w \equiv x)$$

The definitive proposition $(w \equiv x)$ does not imply p merely because p is affirmed. The rule of symbolic logic that any proposition implies an affirmed proposition does not hold in data logic. Therefore, Formula (5) can not be derived in data logic.

Quine cites the additional example:

> Mathematicians may conceivably be said to be necessarily rational and not necessarily two-legged; and cyclists necessarily two-legged and not necessarily rational. But what of an individual who counts among his eccentricities both mathematics and cycling? Is this concrete individual necessarily rational and contingently two-legged or vice versa?" (Quine 1960, p. 199)

The error here is that the individual is not what is necessary (definitive), but the means of deduction. Quine's premises may be expressed using embracings as follows:

$$\text{Mathematician} \subseteq \text{Rational}$$

$$\tilde{}(\text{Mathematician} \subseteq \text{Two-Legged})$$

$$\text{Cyclist} \subseteq \text{Two-Legged}$$

$$\tilde{}(\text{Cyclist} \subseteq \text{Rational})$$

The incidental proposition « Mathematician: (Bernard) » implies the *incidental* ("contingent" in Quine's terms) proposition « Rational: (Bernard) », not that Bernard is definitively ("necessarily" in Quine's terms) rational. Thus, the answer to Quine's question is that Bernard is contingently (incidentally) rational and two-legged, just as he is contingently (incidentally) a mathematician and a cyclist.

Conclusion

The contrasts between inclusion and embracing, deduction and implication, exhaustive quantification and universal quantification, are unified by the definitive operator. For any proposition p, the proposition $!p$ proposes that p is a consequence of how terms are formed (that is, it is a consequence of their plans), rather than a consequence of performances of the terms. For example, if C includes B then in each performance of B, all instances of B have been seen to be also instances of C. When we say that it is *definitive* that C includes B, or, alternatively, that C *must include* B, we mean that in *any* performance, *any* instance of B *must* be an instance of C, by virtue of the way B and C are formed. This is no more than saying that C embraces B, so an embracing is a definitive inclusion.

Readers who are accustomed to symbolic logic should be particularly on guard when manipulating expressions of the form "p & $!q$" and "$!(\tilde{}p \vee q)$". The proposition p & $!q$ is incidental when p is incidental. It therefore implies the proposition p & q, not in general the definitive proposition $!(p$ & $q)$. The definitive alternation $!(\tilde{}p \vee q)$ only implies the implication $p \Rightarrow q$ in general if p is sheath-free.

2.16 CONCLUSION

We have argued that logical reasoning should enforce a fundamental separation between constructive and omissive ideas. We have derived this distinction from the inexhaustibility principle, which states that any constructive class must be able to fail to examine some image. As a practical matter, the separation between constructive and omissive prevents forms of reasoning that lead to paradox in symbolic logic. Thus, we have shown that inexhaustibility leads to the performance type integrity law, which states that an omissive proposition may not imply a constructive proposition. It is therefore impossible to form a problem that leads to a proposition being interchangeable with its negation, $p \Leftrightarrow \tilde{}p$. Most paradoxes of symbolic logic lead to a proposition of the form $p \Leftrightarrow \tilde{}p$ by some means. Since p and $\tilde{}p$ always have different performance types, either "$p \Rightarrow \tilde{}p$" or "$\tilde{}p \Rightarrow p$" violates performance type integrity. The propositions $p \Rightarrow \tilde{}p$ and $\tilde{}p \Rightarrow p$ therefore can not both be affirmed.

We have argued that a logic that describes data must be able to distinguish characteristics of how associations are formed (definitive propositions) from characteristics of populations of the associations (incidental propositions). This distinction is made in data logic by the definitive operator. Thus, if it happens, in some population, that each instance of a class B is also an instance of a class C, then C *includes* B. If, however, B and C are so defined that any instance of B must be an instance of C, then C *definitively includes* B, that is, C *embraces* B.

Data base constraints, such as "any *car* is also a *vehicle*" are definitive; statements in a data base population, such as "item #394612 is a car" are not definitive. Symbolic logic does not distinguish definitive propositions from propositions that are not definitive, and is therefore unable to describe a class whose population changes while the constraints on the class remain the same.

We have argued that the logic of negation is considerably more complex than is recognized by symbolic logic. In particular, we have argued that reasoning from negated propositions is often unreliable. For example, in symbolic logic, the proposition $\tilde{}p \vee q$ implies the proposition $p \Rightarrow q$. By this rule, a false proposition implies every proposition. In data logic, the proposition $(\tilde{}p \vee q)$ does not imply the proposition $p \Rightarrow q$. An incidental proposition p only implies an incidental proposition q in data logic if p and q are logically related. A false proposition (a proposition p such that $\tilde{}p$ is affirmed) does not imply every proposition in data logic.

The different approach to negation allows data logic to accept contradictory propositions. Contradictions arise frequently in practical situations; indeed, a contradiction is often a valuable signal that a mass of data contains some unresolved problem. Symbolic logic can not function in the presence of contradictions, so all such signals must be removed before symbolic logic can be applied. Data logic, in contrast, can manage the data while the contradiction is being resolved, and can assist with determining the source of the problem.

Our presentation now branches in two directions. Readers interested in the further development of data logic, particularly its implications for long-standing problems of philosophy such as paradox, may continue to Chapter 3, Advanced Data Logic. Readers whose interest is more focused on data base issues may skip Chapter 3 and proceed directly to Chapter 4, Applications of Data Logic.

3

Advanced Data Logic

3.1 INTRODUCTION

In this chapter, we apply the techniques of data logic to several advanced problems of logical philosophy. Our aim is to determine how broadly data logic can be applied to abstract reasoning. Because many of these subjects stretch the limits of our understanding, we include some tentative results in this chapter that require further investigation. The results presented here are not used in later chapters, so this chapter may be skipped by readers whose primary interest is the application of data logic to data base design.

In Section 3.2, Postulates, we discuss the requirements that a formal process must satisfy to be an adequate tool for managing proposition tags. We codify these requirements as a set of postulates. Since a piece of data is a proposition tag, the postulates establish the requirements for both a symbolic reasoning process and a data management process.

In Section 3.3, Formal Definitions of Logical Terms, we give rigorous definitions for the logical terms introduced in the last chapter. We show, in particular, how the number of primitive concepts may be reduced by applying plans aggressively. The method of plans also allows data logic to describe its own behavior to a far greater extent than symbolic logic.

In Section 3.4, Axioms, we codify the assumptions of data logic as a set of basic claims called *axioms*. The axioms of data logic are considerably more diverse than the axioms of symbolic logic because the syntax of data logic is expressed in the axioms themselves. In symbolic logic, the syntax of logical expressions is specified outside the logical system.

In Section 3.5, Russell's Paradox, we show how data logic avoids Russell's paradox through performance type integrity. This result allows data logic to employ unrestricted quantification over both associations and recognizers.

In Section 3.6, Foundations of Arithmetic, we show how arithmetic can be developed from data logic. We argue that the definition of the number 1 used in symbolic logic is an inaccurate representation of the number « one » in thought, and so should be changed. We argue that infinite sets should not be admitted into data logic, and show how the natural numbers can be defined as a class without introducing an infinite set of numbers.

In Section 3.7, Comparison with Set Theory, we examine Zermelo's axioms of set theory in detail, and describe where data logic differs. We also discuss Cantor's treatment of infinite sets, and argue that Cantor's results may be interpreted as limitations on the ability to define associations, rather than as statements about the relative magnitude of transfinite numbers.

In Section 3.8, Consistency and Completeness, we show that data logic is consistent and that Gödel's proof of the incompleteness of symbolic logic fails in data logic. We argue, however, that the concepts of consistency and completeness have far less relevance to data logic than they do to symbolic logic. We propose alternative tests for data logic, similar to consistency and completeness, that await further study.

3.2 POSTULATES

Postulates Establish the Symbolic Framework for Data Logic

We turn in the next three sections to writing a set of formal rules that describe data logic. Ultimately, one would like to be able to write a computer program or other formal symbolic procedure that would accept only valid statements of data logic, and would be able to perform all valid forms of reasoning automatically. Although we will not delve deeply into the problems of writing such a program, we will lay out in postulates and axioms the requirements that such a program must satisfy. We believe that such a program is within the capabilities of today's computing technology.

Postulates differ from *axioms* in that postulates describe the engines that manage claims, whereas axioms are claims that are assumed to be affirmed. Continuing the analogy with computer programs, postulates describe the computing environment: aspects of the computer hardware and software needed to manage data. The axioms are claims that are considered to be part of the population of any data base. In general, we can always convert an axiom to a postulate by writing a computer program that implements the axiom rather than stating the axiom as a claim. However, we can not convert a postulate to an axiom because the postulates establish the means used to manipulate claims.

By this reasoning, it is important to minimize the severity of postulates in order to maximize the power of the logical system, even if doing so increases the number of axioms. Here, we differ from modern writers who have argued that the number of axioms should be minimized (Whitehead and Russell 1927). Instead, we return to the original conception of Euclid, who developed geometry from 28 "definitions" and "common notions," but only five postulates (Euclid 300B.C.).

Before we can manipulate claims, we require engines that manipulate the symbols used to express claims. One such engine is the connecting/separating engine that provides conglomerations. Engines that are required for the functioning of logic, and hence for the functioning of data bases, will be called *master engines*.

Each master engine will be described in text as a postulate. In computerized data bases, the postulates establish the requirements the computer system must meet in order to be capable of managing a data base. Since the postulates apply to all data bases, they are very basic. Most are ordinarily guaranteed by the engineering of the computer hardware. In a broader sense, however, the postulates constrain the varieties of hardware that can be used to support data bases. New computer architectures may be tested against the postulates to determine whether or not they are sufficiently powerful to manage data bases. Our approach contrasts with many writers in symbolic logic, who, writing before the invention of computing machines, were content to treat the postulates as assumptions, often not calling them out explicitly.

Fundamental Postulates

The following list contains the postulates that we have introduced so far, along with the section number in brackets where each is discussed:

- **(P1)** It is possible to form an arbitrarily large number of detectors. [1.2]
- **(P2)** Any detector is a binding site. [1.2]
- **(P3)** In any performance of a binding site, an examination results in exactly one outcome, either acceptance or rejection. [1.2]
- **(P4)** It is possible to form a connecting engine that forms a conglomeration from any arbitrarily large collection of symbols. [1.7]
- **(P5)** Any conglomeration of symbols is a symbol. [1.7]
- **(P6)** Two conglomerations t and u are the same symbol if and only if the constituent of t in each position i is the same symbol as the constituent of u in the position i. [1.7]
- **(P7)** Any connecting engine is reversible. [1.7]
- **(P8)** It is possible to form a binding site that accepts proposition tags. [1.12]

Postulates of Deduction

Formal deduction is the introduction of new claims into the population based on formal manipulation of other claims. Formal deduction is executed by engines. One such engine executes incidental deductions:

- **(P9)** It is possible to form a *deductive engine* that transforms a proposition tag "p" and a proposition tag "$p \rightarrow q$" into a symbol "q". [2.15]

We require a *conjoining engine* that forms the conjunction p & q from the two propositions p and q. Symbolic logic dispenses with this engine by defining conjunction in terms of deduction, p & q as $\tilde{}(\tilde{}p \rightarrow q)$, but this formula is incorrect in data logic (see Section 2.15).

> **(P10)** It is possible to form a conjoining engine that transforms a proposition tag "p" and a proposition tag "q" into a symbol "p & q". [2.9]

We require a *substituting engine* that substitutes symbols for exhaustively quantified placetakers. This engine must substitute symbols according to the rules of syntax for propositions, that is, it must substitute only individuals when the placetaker occupies the position of an individual, and only associations of the proper degree when the placetaker occupies such positions.

> **(P11)** It is possible to form a substituting engine that substitutes symbols into exhaustively quantified expressions, in particular, that transforms a proposition tag "$(\forall x)$ B:[x]" and an individual "b" into the symbol "B:[b]". [2.10]

The rules of substitution in quantified settings are rather intricate, and are not described completely by (P11). The difficulties in data logic are the same as those in symbolic logic, and arise when substituting into complex multiply quantified propositions. The interested reader is referred to (Hilbert and Ackermann 1938) or to the more advanced (Kleene 1952).

Conclusion

We have shown how to define processes called *master engines* that execute all the varieties of formal deduction used in data logic. A computer program or other similar process that incorporates these master engines is therefore capable of executing the entire deductive apparatus of data logic.

3.3 FORMAL DEFINITIONS OF LOGICAL TERMS

In this section, we begin to specify data logic in a purely formal way. That is, we will set down symbolic expressions that generate all statements of data logic when the engines assumed in the postulates are applied. We will develop data logic directly from plans. Although this method is somewhat removed from class operations like intersection and union, it makes explicit the issues involved in forming logical statements. The results therefore give insight into the extent to which computers can describe their own operation, and consequently into the scope of computer languages. Truly useful automated reasoning may require that computers be able to describe logical processes, rather than only being able to execute them.

Data logic is able to describe itself much more readily than symbolic logic can. Symbolic logic relies on a system of meta-languages, in which propositions in one meta-language must be described by propositions in a higher meta-language, and so on, resulting in indefinitely many different logical systems. In data logic, there should be no need for this hierarchy of languages, because integrity of the logic is controlled by performance type integrity. There should therefore be only one language, the language of logic, which describes its own operation to the fullest extent possible. Of course, this description can not include the basic operations on symbols that permit a language to exist—these are defined by the postulates. However, characteristics that set logic apart from other languages, such as the definition of a class, should be described within data logic. In this section, we take self-description as far as we have been able to achieve. Further research is needed to prove that this approach, probably with modifications, does indeed suffice to define data logic.

Operations on Plans

Since any recognizer, and any association, is a realization of a plan, we focus attention first on plans. We will assume in this section that a plan is a recognizer. This assumption is only used in Chapter 3, and can be dispensed with by assuming that a plan has a handle. However, the idea that a plan is a recognizer allows us to consider the extent to which we might actually implement a plan on a device such as a computer. A plan of a class might be implemented as a computer program that would determine the individuals that a class tag would accept. The program itself can then be viewed as an individual, a recognizer tag. Notice further that since a recognizer is formed from a plan, we can consider a plan to be itself formed from a plan. Plans of plans will be useful constituents of abstract formulas.

Since propositions are plans, we begin with propositional logic. The most basic operations of propositional logic are conjunction (&), negation (˜), and deduction ($\rightarrow$). All of these operations have been defined for propositions, but we will extend them here more generally to plans. For example, for any two propositions p and q we have the equivalence

$$(\text{Я}p \underset{\cdot}{\subset} \text{Я}q) \equiv (p \rightarrow q) \tag{1}$$

We are able to write Formula (1) as an equivalence (of recognizers) rather than as an interchangeability because we consider the propositions ($\text{Я}p \underset{\cdot}{\subset} \text{Я}q$) and ($p \rightarrow q$) to be recognizers. Formula (1) states therefore that the operation "$\underset{\cdot}{\subset}$" can, in principle, be dispensed with, so that every statement of the form ($x \underset{\cdot}{\subset} y$) may be rewritten equivalently as ($\lambda x \rightarrow \lambda y$), as long as λx and λy are propositions.

Consider further two classes B and C such that C includes B. Since B is formed from a plan λB and C is formed from a plan λC, we may write the inclusion $B \underset{\cdot}{\subset} C$ as

$$\text{Я}\lambda B \underset{\cdot}{\subset} \text{Я}\lambda C$$

This proposition has the same form as the left side of Formula (1). We might reasonably conclude that the two plans λB and λC stand in some relationship to each other that is similar to the relationship of incidental deduction between the propositions p and q in Formula (1). To describe this relationship, we broaden the meaning of *deduction* to cover the relationship between λB and λC as well as the relationship between p and q. We will represent this broader definition of *deduction* using the same symbol "$\rightarrow$". We may therefore define incidental inclusion of both recognizers and associations by the formula

$$(\text{Я}x \underset{\cdot}{\subset} \text{Я}y) \equiv (x \rightarrow y)$$

Here x and y may be any plans, not only propositions. In general, basing definitions on plans will allow us to use the same expressions to describe both the logic of classes and the logic of recognizers.

We extend & and ˜ to cover plans of associations in the same spirit. That is, we define intersection and complement by the formulas:

$$(Яx \cap Яy) \equiv Я(x \ \&\ y)$$

$$\overline{Яx} \equiv Я(\tilde{}x)$$

These formulas have already been discussed where x and y stand for propositions, but we treat them in this section as applying to all plans. Thus, the plan « x & y » may be imagined as the plan « perform plan x and perform plan y ». The realization of « x & y » is therefore the intersection of « $Яx$ » with « $Яy$ ». Similarly, the plan « ˜x » may be imagined as the plan « perform plan x, then accept if x does not accept and reject if x does not reject ». The realization of « ˜x » is therefore the complement of « $Яx$ ».

Method of Definition

We will show how the various terms of data logic may be defined from a small set of ideas called *primitive terms*. For example, union (∪) may be defined from complement (¯) and intersection (∩), so union is not a primitive term. The basic device for defining new terms is equivalence. If a term x is equivalent to a term y, then y may be substituted for x in nearly all contexts. The primary exception is the logic of opposites: °y may not be substituted for °x because equivalence is only concerned with what x and y accept. If x and y reject different ideas, then °x and °y will not be equivalent.

We will define many common ideas using *primitive associations*, which are primitive terms. The proposal methods of primitive associations are determined by considering the performance types of the plans. Recall that a proposition has the same performance type as its topic recognizer. More generally, we say that any plan has the same performance type as its realization.

For example, we say that C is a class if and only if its plan λC is a conformer of the special class *Class*:

$$Class\text{: } [\lambda C]$$

Class is omissive because definitive, hence omissive, propositions will imply that an idea is a class. For example, if it is definitive that C:[d], then C must be a class. If *Class* were constructive, this implication would violate performance type integrity. Since the proposition « C is a class » must be definitive, hence omissive, when C is constructive, λC is a conformer, rather than an instance, of *Class*.

We have, similarly, the omissive class *Recognizer*. When we say that d is a recognizer, we do not mean that an impression bound to d is a recognizer, but that d itself is a recognizer. Thus, we say not that d is a conformer of *Recognizer*, but that the plan of d is:

$$Recognizer\text{: } [\lambda d]$$

Illustration of Definition from Plans

As an illustration of the method we will use, we derive equivalence from primitive terms. Equivalence is defined by the formula

$$(Яx \equiv Яy) \equiv (x \Leftrightarrow y) \tag{2}$$

Formula (2) is not a proper definition of "$\equiv$" because "$\equiv$" is used to relate the left and right sides. To make it proper, we must relate the plans of both sides. That is,

$$\lambda(Яx \equiv Яy) \Leftrightarrow \lambda(x \Leftrightarrow y) \tag{3}$$

To form the right side, we must be able to form the plan of $x \Leftrightarrow y$. Since "$\Leftrightarrow$" may be defined in terms of $\rightarrow$, !, and &, we must form the plans of each of $x \rightarrow y$, $!x$, and $x \,\&\, y$. These plans are formed by the associations:

$$\textit{Definitize}\ [(\lambda x),\ (\lambda !x)]$$

$$\textit{Deduce}\ ([\lambda x],\ (\lambda y),\ (\lambda(x \rightarrow y)))$$

$$\textit{Conjoin}\ [(\lambda x),\ (\lambda y),\ (\lambda(x \,\&\, y))]$$

These associations assemble plans that fit a given criterion. For example, *Definitize* attaches λx to y if y is the plan whose realization is $!x$. The expression $!x$ may therefore be defined to be the realization of the melding of the class *Definitize* [(λx), ( )].

Relationships between plans are definitive, therefore any valid assembly controlled by a primitive association is omissive. By testing each combination of performance types in turn, we may determine the proper proposal methods by the rules given in Section 2.12.

For example, the proposition $!p$ has the same performance type as the proposition p. Therefore, assemblies controlled by *Definitize* must follow the table:

x	*y*	*Definitize*: *x* , *y*
constructive	constructive	omissive
constructive	omissive	constructive
omissive	constructive	constructive
omissive	omissive	omissive

The proper proposal methods are therefore *Definitize*: [(x), (y)], and *Definitize* is omissive.

Using placetakers to represent plans of plans, we may write

$$(!Яx) \equiv Я\mu\textit{Definitize}\ [(x),\ (\ )]$$

$$(Яx \rightarrow Яy) \equiv Я\mu\textit{Deduce}\ [[x],\ (y),\ (\ )]$$

$$(Яx \,\&\, Яy) \equiv Я\mu\textit{Conjoin}\ [(x),\ (y),\ (\ )]$$

It is helpful to express "$\equiv$" in the same way:

$$(Яx \equiv Яy) \equiv Я\mu\textit{Equivalue}\ ((x),\ (y),\ (\ ))$$

We have then,

$$\lambda(Яx \equiv Яy) \equiv \mu\textit{Equivalue}\ ((x),\ (y),\ (\ ))$$

We rewrite Formula (3) using this formula, and using placetakers to represent plans of plans:

$$\mu \textit{Equivalue}\ ((Яx), (Яy), (\ )) \Leftrightarrow \lambda(Яx \Leftrightarrow Яy) \tag{4}$$

We may now build up the definition of "⇔" as follows:

$$\textit{Imply}\ ([x], (y), (z)) \equiv \textit{Definitize}\ [(\mu \textit{Deduce}\ ([x], (y), (\ ))), (z)]$$

$$\textit{Interchange}\ ((x), (y), (z)) \equiv \textit{Conjoin}\ [(\mu \textit{Imply}\ ([x], (y), (\ ))), (\mu \textit{Imply}\ ([y], (x), (\ ))), (z)]$$

$$(Яx \Leftrightarrow Яy) \equiv Я\mu \textit{Interchange}\ ((x), (y), (\ ))$$

Substituting into Formula (4), we obtain

$$\mu \textit{Equivalue}\ ((Яx), (Яy), (\ )) \Leftrightarrow \mu \textit{Interchange}\ ((x), (y), (\ ))$$

We will find it useful to define *Equivalue* according to the stronger condition:

$$\textit{Equivalue}\ ((Яx), (Яy), (\ )) \Leftrightarrow \textit{Interchange}\ ((x), (y), (\ ))$$

Substituting again for "⇔", we have

$$Я\mu \textit{Interchange}\ ((\lambda \textit{Equivalue}\ ((Яx), (Яy), (\ ))), (\lambda \textit{Interchange}\ ((x), (y), (\ ))), (\ )) \tag{5}$$

Here, "λ*Equivalue*" represents the plan of the primitive association *Equivalue*, and "λ*Interchange*" represents the plan of the primitive association *Interchange*. Notice that the only logical operations used in this definition of equivalence are realization (Я) and melding (μ). The rest of the expression consists entirely of associations.

To complete the definition, we must quantify it for any x and for any y. Rather than repeat the entire Formula (5), we consider the general problem of defining the expression

$$!(\forall x)\ (\forall y)\ \mathscr{F}$$

for any given formula $\mathscr{F}$. Prefixing by $(\exists x)$ is defined by:

$$((\exists x)\ y) \equiv Я\mu \textit{Exist}\ [[\lambda x], (\lambda y), (\ )]$$

Notice the use of the plan of a placetaker "λx" on the right side. The symbol "λx" represents that portion of the plan of y that acts as a programmatic position (see Section 1.8). The expression y may or may not contain "x" as a constituent. If y does not contain "x" then prefixing with $(\exists x)$ results in a formula that is interchangeable with y.

We define universal quantification by:

$$(!(\forall x)\ (\forall y)\ \mathscr{F}) \equiv (!\tilde{}(\exists x)\ (\exists y)\ \tilde{}\mathscr{F})$$

Thus, quantification may be defined through an association of plans, and does not require any new operations.

Catalog of Primitive Terms

There are two kinds of primitive terms in data logic: *primitive operators* and *primitive associations*. The primitive operators are logical operations that may not be reduced to combinations of other logical operations. The primitive associations are associations that we will use in definitions, and whose properties will be described further in axioms. There are six primitive operators:

Я (realization)
μ (melding)
. (compounding an impression with a recognizer)
|| (acceptance of an image)
( ) (instantiation)
[ ] (conformalization)

Both instantiation and conformalization are used as proposal methods of primitive associations [as in formula (5)]. Since the highest degree primitive association has degree three, tensor proposal methods need only be provided up to degree three. We will show how proposal methods of associations of higher degree may be formed from primitive associations.

The primitive associations are:

Recognizer [ ]
Proposition [ ]
Position [ ]

Definitize [( ), ( )]
Exist–Impression [( ), ( )]
Negate ([ ], [ ])
Oppose [( ), ( )]
Control [( ), ( )]

Conjoin [( ), ( ), ( )]
Deduce ([ ], ( ), ( ))
Exist [[ ], ( ), ( )]
Localize [( ), ( ), ( )]

All the primitive associations are omissive except *Negate*, which is constructive. Each of the primitive associations is itself formed from a plan. When these plans are needed, they are indicated by a prefixed λ: λ*Recognizer*, λ*Definitize*, etc.

Definitions of Methods of Inference

We will develop the definitions cumulatively, so that we can take advantage of simplifications as we go. A definition will be indicated by a prefix of the form "(D1)". As with postulates, we append the section where the definition is discussed in brackets to the statement of each definition. As a glance at Formula (5) will show, defining everything in primitive terms yields expressions that are inordinately complex. We will therefore depart from the strict practice of forming definitions from only previously defined terms by allowing !, $(\forall x)$, and $\mathrel{\underset{\cdot}{=}}$ to be used before they are defined. Definitions may also be formed without this assumption, but in a much more cumbersome fashion, as shown by the definition of equivalence above. We will generally use $!(\forall x)\,(\forall y)$ rather than $(\mathrm{A}x)\,(\mathrm{A}y)$ as a prefix to definitions and axioms, because the equivalence of the two requires proof.

(D1) $!(\forall x)\,(!\text{Я}x) \mathrel{\underset{\cdot}{=}} \text{Я}\mu\textit{Definitize}\,[(x), (\ )]$ [2.14]

(D2) $!(\forall x)\,({}^{\sim}\text{Я}x) \mathrel{\underset{\cdot}{=}} \text{Я}\mu\textit{Negate}\,([x], [\ ])$ [2.6]

(D3) $!(\forall x)\,(\forall y)\,((\exists\text{Я}x)\,\text{Я}y) \mathrel{\underset{\cdot}{=}} \text{Я}\mu\textit{Exist}\,[[x], (y), (\ )]$ [2.10]

(D4) $!(\forall x)\,(\forall y)\,((\forall\text{Я}x)\,y) \mathrel{\underset{\cdot}{=}} {}^{\sim}(\exists\text{Я}x)\,{}^{\sim}y$ [2.10]

(D5) $!(\forall x)\,(\forall y)\,(\text{Я}x \rightarrow \text{Я}y) \mathrel{\underset{\cdot}{=}} \text{Я}\mu\textit{Deduce}\,([x], (y), (\ ))$ [2.13]

(D6) $!(\forall x)\,(\forall y)\,(\text{Я}x \;\&\; \text{Я}y) \mathrel{\underset{\cdot}{=}} \text{Я}\mu\textit{Conjoin}\,[(x), (y), (\ )]$ [2.9]

(D7) $!(\forall x)\,(\forall y)\,(x \leftrightarrow y) \mathrel{\underset{\cdot}{=}} (x \rightarrow y) \;\&\; (y \rightarrow x)$ [2.13]

(D8) $!(\forall x)\,(\forall y)\,(\text{Я}x \mathrel{\underset{\cdot}{\subset}} \text{Я}y) \mathrel{\underset{\cdot}{=}} (x \rightarrow y)$ [2.13]

(D9) $!(\forall x)\,(\forall y)\,(\text{Я}x \mathrel{\underset{\cdot}{=}} \text{Я}y) \mathrel{\underset{\cdot}{=}} (x \leftrightarrow y)$ [2.13]

(D10) $!(\forall x)\,(\forall y)\,(x \Rightarrow y) \mathrel{\underset{\cdot}{=}} !(x \rightarrow y)$ [2.9, 2.15]

(D11) $!(\forall x)\,(\forall y)\,(x \Leftrightarrow y) \mathrel{\underset{\cdot}{=}} ((x \Rightarrow y) \;\&\; (y \Rightarrow x))$ [2.9]

(D12) $!(\forall x)\,(\forall y)\,(x \subseteq y) \mathrel{\underset{\cdot}{=}} !(x \mathrel{\underset{\cdot}{\subset}} y)$ [1.5, 2.15]

(D13) $!(\forall x)\,(\forall y)\,(x \equiv y) \mathrel{\underset{\cdot}{=}} !(x \mathrel{\underset{\cdot}{=}} y)$ [1.5, 2.15]

(D14) $!(\forall x)\,(;x) \mathrel{\underset{\cdot}{=}} {}^{\sim}!{}^{\sim}x$ [2.14]

Quantification

Quantification of impressions is defined by:

(D15) $!(\forall x)\,((\exists\iota)\,x{:}\iota) \mathrel{\underset{\cdot}{=}} \mu\textit{Exist–impression}\,[(x), (\ )]$ [2.10]

(D16) $!(\forall x)\,((\forall\iota)\,y{:}\iota) \mathrel{\underset{\cdot}{=}} {}^{\sim}(\exists\iota)\,\bar{y}{:}\iota$ [2.10]

Universal and potential quantification are defined as follows:

(D17) $!(\forall x)\,(\forall y)\,((\mathrm{A}\text{Я}x)\,y) \mathrel{\underset{\cdot}{=}} !(\forall\text{Я}x)\,y$ [2.10, 2.15]

(D18) $!(\forall x)\,(\forall y)\,((\mathrm{E}\text{Я}x)\,y) \mathrel{\underset{\cdot}{=}} ;(\exists\text{Я}x)\,y$ [2.15]

(D17) and (D18) are considered to apply when x stands for an impression [normally written $(\mathrm{A}\iota)$, $(\mathrm{E}\iota)$], as well as when x stands for a recognizer and when x stands for an association.

Logical Operators

(D19) $!(\forall x)\,\overline{\text{Я}x} \mathrel{\underset{\cdot}{=}} \text{Я}{}^{\sim}x$ [2.2, 2.6]

(D20) $!(\forall x)\,{}^{\circ}\text{Я}x \mathrel{\underset{\cdot}{=}} \text{Я}\mu\textit{Oppose}\,[(x), (\ )]$ [2.2]

(D21) $!(\forall x)\,(\forall y)\,(x \vee y) \mathrel{\underset{\cdot}{=}} {}^{\sim}({}^{\sim}x \;\&\; {}^{\sim}y)$ [2.9]

(D22) $!(\forall x)\,(\forall y)\,(\text{Я}x \cap \text{Я}y) \mathrel{\underset{\cdot}{=}} \text{Я}(x \;\&\; y)$ [2.4, 2.9]

(D23) $!(\forall x)\,(\forall y)\,(\text{Я}x \cup \text{Я}y) \mathrel{\underset{\cdot}{=}} \text{Я}(x \vee y)$ [2.4, 2.9]

(D24) $!(\forall x)\,(\forall y)\,\Gamma x{:}(y) \leftrightarrow (\exists\iota)\,(x \cap y){:}\iota$ [1.6, 2.10]

Associations

We require further apparatus to be able to manipulate associations of arbitrary degree. We introduce a trio *Localize* that forms the plan of a localization from two plans, the plan of an association and the plan of a recognizer. For example, the assembly Яx(Яy) obeys the formula

$$Я x(Я y) \equiv Я\mu Localize\ [(x), (y), (\ )]$$

We will use *Localize* generally to mean the placement of (y) in the first position of an association x, and *Co-localize* to mean the placement of [y] in the first position of x. The latter operation is called a *co-localization*. A co–localization obeys the formula

$$Я x[Я y] \equiv\ \tilde{}((Я(\tilde{}x))(Я y))$$

Negation is defined by

$$\tilde{}Я x \equiv Я\mu Negate\ ([x], [\ ])$$

So a co-localization is defined by:

$$Co\text{-}localize\ ((x), [y], (\ )) \equiv Negate\ ([Я\mu Localize\ [(\mu Negate\ ([x], [\ ])), (y), (\ )]], [\ ])$$

$$Я x[Я y] \equiv Я\mu Co\text{-}localize\ ((x), [y], (\ ))$$

The full development of localization and co-localization is rather intricate, since it must take account of proposal tensors (see Section 2.12). We will not go through that exercise here. Notice that there are two ways to form a localization of a primitive association: either using the primitive localization operator ( ) or using the association *Localize*. The equivalence of these two methods is guaranteed by an axiom to be discussed in the next section.

If all the positions of an association are filled, then the association may not be localized further. Thus, *B*(*c*) may not be combined with another recognizer *d* to form a new association. An association may therefore be defined to be something that may be localized:

(D25) !(∀x) *Association*: [x] ↔ ((Ay) (*Recognizer*: [y] → (∃ι) μ*Localize* [(x), (y), ( )]:ι)) [2.11]

Notice that we assume in (D25) that *any* recognizer may be assembled into an available position.

The concepts of a class, a correspondence, and a trio may then be defined by:

(D26) ! (∀x) *Class*: [x] ↔ (*Association*: [x] & !(∀y) (∀z) *Localize*: [(x), (y), (z)] → *Recognizer*: [z]) [1.5, 2.11]

(D27) ! (∀x) *Correspondence*: [x] ↔ (*Association*: [x] & !(∀y) (∀z) *Localize*: [(x), (y), (z)] → *Class*: [z]) [1.8, 2.11]

(D28) ! (∀x) *Trio*: [x] ↔ (*Association*: [x] & !(∀y) (∀z) *Localize*: [(x), (y), (z)] → *Correspondence*: [z]) [1.8, 2.11]

We define a plan to be an idea that has a realization:

$$\textbf{(D29)}\quad !(\forall x)\ \textit{Plan}\text{: } [x] \leftrightarrow ((\exists y)\ y \equiv \text{ЯЯ}x) \qquad [1.6]$$

Notice the use of the realization of the realization, because the conformer x of *Plan* is the plan of a plan.

Performance Types

We may define a constructive recognizer to be a recognizer that obeys the inexhaustibility principle. That is, a recognizer d is constructive if and only if it must be possible for d not to accept some impression.

$$\textbf{(D30)}\quad !(\forall x)\ \textit{Recognizer}\text{: } [x] \rightarrow (\textit{Constructive}\text{: } [x] \Leftrightarrow !(\text{E}\iota)\ {}^{\sim}\text{Я}x{:}\iota) \qquad [2.2,\ 2.5]$$

The expression $!(\text{E}\iota)\ {}^{\sim}\text{Я}x{:}\iota$ on the extreme right is omissive when x is constructive and constructive, indeed undescriptive, when x is omissive. Therefore the class *Constructive* is constructive. The proposition *Constructive*: $[x]$ has thus the unusual form of a conformalization of a constructive class. Notice that the placetaker x in (D30) stands for the plan of a constructive recognizer, not the recognizer itself.

A recognizer is omissive if it is not constructive:

$$\textbf{(D31)}\quad !(\forall x)\ \textit{Omissive}\text{: } (x) \leftrightarrow {}^{\sim}\textit{Constructive}\text{: } [x] \qquad [2.2,\ 2.5]$$

Therefore, the class *Omissive* is omissive. We may write the definition of an omissive recognizer more fully, using (D30), as:

$$\begin{aligned} \textit{Omissive}\text{: } (x) &\Leftrightarrow ;(\text{A}\iota)\ \text{Я}x{:}\iota \\ &\Leftrightarrow !;(\forall\iota)\ \text{Я}x{:}\iota \end{aligned}$$

Thus, the proposition that an omissive recognizer is omissive is definitive. Similarly, by inspection of (D30), the proposition that a constructive recognizer is constructive is definitive.

The classes *Constructive* and *Omissive* are subject themselves to performance type integrity. For example, consider the proposition

$$\textit{Constructive}\text{: } [\lambda x] \Leftrightarrow \textit{Omissive}\text{: } (\lambda\bar{x})$$

When x is constructive, λx is constructive, but $\lambda\bar{x}$ is omissive. Therefore, both sides of the implication are omissive. When x is omissive, λx is omissive and $\lambda\bar{x}$ is constructive. In that case, both sides of the implication are constructive. In either case, the implication obeys performance type integrity.

Consider, in contrast, the proposition

$$\textit{Constructive}\text{: } [\lambda C\,] \Rightarrow \textit{Omissive}\text{: } (\lambda C\,)$$

If C is constructive, the left side is omissive while the right side is constructive, so this proposition violates performance type integrity. This result is expected, for if this proposition were permitted, it would be possible to form a class C that is both constructive and omissive. However, if C is omissive, then the left side is constructive while the right side is omissive. In this case, the proposition does obey performance type integrity, which is also expected, since the right side is then definitive. We may show similarly that the following proposition is only admissible when C is constructive:

$$\mathit{Omissive}\text{: } (\lambda C) \Rightarrow \mathit{Constructive}\text{: } [\lambda C]$$

An association is constructive when localizing all positions with omissive recognizers results in a constructive proposition. Since a proposition is assumed to be a recognizer, we may define a constructive association recursively by:

(D32) !(∀*x*) *Association*: [*x*] → (*Constructive*: [*x*] ⇔ ((A*y*) *Recognizer*: [*y*] & *Omissive*: (*y*) → *Constructive*: [Яμ*Localize* [(*x*), (*y*), ( )]])) [2.2, 2.10]

Notice that (D32) only obeys performance type integrity if x is constructive or y is omissive. We will generalize *Omissive*, as we have generalized *Constructive*, to accept plans of associations as well as plans of recognizers. That is, the placetaker x in (D31) may stand for an association.

Concentration

An instance of the concentration of an association R is defined to be the realization of a simple proposition that is controlled by R. To define concentration for associations of arbitrary degree, we broaden the interpretation of the term *controls* so that an association R *controls* any localization of R. Thus, a trio T controls the correspondence $T(\ , b,\ )$ and the class $T(a, b,\ )$ as well as the assembly $T(a, b, c)$. We may then define *controls* recursively by:

(D33) !(∀*w*) (∀*z*) *Control*: [(*w*), (*z*)] ↔ (∃*x*) (∃*y*) *Localize*: [(*x*), (*y*), (*z*)] & *Control*: [(*w*), (*x*)]

That is, Я*w* controls Я*z* if and only if Я*z* ≡ Я*x*(Я*y*, . . .) and Я*w* controls Я*x*. The proposal methods in (D33) are shown for the case where w, x, y, and z all have the same performance type. Other performance types require different proposal methods. The recursion in (D33) is based on the initial statement that any association controls itself, which is guaranteed by an axiom to be discussed in the next section.

We then define concentration by:

(D34) !(∀*x*) (∀*y*) C^1Я*x*:(Я*y*) ↔ *Control*: [(*x*), (*y*)] & *y* [1.8]

For example, considering a correspondence G, we may write

$$\mathrm{C}^1 G{:}(G(u, v)) \Leftrightarrow \mathit{Control}\text{: } [(\lambda G), (G{:}(u, v))]\ \&\ G{:}(u, v)$$

Since G must control $G(u, v)$, we may write more simply

$$\mathrm{C}^1 G{:}(G(u, v)) \Leftrightarrow G{:}(u, v)$$

Notice that (D34) covers assemblies of associations of arbitrary degree, without requiring that the assemblies be broken into pairs as in symbolic logic. For example, in data logic, an assembly of a quartet Q would be written

$$Q(a, b, c, d)$$

In symbolic logic, a tuple such as (a, b, c, d) is defined from ordered pairs, such as:

$$(((a, b), c), d)$$

In data logic, the two expressions $Q(a, b, c, d)$ and $R(S(T(a, b), c), d)$ are different. Indeed, the association Q is a quartet, while the association R is a correspondence.

Limitations Must Be Placed on Reasoning by Self-Description

The description of the syntax of data logic within data logic provides data logic with power that symbolic logic does not possess. This power can, however, be misused to damage the foundations of data logic, much as the ability to overwrite portions of a compiler can damage the effectiveness of a computer language. For example, theory does not prevent affirming that there are no classes:

$$(\forall x)\ \tilde{}\,Class\text{: } [x]$$

If this proposition were affirmed, it would prevent most reasoning from occurring, because no simple propositions could be claimed without contradicting it. Reasoning about plans must therefore be placed under stringent restraints. It remains an area of research to determine what types of reasoning about plans should be allowed and what prohibited. This is entirely a theoretical problem, for we would expect there to be no statements about plans within a typical practical data base.

Conclusion

We have sketched an aggressive program for describing data logic within data logic, rather than relying on meta–languages as symbolic logic does. It appears that six operations can not be described fully within data logic: realization, melding, compounding, acceptance of images, instantiation, and conformalization. It may be that further study will show other areas where data logic can not describe itself. Nevertheless, we have demonstrated that the syntactic structure of logic can be defined extensively as a data structure.

3.4 AXIOMS

Purpose of Axioms

An *axiom* is an assumption of data logic that is considered to be affirmed in all data bases. An example is:

$$(\text{A}x)\ (\text{A}y)\ x \cap y \subseteq x$$

This proposition is assumed to evoke any impression in any system of belief to which data logic applies (it would not apply, for example, to a system of belief that is purposefully illogical). We may imagine actually implementing the axioms by inserting them directly into every data base. The master engines postulated in the prior section will then operate on the axioms to create all the recognized deductions of data logic.

In the discussion that follows, we list all the axioms of data logic. We will not develop new means of deduction, but will formalize those already discussed. We append to each axiom the section where the axiom is discussed, in brackets. There are many more axioms of data logic than of symbolic logic, partly because data logic contains a greater variety of expressions than symbolic logic, but also because the syntax of data logic is expressed in the axioms, while the syntax of symbolic logic is expressed in a metalanguage. True comparison of the relative complexity of the two logics must therefore take into account the rigorous specification of the syntax of symbolic logic, for which Gödel required 40 propositions in addition to the axioms of symbolic logic (Gödel 1931).

In formulating the axioms, we have placed the most emphasis on assuring that each axiom expresses a single, clear idea. We have, secondly, tried to make the axioms a complete description of data logic as developed in the earlier sections. Our treatment of associations of arbitrary degree is less complete than would be desired because certain problems of recursive definition remain unsolved. For example, we do not axiomatize tensor proposal methods, nor do we discuss explicitly the degree of an association. Finally, we have given little attention to minimizing the number of axioms. We have particularly avoided clever constructions that might reduce the number of axioms but would harm their comprehensibility. It is likely, therefore, that other equivalent formulations are possible that contain fewer axioms.

Formation of Propositions

If *C* is a class and *d* is a recognizer then *C*:(*d*) is a proposition (this is the instantiation law):

> **(A1)** !(∀*x*) (∀*y*) (∀*z*) *Class*: [*x*] & *Recognizer*: [*y*] & *Localize*: [(*x*), (*y*), (*z*)] → *Proposition*: [*z*] [1.10]

The assembly *C*(*d*) formed from the primitive localization operator ( ) is equivalent to the assembly *C*(*d*) formed using the primitive association *Localize*:

> **(A2)** !(∀*x*) (∀*y*) Я*x*(Я*y*) ⊂̣ Яμ*Localize* [(*x*), (*y*), ( )] [3.3]
>
> **(A3)** !(∀*x*) (∀*y*) Яμ*Localize* [(*x*), (*y*), ( )] ⊂̣ Я*x*(Я*y*) [3.3]

The proposition *C*:(*d*) is interchangeable with the proposition (∃ι) *C*:|*d*.ι|:

> **(A4)** !(∀*x*) (∀*y*) *Class*: [*x*] & *Recognizer*: [*y*] → (Я*x*:(Я*y*) ⇛ (∃ι) Я*x*:|Я*y*.ι|) [1.5, 2.10]
>
> **(A5)** !(∀*x*) (∀*y*) *Class*: [*x*] & *Recognizer*: [*y*] → ((∃ι) Я*x*:|Я*y*.ι| ⇛ Я*x*:(Я*y*)) [1.5, 2.10]

If a class C accepts the image $d.\iota$, then the recognizer d accepts the impression ι:

(A6) $!(\forall x)\ (\forall y)\ Class\colon [x]\ \&\ Recognizer\colon [y] \rightarrow (!(\forall \iota)\ Яx\colon |Яy.\iota| \rightarrow Яy\colon\iota)$ [1.5]

The negation of the simple proposition $C{:}(d)$ is the simple proposition $\overline{C}{:}[d]$ formed from the primitive co–localization operator [ ]:

(A7) $!(\forall x)\ (\forall y)\ Class\colon [x]\ \&\ Recognizer\colon [y] \rightarrow (\tilde{}(Яx{:}(Яy)) \Rightarrow \overline{Яx}{:}[Яy])$ [2.6]

(A8) $!(\forall x)\ (\forall y)\ Class\colon [x]\ \&\ Recognizer\colon [y] \rightarrow (\tilde{}(Яx{:}[Яy]) \Rightarrow \overline{Яx}{:}(Яy))$ [2.6]

Any association controls itself:

(A9) $!(\forall x)\ Association\colon [x] \rightarrow Control\colon [(x), (x)]$ [3.3]

Any correspondence that satisfies the conditions that define *Control* embraces *Control*. This axiom makes *Control* the *transitive closure* of a projection of *Localize* (see Section 7.5):

(A10) $!(\forall v)\ (!(\forall w)\ (\forall z)\ v{:}[(w), (z)] \leftrightarrow (\exists x)\ (\exists y)\ Localize\colon [(x), (y), (z)]\ \&\ v{:}[(w), (x)]) \rightarrow (v \subseteq Control)$ [3.3]

The realization of a proposition is a recognizer:

(A11) $!(\forall x)\ Proposition\colon [x] \rightarrow Recognizer\colon [Яx]$ [1.10]

Deduction, Inclusion, Implication, and Embracing

If an idea e includes a recognizer d, then e is a recognizer:

(A12) $!(\forall x)\ (\forall y)\ Recognizer\colon [x]\ \&\ (Яx \subsetneq Яy) \rightarrow Recognizer\colon [y]$ [1.5]

If an idea S includes an association R, then S is an association:

(A13) $!(\forall x)\ (\forall y)\ Association\colon [x]\ \&\ (Яx \subsetneq Яy) \rightarrow Association\colon [y]$ [1.5, 2.11]

For any plans r and s, we may form the idea « $r \rightarrow s$ »:

(A14) $!(\forall x)\ (\forall y)\ Plan\colon [x]\ \&\ Plan\colon [y] \rightarrow (\exists z)\ Deduce\colon ([Яx], (Яy), (z))$ [2.13, 3.3]

The idea « $r \rightarrow s$ » is a proposition:

(A15) $!(\forall x)\ (\forall y)\ (\forall z)\ Deduce\colon ([Яx], (Яy), (z)) \rightarrow Proposition\colon [z]$ [2.13]

If p and $(p \rightarrow q)$, then q (this is the direct deduction law):

(A16) $!(\forall x)\,(\forall y)$ *Proposition*: $[x]$ & *Proposition*: $[y] \rightarrow ((Яx \;\&\; (Яx \rightarrow Яy)) \Rightarrow Яy)$ [2.15]

If $r \rightarrow s$ and $s \rightarrow t$, then $r \rightarrow t$:

(A17) $!(\forall x)\,(\forall y)\,(\forall z)$ *Plan*: $[x]$ & *Plan*: $[y]$ & *Plan*: $[z] \rightarrow ((Яx \rightarrow Яy)\;\&\; (Яy \rightarrow Яz) \Rightarrow (Яx \rightarrow Яz))$ [2.13, 3.3]

If $r \rightarrow s$ and $r \rightarrow t$, then $r \rightarrow (s \;\&\; t)$:

(A18) $!(\forall x)\,(\forall y)\,(\forall z)$ *Plan*: $[x]$ & *Plan*: $[y]$ & *Plan*: $[z] \rightarrow ((Яx \rightarrow Яy)\;\&\; (Яx \rightarrow Яz) \Rightarrow (Яx \rightarrow (Яy \;\&\; Яz)))$ [2.13, 3.3]

If $r \rightarrow s$, then $\tilde{}s \rightarrow \tilde{}r$ (this is the contrapositive law):

(A19) $!(\forall x)\,(\forall y)$ *Plan*: $[x]$ & *Plan*: $[y] \rightarrow ((Яx \rightarrow Яy) \Rightarrow (\tilde{}Яy \rightarrow \tilde{}Яx))$ [2.3, 2.9, 2.13, 3.3]

Conjunction and Intersection

Any two plans may be conjoined:

(A20) $!(\forall x)\,(\forall y)$ *Plan*: $[x]$ & *Plan*: $[y] \rightarrow (\exists z)$ *Conjoin*: $[(Яx), (Яy), (z)]$ [2.9, 3.3]

The conjunction of two ideas is a plan:

(A21) $!(\forall x)\,(\forall y)\,(\forall z)$ *Conjoin*: $[(x), (y), (Яz)] \rightarrow$ *Plan*: $[z]$ [3.3]

The conjunction of two propositions is a proposition:

(A22) $!(\forall x)\,(\forall y)\,(\forall z)$ *Proposition*: $[x]$ & *Proposition*: $[y]$ & *Conjoin*: $[(Яx), (Яy), (Яz)] \rightarrow$ *Proposition*: $[z]$ [2.9]

The intersection of two recognizers d and e is the recognizer $d \cap e$. Recall that the plan of $d \cap e$ is the conjunction of the plan of d with the plan of e:

(A23) $!(\forall x)\,(\forall y)$ *Recognizer*: $[x]$ & *Recognizer*: $[y] \rightarrow$ *Recognizer*: $[x \;\&\; y]$ [2.5, 3.3]

The intersection of two associations R and S is the association $R \cap S$. Recall that the plan of $R \cap S$ is the conjunction of the plan of R with the plan of S:

(A24) $!(\forall x)\,(\forall y)$ *Association*: $[x]$ & *Association*: $[y] \rightarrow$ *Association*: $[x \;\&\; y]$ [2.4, 2.11, 3.3]

The conjunction r & s implies r:

(A25) $!(\forall x)\ (\forall y)\ Plan\text{: } [x]\ \&\ Plan\text{: } [y] \rightarrow (\text{Я}x\ \&\ \text{Я}y \Rightarrow \text{Я}x)$ [2.9, 3.3]

The conjunction r & s implies the conjunction s & r:

(A26) $!(\forall x)\ (\forall y)\ Plan\text{: } [x]\ \&\ Plan\text{: } [y] \rightarrow (\text{Я}x\ \&\ \text{Я}y \Rightarrow \text{Я}y\ \&\ \text{Я}x)$ [2.9, 3.3]

Plans may be conjoined in any order interchangeably:

(A27) $!(\forall x)\ (\forall y)\ (\forall z)\ Plan\text{: } [x]\ \&\ Plan\text{: } [y]\ \&\ Plan\text{: } [z] \rightarrow ((\text{Я}x\ \&\ (\text{Я}y\ \&\ \text{Я}z)) \Rightarrow ((\text{Я}x\ \&\ \text{Я}y)\ \&\ \text{Я}z))$ [2.9, 3.3]

(A28) $!(\forall x)\ (\forall y)\ (\forall z)\ Plan\text{: } [x]\ \&\ Plan\text{: } [y]\ \&\ Plan\text{: } [z] \rightarrow (((\text{Я}x\ \&\ \text{Я}y)\ \&\ \text{Я}z) \Rightarrow (\text{Я}x\ \&\ (\text{Я}y\ \&\ \text{Я}z)))$ [2.9, 3.3]

Conjunction distributes with alternation:

(A29) $!(\forall x)\ (\forall y)\ (\forall z)\ Plan\text{: } [x]\ \&\ Plan\text{: } [y]\ \&\ Plan\text{: } [z] \rightarrow (\text{Я}x\ \&\ (\text{Я}y \vee \text{Я}z) \Rightarrow (\text{Я}x\ \&\ \text{Я}y) \vee (\text{Я}x\ \&\ \text{Я}z))$ [2.9, 3.3]

The converse formula $(\text{Я}x\ \&\ \text{Я}y) \vee (\text{Я}x\ \&\ \text{Я}z) \Rightarrow \text{Я}x\ \&\ (\text{Я}y \vee \text{Я}z)$ may be proved from the other axioms.

Negation and Complement

Any plan may be negated:

(A30) $!(\forall x)\ Plan\text{: } [x] \rightarrow (\exists y)\ Negate\text{: } ([x], [y])$ [2.6, 3.3]

The negation of a proposition is a proposition:

(A31) $!(\forall x)\ (\forall y)\ Proposition\text{: } [x]\ \&\ Negate\text{: } ([x], [y]) \rightarrow Proposition\text{: } [y]$ [2.6]

The complement of any recognizer d is the recognizer $\overline{d}$. Recall that the plan of $\overline{d}$ is the negation of the plan of d:

(A32) $!(\forall x)\ (\forall y)\ Negate\text{: } ([x], [y])\ \&\ Recognizer\text{: } [x] \rightarrow Recognizer\text{: } [y]$ [2.5, 3.3]

The complement of an association R is the association $\overline{R}$. Recall that the plan of $\overline{R}$ is the negation of the plan of R:

(A33) $!(\forall x)\ (\forall y)\ Negate\text{: } ([x], [y])\ \&\ Association\text{: } [x] \rightarrow Association\text{: } [y]$ [2.2, 2.11, 3.3]

A plan is interchangeable with the negation of its negation:

(A34) $!(\forall x)\ Plan\text{: } [x] \rightarrow (\text{Я}x \Rightarrow \tilde{}(\tilde{}\text{Я}x))$ [2.9, 3.3]

(A35) $!(\forall x)\ Plan\text{: } [x] \rightarrow (\tilde{}(\tilde{}\text{Я}x) \Rightarrow \text{Я}x)$ [2.9, 3.3]

Opposites

There is an opposite of any association and an opposite of any recognizer:

(A36) !(∀*x*) *Plan*: [*x*] → (∃*y*) *Oppose*: [(Я*x*), (*y*)] [2.2, 2.11]

The opposite of a recognizer is a recognizer:

(A37) !(∀*x*) (∀*y*) *Oppose*: [(*x*), (*y*)] & *Recognizer*: [*x*] → *Recognizer*: [*y*] [2.5]

The opposite of an association is an association:

(A38) !(∀*x*) (∀*y*) *Oppose*: [(*x*), (*y*)] & *Association*: [*x*] → *Association*: [*y*] [2.2, 2.11]

An idea is equivalent to the opposite of its opposite:

(A39) !(∀*x*) *Plan*: [*x*] → (Я*x* ⊆ °°Я*x*) [2.2]

(A40) !(∀*x*) *Plan*: [*x*] → (°°Я*x* ⊆ Я*x*) [2.2]

Melding and Granulation

Any class has a melding:

(A41) !(∀*x*) *Class*: [*x*] → (∃*y*) Я*x* ≡ μ*y* [1.6]

Any melding is a recognizer:

(A42) !(∀*x*) (∀*y*) (*x* ≡ μЯ*y*) → *Recognizer*: [*y*] [1.6]

The melding μ*C* accepts an impression ι if and only if there is some recognizer *d* such that *C* accepts *d*.ι:

(A43) !(∀*x*) *Class*: [*x*] → (!(∀ι) μЯ*x*:ι → (∃*y*) Я*x*:| *y*.ι |) [1.6, 2.10]

(A44) !(∀*x*) *Class*: [*x*] → !(∀ι) ((∃*y*) Я*x*:| *y*.ι |) → μЯ*x*:ι [1.6, 2.10]

Quantification

For any idea « Я*y* » and any programmatic position « *x* », we may form the idea « (∃Я*x*) Я*y* »:

(A45) !(∀*x*) (∀*y*) *Position*: [*x*] & *Plan*: [*y*] → (∃*z*) *Exist*: [[*x*], (Я*y*), (*z*)] [2.10]

The statement of the axioms of quantification is complicated by the need to use *Localize* so that they will apply to associations of any degree. Thus, the embracing Я*x*(Я*y*, . . .) ⊆ (∃Я*z*) Я*x*(Я*z*, . . .) is written:

(A46) !(∀*x*) (∀*y*) (∀*z*) *Position*: [*z*] → (Яμ*Localize* [(*x*), (*y*), ( )] ⊆ (∃Я*z*) Яμ*Localize* [(*x*), (*z*), ( )]) [2.10]

Notice that this embracing only applies if the performance type of the placetaker Я*z* is chosen so that the embracing obeys performance type integrity (such as by choosing the performance type of Я*z* to be the same as the performance type of Я*y*). The axioms to follow that incorporate quantification make similar assumptions about the performance types of placetakers.

The embracing Я*x*(Я*y*, . . .) ⊆ (∃Я*z*) Я*z*(Я*y*, . . .) is written:

(A47) !(∀*x*) (∀*y*) (∀*z*) *Position*: [*z*] → (Яμ*Localize* [(*x*), (*y*), ( )] ⊆ (∃Я*z*) Яμ*Localize* [(*z*), (*y*), ( )]) [2.10]

The implication (Я*w* ⪽ Я*x*) ⇒ ((∃Я*y*) Я*w*(Я*y*, . . .) ⪽ (∃Я*z*) Я*x*(Я*z*, . . .)) is written:

(A48) !(∀*w*) (∀*x*) (∀*y*) (∀*z*) *Position*: [*y*] & *Position*: [*z*] → ((Я*w* ⪽ Я*x*) ⇒ ((∃Я*y*) Яμ*Localize* [(*w*), (*y*), ( )] ⪽ (∃Я*z*) Яμ*Localize* [(*x*), (*z*), ( )])) [2.10, 2.13]

The implication (((∃Я*w*) Я*x*(Я*w*, . . .)) ⪽ Я*y*) ⇒ (∀Я*z*) (Я*x*(Я*z*, . . .) ⪽ Я*y*) is written:

(A49) !(∀*w*) (∀*x*) (∀*y*) (∀*z*) *Position*: [*w*] & *Position*: [*z*] → ((((∃Я*w*) Яμ*Localize* [(*x*), (*w*), ( )]) ⪽ Я*y*) ⇒ (∀Я*z*) (Яμ*Localize* [(*x*), (*z*), ( )] ⪽ Я*y*)) [2.10, 2.13]

For any recognizer *d*, we may form the idea « (∃ι) *d*:ι »:

(A50) !(∀*x*) (∀*y*) *Recognizer*: [*x*] → (∃*y*) *Exist-impression*: [(*x*), (*y*)] [2.10]

The idea « (∃ι) *d*:ι » is a proposition:

(A51) !(∀*x*) (∀*y*) *Exist-impression*: [(*x*), (*y*)] → *Proposition*: [*y*] [2.10]

If a recognizer *e* accepts all impressions, then *e* includes all recognizers:

(A52) !(∀*x*) (∀*y*) *Recognizer*: [*x*] & *Recognizer*: [*y*] → (((∀ι) *y*:ι) ⇒ (*x* ⪽ *y*)) [2.5, 2.14]

If for each impression ι, if a recognizer *d* accepts ι then a recognizer *e* accepts ι, then *e* includes *d*. Conversely, if *e* includes *d*, then for each impression ι, if *d* accepts ι, then *e* accepts ι:

(A53) !(∀*x*) (∀*y*) *Recognizer*: [*x*] & *Recognizer*: [*y*] → (((∀ι) Я*x*:ι → Я*y*:ι) ⇒ (Я*x* ⪽ Я*y*)) [2.10]

(A54) !(∀*x*) (∀*y*) *Recognizer*: [*x*] & *Recognizer*: [*y*] → ((Я*x* ⪽ Я*y*) ⇒ ((∀ι) Я*x*:ι → Я*y*:ι)) [2.10]

The image exhaustion principle $((\forall z)\ (\forall \iota)\ B{:}|z.\iota| \rightarrow C{:}|z.\iota|) \Leftrightarrow (B \subsetneq C)$ follows by applying these axioms to the assemblies $B(z)$ and $C(z)$.

Modal Operators

For any proposition p, we may form $!p$:

(A55) $!(\forall x)$ *Proposition*: $[x] \rightarrow (\exists y)$ *Definitize*: $[(x), (y)]$ [2.14]

If p is a proposition, then $!p$ is a proposition. We leave open the possibility that plans other than propositions might have definitive counterparts:

(A56) $!(\forall x)\ (\forall y)$ *Proposition*: $[x]$ & *Definitize*: $[(x), (y)] \rightarrow$ *Proposition*: $[y]$ [2.14]

The proposition $!p$ implies the proposition p:

(A57) $!(\forall x)$ *Proposition*: $[x] \rightarrow ((!\text{Я}x) \Rightarrow \text{Я}x)$ [2.14]

A definitive proposition evokes any impression:

(A58) $!(\forall x)$ *Proposition*: $[x] \rightarrow ((!\text{Я}x) \Rightarrow !(\forall \iota)\ \text{ЯЯ}x{:}\iota)$ [2.14]

The proposition $!p \vee !q$ implies the proposition $!(p \vee q)$:

(A59) $!(\forall x)\ (\forall y)$ *Proposition*: $[x]$ & *Proposition*: $[y] \rightarrow (!\text{Я}x \vee !\text{Я}y \Rightarrow !(\text{Я}x \vee \text{Я}y))$ [2.14]

If $p \Rightarrow q$, then $(!p) \Rightarrow (!q)$:

(A60) $!(\forall x)\ (\forall y)$ *Proposition*: $[x]$ & *Proposition*: $[y] \rightarrow ((\text{Я}x \Rightarrow \text{Я}y) \Rightarrow ((!\text{Я}x) \Rightarrow (!\text{Я}y)))$ [2.14]

The plan $!(\forall \text{Я}x)\ \text{Я}y$ implies the plan $(\forall \text{Я}x)\ !\text{Я}y$:

(A61) $!(\forall x)\ (\forall y)$ *Position*: $[x]$ & *Plan*: $[y] \rightarrow ((!(\forall \text{Я}x)\ \text{Я}y) \Rightarrow (\forall \text{Я}x)\ !\text{Я}y)$ [2.15]

The plan $(\exists \text{Я}x)\ !\text{Я}y$ implies the plan $!(\exists \text{Я}x)\ \text{Я}y$:

(A62) $!(\forall x)\ (\forall y)$ *Position*: $[x]$ & *Plan*: $[y] \rightarrow (((\exists \text{Я}x)\ !\text{Я}y) \Rightarrow !(\exists \text{Я}x)\ \text{Я}y)$ [2.15]

The proposition $!p$ implies the proposition $!!p$:

(A63) $!(\forall x)$ *Proposition*: $[x] \rightarrow ((!\text{Я}x) \Rightarrow !!\text{Я}x)$ [2.14]

Performance Types

Any idea formed from a plan is either constructive or omissive:

$$\textbf{(A64)}\ \ !(\forall x)\ \textit{Plan}: [x] \rightarrow \textit{Constructive}: [\text{Я}x] \vee \textit{Omissive}: (\text{Я}x) \quad [2.2, 2.5, 2.6]$$

A constructive class must be able not to accept an image (this is the inexhaustibility principle of classes):

$$\textbf{(A65)}\ \ !(\forall x)\ \textit{Constructive}: [x]\ \&\ \textit{Class}: [x]\ \&\ \textit{Position}: [y] \rightarrow\ !(\text{EЯ}y)\ {}^{\sim}(\text{Я}x{:}|\,\text{Я}y\,|) \quad [2.2]$$

A class that must be able not to accept an image is constructive:

$$\textbf{(A66)}\ \ !(\forall x)\ (\forall y)\ \textit{Class}: [x]\ \&\ \textit{Position}: [y] \rightarrow ((!(\text{EЯ}y)\ {}^{\sim}(\text{Я}x{:}|\,\text{Я}y\,|)) \Rightarrow \textit{Constructive}: [x]) \quad [2.2]$$

The analogous inexhaustibility principle of recognizers is given by definition (D30).

The performance type integrity law for classes is deduced from these axioms as follows. Suppose that B and C are both classes, that C is constructive, and that $B \subseteq C$. Then we have the following chain of implications, the axioms used shown to the right:

$$\begin{aligned}
(B \subseteq C) &\Rightarrow (\overline{C} \subseteq \overline{B}) && <\text{A19}\\
&\Rightarrow (((\exists z)\ {}^{\sim}(C{:}|\,z\,|)) \Rightarrow (\exists z)\ {}^{\sim}(B{:}|\,z\,|)) && <\text{A48, A19}\\
&\Rightarrow (((\text{E}z)\ {}^{\sim}(C{:}|\,z\,|)) \Rightarrow (\text{E}z)\ {}^{\sim}(B{:}|\,z\,|)) && <\text{A60, A19}\\
&\Rightarrow ((!(\text{E}z)\ {}^{\sim}(C{:}|\,z\,|)) \Rightarrow\ !(\text{E}z)\ {}^{\sim}(B{:}|\,z\,|)) && <\text{A60}\\
&\Rightarrow\ !(\text{E}z)\ {}^{\sim}(B{:}|\,z\,|) && <\text{A65, A16}\\
&\Rightarrow \textit{Constructive}: (\lambda B)
\end{aligned}$$

That is, if C is constructive and C embraces B, then B is constructive.

A constructive recognizer must not both accept and reject an impression:

$$\textbf{(A67)}\ \ !(\forall x)\ \textit{Constructive}: [x]\ \&\ \textit{Recognizer}: [x] \rightarrow\ !(\forall \iota)\ {}^{\sim}((\text{Я}x \cap {}^{\circ}\text{Я}x){:}\iota) \quad [1.3]$$

The opposite of a constructive idea is constructive:

$$\textbf{(A68)}\ \ !(\forall x)\ (\forall y)\ \textit{Constructive}: [x]\ \&\ \textit{Oppose}: [(x), (y)] \rightarrow \textit{Constructive}: [y] \quad [2.2]$$

The opposite of a constructive idea $\text{Я}x$ is embraced in the complement $\overline{\text{Я}x}$:

$$\textbf{(A69)}\ \ !(\forall x)\ \textit{Constructive}: [x] \Rightarrow ({}^{\circ}\text{Я}x \subseteq \overline{\text{Я}x}) \quad [2.2]$$

If either R or d is constructive, then the association $R(d, \ldots)$ is constructive:

(A70) !(∀*x*) (∀*y*) (∀*z*) *Association*: [*x*] & *Recognizer*: [*y*] & (*Constructive*: [*x*] ∨ *Constructive*: [*y*]) & *Localize*: [(*x*), (*y*), (*z*)] → *Constructive*: [*z*] [2.6]

If both *R* and *d* are omissive, then the association *R*(*d*, . . .) is omissive:

(A71) !(∀*x*) (∀*y*) (∀*z*) *Association*: [*x*] & *Recognizer*: [*y*] & *Omissive*: (*x*) & *Omissive*: (*y*) & *Localize*: [(*x*), (*y*), (*z*)] → *Omissive*: (*z*) [2.6]

The realization of a constructive plan is constructive:

(A72) !(∀*x*) *Plan*: [*x*] & *Constructive*: [*x*] → *Constructive*: [Я*x*] [2.6]

The plan of a constructive idea is constructive:

(A73) !(∀*x*) *Constructive*: [Я*x*] → *Constructive*: [*x*] [2.6]

Conclusion

We have shown how most assumptions of data logic may be reduced to a set of axioms. The axioms of data logic are much more diverse than the axioms of symbolic logic. Theorems are needed to show that this diversity is warranted on the one hand, and sufficient to prove useful results on the other. The axioms of data logic are particularly suited to implementation on a computer, because they are phrased as formal deductions of the form $p \rightarrow q$. A formal deduction process may operate on the premises, form the conclusions, apply the axioms to the conclusions, and so on, to create a logical system. Implementing the axioms in this way would be a valuable test of the applicability of data logic to practical reasoning.

There are several areas where the axiomatization is incomplete. We have not fully described the operations of quantified substitution, and we have not described all aspects of conformalization of associations. It remains to be proved that the performance type integrity law can, indeed, be specified in axioms as we have done, rather than requiring a postulate for its enforcement. However, these topics lie outside the theory of data bases, so they do not hamper application of data logic to practical data base problems.

3.5 RUSSELL'S PARADOX

Data Logic Avoids Russell's Paradox

Russell's paradox in symbolic logic concerns the set *R* of all sets that are not members of themselves. Most ordinary sets are members of *R*; theoretical constructions such as the set of all sets are not members of *R*. In symbolic logic, one can show that *R* is both a member of itself and not a member of itself, establishing a paradox (Russell 1902).

This paradox is resolved in symbolic logic by restricting quantification over sets. That is, placetakers are allowed to stand for individuals, but there are restrictions for when a placetaker is allowed to stand for a set. By avoiding Russell's paradox, data logic dispenses with these restrictions.

In data logic, we consider a class R, rather than a set, defined according to the law

$$(\mathrm{A}x)\ R:(\nu x) \Leftrightarrow \tilde{}(x:(\nu x)) \tag{1}$$

Notice the use of the handle νx to convert the class x to a recognizer. Since the handle has the same performance type as the class, the argument does not depend on use of the handle, but we retain it to keep the distinction clear between x, the class, and νx, the instance.

Formula (1) is well-formed only if it obeys performance type integrity. Since Formula (1) is a bi-directional implication, both the left side and the right side must have the same performance type. The right side, $\tilde{}(x:(\nu x))$, is omissive if x is constructive, while the left side, $R:(\nu x)$, is constructive if x is constructive. Thus, x can not be constructive. If x is omissive, the right side is constructive and the left side has the same performance type as R. Thus, Formula (1) is only well-formed if R is constructive and x is omissive.

Since R and x have different performance types, we can not substitute R for x to form a paradox. That is, we can not form the expression

$$R:(\nu R) \Leftrightarrow \tilde{}(R:(\nu R)) \tag{2}$$

Indeed, Formula (2) is just a version of the liar paradox, which we showed in Section 2.9 could not be formed in data logic, because Formula (2) is fat.

We might alternatively consider conformers, rather than instances, in forming Russell's paradox. That is, we might form a class S such that

$$(\mathrm{A}x)\ S:[\nu x] \Leftrightarrow \tilde{}(x:[\nu x]) \tag{3}$$

If x is constructive in Formula (3), then the left side is omissive while the right side is constructive. Therefore, x can not be constructive. If x is omissive, then the left side has the same performance type as S, while the right side is constructive. Thus, Formula (3) is only well-formed if S is constructive and x is omissive.

Since S and x have different performance types, we can not substitute S for x in Formula (3). That is, we can not form the expression

$$S:[\nu S] \Leftrightarrow \tilde{}(S:[\nu S])$$

Thus, neither the formulation using instances, Formula (1), nor the formulation using conformers, Formula (3), leads to contradiction, so data logic is free from Russell's paradox.

Russell's Paradox in Language

Russell's paradox is often phrased as the word problem:

> The barber shaves all those who do not shave themselves.
> Does the barber shave himself?

In data logic, the premise is written

$$(\text{A}x)\ (barber)\ Shaves{:}\ (x) \Leftrightarrow \tilde{}((x)\ Shaves{:}\ (x)) \tag{4}$$

Given the case of interest, where x is constructive, Formula (4) is fat, because the right side is omissive while the left side is constructive. Thus, the premise is not admissible. One may say only

If the barber shaves x, then x does not shave himself.

The converse, that if x does not shave himself then the barber shaves x, is fat, and is not admissible. Therefore, the premise is malformed and the barber does not shave himself.

We could alter Formula (4) to obey performance type integrity by saying that any *person* who does not shave himself is shaved by the barber:

$$(\text{A}x)\ (barber)\ Shaves{:}\ (x) \Rightarrow \tilde{}((x)\ Shaves{:}\ (x))$$

$$(\text{A}x)\ Person{:}\ (x)\ \&\ \tilde{}((x)\ Shaves{:}\ (x)) \Rightarrow (barber)\ Shaves{:}\ (x)$$

We are now free to state, however, that the barber is not a person.

Conclusion

We have shown that data logic is free from Russell's paradox. Russell's paradox is avoided because its formulation does not obey performance type integrity, and it is therefore not an admissible statement. This is the same method that was used in Section 2.9 to avoid the liar paradox.

3.6 FOUNDATIONS OF ARITHMETIC

Data Logic May Be Used for the Foundations of Mathematics

Symbolic logic has had its most significant success in mathematics. Data logic permits many forms of deduction that symbolic logic prohibits, and prohibits forms that symbolic logic permits (such as the rule of symbolic logic that permits $p \Rightarrow q$ to be deduced from $\tilde{}p \vee q$). The question is raised, therefore, whether the limitations of symbolic logic are necessary to achieve the foundations of mathematics. We believe that they are not, and that mathematics may be developed from data logic, albeit along different lines.

A full development of mathematics from data logic would be well beyond the scope of this book. We will limit ourselves to the key topics of arithmetic and differential calculus. The primary departures made by data logic are the recognition of performance types, the law of performance type integrity, the allowance for incidental contradictions, and limitations on the use of infinities. Assigning performance types to mathematical ideas requires careful thought, since it is often not immediately clear whether an abstract concept should be taken as constructive or omissive.

The Number One

Frege defined the number one to be the class of all one-element classes, a definition which persists in symbolic logic (Frege 1884). In common discourse, however, we do not say that an image is "one," but that an image is one of some class, as in "one car," "one house," etc. As we saw in Section 1.9, two images may be one according to an identity correspondence ΔB but two according to some other identity correspondence ΔC. For example, if a house's identity is defined by its chimney, a large amount of renovation work may be performed on the house and it will still remain « one house ». On the other hand, if a house's identity is defined by its external appearance, a new coat of paint results in another house.

The number « one » is therefore not a class but a correspondence between a class whose instances are to be counted and an identity correspondence that defines what constitutes a unit. A class B is said to have *one* instance according to the identity correspondence ΔC when (i) there is some manifestation of a constructive instance of B that is identical to itself according to ΔC, and (ii) any two images that are both accepted by B and identical to themselves according to ΔC are mutually identical according to ΔC:

$$\begin{aligned}1{:}(\nu B,\ \nu\Delta C) \Leftrightarrow (\exists x)\ &\mathit{Constructive}{:}\ [\lambda x]\ \&\ (\exists\iota)\ B{:}|x.\iota|\ \&\ \Delta C{:}|x.\iota,\ x.\iota| \\ &\&\ ((\forall y)\ (\forall z)\ B{:}|y|\ \&\ \Delta C{:}|y,\ y|\ \&\ B{:}|z|\ \&\ \Delta C{:}|z,\ z| \rightarrow \Delta C{:}|y,\ z|)\end{aligned} \tag{1}$$

The right side of Formula (1) is always constructive, because when x is constructive, $B{:}|x.\iota|$ is constructive, and the right side is a conjunction with $B{:}|x.\iota|$. The number one is therefore constructive. Notice that this argument rests on the requirement that the one instance of B is *constructive*. That is, one must affirm that there is a method for recognizing an instance of B in order to say that there is *one* instance of B. We will see that the ordinary requirements of counting require the number one to be constructive.

The Number Two

The number two is defined similarly. A class B is said to have *two* instances according to the identity correspondence ΔC when (i) there are two manifestations of constructive instances of B that are each identical to themselves according to ΔC, but are not mutually identical according to ΔC, and (ii) any three images accepted by B and identical to themselves according to ΔC are in some way pairwise identical according to ΔC:

$$\begin{aligned}&2{:}(\nu B,\ \nu\Delta C) \Leftrightarrow (\exists u)\ (\exists v)\ \mathit{Constructive}{:}\ [\lambda u]\ \&\ \mathit{Constructive}{:}\ [\lambda v] \\ &\quad \&\ (\exists\iota)\ B{:}|u.\iota|\ \&\ \Delta C{:}|u.\iota,\ u.\iota|\ \&\ (\exists\kappa)\ B{:}|v.\kappa|\ \&\ \Delta C{:}|v.\kappa,\ v.\kappa|\ \&\ \tilde{}\Delta C{:}|u.\iota,\ v.\kappa| \\ &\quad \&\ ((\forall x)\ (\forall y)\ (\forall z)\ B{:}|x|\ \&\ \Delta C{:}|x,\ x|\ \&\ B{:}|y|\ \&\ \Delta C{:}|y,\ y|\ \&\ B{:}|z| \\ &\quad \&\ \Delta C{:}|z,\ z| \rightarrow \Delta C{:}|x,\ y| \vee \Delta C{:}|x,\ z| \vee \Delta C{:}|y,\ z|)\end{aligned} \tag{2}$$

The right side of the equivalence in Formula (2) is always constructive, even if both B and ΔC are omissive. The number two is therefore constructive. The larger positive integers may be defined in a similar fashion. All larger positive integers are constructive.

Equality of Integers

Two integers m and n are said to be *equal* if for any class B and identity correspondence ΔC, B has m instances according to ΔC if and only if B has n instances according to ΔC. That is,

$$m{:}(\nu B,\ \nu\Delta C) \Leftrightarrow n{:}(\nu B,\ \nu\Delta C)$$

Since equality is defined as an implication, a proposition that two integers are equal, written "$m = n$", is an omissive proposition.

When we say that two integers m and n are *unequal*, we mean more than that there is some class B or identity correspondence ΔC such that B has m instances but not n instances, according to ΔC. We mean that *any* class with m instances according to *any* identity correspondence ΔC must not have n instances according to ΔC. This is the property of integers that allows us to say that no class has two different numbers of instances in any given population. This definition of unequality needs to be restricted, however, to populations of B in which ΔC is sheath-free. For example, consider the population

$$\vdash B{:}(d)\ \&\ \Delta C{:}(d,\ d)\ \&\ \tilde{}\Delta C{:}(d,\ d)$$

This population satisfies both Formulas (1) and (2), and thus has both one instance and two instances.

Unequality of integers is therefore defined by:

$$(m \neq n) \equiv ((\mathrm{A}w)\ (\mathrm{A}x)\ (((\mathrm{A}y)\ (\mathrm{A}z)\ \mathit{Constructive}{:}\ [\lambda y]\ \&\ \mathit{Constructive}{:}\ [\lambda z] \\ \&\ w{:}(y)\ \&\ w{:}(z)\ \Rightarrow\ \tilde{}(x{:}(y,\ z)\ \&\ \tilde{}x{:}(y,\ z)))\ \&\ m{:}(\nu w,\ \nu x))\ \Rightarrow\ \tilde{}n{:}(\nu w,\ \nu x)) \qquad (3)$$

Since $m \neq n$ is defined to be an implication, the proposition $m \neq n$ is omissive.

Unequality of Integers Requires That They Be Constructive

By the performance type integrity law, if m is omissive in Formula (3), then n must be constructive. That is, if there were two omissive integers j and k, then j and k could not be unequal. We would then be unable to conclude from the affirmation that some class had j instances that it did not have k instances as well. Such a situation would be useless as a means of counting. There must therefore be at most one number that is omissive; all other numbers must be constructive. The same reasoning extends to rational and real numbers as well as integers.

The Number Zero

The omissive number is the number zero. A class B has zero instances according to ΔC when all manifestations of constructive instances of B are not identical to themselves according to ΔC:

$$0{:}[\nu B,\ \nu\Delta C] \equiv (\forall x)\ (\forall\iota)\ (\mathit{Constructive}{:}\ [\lambda x]\ \&\ B{:}|x.\iota|) \rightarrow \tilde{}\Delta C{:}|x.\iota,\ x.\iota|$$

The right side of the equivalence is a deduction of a proposition from a constructive proposition, so the right side is always omissive. The number zero is therefore omissive.

Notice that the class B could have constructive instances and still have zero instances according to ΔC. For example, suppose that B is the class of animals on a given farm, that B contains many cattle, but no geese. If ΔC represents « Same Goose As », B contains zero instances according to ΔC.

Arithmetic

Following Cantor, we may define the number $m + n$ to be the number of instances in a union of two classes M and N, M with m instances and N with n instances, such that no instance of M is equal to any instance of N, according to some identity correspondence ΔD (Cantor 1895). The expression "1 + 1 = 2" is therefore a shorthand for

$$(\mathrm{A}B)\ (\mathrm{A}C)\ (\mathrm{A}\Delta D)\ (1{:}(\nu B,\ \nu\Delta D)\ \&\ 1{:}(\nu C,\ \nu\Delta D)\ \&\ ((\forall x)\ (\forall y)\ B{:}(x)$$
$$\&\ C{:}(y) \rightarrow\ \tilde{}\Delta D{:}(x,\ y)))\ \Rightarrow\ 2{:}(\nu(B \cup C),\ \nu\Delta D)$$

Theorem 3.1. $1 + 1 = 2$

Proof. Given $1{:}(\nu B, \nu\Delta D)$ and $1{:}(\nu C, \nu\Delta D)$, we may conclude directly that there is at least one instance of B and at least one instance of C:

$$(\exists u)\ B{:}(u)\ \&\ \Delta D{:}(u,\ u)\ \&\ (\exists v)\ C{:}(v)\ \&\ \Delta D{:}(v,\ v)$$

Since u is an instance of B and v is an instance of C, they are not identical according to ΔD:

$$\tilde{}\Delta D{:}(u,\ v)$$

Moreover, given three instances x, y, and z of $B \cup C$, each must be either an instance of B or an instance of C. Since any two instances of B or of C are identical according to ΔD, at least two of x, y, and z are identical according to ΔD.

Conjoining these results yields the expression, Formula (2), for $2{:}(\nu(B \cup C), \nu\Delta D)$. Notice that reasoning by contradiction was not used in this proof, so it holds even in the presence of sheaths. Q.E.D.

Theorem 3.2. $2 \neq 1$

Proof. Suppose $2{:}(\nu B, \nu C)$. Then, from Formula (2), we have

$$(\exists u)\ (\exists v)\ \mathit{Constructive}{:}\ [u]\ \&\ \mathit{Constructive}{:}\ [v]\ \&\ B{:}(u)\ \&\ \Delta C{:}(u,\ u)$$
$$\&\ B{:}(v)\ \&\ \Delta C{:}(v,\ v)\ \&\ \tilde{}\Delta C{:}(u,\ v)$$

If $1{:}(\nu B, \nu C)$ then, by Formula (1), $\Delta C{:}(u, v)$, contradicting the last term. Since ΔC is assumed to be sheath-free relative to constructive instances of B [by Formula (3)], we may conclude that $\tilde{}1{:}(\nu B, \nu C)$. Notice how this proof relies on preventing the contradiction $\Delta C{:}(u, v)\ \&\ \tilde{}\Delta C{:}(u, v)$. Q.E.D.

The Class of Positive Integers

We may define the class $\mathbb{N}$ of positive integers to be the class of correspondences that are either the number 1 or are equivalent to $x + 1$ for some positive integer x. We clearly want the statement "x is a positive integer" to be definitive when affirmed, hence omissive. Since each positive integer is constructive, νx must therefore be a conformer of $\mathbb{N}$. We write, therefore,

$$(\mathrm{A}y)\ \mathbb{N}{:}[\nu y] \Leftrightarrow (y \equiv 1) \vee (\exists x)\ y \equiv x + 1\ \&\ \mathbb{N}{:}[\nu x] \tag{4}$$

Using the positive integers as a base, we may define negative integers, multiplication, and rational numbers (as fractions) in the same way as in symbolic logic (Cantor 1895, Zuckerman 1974).

At current writing, it would seem that one could choose $\mathbb{N}$ to be either constructive or omissive. Thus, Formula (4) indicates that $\mathbb{N}{:}[\nu y]$ must be omissive for any positive integer y. Since all positive integers are constructive, $\mathbb{N}{:}[\nu y]$ is omissive whatever the performance type of $\mathbb{N}$, so Formula (4) is satisfied in either case.

The class of integers $\mathbb{Z}$ must, however, be omissive. Since the number zero is omissive, the proposition $\mathbb{Z}{:}[\nu 0]$ has the same performance type as $\mathbb{Z}$. Since we want to consider the integers to contain 0 definitively, $\mathbb{Z}$ must be omissive.

Data Logic Avoids Infinity

The positive integers are commonly considered to be an infinite set. In data logic, there can be no infinite assembly of images, since an image requires time to be conceived. Any infinite assembly of images could not be formed in a finite period of time, and is therefore inconceivable. We may only imagine, therefore, a finite number of images, and a class may only have a finite number of instances. Unlike symbolic logic, however, data logic does not require that all instances of a class be exhibited. Thus, a class may be defined so that it is impossible to exhibit all its instances.

The class $\mathbb{N}$ is said to be *insatiable*, meaning that there is no population of simple propositions of the form $\mathbb{N}{:}[x]$ that is obedient to Formula (4): there will always be some highest number z in such a population, in which case the positive number $z + 1$ is not in the population. A class, we recall, is a conceptual mechanism that accepts images. The class $\mathbb{N}$ is therefore the mechanism that accepts any positive number that is presented to it, the test that determines whether or not an image is a positive number. The class $\mathbb{N}$ is not an infinite assembly of all possible positive numbers.

A finite population of $\mathbb{N}$ is permitted because a population may contain an existential quantification in data logic that is not satisfied by any recognizer in the population. Thus, the following is a valid population of $\mathbb{N}$:

$$\mathbb{N}{:}[\nu 1]\ \&\ \mathbb{N}{:}[\nu 2]\ \&\ \mathbb{N}{:}[\nu 3]\ \&\ (\forall y)\ (\exists z)\ \mathbb{N}{:}[\nu y] \rightarrow (z = y + 3)\ \&\ \mathbb{N}{:}[\nu z]$$

The quantified expression on the right is sufficient to satisfy the rule, Formula (4), that each conformer x of $\mathbb{N}$ have a successor $x + 1$, even though the successors to 3 are not exhibited in the population.

Although it is fashionable to presuppose infinite sets as a prerequisite to mathematical discussion, there is often no need to do so. For example, instead of saying "let x be a member of the infinite set of rational numbers," one should say "let x be a rational number." The latter statement does not presuppose an infinite set of rational numbers, but only a process for determining whether or not a candidate image is a rational number. Indeed, several thinkers have argued that infinite collections are contrary to proper reasoning [see, for example, (Poincaré 1908)]. Gauss says, "I object . . . to the use of an infinite magnitude as a completed idea, which in mathematics is never allowed. Infinity is only a figure of speech, while one speaks properly of a bound that may grow without limitation, however close one comes by fixed quantities" (Gauss 1831).

Conclusion

We have shown how data logic may be used to develop the basic apparatus of arithmetic. We will extend the methods developed above to cover real numbers and differential calculus in the next section. We argue, therefore, that data logic is a suitable means for developing the foundations of mathematics.

Data logic differs from symbolic logic in the treatment of infinity. While symbolic logic permits infinite sets, data logic permits only finite sets. Unending processes are considered in data logic to be *insatiable* classes. It is impossible to form the *set* of all instances of an insatiable class in data logic.

Existence arguments about instances of insatiable classes in data logic (for example, to resolve the question of whether the class of prime integers is insatiable) must include a procedure that calculates the desired instance (in this case, a formula that gives a prime number greater than any given integer). Arguments that do not contain such a procedure, sometimes called "nonconstructive" arguments, are usually not admissible proofs in data logic. This restriction makes it possible that many proofs in branches of mathematics such as general topology and transfinite set theory are not valid proofs in data logic.

3.7 COMPARISON WITH SET THEORY

Comparison of Data Logic with Zermelo's Axioms

Zermelo defined set theory rigorously from seven axioms (Zermelo 1908). These axioms continue to be the basis of modern set theory—see, for example, (Zuckerman 1974). We examine each of these axioms in turn, and discuss to what extent they apply to sets and to classes in data logic. We will paraphrase the axioms somewhat to accommodate them to the terms we have been using. We have translated the axioms from the original article in *Mathematische Annalen* 65:261–281.

> (Z1) If each member of a set S is also a member of a set T, and vice versa, then $S = T$. Or more briefly: Each set is determined by its members.

Recall that a set is a literal class in data logic, and the members of the set are conformers of the class. While two literal classes that have the same conformers are equally extensive

($S \doteqdot T$), they need not be equivalent ($S \equiv T$). Thus, classes in general are not determined by their members. Two *sets* that have the same members are equivalent in data logic, as they are in symbolic logic.

> (Z2) There is an (artificial) set $\varnothing$ that has no member. If b is any object within the given range, there is a set $\{b\}$ that has b and only b as a member; if b and c are any two objects within the range, there is a set $\{b, c\}$ that has b and c as members, but no other object different from both.

Zermelo presupposes an infinite "range" of "objects," which establishes the area of discussion. Only objects within the range may be members of sets. Each set is also an object according to Zermelo. In data logic, an "object" is a recognizer. A set is not a recognizer in data logic, but each set is usually assumed to have a handle which is a recognizer. A set is not required to have a handle in data logic, however; a set that has no handle would not be considered part of Zermelo's "range," and could therefore not be a member of any set.

Zermelo states explicitly that the range is not a set. In data logic, the range is a class, and sets are collections of conformers of the class. It is natural to define the range to be the class R of all recognizers, defined by

$$(\mathrm{A}x)\ \mathit{Recognizer}\text{: } [x] \Leftrightarrow R\text{:}[Я x]$$

The range may also be defined to be less extensive, such as the class of recognizers that are relevant to some topic of interest. Since each recognizer requires time to be conceived, there can only be a finite number of recognizers in any population. Thus, there are only a finite number of objects in data logic, so all sets in data logic are finite.

The set $\varnothing$ is defined in data logic by the formula

$$(\mathrm{A}x)\ \tilde{}\varnothing\text{:}(x)$$

Notice that $\varnothing$ is a constructive class with no *instances*. The statement that a class must have no conformers would violate inexhaustibility.

The set $B = \{b\}$ is defined by the formula

$$(\mathrm{A}x)\ B\text{:}[x] \Leftrightarrow (x \equiv b)$$

The set $\{b, c\}$ is defined similarly:

$$(\mathrm{A}x)\ C\text{:}[x] \Leftrightarrow ((x \equiv b) \vee (x \equiv c))$$

Notice that a set in data logic is defined by a definitive list of members, so that the proposition that a recognizer is a member of a set is an inherently definitive proposition.

Although we have used equivalence in defining sets, one may also define sets using a correspondence ΔR, which represents « ① *Is The Same Object As* ② ». Two recognizers may then be the same object yet not be equivalent, and two recognizers may be not equivalent yet be the same object. Since the members of a set are definitively members of the set, we consider conformalizations of ΔR, ΔR:$[x, y]$, and assume that ΔR:$[x, y] \Rightarrow$!ΔR:$[x, y]$. In this more general formulation, the sets $B' = \{b\}$ and $C' = \{b, c\}$ are defined by:

$$(\mathrm{A}x)\ B':[x] \Leftrightarrow \Delta R:[x, b]$$

$$(\mathrm{A}x)\ C':[x] \Leftrightarrow (\Delta R:[x, b] \vee \Delta R:[x, c])$$

(Z3) If the class-predicate $F(\ )$ is definite [that is, if it is either true or false] for all members of a set S, then there is a subset S_F of S such that all members x of S for which $F(x)$ is true, and only such objects x, are members of S_F.

We may define S_F by the formula

$$(\mathrm{A}x)\ S_F:[x] \Leftrightarrow S:[x]\ \&\ F:[x]$$

Notice that the class-predicate F is, in data logic, nothing other than a class (namely, the class of recognizers x for which $F(x)$ is "true"). If S is a set and F is a class, then S_F is always a class, but S_F is only a set if the conformers of S_F are definitively conformers of F. If some member d of S is only incidentally a conformer of F, then the expression $S:[d]$ & $F:[d]$ is not inherently definitive, and S_F is not a set.

(Z4) (Axiom of the power set) For each set S there is another set $\mathcal{P}S$, called the "power set" of S, such that all the subsets of S, and only these objects, are members of $\mathcal{P}S$.

The axiom (Z4) behaves very differently in data logic than it does in set theory. We may define the *power class* $\mathcal{P}S$ by the formula

$$(\mathrm{A}x)\ \mathcal{P}S:[\nu x] \Leftrightarrow (x \subsetneq S)$$

The class $\mathcal{P}S$ is then the class of subclasses of S, and has the same performance type as S.

If S is an insatiable class, then there may be subclasses of S that are not sets in data logic, because all sets in data logic are finite. For example, the class of even integers is a subclass of the class of integers, but it is not a set. Moreover, there may be "infinite subsets of S" in set theory that are not subclasses of S in data logic.

For example, suppose that we form the class $\mathbb{Z}$ of the integers according to the rules of mathematics. We know then that we can form many insatiable subclasses of $\mathbb{Z}$: the class of even integers, the class of integers greater than 6, and so on. We may therefore form the class $\mathcal{P}_1\mathbb{Z}$ of all subclasses of $\mathbb{Z}$ that may be defined by mathematical formulas of finite length. Now consider a person, Joe, who likes certain integers and dislikes others. Imagine that Joe is able to form a definite opinion about any integer that he is asked about, so that whether or not Joe likes any number may be determined definitely by asking him. The idea *Joe Likes The Integer* ( ) is therefore a class, and it is a subclass of $\mathbb{Z}$. However, supposing that Joe does not follow a fixed pattern in what he likes, it is not at all certain that the class *Joe Likes The Integer* ( ) is a mathematically formulatable subclass of $\mathbb{Z}$. It may therefore not be a member of $\mathcal{P}_1\mathbb{Z}$.

We may form a new class of subclasses $\mathcal{P}_2\mathbb{Z}$, which includes the class $\mathcal{P}_1\mathbb{Z}$, and contains in addition the class *Joe Likes The Integer* ( ) and other classes formed from it (such as the even integers Joe likes, the integers Joe does not like, etc.). We may continue to define alternative classes of subclasses for each new class of integers that we can imagine. It is not certain that this process will ever terminate, that is, that we can ever define a valid procedure in data logic that will form all the insatiable subclasses of $\mathbb{Z}$ that are supposed in set theory.

(Z5) For each set S there is a set $\mathcal{U}S$ such that all objects that are members of the members of S, and only these objects, are members of $\mathcal{U}S$.

The class $\mathcal{U}S$ is defined by

$$(\mathrm{A}x)\ \mathcal{U}S{:}[x] \Leftrightarrow (\exists y)\ y{:}[x]\ \&\ S{:}[y]$$

$\mathcal{U}S$ is a set if S is a set and all the members of S are sets (rather than its members being merely classes).

(Z6) (Axiom of choice) If S is a set of mutually disjoint sets, each of which is different from $\varnothing$, then there is at least one subset T of $\mathcal{U}S$ such that T has one and only one member in common with each member of S.

The axiom of choice has engendered much controversy in mathematics [see (Zuckerman 1974) for a discussion of its implications]. The axiom of choice is contrary to the spirit of data logic, since it assumes the existence of a class T without describing a way to form it. We therefore do not include the axiom of choice in data logic, neither when S or T is a set nor when S or T is a class.

(Z7) (Axiom of infinity) The range contains at least one set Z that has $\varnothing$ as a member and such that for each member x of Z, $\{x\}$ is also a member of Z.

The class Z may be defined in data logic as follows:

$$Z{:}[\nu\varnothing]\ \&\ (\mathrm{A}x)\ (Z{:}[\nu x]\ \Rightarrow\ ((\exists y)\ Z{:}[\nu y]\ \&\ (\mathrm{A}z)\ (y{:}[z] \Leftrightarrow (z \equiv x))))$$

Z is an insatiable class, but it is not a set because all sets in data logic are finite. In set theory, Z is often taken to be a definition of the class of positive integers. While Z may be placed in *one-to-one all-to-all* correspondence with the positive integers in data logic, Z is not equivalent to the class of positive integers, because the instances of Z are not numbers.

Real Numbers

A real number is best defined as an unbounded series of rational numbers with ever smaller increments between the members, as is achieved by expressing the number as a decimal expansion: 3, 3.1, 3.14, 3.141, . . . We may index the series by positive integers, so a real number L is a correspondence from $\mathbb{N}$ to $\mathbb{Q}$, the class of rational numbers, that is, $L \subseteq \mathbb{N} \times \mathbb{Q}$.

Since L is insatiable, L can not be defined by exhibiting its attachments. L must therefore be defined by an inductive process that establishes how the rational number that attaches to each index i is to be computed. The number e, for example, is a valid correspondence of this kind, since the rational number that attaches to the index i is defined to be:

$$\sum_{j=0}^{i} \frac{1}{j!}$$

The series *L converges* when it meets Cauchy's condition (Cauchy 1821):

$$(\mathrm{A}\varepsilon)\ (\exists N)\ (\mathrm{A}x)\ (\mathrm{A}y)\ \mathbb{Q}{:}[\varepsilon]\ \&\ \varepsilon > 0\ \&\ x > N\ \&\ y > N \Rightarrow |x.L - y.L| < \varepsilon$$

Here, ">" indicates comparison of quantity. The proposition $m > n$ is omissive, like the proposition $m = n$. The class of convergent correspondences is the class of real numbers, $\mathbb{R}$.

The definition of the real numbers hinges upon the definition of a series. We assume that all series that are defined by ordinary mathematical formulas of finite length are valid series, so that if they converge, they are real numbers. This definition is similar to Turing's definition of a "computable number" (Turing 1937). However, it is not so clear that an unbounded progression whose members are not strictly determined should be considered to be a real number, even if the progression converges [for the definition of the real numbers in symbolic logic, see (Dedekind 1872) or (Zuckerman 1974)].

For example, recalling Joe from our discussion above, let $J(h)$ have the value 1 if Joe likes the integer h, and 0 if Joe does not like h. Then consider the partial sums

$$\sum_{h=0}^{i} \frac{J(h)}{2^h}$$

This progression converges according to Cauchy's criterion, but it is not clear that it should be considered to be a valid series, because there is no formula that defines $J(h)$. This argument is made more potent by recognizing that the theory of power series, hence the theory of complex analytic functions, is concerned entirely with series in which the terms are defined by formula. Indeed, Cauchy defined a series to be "an indefinite succession of quantities that are derived one after another according to a definite law," and he was able to derive most of calculus with this restriction (Cauchy 1821).

These observations call into question the uniqueness of the real numbers. If we restrict the real numbers to series whose terms are defined by formula, it is not at all clear that all the real numbers in symbolic logic are real numbers to data logic. The series defined from $J(h)$ above is an example: it is certainly a real number to symbolic logic, but it is not certain that it is a real number to data logic. We may imagine adding a finite number of declared classes, such as J, and extending the definition of the real numbers to incorporate series formed using these classes. We might thereby arrive at several alternative definitions of the real numbers, each of which satisfies many of the requirements of calculus. It is not certain that we could ever attain all of the real numbers recognized by symbolic logic using this process, so that the real numbers as viewed in symbolic logic may be unattainable. If we can derive calculus using the real numbers as defined in data logic, it is likely that there are several workable definitions of the real numbers, each with a different population.

Differential Calculus

Derivatives are defined using the same methods as symbolic logic (Spivak 1967). For example, the formula of calculus

$$\frac{d(x^2)}{dx} = 2x$$

is an abbreviation for

$$\lim_{h \to 0} \frac{(x + h)^2 - x^2}{h} = 2x$$

which becomes in data logic

$$(\mathrm{A}x)\ (\mathrm{A}\varepsilon)\ (\exists\delta)\ (\mathrm{A}h)\ \mathbb{R}:[x]\ \&\ \mathbb{Q}:[\varepsilon]\ \&\ 0 < h < \delta \Rightarrow \frac{(x + h)^2 - x^2}{h} - 2x < \varepsilon$$

This statement obeys performance type integrity because both sides of the implication are omissive.

It is easy to see how these formulas may be extended to define derivatives of higher order, and so Taylor series. Existence of solutions to equations may be proved by describing explicitly a sequence that converges to the solution. For example, the fundamental theorem of algebra may be proved by demonstrating the convergence of any numerical root-finding method.

Cantor's Theorem

Cantor's theorem states that the set of subsets of a set has more members than the set itself (Cantor 1895). Paradox results when the theorem is applied to the set of all sets. In data logic, Cantor's theorem is most evocative when applied to classes, since it is true trivially for finite sets, the only kind of sets admissible in data logic.

Recall that we defined the power class $\mathcal{P}B$ to be the class of subclasses of a class B:

$$\mathcal{P}B:[\nu S] \Leftrightarrow (S \subseteq B)$$

If B is constructive, then $\mathcal{P}B:[\nu S]$ has the complementary performance type to S, so $\mathcal{P}B$ is constructive. If B is omissive, then $\mathcal{P}B:[\nu S]$ is always omissive, so $\mathcal{P}B$ is omissive. We will assume that B is omissive, and we will consider conformers of B, since this formulation fits the mathematical classes such as $\mathbb{Q}$ and $\mathbb{R}$ with which Cantor was primarily concerned.

Cantor defined "more members" as follows. Suppose that there is a correspondence G that attaches each conformer of a class A to exactly one conformer of a class B, and such that each conformer of B attaches to at most one conformer of A. If A and B are finite sets, the existence of such a correspondence G would imply that B had at least as many members as A. If we could establish that B had a member that was not attached to by G, then B would have a greater number of members than A.

The same procedure does not apply directly to infinite sets in set theory. For example, the correspondence that attaches each positive integer n to the even positive integer $2(n + 1)$ attaches to each even positive integer except 2. We can not conclude, however, that there are more even positive integers than there are positive integers.

Cantor argued that if *all* correspondences G that meet the tests above leave some conformer of B unattached, then B should be said to have "more members" than A. Thus, since the correspondence that attaches each positive integer n to the even positive integer $2n$ (rather than $2(n + 1)$) attaches to all the even positive integers, we would not conclude that there are more even positive integers than there are positive integers.

Cantor's Proof Fails in Data Logic

Suppose, then, that there is a correspondence G from B to $\mathcal{P}B$. We seek to show that there is a conformer of $\mathcal{P}B$, that is, a subclass of B, that G does not attach to. Cantor considered the class C defined by

$$(\mathrm{A}x)\ C{:}[x] \Leftrightarrow B{:}[x]\ \&\ (\exists y)\ G{:}[x,\ \nu y]\ \&\ \tilde{}y{:}[x] \tag{1}$$

The argument is clearest when G is taken to be omissive, and all proposal methods of G are conformalizations as shown. Then Formula (1) obeys performance type integrity only if x is omissive and C has the complementary performance type to y.

Cantor then supposed that G attached some recognizer d to νC. Substituting, we would then obtain

$$C{:}[d] \Leftrightarrow B{:}[d]\ \&\ \tilde{}C{:}[d]$$

This substitution, however, is invalid in data logic, because Formula (1) only applies if y and C have complementary performance types, and here νC (which has the same performance type as C) is substituted for y. Therefore G may attach d to νC, and, assuming that C is constructive, d is not a conformer of C.

Critique of Reasoning About Relative Magnitudes of Infinities

We may draw several conclusions from this line of reasoning. First, there are sets in set theory that are not classes in data logic: the set C as defined in set theory contains the recognizer d, but that set C can not be defined in data logic because of performance type integrity. Therefore, a power set as defined in set theory may contain sets that the power class as defined in data logic does not contain.

It is possible to remove the obstacle of performance type integrity by changing the proposal methods in Formula (1). For example, suppose that B, G, and C are constructive and that the proposal methods are all taken as instantiations rather than conformalizations. Then we have

$$(\mathrm{A}x)\ C{:}(x) \Leftrightarrow B{:}(x)\ \&\ (\exists y)\ G{:}(x,\ \nu y)\ \&\ \tilde{}y{:}(x) \tag{2}$$

Both sides are now constructive, so performance type integrity is obeyed. We may therefore substitute d for x to obtain

$$C{:}(d) \Leftrightarrow B{:}(d)\ \&\ G{:}(d,\ \nu C)\ \&\ \tilde{}C{:}(d)$$

Since the proposition $C{:}(d)$ is constructive, it is incidental, and we are free to conclude that Formula (2) is merely contradictory, and that C (or B or G) has a nonempty sheath. Thus, contradictions in set theory can be benign in data logic, if they involve entirely incidental propositions.

We may make Formula (2) more severe by supposing that B, C, and G are sheath-free. Then Formula (2) implies a contradiction of a definitive proposition, which is forbidden. We may conclude, then, that there is no correspondence G that satisfies Formula (2). However, since we never provided a means of forming G, this result is not contradictory. In symbolic logic, it is assumed that any arbitrary pairing, even of infinite sets, is a correspondence (a ''binary relation'' in set theory). This assumption is not valid in data logic.

Just as there may be sets in symbolic logic that are not classes in data logic, there may also be binary relations in symbolic logic that are not correspondences in data logic. Cantor's reasoning, therefore, that if all one-to-one correspondences between a class A and a class B leave some conformer of B unattached, then B has ''more members'' than A, is suspect. It could be that there is some abstract matching that attaches each conformer of B to each conformer of C, but that matching may be missed because it is not a correspondence.

We suggest, therefore, that Cantor's theorem is not a statement about the relative sizes of two classes, but a statement that limits the ability to choose a correspondence G. We argue, then, that the mere *undefinability* of a correspondence should not be used as a test of relative magnitude. For example, Cantor's theorem shows that there is no *one-to-one all-to-all* correspondence between the class of classes *Class* and its power class. Since we have no method for forming such a correspondence, there is no contradiction. This result therefore does not demonstrate that the two classes have a different number of members.

Application to the Real Numbers

Cantor's method is applied in symbolic logic to show that there are ''more'' real numbers than integers, as follows. Let G be a *one-to-one* correspondence from $\mathbb{N}$ to the class of real numbers between 0 and 1. For any integer i, we consider the decimal expansion of $i.G$, and form a real number r as follows: Define the digit in the ith position of the decimal expansion of r to be different from the digit in the ith position of $i.G$ (to make the procedure definite, add one to the digit unless it is 9, in which case use 0). The real number r is then not attached to by G.

This argument hinges upon the nature of the correspondence G. If G is defined according to a definite formula of mathematics, then the number r is a real number. However, if G is defined in some other way, external to the methods used to create the real numbers, then r might not be a real number, and the proof would fail. Turing used a similar argument to show that the class of computable real numbers is countable (Turing 1937).

Conclusion

Data logic differs from set theory in several key points: Data logic only recognizes finite sets, while set theory permits infinite sets. ''Infinite sets'' are treated in data logic as insatiable classes. Data logic denies the axiom of choice. Data logic insists that insatiable classes be defined according to a method that determines when a given recognizer is a conformer of the class. This is similar to the requirement of ''predicative definition'' used by some writers. Data logic recognizes the axiom of the power set in a modified form: since data logic requires rules of formation while set theory does not, there may be infinite subsets according to set theory that are not subclasses according to data logic.

We have applied data logic to the construction of the real numbers and to differential calculus, showing that data logic is applicable to branches of mathematics beyond arithmetic. Data logic predicts that there may be viable definitions of the real numbers that are far less extensive than the real numbers as defined by symbolic logic.

We have applied data logic to Cantor's theorem, and have shown that it does not lead to paradox as it does in symbolic logic. We have argued that Cantor's proof of the existence of higher infinities is unconvincing in data logic, so that there might be no uncountable infinities in thought.

3.8 CONSISTENCY AND COMPLETENESS

Consistency

In symbolic logic, a system of axioms is said to be *consistent* if it does not lead to contradiction when applied to itself. The consistency of data logic is assured by performance type integrity: all axioms are definitive, and only omissive propositions may be definitive, so all axioms are omissive. By performance type integrity, only omissive propositions may follow from omissive propositions, so all consequences of the axioms alone are omissive. The negation of an omissive proposition is always constructive, so contradictions always involve conjoining an omissive proposition with a constructive proposition. Since no constructive propositions may be deduced from the axioms alone, there can be no such contradictions, and data logic is consistent.

The definition of consistency used in symbolic logic is not, however, powerful enough to test the applicability of data logic in real situations. For example, even though the definition of the number 1 is an omissive proposition, the proposition that a given class has one instance is constructive. It remains unknown whether this constructive proposition could be contradicted by an omissive proposition derived from the axioms.

Investigation of the consistency of data logic should therefore proceed along different lines than the investigations of the consistency of symbolic logic. The most important problem is to identify to what extent propositions may be included in a logical system without fear of contradiction. This question has immediate relevance to data bases, because propositions are usually processed to assure that they do not contradict the contents of the data base before they are added to the population. If we can be certain that a given proposition will not cause a contradiction, or if we can place limits on the extent to which we must process the proposition to determine if it causes a contradiction, then we can design data base management systems to handle such propositions on a regular basis.

Completeness

An axiom system in symbolic logic is said to be *complete* if every true proposition is provable, that is, may be deduced from the axioms. Data logic is certainly not complete in this sense, for propositions may be affirmed that are independent of the axioms, such as the proposition « any car is also a vehicle ». Symbolic logic, which was developed for mathematics, attempts to establish a framework in which all contentions can be traced to their ultimate assumptions. Completeness is thus very important to symbolic logic, because it strikes to the core of its claim to legitimacy. Data logic, in contrast, is concerned primarily with manipulating claims that often have no logical basis, but represent opinions. Data logic is far more concerned with assuring that the patterns of deduction are accurate. In data logic, we would rather exclude a pattern of deduction if it is suspect, even at the cost of being unable to prove a grand result as a consequence. The more important question to data logic is therefore not completeness or incompleteness of the logical system, but a description of the limitations of proof, to know what topics data logic can, and can not, address.

To that end, we examine Gödel's proof of the incompleteness of symbolic logic (Gödel 1931). We show that the proof fails in data logic. This shows that a proposition of particular interest, namely the proposition that says of itself that it is not provable, does not lead to paradox in data logic. However, the more difficult question of what propositions can indeed be proved remains open.

By systematically defining the syntactic requirements for a proof, Gödel formed a class *Proof* that accepts any valid proof. A proof is a conjunction of omissive propositions, so any proof is omissive. If s is a proof, then s is definitively a proof, so the proposition « s is a proof » is omissive only when s is omissive. The class *Proof* is therefore omissive, and s is an instance of *Proof*.

The proposition « s is a proof of p » may be described using a correspondence ( ) *Is A Proof Of* ( ). The proposition « (s) *Is A Proof Of*: (p) » is definitive only if s and p are both omissive, so *Is A Proof Of* is omissive.

Gödel then considered the proposition that says of itself that it is unprovable:

$$p \Leftrightarrow \tilde{}(\exists x)\ (x)\ \textit{Is A Proof Of}:\ (p) \quad (1)$$

This definition is well-formed in symbolic logic, showing that p is true but unprovable.

In data logic, if p is constructive, then p is unprovable because only omissive propositions may have proofs. Thus, Formula (1) is satisfied, but this is uninformative. If p is omissive, then the right side of Formula (1) must be omissive by performance type integrity. This can only occur when x is constructive, but if x is constructive, then x is not a proof, because all proofs are omissive. Therefore, there can be no omissive p that satisfies Formula (1), and there is no paradox.

We can weaken Formula (1) by replacing the interchangeability by an implication,

$$\tilde{}(\exists x)\ (x)\ \textit{Is A Proof Of}:\ (p) \Rightarrow p \quad (2)$$

That is, we consider a proposition p that may only be affirmed if it is unprovable. In Formula (2), p may be omissive, showing that there may be definitive propositions that are not provable. This is as expected, because there may be definitive propositions that describe characteristics of experience, so can not be derived logically from the axioms alone, such as the definitive proposition « any car is also a vehicle ».

Conclusion

We have shown that data logic is consistent because of performance type integrity. We have shown further that Gödel's proof of the incompleteness of symbolic logic does not apply to data logic. This result suggests, but does not demonstrate, that by restricting infinities and applying performance type integrity, data logic may furnish a consistent framework for countable systems, including arithmetic.

Additional issues are raised in data logic beyond the questions of consistency and completeness of the logical system. For example, it would be useful to have criteria for determining that a set of propositions (such as a data base population) will not lead to contradiction. It would also be useful to characterize the propositions that *can* be proved in data logic, to judge how widely data logic can be applied. Here data logic may be contrasted with symbolic logic, where the emphasis has been on discovering propositions that can *not* be proved.

3.9 CONCLUSION

We have identified the fundamental assumptions of data logic in a set of postulates, axioms, and formal definitions. We have shown how data logic gives formal proofs of basic results in arithmetic, demonstrating that data logic is sufficiently powerful to manage abstract reasoning. We have shown how data logic avoids Russell's paradox and predicts characteristics of infinite systems that differ from the predictions of data logic. Thus, data logic is able to make predictions about the most advanced realms of logical philosophy.

Data logic argues for a thorough reexamination of the treatment of the infinite in abstract mathematics. Many infinite constructions, particularly in calculus and modern algebra, are properly insatiable classes rather than infinite sets. Although we do not currently foresee problems with the computational methods of calculus (such as Taylor series, for example), we do question whether the many nonconstructive existence theorems which are often found in modern calculus texts are provable, or are even needed.

Data logic further recommends a reappraisal of the methods used for founding mathematics. The primary departure from symbolic logic is to assign performance types to all basic mathematical concepts. Consistency of the logical system will then be assured by performance type integrity. However, certain types of proof may involve reasoning that would violate performance type integrity, and such proofs should be reexamined. This is particularly likely to occur in proofs that involve paradoxes, such as undecidability or incomputability theorems. It is likely that many such proofs will fail in data logic (as with Gödel's incompleteness theorem), casting doubt on the hypotheses.

CONCLUSION TO PART 1

We have argued that a theory of data should be founded on a study of thought, rather than on a study of consistent symbolic systems or a study of computing technology, as other theories have been. We have seen that data has both a symbolic component and a mental component: data is expressed using symbols that are selected for their permanence and reproducibility (such as alphanumeric characters, for example), and data represents thoughts that can be claimed (propositions).

How data behaves in thought can be very different from how physical systems behave. In particular, data can intentionally represent opinions that conflict with the physical world. One may, for example, use a farm management system to maintain a complete record of a unicorn breeding farm. To a data management process, there is no difference between this fictitious farm and a real farm that breeds cattle; both will be managed equally well.

We have studied thought to determine what conclusions it is proper to draw from a given symbolic cluster of data. The symbols themselves do not provide the answer: we can not look at the proposition tag *Unicorn*:(*Sam*), for example, and know from its appearance that it is interchangeable with the double negation ~~*Unicorn*:(*Sam*). We only reach this conclusion by examining how negation behaves in thought.

We have developed a new system of logic, *data logic*, specifically for the management of data. Finite symbolic logic may be viewed as a simplified subset of data logic, one where propositions are true if and only if they are definitive (since $p \Leftrightarrow\ !p$), where logical deduction is equivalent to alternation with a negation $((\tilde{}p \vee q) \Leftrightarrow (p \rightarrow q))$, and where performance types and proposal methods are chosen so that all propositions obey performance type integrity. We have seen that two of the assumptions of symbolic logic are incompatible: we can not assume both that all true propositions are definitive and that performance types can be so chosen to avoid performance type integrity, because this combination leads to the liar paradox.

PART 2
Theory of Data Bases

INTRODUCTION TO PART 2

In the next two chapters, we apply the principles of data logic to the study of data bases. Before proceeding, we take this opportunity to survey the consequences of data logic to the design and operation of data bases. The consequences are of three kinds: areas where data logic explains phenomena that have not been fully understood, areas where data logic provides ways of enhancing current capabilities, and areas where data logic presents new opportunities for managing data that have yet to reach implementation.

Data logic explains how a class can remain the same while its population changes. Thus, a class is defined to be a process that accepts images, while the population is the set of images that the process has accepted in some given set of performances. The set of images accepted may change each time the class is performed, while the process that defines the class remains the same. In practical data designs, data logic emphasizes the criteria used to determine acceptance in a class. That is, data logic focuses on the "data definition" of a class.

Data logic explains why a constraint can not be deduced from an examination of past populations of a data base. Thus, a data base constraint is defined in data logic to be a definitive proposition, that is, a proposition that supervises any population that the data base might contain. A data base design is therefore seen as a collection of controlling principles, which is different from a mere list of past coincidences. Thus, data logic explains why a data base design project always involves a debate, which can not be settled by appealing to the existing body of data. Any given body of data can be explained by any number of hypothetical principles; a debate is required to choose which principles are to be considered immutable.

Data logic provides formulas for many of the common constraints in practical data base designs. By expressing these constraints in logic, one may prove theorems about them. This ability opens the way to a science of data structures, since data logic can predict how a data structure will behave before it is implemented.

Expressing data base constraints in logic shows further that there are many constraints, similar to those in current use, that are not implemented by today's data base management systems. Data logic thus provides a framework for advancing the variety of data structures available to the designer.

For example, we show in Section 4.7 that a *from all* constraint may be written as an embracing of classes of the form $B \subseteq \pi^1 G$. A *from all* constraint is very common in data base design: it says that any instance of B must attach by G to something. Since this constraint, a common one, is an embracing of classes of the form $B \subseteq C$, we suggest that any embracing of classes of the form $B \subseteq C$ should be allowed in a data base design. Today, no major data model is this permissive: most do not permit any such embracing except in the case of a *from all* constraint. In the areas of artificial intelligence and object-oriented design, many systems do allow embracings of classes, but restrict them to form a hierarchy. That is, these systems prohibit both $B \subseteq C$ and $B \subseteq D$ from being declared in the same schema. The evidence from data logic is that these prohibitions are purely operational, and could be eliminated with improved technology.

Unfortunately, many of the simplest embracings can not be implemented in the major data base management systems today. An example is an embracing of correspondences, such as *Repairs* $\subseteq$ *Services* (if someone repairs something then he must service it, but it is possible for someone to service something without repairing it, as with a periodic reading of a meter). Most data base management systems would be unable to maintain both the correspondences *Repairs* and *Services* simultaneously, or else they would be unable to guarantee that each occasion of repairing was also an occasion of servicing.

These examples illustrate the basic method we will use to propose new forms of data base constraints. We analyze commonly used constraints, and argue that any constraints similar in form should be allowed. By repeated application of this method, we reach a form of constraint called a *positive embracing*, which is far more diverse than the constraints that are supported by current data base management systems. We argue that new data base management systems are needed that will accept the full variety of positive embracings, and we analyze some of the problems that such systems will have to face.

These additional forms of constraints require new notations for their presentation. The difficulties in developing an effective notation should not be underestimated: even small data base designs often exceed 100 constraints. Each constraint must be fully comprehended, and its consequences thoroughly explored, before undertaking system development. A change in constraint, such as a decision to make a correspondence *to many* that has been *to one*, can require changes to all programs that use the correspondence. The only effective way to communicate so many constraints to users and developers alike is through a notation that is at once evocative, rigorous, and easy to use.

Current data design notations can not express the full variety of constraints predicted by data logic. Diagrams based on relational tables are generally awkward for presenting constraints such as embracings that involve more than one relation. Network diagrams such as Bachman diagrams or entity-relationship diagrams work well for correspondences, but are unable to manage the full variety of trios and higher degree associations predicted by data logic. Network diagrams, too, have no way of expressing embracings.

In Chapter 5, we propose a new notation which we call *extended associative notation*. It is based on the Associative Data Model (Jones 1976, Jones and Curtice 1988), which the authors and our colleagues have used with over 3000 people for over 20 years. The Associative Data Model expresses the associations that each class participates in, rather than expressing the totality of all associations at once (the totality can of course be formed mechanically by going through all the classes). Extended associative notation can therefore express data designs of arbitrary size and complexity without the bewildering diagrams that result from trying to put all the associations on one chart. Extended associative notation is also able to express associations of arbitrary degree, with or without null values, within its normal syntax.

4

Application of Data Logic to Data Bases

4.1 INTRODUCTION

We defined a data base in Chapter 1 to be a binding site whose occupants are claims. In Section 4.2, Components of a Data Base, we expand this definition to incorporate data base constraints, such as "a hospital admission event must be for one person." Data bases make a clear distinction between a *schema* which contains constraints and a *data base population* which contains claims. Applying data logic, we see that the constraints in a schema are all definitive. That is, constraints describe how the data is structured, not only how particular populations behave. In contrast, no claim in a data base population is definitive.

In Section 4.3, Affirmation and Denial, we discuss the consequences of applying data logic to the claims in a data base population. We show that data logic accommodates a freer approach to individuals than is common in current data base management systems. In particular, data logic allows an individual to be an instance of many class tags simultaneously.

We show how data logic predicts that there are two forms of « or » that apply to data bases. In *resolved alternation*, the claim "*p* or *q*" means that either "*p*" or "*q*" (or both) are affirmed. That is, "*p* or *q*" means that we can deduce the symbol "*p*" or the symbol "*q*" from the data base population. Resolved alternation is the form of alternation used in symbolic logic.

In unresolved alternation, the claim ''p or q'' means that either « p » or « q » (or both) are affirmed, but that it may not be possible to determine which is affirmed by examining the population. That is, ''p or q'' may be affirmed yet it may be impossible to deduce either ''p'' or ''q'' from the data base population. An example is the proposition « the cat went outside or the cat is still indoors ». We can affirm this proposition without knowing where the cat is.

We discuss how a proposition may be *denied*. Current data base management systems are usually unable to manage denials. We show, however, that denied propositions are a natural consequence of data logic, and argue that such propositions should be incorporated into future data base management systems.

Data logic distinguishes a proposition that is *denied* from one that is *not affirmed*. Similarly, it distinguishes a proposition that is *affirmed* from one that is *not denied*. We show that it is possible to state formally that a given proposition is neither affirmed nor denied. For example, the proposition « there are nine planets in the solar system » is usually neither affirmed nor denied in a typical personnel data base.

In Section 4.4, Population Diagrams, we introduce a notation for presenting incidental claims as pictures. We will use population diagrams extensively in succeeding chapters to illustrate a sample population of a data structure.

In Section 4.5, Forms of Data Base Constraints, we argue that all forms of *positive embracings* should be permitted in data base designs. Positive embracings incorporate most constraints in common use, including parent/daughter, functional dependencies, multivalued dependencies, foreign key constraints, and so on. We also argue that constraints that are not positive embracings should not be allowed in data base designs. By this method, all data base schemas can be brought into a single unified theoretical framework.

In Section 4.6, Design of Individuals, we discuss the interaction of the design of recognizers with the design of associations. In particular, we discuss *stationing*, which is the design of associations and recognizers so that claims may be conjoined freely, and *relative unity*, which limits the breadth of interpretation of individuals.

In Section 4.7, Characters, we discuss four varieties of constraints that are of central importance to data theory: *from all, from one, to one*, and *to all*. The *from one* and *to one* constraints are similar to functional dependencies; the *from all* and *to all* constraints are sometimes referred to as ''onto'' or ''surjective'' mappings. These four constraints are called *character constraints*, and the expression that encodes which constraints are obeyed by a correspondence is called a *character*.

We show how each character constraint may be expressed as a positive embracing. The embracing format has several advantages: it provides a vehicle for proof, since embracings obey specific rules of data logic. It also provides a unified framework for the four varieties of character constraints: rather than being different concepts, the character constraints are special cases of one concept, a positive embracing. The embracing format shows further that the four constraints are intimately related. Thus, *from one* and *to one* are *converses* of each other, while *from one* and *from all* are related by a duality in the syntax of an embracing. The four character constraints are therefore a conceptual unit.

Correspondence characters describe a correspondence *relative to* a pair of classes. For example, we can not say that a correspondence G is *from all*, only that G is *from all* from a class B to a class C. This constraint means that any instance of B attaches to some instance of C through G. Data logic permits the same correspondence to be declared relative to many pairs of classes. That is, G may attach an individual d to some instance c of C, but d need not be an instance of B. It is possible, and permitted in data logic, for G to be *from all* from B to C, yet not to be *from all* from some other class D to C or to some other class E. In data logic, a correspondence may obey simultaneous constraints relative to many different classes.

In Section 4.8, Constraints of Higher Degree Associations, we begin a study of associations of degree higher than two that will culminate in the exhaustive treatment of trios in Chapter 9. These associations require additional study because of the presence of what are called "null values" in the relational model, which data logic permits in all positions. We show that the constraints of a trio may be relative both to a *triple* of classes and to a triple of correspondences. Null values are seen to be present unless they are prohibited by a constraint. We show that the constraints that prohibit null values are *from all* constraints, and are therefore handled by the theory of character constraints and positive embracings.

4.2 COMPONENTS OF A DATA BASE

A Data Base May Be Associated with a Data Base Design

In Section 1.12, we defined a *data base* to be a binding site whose occupants are proposition tags, called *claims*. A "tuple" in the relational data model is such a proposition tag. For example, the tuple (Sarah, accounting department) in the "Works In" relation represents the proposition « Sarah works in the accounting department ». We write this proposition as "*Works In*: (*Sarah*, *accounting department*)", or equivalently, as "(*Sarah*) *Works In*: (*accounting department*)".

We write the binding site that accepts claims, that is, the software and hardware apparatus that permits claims to be stored, as "*Claim*"; different data bases are indicated by subscripts: "$Claim_1$", "$Claim_2$", and so on. The population of *Claim* consists of the incidental claims that comprise the data base population. It does not include the constraints and other material that form the *data base design*.

A data base design has two components: a collection of *declared association tags* that establish what association tags will be recognized in the data base, and a collection of *schema elements* that establish the constraints that the data base must obey. These collections, like the collection of claims, are subject to change. We therefore describe these collections using two binding sites, *Declared Association* and *Schema*: We define a *declared association tag* to be an occupant of the binding site *Declared Association*, and we define a *schema element* to be an occupant of the binding site *Schema*. We will distinguish different binding sites using subscripts, as in $Declared\ Association_2$, or $Schema_4$.

We define a *data base design* to be a pair of binding sites ($Declared\ Association_i$, $Schema_i$), and a *data base* to be a triple of binding sites ($Declared\ Association_i$, $Schema_i$, $Claim_i$). What we call a *data base design* is referred to more specifically by some writers as a "logical" or "conceptual" data base design, in contrast to a "physical" data base design that includes a description of how the data base is implemented on a computer. When we refer to the *population of a data base*, we will mean the population of $Claim_i$. We will concentrate on describing how any chosen data base behaves, rather than on comparing different data bases. We will therefore usually drop the subscripts, and write "*Claim*", "*Declared Association*", and "*Schema*".

A Claim May Contain an Association Tag That Is Not Declared

It has been customary in data base applications to define all the association tags that a data base will accept beforehand, as part of the design of the data base. This restriction is similar to requiring predefinition of variables in a compiler, and has the similar consequence of permitting more efficient structuring of storage before the storage space is used. In knowledge base systems, however, a different approach has been taken, which permits claims to be added that contain undeclared association tags (Frost 1986). From a logical standpoint, there is no need to require predefinition of allowable association tags. We might, for example, implement a data base using a syntactic parser that accepts any symbol of the form "X:(y)" as a valid proposition tag, and dutifully records X as a class tag and y as an individual, even if neither X nor y has been declared beforehand.

If undeclared association tags like "X" are permitted, then undeclared association tags behave just as unconstrained declared association tags: any population of an undeclared association tag is allowed. There is no logical difference, for example, between allowing claims of the form B:(x) without declaring B, and declaring B without placing any constraints on B.

The decision whether or not to permit claims that incorporate undeclared association tags is therefore operational, not theoretical. We would argue that the requirement to declare all association tags in advance is largely a limitation of today's technology, rather than a fundamental need. In many applications, users would be happy to be able to insert new claims into the data base outside the bounds of the schema, but the current technology prohibits them from doing so. Data logic can accommodate either approach, but we will assume that claims are allowed to incorporate association tags that are not derived from the declared association tags. Notice that any knowledge base is therefore a data base under our definition.

A Schema Contains Constraints and Relaxations

We define a *schema* to be a binding site that accepts only definitive proposition tags and negations of definitive proposition tags. Each such proposition tag will be called a *schema element*. For example, the proposition tag *Any employee must be assigned to one department* is a definitive proposition tag, but the proposition tag *An employee might be covered under many benefit plans* is a negation of a definitive proposition tag, namely, the proposition tag *An employee must be covered under at most one benefit plan*.

A definitive schema element is called a *constraint*, or, more precisely, a *declared constraint*. A schema element that is the negation of a definitive proposition is called a *relaxation*, or, more precisely, a *declared relaxation*. Other proposition tags formed from the schema elements by applying logical laws are called *derived constraints*, and *derived relaxations*, as appropriate. We will assume that each association tag that appears in the schema is declared. That is, if an association tag R is used in a constraint or a relaxation, then R must be declared; if R is only used in claims, then R need not be declared.

A schema element is a specific statement that contains association tags with prescribed interpretations. A format for a schema element where no particular interpretation is assigned will be called a *data structure*. For example, the particular constraint $B \subseteq C$ for some declared association tags B and C is a schema element, while the general embracing $x \subseteq y$, where x and y stand for two unspecified classes, is a data structure.

"Same Data Base Design" Is Defined by Binding Sites

We consider under what circumstances we would say that two data base designs are "different." As a particularly severe test case, suppose that two data base designs have the same set of declared association tags and the same set of schema elements. Can we conclude that they are the same data base design? We argue that we can not. For example, suppose that two data bases are under design, one for a manufacturing facility, and the other for a sales office. It is agreed at the outset that the designs will be loosely integrated. In particular, it is agreed that both the manufacturing organization and the sales organization will report operating financial information using a standard list of *corporate accounts*. At the outset of the design process, we may establish two data base designs, each containing nothing but the one class tag *Corporate Account*. Even though each data base design contains exactly the same association tags and exactly the same constraints, they are different data base designs: one is the manufacturing data base design, and the other is the sales data base design. The two data base designs have, incidentally, the same population.

Suppose now that a design meeting is convened and that various additional association tags and constraints are added to the manufacturing data base design, such as *Part, Machine Tool*, and the like. Does this create a new data base design? Certainly the *population* of the binding site *Declared Association* has changed, but that does not require that we view it as a new data base design. Indeed, in the process of designing a data base, one will ordinarily permit a certain amount of latitude for design changes before declaring that a new design has been created. A new design is akin to a new version of a software program. One does not ordinarily create a new version until a significant body of modifications has been made, and until the program satisfies various standards of internal integrity. In the same way, a new data base design is formed only when it is desirable to do so for project management reasons, not automatically any time a change is made.

The data base design ($Declared\ Association_i$, $Schema_j$) is therefore the same data base design as ($Declared\ Association_k$, $Schema_l$) if and only if $Declared\ Association_i$ and $Declared\ Association_k$ are the same binding site, and $Schema_j$ and $Schema_l$ are the same binding site.

Claims Are Supervised by a Data Base Design

The population of a data base is the set of occupants of a binding site $Claim_i$. In practical data bases, claims differ from schema elements in that each claim is *incidental*. That is, a claim does not contain the symbol "!" in its expression (notice that this restriction also prohibits alternations such as $p \vee !q$ from being claims). We call this rule the *incidental claim restriction*, and we will follow it throughout. The incidental claim restriction has the practical advantages of providing a ready test of whether a candidate proposition tag should be considered a member of a data base population or a schema element, and of simplifying the allowable syntax of claims.

When a binding site $Claim_i$ is combined with two binding sites $Declared\ Association_i$ and $Schema_i$ to form a data base, we say that the schema $Schema_i$ *supervises* the data base. That is, the population of $Claim_i$ is constrained so that it does not contradict the contents of $Schema_i$. We say, equivalently, that each population of $Claim_i$ *obeys* (does not contradict) each schema element.

Varieties of Individuals

Two varieties of individuals are used in data bases: a *hidden* individual is an arbitrary tag that is never reported to users, while an *exposed* individual is a tag whose physical appearance is significant. An exposed individual can not be changed at will. For example, a person's name is an exposed individual: we can not choose to represent the name « Joe » by the tag "Susan" without causing confusion. There is a commonly understood way of representing the name « Joe » that the data base must follow, namely, the text "Joe", the ASCII characters "Joe", or some similar method. Other examples of exposed individuals are a mailing address, a digitized image (such as a photograph of Joe), and a string of numerals used to represent a number.

Hidden individuals are under the complete control of the data designers and administrators, and may therefore be defined to serve whatever needs arise. Exposed individuals, in contrast, inevitably acquire usages and interpretations that are beyond the control of the data base, and that can hamper the operation of a system. For example, the data base can not change a person's name. If two people with the same name are to be distinguished, each person must be represented by a different (symbolic) individual, different from the person's name. These individuals, these "person tags," should be hidden.

For embracings to work properly, hidden individuals must be assigned with greater care than has been common in data bases today. The population of a class should not intermix hidden and exposed individuals: the population should consist entirely of hidden individuals, or entirely of exposed individuals. A class tag whose population consists entirely of hidden individuals is called an *interior* class tag, and a class tag whose population consists entirely of exposed individuals is called an *exterior* class tag.

Hidden individuals should be chosen so that an individual always has the same interpretation, whatever class tag the individual may be an instance of. For example, the symbol "10398" should not be used both as a customer identifier and as a part number, except in the special case where "10398" represents an image that is both a customer and a part (which could occur, for example, if the customer provided a service that was a component of some final product).

Data bases today are usually designed with the weaker assumption that an individual represents the same recognizer each time it is used as an instance of a given class tag. Thus, in the method that is common today, "10398" would not be used to represent two different customers, or to represent two different parts, but it would be assumed that if "10398" appeared in both the *Customer* file and the *Part* file, that it was only a coincidence, and that the same recognizer was not meant. When individuals are to be allowed to be instances of several class tags simultaneously, however, which occurs with embracings, individuals must be assigned uniquely over all interior class tags.

Conclusion

We have expanded the definition of *data base* given earlier to incorporate a *data base design*. Specifically, we have defined a *data base* to be a triple of binding sites (*Claim*, *Declared Association*, *Schema*). The population of each binding site can change without there being a new data base. The occupants of *Claim* are pieces of data (they are "records" in a file management system, for example). The occupants of *Declared Association* are the association tags used in forming claims (they are "attribute names," "domain names," and "relation names" in the relational data model, for example). The occupants of *Schema* are constraints or relaxations that determine what claims are allowed (the schema elements determine if a correspondence is *one-to-one, one-to-many*, or otherwise, for example).

4.3 AFFIRMATION AND DENIAL

Data logic suggests new approaches for managing data base populations. In particular, data logic suggests that pieces of data should be managed as propositions rather than as records. Thus, since a piece of data is a proposition tag, it should be possible to include the basic logical operations of « and », « or », and « not » in data base populations. We are accustomed to forming the « and » of two pieces of data; we do so by placing each piece of data in a data base population. This action is ordinarily interpreted to mean that both propositions are affirmed. Data logic suggests that it is just as natural to permit propositions to be joined by « or ». Thus, one may list alternatives in a data base, and claim that at least one of the alternatives holds, but that which one is unknown.

Negation must be approached more cautiously, because one must consider carefully whether the idea « not » is to be managed as an opposite or as a complement. We discuss briefly how propositions in a data base population could be denied, and suggest that opposites may be a more effective method than complements in a population that is subject to updates. Populations that employ « or » and « not » are managed today in some knowledge base and artificial intelligence environments (Frost 1986). Data logic enables these populations to be analyzed with the same assurance as conventional data bases.

Elementary Logic of Affirmation

A proposition tag p is said to be *affirmed* if p may be deduced, using the laws of data logic, from the claims in a data base population. We write the statement that p is affirmed as "$\vdash p$". If the proposition tag "p" is affirmed, we will also say that the proposition « p » is affirmed. Similarly, if the proposition tag "p" is claimed, we will also say the the proposition « p » is claimed.

The logic of affirmed propositions may be determined as follows. A proposition p is affirmed if p may be deduced from the conjunction of all the claims in the data base population. This conjunction is called the *comprehensive proposition*, and is written "$\dashv$".

That is, if $q_1, \ldots, q_n$ are all the claims in the data base population,

$$\dashv \leftrightarrow q_1 \ \& \ q_2 \ \& \ \ldots \ \& \ q_n$$

This is a bi-directional incidental deduction, not a definitive interchangeability, because the proposition tags $q_1, \ldots, q_n$ may be only incidentally claims. Each time a new claim is added, or an old claim deleted, $\dashv$ indicates a different conjunction.

Whatever population the data base may contain, a proposition p is affirmed if and only if p may be deduced from $\dashv$. Thus, we have

$$(\vdash p) \Leftrightarrow (\dashv \rightarrow p)$$

We may now determine the logic of affirmation from the logic of deduction:

$$\begin{aligned} \vdash (p \ \& \ q) &\Leftrightarrow (\dashv \rightarrow p \ \& \ q) \\ &\Leftrightarrow (\dashv \rightarrow p) \ \& \ (\dashv \rightarrow q) \\ &\Leftrightarrow (\vdash p) \ \& \ (\vdash q) \\ \vdash (p \vee q) &\Leftrightarrow (\dashv \rightarrow p \vee q) \\ &\Leftarrow (\dashv \rightarrow p) \vee (\dashv \rightarrow q) \\ &\Leftarrow (\vdash p) \vee (\vdash q) \end{aligned}$$

Notice that $\vdash (p \vee q)$ does not generally imply that $(\vdash p) \vee (\vdash q)$.

Alternations May Be Resolved or Unresolved

The alternation $(\vdash p) \vee (\vdash q)$ is called a *resolved* alternation, because it states that either p is affirmed or q is affirmed (or both). That is, by further analysis of the contents of the data base, one could determine which of the propositions p or q is affirmed. The alternation $\vdash (p \vee q)$, in contrast, is called an *unresolved* alternation. Data logic allows a data base to retain an unresolved alternation without retaining sufficient information to affirm either proposition alone. For a proposal on a way to extend the relational data model to incorporate certain forms of unresolved alternation, see (Liu and Sunderraman 1990).

Current computer systems are generally only equipped to manage resolved alternations, when they can manage alternations at all. Implementing unresolved alternations may improve the ability of computer systems to handle data that is incompletely specified. For example, suppose that an investigation is being conducted to determine the perpetrator of some offense. Suppose that the suspects have been narrowed down to three: Ralph, Sarah, and Bill. Given an ability to retain unresolved alternations, we may add the following proposition to the data base:

$$\vdash (\mathit{Ralph}) :\mathit{Did\ It} \vee (\mathit{Sarah}) :\mathit{Did\ It} \vee (\mathit{Bill}) :\mathit{Did\ It}$$

Suppose that Ralph gives the investigators an alibi, and the investigators conclude that Ralph is innocent. They may then add the claim

$$\vdash ((\mathit{Ralph}) :{}^{\circ}\mathit{Did\ It})$$

The computer may then conclude that Sarah or Bill committed the offense. Note the use of the opposite of *Did It* to indicate that the investigators have made a constructive judgment that Ralph did not commit the offense. We will return to this use of the opposite later in this section.

Although this example is simple, it can be generalized to manage automatically the vast range of possibilities that are common in a real investigation. Such investigations often turn up contradictory results that must be untangled by further inquiry. Proper use of sheaths (see Section 2.7) will aid in resolving these contradictions. Of course, the same methods can be used for less onerous examples than criminal investigations, such as searching for a cause of a disease.

Resolute Associations Do Not Exhibit Unresolved Alternations

In some applications, it is important to prohibit unresolved alternations. For example, consider an auto parts store that stocks three varieties of headlights. Suppose that when headlights are received into inventory, they are placed in one of three inventory locations, a, b, and c. Upon delivery of a dozen assorted headlights to the auto parts store, we may conclude that each headlight will be received into a, into b, or into c, an unresolved alternation. However, a headlight has not been received into inventory until a choice of a, b, or c is made. Thus, if h represents a headlight, the claim

$$\vdash (h)\ \textit{Is Stocked In}{:}\ (a) \vee (h)\ \textit{Is Stocked In}{:}\ (b) \vee (h)\ \textit{Is Stocked In}{:}\ (c)$$

is not a valid inventory record.

An association whose population is prohibited from containing unresolved alternations is said to be *resolute*. A resolute correspondence G is defined in data logic to be a correspondence that obeys the formula

$$(\mathrm{A}x)\ (\mathrm{A}y)\ G{:}(x,\ y) \Rightarrow \vdash G{:}(x,\ y)$$

For example, the correspondence ( ) *Is Stocked In* ( ) cited above is resolute. Associations of any degree may be resolute. For example, a resolute class is a class B that obeys the formula

$$(\mathrm{A}x)\ B{:}(x) \Rightarrow \vdash B{:}(x)$$

We will generally assume that associations are not resolute, so that we may explore the effects that data base constraints may have on unresolved alternations.

Logic of Constraints

When a constraint is part of a data base schema, the constraint applies to any proposition that is affirmed. Thus, the statement that the constraint p is in the schema may be written $\dashv \Rightarrow p$, or, more simply, $!\vdash p$. Notice that logical deductions from the physical contents of a schema are also considered to be part of the schema. For example, if the schema contains the constraints $!\vdash B \subseteq C$ and $!\vdash C \subseteq D$, then it is considered to also contain the constraint $!\vdash B \subseteq D$.

The interaction of constraints with claims is therefore described by the formulas

$$((\vdash p) \;\&\; !\vdash q) \Rightarrow (\vdash p) \;\&\; \vdash q$$

$$\Rightarrow \vdash (p \;\&\; q)$$

In particular,

$$((\vdash p) \;\&\; !\vdash (p \rightarrow q)) \Rightarrow (\vdash p) \;\&\; \vdash (p \rightarrow q)$$

$$\Rightarrow \vdash (p \;\&\; (p \rightarrow q))$$

$$\Rightarrow \vdash q \qquad (1)$$

The form $!\vdash p$ is important when comparing two different data base designs. For example, if the schema for data base 1 contains the constraint p, but the schema for data base 2 does not, then we would write: $!\vdash_1 p \;\&\; \tilde{}!\vdash_2 p$. In this book, we do not emphasize the logical formalisms required when comparing different data base designs. When attention is focused on one schema, the proposition $!\vdash p$ acts on a data base in the same way as the simpler $!p$. We will therefore use this simpler form unless extra precision is needed. Thus, we will write the constraint "C embraces B" as "$B \subseteq C$", rather than the more precise "$!\vdash (B \subseteq C)$".

By Formula (1) then,

$$(\vdash B{:}(d) \;\&\; (B \subseteq C)) \Rightarrow (\vdash B{:}(d)) \;\&\; !\vdash (B \subseteq C)$$

$$\Rightarrow \vdash C{:}(d)$$

That is, if it is affirmed that d is an instance of B, and C embraces B according to the schema, then it is affirmed that d is an instance of C. Notice that it is not necessary for d to be *claimed* to be an instance of C. That is, one need not physically store the proposition tag "$C{:}(d)$". Data logic is insensitive to whether or not individuals are stored redundantly. If the class C embraced the class B, one could store only those instances of C that were not instances of B, for example, as long as the data base management system produced all the instances of B when asked for the instances of C.

Existential Quantifications May Be Resolved or Unresolved

Data logic also permits existential quantifications within a data base population. For example, we may imagine inserting the claim "$(\exists x)\ G{:}(b, x)$", « *b Gs* something », into a population. There are two forms of this expression, *resolved* and *unresolved*. The resolved form, « *b Gs* something », means that there is some individual d in the data base population such that $G{:}(b, d)$ is affirmed. A resolved existential quantification is thus a deduction from other information in the data base. In the *unresolved* form, the statement « *b Gs* something » might be affirmed without there being any individual d that b attaches to. An unresolved existential quantification is thus similar to a "present but value unknown" indicator (Maier 1983).

In data logic, a resolved existential quantification is written with the affirmation symbol "$\vdash$" following the quantifier:

$$(\exists x) \vdash G{:}(b, x)$$

The unresolved form is written with the affirmation symbol preceding the quantifier:

$$\vdash (\exists x)\ G{:}(b, x)$$

A resolute correspondence does not permit unresolved existential quantifications in its population. We will generally assume that unresolved existential quantifications are permitted.

Populations May Contain Denials

In many applications, it would be useful to retain not only the recognizers that have been affirmed to be instances of a given class, but also to retain recognizers that have been *denied* to be instances of the class. This ability is of little use if we imagine that a recognizer *d* is denied to be an instance of a class *B* if and only if *d* is not affirmed to be an instance of *B*: in that case, the denials can be calculated from the population of *B*. However, in many cases, the conditions for being denied are more stringent than the conditions for being not affirmed.

For example, suppose a study group is conducting a survey of the buildings in a given city to determine which buildings are safe (according to some criteria, such as fire-resistance), and which buildings are unsafe. A judicious definition of "safe" and "unsafe" is bound to leave leeway for buildings that are not well enough protected to be declared "safe", yet are not sufficiently poorly protected to be declared "unsafe".

The classes *Safe* and *Unsafe* are opposites of each other. Both *Safe* and *Unsafe* are constructive classes. They therefore obey the inexhaustibility principle of data logic, which states that any two constructive opposites *B* and °*B* must permit an image to be accepted by neither class (that is, an image that is neither safe nor unsafe).

We write the proposition that it is affirmed that a building *b* is safe as $\vdash$ *Safe*:(*b*). It is *denied* that *b* is safe if it is affirmed that *b* is unsafe: $\vdash$ *Unsafe*:(*b*). We write this denial equivalently as "▼ *Safe*:(*b*)". Denial is defined in data logic by the formula

$$\blacktriangledown\ B{:}(b) \Leftrightarrow\ \vdash {}^{\circ}B{:}(b)$$

Denial obeys a rigorous logic, derived from data logic. In particular, one may state formally that a proposition is neither affirmed nor denied. Such a statement is not allowed in symbolic logic, because all propositions are either "true" or "false" in symbolic logic.

For example, imagine a data base that records the location of shipments. Suppose that shipment *s* has been delivered to Denver. The data base then records

$$\vdash (s)\ Is\ At{:}\ (Denver)$$

Since a shipment can not be two places at the same time, the data base may also deny that *s* is at Atlanta:

$$\blacktriangledown\ (s)\ Is\ At{:}\ (Atlanta)$$

Now consider a shipment *t* whose whereabouts are unknown. The data base then does not affirm or deny the location of *t*. So we have

$$\tilde{\ }\vdash (t)\ Is\ At{:}\ (Denver)\ \&\ \tilde{\ }\blacktriangledown\ (t)\ Is\ At{:}\ (Denver)$$

A proposition such as (t) *Is At*: (*Denver*) that is neither affirmed nor denied is called an *alien* proposition.

Denials remain a research area, and we will not normally consider denials in our discussions of data structures. However, data logic does open these propositions to serious study, and we see no obstacle to implementing them under experimental conditions.

Comparison with Intuitionistic Logic

The result that there are propositions that are neither affirmed nor denied is similar to the view of intuitionistic logic, which states that there may be propositions p such that neither p nor $\tilde{}p$ are true. Intuitionistic logic bases its view on consideration of mathematical proof: a proposition is only considered to be "true" in intuitionistic logic if it can be proved. Certainly there are propositions p for which no proof is known of either p or $\tilde{}p$; Fermat's last theorem is an example. In intuitionistic logic, then, neither p nor $\tilde{}p$ would be true.

We sympathize with this critique of symbolic logic, but we believe that redefinition of negation is the wrong approach. In data logic, the proposition $\vdash p$ may be used to mean that p has been demonstrated. The proposition $\blacktriangledown\ p$ would then mean that $\tilde{}p$ has been demonstrated, and the proposition $\tilde{}\vdash p$ would mean that p has not been demonstrated. Thus, data logic incorporates the major thrust of intuitionistic logic, the clear distinction between a demonstration of $\tilde{}p$ ($\blacktriangledown\ p$) and the lack of a demonstration of p ($\tilde{}\vdash p$). At the same time, data logic maintains the useful interchangeability of p with $\tilde{}\tilde{}p$, which intuitionistic logic denies. For further discussion of intuitionistic logic, see (Heyting 1966) or (Kleene 1952).

Quine's Criticisms of Belief Operators

The logical operator $\vdash$ is a means of introducing "belief" into logic. Quine has criticized operators of this kind, and we respond to some of his criticisms below. In *From a Logical Point of View*, Quine cites the following proposition, referring to figures from ancient history (Quine 1980, pp. 139–159):

Philip is unaware that Tully denounced Catiline (2)

The person named "Tully" was also named "Cicero" ("Tullius" was Cicero's middle name). Substitution of one for the other yields

Philip is unaware that Cicero denounced Catiline

Yet Philip may be aware of Cicero's actions without knowing that Cicero and Tully were the same man. Quine argues that the error is in permitting substitution following a modal expression such as « is unaware that », but this conclusion is overly severe. The proper formulation is seen by writing the expressions in data logic. Thus, writing "$\vdash$" for « Philip is aware that », Formula (2) is

$$\tilde{}\vdash (\mathit{Tully})\ \mathit{Denounced}\colon (\mathit{Catiline})$$

The statement that Philip *is aware that* Tully and Cicero were the same man is written

$$!\vdash (\mathit{Tully} \doteqdot \mathit{Cicero}) \qquad (3)$$

From Formulas (2) and (3) we may deduce that Philip is unaware that Cicero denounced Catiline:

$$\neg\vdash \textit{(Cicero) Denounced: (Catiline)}$$

Notice, however, that the argument hinges on whether or not Philip is aware that Tully and Cicero were the same man. If he is not aware of this, then there is no contradiction. In data logic, unlike symbolic logic, there is no absolute authority of reality that supersedes belief. Philip is free to believe in images that are unreal if he chooses, while continuing to think logically.

Conclusion

Data logic distinguishes between *unresolved alternation* of propositions, where "p or q" may be affirmed without p or q being affirmed, and *resolved alternation* of propositions, where "p or q" can only be affirmed if one or both of p and q is affirmed. Most current automated systems of reasoning do not support alternation, and those that do usually support only resolved alternation. Unresolved alternation addresses situations that are incompletely understood, or situations where a reasoning process must consider several possibilities in parallel.

We have shown how affirmation and denial may be described in data logic. This treatment differs from symbolic logic because affirmation in data logic is itself an operation that can be subjected to logical analysis. Thus, we can write in data logic that a proposition is not affirmed, and we can contrast this statement with the statement that a proposition is denied. We are therefore able to consider propositions that are neither affirmed nor denied, which are propositions that bear no logical relation to the claims in a given data base population.

These principles have enticing implications for systems of automated reasoning. We showed in Chapter 3 that reasoning can be modelled by a deductive engine that forms new claims from claims that are already resident in a data base population. Thus, we can imagine a reasoning process that not only forms new conclusions, but is able to "show its work" by entering intermediate results directly into the data base population. These results may include denials as well as affirmations. They can even include statements that a given proposition can not be decided based on existing claims (such a proposition would be affirmed to be neither affirmed nor denied).

4.4 POPULATION DIAGRAMS

Population Diagrams Illustrate Data Base Populations

In this section, we introduce a pictorial technique for illustrating a sample population of a schema. It has become common for such illustrations to be written as tables, but tables do not express denials or unresolved alternations well, and tables are often less comprehensible than pictures when many symbols must be considered simultaneously.

Figure 4.1 shows the basic symbols used in population diagrams. A hidden individual, such as "b" in the figure, is shown surrounded by a double rectangle. An exposed

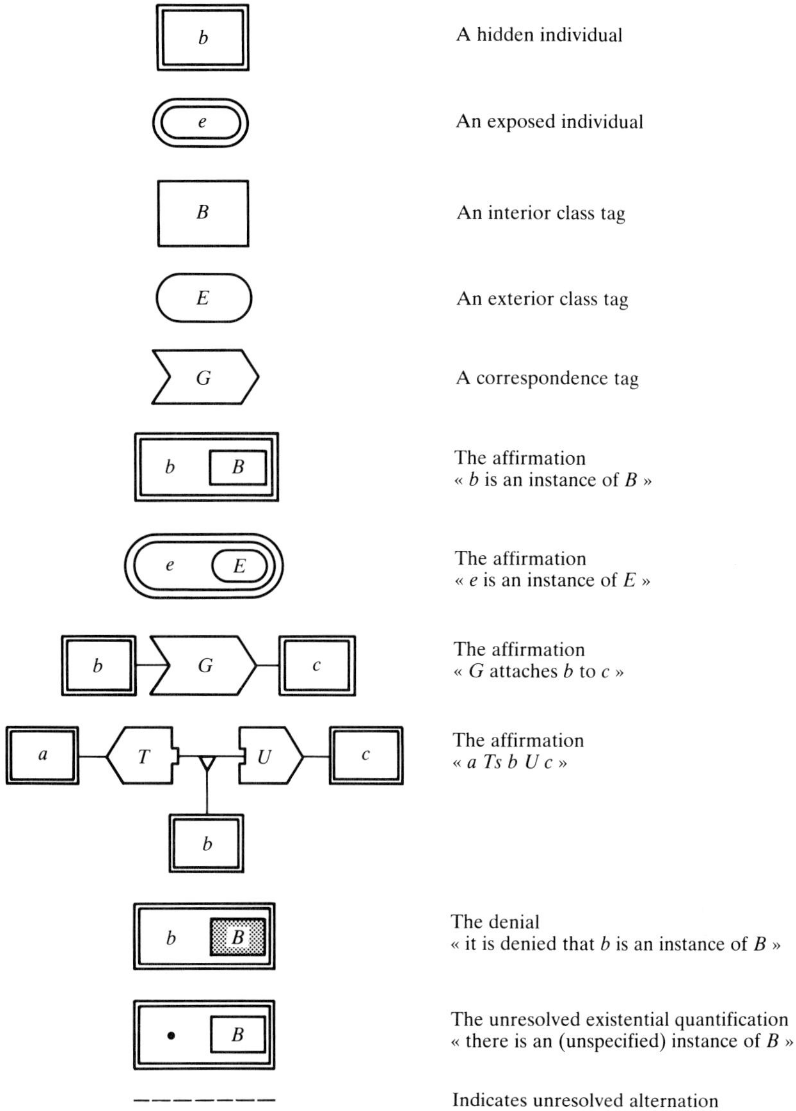

Figure 4.1 Components of population diagrams.

individual, such as "*e*" in the figure, is shown surrounded by a double oval. An interior class tag, such as "*B*" in the figure, is shown surrounded by a single rectangle. An exterior class tag, such as "*E*" in the figure, is shown surrounded by a single oval. The simple proposition $\vdash B$: (b) is written by enclosing the rectangle that surrounds the class tag B within the double rectangle that surrounds the individual b. A similar form is used for the simple proposition $\vdash E$: (e), using ovals instead of rectangles. Denial is expressed by shading, or, on video terminals, by reverse video. Unresolved existential quantification is shown by a dot inside a double rectangle. We will illustrate the basic forms of population diagrams using interior class tags. The similar diagrams for exterior class tags may be formed by converting rectangles to ovals.

A population diagram may represent many simple propositions, which are all assumed to be conjoined. A population diagram may be simplified by including more than one class tag within a double rectangle, but a double rectangle may contain no more than one individual. An individual may, however, appear in several double rectangles. Thus, $\vdash (B{:}(b) \vee C{:}(b))$ may be written in the two equivalent ways shown in Figure 4.2.

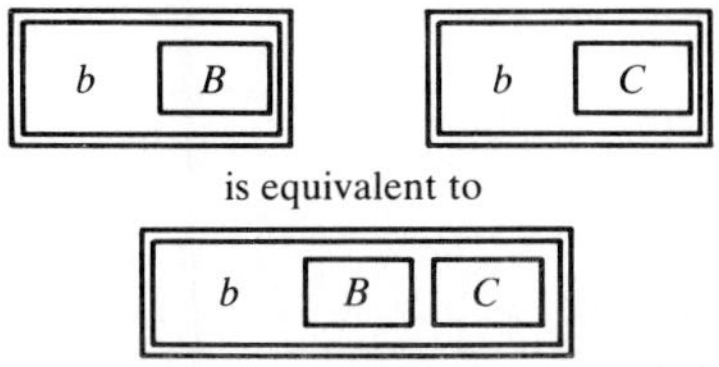

Figure 4.2

Unresolved alternation is expressed by a dashed line. Thus, Figure 4.3 indicates $\vdash (B{:}(b) \vee C{:}(c))$. Unresolved alternations may be simplified when one individual is involved. Thus, $\vdash (B{:}(b) \vee C{:}(b))$ may be written as shown in Figure 4.4.

Resolved alternations are not shown in population diagrams. Since $\vdash p \vee \vdash q$ states that p is in the population or q is in the population, the proposition tags that are in the population (p, q, or both) are shown directly.

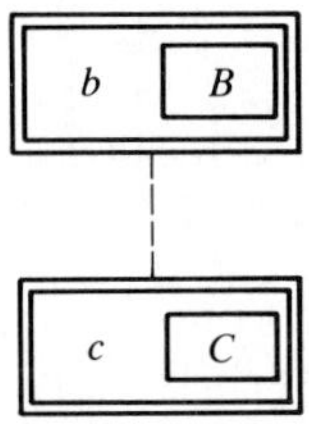

Figure 4.3 An unresolved alternation.

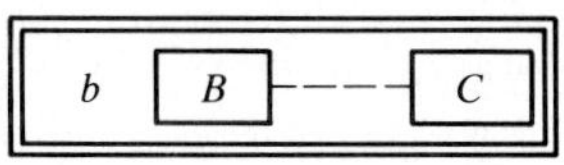

Figure 4.4 Abbreviated form for an unresolved alternation.

Correspondences

A correspondence tag is surrounded by a *chevron*, such as the correspondence tag ''*G*'' in Figure 4.1. A simple proposition controlled by a correspondence is written by connecting the chevron to the double rectangles that surround the individuals that are attached. Thus, Figure 4.1 illustrates the affirmation $\vdash G{:}(b, c)$, « *G* attaches *b* to *c* ». A correspondence may also attach a recognizer to itself. Thus, « $\vdash G{:}(b, b)$ » is written as shown in Figure 4.5.

Notice that the positioning of lines on the page has no significance, and that lines may be straight, bent, or curved, as needed. Denials are shown by shading the chevron. Unresolved alternation may be shown by attaching chevrons with dashed lines.

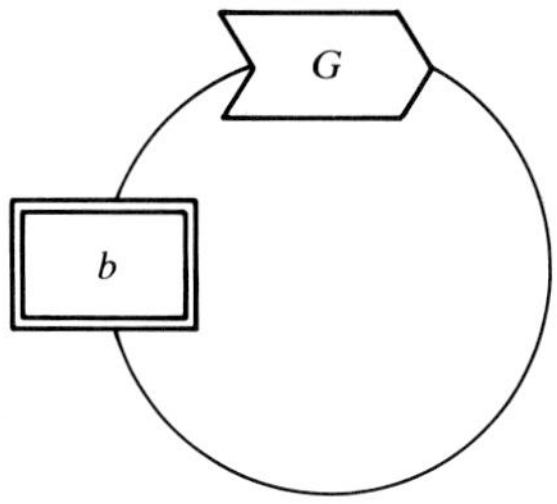

Figure 4.5 An attachment of an individual to itself.

Lines may be bunched together to save space. Thus, the proposition

$$\vdash (G{:}(b_1, c_1)\ \&\ G{:}(b_1, c_2)\ \&\ G{:}(b_2, c_1)\ \&\ G{:}(b_2, c_2))$$

may be shown in the abbreviated form shown in Figure 4.6. When lines are bunched in this fashion, the diagram is interpreted to read that *all* individuals attached to the left side of the chevron attach to *all* individuals attached to the right side of the chevron.

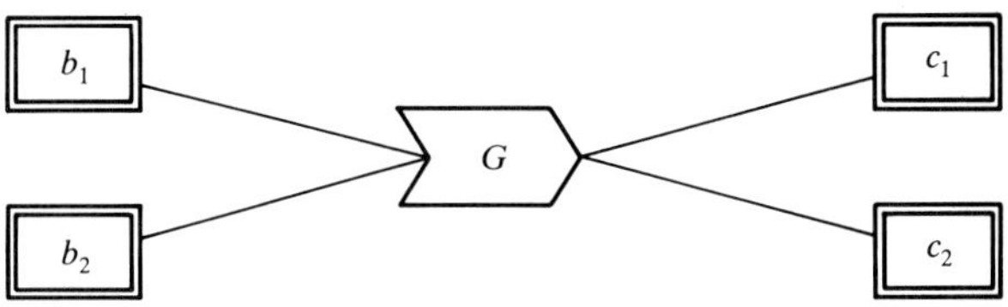

Figure 4.6 Abbreviated form for several attachments.

The class tags that an individual is an instance of may be written within the same double rectangle that shows its attachments. Thus, the following expression is shown in Figure 4.7:

$$\vdash (B{:}(b_1)\ \&\ B{:}(b_2)\ \&\ C{:}(c_1)\ \&\ C{:}(c_2)\ \&\ G{:}(b_1, c_1)\ \&\ G{:}(b_1, c_2)\ \&\ G{:}(b_2, c_2))$$

Notice how the fairly lengthy expression in data logic notation may be expressed concisely as a population diagram.

Dashed lines that express unresolved alternation may be bunched in a similar way. Thus, the affirmation

$$\vdash (G{:}(b_1, c_1) \vee G{:}(b_1, c_2))$$

may be drawn as shown in Figure 4.8.

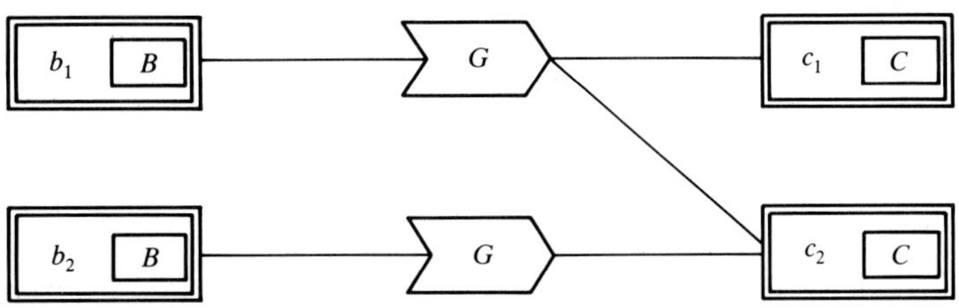

Figure 4.7

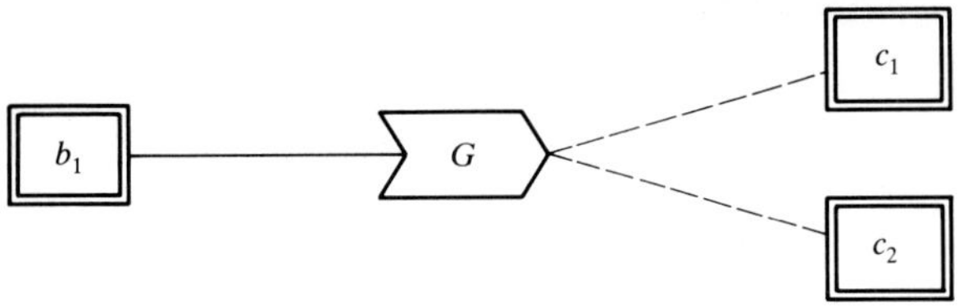

Figure 4.8 Abbreviated form for an unresolved alternation.

Trios

A trio is written in one of the two forms

$$T{:}(\ ,\ ,\ ) \text{ or } (\ )T{:}(\ )U(\ )$$

Of these two, the former is the easier one to manipulate in proofs and the latter is the easier one to illustrate. Usually, the latter form is to be preferred in all but theoretical work, because it can be constructed directly from linguistic expressions. For example, a common linguistic representation of a trio is a verb followed by a prepositional phrase, as in

(*Joe*) *Pays*: (*Harry*) *For* (*the meatloaf*)

Trios and higher order associations are drawn as hexagonal *tiles* rather than chevrons, and the tile may be broken up to show parts of the trio tag, as shown in Figure 4.9. The dovetailed edges of the shapes surrounding *Pays* and *For* indicate that they are constituents of the trio tag *Pays For* rather than correspondence tags in their own right. The small triangle serves as a connector whose one free corner establishes a position for a third symbol in the representation of an attachment, as shown in Figure 4.10.

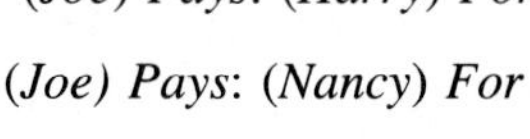

Figure 4.9 A trio tag.

The connector is necessary to identify triples properly. For example, the three expressions

(*Joe*) *Pays*: (*Harry*) *For* (*meatloaf*)

(*Joe*) *Pays*: (*Nancy*) *For* (*light bulbs*)

(*Ralph*) *Pays*: (*Harry*) *For* (*light bulbs*)

are shown in Figure 4.11.

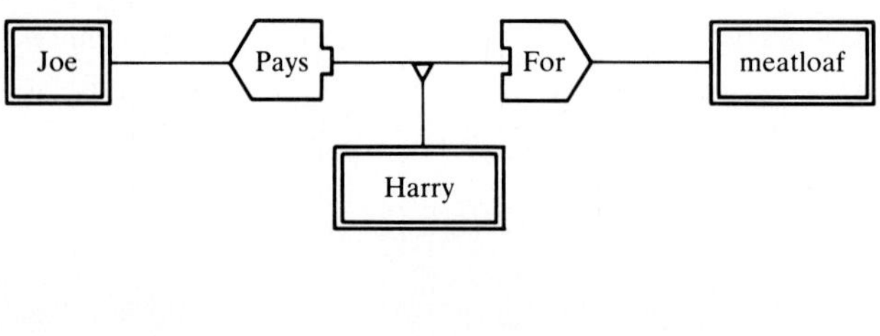

Figure 4.10 An assembly controlled by the trio *Pays For*.

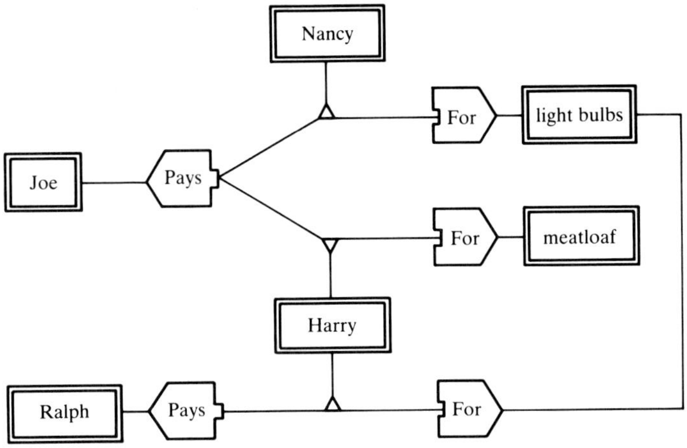

Figure 4.11

4.5 FORMS OF DATA BASE CONSTRAINTS

Design Techniques Should Be Limited

Data logic provides a far greater variety of data base constraints (that is, definitive propositions) than are used in data base designs today. Yet the ability of data logic to describe a constraint does not imply that the constraint would be useful in practical data bases. Data base designs must meet additional criteria beyond being logically sound. Most importantly, the effects of incorporating a candidate schema element must be clearly understood so that the designer, and the data base users, can properly weigh the alternatives of including, omitting, or modifying each proposed schema element.

We have isolated a particular form of constraint, called a *positive embracing*, that we feel we have analyzed sufficiently thoroughly that we can advocate its use in practical design situations. Other forms of constraints are possible, but we do not feel that they are well enough understood that they should be adopted in production environments. In this section, we define positive embracings, and we discuss briefly some other forms of constraints, and the difficulties they present.

Embracings Are Fundamental

We will develop the definition of a positive embracing gradually by examining common constraints, and generalizing from their form. We will say that a constraint is *admissible* if the constraint is a candidate for implementation in practical data base designs.

The most fundamental form of data base constraint is the embracing of associations $R \subseteq S$. This embracing may be written equivalently as

$$(\mathrm{A}x_1) \ldots (\mathrm{A}x_r)\ R{:}|x_1, \ldots, x_r| \Rightarrow S{:}|x_1, \ldots, x_r| \qquad (1)$$

We argue that constraints that are similar to Formula (1) should be allowed into schemas, but that constraints that are not similar should be prohibited until they are understood more thoroughly.

For example, all the quantifiers in Formula (1) are over images. We will allow only quantification over images in a schema element. Quantification over associations, impressions, or recognizers, is prohibited.

The quantifiers $(\mathrm{A}x_1) \ldots (\mathrm{A}x_r)$ form a *prefix* on the extreme left of Formula (1). All the quantifiers in the prefix of Formula (1) are universal. We will allow only universal quantifiers in the prefix of a schema constraint. Notice that R or S may still be defined using quantifiers: such quantifiers are not part of the prefix.

The remainder of Formula (1), following the prefix, is an implication. We will require that the portion of a constraint that follows the prefix consist entirely of a single implication. This rule prohibits, in particular, an alternation such as « it must be that C includes B or E includes D »: $!((B \subseteq C) \vee (D \subseteq E))$, which would be:

$$(\mathrm{A}x)\ (B{:}|x| \rightarrow C{:}|x|) \vee (D{:}|x| \rightarrow E{:}|x|)$$

Such an alternation is not allowed.

Based on the requirements we have introduced so far, then, an admissible schema constraint must be an entirely universally quantified implication. We turn next to determining what forms the implication can take.

Embracings of Classes

The number of universal quantifiers in the prefix is called the *degree* of Formula (1). The simplest expression would contain no quantifiers, be of degree zero, and so would be simply an implication of propositions "$p \Rightarrow q$". Allowing unquantified implications into the schema would open the entire field of definitive reasoning into data base design, which would be too broad an arena. We therefore require that the degree of a data base constraint be at least one.

An admissible constraint of degree one is an embracing of classes: $(\mathrm{A}x)\ B{:}|x| \Rightarrow C{:}|x|$, or equivalently, $B \subseteq C$. Intersection and union can be introduced by conjoining embracings:

$$(B \subseteq C)\ \&\ (B \subseteq D) \Leftrightarrow (B \subseteq C \cap D) \tag{2}$$

$$(B \subseteq D)\ \&\ (C \subseteq D) \Leftrightarrow (B \cup C \subseteq D) \tag{3}$$

Notice that data logic does allow an individual to be an instance of more than one class tag. For example, a person tag could be an instance of the class tags *Employee, U.S. Citizen*, and *PTA Member*. Populations that obey the embracings in Formulas (2) and (3) are illustrated in Figure 4.12.

A class such as $C \cap D$ is called a *derived class*, because it is formed from other classes (namely C and D) using a logical operation (in this case, intersection). An association of any degree formed by applying logical operations to declared associations is called a *combination*. The embracing $B \subseteq C \cap D$ may therefore be viewed as an embracing of the form of Formula (1), where S is the combination $C \cap D$. Our method for generalizing constraints will be to allow combinations of various kinds in the places of R and S.

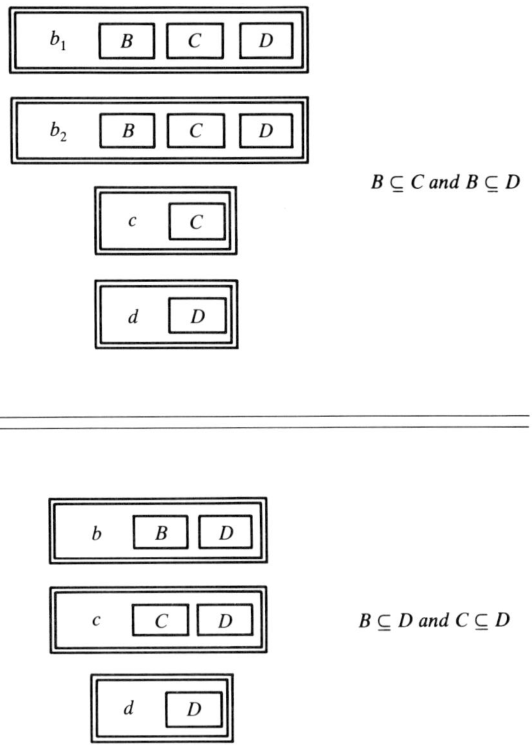

Figure 4.12 Sample populations constrained by embracings.

Conjunction of embracings always introduces intersection on the right side or union on the left side, as shown in Formulas (2) and (3). However, we will find that many important constraints arise in dual pairs: if the constraint $\mathcal{F} \subseteq \mathcal{G}$ is valuable, the *dual* constraint $\mathcal{G} \subseteq \mathcal{F}$ is usually seen to be valuable as well. We will therefore permit intersections to be introduced on the left side and unions to be introduced on the right side. That is, we will permit embracings of the form

$$\boxed{B_1 \cap \ldots \cap B_m \subseteq C_1 \cup \ldots \cup C_n} \tag{4}$$

More complex combinations of unions and intersections of classes are also allowed, but they can always be reduced to embracings of the form of Formula (4) by removing unions on the left side and removing intersections on the right side.

Embracings of the form $B_1 \cap \ldots \cap B_m \subseteq C$ are similar to "Horn clauses," which are discussed in advanced works on data design and artificial intelligence (Maier 1983, Genesereth and Nilsson 1987). Positive embracings go beyond Horn clauses by permitting unions on the right side. Implementation of constraints with unions on the right side may require an ability to manage unresolved alternations. For example, if we have the embracing $B \subseteq C \cup D$ and the affirmation $\vdash B{:}(b)$, then we can conclude $(\vdash (C \cup D){:}(b)) \Rightarrow \vdash (C{:}(b) \vee D{:}(b))$. That is, if $C \cup D$ embraces B, we can not determine without additional information whether an instance of B is an instance of C or of D, but we can conclude the unresolved alternation « b is an instance of C or b is an instance of D ». The unresolved alternation may be avoided by requiring a user to specify at the time a new instance b of B is added whether b is also an instance of C or an instance of D (or both). For an example of an embracing that uses unions on the right side, see Section 7.4.

Embracings of Correspondences

The general expression of degree two in the form of Formula (1) is written

$$(\text{A}x)\ (\text{A}y)\ G{:}|x,\ y| \Rightarrow H{:}|x,\ y| \tag{5}$$

This constraint is also written "$G \subseteq H$"; a sample population is illustrated in Figure 4.13. There, both G and H attach b_1 to c_1 and b_2 to c_2. H also attaches b_1 to c_2.

Most current data base management systems do not allow embracings of correspondences, such as Formula (5), but we argue that they follow naturally from data logic, and therefore should be permitted. The embracing $G \subseteq H$ can be implemented by controlling additions and deletions to G and H. The embracing $G \subseteq H$ does not restrict additions to H or deletions from G: such updates may be managed as if the embracing were not present. Upon receiving a request to add an attachment $G(b, c)$ to the population of G, the data base management system must also add the attachment $H(b, c)$ to the population of H. Similarly, upon receiving a request to delete the attachment $H(b, c)$ from the population of H, the data base management system must also delete the attachment $G(b, c)$ from the population of G.

We note the similarity of this method of implementing embracings to the controlled redundancy found in distributed data bases. Indeed, the statement that the file of corporate accounts at the Denver office must be maintained so that it has the same contents as the file of corporate accounts at the Atlanta office is a bi-directional embracing: *Account At Denver* $\equiv$ *Account At Atlanta*. Techniques developed to manage this sort of redundancy may be

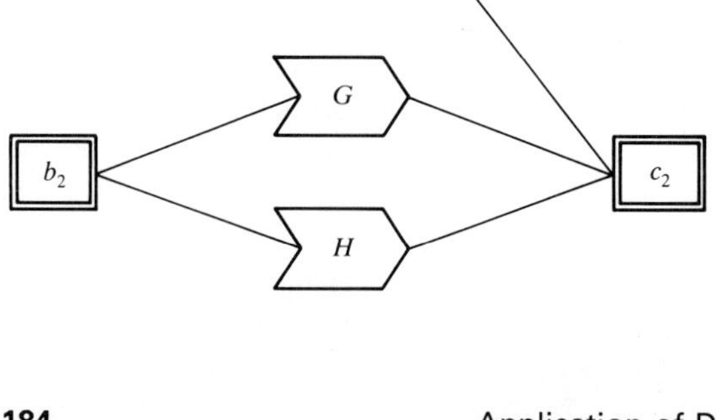

Figure 4.13 The embracing $G \subseteq H$.

helpful in implementing embracings. Conversely, embracings may be helpful in describing how complex data bases can be distributed.

Logic of Embracings of Correspondences

Correspondences (and associations of higher degree) exhibit permutations in the order of placetakers. Thus, the following is a different embracing from the embracing shown in Formula (5):

$$(\mathrm{A}x)\ (\mathrm{A}y)\ G{:}|x,\ y| \Rightarrow H{:}|y,\ x| \tag{6}$$

The different order of placetakers following "H" in Formula (6) is expressed by saying that the converse of H, H^*, embraces G (see Section 2.11). Thus, we may write Formula (6) as "$G \subseteq H^*$". The converse is shown in a population diagram by changing the chevrons to point in the opposite direction, as shown in Figure 4.14.

Correspondences may be intersected and united as classes may be. Thus, the analog of Formula (4) is

$$\boxed{G_1 \cap \ldots \cap G_m \subseteq H_1 \cup \ldots \cup H_n} \tag{7}$$

Or, as an implication,

$$(\mathrm{A}x)\ (\mathrm{A}y)\ G_1{:}|x,\ y|\ \&\ \ldots\ \&\ G_m{:}|x,\ y| \Rightarrow H_1{:}|x,\ y| \vee \ldots \vee H_n{:}|x,\ y|$$

It is understood that any of the correspondences may also appear as a converse, as in $G_1 \cap G_2^* \subseteq H_1^* \cup H_2$.

A simple embracing of the form of Formula (7), $F \cap G \subseteq H \cup J$, is illustrated in Figure 4.15. In that figure, since both F and G attach b_1 to c_2, either H or J (H is shown) attaches b_1 to c_2. Similarly, since both F and G attach b_2 to c_4, either H or J (J is shown) attaches b_2 to c_4. Notice that the union $H \cup J$ could also be unresolved: from $\vdash F{:}(d,\ e)$ and $\vdash G{:}(d,\ e)$ we could conclude only $\vdash (H \cup J){:}(d,\ e)$. It might then be that neither $H{:}(d,\ e)$ nor $J{:}(d,\ e)$ is affirmed.

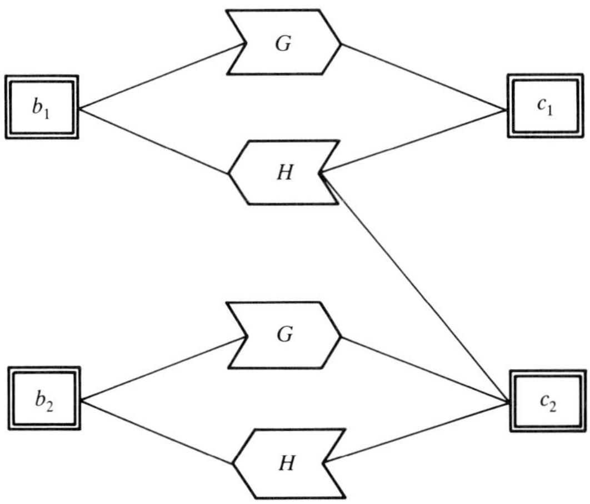

Figure 4.14 The embracing $G \subseteq H^*$.

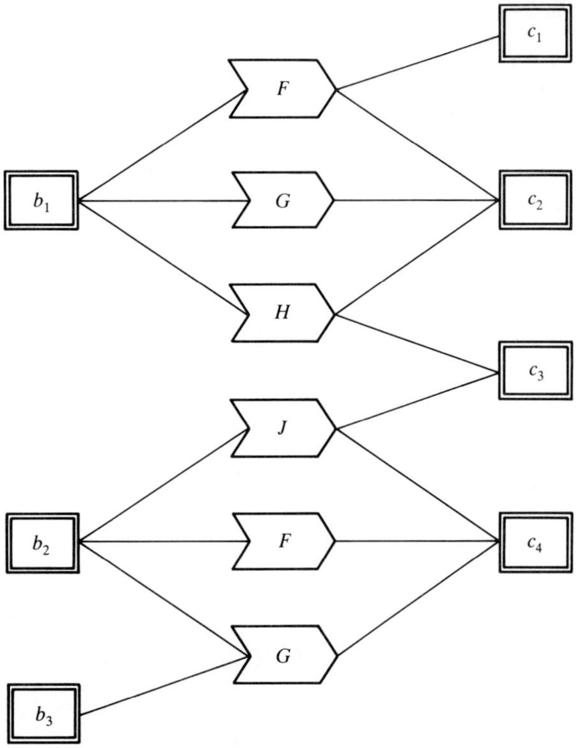

Figure 4.15 The embracing $F \cap G \subseteq H \cup J$.

Composition of Correspondences

The *composition* of two correspondences H and J is written "$H \circ J$", and is defined by

$$(\text{A}x)\ (\text{A}z)\ H \circ J{:}|x, z| \Leftrightarrow (\exists y)\ H{:}|x, y|\ \&\ J{:}|y, z| \tag{8}$$

That is, $H \circ J$ attaches x to z if there is some image y such that H attaches x to y and J attaches y to z. Composition is a very common operation in practical data base management.

A composition attaches two individuals if there is an *attachment path* between them consisting of two attachments to the same individual, as shown in Figure 4.16. There, $H \circ J$ attaches a_1 to both c_1 and c_2, but attaches a_2 only to c_2. $H \circ J$ does not attach a_3 to any individual even though H attaches a_3 to an individual b_3, because J does not attach any individual to b_3, so there is no attachment path from a_3 that involves both an attachment by H and an attachment by J.

Notice that composition uses *unresolved* existential quantification. This means that $H \circ J$ may attach two individuals even if there is no declared attachment path between them, when an attachment path can be deduced by exhaustion of a set of unresolved alternatives. For example, consider the population illustrated in Figure 4.17:

$$\vdash (H{:}(a_1, b_1)\ \&\ J{:}(b_1, c_1)) \vee (H{:}(a_1, b_2)\ \&\ J{:}(b_2, c_1))$$

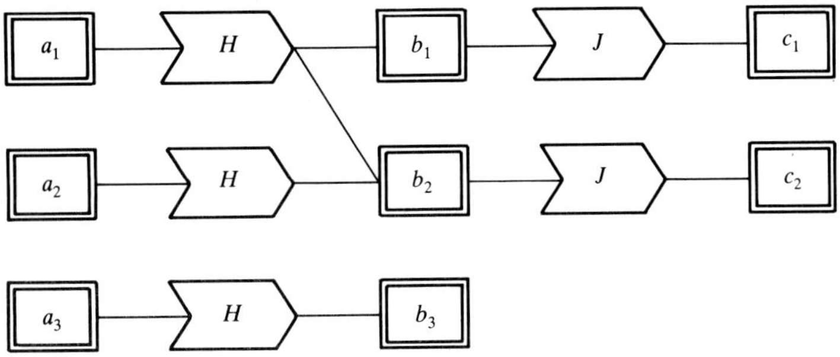

Figure 4.16

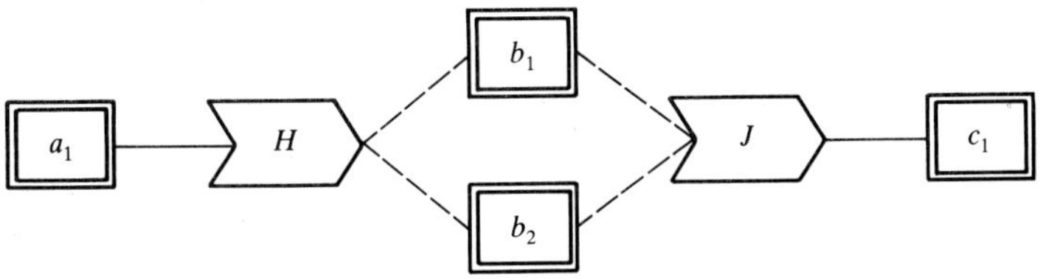

Figure 4.17 An attachment path incorporating unresolved alternation.

Since there is an attachment path either through b_1 or through b_2, $H \circ J$ does attach a_1 to c_1.

Existential Quantification Is Allowed

The expression that defines composition, Formula (8), includes an existential quantification over images: "$(\exists y)$". We will permit existential quantification over images on either side of an implication, but we do not allow the same quantified placetaker to appear on both sides of an implication. Thus, the following expression is permitted:

$$(\text{A}x)\ ((\exists y)\ H{:}|x,\ y|) \Rightarrow (\exists z)\ J{:}|z,\ x|$$

But the following expression is prohibited:

$$(\text{A}x)\ (\exists y)\ (H{:}|x,\ y| \Rightarrow J{:}|x,\ y|)$$

Allowing existential quantification permits compositions and projections to be incorporated into schema constraints. For example, the following expressions are all permitted:

$$(\text{A}x)\ B{:}|x| \Rightarrow (\exists y)\ G{:}|x,\ y| \qquad (B \subseteq \pi^1 G)$$

$$(\text{A}x)\ (\text{A}z)\ F{:}|x,\ z| \Rightarrow (\exists y)\ G{:}|x,\ y|\ \&\ H{:}|y,\ z| \qquad (F \subseteq G \circ H)$$

$$(\text{A}x)\ (\text{A}z)\ ((\exists y)\ G{:}|x,\ y|\ \&\ H{:}|y,\ z|) \Rightarrow F{:}|x,\ z| \qquad (G \circ H \subseteq F)$$

Each of these expressions has special properties which will be discussed in Part 3.

Associations Are Required to Be Constructive

Only constructive associations are declared in practical data base designs. Thus, one would not make a file of individuals that are "not a part" or "not a customer." This reasoning does not prohibit denials: the class « *Non-Customer* », the opposite of « *Customer* », is a constructive class whose instances have been determined not to be customers. We might exclude images such as pieces of cloth that are obviously not customers from being instances of « *Non-Customer* », and restrict « *Non-Customer* » to human beings or businesses who are not customers, for example. We may not exclude such images from the omissive class « *Not A Customer* », the complement of « *Customer* », because a complement is defined to accept every image that the class does not accept. There is therefore no benefit to including both a file *Customer* and the file *Not A Customer* in the same data base: the contents of *Not A Customer* must always be all the individuals that are not instances of *Customer*.

Given that all declared associations are constructive, all the combinations discussed so far in this section are also constructive. That is, any intersection, union, or projection of constructive associations is constructive. The entire variety of constraints that we have discussed in this section, therefore, employs only constructive associations.

Definition of a Positive Embracing

We may formalize this discussion as follows: We assume first that all declared associations are constructive. We define a *positive combination* to be any expression that may be formed using declared associations, conjunction, alternation, and existential quantification over images (in particular, negation can not be used in forming a positive combination). Each available position in a positive combination is occupied by a placetaker defined over images. For example, all the following are positive combinations:

$$B{:}|x| \;\&\; G{:}|x, y|$$

$$(\exists y)\; F{:}|x, y| \;\&\; T{:}|x, y, z|$$

$$G{:}|x, y| \vee (B{:}|w| \;\&\; (\exists z)\; Q{:}|w, x, y, z|)$$

A positive combination is an association whose degree equals the number of different placetakers that are not existentially quantified. A *positive embracing* is an embracing of a positive combination in another positive combination of the same degree.

We recommend that the admissible constraints be limited to positive embracings, and, conversely, that all positive embracings be admissible as schema constraints. Similarly, a relaxation should be admissible if and only if it is a negation of a positive embracing. The limitation of schema constraints to positive embracings will be called the *positive design restriction*.

Discussion of Negation

Constraints that involve negation are prohibited because the effects of including them can be both severe and unpredicted. Consider, for example, the embracing $C \subseteq \overline{C}$, for some class C. This embracing states that any instance of C must also not be an instance of C. It is difficult to imagine a practical situation where such a class would be useful.

We would therefore like to assure that no schema contains an embracing of the form $R \subseteq \overline{R}$, for any declared association R. Since embracings may be combined to form chains of deductions, we may form an arbitrarily long chain $R \subseteq S_1$, $S_1 \subseteq S_2$, . . . , $S_n \subseteq \overline{R}$ that will eventually lead to the embracing $R \subseteq \overline{R}$. A designer might have specified all but one of the embracings in this chain, and might easily not realize that by adding one more embracing he had made each assembly controlled by R contradictory.

We may make this example arbitrarily more complex, by making n arbitrarily large, or by converting the associations S_i to complex combinations whose interactions are arbitrarily difficult to follow. We feel that at the present state of knowledge it is best to prohibit such chains from developing by restricting the types of constraints permitted in a schema. Notice that this restriction is based on engineering concerns rather than on the fundamental nature of data. If better methods are devised for managing negation in the future, the restrictions may be relaxed.

One way to relax the restraint is to allow opposites to be included in embracings. That is, one could allow the embracing $B \subseteq {}^{\circ}C$, even though $B \subseteq \overline{C}$ is prohibited. Opposites could be incorporated without violating the positive design restriction because opposites are constructive. Allowing opposites presents some similar problems to allowing complements: the embracing $B \subseteq {}^{\circ}C$ implies the embracing $B \subseteq \overline{C}$, so one could still inadvertently cause a contradiction $B \subseteq \overline{B}$ using opposites. However, if an embracing $B \subseteq {}^{\circ}C$ causes an undesirable contradiction, one may repair the contradiction by narrowing the definition of ${}^{\circ}C$ so that it no longer embraces B. Since there may be images that are accepted neither by C nor by ${}^{\circ}C$, the definition of ${}^{\circ}C$ may be changed without changing the definition of C. This same method can not be applied to the embracing $B \subseteq \overline{C}$, because any narrowing of $\overline{C}$ requires a complementary expanding of C.

Exclusive Or

A common constraint excluded by the positive design restriction is the ''exclusive or,'' that is, a constraint of the form ''every A must be either a B or a C, not both.'' An ''exclusive or'' is actually two independent statements, the constraint ''every A must be either a B or a C'', that is, ''$A \subseteq B \cup C$'', and the constraint ''an A can not be both a B and a C'', that is, ''$A \subseteq \overline{B \cap C}$''. It is the latter constraint, the ''not both,'' that violates the positive design restriction.

The ''exclusive or'' constraint is often overused in contemporary data designs. Consider, for example, a case where every instance of a class B must be associated with exactly one status, either ''on'' or ''off''. It is far better to model this situation as a correspondence from B to a class *Status* that assigns each instance of B to one status than to declare an ''exclusive or'' constraint ''every B is either on or off'' in the schema. When a correspondence is used, it is a simple matter to add a new status ''out of service'' if the need arises. When an ''exclusive or'' is used, adding a new status requires a schema change.

In the presence of embracings, ''exclusive or'' constraints can also lead to unpredicted contradictions as illustrated above. The simplest such form is the combination of constraints ''every B is also a C'' and ''every A must be either a B or a C, not both.'' Here, a user who tried to add an individual d that is both an A and a B would meet with a contradiction: d would have to be a C because of the embracing, but the ''not both'' clause of the ''exclusive or'' constraint prohibits d from being both a B and a C.

''Exclusive or'' constraints can have unexpected consequences for deletions as well. For example, if every instance of A must be either a B, a C, or a D, and we delete the record that a given individual a_1 is a D, it is unresolved whether a_1 is subsequently a B, a C, or no longer an A. For further discussion of ''exclusive or'' constraints and their effects, see (Jones and Curtice 1988).

Conclusion

We have defined the admissible constraints to be positive embracings. A positive embracing is a logical formula of the form $\mathcal{F} \subseteq \mathcal{G}$, where $\mathcal{F}$ and $\mathcal{G}$ are formed using the operations &, $\vee$, and $(\exists x)$. Negation is excluded. We have argued that all forms of positive embracings should be allowed in data base designs. This is a major expansion of the variety of data structures available today.

4.6 DESIGN OF INDIVIDUALS

Stationing

In practical data bases, we want to be able to combine claims as freely as possible as a means to gaining new insights. In particular, we want to be able to conclude the conjunction $\vdash (p \,\&\, q)$ from the two claims $\vdash p$ and $\vdash q$. If the individuals or association tags in the data base are interpreted improperly, conjunctions of claims can be misleading.

For example, consider a device that measures the temperature of a vat. Let ''p'' represent the proposition « the temperature of vat 7 is 20°C » and let ''q'' represent the proposition « the temperature of vat 7 is 30°C ». Both propositions may be claimed at different times. If the claims were registered in the data base without recording the time each measurement was made, the data base would contain $\vdash p$ and $\vdash q$. It would be improper to conclude $\vdash (p \,\&\, q)$, that is, that the temperature of vat 7 was both 20°C and 30°C, because the two affirmations described different impressions.

This example is logically valid, but it is poor experimental procedure and poor data base design. It is better to include the time of measurement explicitly into each proposition: « the temperature of vat 7 at 9:00 was 20°C », and « the temperature of vat 7 at 10:00 was 30°C ». The two propositions may then be conjoined without contradiction.

The process of determining and declaring the parameters that render the interpretation of a proposition tag unambiguous will be called *stationing*. Stationing is part of data base design—the designer must declare that for a temperature reading to be unambiguous, a vat identifier and a time are required. Stationing is a sensitive process that can occupy much thought. For example, it may be that several readings are performed simultaneously on the same vat, perhaps at different depths in a vat that is being heated. It may then be necessary to identify the measuring device, the depth, or both, for the temperature reading to be useful.

Relative Unity

Combining simple propositions by conjunction can run afoul of the uncertainty principle of impressions, which states that any recognizer that accepts one impression must be capable of accepting many impressions. The conjunction « d is an instance of B and d is an instance of C », written "B:(d) & C:(d)", does not therefore imply that d is an instance of $B \cap C$, written "$B \cap C$:(d)", because B and C could accept different manifestations of d.

The uncertainty principle of impressions makes it impossible to resolve this difficulty by refining the recognizer d to accept fewer impressions: it will always be possible for B and C to accept different manifestations of d, however much we refine d. The same difficulty applies to more complex expressions that involve d. In particular, given $\vdash G$:(d, e) and $\vdash G$:(d, f), we can not conclude that the same manifestation of d attaches to both a manifestation of e and a manifestation of f.

Although we can not restrict d so that it accepts only one impression, we can insist that all manifestations of d be the same according to some identity correspondence. That is, for any individual d and declared association tag B, we require that

$$(\mathrm{A}\iota)\ (\mathrm{A}\kappa)\ B{:}|d.\iota|\ \&\ B{:}|d.\kappa| \Rightarrow \Delta B{:}|d.\iota,\ d.\kappa|$$

This rule will be called the *relative unity principle*. It states that any two manifestations of d that are both accepted by a class B must be the same instance of B. The relative unity principle establishes a requirement that the definitions of recognizers and associations be coordinated.

For example, let "Joe" represent some person « Joe », and consider the conjunction:

$$\vdash \textit{Employee}{:}\ (\textit{Joe})\ \&\ \textit{Basketball Player}{:}\ (\textit{Joe})\ \&\ \textit{Landowner}{:}\ (\textit{Joe}) \qquad (1)$$

We can not conclude from this affirmation that there is a manifestation of « Joe » that is at once an employee, a landowner, and a basketball player. For example, Joe might have played basketball in school, stopped playing when he went to work, and bought some land after leaving the company. The conjunction in Formula (1) describes this situation accurately, just as it describes Joe buying a house, working, and playing on the company basketball team, all at once. The data base does not distinguish between these possibilities.

Whatever happens, however, the tag "Joe" always represents the same *person*. Thus, we may conclude correctly that the same *person* has been an *employee*, a *basketball player*, and a *landowner*. Although we have distinguished the manifestations of « Joe » by time in this example, other images could be distinguished by space, as with the vat whose temperature varies by depth.

As a further example, suppose that a bank performs various services for its customers for which it charges a fixed rate: m dollars for a bad check, n dollars for a duplicate statement, and so on. Imagine that each of these services is assigned a tag: "b" for bad check, "d" for duplicate statement, and so on. Each of these tags is an instance of the class *Service*. Now suppose that the correspondence « *Same Service As* » is defined so that two *services* are only the same if they have the same price. So far, there is no difficulty, because all the *services* have a fixed price.

Now consider a service with a variable price: a new set of checkbooks might have one price for ordinary checks, and a higher price for deluxe checks. Suppose that the service of providing a new set of checkbooks is represented by one tag "c", regardless of which variety of checkbook is ordered. Here, two different *services* are represented by the same tag "c", so "c" violates the relative unity principle.

This difficulty can be remedied by assigning two different tags: "c_1" for ordinary checks, and "c_2" for deluxe checks. Services with more complex pricing, such as a currency exchange fee of 1 percent up to $1000, 0.5 percent up to $10,000, with adjustments for higher dollar amounts based on such parameters as settlement time, could not be managed well by the design discussed. Even though this offering is a service, the idea of "same price" is not sufficiently precise to determine when two customers have received the same service. This example illustrates how one must carefully consider the definition of a class B, the way the instances of B are to be represented, and the definition of the identity correspondence *Same B As* interdependently in data design.

Conclusion

For data bases to function properly, individuals must be assigned to recognizers in a fashion that is coordinated with the definitions of the declared association tags. One such need is described by *stationing*, which requires that a claim not be interpreted so broadly as to represent two propositions that can not be conjoined. Another is *relative unity*, which requires that an individual not be interpreted so broadly that it represents two instances of a declared class.

4.7 CHARACTERS

Certain embracings are so commonplace in data base design that we will single them out for special attention. These are the characteristics of correspondences we call *from one*, *to one*, *from all*, and *to all*. In this section, we give rigorous definitions of these constraints in terms of data logic, which allows them to be applied to all populations, including those that use unresolved alternation or unresolved existential quantification. Character constraints have been formulated in symbolic logic by (Fagin 1982) and (Grant and Jacobs 1982).

Basic Characteristics of *to one*

A correspondence G is said to be *to one* relative to the pair of classes (B, C) if for any image x accepted by B, and any two images y_1 and y_2 both accepted by C, if $G{:}|x, y_1|$ and $G{:}|x, y_2|$, then y_1 and y_2 must be the same C. A statement that a correspondence is *to one* is similar to a "functional dependency" in the relational data model. A typical population of a *to one* correspondence is shown in Figure 4.18.

Reduced Correspondences

The relative nature of a constraint such as *to one* may be represented by a *reduced correspondence*. The correspondence G reduced to the pair of classes (B, C) is defined to attach x to y whenever

$$(\exists x')\ (\exists y')\ \Delta B{:}|x, x'|\ \&\ G{:}|x', y'|\ \&\ \Delta C{:}|y, y'|$$

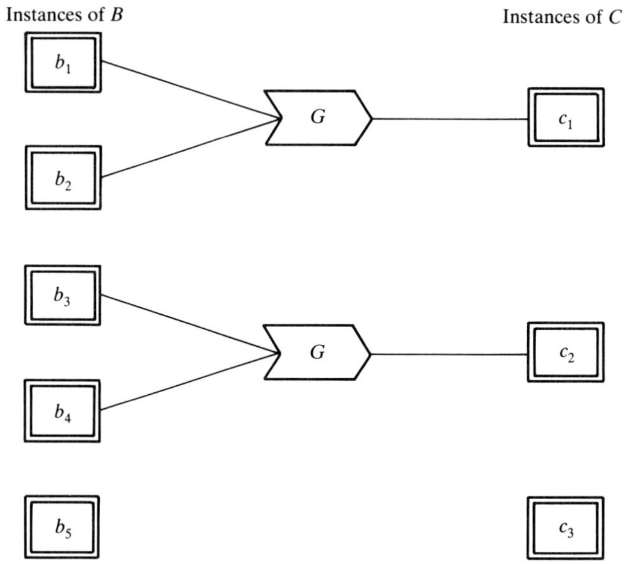

Figure 4.18 A *to one* correspondence.

When B and C are understood, this correspondence is written $\dot{G}$. Thus, $\dot{G}$ attaches x to y if and only if there is some x' that is the same B as x, some y' that is the same C as y, and G attaches x' to y'. See Section 1.9 for further discussion of the identity correspondences ΔB, « *Same B As* », and ΔC, « *Same C As* ».

The combination of a correspondence G with two classes B and C is called a *correspondence complex*, and is written $(G; B, C)$. The class B is called the *source* of the correspondence complex, and the class C is called the *destination*. We will often refer to the classes B and C as a "pair" (B, C) to indicate that G is relative to B in its first position, and to C in its second position. Actually, a correspondence complex is not a pair but an assembly of plans (see Section 3.3). Notice that the reduced correspondence $\dot{G}$ is equivalent to the composition

$$\boxed{\dot{G} \equiv \Delta B \circ G \circ \Delta C}$$

A Correspondence May Be Declared Relative to Several Pairs of Classes

It has been common in practice for every correspondence to be declared relative to only one pair of classes. Indeed, it is common for a correspondence to be embraced in a Cartesian product of classes:

$$(\mathrm{A}x)\ (\mathrm{A}y)\ G{:}|x,\ y| \Rightarrow B{:}|x|\ \&\ C{:}|y|$$

That is,

$$G \subseteq B \times C$$

This restriction has hampered the extension of data base principles to new areas such as artificial intelligence, and we recommend that it be abolished. Consider, for example, the correspondence *Consumes* that organizes living creatures into food chains. We have then:

foxes consume rabbits
rabbits consume grass
grass consumes carbon dioxide

Imagine that we have a class of foxes, of rabbits, and of blades of grass whose habits we are studying. Most data models would recommend that we form a class *Consumers* that would include foxes, rabbits, and grass, and a class of *Consumed Things* that would include rabbits, grass, and carbon dioxide. They would then recommend embracing the correspondence tag *Consumes* in the Cartesian product (*Consumers*) × (*Consumed Things*). But this is an artificial construction that does not advance our understanding beyond what we could gather from the correspondence *Consumes*. Furthermore, it obscures the interdependencies that cause the formation of a food chain: foxes do not consume carbon dioxide, for example, but if we view *Consumes* solely as relating *Consumer* to *Consumed Thing*, we can not declare this constraint.

The proper method for managing this correspondence is to permit any two individuals to attach by *Consumes* and then to restrict their behavior based on the class tags that the individuals are instances of. For example, if we do not consider the action of certain microorganisms, then anything that grass consumes is inanimate (water, carbon dioxide, trace elements, etc.) We may write this constraint as

$$(\mathrm{A}y)\ (\exists x)\ \mathit{Grass}{:}|x|\ \&\ |x|\mathit{Consumes}{:}|y| \Rightarrow \mathit{Inanimate}{:}|y|$$

or equivalently in embracing form, as

$$\pi^2(\Delta \mathit{Grass} \circ \mathit{Consumes}) \subseteq \mathit{Inanimate}$$

This is a constraint upon the correspondence *Consumes* relative to the class *Grass*. It does not affect attachments controlled by *Consumes* of individuals that are not instances of *Grass*.

Logical Formulation of *to one*

The *to one* constraint may be expressed as the implication

$$(\mathrm{A}x)\ (\mathrm{A}y)\ (\mathrm{A}z)\ \dot{G}{:}|x, y|\ \&\ \dot{G}{:}|x, z| \Rightarrow \Delta C{:}|y, z| \qquad (1)$$

where $\dot{G}$ is the correspondence G reduced to the pair of classes (B, C). This is equivalent to the implication

$$(\mathrm{A}y)\ (\mathrm{A}z)\ ((\exists x)\ \dot{G}^*{:}|y, x|\ \&\ \dot{G}{:}|x, z|) \Rightarrow \Delta C{:}|y, z|$$

Using composition, the *to one* constraint may therefore be written

$$\boxed{\dot{G}^* \circ \dot{G} \subseteq \Delta C}$$

This is a particularly convenient way of expressing the *to one* constraint as an embracing. The correspondence $\dot{G}^* \circ \dot{G}$, a composition of a correspondence with its converse, is called a *retroactive correspondence*. The retroactive correspondence $\dot{G}^* \circ \dot{G}$ attaches two recognizers if they each attach to the same recognizer (perhaps along with others) by $\dot{G}^*$.

This definition of *to one* goes beyond the functional dependency of the relational data model in several ways. It makes explicit the relationship between the *to one* constraint and the associations the constraint is relative to. Thus, it would be ambiguous to say that B determines C without referring to G, should there be several correspondences that attach instances of B to instances of C. For example, an internal auditor might be employed by only one department, but might review material from several departments. Here there are two correspondences, *Is Employed By* and *Reviews Material From*. The correspondence *Is Employed By* relative to *Internal Auditor* and *Department* is *to one*, while the correspondence *Reviews Material From* relative to the same two classes *Internal Auditor* and *Department* is not *to one*.

Formula (1) shows further that the correspondence G may be *to one* relative to one pair of classes but not *to one* relative to another. For example, imagine that the correspondence *Works For* applies to independent contractors as well as to employees. We might require that an *employee* must *work for* exactly one *department*, but an independent contractor might *work for* several *departments*. Figure 4.19 shows a correspondence G that is *to one* relative to the pair of classes (B, C) but not to the pair of classes (B, D).

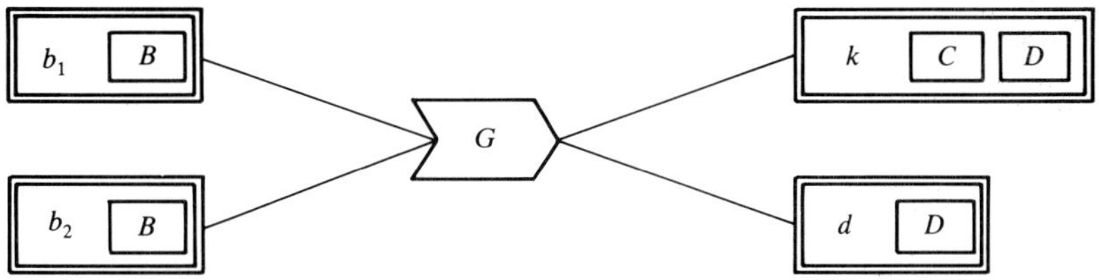

Figure 4.19 The correspondence G is *to one* relative to (B, C) but is not *to one* relative to (B, D).

We also depart from common practice by allowing a *to one* correspondence tag to attach an individual to more than one individual, as long as the target individuals are identical according to the identity correspondence tag of the destination class tag. For example, we might identify people both by Social Security number and by driver's license number. Suppose that Ronald Luria is identified both by Social Security number m and by driver's license number n. Then, so long as we have affirmed that m and n represent the same *person*, $\vdash \Delta Person: (m, n)$, a correspondence G that is *to one* to *Person* may attach an individual to both m and n: $\vdash G{:}(b, m)\ \&\ G{:}(b, n)$.

A Correspondence Complex That Is Not *to one* Is *to many*

A correspondence complex that is not *to one* is said to be *to many*. The statement that a correspondence complex $(G; B, C)$ is *to many* is a relaxation. Specifically, it is the proposition

$$;(\exists x)\ (\exists y)\ (\exists z)\ \tilde{}(\dot{G}{:}|x, y|\ \&\ \dot{G}{:}|x, z| \rightarrow \Delta C{:}|y, z|)$$

In sheath-free situations, this proposition may be written more simply as

$$;(\exists x)\ (\exists y)\ (\exists z)\ \dot{G}{:}|x,\ y|\ \&\ \dot{G}{:}|x,\ z|\ \&\ {}^{\sim}\Delta C{:}|y,\ z|$$

That is, « it is possible for G to attach some x to some two images y and z that are not the same C ».

A correspondence complex *appears to many* if the existence of some such images x, y, and z are affirmed in the population. That is, $(G;\ B,\ C)$ appears *to many* if

$$\vdash (\exists x)\ (\exists y)\ \dot{G}{:}(x,\ y)\ \&\ \dot{G}{:}(x,\ z)\ \&\ {}^{\sim}\Delta C{:}(y,\ z)$$

The phenomenon of appearing *to many* furnishes an example of the application of the relative unity principle discussed in the last section. Suppose that the individual "d" represented two images $d.\iota$ and $d.\kappa$ that were not the same B. Then G could attach $d.\iota$ to some image $e.\lambda$ and $d.\kappa$ to some image $f.\mu$, even if G attached any given image to only one image. This would appear in the data base as $\vdash G{:}(d,\ e)\ \&\ G{:}(d,\ f)$. Thus, without the relative unity principle, G could appear *to many* yet be *to one*.

With the relative unity principle, any correspondence complex that appears *to many* is *to many*. This is shown as follows. Suppose that

$$\vdash G{:}(b,\ c_1)\ \&\ G{:}(b,\ c_2)\ \&\ B{:}(b)$$

Converting to images, we have

$$\vdash (\exists \iota)\ (\exists \kappa)\ G{:}|b.\iota,\ c_1.\kappa|\ \&\ (\exists \lambda)\ (\exists \mu)\ G{:}|b.\lambda,\ c_2.\mu|$$

Since b is an instance of B, $b.\iota$ and $b.\lambda$ are the same B by the relative unity principle. That is,

$$\vdash \Delta B{:}|b.\iota,\ b.\lambda|$$

Therefore $b.\iota$ attaches to $c_2.\mu$ by the correspondence $\Delta B \circ G$. Since it is this correspondence that is used in defining the *reduced* correspondence $\dot{G}$, $b.\iota$ attaches to both $c_1.\kappa$ and $c_2.\mu$ by $\dot{G}$. Thus, any correspondence complex that appears *to many* is *to many*.

Effect of the *to one* Constraint on Populations

By formulating the *to one* constraint as a definitive proposition of data logic, the constraint applies to any population, however the population may change. A population is said to *appear to one*, in contrast, if each individual in *some chosen* set of populations attaches *to one*. That is, G *appears to one* relative to $(B,\ C)$ if

$$\vdash (\forall x)\ (\forall y)\ (\forall z)\ \dot{G}{:}(x,\ y)\ \&\ \dot{G}{:}(x,\ z) \rightarrow \Delta C{:}(y,\ z)$$

A population may appear *to one* yet not be *to one*. A correspondence tag with no population, for example, appears *to one* because every instance of B attaches to no instance of C by G, hence it attaches to at most one instance of C by G. A correspondence tag is only *to one*, however, if it is declared to be *to one* in the schema.

The formulation of *to one* in data logic also permits analysis of the effect of a *to one* constraint on unresolved alternations and unresolved existential quantifications. Consider, for example, the affirmation

$$\vdash (\dot{G}{:}(b,\ c_1) \vee \dot{G}{:}(b,\ c_2))$$

That is, « b » attaches to « c_1 » or to « c_2 », but it is not stated which. This claim is permitted when G is *to one* relative to (B, C). The effect of *to one* is to require that b not attach to both c_1 and c_2 (presuming that they are different instances of C), but it is still possible for it to be unknown whether « b » attaches to « c_1 » or to « c_2 ».

For example, suppose it has been determined that John of York, a historical figure, was born on March 12, 1168 or March 13, 1168, though the exact date is unknown. The unresolved "or" combines the two candidate birthdates into what might seem to be a list of dates. Nevertheless, John of York bears a *to one* relationship to his birthdate just like everybody else.

Similarly, consider the affirmation

$$\vdash ((\exists x)\ \dot{G}{:}|b,\ x|) \qquad (2)$$

That is, there is some unspecified image « x » that b attaches to. The effect of *to one* is to require that there be exactly one such « x » (one instance of « C »), but the image « x » need not be known. Therefore, Formula (2) is permitted by a *to one* correspondence complex.

The Converse of a *to one* Correspondence Complex Is *from one*

A correspondence G is said to be *from one* relative to (B, C) if its converse G^* is *to one* relative to (C, B). A typical population of a *from one* correspondence complex is shown in Figure 4.20.

A correspondence complex that is denied to be *from one* is said to be *from many*. The decisions of whether a correspondence is *to one* or *to many*, *from one* or *from many*, are called *single/multiple* decisions: the two decisions *from one* and *to one* are called *single*, while the two decisions *from many* and *to many* are called *multiple*. These descriptions are often combined—a correspondence complex that is *from one* and *to many* is said to be

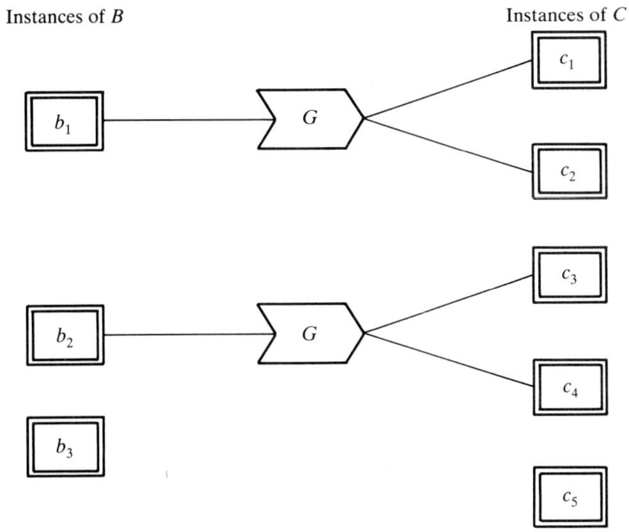

Figure 4.20 A *from one* correspondence complex.

one-to-many, a correspondence complex that is *from one* and *to one* is said to be *one-to-one*, and so on.

A correspondence complex behaves as if it were *many-to-many* unless it is constrained to be *to one* or *from one* by embracings. However, a correspondence complex $(G; B, C)$ is not precisely *to many* unless it is explicitly denied that $(G; B, C)$ is *to one*. That is, $(G; B, C)$ is not *to many* unless the relaxation « G is *to many* relative to (B, C) » may be derived from the occupiers of the binding site *Schema*, or from the appearance of the data base population. If the designer has not declared that $(G; B, C)$ is *to one*, and has not declared that $(G; B, C)$ is *to many*, then the question of whether $(G; B, C)$ is *to one* or *to many* is said to be *undetermined*.

From all

Another common constraint is the statement that any image accepted by a class B attaches to some image accepted by a class C by a correspondence G. A correspondence G that satisfies this constraint is said to be *from all* relative to (B, C). A typical population of a *from all* correspondence complex is shown in Figure 4.21.

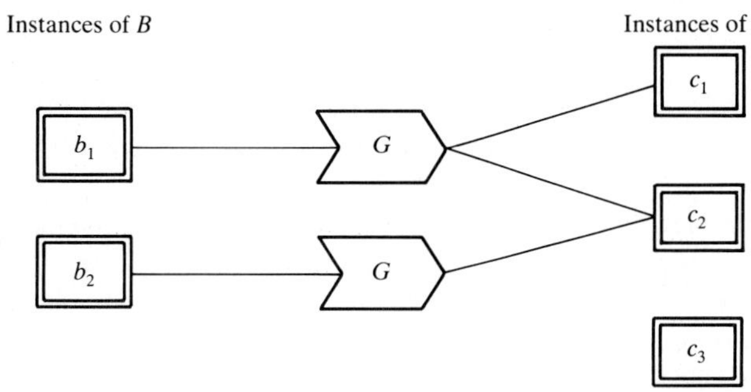

Figure 4.21 A *from all* correspondence complex.

The *from all* constraint is written in data logic as

$$(\mathrm{A}x)\ B{:}|x| \Rightarrow (\exists y)\ (\exists x')\ \Delta B{:}|x, x'|\ \&\ G{:}|x', y|\ \&\ C{:}|y|$$

This expression may be simplified using the reduced correspondence $\dot{G}$:

$$(\mathrm{A}x)\ B{:}|x| \Rightarrow (\exists y)\ \dot{G}{:}|x, y|$$

and may be simplified further using embracing notation:

$$\boxed{B \subseteq \pi^1 \dot{G}}$$

The class $\pi^1\dot{G}$ is called the *scope* of the correspondence $\dot{G}$. It represents the class of images that attach to some image by $\dot{G}$. A scope is often represented in English by adding the suffix "-er" to a verb. For example, the scope of the correspondence *Purchases* is the class *Purchaser*.

The scope of the converse $\dot{G}^*$, or $\pi^2\dot{G}$, is called the *counterscope* of the correspondence $\dot{G}$. It represents the class of images that are attached to by some image by $\dot{G}$. Thus, the counterscope of the correspondence *Purchases* is the class *Something That Is Pur-*

chased. Any correspondence is embraced trivially in the Cartesian product of its scope with its counterscope:

$$F \subseteq \pi^1 F \times \pi^2 F$$

The unresolved alternation

$$\vdash (G{:}(b, c_1) \vee G{:}(b, c_2)) \tag{3}$$

is permitted in a *from all* correspondence complex, since Formula (3) states that « b » attaches to at least one of « c_1 » or « c_2 », and therefore « b » attaches to some instance of C. Similarly, the following affirmation is permitted:

$$\vdash ((\exists y)\ G{:}(b, y)\ \&\ C{:}(y))$$

Thus, an individual such as b may participate in a *from all* correspondence complex without any claim that there is an individual that b attaches to.

To all

A correspondence G is said to be *to all* relative to a pair of classes (B, C) if G^* is *from all* relative to (C, B). A *to all* correspondence complex is said in mathematics to be "surjective" or "onto." A typical population of a *to all* correspondence complex is illustrated in Figure 4.22.

A correspondence complex that is denied to be *from all* is said to be *from some*, and a correspondence complex that is denied to be *to all* is said to be *to some*. A correspondence complex that is *from some* may exhibit instances of the source class that attach to no instances of the destination class. For example, if the correspondence G is *from some* relative to (B, C), then there may be an instance b of B such that G attaches no instance of C to b. Such an instance b is called an *orphan* of the correspondence complex $(G; B, C)$. For example, b_3 is an orphan in Figure 4.22.

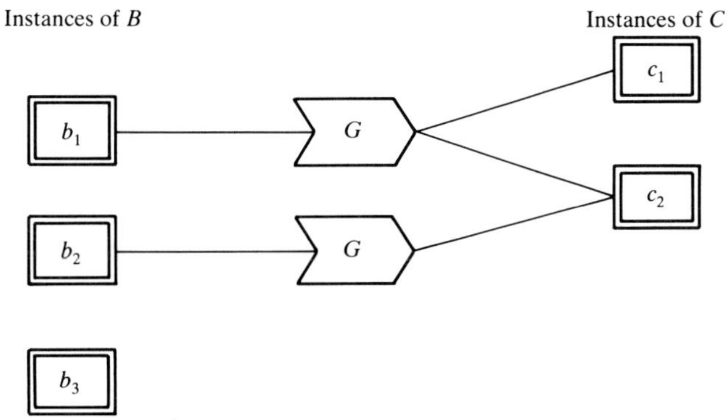

Figure 4.22 A *to all* correspondence complex.

The descriptions of *from all/from some* and *to all/to some* are often combined. For example, a correspondence complex that is *from all* and *to some* is said to be *all-to-some*. The two decisions *from all* and *to all* will be called *mandatory*, while the two decisions *from some* and *to some* will be called *optional*.

Characters

The decisions about whether a correspondence complex is *from all* or *from some*, *to one* or *to many*, *from one* or *from many*, and *to all* or *to some*, are basic to data base design. We call each of these decisions a *character decision*. The outcome of a character decision is a *choice* of whether or not to *restrict* a correspondence. Thus, the choices that incorporate the words *all* or *one* involve adding an embracing to the schema and are therefore restrictive. On the other hand, the choices that incorporate the words *some* or *many* involve adding a denial of an embracing and are called *permissive*.

The four character decisions are grouped together into an analytical device called the *character* of a correspondence complex. It is broken into the *optionality* of the correspondence complex, which incorporates the decisions of *all* versus *some*, and the *multiplicity* of the correspondence complex, which incorporates the decisions of *one* versus *many*.

We adopt a special notation for characters, as follows. The character of G relative to (B, C) is written

$$\text{chr}\ (G;\ B,\ C)$$

When all the character decisions are undetermined, we write

$$\text{chr}\ (G;\ B,\ C) = \text{“}\mathring{]}\mathring{<}\mathring{>}\mathring{[}\text{”}$$

A character is always written enclosed in quotation marks. The raised circles indicate that the decisions are undetermined. Each of the four symbols inside the quotation marks is called a *bracket*. Each bracket stands for the permissive choice of a character decision, as follows:

$]$ stands for *from some*
$<$ stands for *to many*
$>$ stands for *from many*
$[$ stands for *to some*

The direction of the angle brackets $<$ and $>$ is meant to reflect the fanning out of lines of attachment in population diagrams. Thus, if G is *one-to-many*, and attachments are read left to right as in $(b)G{:}(c)$, each instance of the scope of G (on the left) will be seen to be associated with many instances of the counterscope of G (on the right), so the symbol for *to many* is $<$.

The direction of the square brackets $]$ and $[$ is inspired by the direction of the angle brackets, noting that in a *one-to-many all-to-all* correspondence complex, there may be more instances of the class that the symbol $<$ opens towards (the right side, hence the destination class) than there are of the class that it closes upon (the left side, the source class). Similarly, in a *one-to-one all-to-some* correspondence, there may be more instances of the destination class than there are of the source class. Therefore the bracket for *to some*, $[$, opens to the right, towards the destination class.

A *character tag*, which we will usually refer to as simply a *character*, is a string of brackets. When a permissive character choice is made, the corresponding bracket is included as part of the character, and when a restrictive character choice is made, the corresponding bracket is omitted. For example, the following expression:

$$\text{chr}\ (G;\ B,\ C) = \text{“}]>\text{”}$$

is equivalent to the expression

$$G \text{ is } \textit{many-to-one some-to-all} \text{ relative to } (B, C)$$

With one exception to be discussed in Section 6.6, the order of brackets: **]** then < then > then **[** is always followed in writing characters. This order will be called *standard order*. The reason for ordering brackets in this way is based on considerations of the composition of correspondences, and will be discussed in Section 6.5. A *one-to-one all-to-all* correspondence complex has no brackets in its character, so its character is written as the empty set $\varnothing$.

This notation for characters vastly simplifies lexical expression of the schema and can be a valuable aid in proofs. For example, the one expression

$$\text{chr}\ (G;\ B,\ C) = \text{``<>''}$$

is equivalent to the logical expression

$$(\mathrm{A}x)\ B{:}|x| \Rightarrow (\exists y)\ (\exists x')\ \Delta B{:}|x, x'|\ \&\ G{:}|x', y|\ \&\ C{:}|y|$$

$$\&\quad {}^{\sim}(\mathrm{A}x)\ (\mathrm{A}x')\ (\mathrm{A}x'')\ (\mathrm{A}y)\ (\mathrm{A}y')\ (\mathrm{A}z)\ (\mathrm{A}z')\ \Delta B{:}|x, x'|\ \&\ \Delta B{:}|x, x''|\ \&\ G{:}|x', y|\ \&\ G{:}|x'', z|\ \&\ \Delta C{:}|y, y'|\ \&\ \Delta C{:}|z, z'| \Rightarrow \Delta C{:}|y, z|$$

$$\&\quad {}^{\sim}(\mathrm{A}x)\ (\mathrm{A}x')\ (\mathrm{A}x'')\ (\mathrm{A}y)\ (\mathrm{A}y')\ (\mathrm{A}z)\ (\mathrm{A}z')\ \Delta C{:}|x, x'|\ \&\ \Delta C{:}|x, x''|\ \&\ G{:}|y, x'|\ \&\ G{:}|z, x''|\ \&\ \Delta B{:}|y, y'|\ \&\ \Delta B{:}|z, z'| \Rightarrow \Delta B{:}|y, z|$$

$$\&\quad (\mathrm{A}x)\ C{:}|x| \Rightarrow (\exists y)\ (\exists x')\ \Delta C{:}|x, x'|\ \&\ G{:}|y, x'|\ \&\ B{:}|y|$$

Character Decisions Exhibit Duality

The *to one* constraint, we recall, is defined by the embracing

$$\dot{G}^* \circ \dot{G} \subseteq \Delta C$$

Conversely, the *from one* constraint may be written as

$$\dot{G} \circ \dot{G}^* \subseteq \Delta B \tag{4}$$

The *from all* constraint, we recall, is defined by the implication

$$(\mathrm{A}x)\ B{:}|x| \Rightarrow (\exists y)\ \dot{G}{:}|x, y|$$

This is equivalent to the implication

$$(\mathrm{A}x)\ (\mathrm{A}z)\ \Delta B{:}|x, z| \Rightarrow (\exists y)\ \dot{G}{:}|x, y|\ \&\ \dot{G}^*{:}|y, z|$$

Or, using composition,

$$\boxed{\Delta B \subseteq \dot{G} \circ \dot{G}^*}$$

This expression for the *from all* constraint differs from the expression for the *from one* constraint [Formula (4)] only in the direction of the embracing symbol. Because we may convert between *from all* and *from one* by reversing the direction of embracing, we say that *from all* and *from one* are *dual* constraints. We will often find that a characteristic of *from all* correspondence complexes has a dual characteristic that is obeyed by *from one* correspondence complexes.

Similarly, the *to all* constraint

$$\Delta C \subseteq \dot{G}^* \circ \dot{G}$$

is dual to the *to one* constraint

$$\dot{G}^* \circ \dot{G} \subseteq \Delta C$$

The four character constraints are therefore intimately interrelated: the ''*from*'' constraints to the ''*to*'' constraints by converse, and the ''*one*'' constraints to the ''*all*'' constraints by duality. The close interrelationships of the character constraints, and the simplicity of their expressions as embracings, help to explain why these constraints are so common in practical data base designs.

Conclusion

We have shown how the basic constraints of *from all*, *to one*, *from one*, and *to all* may be expressed as positive embracings. These constraints are combined into a *character*, which has a special lexical expression as a sequence of *brackets*. Each bracket represents a relaxation that is a negation of a character constraint: **]** represents *from some*, < represents *to many*, > represents *from many*, and **[** represents *to some*.

4.8 CONSTRAINTS OF HIGHER DEGREE ASSOCIATIONS

Trios Are Declared Relative to Both Classes and Correspondences

While a correspondence is declared relative to a pair of classes, an association of degree three, a *trio*, may be declared not only relative to classes, but relative to correspondences as well.

For example, consider the trio (*x*) *Pays* (*y*) *For* (*z*). We may make this trio more specific by focusing attention on the case when *x* is a *Customer, y* is a *Vendor*, and *z* is a *Product*. We do not require in general that anyone who *pays* someone *for* something need be a *customer*, nor that anyone who *is paid for* something need be a *vendor*. Just as a correspondence may be declared relative to many different pairs of classes, so also a trio may be declared relative to many triples of classes. Thus, people who are not identified as *customers* may *pay for* items, as in a cash sale where the payer's identity is unknown. Organizations other than *vendors* may receive payments, such as banks. Items other than *products* may be *paid for*, such as financial services (we assume that a *Product* is some tangible good). There may therefore be claims of the form (*x*) *Pays* (*y*) *For* (*z*) in the population that do not represent a *Customer* paying a *Vendor* for a *Product*.

We may restrict attention further: to a case where (*x*) *Has An Account With* (*y*), (*y*) *Distributes* (*z*), and (*x*) *Purchases* (*z*). Again, there may be claims controlled by *Pays For* in which these additional correspondences do not apply: a *customer* may pay a *vendor* in cash and have no *account*, a *vendor* may receive payment for items that it does not distribute, and a *customer* may pay a *vendor* on behalf of another and therefore not purchase the *product*. Using relative associations, we may thereby focus the trio into the *reduced* form:

« a *customer pays* a *vendor* that he *has an account with for* a *product* that the *customer purchases* and that the *vendor distributes* »

It is very common in data base design to focus higher degree associations in this way, so as to be certain what images participate in the association. It is not necessary to adopt all three correspondences. Indeed, it is more common to declare a trio relative to fewer than three. The collection of a trio, together with three classes and up to three correspondences that the trio is declared relative to, is called a *trio complex*.

Trio Complexes Are New Data Structures

Trio complexes include many new data structures which are not recognized by today's data base management systems. For example, imagine a large organization that is involved with building a space station. Various *people*, all astronauts, are assigned *roles* on various *projects*. The *roles* are very specific and all of the form ''operator of device *x*''. People must be trained and qualified to operate devices.

We may begin to describe this problem using the three correspondence complexes *Person Is Assigned To Project, Person Is Qualified For Role,* and *Project Requires Role*. These correspondence complexes form a delta in a network diagram, as shown in Figure 4.23. Each of the correspondence complexes is *many-to-many some-to-some*: A *person* on an extended leave might *be assigned to* no *project*, and a *project* in the planning stage might have no *people assigned*. A passenger might *be qualified for* no *role*, and a *role* that involves operating newly acquired equipment might have no *qualified person*. A *project* might be entirely administrative, and would therefore not require any of the operational

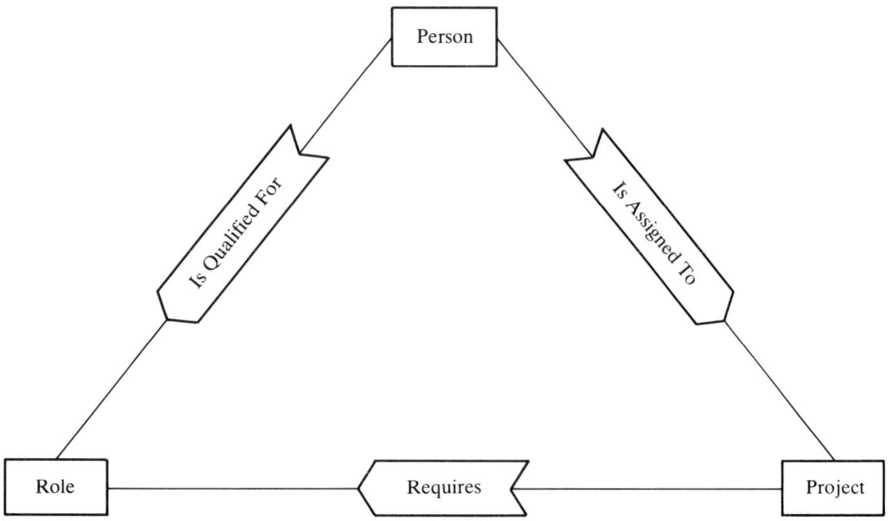

Figure 4.23

roles that we are considering, while a *role* might involve operating a type of equipment that is not currently being used on any *project*.

We represent the information of which *person* performs which *role* in which *project* using a trio *Person* ① *Performs Role* ② *In Project* ③. For a *person* to *perform* a *role in* a *project*, we suppose that the following rules are to be obeyed:

(i) The *person* must be *assigned* to the *project*.
(ii) The *project* must *require* the *role*.
(iii) The *person* must be *qualified for* the *role*.

Because these rules are to be obeyed, the trio *Performs In* is said to be *situated within* the correspondences *Is Assigned To, Is Qualified For,* and *Requires*. A trio need not in general be situated within the correspondences that it is declared relative to, but it is a helpful assumption that avoids the need to introduce the formalism of a reduced trio.

A sample population that satisfies rules (i) to (iii) is shown in the following tables. We imagine an extract for a particular *project*, *project* number 256:

Person	*Is Qualified For*	*Role*
Alice		Device 1
Alice		Device 2
Mike		Device 1
Mike		Device 3
Tony		Device 5
Phoebe		Device 4

Project	*Requires*	*Role*
256		Device 1
256		Device 2
256		Device 3
256		Device 4

Person	*Is Assigned To*	*Project*
Alice		256
Mike		256
Tony		256

Person	*Performs*	*Role*	*In*	*Project*
Alice		Device 2		256
Mike		Device 1		256
Mike		Device 3		256

If we were to attempt to describe this data structure as a single table (*Person*, *Role*, *Project*) in the relational data model, we would be forced to introduce "null values" in each of the three columns. Thus, nobody *performs* the *role* "Device 4" in the *project*, even though the *project requires* the *role* (the project leader may be waiting for an expert in Device 4 to be transferred to the *project*). Tony *performs* no *role* in the *project*, even though he *is assigned to* the *project* (he might have been recently *assigned* to the *project*, and is undergoing training for a future *role*). Although we have only illustrated one *project*, it is possible for a person to be *qualified for* a *role*, but for there to be no *project* that the *person performs* the *role* in. For example, Alice might be used on all her *projects* only as an operator of Device 2, even though she is also *qualified* to operate Device 1.

Alternatively, describing the data structure as four separate tables in the relational data model would fail to enforce the rules (i) to (iii). The effects of these rules are made particularly clear by considering deletions. For example, if a *person* is no longer *assigned to* a *project*, then the *person* can no longer *perform* a *role* in the *project*. Specifically, suppose Alice is reassigned and is no longer on the staff of *project* 256. The population above showed Alice *performing* the *role* of operator of Device 2 in *project* 256. Now that Alice is not available to the *project*, she can not retain this *role* or any others in *project* 256. All the triples that mention Alice *performing* a *role* in *project* 256 must therefore be deleted. Similarly, if a *person* is no longer *qualified for* a *role*, the *person* can no longer *perform* that *role* in any *project*. If the scope of a *project* is changed, making a *role* unnecessary, no person can *perform* that *role* in the *project*.

Rules such as (i), (ii), and (iii) have typically been considered to be procedures that lie outside the data base management system. We argue that data base management systems should be made more powerful so that they can manage integrity constraints such as these automatically. Any programs that use data about *Performs In* would thereby be assured of a properly formed population.

We may extend this example by adding a second trio complex to the data base. Imagine that *people* may attend *refresher courses* from time to time on the operation of the equipment for the various *roles*. We may set up a delta for this new trio complex using the following three correspondence complexes:

> *Person Is Qualifed For Role*: This is exactly the same correspondence that we used earlier. We will suppose that a *person* does not attend a *refresher course* unless he is *qualified* for the *role*. People seeking initial qualification are sent to other types of training courses.
>
> *Person Is Assigned To Refresher Course*: This is the same correspondence, *Is Assigned To*, that was used to associate people with projects, but here it is declared relative to a different pair of classes: (*Person*, *Refresher Course*) rather than (*Person*, *Project*). This use of the same correspondence indicates an opportunity to use the same programs to manage assignments to *refresher courses* as are used to manage assignments to *projects*.
>
> *Refresher Course Refreshes Role*: This is a *many-to-many all-to-some* correspondence complex that indicates what the course covers. Notice that a given *refresher course* might *refresh* many *roles* (it might cover a family of related machines, for example).

The resulting two deltas are illustrated in Figure 4.24.

The information about which *person* takes which *refresher course* for which *role* is retained in the trio *Refresher Course Instructs Person In Role*. We imagine that a *refresher course* might not *instruct* each student in each *role* covered by the course. For example, the *refresher course* might involve operating simulators of Devices 3, 4, and 5, but since the number of simulators and the time available are limited, one third of the class is instructed in each of the three devices.

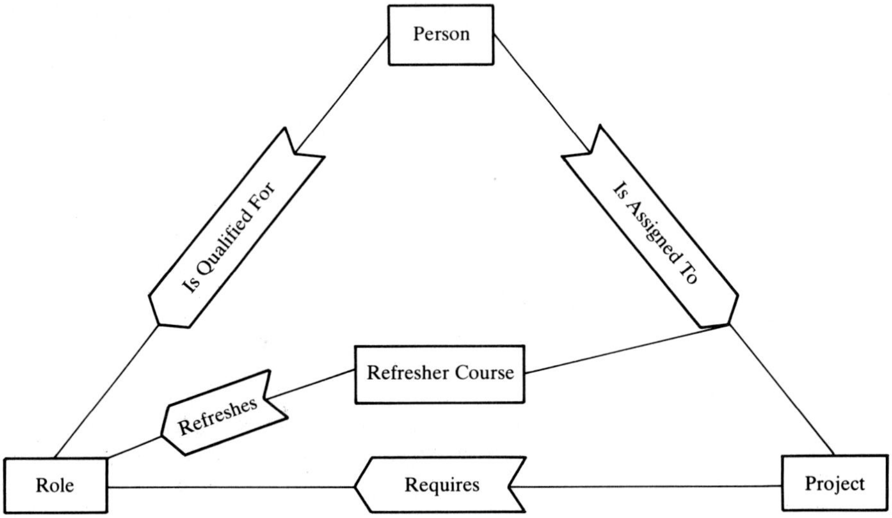

Figure 4.24

We will suppose that the trio ① *Instructs* ② *In* ③ is situated within these three correspondence complexes. That is, the trio complex obeys the rules:

> For a *refresher course* to *instruct* a *person in* a *role*, the *person* must be *qualified for* the *role*.
>
> For a *refresher course* to *instruct* a *person in* a *role*, the *person* must be *assigned to* the *refresher course*.
>
> For a *refresher course* to *instruct* a *person in* a *role*, the *role* must be *refreshed* by the *refresher course*. That is, training on the associated device must be an element of the course curriculum.

The way that these two trio complexes interact is illustrated by making selected changes to the populations of the four correspondences shown in Figure 4.24. For example, suppose Alice is scheduled for *refresher course* 131 on Device 1. Suppose that Alice is later transferred out of *project* 256. This transfer has no effect on the *Instructs In* trio—she remains scheduled for *refresher course* 131 on Device 1. Alternatively, suppose Alice loses her qualification for operating Device 1. She remains *assigned to refresher course* 131, but she can no longer conduct refesher exercises on Device 1. Thus, the entry *''refresher course* (131) *instructs* (Alice) *in* (Device 1)'' is automatically deleted. Similarly, she remains *assigned to project* 256, but the record of her *performing* as operator of Device 1 in *project* 256 is deleted. Notice how two similar operations, each a deletion of an attachment of ''Alice'', have different consequences based on where the controlling correspondence is located in the two trio complexes.

Sometimes, trio complexes such as these have been implemented using dummy instances. For example, to avoid the idea of a *person performing* no *role* on a *project*, one might assign a dummy *role* ''No role'' to each such *person*. This immediately raises the question of whether a *person* could *perform* a normal *role* in addition to *performing* ''No role'' (recall that a *person* can *perform* many *roles* in a *project*). Since this is probably not what was intended, special programs must be developed to manage ''No role''.

The dummy *role* is now propagated by the action of the embracings. Thus, if Nancy *performs* ''No role'' on some *project,* then Nancy must be *qualified for* ''No role''. The dummy ''No role'' also propagates to the *Instructs* trio complex. Since a *person* may be *qualified for* ''No role'', it is possible for a *person* to take a *refresher course* in ''No role''.

Special programs must be put in place for managing queries that combine results from both trio complexes. For example, a query to list all *people* who are taking *refresher courses* in *roles* that they *perform* in a given *project* must exclude those *people* who are taking *refresher courses* in ''No role''.

These additional appearances of ''No role'' are ripe for abuse. It is likely that the tag ''No role'' will be seized by users of one trio complex for different purposes than the other trio complex. For example, the meaning of ''No role'' in the *Instructs* trio complex may drift toward « the *role* could be any one of the *roles* covered by the course, the actual *role* to be decided by the instructor », while the meaning of ''No role'' in the *Performs* trio complex drifts toward « the *person performs* a nontechnical administrative *role* ». The status of the tag ''No role'' as a dummy makes it particularly ripe for this sort of abuse, since it is in the nature of a dummy to incorporate everything that is not handled elsewhere. We recommend that dummies be avoided for these reasons, and that data base management systems manage embracings directly instead.

Formal Specification of Trio Complexes

We describe declaration of trios formally as follows: a trio T may be declared relative to a triple of classes (A, B, C) and a triple of correspondences (F, G, H). The resulting *trio complex* is written $(T; A, B, C; F, G, H)$. The *reduced trio* $\dot{T}$ relative to this complex is defined by

$$\dot{T}{:}|x, y, z| \equiv (\exists x')\,(\exists y')\,(\exists z')\ \Delta A{:}|x, x'|\ \&\ \Delta B{:}|y, y'|\ \&\ \Delta C{:}|z, z'|\ \&\ \Delta A \circ F \circ \Delta B{:}|x, y| \\ \&\ \Delta B \circ G \circ \Delta C{:}|y, z|\ \&\ \Delta C \circ H \circ \Delta A{:}|z, x|\ \&\ T{:}|x', y', z'|$$

Notice that F is considered relative to (A, B), G relative to (B, C), and H relative to (C, A). A triple of classes (A, B, C) is required when declaring trio constraints, because the classes determine the forms of identity to be used in each position. Any or none of the correspondences F, G, and H may be declared as well.

Trio Constraints Are Described As Characters of Elision Correspondences

Assemblies controlled by a trio complex may be viewed as triples that may contain unfilled positions. For example,

$(a, \ , \ )$ indicates $A{:}(a)$

$(a, b, \ )$ indicates $\dot{F}{:}(a, b)$

$(a, \ , c)$ indicates $\dot{H}^*{:}(a, c)$

(a, b, c) indicates $\dot{T}{:}(a, b, c)$

$$(\ , b, c) \text{ indicates } \dot{G}{:}(b, c)$$
$$(\ , \ , c) \text{ indicates } C{:}(c)$$

This manner of presentation inspired the term "null value" in the relational model, which refers to the unfilled positions in the sequences above. We will prefer to refer to an unfilled position as an *optional* choice. If the triple contains two filled positions and one unfilled position (such as (, b, c)), we will call the relaxation a *downstream optional*, for reasons to be explained in the next chapter. Over 90 percent of the trio complexes that we will discuss in this book contain downstream *optionals*.

The constraints peculiar to trios involve the relationships of one position with the projection onto the other two positions. For example, the statement that there may be no instances of the trio complex of the form (a, b,) is a *mandatory* constraint:

$$(\text{A}x)\ (\text{A}y)\ \dot{F}{:}|x, y| \Rightarrow (\exists z)\ \dot{T}{:}|x, y, z|$$

Alternatively, the statement that for any pair (a, b) there is at most one instance c such that (a, b, c) is an instance of the trio complex is a *single* constraint:

$$(\text{A}x)\ (\text{A}y)\ (\text{A}z)\ (\text{A}z')\ \dot{T}{:}|x, y, z|\ \&\ \dot{T}{:}|x, y, z'| \Rightarrow \Delta C{:}|z, z'|$$

Other similar constraints are formed by considering the pairs (a, c) or (b, c).

These constraints may be expressed by considering the concentrations of the correspondences of the trio complex, that is, the classes of their assemblies. An assembly controlled by the correspondence $\dot{F}$ may be represented as "$\dot{F}(a, b)$". We have then

$$\boxed{(\text{A}x)\ (\text{A}y)\ \text{C}^1\dot{F}{:}|\dot{F}|x, y|| \Leftrightarrow \dot{F}{:}|x, y|}$$

That is, $\dot{F}$ attaches an image $a.\iota$ to an image $b.\kappa$ if and only if the assembly manifestation $\dot{F}|a.\iota, b.\kappa|$ is accepted by the concentration $\text{C}^1\dot{F}$. Extending this technique, we define the *elision correspondence* ${}_{12}\dot{T}_3$ to be the correspondence

$$\boxed{(\text{A}x)\ (\text{A}y)\ (\text{A}z)\ {}_{12}\dot{T}_3{:}|\dot{F}|x, y|, z| \Leftrightarrow \dot{T}{:}|x, y, z|}$$

The elision correspondence may be thought of as rewriting the triples (a, b, c) as pairs ((a, b), c). That is, $\dot{T}$ accepts $a.\iota$, $b.\kappa$, and $c.\lambda$ if and only if ${}_{12}\dot{T}_3$ accepts $\dot{F}|a.\iota, b.\kappa|$ and $c.\lambda$. The subscripts on $\dot{T}$ indicate the arrangement of the individuals within the parentheses, distinguishing ((a, b), c) for ${}_{12}\dot{T}_3$ from (a, (b, c)) for ${}_1\dot{T}_{23}$ or ((c, a), b) for ${}_{31}\dot{T}_2$.

The scope of the elision correspondence ${}_{12}\dot{T}_3$ is embraced in the concentration $C^1\dot{F}$:

$$\boxed{(\text{A}x)\ (\text{A}y)\ (\text{A}z)\ {}_{12}\dot{T}_3{:}|\dot{F}|x, y|, z| \Rightarrow \dot{F}{:}|x, y|}$$

That is, if $\dot{T}$ assembles x to y to z then $\dot{F}$ attaches x to y. This embracing always holds because we are considering the reduced trio $\dot{T}$, which has already been restricted to assemble only individuals that are attached by $\dot{F}$. It would not apply in general if the unreduced trio T were substituted for $\dot{T}$ in the formula. Data base management systems that do not implement embracings have been unable to express this constraint. This has been a prime reason why downstream *optionals* have not been implemented effectively.

The character decisions of the elision correspondences are basic to describing trio complexes. For example, stating that ${}_{12}\dot{T}_3$ is *from some* permits assemblies of the form

$$(a,\ b,\ )$$

Stating that $_{12}\dot{T}_3$ is *from all* prevents such assemblies. That is, if $_{12}\dot{T}_3$ is *from all*, there must always be some individual in the third position (unless unresolved alternations are permitted, in which case the third position must be occupied, but its contents could be unresolved).

Stating that $_{12}\dot{T}_3$ is *to many* permits populations of the form

$$(a,\ b,\ c_1)$$
$$(a,\ b,\ c_2)$$

Stating that $_{12}\dot{T}_3$ is *from many* permits populations of the form

$$(a_1,\ b_1,\ c)$$
$$(a_1,\ b_2,\ c)$$
$$(a_2,\ b_1,\ c)$$

Stating that $_{12}\dot{T}_3$ is *to some* permits populations of the form

$$(\ ,\ ,\ c)$$

Each of the elision correspondences has a character. When a correspondence is declared relative to three correspondences, three characters should be declared:

$$\text{chr}\ ({}_{12}\dot{T}_3;\ \text{C}^1\dot{F},\ C)$$
$$\text{chr}\ ({}_{23}\dot{T}_1;\ \text{C}^1\dot{G},\ A)$$
$$\text{chr}\ ({}_{31}\dot{T}_2;\ \text{C}^1\dot{H},\ B)$$

The character decisions in trios are not independent as they are in correspondences, but are subject to a variety of interdependencies. These interdependencies, along with other characteristics of trios, will be explored in Chapter 9.

Associations of Degree Greater than Three

The technique of elision correspondences for describing constraints may be extended readily to associations of higher degree, although the difficulty of describing associations increases rapidly with increasing degree. Quartets may be declared not only relative to classes and correspondences, but relative to trios as well. Indeed, a general association R of degree r may be declared relative to associations for all possible projections of R, up to $2^r - 2$ possible associations. However, only a sequence of r classes is required, to establish the means of defining identity in each position.

For example, a quartet $Q(w, x, y, z)$ may be declared relative to all the following associations:

$A(w)$	$F(w, x)$	$T(w, x, y)$
$B(x)$	$G(x, y)$	$U(x, y, z)$
$C(y)$	$H(y, z)$	$V(y, z, w)$
$D(z)$	$I(w, y)$	$W(z, w, x)$
	$J(x, z)$	
	$K(w, z)$	

Four trio complexes, for T, U, V, and W, must then be declared as part of declaring Q.

Additionally, one must declare the characters of seven elision correspondences formed from Q:

$$\text{chr}\ ({}_{123}\dot{Q}_4;\ \mathrm{C}^1\dot{T},\ D)$$

$$\text{chr}\ ({}_{412}\dot{Q}_3;\ \mathrm{C}^1\dot{W},\ C)$$

$$\text{chr}\ ({}_{341}\dot{Q}_2;\ \mathrm{C}^1\dot{V},\ B)$$

$$\text{chr}\ ({}_{234}\dot{Q}_1;\ \mathrm{C}^1\dot{U},\ A)$$

$$\text{chr}\ ({}_{12}\dot{Q}_{34};\ \mathrm{C}^1\dot{F},\ \mathrm{C}^1\dot{H})$$

$$\text{chr}\ ({}_{13}\dot{Q}_{24};\ \mathrm{C}^1\dot{I},\ \mathrm{C}^1\dot{J})$$

$$\text{chr}\ ({}_{14}\dot{Q}_{23};\ \mathrm{C}^1\dot{K},\ \mathrm{C}^1\dot{G})$$

Notice how the number of character decisions increases exponentially with the degree of the association. This pattern makes selection of relative associations particularly important in higher degrees. In practice, a quartet would invariably be declared relative to fewer associations than the maximum 14 shown in this example. We will discuss how to simplify the declaration of associations of high degree in Section 5.7.

Conclusion

Just as the properties of correspondences were described in Section 4.7 by introducing a *correspondence complex*, so the properties of trios may be described by introducing a *trio complex*. A trio complex contains one trio, three classes, and up to three correspondences. Schema elements that describe a trio complex are formed from the character constraints of *elision correspondences*, which relate the populations of the associations in the trio complex to each other.

4.9 CONCLUSION

Nearly all data base constraints in common use are unified by the format of a *positive embracing*. These constraints include, in particular, the *character constraints* of *from all*, *to one*, *from one*, and *to all*. We have recommended that all forms of positive embracings should be handled by data base management systems of the future. Constraints that incorporate negation are not positive embracings, and we have recommended that these constraints be avoided.

The foundational development of data as a collection of claims (rather than a collection of records) indicates an opportunity to apply propositional logic to the contents of a data base population. Thus, claims may be denied as well as being affirmed. Claims may include an *unresolved alternation* where several alternatives are presented but none is chosen.

Positive embracings furnish a framework for describing trios, which are not described thoroughly by other current techniques. In particular, we have shown that a trio can be described by forming the characters of *elision correspondences*, which relate the concentration of the trio to classes and correspondences in a trio complex.

5

Extended Associative Notation

5.1 INTRODUCTION

The new capabilities afforded by data logic require new data design notations. Two needs are particularly acute: the need to include correspondences and trios explicitly in data designs, and the need to develop a notation for expressing embracings.

Data logic indicates that correspondences, trios, and other associations of higher degree should be represented with tags just as classes are. These tags should be verbs, not nouns, so that data base claims can be read as complete sentences. Thus, a customer *purchases* a product, a vendor *sells* a product, a customer *has a sales agreement with* a vendor, and a customer *buys* a product *from* a vendor. The correspondence tags ''*Purchases*'', ''*Sells*''; and ''*Has A Sales Agreement With*'', and the trio tag ''*Buys From*'', should be recognized as constituents of a data base design of the same importance as the class tags ''*Customer*'', ''*Product*'', and ''*Vendor*''.

There are three reasons to name correspondences explicitly in a data base design: there can be more than one correspondence between the same two classes, the same correspondence may appear relative to more than one pair of classes, and a correspondence may appear in an embracing. Thus, a customer may *own stock in* a vendor in addition to *having a sales agreement with* the vendor. If the correspondences were not named, one could not determine whether an attachment of a customer to a vendor indicated an owning of stock or a sales agreement.

A correspondence such as *Purchases* might apply to services as well as to products. That is, a data base may contain two correspondence complexes, *Customer Purchases Product* and *Customer Purchases Service*, for the same correspondence *Purchases*. In an object-oriented operating environment, the correspondence *Purchases* could then be associated with a set of procedures that would apply automatically to the purchasing of both products and services.

The correspondence *Purchases* may also appear in an embracing. Suppose, for example, that any *purchase* is always associated with a total price. This rule applies to the correspondence *Purchases*, whatever classes it is relative to. It therefore applies to both the correspondence complexes *Customer Purchases Product* and *Customer Purchases Service*. Moreover, if we add a new correspondence complex *Customer Purchases Fixed Asset*, the rule applies to this correspondence complex as well.

New notations are also needed for positive embracings. The data logic notation introduced in earlier chapters was designed for close reasoning by data base experts. Data base design, in contrast, requires rapid communication of ideas to a wide audience. Mathematical or highly abbreviated notations, however useful for careful work, are very poor presentation devices. Presentation of data designs should rely on the more immediately accessible avenues of pictures and natural language.

We introduce a pictorial notation in this chapter, called *extended associative notation*, which is geared to solving the twin problems of explicit definition of associations and support for embracings. Extended associative notation is based on the Associative Data Model notation discussed in (Jones and Curtice 1988) and (Jones 1976). Associative Data Model notation has been used by the authors and our colleagues for over 20 years, and with over 3000 people, to design practical data bases. Elements of the Associative Data Model are included by permission of QED Information Sciences, Inc., 170 Linden Street, Wellesley, MA 02181.

In today's world of ready access to technology, it is shameful that most data designs today are prepared on paper, or on design aids that are little more than mechanical drawing programs. Data base designs should not be prepared on paper, but should be supported by a highly functional *design management device*, which takes an active role in their development and presentation. The design management device should be able to present a precise and intelligible narration in natural language of any data base design, for example. It should be able to present a sample population diagram of any portion of the schema on request. It should be able to convert an extended associative notation design into a network notation on request. We begin to discuss how these functions of the design management device can be performed in this chapter, but implementation of these capabilities remains beyond the scope of this book.

In Section 5.2, Basic Components, we present an overview of the basic shapes used in extended associative notation and their interpretation. In Section 5.3, Characters, we discuss the presentation of simple varieties of constraints and relaxations. Extended associative notation (like Associative Data Model notation) is equipped with many shorthands for frequently occurring constraints, particularly the character constraints, *from all, from one, to one,* and *to all*. Extended associative notation contains a more formal approach to correspondences than Associative Data Model notation, allowing correspondence tags to be written inside a special shape.

In Section 5.4, Comparison with Other Notations, we present a brief comparison of extended associative notation with other contemporary data design notations. This discussion is designed as an aid to the reader who may be familiar with other techniques, and is not a thorough critique of the differences between design notations. We show how any design developed using the hierarchical data model or the network data model may be converted to extended associative notation, and we begin the discussion of how designs developed using the relational data model may be converted. We will postpone the conversion of relational data model designs that include trios to Section 9.3.

In Section 5.5, Embracings, we present a notation for expressing embracings within a data base design. This is a new capability of extended associative notation. It is not supported by Associative Data Model notation, nor by most other data design notations. We show how logical operations such as *and* and *or* can be shown as text, and show how logical formulas can be expressed.

In Section 5.6, Trios of the First Stable State, we present the primary form of extended associative notation for associations of degree three and higher.We consider more intricate forms in Section 5.7, Other Forms of Trios, and Quartets. Trios will be discussed in detail in Chapter 9, after we have developed enough technical apparatus to understand them fully. We present the notation for trios here so that extended associative notation will be completely specified in Chapter 5.

In Section 5.8, Case Study: Books, we present an imaginary case study that illustrates the process of designing a data base. A real data design project is far from the straightforward exercise in analyzing well-understood requirements that one might expect from reading books on data theory. A real data design project requires creating a rigorous framework from poorly understood, vaguely defined, and often contradictory conceptions of the way things should be done. It is a challenging and above all a creative task.

5.2 BASIC COMPONENTS

The basic components of extended associative notation are illustrated in Figure 5.1.

Notation for Classes and Correspondences

Association tags in extended associative notation are placed inside special shapes, the shape indicating the degree of the association. A class tag, for example, is placed inside a rectangle as shown in Figure 5.1. This notation agrees with the network notation of Bachman and the entity-relationship notation of Chen (Bachman 1983, Chen 1976). In Chen's technique, classes are called ''entities.'' We prefer to avoid the term ''entity,'' because it means precisely « something that exists ». A class, in contrast, need not exist, but may be purely imaginary, such as the class « *Unicorn* ».

A class tag in extended associative notation is a countable noun phrase, that is, a phrase that can be preceded by the indefinite article ''a'' or ''an.'' Thus ''milk carton'' and ''pair of socks'' are valid class tags, while ''air'' and ''Nassau, Bahamas'' are avoided. It is important to use countable noun phrases as class tags, because extended associative notation uses the class tags to form complete sentences that describe a data base design,

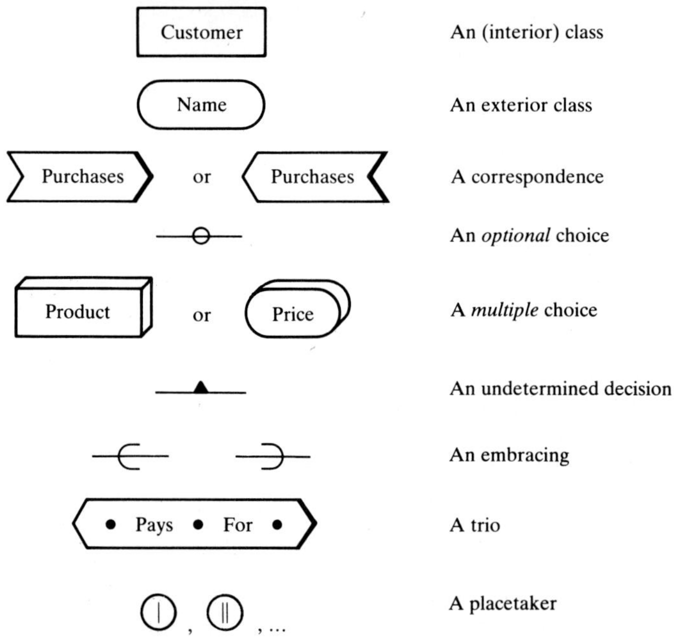

Figure 5.1 Components of extended associative notation.

and these sentences will be ungrammatical unless the tags are the proper part of speech.

A correspondence tag is placed inside a *chevron*. The chevron, unlike the rectangle, is directed. The direction is used to distinguish the individual in the first position from the individual in the second, that is, to distinguish between the two different expressions:

(*United Motors*) *Purchases*: (*Sunnyvale Golf Club*)
(*Sunnyvale Golf Club*) *Purchases*: (*United Motors*)

A chevron need not point from left to right. It may point from right to left, in which case it identifies the converse of a correspondence. A correspondence tag in extended associative notation is a transitive verb phrase, that is, a phrase that takes one subject and one object, such as ''*Purchases*'', ''*Carries*'', and so on. Intransitive verbs such as ''sleeps'' are best converted into nouns and used as class tags, in this case the class tag ''*Sleeper*''. The subject of the verb phrase is viewed as fitting into the open end of the chevron, and the object as following the pointed end, to form a complete sentence.

Notation for Trios and Associations of Higher Degree

An association of degree higher than two is shown inside a hexagonal *tile* shape. Figure 5.1 illustrates the trio « ① *Pays* ② *For* ③ ». The various positions of the association are shown as dots inside the tile. The dots are often replaced by other symbols such as ''+'' and ''−'' when a tile appears in context with other associations.

A trio tag usually consists of a verb such as *Pays* and an auxiliary phrase of some kind, either a prepositional phrase such as *For*, or a construction with an infinitive, as in

( ) *Pays* ( ) *To Supply* ( ). Trios, quartets, and associations of higher degree are shown in a tile as in Figure 5.1, with as many dots as there are positions to be substituted (that is, the number of dots equals the degree of the association).

Notation for Character Decisions

Characters are shown attached to a vertical line drawn beneath a class tag. A typical pattern is shown in Figure 5.2. This figure illustrates the correspondence complex (*Offers*; *Company*, *Product*). That is, it concerns *offerings* of *products* by *companies*, not *offerings* more generally (say, of *services* by *individuals*), nor different correspondences between *Company* and *Product* (such as *Company Advertises Product*).

The illustration shown in Figure 5.2 of three shapes connected by a staircase of vertical and horizontal lines is called a *cascade*. Each position in the cascade is called a *level*. Thus, in Figure 5.2, "*Company*" is on the first level, "*Offers*" is on the second level, and "*Product*" is on the third level. A cascade can also continue further down and to the right than is shown in Figure 5.2.

Marks on the cascade illustrate character decisions (and other decisions) for the correspondence complex. Thus, in Figure 5.2, the small "o" beside *Offers* indicates that a *company* may *offer* nothing (as a holding company would, for example). The three-dimensional box surrounding "*Product*" shows that a company may *offer* many *products*. Note that the illustration shown in Figure 5.2 is silent about how a *product* relates back to a *company*: it is not said whether or not there may be a *product offered* by no *company*, or whether a *product* could be *offered* by many *companies*. These decisions are shown on a different cascade.

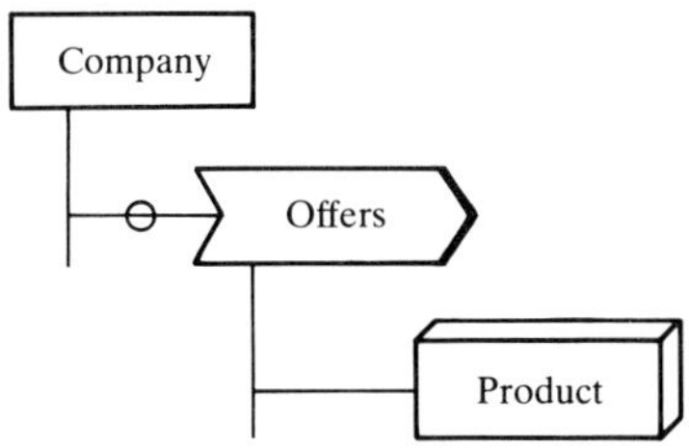

Figure 5.2 A cascade.

Notation for Embracings

An embracing is shown by a "C" shape underneath an association tag. For example, the embracing "any *corporation* is also a *company*", which would be written in data logic notation as "*Corporation* $\subseteq$ *Company*", is shown in Figure 5.3.

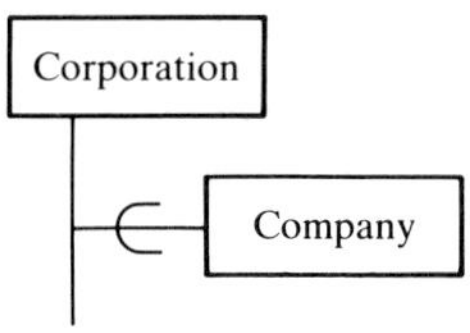

Figure 5.3 An embracing.

5.3 CHARACTERS

Treatment of Correspondences

The extended associative notation for characters is an extension of the Associative Data Model notation introduced in (Jones 1976) and (Jones and Curtice 1988). Associative Data Model notation expresses characters, but does not express correspondences explicitly. In extended associative notation, correspondences are given tags just as classes are, and additional questions are asked about how the correspondences and the classes are interrelated.

Notation for Classes

All declared relationships that a class participates in are shown attached to a vertical line beneath the class tag. The definition of the class is shown to the right of the class tag. The definition of the class « *B* » is text supplied by the designer that begins with the phrase "A/An *B* is". The definition shown is the meaning of the symbol *B* for the purposes of the data base. For example, if "*account*" means a client (as in an advertising account), then it should be so defined. It should not be defined using the definition of the word "account" in a dictionary of English. Tags that are used in the data base design are written in italics (*account*) to distinguish them from words used with their ordinary meaning. The definition should also identify when two images are the same *B*, so that it will be clear what is meant by saying that a class associates with *one* instance of *B*.

The basic format for declaring a correspondence complex (*G*; *B*, *C*) is shown in Figure 5.4. Notice that a correspondence complex is declared using two cascades called *reversals* of each other. Each of the shaded triangles (six in all) shows a decision that should be made when declaring a correspondence complex. Removing a shaded triangle indicates a constraint; replacing a shaded triangle with another symbol indicates a relaxation.

The diagram shown beneath "*G*" presents the definition of *G* and provides a cross-reference to the classes that *G* is declared relative to. It will also be used to show embracings. It does not express any design decisions.

The correspondence *G* is shown with two *position designators* "|" and "||", which serve to identify the source classes and the destination classes of each of the correspondence complexes that *G* is declared in. Thus, the source class tag "*B*" is shown beneath the position designator "|", and the destination class tag "*C*" is shown beneath the position designator "||". The design management device inserts an *explanation* to the right of each class tag, as shown, that describes how the class relates to the correspondence. The definition of the correspondence *G* is provided by the designer, and is shown to the right of the tile containing the tag "*G*".

We will illustrate the various decisions using the example « a *person purchases* a *car* ». That is, *Person* takes the place of *B*, *Purchases* takes the place of *G*, and *Car* takes the place of *C*.

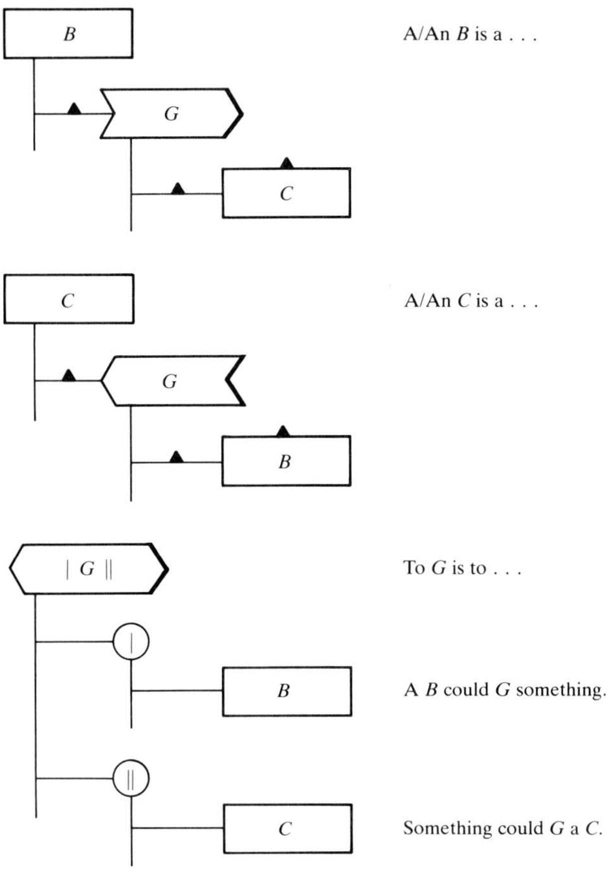

Figure 5.4 A correspondence complex.

Agency Decisions

The first shaded triangle, shown below ''*B*'' and directly to the left of ''*G*'', is called an *agency decision*. It expresses the answer to the question

> Must any *B G* something?
>
> Must any *person purchase* something?

The outcome of a decision is called a *choice*. If the answer to this question is yes, we say that the choice is ''*mandatory*'', if the answer is no, we say that the choice is ''*optional*''.

At this point, we do not ask if a *person* must *purchase* a *car*, but only if there must be something (perhaps a *car*, perhaps something other than a *car*) that a *person purchases*. Normally, a *person* could be represented in the data base without having made any purchases. Thus, in the example, we would expect the agency choice to be *optional*.

The two potential choices are illustrated in Figure 5.5. Each choice is described by an explanation in natural language that is shown to the right of the choice. Explanations are unambiguous text expressions that are generated by the design management device. An explanation may be supplemented by additional text on the right side.

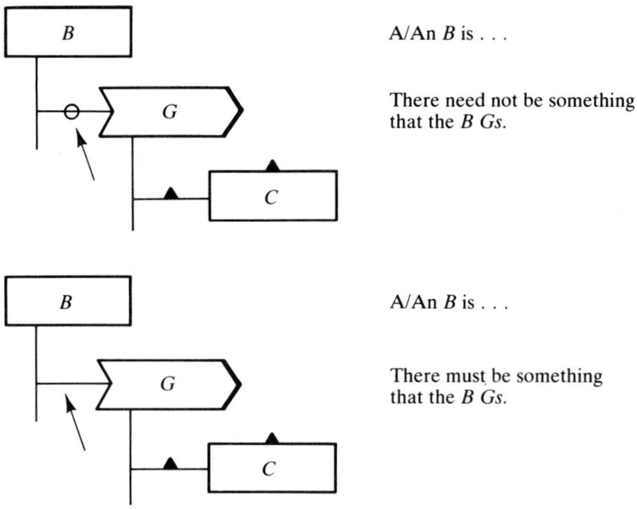

Figure 5.5 The two potential choices in an agency decision.

The design management device substitutes the appropriate class tag and correspondence tag for ''*B*'' and ''*G*'', respectively, when forming the explanation. Thus, in the example we are using, the two choices would be explained as:

> There need not be something that the *person purchases* (the choice we would expect).
>
> There must be something that the *person purchases* (this choice would limit the *people* in the data base to people who are *purchasers*).

Explanations use the term ''something'' to mean « some image ». Using the term ''image'' in documentation is often awkward, and we avoid it. It is important for the designer to remember, however, that ''something'' refers to an idea, not a physical thing (at best, it refers to a way of perceiving a physical thing, but there may also be no physical thing at all).

A *mandatory* agency choice is written in data logic notation as the formula

$$(\mathrm{A}x)\ B{:}|x| \Rightarrow (\exists x')\ (\exists y)\ \Delta B{:}|x,\ x'|\ \&\ G{:}|x',\ y|$$

For example, if every *person* must *purchase* something, we would write

$$(\mathrm{A}x)\ \mathit{Person}{:}|x| \Rightarrow (\exists x')\ (\exists y)\ |x|\ \mathit{Is\ The\ Same\ Person\ As}{:}\ |x'|\ \&\ |x'|\ \mathit{Purchases}{:}\ |y|$$

The *mandatory* agency choice can also be written as the embracing

$$B \subseteq \pi^1(\Delta B \circ G)$$

$$Person \subseteq \pi^1(Is\ The\ Same\ Person\ As \circ Purchases)$$

An *optional* agency choice is a denial of this constraint.

Targeting Decisions

The decision shown to the left of the class tag "*C*" in Figure 5.4, in the cascade under "*B*", is called a *targeting decision*. It expresses the answer to the question

If a *B Gs* something, must the *B G* some *C*?

If a *person purchases* something, must the *person purchase* some *car*?

If the answer to this question is yes, we say that the choice is "*mandatory*", if the answer is no, we say that the choice is "*optional*".

Note that the question is not "if a *person purchases* something, must that thing be a *car*?", that is, "are *cars* the only things that a *person* can *purchase*?". Rather, the question is whether any *purchaser purchases* a *car*, perhaps in addition to *purchasing* other items.

The notation for the two targeting choices is shown in Figure 5.6. We do not repeat the explanations given earlier to conserve space, although all explanations would be included in a final data design.

In our example, the two targeting choices would be explained as:

What the *person purchases* need not include a *car* (if purchases of items that are not cars are included in the data base).

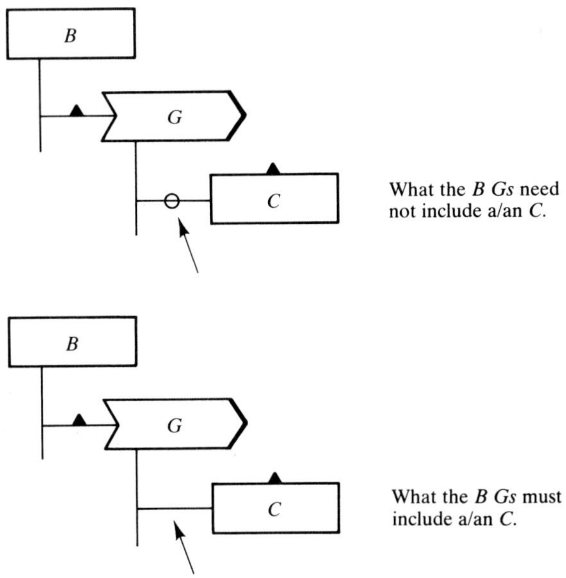

Figure 5.6 The two potential choices in a targeting decision.

What the *person purchases* must include a *car* (if only purchasers of cars are included in the data base, as a data base for a car dealership might be).

The *mandatory* targeting choice is written in data logic notation as the formula

$$(\mathrm{A}x)\ (\exists x')\ (\exists y)\ \Delta B{:}|x, x'|\ \&\ G{:}|x', y| \Rightarrow (\exists x'')\ (\exists z)\ \Delta B{:}|x, x''|\ \&\ G{:}|x'', z|\ \&\ C{:}|z|$$

This formula may also be written as the embracing

$$\pi^1(\Delta B \circ G) \subseteq \pi^1(\Delta B \circ G \circ \Delta C)$$

Mandatory/Optional **Character Decisions**

The character constraint of *from all* is the conjunction of a *mandatory* agency choice with a *mandatory* targeting choice. For example, a *person* must *purchase* a *car* if and only if a *person* must *purchase* something (an agency choice) and a *person* who *purchases* something must *purchase* a *car* (a targeting choice). Thus, if both the agency choice and the targeting choice are *mandatory*, the correspondence G is *from all* relative to (B, C).

Conversely, if either the agency choice or the targeting choice is *optional*, the character choice is *from some*. In the example, a *person* might *purchase* no *car* if and only if a *person* might not *purchase* anything (an agency choice) or a *person* who *purchases* something might *purchase* no *car* (a targeting choice).

This result is easily proved using embracings. Recall that the *from all* constraint may be expressed as the embracing $B \subseteq \pi^1(\Delta B \circ G \circ \Delta C)$ (see Section 4.7). The *mandatory* agency choice is the embracing $B \subseteq \pi^1(\Delta B \circ G)$, and the *mandatory* targeting choice is the embracing $\pi^1(\Delta B \circ G) \subseteq \pi^1(\Delta B \circ G \circ \Delta C)$.

Single/Multiple **Decisions**

The shaded triangle shown on top of the rectangle enclosing the class tag "C", in the cascade under "B", is called a *single/multiple decision*. It expresses the answer to the question

> Might a B G many Cs?
>
> Might a *person purchase* many *cars*?

If the answer to this question is no, we say that the choice is "*single*"; if the answer is yes, we say that the choice is "*multiple*". Equivalently, we say that G is *to one* relative to (B, C) if the choice is *single*, and that G is *to many* relative to (B, C) if the choice is *multiple*. The two potential choices are illustrated in Figure 5.7.

In our example, the two choices would be explained as

> There might be many *cars* that the *person purchases* (the decision we would expect).
>
> There must be at most one *car* that the *person purchases*.

The *single* choice, that is, the *to one* constraint, is written in data logic notation as follows, where "$\dot{G}$" indicates the reduced correspondence $\Delta B \circ G \circ \Delta C$ (see Section 4.7):

$$\dot{G}^* \circ \dot{G} \subseteq \Delta C$$

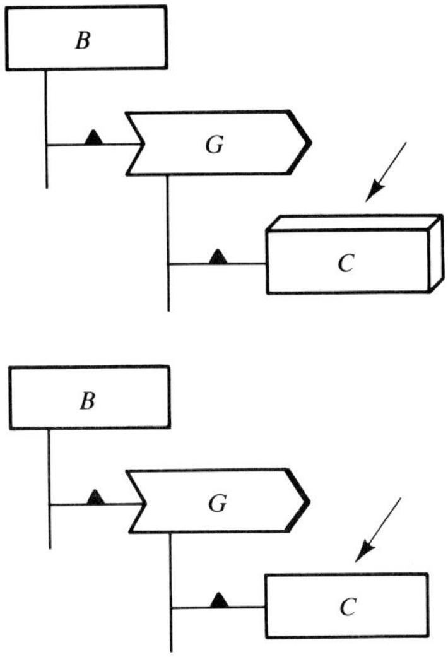

Figure 5.7 The two potential choices in a *single/multiple* decision.

Reversal

The cascade we have been working with has a reversal, shown in Figure 5.8. A correspondence complex is declared using two cascades that reverse each other. Thus, in Figure 5.8, the order of classes down the cascade is reversed: *C* then *B*, rather than *B* then *C*. The chevron also points in the opposite direction: right-to-left rather than left-to-right. The cascade is always read in the direction that the chevron points. Thus, the cascade in Figure 5.8 continues to represent "a *B Gs* a *C*".

The decisions shown on a reversal are described in the same pattern shown earlier. Thus, the two agency choices are explained as

> There need not be something that *Gs* the *C*.
> There must be something that *Gs* the *C*.
>
> There need not be something that *purchases* the *car*.
> There must be something that *purchases* the *car*.

Notice that the agency decision shown in Figure 5.8 asks whether there must be something that *purchases* a *car*, while the agency decision for its reversal, Figure 5.5, asks whether there must be something that a *person purchases*. These decisions are entirely independent.

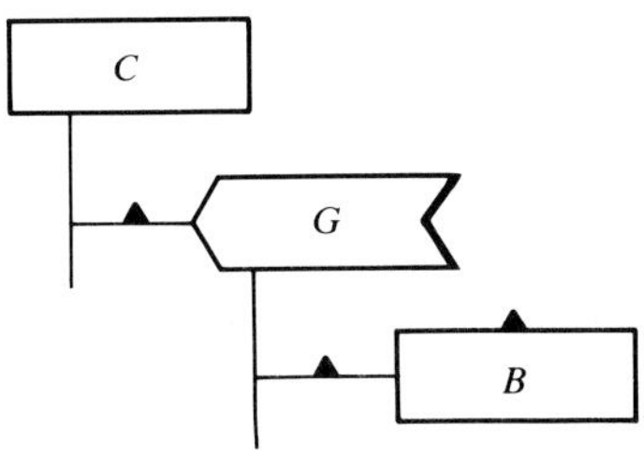

Figure 5.8 A reversal.

A similar pattern is followed by the targeting choices:

What *Gs* the *C* need not include a *B*.
What *Gs* the *C* must include a *B*.

What *purchases* the *car* need not include a *person*.
What *purchases* the *car* must include a *person*.

The correspondence *G* is *to all* relative to (*B*, *C*) if both the agency choice and the targeting choice are *mandatory*. *G* is *to some* relative to (*B*, *C*) if either the agency choice or the targeting choice is *optional*.

The *single/multiple* choices are

There might be many *Bs* that *G* the *C*.
There must be at most one *B* that *Gs* the *C*.

There might be many *people* that *purchase* the *car*.
There must be at most one *person* that *purchases* the *car*.

The correspondence *G* is *from one* relative to (*B*, *C*) if the choice is *single*, and *G* is *from many* relative to (*B*, *C*) if the choice is *multiple*.

Figure 5.9 shows a completed declaration of our running example. We imagine that it is a sales data base for a car dealership, so purchases of things other than cars are not recorded, and cars that are unsold are not recorded. The dealership does sell to institutions, which are not people, and it does not make joint sales to several people—the policy is that one *person* must be listed as the purchaser.

The data structures that incorporate a given class tag are shown off the vertical line that extends down from the class tag at the extreme left of the diagram. Thus, Figure 5.10 shows the two correspondence complexes *Person Purchases Car* and *Company Employs Person*. The complete diagram beneath a class tag *B* is called the *template* for *B*.

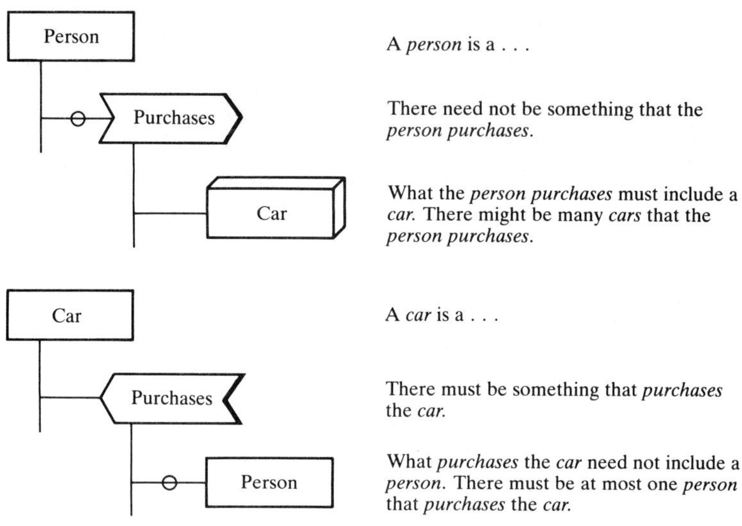

Figure 5.9 A correspondence complex.

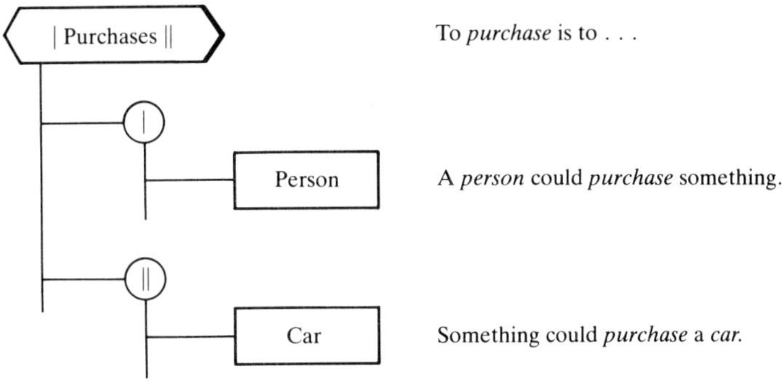

Figure 5.9 *(continued)*

The vertical line that extends down from a chevron can also be extended. For example, suppose that the car dealership is affiliated with an appliance store, and the car dealership gathers information about which of its customers purchase dishwashers. Not all of the « *purchasers* » then *purchase dishwashers*, although they all *purchase cars*. This data structure is shown in Figure 5.11. It is reversed to both *Car* and *Dishwasher*.

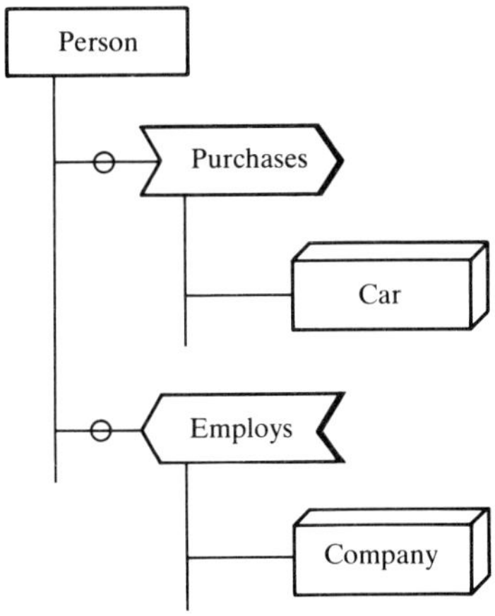

Figure 5.10 The *Person* template.

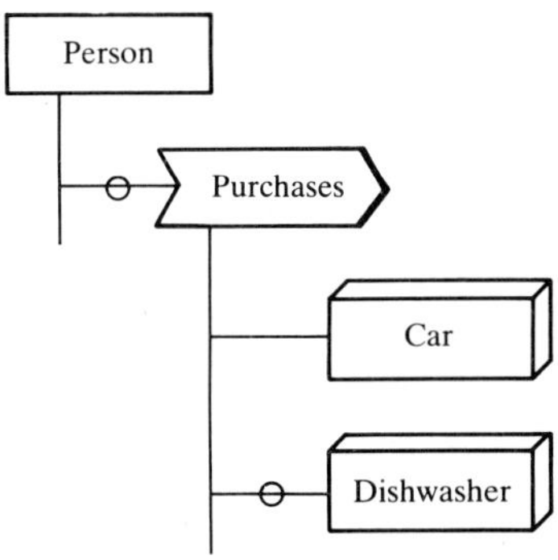

Figure 5.11 A *person* may *purchase* both *cars* and *dishwashers*.

The template for the correspondence tag *Purchases* shows both *Car* and *Dishwasher* as destinations, as shown in Figure 5.12.

Loops

We note that *B* and *C* may be the same class tag. This occurs in many classification schemes, such as a bill of materials, as shown in Figure 5.13. A correspondence complex where the two relative classes are the same class, that is, a correspondence complex of the form (*G*; *B*, *B*), will be called a *loop*. Some data models require rewriting a loop in a factored form, usually by creating a "usage record" that is in effect a concentration of *Goes Into*. We feel such a restriction needlessly complicates the fairly direct idea of a recursively applicable association.

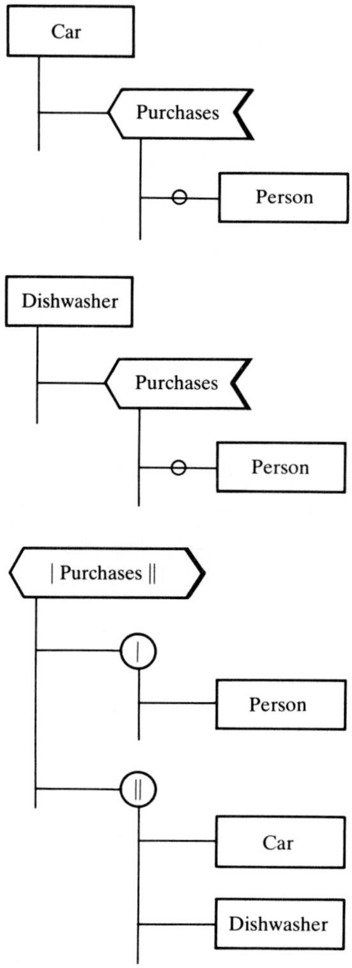

Figure 5.12 Reversals for Figure 5.11.

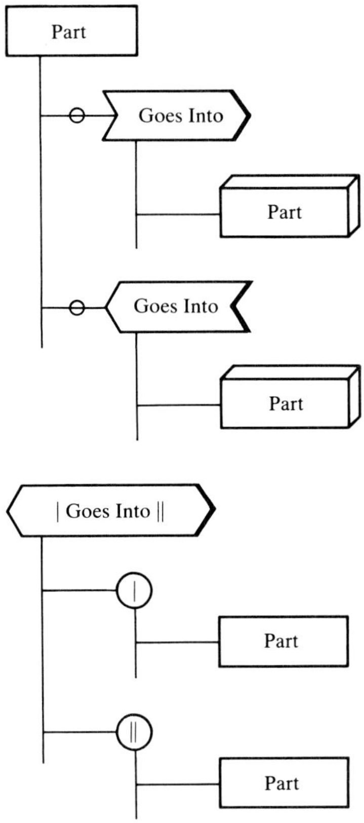

Figure 5.13 A loop.

Exterior Class Tags

An exterior class tag, that is, a class tag where the physical appearance of its instances is significant, is shown inside an oval. Examples are codes of various kinds, administrative identification strings such as license plate numbers, textual descriptions, measurements, and pictures. For example, the most recent daily balance of a checking account might be shown inside an oval as illustrated in Figure 5.14.

Figure 5.14 shows that an *account* must be associated with one *balance of account*, and that there may be many accounts with the same balance. *Optional* and *multiple* decisions may also be shown with ovals. For example, a truck might have many license plates from different states, or none if it is unregistered. This data structure is shown in Figure 5.15. We may view an instance of *License Plate* as a number with an associated state of registration or as a picture of a physical license plate.

In certain practical situations, it is desirable to write an exterior class tag inside a rectangle, as if it were an interior class tag. This indicates that the instances of the exterior class tag are to be relied on to represent accurately the recognizers of interest to the data base. This method should be used with caution, because the needs for which the exposed individuals were developed may differ in subtle but significant ways from the needs of the

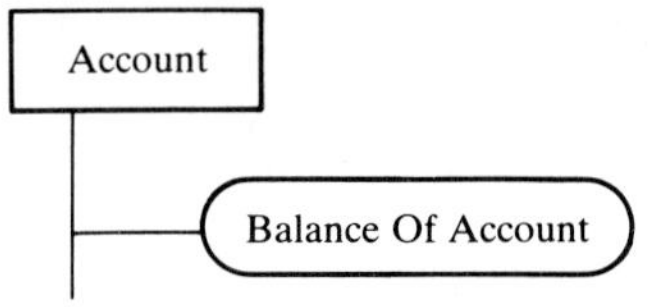

Figure 5.14 An exterior class tag. *"Balance of Account"*.

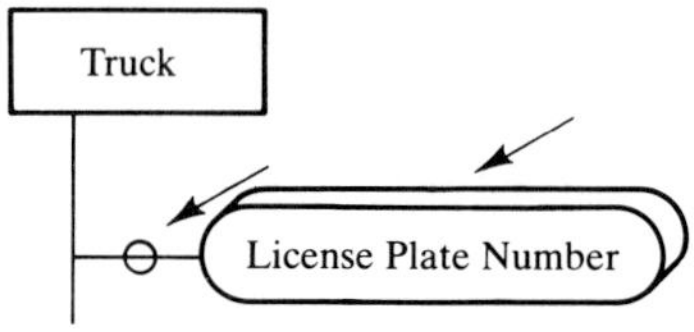

Figure 5.15 *Optional and multiple* character choices for exterior class tags.

data base under design. It is far better, as a rule of thumb, to assume that any exposed individuals will have been defined in some way differently than is needed than to blindly incorporate exposed individuals into a data design merely because they have been successful in other settings. For further discussion of the application of ovals, see (Jones and Curtice 1988).

Conclusion

Extended associative notation provides a direct, visual way of expressing the character decisions of *from all/from some*, *to one/to many*, *from one/from many*, and *to all/to some*. These methods are similar to Associative Data Model notation. They differ in that correspondence tags are written explicitly in extended associative notation, whereas they are omitted in Associative Data Model notation. Writing the correspondence tag explicitly allows extended associative notation to express additional design decisions called *agency* and *targeting* decisions.

5.4 Comparison with Other Notations

In this section, we compare extended associative notation to other data design notations that are used widely. Since our purpose is to help orient the reader who is familiar with one of the other major data models, we will contrast extended associative notation with the other data models using the terms of the other data models. We can only include an overview of the major points. This section should not be construed as a detailed study of conversion between notations.

Since the notations used for the various data models have many variations, we have used Tsichritzis and Lochovsky's book *Data Models* (1982) as a standard. The example we will use to illustrate the various notations is a simplified version of that used in Tsichritzis, to whom the reader is referred for more detailed discussions of the various data models. A discussion of the relationship between Associative Data Model notation and other data models may be found in (Jones and Curtice 1988).

The Hierarchical Data Model

A sample hierarchical data model diagram is shown in Figure 5.16. The equivalent extended associative notation is shown in Figure 5.17.

The symbols inside the rectangles, called "record types" in the hierarchical data model, are called *class tags* in extended associative notation. Thus, "HOSPITAL" is a class tag. Class tags are also shown inside rectangles in extended associative notation.

The arrows in a hierarchical data model diagram indicate *one-to-many correspondences* in extended associative notation. Thus, *one* HOSPITAL may have *many* WARDS. The idea of "many WARDS" is shown by enclosing *Ward* in a three–dimensional box shape in Figure 5.17. In extended associative notation, each correspondence is given a name, or *correspondence tag*. This would be akin to giving a name to each line in a hierarchical data model diagram. Thus, we have given the name *Contains* to the line from HOSPITAL to WARD. In extended associative notation, the same name could be given to many lines, but we have not shown this capability in this example.

In the hierarchical data model, there can not be two lines that connect the same two rectangles. This is permitted in extended associative notation, where it would mean that there may be two *one-to-many* correspondences between the same two record types *B* and *C*. The two correspondences would have different correspondence tags to distinguish between them, and they could attach different instances of *B* and *C* to each other (one could attach an instance *b* to the instances c_1 and c_2; the other could attach *b* to the instances c_2 and c_3, for example).

In extended associative notation, a correspondence tag can be declared relative to the same class tag in both positions. This would be akin to a line in a hierarchical diagram connecting a record type to itself. Such a correspondence can be used to show hierarchical breakdowns within a record type, such as a PART that is a component of another PART, which is itself a component of yet another PART, and so on.

In the hierarchical data model, a record type can have at most one "parent," which is connected directly above the record type. For example, HOSPITAL is the parent of WARD. Conversely, WARD is a "child" of HOSPITAL. In extended associative notation, a class tag may have many "parents," that is, there may be many class tags to which a given class tag corresponds *to one*.

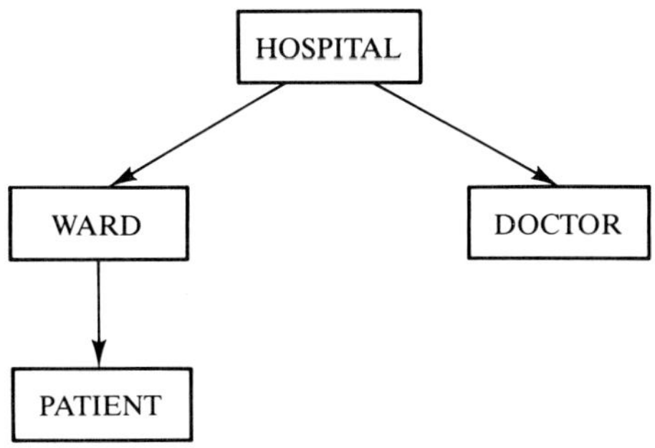

Figure 5.16 Hierarchical data model notation. [Adapted by permission from Figure 7.2-1 Tsichritzis and Lochovsky, *Data Models* © 1982, p. 149. Reprinted by permission of Prentice-Hall, Inc., Englewood Cliffs, N.J.]

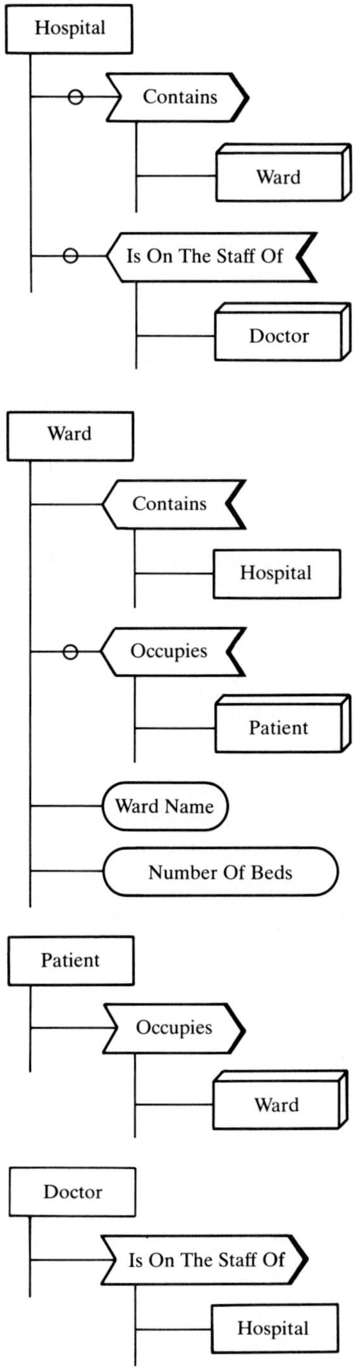

Figure 5.17 Extended associative notation for Figure 5.16.

In the hierarchical data model, a record type may be associated with additional "data items" or "data elements" that are normally shown in text:

WARD (Ward Code, Name, Number Of Beds)

Here, "Name" and "Number Of Beds" are data items. Writing these data items together with WARD in this form indicates that a WARD is associated with one Name and one Number Of Beds. In extended associative notation, data items like "Name" and "Number Of Beds" whose instances are exposed to outside use are shown inside ovals, as illustrated in Figure 5.17.

In the hierarchical data model, a child is usually considered to correspond *from all* to its parent and a parent is usually considered to correspond *from some* to its child. That is, *all* WARDS are associated with a HOSPITAL, but *some* HOSPITALS may have no WARDS. The idea of "some HOSPITALS" is shown in extended associative notation by a small "o" beneath HOSPITAL and before *Contains*. In extended associative notation, decisions of *some* versus *all* can be made for both a child and its parent. Thus, one could specify that *some* instances of a child have a parent instance, or that *all* instances of a parent have a child instance.

Extended associative notation also permits *many-to-many* correspondences to be declared. For example, a *patient* might have many *doctors*, and a *doctor* might have many *patients*. This correspondence would not be represented directly in a hierarchical data model diagram, but it can be shown on an extended associative notation diagram (see Figure 5.19).

Any design produced by a hierarchical diagramming technique may be converted to extended associative notation by the method we have sketched. Other capabilities provided by extended associative notation include direct representation of trios and higher order associations, embracings, and logical constructions involving "and" and "or."

The Network Data Model

The network data model uses similar diagrams to the hierarchical data model. The primary departure made by the network data model is to drop the restriction that a child may have only one parent. Network data model diagrams can therefore be networks, hence the name, while hierarchical data model diagrams are always trees.

Using the network data model, the example may be extended to include a *many-to-many* correspondence from *Doctor* to *Patient*, as shown in Figure 5.18. The extended associative notation diagram for this example is the same as shown in Figure 5.17, except that the templates for *Patient* and *Doctor* are changed as shown in Figure 5.19.

In the network data model, a line that connects two classes is called a "data set" or a "DBTG set type." Each line is labelled, usually by a nominal phrase. These nominal phrases are correspondence tags, and in extended associative notation they should be converted to verbs. For example, the data set HOSPITAL WARD is shown in extended associative notation as the verb *Contains*. Verbs permit extended associative notation diagrams to be read as complete sentences: "a hospital may contain many wards."

Notice that the "intersection" class tag "DOCTOR PATIENT" is not used in extended associative notation. Instead, the *many-to-many* correspondence is represented directly. Bachman, the founder of the network data model, has extended the model to include all 16 correspondence characters (Bachman 1983), so that DOCTOR and PATIENT could be connected directly.

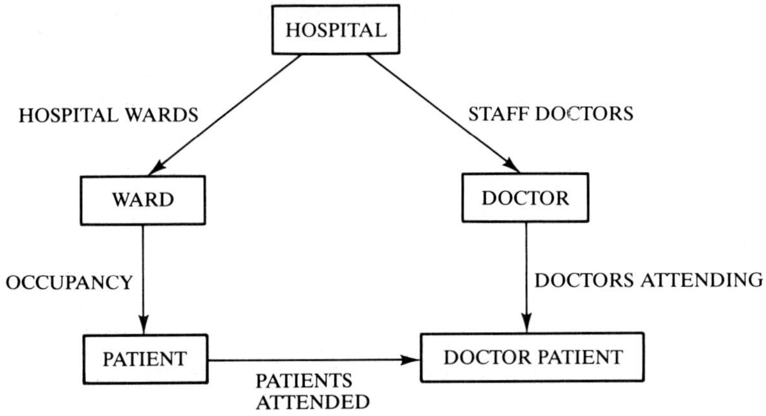

WARD (Ward Code, Name, Number Of Beds)

Figure 5.18 Network data model notation. [Adapted by permission from Figure 6.2-1 Tsichritzis and Lochovsky, *Data Models* © 1982, p. 121. Reprinted by permission of Prentice-Hall, Inc., Englewood Cliffs, N.J.]

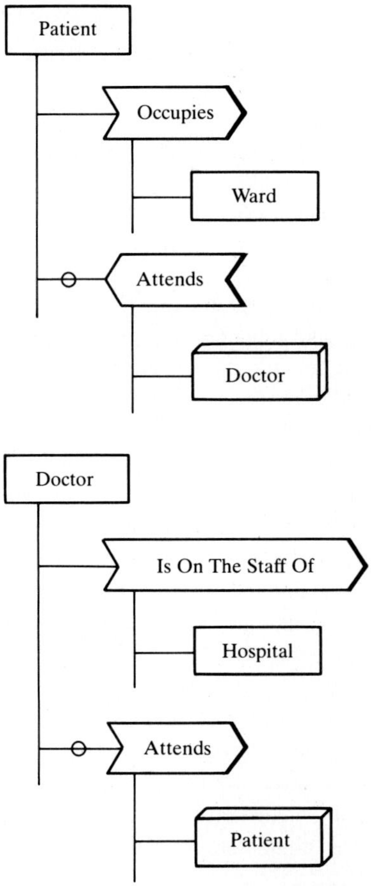

Figure 5.19 Extended associative notation for Figure 5.18.

Any design developed using the network data model may be converted to extended associative notation, using the method we have sketched. Other capabilities provided by extended associative notation include direct representation of trios and higher order associations, embracings, and logical constructions involving ''and'' and ''or.''

The Relational Data Model

The relational data model is the least clearly defined of the major data models, with many alternative formulations available. We have followed the treatments in (Maier 1983) and (Date 1986).

The example we have been working with would be presented in the relational data model as follows:

WARD (Ward Code, Hospital Code, Ward Name, Number of Beds)
DOCTOR (Doctor Number, Hospital Code)
PATIENT (Patient Number, Ward Code)
ATTENDING DOCTOR (Doctor Number, Patient Number)

The underlined text indicates the ''key'' portion of each relation scheme. This example would be shown as Figure 5.20 in extended associative notation (beware—this is not the same as Figures 5.17 and 5.19).

The noun phrases found inside the parentheses of the relational specification are called ''attribute names'' in the relational data model. Thus, ''Ward Code'', ''Hospital Code'', and ''Ward Name'' are all attribute names. An attribute name is called a *class tag* in extended associative notation. Class tags in extended associative notation usually omit qualifiers such as ''code'', ''number'', and so on, that describe how an image is represented. Thus, the attribute name ''Ward Code'' is written ''*Ward*'' in extended associative notation.

The text found outside a pair of parentheses in the relational specification is called a ''relation name''. A relation name is called an *association tag* in extended associative notation. Association tags are usually verbs in extended associative notation. Verbs permit extended associative notation designs to be read as complete sentences: ''a hospital may contain many wards.'' In our illustration, the relation name WARD is renamed *Contains* (precisely, only the first two columns of the relation), the relation name DOCTOR is renamed *Is On The Staff Of*, the relation name PATIENT is renamed *Occupies*, and the relation name ATTENDING DOCTOR is renamed *Attends*. The entire text consisting of a relation name together with its attribute names is called a ''relation scheme''. For example, ''PATIENT (Patient Number, Ward Code)'' is a relation scheme.

Extended associative notation distinguishes *interior* class tags, whose instances represent things that data is kept about, from *exterior* class tags, whose instances are symbols with predetermined meanings. For example, hospital codes and ward codes would be treated in extended associative notation as arbitrary identifiers of « hospitals » and « wards », so ''*Hospital*'' and ''*Ward*'' are interior class tags. Ward names and counts of the number of beds in a ward are represented by strings of characters that can not be changed without changing their meaning, so ''Ward Name'' and ''Number Of Beds'' are exterior class tags. As shown in Figure 5.20, interior class tags like ''Hospital'' and

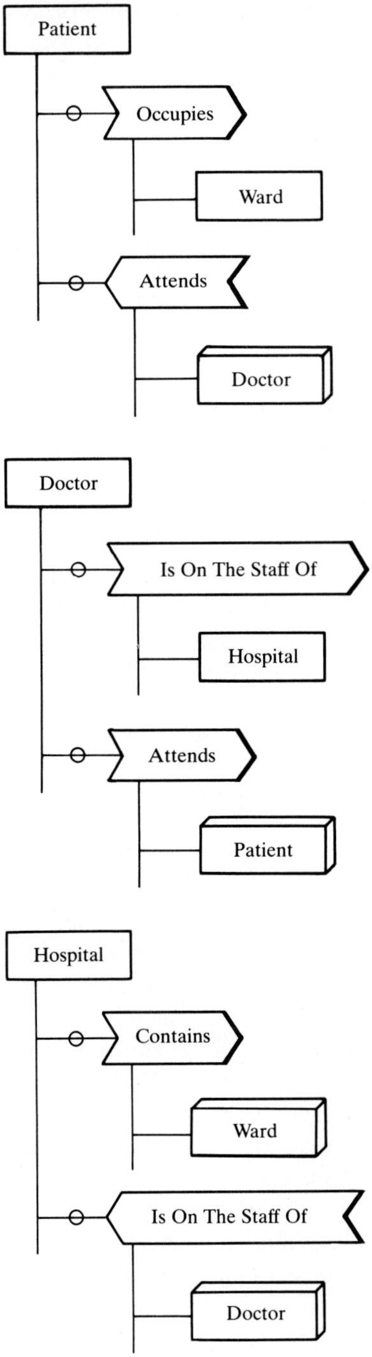

Figure 5.20 Extended associative notation for relational data model example.

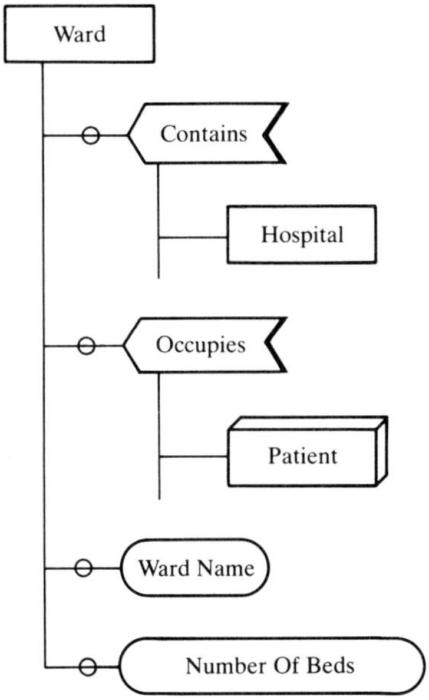

Figure 5.20 *(continued)*

''Ward'' are shown in extended associative notation inside rectangles, while exterior class tags like ''Ward Name'' and ''Number Of Beds'' are shown inside ovals.

Four *cascades* are shown beneath the class tag *Ward* in extended associative notation: *Contains–Hospital, Occupies–Patient, Ward Name,* and *Number Of Beds*. Three of these cascades are shown in the one relation scheme ''WARD (Hospital Code, Ward Name, Number of Beds). In general, all non–key attribute names in a relation scheme are shown in separate cascades in extended associative notation. The remaining cascade, *Occupies–Patient,* is a *reversal* of the association between *Patient* and *Ward* shown in the relation scheme PATIENT. In extended associative notation, all association tags between two class tags (that is, all *correspondence tags*) are shown twice, beneath each of the class tags.

In some formulations of the relational data model, an attribute name may only appear in one relation scheme. In extended associative notation, in contrast, the same class tag may appear in several correspondence complexes. Thus, a hospital may both contain a ward and have doctors on its staff. In the relational data model, this situation may be represented by forming a ''domain'', a set of allowable hospital codes, and assigning the two attribute names ''Hospital Code'' in relation scheme WARD and ''Hospital Code'' in relation scheme DOCTOR to the same domain. Extended associative notation takes a different approach: it concentrates on the images that are represented, « hospitals » in this case, not on the symbols, hospital codes.

When a domain is used in a relational data model design to indicate that the same image can be represented by values of two attribute names, then the class tag in extended associative notation takes the place of the domain name in the relational data model. However, domains can also be used to describe operational characteristics of data rather than what the data represents. Such are the domains ''floating point number'' or ''forty character string.'' These operational domains are generally not written in extended associative notation. See, however, (Jones and Curtice 1988) for a discussion of how they may be represented in Associative Data Model notation.

Some formulations of the relational data model permit "foreign keys", which in extended associative notation are called "*from all*" and "*to all*" constraints. For example, according to the treatment of Date, if "Ward Code" in the relation scheme PATIENT is a foreign key matching the attribute name "Ward Code" in the relation scheme WARD, then each instance of "Ward Code" in PATIENT must be an instance of "Ward Code" in WARD. In extended associative notation, this rule would be described by saying that each *ward* is *contained* in at least one *hospital*. That is, we would say that the correspondence *Contains* is *to all*. The constraint would be shown by removing the small "o" below *Ward* and before *Contains* in the *Hospital* template in Figure 5.20.

Date requires further that a foreign key be a primary key in the target relation. Thus, matching "Ward Code" in PATIENT to "Ward Code" in WARD is only permitted because "Ward Code" is key in WARD. This rule prevents us from declaring, for example, that a *hospital* must *contain* at least one *ward*. To do so, we would need to declare that "Hospital Code" was a foreign key in DOCTOR, matching "Hospital Code" in WARD, but "Hospital Code" is not key in WARD, so this is prevented. If we make "Hospital Code" key in WARD, WARD is not in second normal form, since "Ward Code" determines "Hospital Code".

In extended associative notation, *from all* and *to all* constraints are declared directly, not through foreign keys. Thus, the first "o" under *Ward* shows that a *ward* need not be *contained* in any *hospital*. To declare that each *ward* must be *contained* in a *hospital*, remove the "o". Similarly, the next "o" indicates that a *ward* need not be *occupied* by any *patient*. To declare that a *ward* must be *occupied* by at least one patient, remove the "o". Similar descriptions apply to the "o" symbols before *Ward Name* and *Number of Beds*. In extended associative notation, each of these decisions may be made independently.

The relational data model includes many implied interrelationships between the character decisions of extended associative notation. For example, suppose we declare that each *ward* is contained in at least one *hospital* (that is, there are no *wards* that are *occupied* by *patients* but are not *contained* in *hospitals*). We must then conclude that each *ward* has a name and has a number of beds. This unusual deduction is a consequence of the attribute names used in the relation scheme WARD.

In the relational data model, designating certain attribute names as "key" (shown by underlines in the example) indicates the "functional dependencies" of the schema. In extended associative notation, functional dependencies are called *from one* and *to one* constraints. For example, since "Doctor Number" is key in DOCTOR, we can conclude that all other attribute names in DOCTOR (in this case, "Hospital Code") correspond *to one* to the attribute name "Doctor Number" (each doctor is on the staff of at most *one* hospital). In extended associative notation, functional dependencies are shown directly, and are not shown by choosing certain class tags to be "key." Thus, this functional dependency is shown by enclosing *Hospital* in a single rectangle below *Doctor–Is On The Staff Of*.

Failure to obey a functional dependency is also shown explicitly in extended associative notation. For example, since both "Doctor Number" and "Patient Number" are key in ATTENDING DOCTOR, we may conclude that the class tags *Doctor* and *Patient* correspond *many–to–many*. That is, a doctor may attend many patients, and a patient may be attended by many doctors. These "many" characteristics are shown by three-dimensional boxes in extended associative notation: the rule that a *doctor* may *attend* many *patients* is shown by a three-dimensional box around *Patient* beneath *Doctor–Attends*, and the rule that a *patient* may be *attended* by many *doctors* is shown by a three-dimensional box around *Doctor* beneath *Patient–Attends*.

In the relational data model, a relation scheme contains exactly one sequence of attribute names. For example, ATTENDING DOCTOR contains the pair of attribute names (Doctor Number, Patient Number). In extended associative notation, the same association tag may attach instances of several sequences of class tags. For example, extended associative notation permits the correspondence complex *Nurses Attend Patients* to appear in the same data base as the correspondence complex *Doctors Attend Patients*. In extended associative notation, the same association tag *Attends* may obey different constraints within the two correspondence complexes. For example, it could be that a *patient* could have at most one attending *doctor*, but could have many attending *nurses*.

In the relational data model, relations are altered by a process of "normalization" that determines, once the functional dependencies are known, the proper tabular form of relations, and the attribute names that should be key. Most issues handled by normalization in the relational data model arise in associations of degree three and higher, and will be discussed in Chapter 9. Normalization is hindered, in particular, by the presence of "null values." Extended associative notation, in contrast, allows null values to be permitted or prohibited in any or all columns of a relation.

Any design developed using the relational data model may be converted to extended associative notation, using the methods we have sketched and the methods to be discussed in Chapter 9. Care must be used, however, to represent the *from all/from some* and *to all/to some* decisions properly, since these decisions are not shown directly in relational data model notation. The relational data model has difficulty with *from some* and *to some* decisions in relationships of degree greater than two, since such decisions can require "null values". Other capabilities provided by extended associative notation include declaration of embracings and logical constructions using "and" and "or", which will be discussed in later sections of this chapter.

5.5 EMBRACINGS

Simple Embracings

An embracing of classes, $B \subseteq C$, is shown in Figure 5.21. The embracing is shown in both the template for the class B and the template for the class C. As with the character brackets $\lceil$ and $<$, the embracing symbol opens to the class that may have more instances. Thus, in both templates the embracing symbol faces toward "C". The design management device assures that the two templates are maintained in tandem. The embracing $B \subseteq C$ is explained by the phrase "Any B is also a/an C", which is shown beside both templates.

A bi-directional embracing, that is, an equivalence, $B \equiv C$, is shown by writing the embracing symbols side-by-side, as shown in Figure 5.22. As with a single embracing, both $B \equiv C$ and $C \equiv B$ are shown.

An embracing of correspondences is shown similarly. The position designators "|"

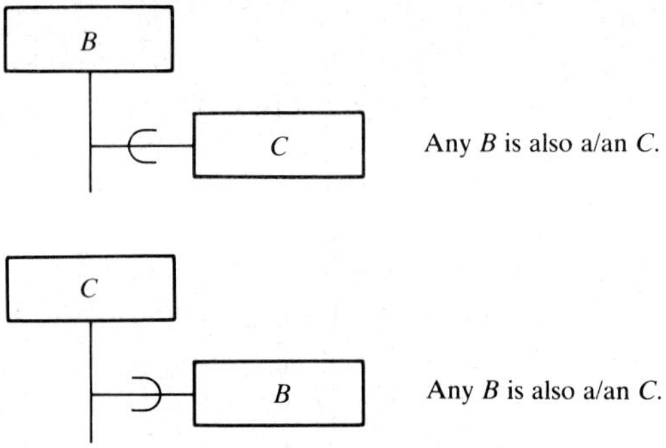

Figure 5.21 An embracing of classes.

and "||" are used to show the orientation of the correspondences. Thus, Figure 5.23 shows the two embracings $F \subseteq G$ and $H^* \subseteq F$.

The position designators "|" and "||" retain their meaning throughout a template, but can not be compared across templates. Thus, in Figure 5.23, the embracing of "|| *H* |" in "| *F* ||" in the template for *F* states that for any images *x* and *y*, if *F*:|*x*, *y*|, then *H*:|*y*, *x*| (here "*x*" is used for "|" and "*y*" is used for "||"). This same constraint is shown in the template for *H* as "| *H* ||" being embraced in "|| *F* |". The position designator "|" in the template for *H* therefore designates a different position than the position designator "|" in the template for *F*.

Combinations

More complex embracings are shown in extended associative notation using *combinations*. A *combination* is an expression formed by combining initial association tags with logical operations. For example, a combination is used to represent the intersection of two classes, or the composition of two correspondences. Data logic notation represents combinations by special symbols: "$\cap$" for intersection, "$\circ$" for composition, and so on.

The first priority for a design notation must be that the meaning of each piece of notation should be immediately clear to a user with a minimum of training. This is a

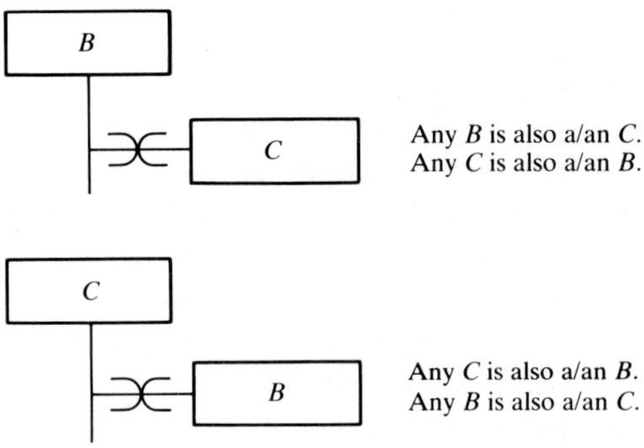

Figure 5.22 An equivalence of classes.

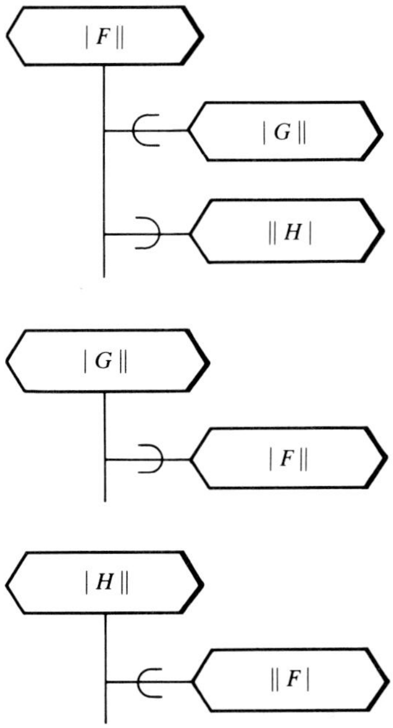

Figure 5.23 Embracings of correspondences.

particularly important requirement in the case of combinations, because it is easy to create very complicated combinations. We suggest that complicated combinations be broken apart into *modules* in such a way that each module contains only one logical operation. For example, consider the embracing

$$(F \circ G) \cap H \cap I \subseteq J \cup (K \circ L)$$

Rather than trying to declare this embracing in one picture, we would advise breaking it into three constraints:

$$E \equiv F \circ G$$

$$M \equiv K \circ L$$

$$(E \cap H \cap I) \subseteq (J \cup M)$$

New names, E and M, are given to each of the two compositions $F \circ G$ and $K \circ L$. By this method, each declared embracing contains only one logical operation on either side of the embracing symbol.

To emphasize that we view extended associative notation as being implemented on a design management device, we have taken the additional step of describing how such a device might function. We have kept the discussion as generic as possible, so as not to prejudice the software solution. We will suppose that each logical operation is associated with a *tool* in the design management device that manages the formation of combinations using that logical operation. Thus, there is an AND tool, an OR tool, and a COMPOSE tool, for example.

Combinations of Classes

Figure 5.24 illustrates the method for forming the class tag *Chair and Wheeled Object*, that is, « _____ Is A Chair With Wheels », from the class tags *Chair* and *Wheeled Object*. This combination represents the intersection « *Chair* ∩ *Wheeled Object* ». An image is accepted by the intersection if it is accepted both by *Chair* and by *Wheeled Object*.

In forming combinations by "and", the first element chosen establishes the outline shape of the new combination: it will be a rectangle for classes, a tile for associations of degree two or higher. The choice of tool determines how the association tags are to be combined (in this case, by "and"). The CREATE COMBINATION tool forms the extended associative notation diagram at the bottom of Figure 5.24. Notice that the word "and" is written in lower case inside the rectangles to identify it as a notational word supplied by the design management device.

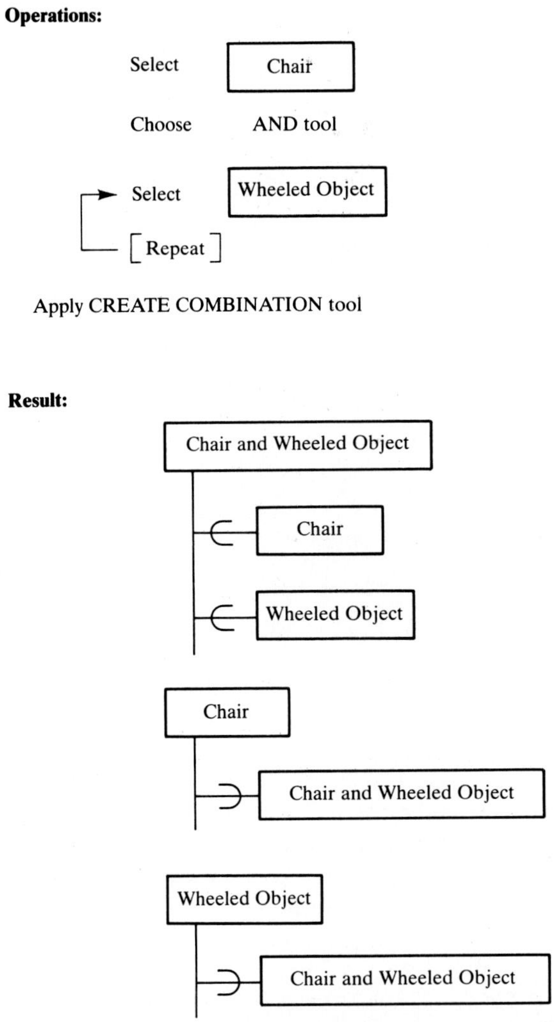

Figure 5.24 Combination using AND.

By definition, any image accepted by *Chair and Wheeled Object* is accepted by *Chair* and by *Wheeled Object*. Thus, the combination *Chair and Wheeled Object* is embraced in both *Chair* and *Wheeled Object*, and the design management device inserts these embracings automatically.

The AND tool can be used repeatedly to form intersections of arbitrarily many classes. Thus, the class of red chairs with wheels may be represented by the combination *Chair and Wheeled Object and Red Object*.

A similar procedure is followed for forming unions. The class of images that are either office furniture or aids for the disabled (or both) is written *Office Furniture or Aid For The Disabled*, the word "or" indicating union. Figure 5.25 illustrates the procedure for forming the union. By definition, a union $B \cup C$ embraces both B and C. These embracings are established automatically by the design management device.

A complex embracing $\mathcal{F} \subseteq \mathcal{G}$, where $\mathcal{F}$ and $\mathcal{G}$ are logical formulas, is expressed in

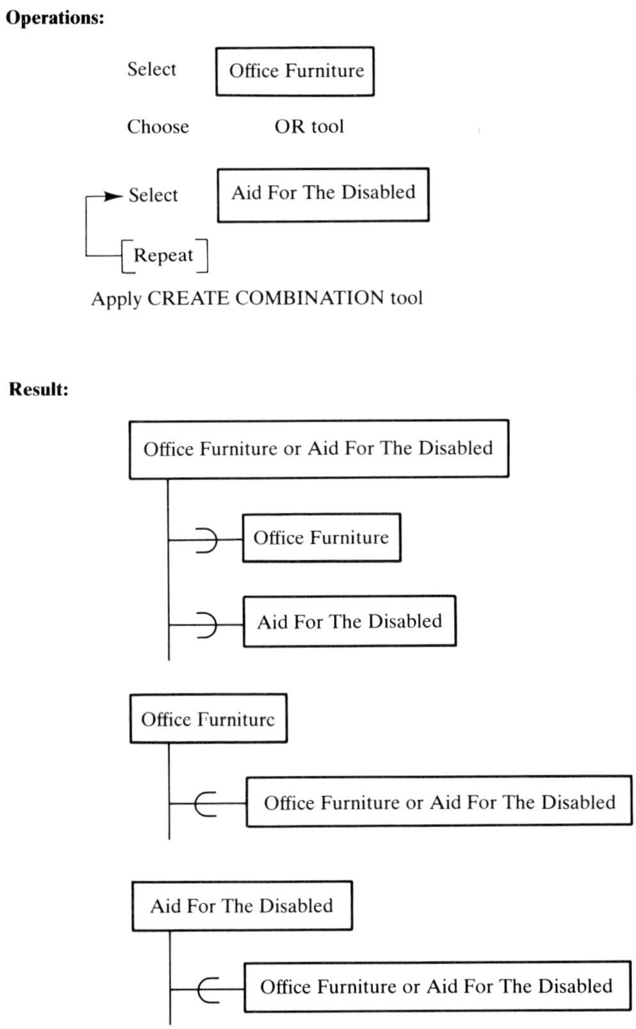

Figure 5.25 Combination using OR.

extended associative notation by decomposing $\mathscr{F}$ and $\mathscr{G}$ into modules so that each module contains only one logical operation. Logic may also provide a way to simplify the embracing. For example, the embracing $B \subseteq C \cap D$ is equivalent to the two embracings $B \subseteq C$ and $B \subseteq D$ (see Section 2.4). Each module is then declared as a combination, as shown in Figures 5.24 and 5.25. The combinations are then embraced in each other. For example, the embracing

$$\textit{Chair} \cap \textit{Wheeled Object} \subseteq \textit{Office Furniture} \cup \textit{Aid For The Disabled}$$

is shown in extended associative notation in Figure 5.26.

Combinations of Correspondences

Forming AND and OR combinations of correspondences requires the use of position designators to show the orientation of each correspondence. For example, the combination "| *Acquires* || *and* || *Sells To* |" represents the correspondence that attaches a company c to a company d if c acquires d and d sells to c (that is, d is a regular supplier to c). This correspondence is written in data logic notation as *Acquires* $\cap$ (*Sells To*)*. The formation of this combination is illustrated in Figure 5.27. The orientation of each correspondence is specified by selecting the position designator that is to occupy the first position in the combination.

The embracings $F \cap G \subseteq F$ and $F \cap G \subseteq G$ are supplied automatically by the design management device. Unions of correspondences are formed in the same way, but by applying the OR tool instead of the AND tool.

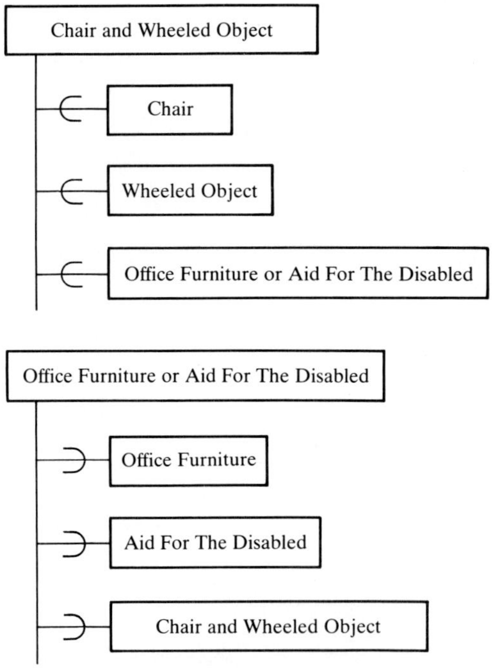

Figure 5.26 An embracing of combinations.

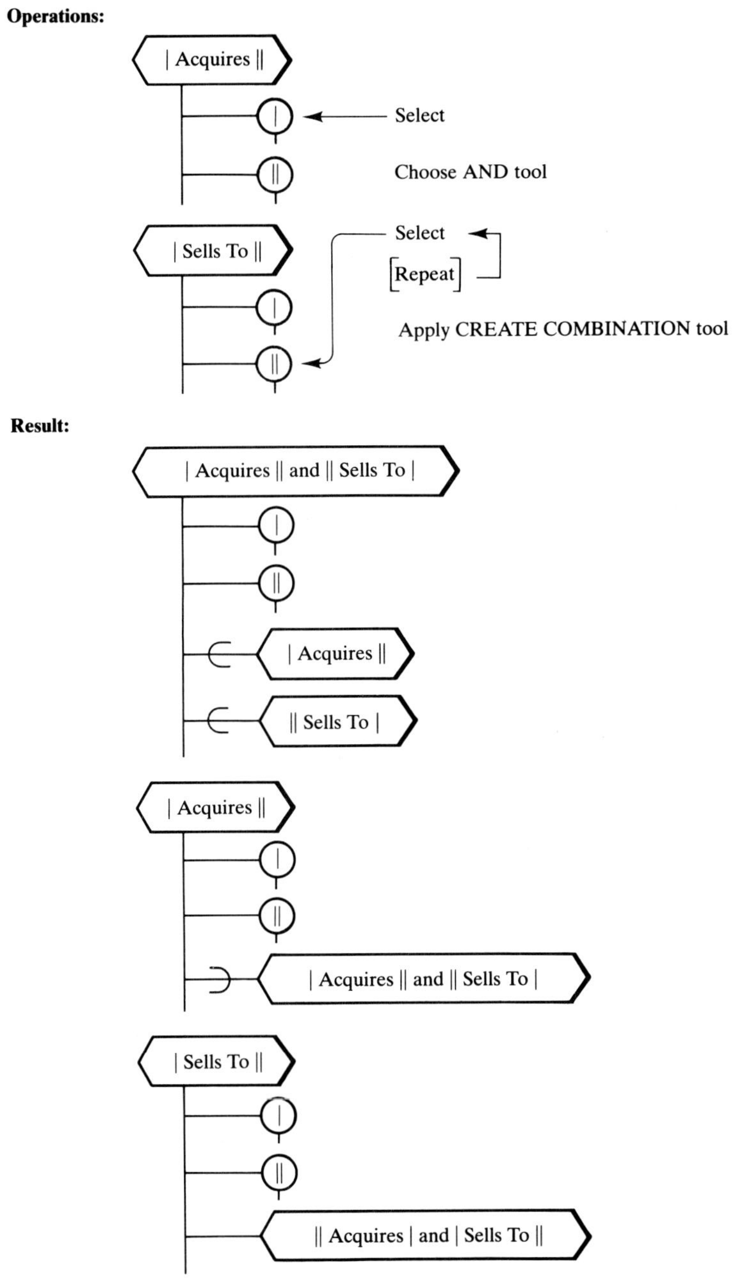

Figure 5.27 A combination of correspondences.

Other special combinations are formed similarly: The identity correspondence ΔB for a class B is written "| *is the same B as* ||". The Cartesian product $B \times C$ is written "*a B|and a C* ||".

Paths

Composition of correspondences is often used in forming data base constraints. In extended associative notation, these constraints usually involve reduced correspondences, and are formed so that the destination class of a correspondence complex is also the source class of the correspondence complex it is composed with. Thus, the general form of a composition alternates identity correspondences with declared correspondences:

$$\Delta A \circ F \circ \Delta B \circ G \circ \Delta C \circ H \circ \ldots \circ \Delta E$$

A composition usually begins and ends with an identity correspondence. We will discuss paths in more depth in Section 6.4.

In extended associative notation, a path is shown by *extending* the correspondence complexes to form a long cascade that is then converted into a composition correspondence. The process of extending a correspondence complex is illustrated in Figure 5.28. Notice the small hollow rectangle in the template at the bottom of the figure, which indicates an extension.

A composition is formed by selecting an extended cascade and applying the CREATE COMPOSITION tool. Figure 5.29 illustrates the procedure. The general form for a composition $\Delta B \circ G \circ \Delta C \circ H \circ \Delta D$ is "*B| Gs some C that Hs D*||". The places of "|" and "||" in the combinations are altered as needed for converse correspondences.

Projection

The class of images that *own* something, that is, the class of *owners*, is the projection onto the first position of the correspondence *Owns*, written $\pi^1 Owns$ in data logic notation. In extended associative notation, this class is represented by the combination "*a thing| where | Owns something*". The word "something" is used to indicate a projection. The projection of the reduced correspondence *Person Owns Car* is represented by the combination "*a Person| where| Owns some Car*". Formation of these combinations is illustrated in Figure 5.30. In the projection of a reduced correspondence, the design management device supplies the embracing in the appropriate relative class.

Synonyms

It is often valuable to give a complex combination a *synonym* that can be used in its place in other portions of the design. Combinations must be given a synonym when declaring logical expressions with many modules: to declare the logical expression $F \cap (G \circ H)$, for example, $G \circ H$ is given the synonym "*I*", and the combination $F \cap I$ is formed.

A synonym is declared in extended associative notation by a bi-directional embracing. Figure 5.31 shows the declaration of "*Owner*" as a synonym for "*a Person| where| Owns something*".

Operations:

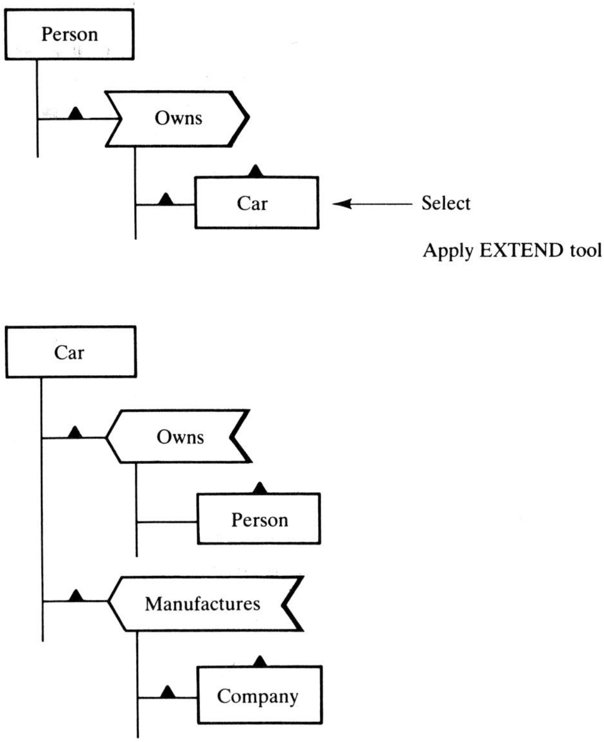

Result:

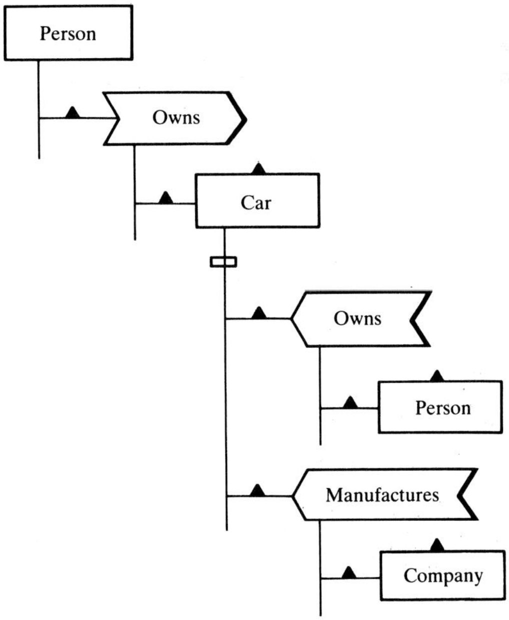

Figure 5.28 Extending a cascade.

Operations:

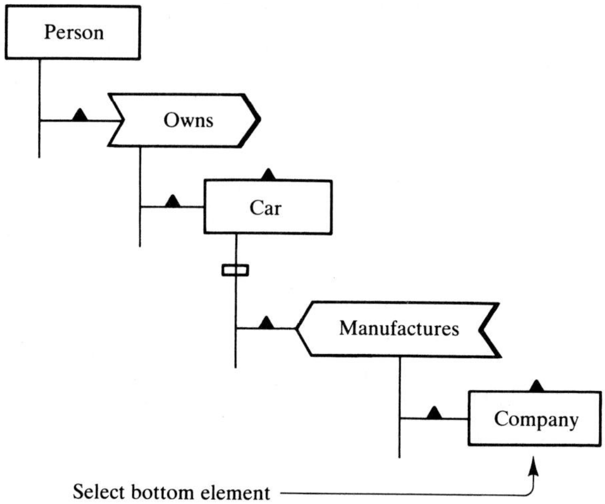

Apply CREATE COMPOSTION tool

Result:

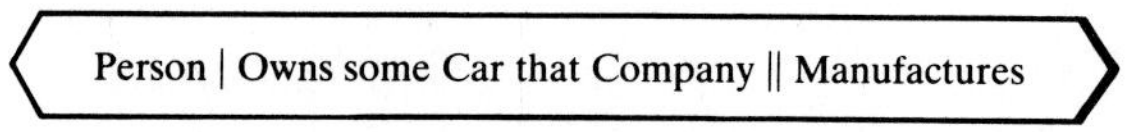

Figure 5.29 A composition.

Conclusion

We have discussed how both simple and complex embracings may be expressed in extended associative notation. Embracings of the form $R \subseteq S$, where both R and S are declared association tags, may be expressed directly. We recommend that synonyms be used liberally to express complex embracings, so that each embracing remains readily comprehensible.

5.6 TRIOS OF THE FIRST STABLE STATE

Overview of Trio Complexes

Every student of data has encountered trios in one form or another. The scenario encountered most frequently occurs after a correspondence is formed. Imagine that two classes, *Person* and *Project*, have been related by a correspondence « a *person* works on a *project* ». Suppose it is now required to show the *role* of each *person* on each *project*: *Role* is a third class that needs to be associated with the other two. Most data analysts at this juncture typically resort to extensive trial and error. The design group will try connecting

Operations:

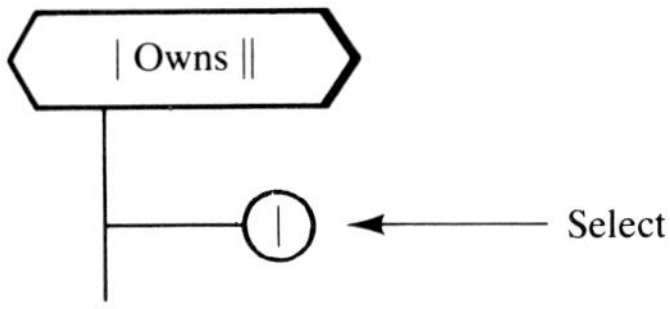

Apply CREATE PROJECTION tool

Result:

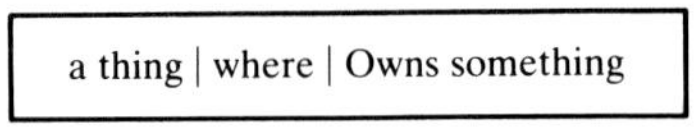

Operations:

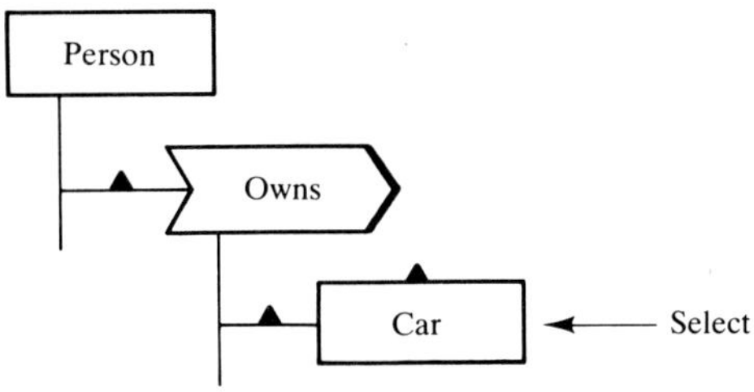

Apply CREATE PROJECTION tool

Result:

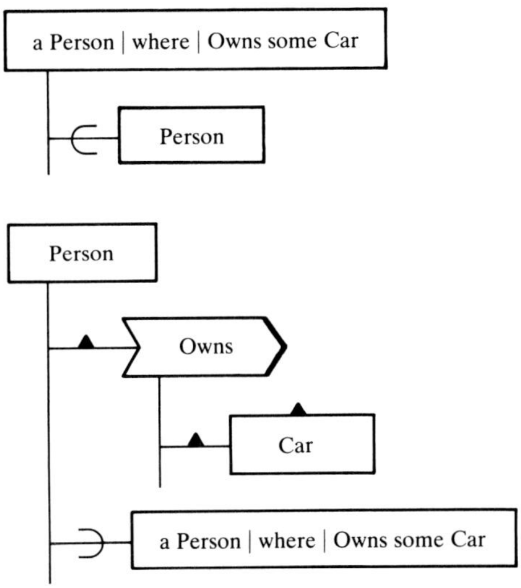

Figure 5.30 A projection.

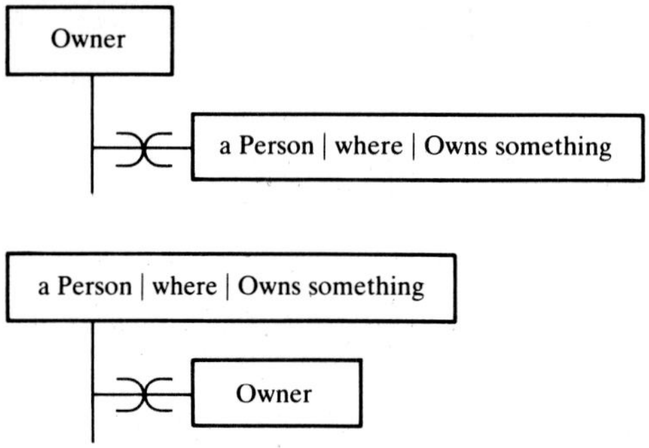

Figure 5.31 A synonym.

Person–Project to *Role*. If that does not work, they try forming *Person–Role* and connecting it to *Project*. Or they try forming *Project–Role* and connecting it to *Person*. Or they form a *Person–Role–Project* triple. There is probably some creativity devoted to inventing ''null'' objects of various kinds during the discussions. In many cases, one of the structures is found to work. In other cases, nothing seems to work.

Although most modern data design techniques provide some facility for handling trios, none can express the full variety of possible forms that a trio complex can exhibit. A fully reversed trio complex, that is, a trio declared relative to three classes and three correspondences, may be visualized as the network drawing shown in Figure 5.32.

The boxes *A, B,* and *C* represent classes, the boxes *F*, *G*, and *H* represent correspondences, and the box *TU* represents a trio. The whole picture is called a *trio complex*, which is what one must consider when designing a trio. The brackets show character decisions that must be made as part of the declaration. Figure 5.32 shows all the possible brackets, and therefore illustrates the most permissive trio complex possible. Other varieties of trio complexes are formed by deleting brackets from Figure 5.32.

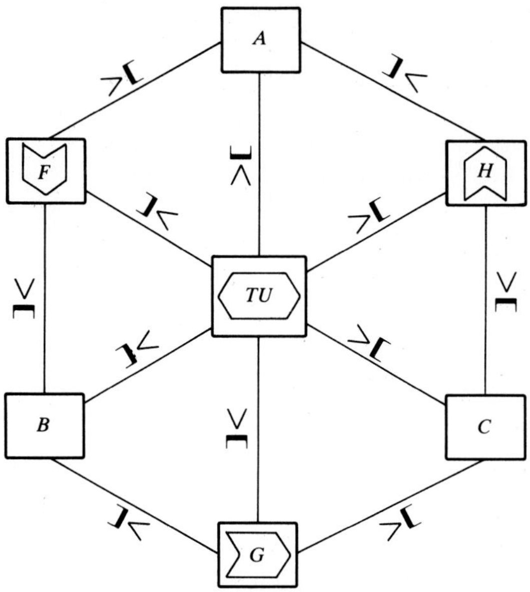

Figure 5.32 A trio complex.

There are 24 character decisions to be made in declaring a fully reversed trio complex, and each combination of different decisions yields a different data structure with different constraints on its population. There are a total of 30,660 different varieties of trio complexes as shown on Figure 5.32, whereas there are only 16 varieties of correspondence complexes (the 16 different characters).

Many data models limit which brackets may be declared on Figure 5.32. For example, the [brackets between the trio *T* and the correspondences *F*, *G*, and *H* identify "null values," which are usually prohibited in the relational data model (Date 1986). Over 98 percent of the varieties of trio complexes that can be declared in extended associative notation have at least one [bracket in a "null value" position, showing that trio complexes with "null values" are not an aberration, but the dominant form.

Other data models, such as the entity–relationship model, can express the picture in Figure 5.32, but do not express all the interrelationships between the associations (see (Tsichritzis and Lochovsky 1982) or (Chen 1976) for a description of the entity–relationship model). For example, the path from *TU* through *F* to *A* can be defined as a correspondence (specifically, a composition of two elision correspondences). So can the path from *T* to *A*. These two paths are equivalent, that is, they are related by a bi–directional embracing. Data models without embracings can not express this constraint.

One might think that the *T*–to–*A* correspondence could be deleted from Figure 5.32 because it can be computed from the path *T*–to–*F*–to–*A*. However, there are trio complexes that we call *pineal* in which the character of the *T*–to–*A* correspondence constrains the potential populations of the *T*–to–*F*–to–*A* path, so that removing the *T*–to–*A* correspondence would change the data structure. We will discuss this type of interaction between the characters of different correspondences, called a *composition cone constraint*, in Chapter 8. There are over 11,000 forms of pineal trio complexes.

To ease the burden of declaring the complete diagram shown in Figure 5.32, we introduce simpler forms of trio notation called *stable states*. These are alternative forms that may be used to save time, but are completely equivalent to a full reversal. In a stable state, some of the bracket decisions shown in Figure 5.32 are defaulted in a regular way. There are four stable states, corresponding to the number of [brackets between the trio *T* and the correspondences *F*, *G*, and *H*. If there are no such brackets, the trio is in the *base state*, if there is one it is in the *first stable state*, and so on. Each of these brackets corresponds to a statement of the form « it is possible for *F* to attach *x* to *y* without there being a *z* such that *T* assembles the triple (*x*, *y*, *z*) ». In each such case, a correspondence may have attachments that can not be deduced from the population of the trio *T*. The behavior of these additional attachments complicates declaration of the trio complex.

Tile–Relative Notation

Consider a correspondence tag *G* that is declared relative to the pair of class tags (*B*, *C*). The correspondence tag "*G*" appears, then, twice on the second level, once under *B* and once under *C*, as shown in Figure 5.33.

The direction of the chevron serves to distinguish the image « a *B Gs* a *C* », which is intended, from the image « a *C Gs* a *B* », which is not. Another way to make this distinction is to use *tile–relative notation*, which distinguishes *B* from *C* by the fact that *B* appears *above G* in the diagram, and *C* appears *below G*. In tile–relative notation, the class

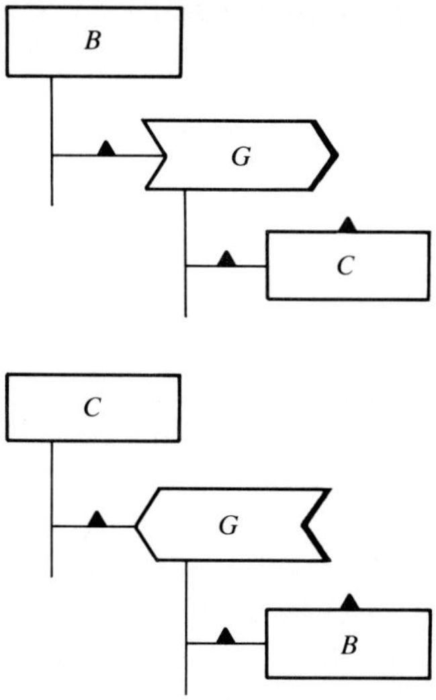

Figure 5.33

tag one step above G (namely B) is indicated by "–", and the class tag one step below G (namely C) is indicated by "+". When we use this approach, the correspondence tag G is shown inside a tile rather than a chevron. The correspondence complex (G; B, C) is shown using tile–relative notation in Figure 5.34.

The chevron notation and the tile–relative notation are equivalent for correspondences. The tile–relative notation, however, can be generalized to associations of arbitrarily high degree, while the chevron notation can not.

A trio is often represented as a combination of a transitive verb with an auxiliary phrase, either a prepositional phrase or an infinitive, as in

① *Pays* ② *For* ③

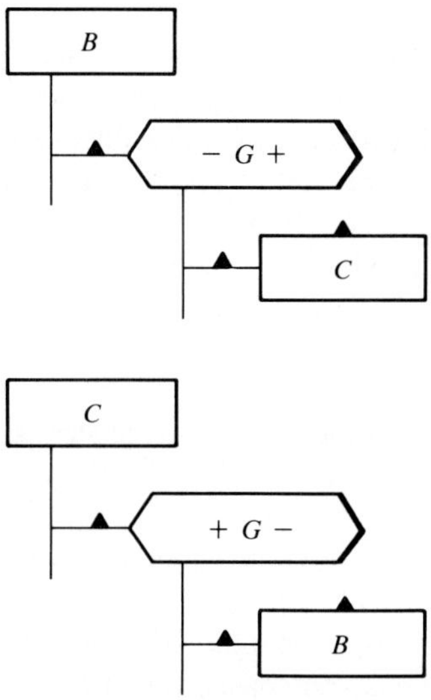

Figure 5.34 Tile-relative notation for Figure 5.33.

This trio may be written in data logic notation as

( ) *Pays* ( ) *For* ( )

Some trio tags do not separate so cleanly. For example, the proposition

Joe lends Sally the truck

may be viewed as an instance of the trio *Lends*(, ,), written

(*Joe*) *Lends*: (*Sally*) (*the truck*)

In extended associative notation, these trio tags would be written as shown in Figure 5.35. The small dots will be replaced by "+" signs or "−" signs that depend upon the place that the trio tag occupies in the diagram.

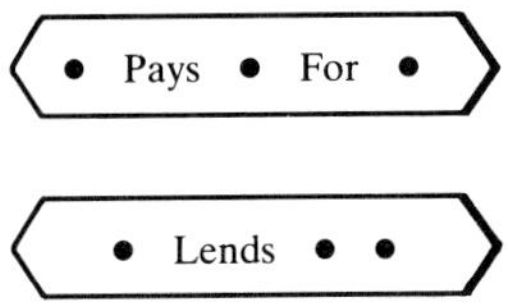

Figure 5.35 Trio tags.

Relative Declaration

In extended associative notation, a trio tag ( )*T*( )*U*( ) is always declared relative to a triple of class tags (*A*, *B*, *C*) as in

« an *A Ts* a *B U* a *C* »

A trio tag may also be declared simultaneously relative to up to three correspondence tags:

« an *A Fs* a *B* »

« a *B Gs* a *C* »

« a *C Hs* an *A* »

When we say that a trio tag is declared *relative* to these association tags, we mean that the assemblies of the trio tag are restricted to those cases where the individuals are also instances of the relative class tags, and appear in attachments governed by the relative correspondence tags. For example, if we say that, given individuals *a* and *b*, there is at most one individual *c* such that $T:(a, b, c)$ relative to *A*, *B*, *C*, and *F* above, we mean that if $A:(a)$ and $B:(b)$ and $F:(a, b)$, then there is at most one individual *c* such that $\dot{T}:(a, b, c)$ and $C:(c)$. In data logic notation, we are considering the reduced association $\dot{T}$ defined by

$$(\mathrm{A}x)\ (\mathrm{A}y)\ (\mathrm{A}z)\ \dot{T}:|x, y, z| \Leftrightarrow (\exists x')\ (\exists y')\ (\exists z')\ \Delta A:|x, x'|\ \&\ \Delta B:|y, y'|\ \&\ \Delta C:|z, z'|\ \&\ |x|\Delta A \circ F \circ \Delta B:|y|\ \&\ T:|x', y', z'|$$

The combination of the trio tag *T* with the association tags that it is declared relative to (in this case, *A*, *B*, *C*, and *F*) is called a *trio complex*. The three classes *A*, *B*, and *C* must always be specified when declaring a trio. Any combination of the correspondence tags *F*, *G*, and *H* may be specified as well. If no correspondence is declared, the trio is said to be in the *base state,* if one, the *first stable state*, if two, the *second stable state*, and if all three, the trio is said to be *fully reversed*. Techniques for deciding which correspondences to specify, as well as more precise definitions of a *trio complex* and a *stable state*, will be discussed in the in–depth analysis of trios in Chapter 9. We will confine ourselves in this chapter to showing how each of the stable states may be expressed in extended associative notation.

Notation for the First Stable State

Since the base state is somewhat atypical, we begin with the first stable state. The first stable state occurs when a trio tag ( )*T*( )*U*( ) is declared relative to a triple of class tags (*A*, *B*, *C*) and one correspondence tag ( )*F*( ), and when *F* is itself declared relative to (*A*, *B*). We will use the general symbols *A*, *B*, *C*, *F*, and *T* to show the formal notation for a first stable state trio. We will also show an illustration alongside:

« A *person operates* a *truck*, and may *use* the *truck to carry* an *item* »

That is,

$$A \equiv Person$$

$$B \equiv Truck$$

$$C \equiv Item$$

$$F \equiv Operates$$

$$T \equiv Uses$$

$$U \equiv To\ Carry$$

This trio is declared using the format shown in Figure 5.36. Notice that the trio tag ()*T*()*U*() is drawn preceded by a double minus sign, indicating *A*, followed then by a single minus sign, indicating *B*, and finally a single plus sign, indicating the class tag *C*, which appears below.

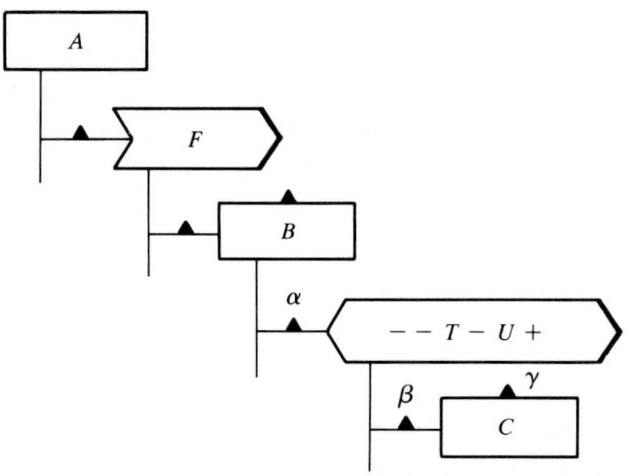

Figure 5.36 A trio complex (first stable state).

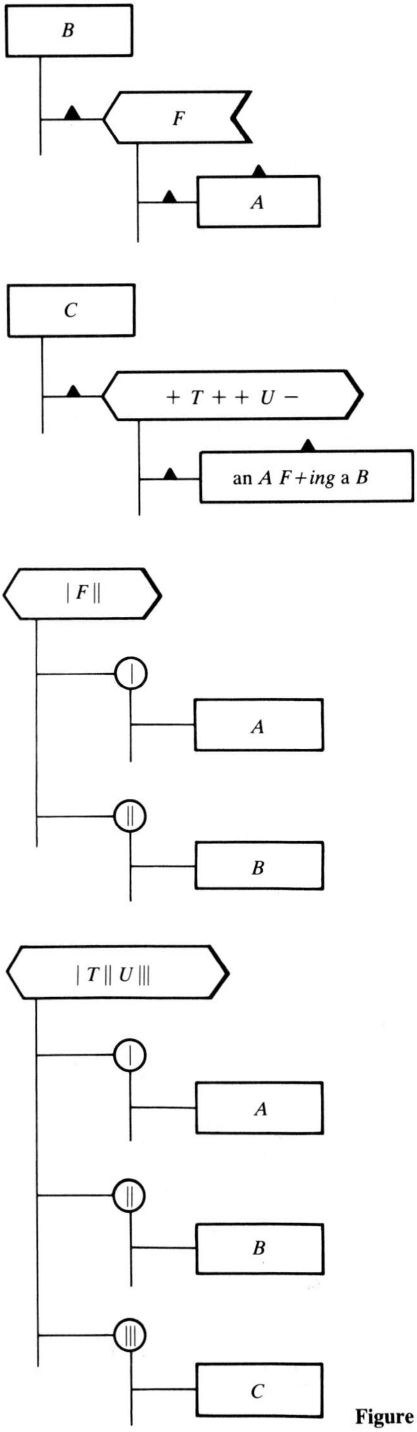

Figure 5.36 *(continued)*

The "$-$" markers are required when the trio tag is declared relative to a loop « a *B Ts* a *B U* a *C* ». The "$-$" markers then distinguish instances of positions one and two, which are declared relative to the same class. If the two class tags are different, one may remove the minus signs as shown in Figure 5.37.

A first stable state trio complex may be illustrated as the network diagram shown in Figure 5.38. It includes one of the corners (in this case, the upper left corner) of the network diagram for a fully reversed trio complex shown earlier in Figure 5.32. This diagram shows that the classes *A* and *B* are associated via the correspondence *F*, and that *C* is associated via the trio *TU* (precisely, via the elision correspondence ${}_{12}TU_3$) with the correspondence *F*.

The translation between these network diagrams and extended associative notation is performed as follows: the tags inside the rectangles in the network diagrams are association tags, which are drawn inside shapes of various kinds (rectangles, chevrons, hexagons) in extended associative notation. The lines in the network diagrams indicate places where character decisions are required (the outcomes of the decisions may be shown as brackets on the network diagram). These decisions are shown as shaded triangles in extended associative notation (the two notations are not identical, because extended associative notation distinguishes agency from targeting decisions, while the network diagrams show only *some/all* character decisions).

The extended associative notation for a trio complex, Figure 5.36, contains three new decisions α, β, and γ, which are called *downstream* decisions because they appear below the third level in a cascade. We will describe each of these decisions in turn. The decision α is the agency decision

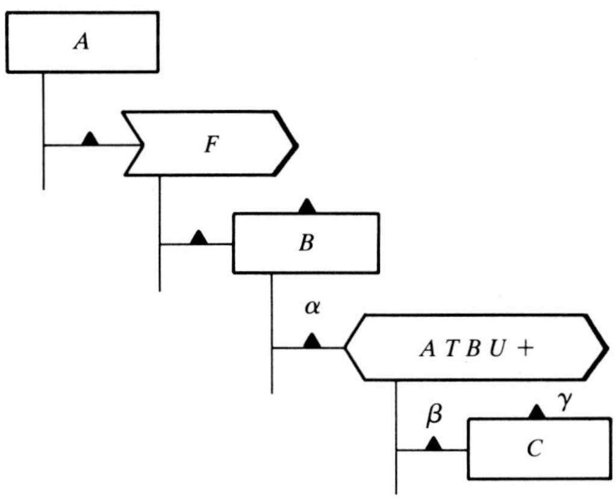

Figure 5.37 Alternate notation for a cascade.

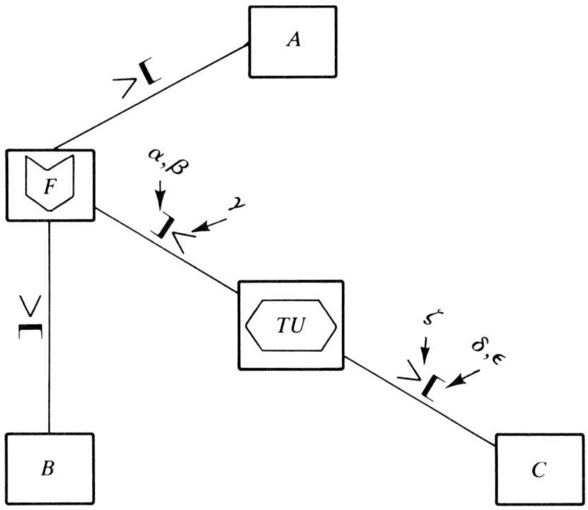

Figure 5.38 A first stable state trio complex.

If $A{:}|x|$, $B{:}|y|$, and $|x|F{:}|y|$, must there be some x', y', and z such that $\Delta A{:}|x, x'|$, $\Delta B{:}|y, y'|$, and $|x'|T{:}|y'|U|z|$?

If a *person operates* a *truck*, must there be something that the *person uses* the *truck to carry*?

If the answer to this question is no, the shaded triangle α is replaced by a small circle; if the answer is yes, the shaded triangle is removed. If α is *mandatory*, the explanation is

If an *A Fs* a *B*, there must be something that the *A Ts* the *B U*.

If a *person operates* a *truck,* there must be something that the *person uses* the *truck to carry*.

If α is *optional*, "must" is changed to "need not", and the explanation is

If an *A Fs* a *B*, there need not be something that the *A Ts* the *B U*.

If a *person operates* a *truck*, there need not be something that the *person uses* the *truck to carry*.

The decision β is the targeting decision

If $A{:}|x|$, $B{:}|y|$, $|x|\dot{F}{:}|y|$, and there are some x', y', and z such that $\Delta A{:}|x, x'|$, $\Delta B{:}|y, y'|$, and $|x'|T{:}|y'|U|z|$, must there be x'', y'', and z' such that $\Delta A{:}|x, x''|$, $\Delta B{:}|y, y''|$, $|x''|T{:}|y''|U|z'|$ and $C{:}|z'|$?

If a *person operates* a *truck*, and the *person uses* the *truck to transport* something, must the *person use* the *truck to carry* an *item*?

If the answer to this question is no, the shaded triangle β is replaced by a small circle; if the answer is yes, the shaded triangle is removed. If β is *mandatory*, the explanation is

If an *A Fs* a *B*, what the *A Ts* the *B U* must include a/an *C*.

If a *person operates* a *truck*, what the *person uses* the *truck to carry* must include an *item*.

If β is *optional*, the explanation is

If an *A Fs* a *B*, what the *A Ts* the *B U* need not include a/an *C*.

If a *person operates* a *truck*, what the *person uses* the *truck to carry* need not include an *item*.

The decision γ is the *single/multiple* decision

If $A{:}|\,x\,|$, $B{:}|\,y\,|$, and $|x|\,\dot{F}{:}|y|$, must there be at most one z such that $\Delta A{:}|\,x, x'\,|$, $\Delta B{:}|\,y, y'\,|$, $|x'\,|\,T{:}|\,y'\,|\,U\,|\,z\,|$ and $C{:}|\,z\,|$ (that is, must any two such images z and z' be the same C, $\Delta C{:}|\,z, z'\,|$)?

If a *person operates* a *truck*, must there be at most one *item* that the *person uses* the *truck to carry*?

If γ is *single*, the explanation is

If an *A Fs* a *B*, there must be at most one *C* that the *A Ts* the *B U*.

If a *person operates* a *truck*, there must be at most one *item* that the *person uses* the *truck to carry*.

If γ is *multiple*, the explanation is

If an *A Fs* a *B*, there might be many *Cs* that the *A Ts* the *B U*.

If a *person operates* a *truck*, there might be many *items* that the *person uses* the *truck to carry*.

The Trio Tag May Appear Beneath Either a Correspondence Tag or Its Reversal

The tile containing the trio tag *TU* may be written beneath the cascade $A \rightarrow F \rightarrow B$, as in Figure 5.36, or beneath the reversal cascade $B \rightarrow F^* \rightarrow A$, as shown in Figure 5.39. The decisions α, β, and γ in Figure 5.39 must be the same as the decisions α, β, and γ shown in Figure 5.36. Although in principle the fourth and fifth levels of Figure 5.39 are redundant with the same levels in Figure 5.36, there is often benefit in showing both forms simultaneously. The design management device should be able to show the trio tag under either or both appearances of the correspondence tag on request.

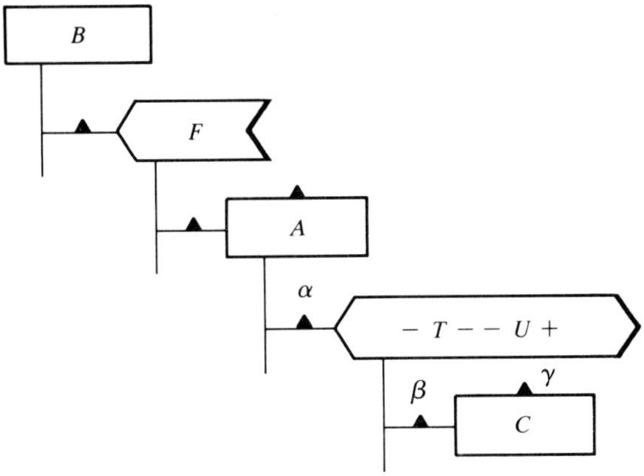

Figure 5.39 Tile shown beneath reversal of *F*.

Many Class Tags May Appear at the Fifth Level

Just as several class tags may appear on the third level beneath a chevron, so several class tags may appear on the fifth level beneath a tile. For example, Figure 5.40 shows the two trio complexes:

« an *A Ts* a *B U* a *C* »

« an *A Ts* a *B U* a *D* »

For example, suppose that a *truck* could *carry* one or more *spare tires*, which are not considered to be *items*. There are then two trio complexes:

A *person uses* a *truck to carry* an *item*

A *person uses* a *truck to carry* a *spare tire*

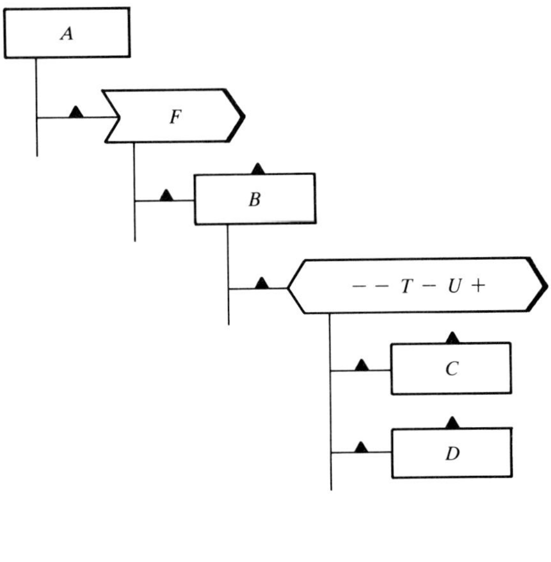

Figure 5.40 Two trio complexes of the trio *TU*.

The structure shown in Figure 5.40 allows the designer to specify if a *person* might *use* a *truck to carry* zero *spare tires*, or many *spare tires*, without changing the decisions for a *person using* a *truck to carry items*.

Axial and Facial Decisions

The first stable state trio shown in Figure 5.36 can be thought of as a correspondence between *AB* pairs and the class *C*. In data logic, the idea of an *AB* pair is ambiguous, because different correspondences yield different classes of *AB* pairs. More specifically, a trio establishes a correspondence between the concentration $C^1\dot{F}$ and the class *C* (this correspondence is precisely the elision correspondence ${}_{12}\dot{T}_3$). The decisions α, β, and γ discussed above pertain to one direction of declaring this correspondence: the declaration from *AB* to *C*. These decisions are called *axial* decisions.

The reversal of the elision correspondence is shown in Figure 5.41. The concentration $C^1\dot{F}$ is expressed by the present participle of the verb *F*. Thus, the class of assemblies of a *person operating* a *truck* (loosely, *person-truck* pairs) is written "*a Person Operating a Truck*" in extended associative notation. Note that the word "*a*" is written in lower case to show that it is part of the notation, to distinguish it from the words "*Person*", "*Operate*", and "*Truck*" that are supplied by the designer.

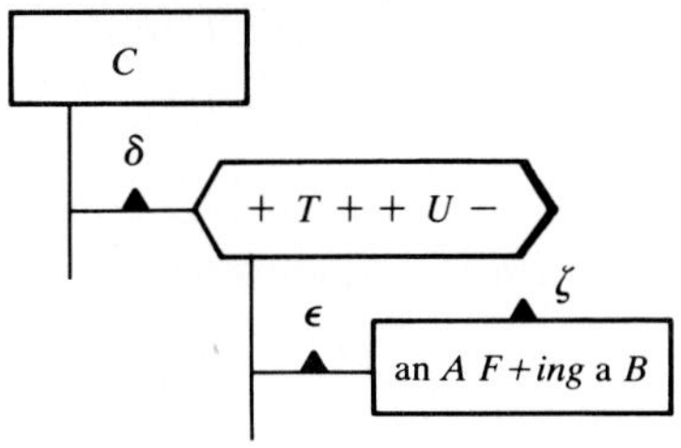

Figure 5.41 Facial decisions.

The decisions δ, ϵ, and ζ shown in Figure 5.41 are called *facial* decisions, by virtue of the analogy of a trio to a three-dimensional array. The relative correspondences may then be viewed as two-dimensional arrays that appear as the *faces* of the trio array (see Figure 5.42). The facial decisions describe how the trio maps individuals to these faces. Facial decisions are also shown in the network diagram for a first stable state trio complex, Figure 5.38.

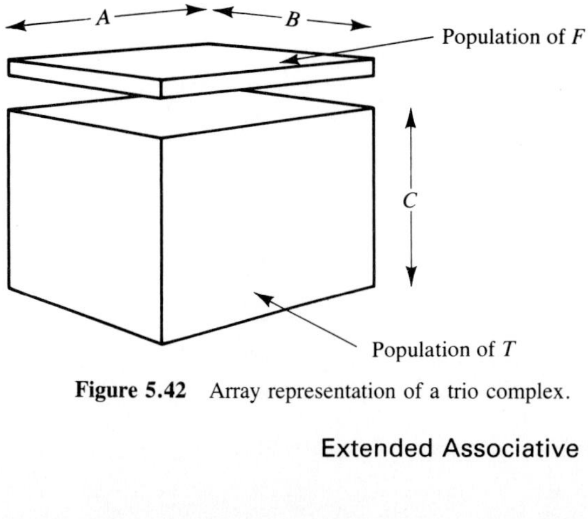

Figure 5.42 Array representation of a trio complex.

The decision δ expresses the answer to the question

If $C{:}|z|$, must there be images x and y such that $|x|T{:}|y|\ U|\ z|$?

Must there be images x and y for any *item* such that x *uses* y *to carry* the *item*?

If δ is *mandatory*, the explanation is

There must be something that *Ts* something *U* the *C*.

There must be something that *uses* something *to carry* the *item*.

If δ is *optional*, the explanation is

There need not be something that *Ts* something *U* the *C*.

There need not be something that *uses* something *to carry* the *item*.

The decision ϵ expresses the answer to the question

If $C{:}|z|$ and there are images x and y such that $|x|T{:}|y|\ U|\ z|$, then must there be images x' and y' such that $\Delta A{:}|x, x'|$, $\Delta B{:}|y, y'|$, and $|x'|F{:}|y'|$?

If something uses something to carry an *item*, must there be a *person* that *uses* a *truck to carry* the *item*?

If ϵ is *mandatory*, the explanation is

What *Ts* something *U* the *C* must include an assembly of a/an *A F+ing* a *B*.

What *uses* something *to carry* the *item* must include an assembly of a *person operating* a *truck*.

If ϵ is *optional*, the explanation is

What *Ts* something *U* the *C* need not include an assembly of a/an *A F+ing* a *B*.

What *uses* something *to carry* the *item* need not include an assembly of a *person operating* a *truck*.

The decision ζ expresses the answer to the question

If $C{:}|z|$, must there be at most one image x and at most one image y such that $\Delta A{:}|x, x'|$, $\Delta B{:}|y, y'|$, $|x|F{:}|y|$, and $|x'|T{:}|y'|U|z|$ (that is, must any two such images x_1 and x_2 be the same A, and any two such images y_1 and y_2 be the same B)?

For any *item*, must at most one *person use* at most one *truck to carry* the *item*?

If ζ is *single*, the explanation is

There must be at most one *A* and at most one *B* where the *A Fs* the *B* and the *A Ts* the *B U* the *C*.

There must be at most one *person* and at most one *truck* where the *person operates* the *truck* and the *person uses* the *truck to carry* the *item*.

If ζ is *multiple*, the explanation is

> There might be many *As* or many *Bs* where the *A Fs* the *B* and the *A Ts* the *B U* the *C*.
>
> There might be many *people* or many *trucks* where the *person operates* the *truck* and the *person uses* the *truck to carry* the *item*.

Notice that the design management device should have a sufficient command of the syntax of English to supply the irregular plural *people*.

The example we have been working with is shown in full in Figure 5.43.

Conclusion

We have shown how a trio tag may be declared relative to one correspondence tag in extended associative notation. We expect that this form of presentation, called the *first stable state*, will be the most common means of declaring a trio in practical design situations. Even so, many data base management systems are incapable of handling all forms of first stable state trio complexes because implementation can require ''null values'' in one of the three positions.

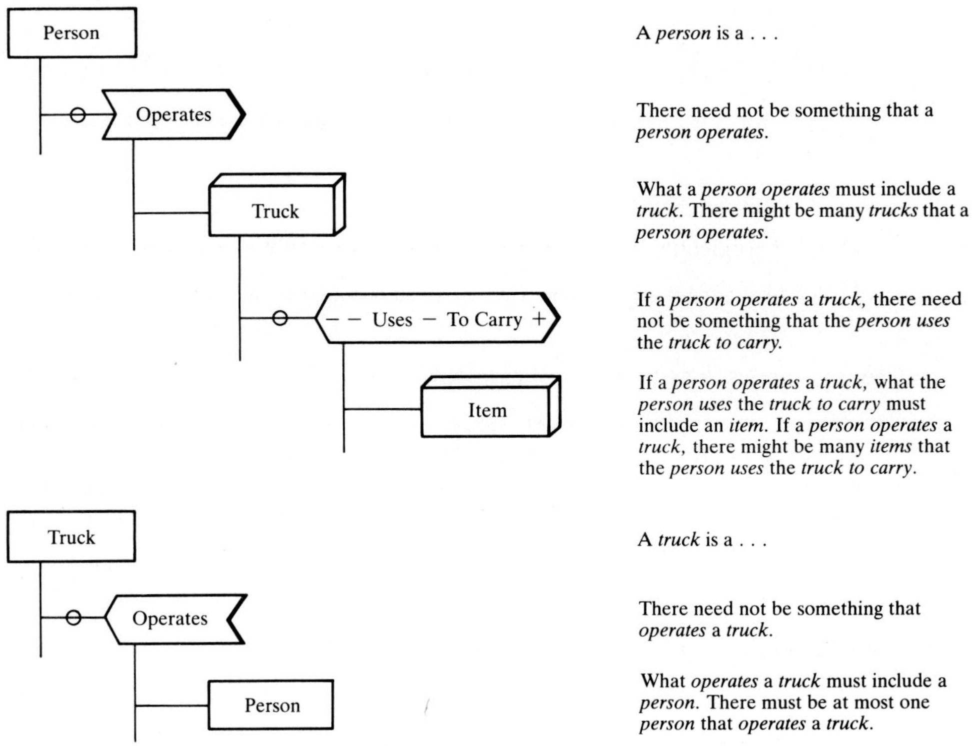

Figure 5.43 A first stable state trio complex.

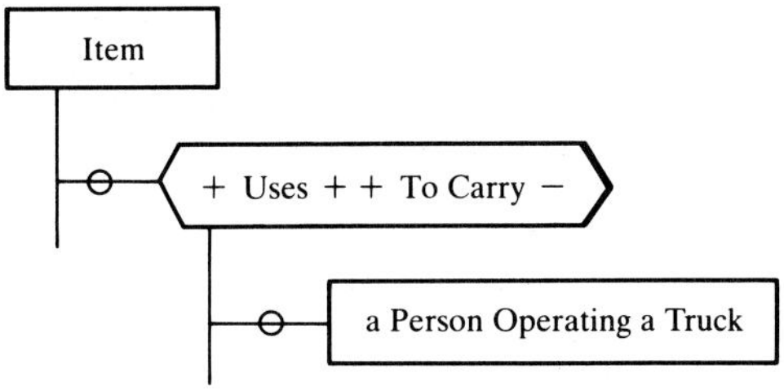

An *item* is a . . .

There need not be something that *uses* something *to carry* the *item.*

What *uses* something *to carry* the *item* need not include an assembly of a *person operating* a *truck*. There must be at most one *person* and at most one *truck* where the *person operates* the *truck* and the *person uses* the *truck to carry* the *item.*

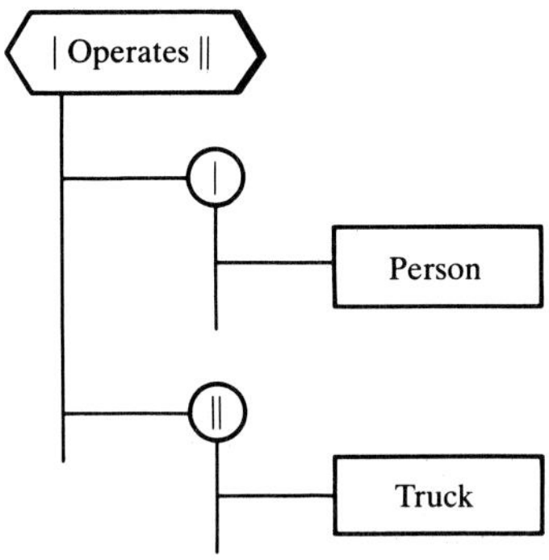

To *operate* is to . . .

A *person* could *operate* something.

Something could *operate* a *truck.*

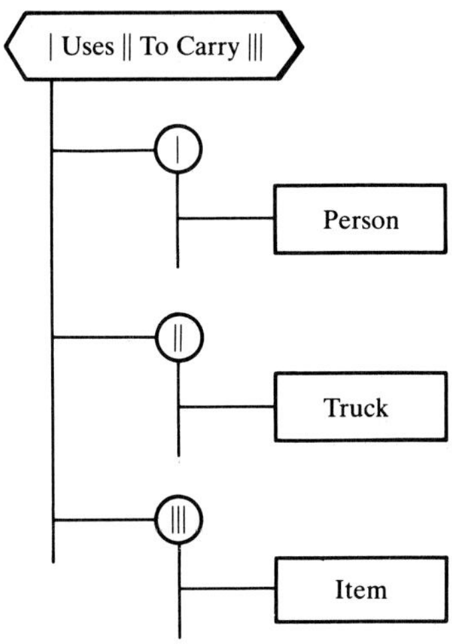

To *use to carry* is to . . .

A *person* could *use* something *to carry* something.

Something could *use* a *truck to carry* something.

Something could *use* something *to carry* an *item.*

Figure 5.43 *(continued)*

5.7 OTHER FORMS OF TRIOS, AND QUARTETS

Network Illustration of the First Stable State

As we recall, a first stable state trio complex may be illustrated as the network drawing shown in Figure 5.44. This drawing shows that the classes *A* and *B* are associated via the

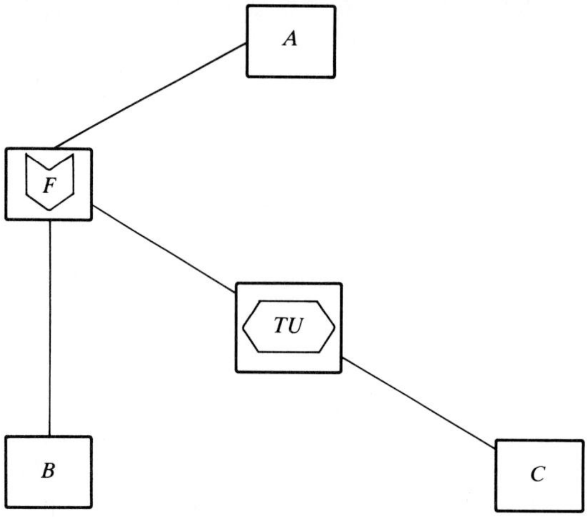

Figure 5.44 A first stable state trio complex.

correspondence F, and that C is associated via the trio TU (precisely, via the elision correspondence ${}_{12}TU_3$) with the correspondence F.

Now suppose that instead of declaring the the trio TU relative to the correspondence F, we choose to declare TU relative to a different correspondence G, between B and C. The resulting first stable state trio complex is illustrated in Figure 5.45. Here B and C are associated via G, and the remaining class, A, is associated via TU with the concentration of G, instead of with the concentration of F as in Figure 5.44.

In extended associative notation, declaring TU relative to G rather than F changes the positions of the classes in the diagrams, and changes the "+" and "−" markings inside

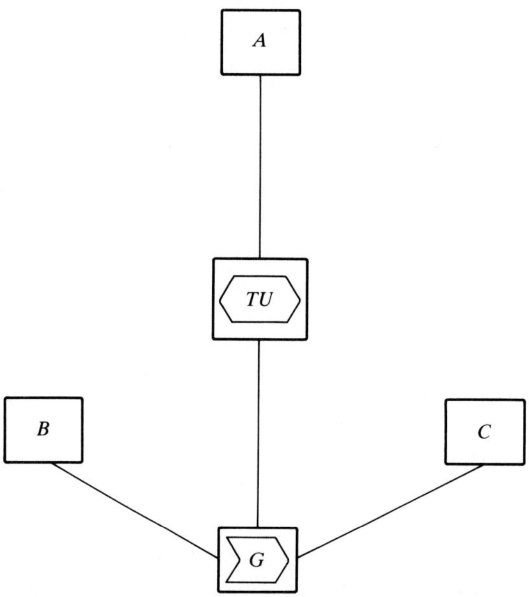

Figure 5.45 A first stable state trio complex.

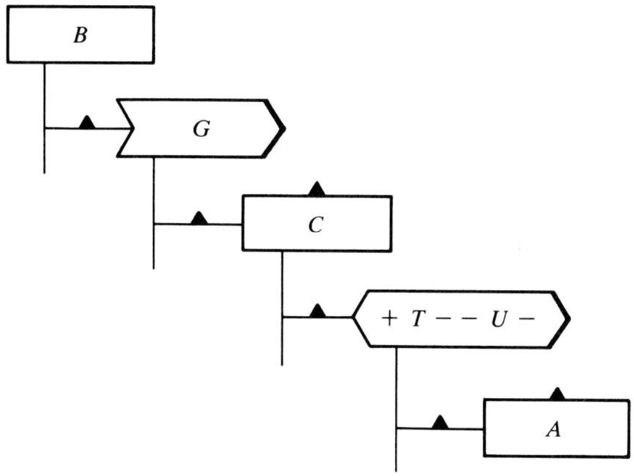

Figure 5.46 Extended associative notation for Figure 5.45.

the tiles. The central cascade in the extended associative notation for this trio complex is shown in Figure 5.46.

Continuing along the same line, we could choose to declare a correspondence *H* between *C* and *A* instead of *F* or *G*. This choice would give us a structure of the form shown in Figure 5.47. Each of the structures discussed so far is a first stable state trio complex.

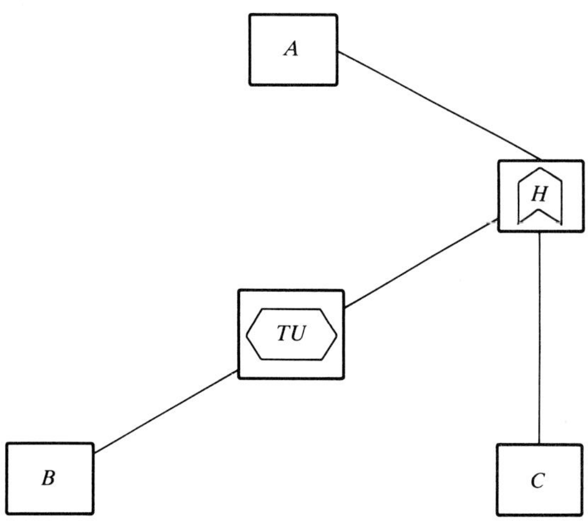

Figure 5.47 A first stable state trio complex.

Network Illustration of the Second Stable State

Now suppose that *TU* is declared relative to two correspondences, say *F* and *G*. This form of declaration is called a *second stable state*. It is illustrated in Figure 5.48. There are three different forms of second stable state, according to which pair of correspondences *F* and *G*, *F* and *H*, or *G* and *H* is declared. Each form may be interconverted into any other by altering the positions of the class tags and the "+" and "−" signs inside the tile, or alternatively, by rewriting the trio tag itself.

We would expect Figure 5.48 to be a combination of Figures 5.45 and 5.47, which show *TU* declared relative to *F* alone, and *TU* declared relative to *G* alone. Notice that Figure 5.48 is not simply a disjoint union of the two figures, because the symbol "*TU*" is recognized to be the same in both figures, and is therefore written only once in their combination. Notice, however, that there is no redundancy in the *lines*—no line in Figure 5.48 appears both in Figure 5.45 and in Figure 5.47. One additional line appears in Figure 5.48, from *B* to *TU*, which is required to describe interactions between the two component figures.

Since no line in Figure 5.48 appears in both Figure 5.45 and Figure 5.47, each decision required to declare *TU* relative to *F* is different from each decision required to declare *TU* relative to *G*. Since each line that appears in either Figure 5.45 or Figure 5.47 appears in Figure 5.48, all the decisions required to declare *TU* relative to *both F* and *G* are required to declare *TU* relative to *F* alone or to declare *TU* relative to *G* alone. The additional line, from *B* to *TU*, requires some further decisions.

In extended associative notation then, the declaration of *TU* relative to both *F* and *G* includes all the notation for declaring *TU* relative to *F*, all the notation for declaring *TU* relative to *G*, and adds additional decisions, called *pineal* decisions, for the line from *B* to *TU*. Figure 5.49 shows the cascades in the extended associative notation for a second stable state trio complex. Notice that the pineal decisions are expressed using the concentration of *TU* because no correspondence between *A* and *C* is declared.

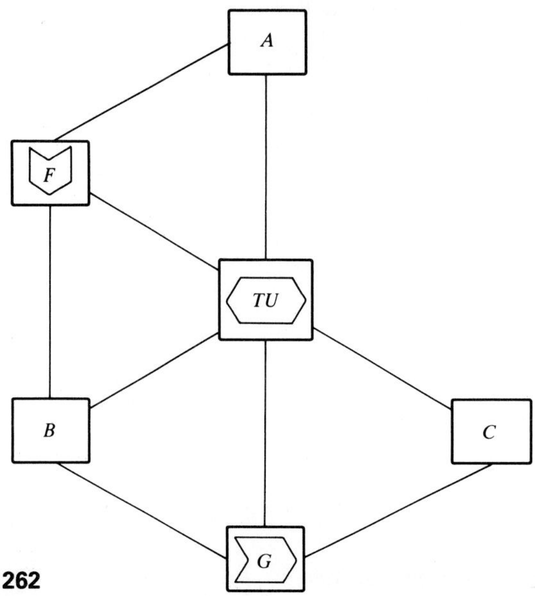

Figure 5.48 A second stable state trio complex.

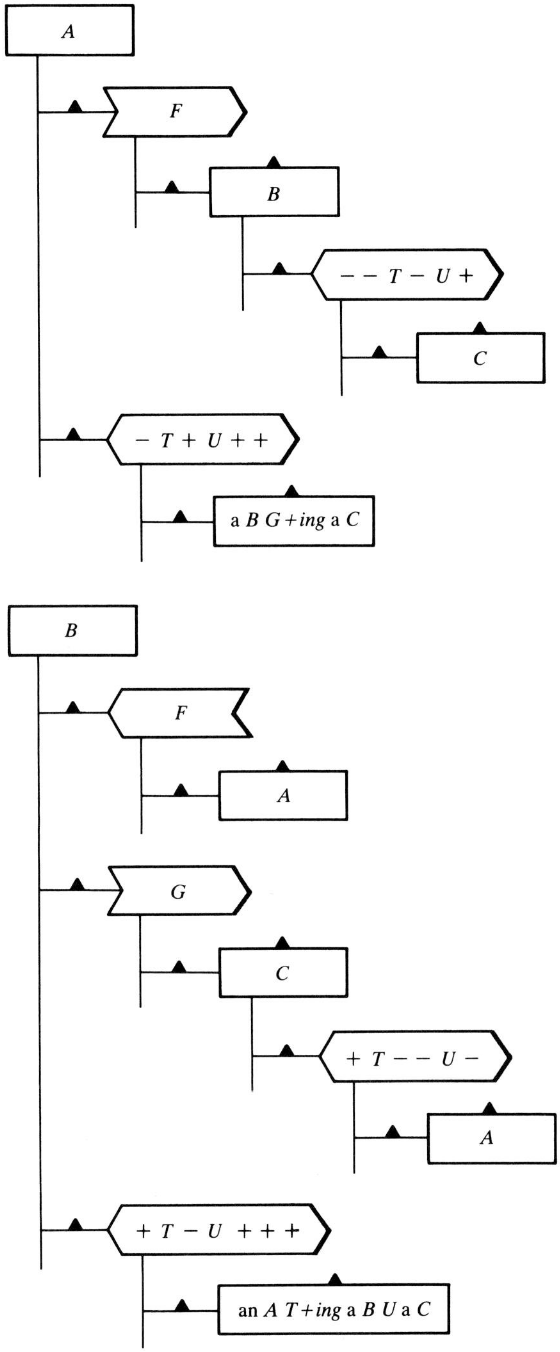

Figure 5.49 A second stable state trio complex.

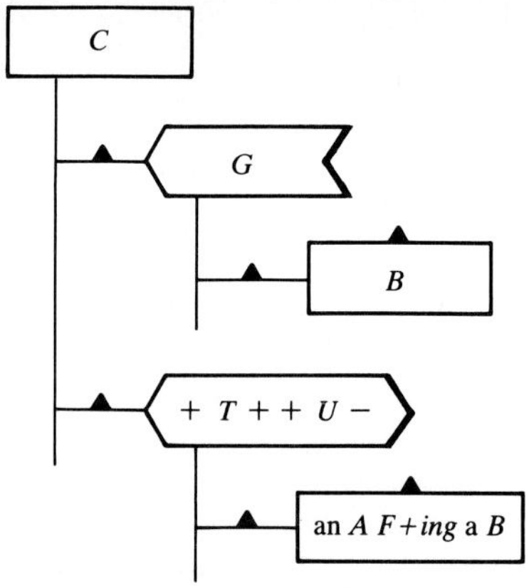

Figure 5.49 *(continued)*

Character Decision Interdependencies

Figure 5.48 also differs from Figures 5.45 and 5.47 in possessing *cycles*, that is, closed paths in the network drawing. For example, the path $A \rightarrow F \rightarrow TU \rightarrow A$ is a cycle. Each cycle in Figure 5.48 is constrained by an embracing that interrelates some of the decisions in declaring *TU* relative to *F* with some of the decisions in declaring *TU* relative to *G*. For example, if the following population of $\dot{T}U$ is permitted:

$$\vdash (a)\dot{T}:(b)U(c_1)$$

$$\vdash (a)\dot{T}:(b)U(c_2)$$

that is, if an "*AB* pair" can associate with more than one *C*, then an *A* can associate with more than one *C* via $\dot{H}*$ (recall that the reduced trio $\dot{T}U$ was defined so that any assembly of $\dot{T}U$ projects to an attachment of $\dot{H}*$). This example illustrates how the character decisions in a second stable state trio complex are not independent of each other. These *character decision interdependencies* will be discussed in detail in Chapter 9.

Fully Reversed Trio Complexes

The most complex state of a trio is a fully reversed trio complex, in which a trio is declared relative to three correspondences *F*, *G*, and *H*. The comparable network diagram is shown in Figure 5.50.

Figure 5.50 shows the high degree of symmetry possessed by a fully reversed trio complex. The diagram may be rotated 120°, or flipped about a vertical axis, without any change in shape. The comparable property of extended associative notation is that the structures under each class tag, *A*, *B*, and *C*, look identical in the sense that the shapes are the same; only the tags within the shapes and the "+" and "−" signs differ. Thus, to illustrate the fully reversed trio complex, it suffices to show the structure beneath any one of the class tags. The structure beneath the class tag *A* is shown in Figure 5.51. In the full reversal, diagrams comparable to Figure 5.51 beneath *B* and *C* are prepared as well.

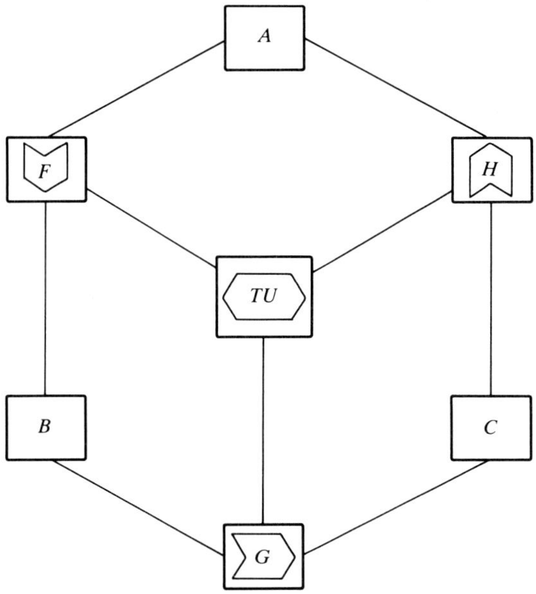

Figure 5.50 A fully reversed trio complex.

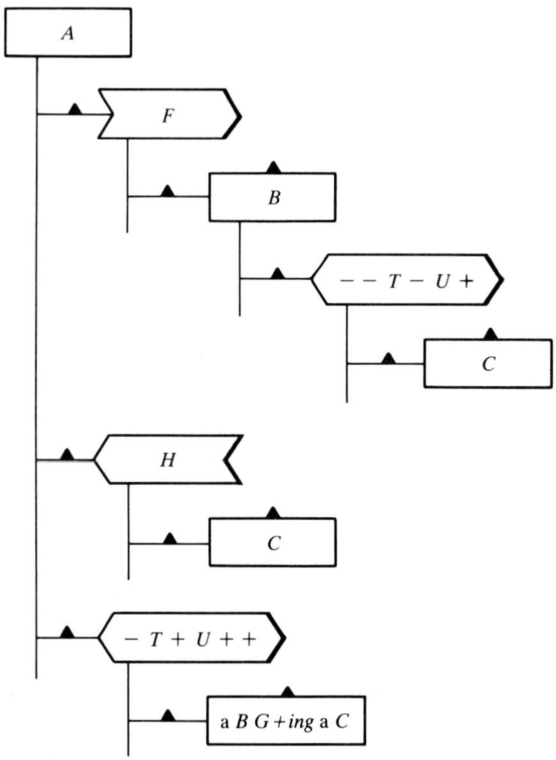

Figure 5.51 A fully reversed trio complex.

The Base State

In the *base state*, no correspondences are declared. The base state is valuable for converting between notations, because a third order relation without null values in the relational data model may be expressed as a base state trio complex. The network diagram for a base state trio complex is shown in Figure 5.52. The concentration of the trio is used in declaring a base state trio complex in extended associative notation, as shown in Figure 5.53.

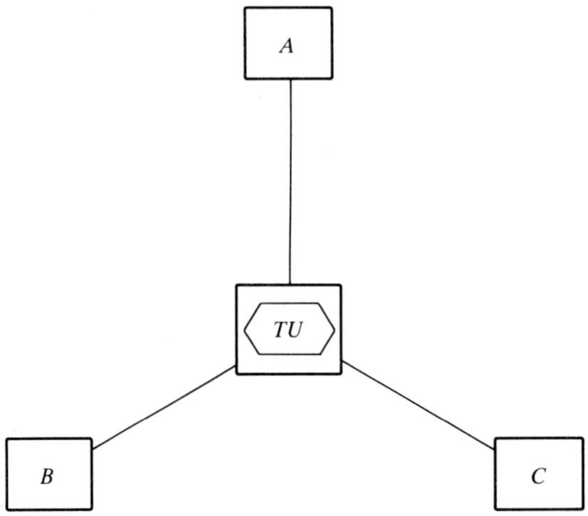

Figure 5.52 A base state trio complex.

Determination of Stable State

One may determine with relative ease the lowest possible stable state that a trio complex may be declared in. A trio may, however, exhibit additional constraints that are best expressed by writing the trio in a higher state than the minimum. In practice, we advise trying the lowest order state first, and questioning seriously the requirements to increase the order. Generally speaking, we find the base state to have only a small advantage over the first stable state, and we usually prefer to use the first stable state even when the trio could theoretically be written in the base state. We find the second and third stable states to be considerably more difficult than the first stable state, and we will normally devote additional design effort to reconceptualizing the problem before declaring a trio in these forms.

The minimum order stable state is determined from the optionality of the elision correspondences ${}_{12}\dot{T}_3$, ${}_{23}\dot{T}_1$, and ${}_{31}\dot{T}_2$. That is, the crucial decisions are found on the fourth and fifth levels of the extended associative notation expression of the trio complex, as illustrated in Figure 5.54.

That is, if either α or β is *optional*, then ${}_{12}\dot{T}_3$ is *from some*, if either γ or δ is *optional*, then ${}_{23}\dot{T}_1$ is *from some*, and if either ϵ or ζ is *optional*, then ${}_{31}\dot{T}_2$ is *from some*. The number of these elision correspondences that are *from some* equals the minimum order of stable state which *TU* may be declared in.

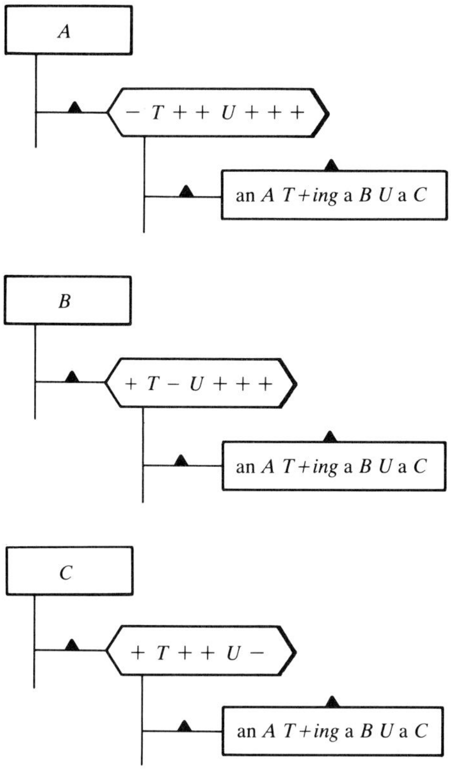

Figure 5.53 A base state trio complex.

To illustrate, consider the trio *Person Pays Shop For Appliance*. That is, in the algebraic symbols we are using, $A \equiv$ *Person*, $B \equiv$ *Shop*, $C \equiv$ *Appliance*, $T \equiv$ *Pays*, and $U \equiv$ *For*. Also assume that *Person Visits Shop* (so $F \equiv$ *Visits*), *Shop Stocks Appliance* (so $G \equiv$ *Stocks*), and *Appliance Pleases Person* (so $H \equiv$ *Pleases*). The questions to determine the stable state of the trio complex are then:

> If a *person visits* a *shop*, must there be an *appliance* such that the *person pays* the *shop for* the *appliance*?
>
> Surely not.
>
> If a *shop stocks* an *appliance*, must there be a *person* such that the *person pays* the *shop for* the *appliance*?
>
> Maybe eventually.
>
> If an *appliance pleases* a *person*, must there be a *shop* such that the *person pays* the *shop for* the *appliance*?
>
> Surely not.

Thus *Person Pays Shop For Appliance* must probably be shown in the fully reversed form, because all three questions are answered negatively. However, the trio complex could be reduced to the second stable state if the middle question above can be answered in the affirmative. For example, we could create a phantom *person* called "available for sale",

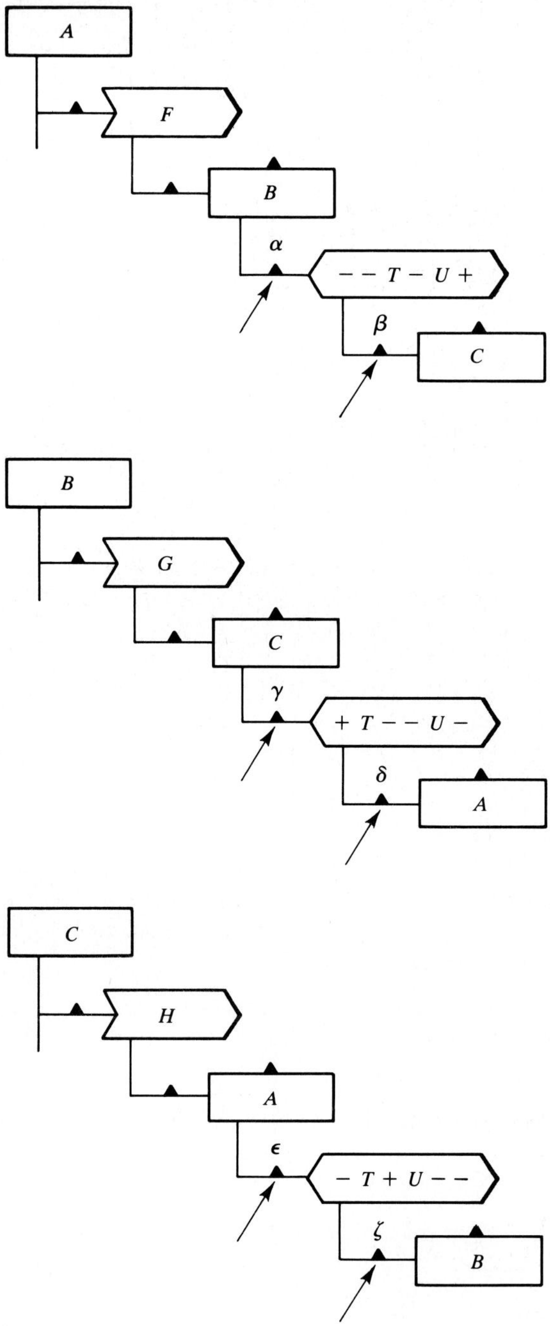

Figure 5.54 Decisions that determine the stable state.

and say that any item that is *stocked* is first sold to ''available for sale'', then perhaps later is resold to some other *person*. If the store does extensive bargaining, the sale to ''available for sale'' might indicate the initial asking price, whereas subsequent sales would indicate the agreed price.

Notice that one does not have to write the entire diagram shown in Figure 5.54 to determine the minimum order stable state. One should instead ask the three questions:

$$\begin{array}{|l|}\hline \text{If } \dot{F}{:}|x, y|, \text{ must there be a } z \text{ such that } |x|\dot{T}{:}|y|U|z|? \\ \text{If } \dot{G}{:}|y, z|, \text{ must there be an } x \text{ such that } |x|\dot{T}{:}|y|U|z|? \\ \text{If } \dot{H}{:}|z, x|, \text{ must there be a } y \text{ such that } |x|\dot{T}{:}|y|U|z|? \\ \hline \end{array} \qquad (1)$$

The number of ''no'' answers gives the minimum order stable state. Moreover, the correspondences that must be declared are given by the questions for which the answer is ''no.'' For example, if the answer to the first question, which concerns $\dot{F}$, is ''no,'' then F must be declared, and indeed one or both of α or β is *optional* in Figure 5.54.

It is important to interpret $\dot{T}U$ properly in the questions above as the *reduced* trio relative to $(A, B, C; F, G, H)$, not the original unreduced trio TU. Thus, the first question reads, fully written,

$$\begin{gathered}\text{If } \Delta A{:}|x, x'|,\ F{:}|x', y'|, \text{ and } \Delta B{:}|y', y|, \text{ must there be a } z \text{ such that} \\ |x|T{:}|y|U|z|,\ C{:}|z|,\ \Delta B \circ G \circ \Delta C{:}|y, z| \text{ and } \Delta C \circ H \circ \Delta A{:}|z, x|?\end{gathered} \qquad (2)$$

The designer should therefore have three correspondences F, G, and H in mind before asking the Questions (1). A common simplifying procedure is to use correspondences that embrace the appropriate projections of the trio. For example, if we have the embracings:

$$\begin{gathered}\pi^{23}TU \subseteq \dot{G} \\ \pi^{31}TU \subseteq \dot{H}\end{gathered} \qquad (3)$$

then Question (2) may be simplified to read:

$$\begin{gathered}\text{If } \Delta A{:}|x, x'|,\ F{:}|x', y'|, \text{ and } \Delta B{:}|y', y|, \text{ must there be a } z \text{ such that} \\ |x|T{:}|y|U|z| \text{ and } C{:}|z|?\end{gathered} \qquad (4)$$

The designer should be on guard against redefining the correspondences once a trio has been declared. Doing so may not only alter the design decisions, but may also change the order of the stable state of the trio. For example, consider a trio initially declared using the embracings in Formula (3), and imagine that Question (4) was answered in the affirmative, so that F was not declared. Now suppose that G is redefined so that it no longer embraces $\pi^{23}TU$. The answer to Question (4) is now invalid because it relied on a simplification that assumed G embraced $\pi^{23}TU$. The new interpretation of G might therefore require declaration of F. Of course, such changes do occur in the course of a design. If the relative associations of a trio are reinterpreted, we recommend reverifying the stable state of the trio by asking all three Questions (1) afresh.

Notation for a Trio Complex That Contains Two Ovals

Ovals obey the following basic rule, called the *oval placement rule*:

An oval never appears at the top of a cascade.

The forms of trio complexes that contain ovals may all be formed by applying the oval placement rule *after* the normal techniques for describing trios, as illustrated in Figures 5.55 and 5.56. In Figure 5.55, it is assumed that the interior class tag *A* does not bear a separate relationship with the exterior class tag *E* beyond the relationship shown in the cascade. That is, it is assumed that an instance of *A* only associates with an instance of *E* through an instance of *D*.

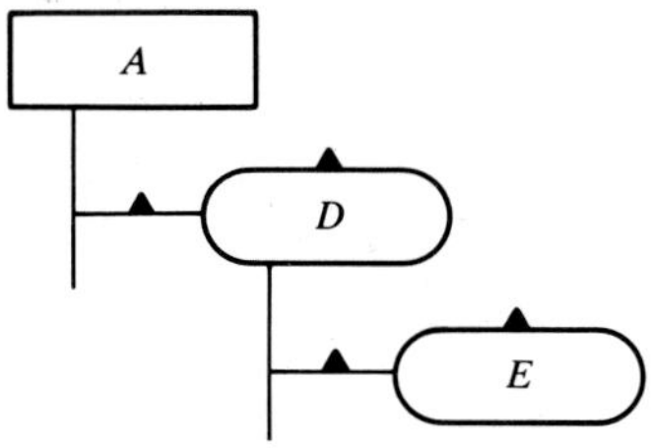

Figure 5.55 A trio complex with two exterior class tags.

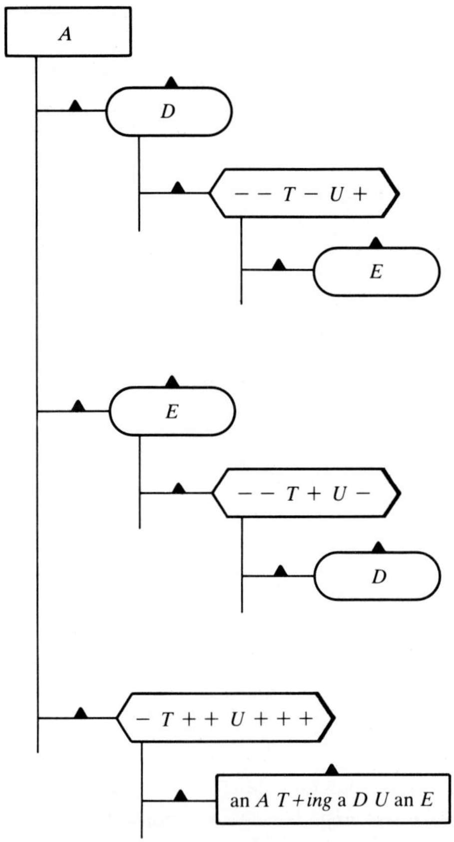

Figure 5.56 A trio complex with two exterior class tags.

If a second relationship with E is to be shown, then the cascade in Figure 5.55 must be reversed as shown in Figure 5.56. A trio tag TU must then be shown explicitly to link the three cascades together.

Trio Complexes That Contain One Oval

There are two forms of a first stable state trio complex using one oval, shown in Figures 5.57 and 5.58. In Figure 5.57, it is assumed that the only correspondence from A to D is through instances of B. In Figure 5.58, it is assumed that the trio TU is not to be declared relative to a correspondence from A to B. If either assumption is not justified, the trio should be expressed in the second stable state, shown in Figure 5.59. The fully reversed form is formed by adding the cascade $B \rightarrow D \rightarrow TU \rightarrow A$ to Figure 5.59.

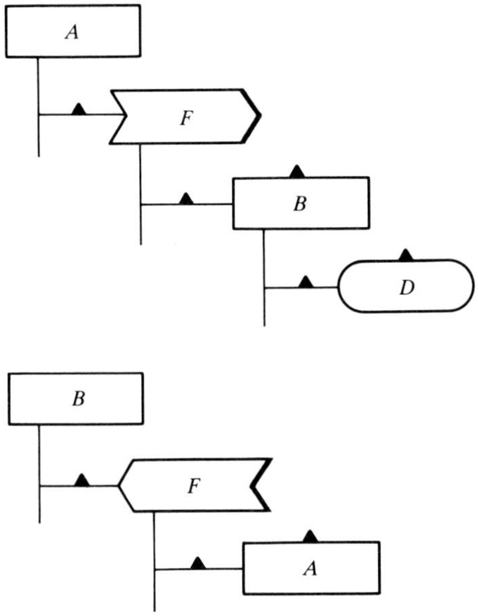

Figure 5.57 A first stable state trio complex with one exterior class tag.

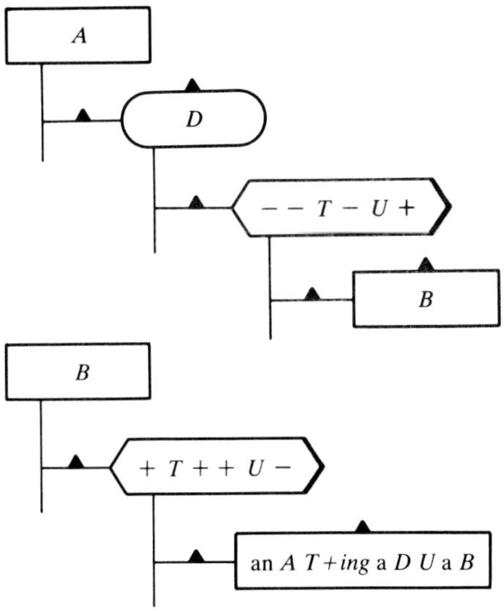

Figure 5.58 A first stable state trio complex with one exterior class tag.

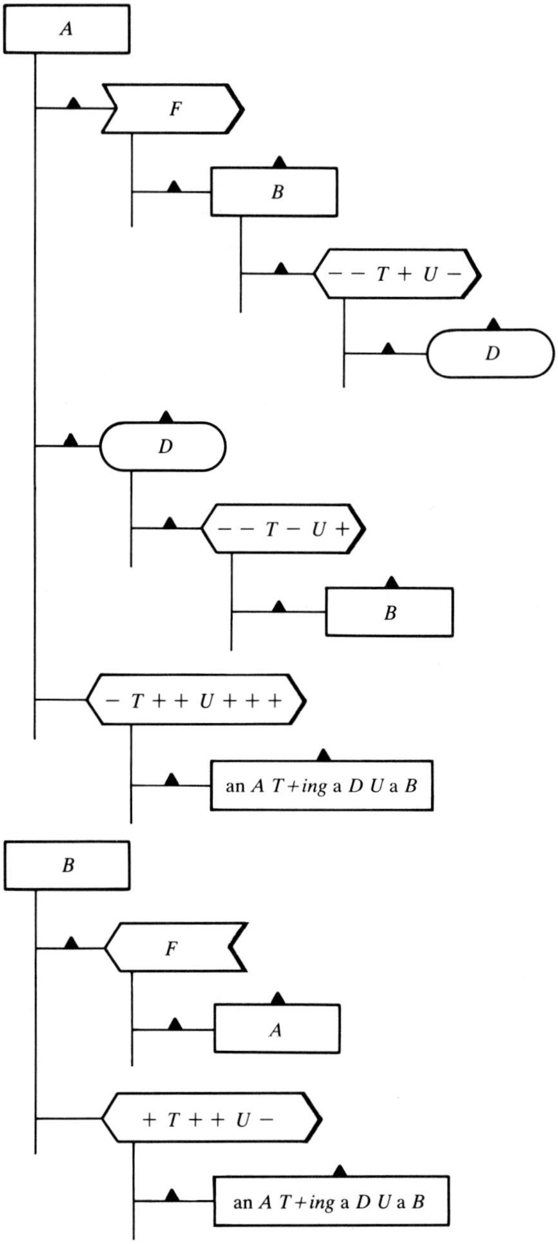

Figure 5.59 A second stable state trio complex with one exterior class tag.

Embracings of Trios

Embracings that involve trios may be expressed in extended associative notation using the same techniques as were discussed in Section 5.5 for expressing embracings of correspondences. For example, the embracing, « if a *person pays* something *for* an *item*, then the *person purchases* the *item* » is shown in Figure 5.60.

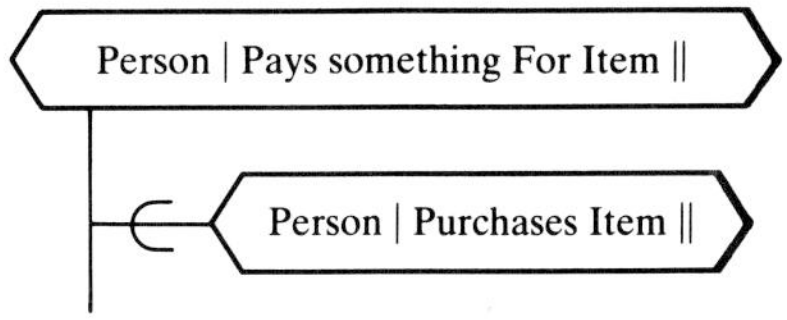

Figure 5.60 An embracing using the trio *Pays For*.

Notation for Quartets and Higher Degree Associations

Quartets may be declared using the same methods as trios, although there are many more varieties of stable states. We postpone detailed investigation of stable states to Chapter 9. The designer is urged to exercise great care when declaring a quartet, and especially an association of higher degree. It is well worth the effort to consider first whether the association may be written more simply in another way. We find that quartets, in addition to being hard to design, can be very confusing to users and developers alike. Restructuring is usually the best policy.

A quartet is encountered in practice most frequently as an extension to a trio complex. The initial cascade is then of the form shown in Figure 5.61. The cascade is reversed by recognizing the tile containing *QRS* as the elision corresponence ${}_{123}QRS_4$. We therefore follow the rules for declaring a correspondence, and add a reversal to the concentration of the relative association for positions (①, ②, ③), that is, the concentration of the trio *TU*. This reversal is shown in Figure 5.62.

Another kind of stable state of a quartet is two correspondences in correspondence with each other. It is declared as shown in Figure 5.63.

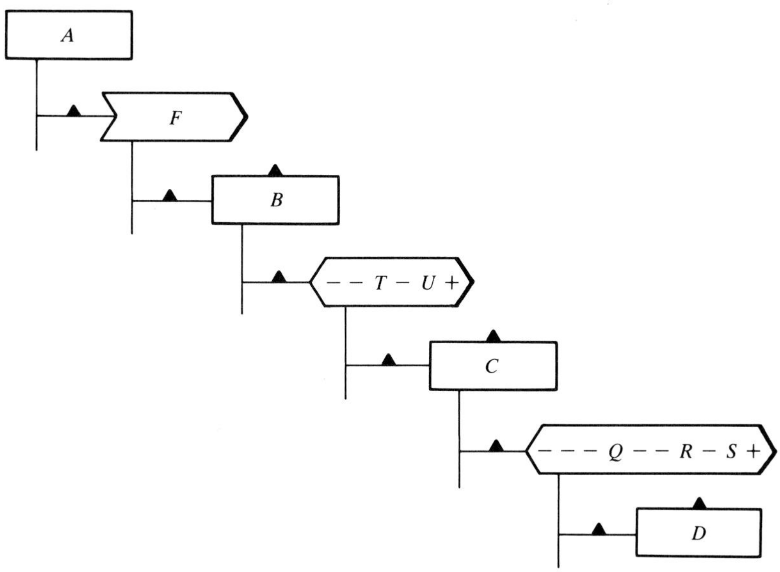

Figure 5.61 A quartet complex.

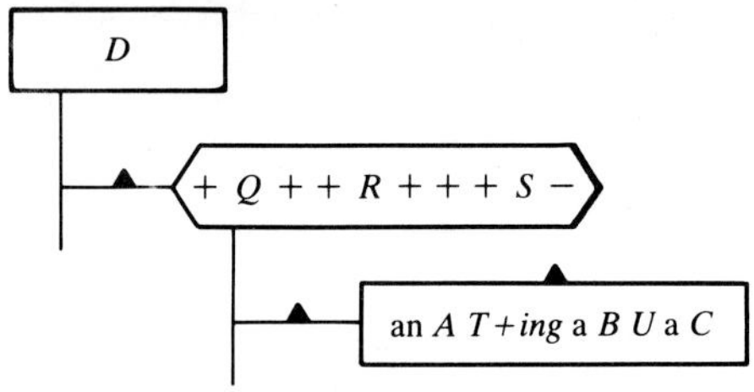

Figure 5.62 Reversal using the concentration of the trio *TU*.

Conclusion

Extended associative notation permits designing trio complexes with null values in all positions. Designing trio complexes becomes progressively more difficult with the variety of null values that may be allowed. Thus, a trio complex that can have null values in all positions, and in all combinations of positions, must be *fully reversed.* If fewer forms of null values are required, the trio complex may be written in a simpler form, namely, the *first stable state,* the *second stable state*, or the *base state.*

In purely theoretical terms, the fully reversed form suffices for declaring all trio complexes. The other forms are provided as a shorthand that can significantly reduce the time required to design and to present a trio complex. Since the forms are equivalent, however, the design management device should convert a trio in any stable state to a fully reversed form on request, and should convert a trio to the minimum degree stable state possible on request as well. We will discuss these conversions, stable states, and associations of high degree in general, in Chapter 9.

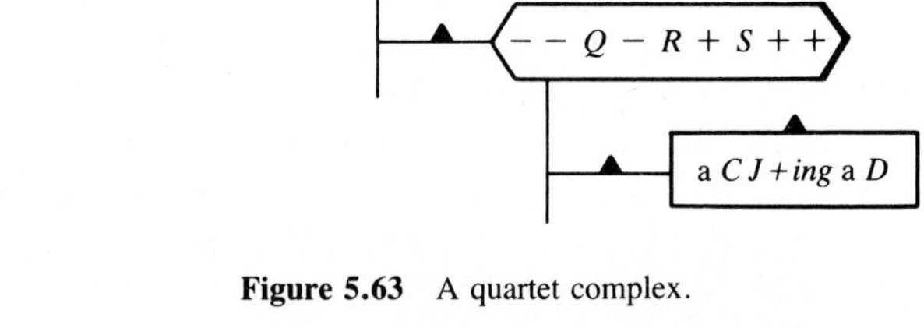

Figure 5.63 A quartet complex.

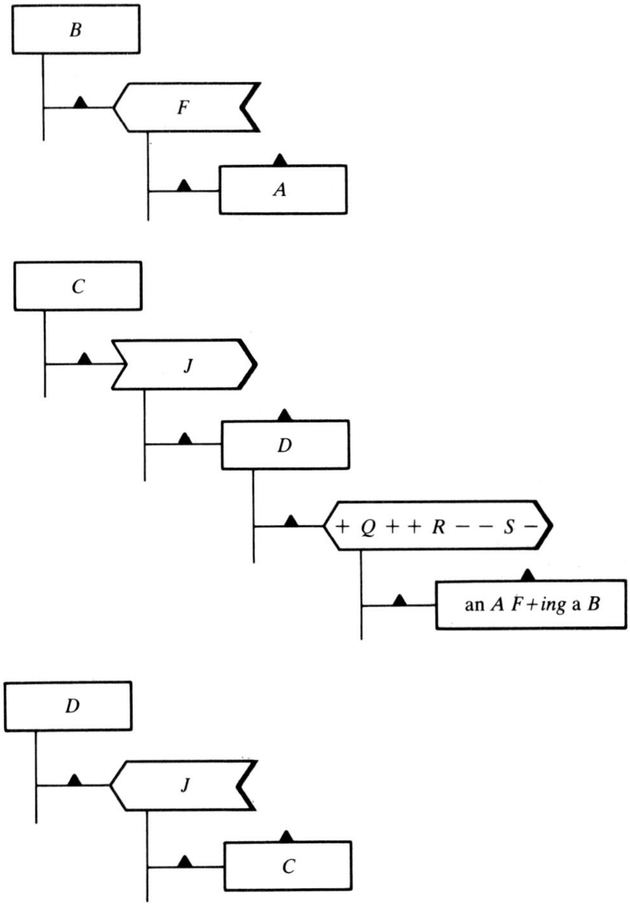

Figure 5.63 *(continued)*

5.8 CASE STUDY: BOOKS

Data base design is all too often portrayed as a fairly simple process. One is given the impression that a reasonably correct form of a schema may be determined easily, after which various transformations can be applied that convert the schema into an acceptable form. In practice, the design of a schema is an activity that regularly stretches out over several months and regularly involves dozens (and sometimes hundreds) of people. The design transformations (such as normalization in the relational model), on the other hand, can be performed typically by a skilled data practitioner in a matter of days once the data requirements are understood.

To illustrate why designing a schema requires so much effort, an imaginary design session using extended associative notation is reproduced below. We feature primarily the basic apparatus of cascades in this case study. Embracings will be applied more extensively in the case study on time in Chapter 6.

Initially the page is blank, and a meeting is convened to discuss the need for a data base covering the group's collection of books.

The subject of the discussion is « a book ». It has a title, represented as text. It is agreed that a book must have exactly one title. Since the title is exposed, ''Title'' is written inside an oval (Figure 5.64).

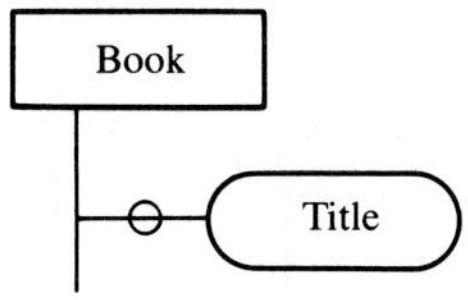

Figure 5.64

Most *books* have exactly one International Standard Book No. (ISBN). Since that number is used for placing orders for copies of *books*, it distinguishes various editions and kinds of binding. The group does not wish to worry about such fine distinctions as the type of binding. Periodicals, manuscripts, and old books have no ISBN. Although the ISBN is an exposed tag, it is a sufficiently provocative concept that the designer elects to draw it inside a rectangle (Figure 5.65).

The designer recognizes that it has not been discussed how a *book* with no ISBN would be identified. He therefore places the *optional* choice below the correspondence tag *Identifies*. This allows the decision as to whether or not a *book* must be *identified* to be made later (shown by the shaded triangle to the left of ''*Identifies*'').

The group needs to know how many copies of the *book* they have. The number may be zero (Figure 5.66).

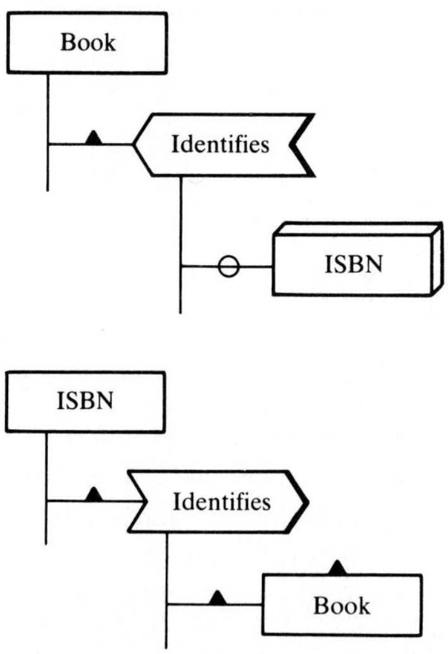

Figure 5.65

Figure 5.66

Actually the group needs to know a lot about each copy. Thus they erase the *Number Of Copies In Inventory* oval and add a new class called *Copy*. As before, they may have no *copy* of the *book* (Figure 5.67).

The designer chooses to define any replicate of a book to be a *copy*. Thus, if a *book* has a replicate, then the *book* has a *copy*. The designer therefore places the *optional* symbol aside *Replicates* to show that a *book* need not have any replicate, and shows the decision below *Replicates* as *mandatory*, indicating that there can be no replicate of a *book* without there being a *copy*.

For each *copy*, the group requires a record of the purchase order line item on which the *copy* was acquired. Some *books* are obtained as gifts, not purchased. There is no purchase order for donated *books* (Figure 5.68).

They need to know each occasion when a *copy* moved. They also want the data base to cover *books* received via interlibrary loan, *books* that they don't own. The designer chooses to call each occasion of moving a *copy* a *transfer* (Figure 5.69).

There is a need to know the cost of each *transfer*. It is ventured that the cost of *transfers* between two given locations does not vary significantly and so could be handled by a standard cost. Argument ensues about whether they need to call in an accountant to determine whether standard costing in this fashion will be acceptable. Then the supervisor of the bindery speaks up and says that in his shop, the act of binding a copy and the release of the copy from the bindery are treated as one operation. He does not keep an inventory of bound copies, but returns them as soon as his job is complete. He would like, he says, to record the cost of binding on the transfer out of the bindery of the copy. There is general

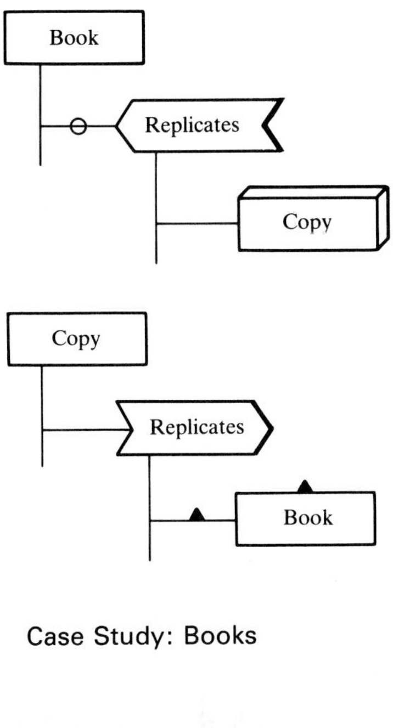

Figure 5.67

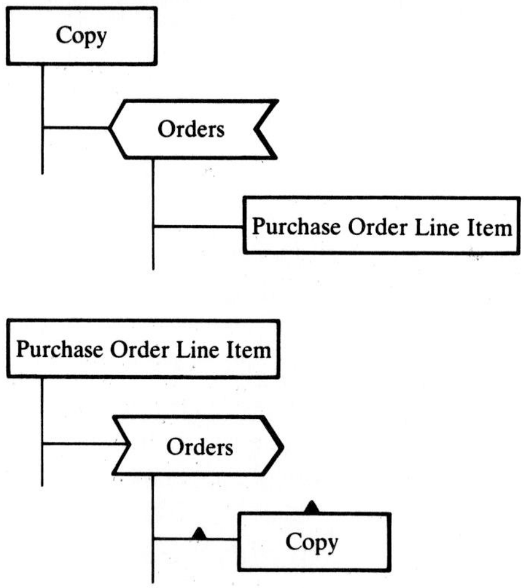

Figure 5.68

agreement that doing so would make everyone's job easier, and similar ideas are voiced from the restoration and cataloging departments. Since the cost of binding differs from copy to copy, the standard cost issue becomes moot (Figure 5.70).

While *transfers* move *books* from place to place within the confines of the library system, *books* are also used by outside patrons. That is, a *copy* will circulate. Associated with each *copy* is a chain of circulation transactions extending back in time. An embracing guarantees that the entire chain points to the same *copy* (Figure 5.71).

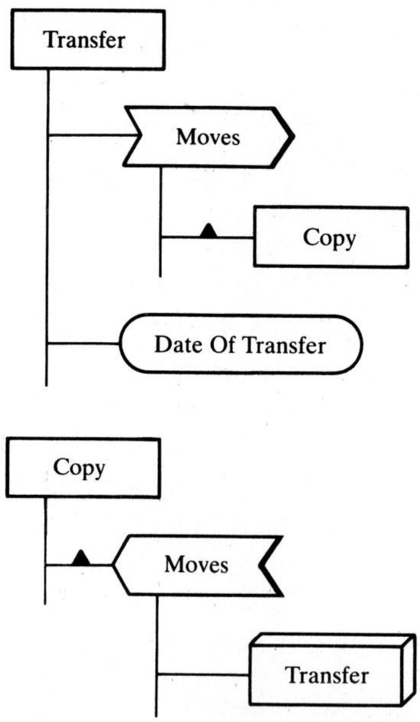

Figure 5.69

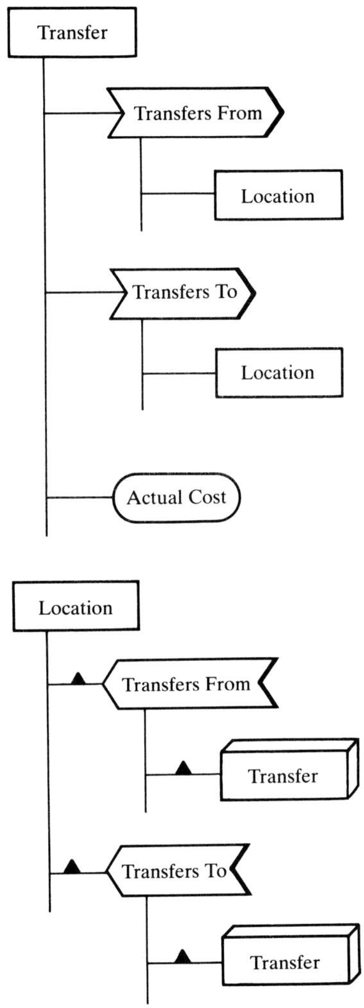

Figure 5.70

The *circulation transaction* moves the *copy* to a *circulation status* (out, in, at bindery, interlibrary loan, etc.). Considerable confusion ensues over the difference between a *transfer* and a *circulation transaction*, since some people consider the sister library to be part of the library system while others view it as analogous to a patron, existing outside the system. In this confusion it is decided that there may be a purchase order line item associated with any *circulation transaction*, which would record the cost of ordering the *copy* (see Figure 5.68), along with costs that might arise from other kinds of *transfers* (Figure 5.72). Each *copy* now has at least one *circulation transaction* that records how the *copy* was acquired.

It is questioned whether *Purchase Order Line Item* should be generalized to include other financial transactions like receipt of fines, postage, etc. Discussion begins to drift towards issues of auditability, money collections, and such. Unlike the discussion of copy

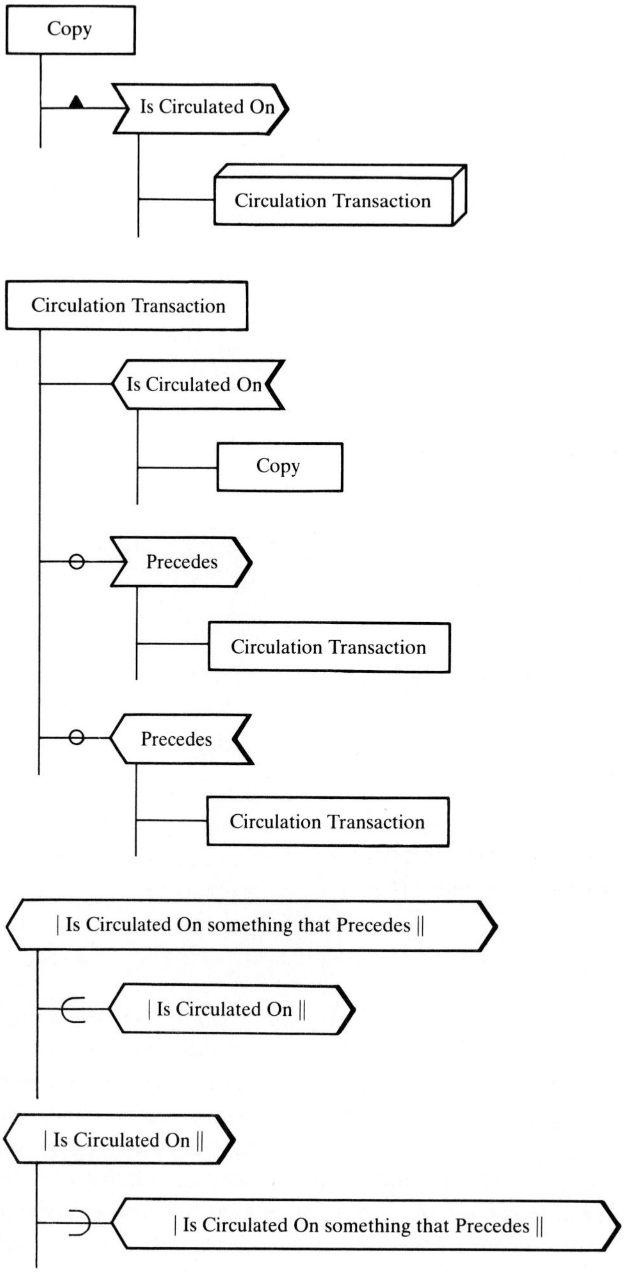
Copy
Is Circulated On
Circulation Transaction
Circulation Transaction
Is Circulated On
Copy
Precedes
Circulation Transaction
Precedes
Circulation Transaction
Is Circulated On something that Precedes	
Is Circulated On	
Is Circulated On	
Is Circulated On something that Precedes	

Figure 5.71

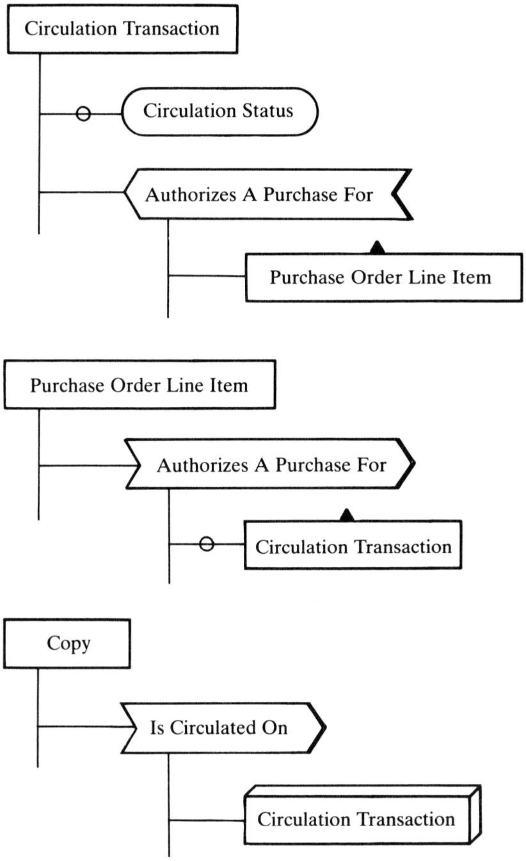

Figure 5.72

transfers, which clarified the distinction between a *book* and a *copy,* these new discussions shed no new light on *books* or *copies*. The discussion leader returns attention to *book*.

On re-examination of *book*, it is evident the group neglected to indicate the author. Discussion follows: there could be many authors; an author is not necessarily a person, but could instead be a corporate author; need to indicate the primary author; if the author uses a pen name, record the pen name in *author*, the real name, if known, in a separate element (Figure 5.73).

The relationship between *books* and ISBNs is re-examined. Although ISBN is shown associated with *Book,* the question is raised: "Shouldn't an ISBN be a property of each *copy*?" Someone asks whether an ISBN may point to no *copies*. For example, the *book* is one we have ordered or hope to acquire when funds are available.

A heated discussion ensues concerning the role of the ISBN in the group's plans for the future. The heat is normal: the group is grappling with two concepts — « *Book* » and « *International Standard Book Number* » — that are quite similar in meaning. Resistance to making unduly fine distinctions is met with equal resistance to smearing distinct concepts into one. The first outcome of the discussion is to reach agreement on which *books*

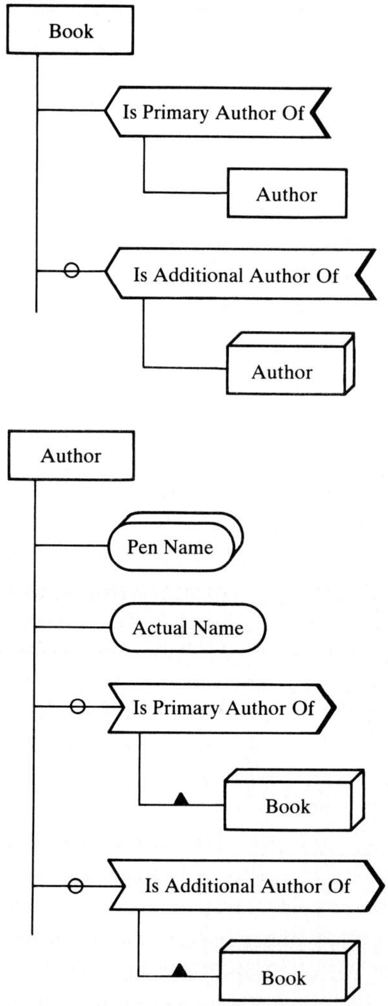

Figure 5.73

they are interested in: If the library anticipates it may order a copy of the *book* some day, they want an identifier for the *book* in the data base.

It is, of course, evident to everyone that each ISBN could point to several *copies*, since the library often has several identical copies of a book. The discussion leader, however, reports concern that there is a problem hidden here. He shows how one ISBN can point to two *copies,* where each is a copy of a different *book*. The two *books* so indicated could have different titles, different authors, etc. Is this correct? Heated debate resumes, focusing now on special cases, such as:

(i) "Chilton's Auto Repair Manual" for "Buick, Ford, VW" in model year "1962, 1963, 1964, . . ." Is this one *book*, or is it several series of *books* (VW62, VW63, VW64, . . .), or is it several sets of *books* (all the '62 models, all the '63 models, etc.)?

(ii) Is Volume 3 of an encyclopedia a *book*?

(iii) The English translation versus the French original of a book.

The significant decision is this: "No matter what the ISBN people do in such cases, we need to have the flexibility to choose the opposite possibility." In other words, we want to be able to see two *books* where they see one. The idea of using ISBNs as hidden tags for *books* is abandoned, and it is decided that a separate tagging scheme for *books* will be developed. The representative from the data processing department urges a tentative decision that the ISBN will be used as a default for most *books*, but a chorus of voices from the user community stresses that a procedure must be in place for assigning a new tag when one is needed. The group is finally certain that *book* and ISBN are intentionally distinct ideas, the idea of associating an ISBN with each *copy* is abandoned, and armed now with the ability to define a new *book* tag whenever one is required, the group agrees that each *copy replicates* exactly one *book* (Figure 5.74).

After a short break, the group turns to subject indexing. At first they assign a Dewey Decimal Number and a set of index terms to some *books*. An index term is a text string one or more words long. A requester can supply one or more index terms linked by logical connectives (AND, OR). The system combines the various sets of *books* pointed to by those terms, following the prescriptions given by the logical connectives. The resulting subset of *books* is retrieved, and their titles, etc., are presented to the requester.

Discussion follows on synonymous index terms—alternate spellings such as "color" and "colour," abbreviations, renamings such as "Zimbabwe" for "Rhodesia." It is decided that all the synonyms should retrieve the same *index item* (for example, a request for books on the history of Zimbabwe would retrieve the same list as a request for books on the history of Rhodesia). A *book* therefore relates to *index items*, not directly to *index terms*.

After pondering how such a retrieval system would work, the group decides the *book* is too large a chunk of text to index. They think of collections (e.g., bound volumes of periodicals) that contain articles on many subjects. They decide to call the indexed portion of a *book* a *unit*. They decide that *units* can be broken into smaller *units*. The result is a hierarchy of *units*, each of which may be indexed (Figure 5.75).

The discussion leader concludes that we have learned as much as we are likely to about *book* and adjourns the meeting. The final outcome is shown in Figure 5.76. The figure shows all the cascades under classes that were developed, along with the embracing of correspondences that described circulation transactions. The complete diagram would include, in addition, cascades for all the correspondences, definitions of all the classes and all the correspondences, and explanations for each decision, but these are omitted to conserve space.

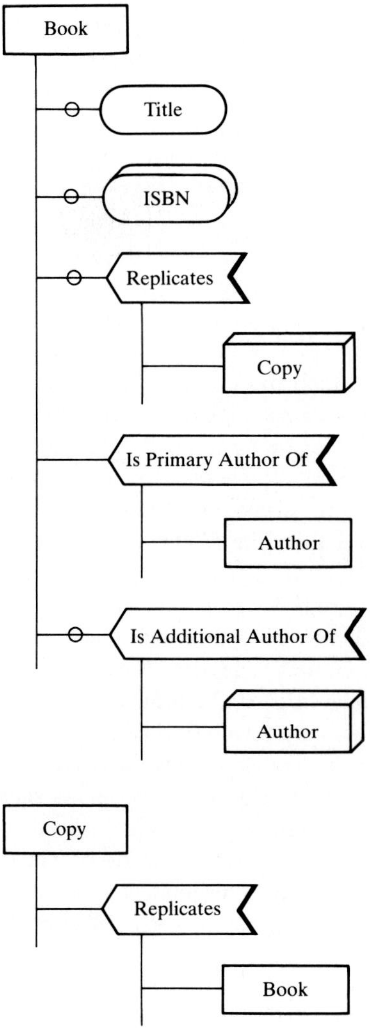
Book
Title
ISBN
Replicates
Copy
Is Primary Author Of
Author
Is Additional Author Of
Author
Copy
Replicates
Book

Figure 5.74

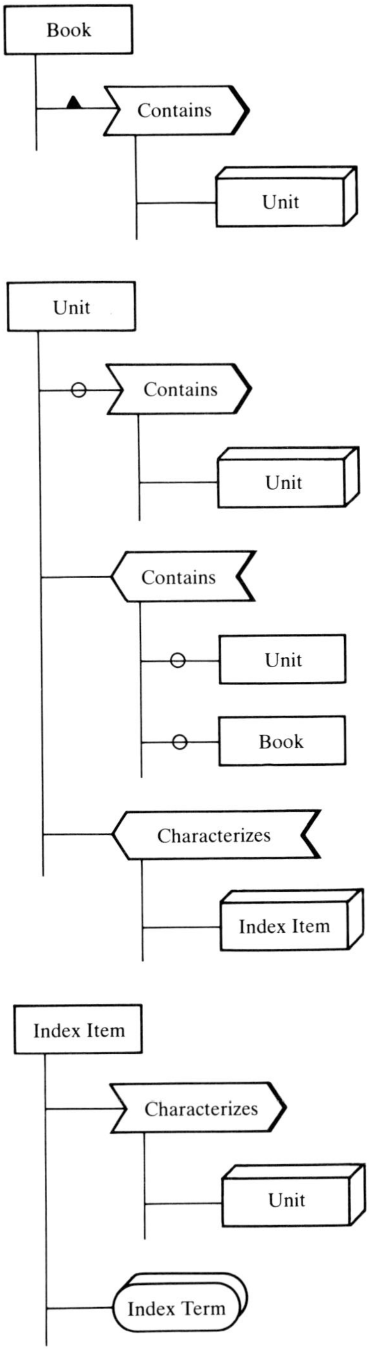
Book
Contains
Unit
Unit
Contains
Unit
Contains
Unit
Book
Characterizes
Index Item
Index Item
Characterizes
Unit
Index Term

Figure 5.75

Conclusion

This case study illustrates how much discussion can be required in practical situations to come to an understanding of even something as superficially simple as a « book ». We found in the end that « book » was a loose concept, and that we needed three different class tags, *Book, Copy,* and *Unit,* to handle the problems that arose.

Notice that the class tags *Copy* and *Unit* were not used by the participants before this meeting. They could not therefore have been determined by analysis of existing procedures or official documents. This is a typical example of data design as a creative art, establishing new, more rigorous ideas so that automatic solutions can operate reliably.

Notice also how it was crucial to investigate seemingly peripheral topics, such as copy transfers and subject indexing. Part of the training of a data base designer is to know the difference between an investigation that is leading nowhere and an investigation that is making progress. Thus, the discussion of *Purchase Order Line Item* was stopped before it got out of hand. The discussion of *Circulation Transaction*, on the other hand, though allowed to go on into historical issues seemingly prematurely, eventually brought clarification to the ordering process and helped to distinguish between *book* and ISBN. Notice further that no use was made of normalization techniques throughout the entire discussion. This is typical of design sessions conducted using the Associative Data Model.

It is tempting upon emerging from such a meeting to believe that the group has reached understanding on all points discussed. However, in the design as it stands, the only classes of which there is moderately good understanding are *Book, Copy,* ISBN, and possibly *Unit.* The other classes have only been touched upon, and, most importantly, have only been viewed in the context of how they relate to books, copies, and the like. As the discussion of « book » shows, it is necessary to view an idea from several angles before it will be clear how it should be represented. Thus the design as it stands is really only a start.

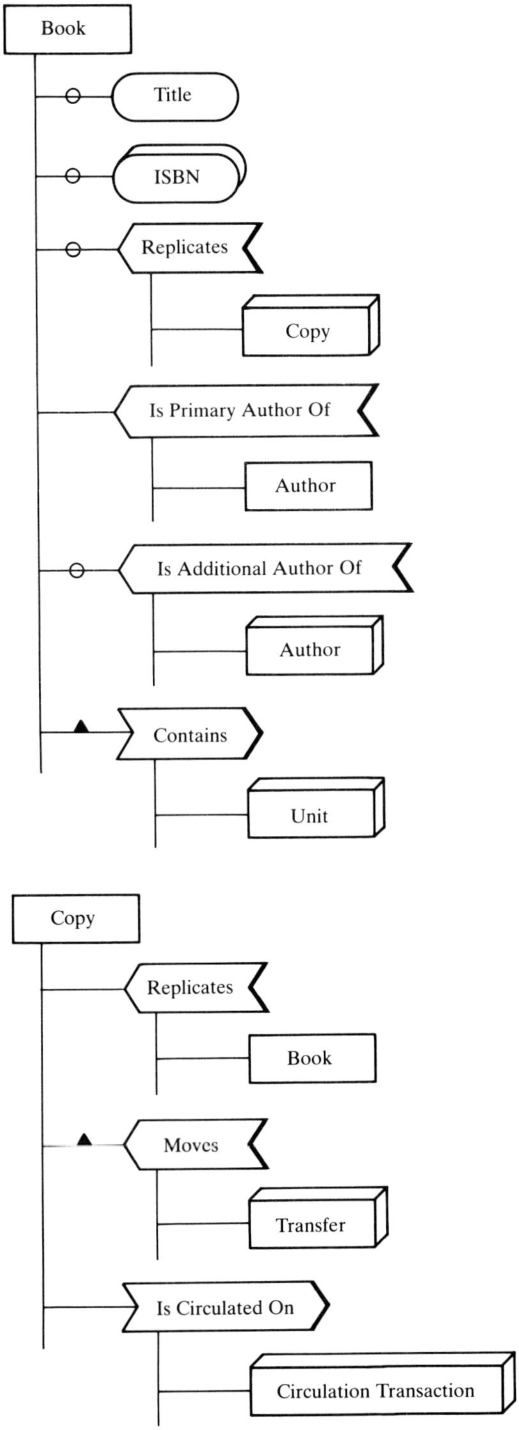

Book
Title
ISBN
Replicates
Copy
Is Primary Author Of
Author
Is Additional Author Of
Author
Contains
Unit
Copy
Replicates
Book
Moves
Transfer
Is Circulated On
Circulation Transaction

Figure 5.76

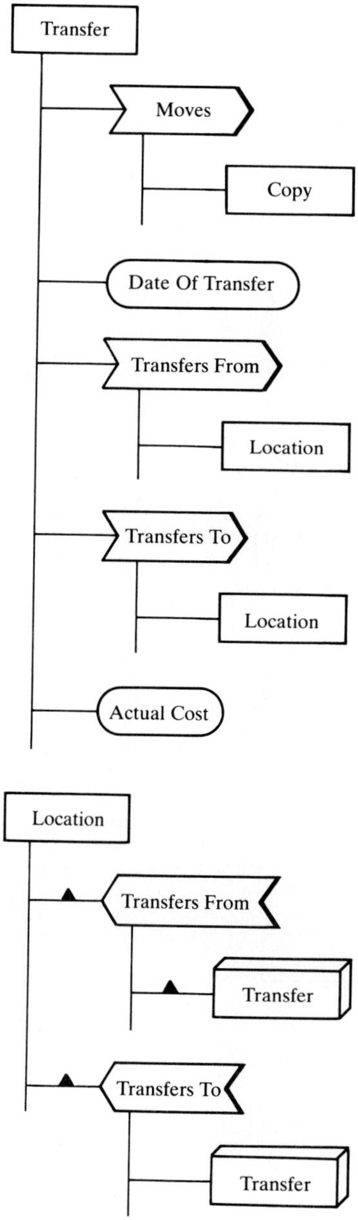

Figure 5.76 *(continued)*

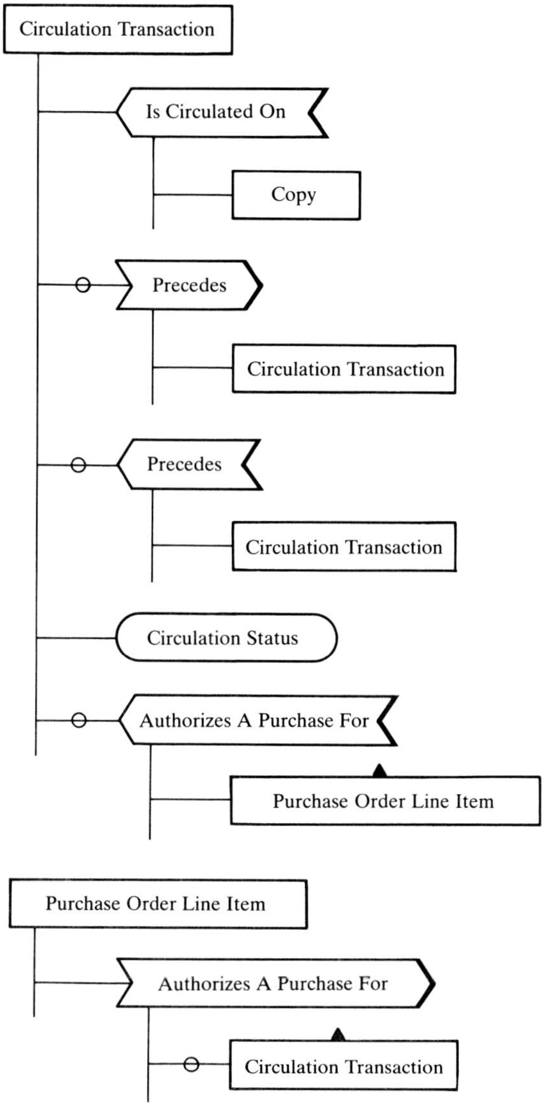

Figure 5.76 *(continued)*

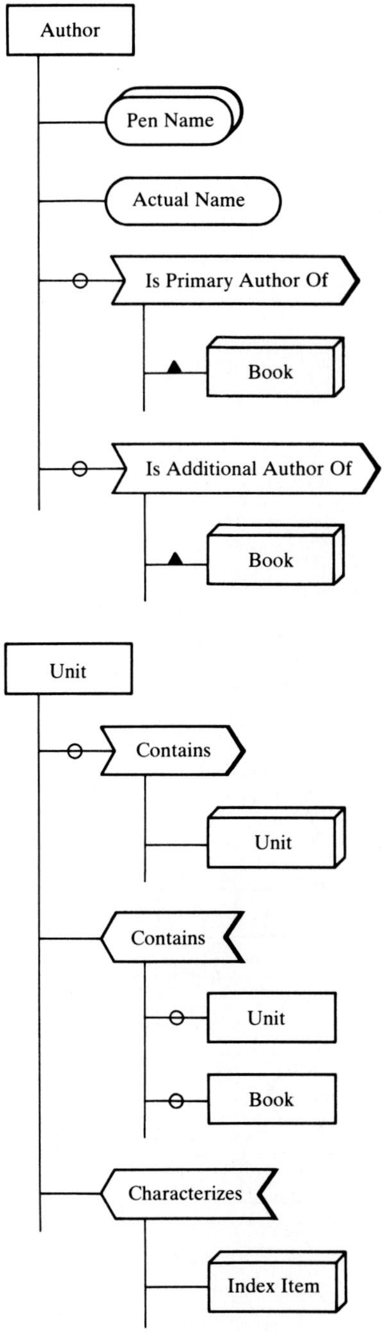

Figure 5.76 *(continued)*

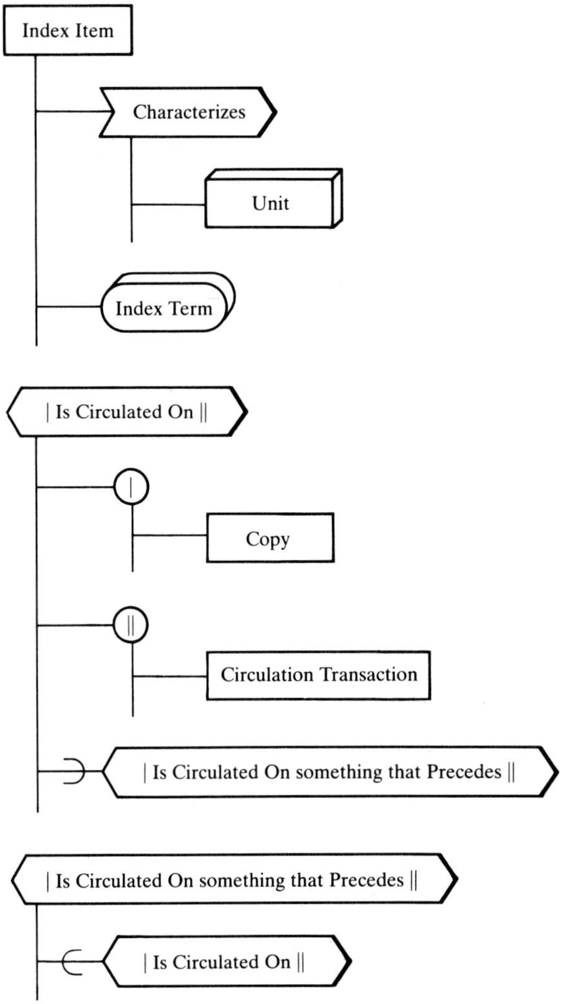

Figure 5.76 *(continued)*

5.9 CONCLUSION

We have described a notation for presenting schema constraints to a wide audience. Data bases are not designed by system engineers alone, but by teams of data designers, users, and process designers. Extended associative notation is a language that is at once precise and evocative enough to serve the needs of all participants in a design effort.

Extended associative notation is designed to facilitate declaration of the most common constraints. Associative Data Model notation, on which extended associative notation is built, contains special facilities for representing character decisions. Extended associative notation adds the ability to show and to define correspondences, trios, and associations of higher degree directly in a data design. Extended associative notation incorporates the additional design decisions of agency decisions and targeting decisions. It provides facilities for declaring embracings, and includes linguistic devices that permit complex formulas to be expressed in a modular way. Extended associative notation also includes an automatic documentation facility that generates natural language explanations for all constraints.

Extended associative notation can express many forms of constraints that are not supported by current data base management systems. We believe that it is important for a data specification language such as extended associative notation to be ahead of the abilities of automated packages. A data design is usually created many years before a system becomes operational, so it must not be constrained to the limitations of current technology, but must look ahead to capabilities that may be years in coming to production. A good data design always reflects the user requirements in the most accurate way possible, even if those requirements will be difficult to implement.

CONCLUSION TO PART 2

We have shown how data logic unifies the capabilities of the major data models within a common framework. By expressing results about data in data logic, therefore, we can describe data without being constrained by any particular data base management system. Data logic also provides a standard language that can be used to compare the effectiveness of different data management implementations.

We have shown how schemas designed using data logic can be expressed in the graphical form of extended associative notation. This notation is a concise and easy to understand language specifically geared to practical data design. Extended associative notation includes abilities to handle such data structures as embracings and trio complexes that reach beyond the current state of computing technology.

We have argued that data base management systems need to be enhanced markedly beyond their current abilities. The current architectures based on records or on tuples are inadequate to handle unresolved alternation, denial, and relative associations (which cause "null values" in a tuple-based system). Data management for the future should incorporate reasoning abilities similar to those found in artificial intelligence systems. Logic programming, expert systems, and knowledge bases are all founded on data logic just as data bases are, and future data management systems should support all these capabilities.

PART 3
Data Structures

INTRODUCTION TO PART 3

In the remaining chapters, we investigate the varieties of data structures that may be designed using positive embracings. This investigation will tend to become technical as we explore complex structures. Readers who do not have an extensive background in data bases may prefer to concentrate on the chapter introductions and the two case studies, which illustrate the most significant findings without the technical justification.

Data logic permits a far wider variety of data structures than other contemporary theories. In particular, embracings allow updates to one association to affect other associations in unfamiliar ways. We must, therefore, abandon the prejudice that each association should be independent of every other. The building blocks of data structures are properly not associations, but groups of associations that are interrelated by embracings.

Our discussion will culminate in an exhaustive study of trio complexes, that is, declarations of associations of degree three. Trio complexes are familiar data structures that are present in most data designs of significant size. Trios are also the lowest degree associations that present the problems of "null values." In data logic terms, null values occur when a trio T is declared relative to a correspondence F, and $F{:}(x, y)$ may be claimed without there being an individual z such that $T{:}(x, y, z)$. Null values have been a serious problem for data bases designed according to the relational data model.

There is an internal embracing in a trio complex, which may be described loosely by the following argument: the assemblies of a trio T are similar to triples (a, b, c). We may determine the triples that begin with some individual a in two ways: either by proceeding from a to the pairs (a, y) and then to the triples (a, y, z), or by proceeding from a to the pairs (a, z) (leaving out individuals in the second position) and then to the triples (a, y, z). We should get the same answer whichever path we choose, namely, the triples that begin with a. When the data structure of a trio is formulated, this equivalence of the two paths appears as a bi-directional embracing of correspondences.

Before we can study trio complexes, therefore, we must investigate the properties of embracings in more detail. Chapter 6, Analysis of Character Constraints, studies the properties of correspondences in detail, and uses embracings to prove theorems about data structures. Most of the topics discussed will be familiar to data base practitioners, although we include some basic theorems about embracings that may be unfamiliar.

Chapter 7, Embracings of Correspondences, discusses some simple varieties of embracings of degree two. Most of these embracings are not supported by current data base management systems, and will be unfamiliar to data base practitioners. At the end of the chapter, we present a case study on the representation of time, where we show how embracings can be put to use.

Chapter 8, Composition Cones, discusses one particular variety of embracings in detail: the bi-directional embracing $F \circ G \equiv H$. That is, we consider two correspondences F and G whose composition is equivalent to another correspondence H. In data logic, it is possible for H to obey constraints that constrain the behavior of F and G. We will see that such constraints, called *composition cones*, give a much more diverse variety of potential populations for F and G than would be predicted from the characters of F and of G alone.

In Chapter 9, Associations of High Degree, we apply the results gained in earlier chapters to the study of associations of degree three and higher. We show how data logic predicts the degeneracy of many such associations (such as the Student-Course-Teacher example found in many introductory texts) without the need for ''normalization'' procedures. We then discuss how to represent those associations of higher degree that can not be reduced to correspondences. Extended associative notation allows up to 36 partially independent decisions to be made when declaring a trio. At the end of the chapter, we present a case study that examines all 36 decisions in turn.

6

Analysis of Character Constraints

6.1 INTRODUCTION

In this chapter we show how characters may be treated as objects in their own right, independent of the correspondences that exhibit the character. The relational algebra of symbolic logic can not describe characters independently, because to do so requires quantifying over associations, which requires what is called the second-order predicate calculus, and relational algebra is restricted to the simpler first-order predicate calculus. There are no such orders in data logic to restrict analysis. By studying characters without referring to particular correspondences, we are able to prove general theorems about data that must be obeyed by any schema.

In Section 6.2, Permissiveness Ordering of Characters, we show how operations on characters as sets of brackets are related to the populability of correspondences. For example, any population of a *one-to-one all-to-all* correspondence G continues to be a population of G if the constraints on G are changed so that G becomes *one-to-many all-to-all*. We show further that *one-to-one*, *one-to-many,* and *many-to-one* correspondences can be classified completely by their potential populations.

In Section 6.3, Loops, we examine correspondence complexes where the correspondence tag is declared relative to the same class tag in both positions: (G; B, B). These data structures are not recognized by many data models, but they are predicted by data logic, and they may be declared in extended associative notation.

In Section 6.4, Multicorrespondence Data Structures, we discuss the typical data structures of *cycles*, *paths*, and *hubs*. These patterns are named for their appearance in network drawings. Many interactions between correspondences may be described by their action on such patterns. For example, we show in Section 6.5, Elongation Factoring and Mantles, how a correspondence may be *factored* into a path in such a way that the character of each constituent correspondence of the path consists of exactly one bracket from the factored correspondence. This factoring, called an *elongation factoring*, determines the standard ordering of brackets in a character: **]**, <, >, **[**.

In Section 6.6, Bundlings, we analyze a particular variety of correspondences called *bundlings*, which obey a constraint similar to a "multivalued dependency" in the relational data model. We show how bundlings may be re-expressed as a path of length two, and show how bundlings can be considered to be the simplest form of *many-to-many* correspondences.

6.2 CLASSIFICATION OF POPULATIONS

Characters May Be Manipulated as Sets

A character, though written as a sequence of brackets, is really a set of brackets, written in a standard order for convenience. (See, however, the positional character notation, which does make distinctions based on the positions of the brackets in sequence, Section 6.6.) As sets, characters are subject to the common operations of intersection, union, and inclusion. Thus we may write quite properly:

"**]**<" ∩ "<**[**" = "<"

"<>" ∪ "**]**>" = "**]**<>"

"**]**" ⊂ "**]**<"

These operations have important uses. Intersection of characters is used as a mask to extract portions of a character for study. Thus, chr $(G; B, C)$ ∩ "**]**" represents the *from some/from all* bracket decision for G relative to (B, C). It is either equal to "**]**", if G is *from some* relative to (B, C), or equal to $\varnothing$, if G is *from all*. Union of characters is used in the study of composition, discussed in the next chapter. We will discuss inclusion of characters in this section.

Inclusion of Characters Indicates Inclusion of Potential Populations

The key result about inclusion of characters is contained in the following theorem:

Theorem 6.1. Let G and H be two correspondences, constrained in no way other than by their characters. Suppose chr $(G; B, C) \subset$ chr $(H; B, C)$. Then any population of $(G; B, C)$ may be transformed into a population of $(H; B, C)$ by replacing all appearances of the association tag "G" with the association tag "H".

That is, if we have any population diagram for a correspondence G of character α relative to (B, C), we can convert this diagram to a population diagram for a correspondence H of character β relative to (B, C) just by erasing all the occurrences of the letter

"*G*" and replacing them with the letter "*H*", provided $\alpha \subset \beta$. We use the two tags *G* and *H* to keep the two correspondence characters straight. Theorem 6.1 can also be used to study the effect of changing the character of a correspondence *G* from α to β. Then, *H* indicates « *G* with the new character β ».

The clause ". . . constrained in no way other than by their characters" in the statement of Theorem 6.1 is needed because *H* may appear in other embracings that would further constrain its potential populations (for example, *H* might be embraced in another correspondence *J*). This clause can be dispensed with by requiring that *G* obey all the constraints formed by replacing "*H*" with "*G*" in the constraints that involve "*H*". For example, if *J* embraced *H*, then Theorem 6.1 would only apply if *J* embraced *G* as well. Notice that this additional requirement is satisfied automatically if *H* indicates « *G* with a different character ».

Proof of Theorem 6.1. Every bracket in chr (*G*; *B*, *C*) represents the *denial* of a constraint. Thus, **]** $\in$ chr (*G*; *B*, *C*) means that *G* is not *from all* relative to (*B*, *C*), $< \in$ chr (*G*; *B*, *C*) means that *G* is not *to one* relative to (*B*, *C*), and so on. If chr (*G*; *B*, *C*) $\subset$ chr (*H*; *B*, *C*) then there are more brackets in chr (*H*; *B*, *C*) than in chr (*G*; *B*, *C*). Hence there are *fewer* constraints.

For example, suppose that chr (*H*; *B*, *C*) equals chr (*G*; *B*, *C*) except that chr (*H*; *B*, *C*) contains **]** while chr (*G*; *B*, *C*) does not. Then *H* permits a population that includes any number of orphans, including zero, while *G* requires that there be no orphans. Thus any population of *G* can also be a population of *H*. Similarly, suppose that chr (*H*; *B*, *C*) equals chr (*G*; *B*, *C*) except that chr (*H*; *B*, *C*) contains $<$ where chr (*G*; *B*, *C*) does not. Then *H* permits populations where instances of *B* attach to many instances or to one instance of *C*, while *G* requires that instances of *B* attach to at most one instance of *C*. Thus any population of *G* can also be a population of *H*. The required properties of the other bracket symbols, $>$ and **[**, follow from the discussion of **]** and $<$ by considering the converse correspondences *G** and *H**. Q.E.D.

By virtue of Theorem 6.1, we say that a character β is *more permissive* than a character α if $\alpha \subset \beta$ (and $\alpha \neq \beta$), and we say conversely that β is *less permissive* than α. Alternatively, we say that β is *less restrictive* than α, and that α is *more restrictive* than β. We may view these ideas in a practical sense as saying that we may change a schema in the course of developing the design by making correspondences *more permissive* and be certain that the populations of the old design can be accommodated in the new design. Notice that relative permissiveness is defined by set inclusion, not by counting brackets. For example, "**]**$<$" is not more permissive than "**[**", because "**]**$<$" does not contain "**[**" as a set.

Method for Classifying Correspondence Complexes

Characters may be studied by examining their potential population diagrams. We will study a correspondence complex of the form (*G*; *B*, *C*). We assume that *B* and *C* are different class tags, that is, we assume that *B* and *C* are not identical. Such correspondence complexes are said to be *pillared*. Correspondence complexes where the two class tags are identical, such as (*G*; *B*, *B*), are called *loops*, and will be discussed in Section 6.3. We will devote the remainder of this section to a detailed study of the potential populations exhibited by each character. This will furnish a means of classifying all pillared correspondence complexes that are not *many-to-many*.

Each character α has a *converse*, written α^*, formed by turning α upside down. Thus, the converse of “**]**” is “**[**”, the converse of “>**[**” is “**]**<”, and the converse of “<>” is “<>”. If the correspondence complex (G; B, C) has the character α, then the converse correspondence complex (G^*; C, B) has the character α^*. We need not examine both a character and its converse, because a population diagram for the converse of a character α may be formed by turning a diagram for the character α upside down. Six characters may therefore be ignored by virtue of the converses:

“**]**” ↔ “**[**”

“>” ↔ “<”

“**]**>” ↔ “<**[**”

“**]**>**[**” ↔ “**]**<**[**”

“>**[**” ↔ “**]**<”

“**]**<>” ↔ “<>**[**”

Classification Excludes Unresolved Alternations

Claims that incorporate unresolved alternations are far less affected by character constraints than resolute claims. For example, the population illustrated in Figure 6.1 is permitted by any character of G. This population diagram indicates that b_1 or b_2 attaches to c_1 or to c_2. Even if G were *one-to-one all-to-all,* this population would be allowed, for it could be that b_1 attaches to c_1 and that b_2 attatches to c_2. If the lines in Figure 6.1 had been solid instead of dashed, the diagram would be prohibited in a *one-to-one all-to-all* correspondence complex, because an instance of B would attach to many instances of C and an instance of C would attach to many instances of B.

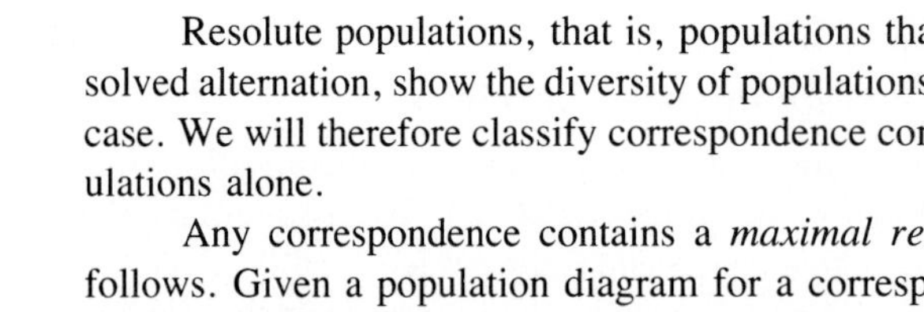

Figure 6.1 Unresolved alternation.

Resolute populations, that is, populations that do not contain claims that use unresolved alternation, show the diversity of populations far more clearly than the more general case. We will therefore classify correspondence complexes based upon their resolute populations alone.

Any correspondence contains a *maximal resolute subcorrespondence*, formed as follows. Given a population diagram for a correspondence G, erase all the dashed lines from the diagram. This may leave some individuals unattached that were attached before by dashed lines only. If orphans are permitted, these individuals are retained. If orphans are prohibited, erase these individuals as well. The resulting populations are the populations of the maximal resolute subcorrespondence $\acute{G}$. If G obeys other constraints, $\acute{G}$ is so defined to obey these constraints as well.

For example, Figure 6.2 shows a potential population of a correspondence complex $(G; B, C)$ of character ''<[''. The associated population of the maximal resolute subcorrespondence $\acute{G}$ is shown in Figure 6.3.

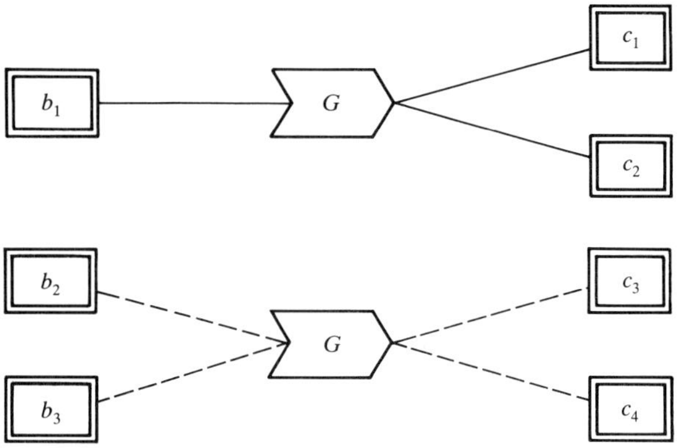

Figure 6.2 *G* has character ''<['' relative to (B, C).

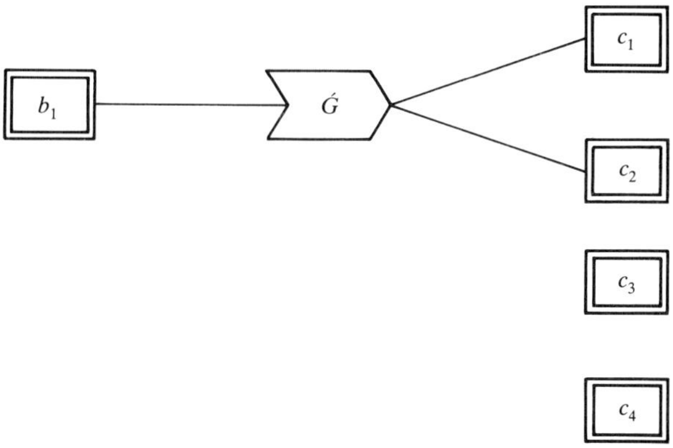

Figure 6.3 Maximal resolute subcorrespondence of *G*.

The individuals b_1 and b_2 are erased because G is *from all*, but the individuals c_3 and c_4 are retained because G is *to some*. The classification of a given population that contains unresolved alternations is defined to be the classification of the associated population of the maximal resolute subcorrespondence.

Similarity and Logical Measures

Many characters exhibit *similarity*, which means that all potential population diagrams appear alike, and differ only in sizing factors that are related to the number of instances in the population. A data structure can only be said to be understood if its potential resolute populations can be classifed completely by similarity. Once we can reach such an understanding, not only can we generate all potential resolute populations, but we can also develop measures of data base populations.

Those measures that are available today are usually expressed in terms of physical factors such as storage utilization. For example, one might measure the total number of bytes occupied by a given population. Such measures, however, mix implementation characteristics with design characteristics to give an unclear picture. For example, a list of 1000 six-character part numbers may take twice the physical storage space as a list of 1000 three-character part numbers, but each is logically the same number of instances. We introduce a variety of *logical measures* of populations below that are independent of the symbols chosen as individuals. These logical measures can be used to compare populations of a data base at different times, and so give a picture of data base growth.

Classification of Correspondence Complexes

1. chr $(G; B, C) = \varnothing$

A *one-to-one all-to-all* correspondence complex has a typically monotonous appearance. A population diagram of a resolute *one-to-one all-to-all* correspondence complex is completely characterized by the number of instances of either class (which must equal the number of instances of the other class as well as the number of attachments). Thus, all *one-to-one all-to-all* correspondence complexes are similar, and their populations are described by one number. In Figure 6.4, this number is three.

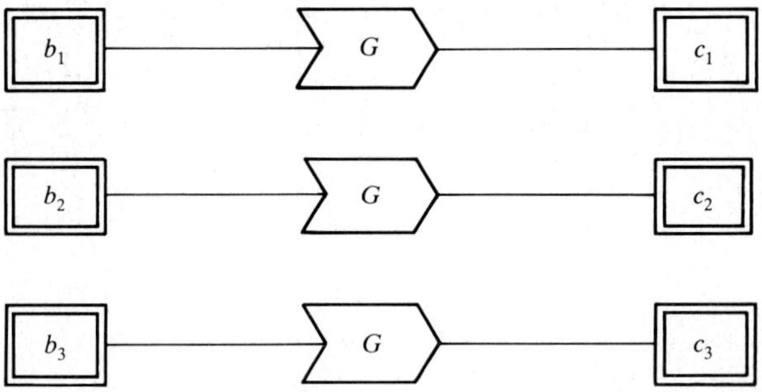

Figure 6.4 Character $\varnothing$.

2. chr $(G; B, C)$ = "]"

There are two types of instances of the source class B: the instances of the scope of G, b_1 and b_2, and the instances of the orphan class, b_3. Other than the orphans, G appears the

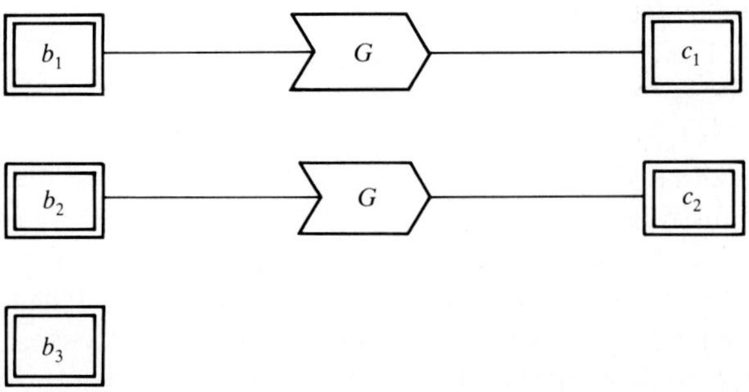

Figure 6.5 Character "]".

same as a *one-to-one all-to-all* correspondence. Since the orphans participate in no attachments via G, they are all similar. Thus, all *one-to-one some-to-all* correspondence complexes are similar, and their populations are described by two numbers, the number of attachments and the number of orphans.

3. chr (G; B, C) = ">"

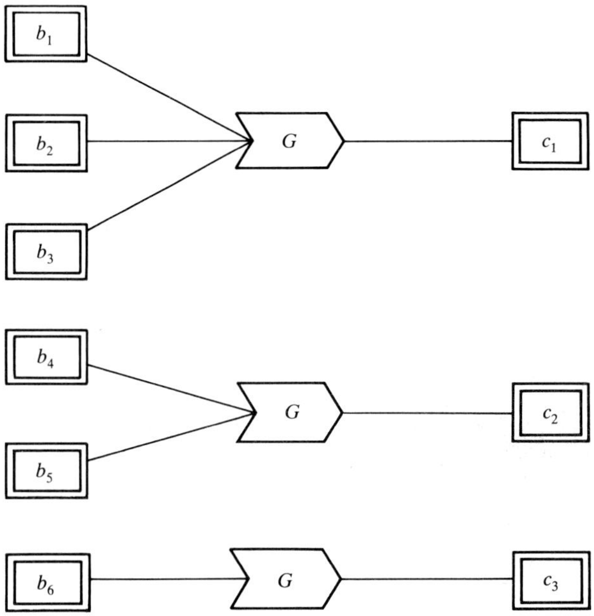

Figure 6.6 Character ">".

There are two types of instances of the destination class: the instances that attach to many instances of the source class, namely c_1 and c_2, and the instances that attach to one instance of the source class, namely c_3 and c_4. The instances of the destination partition the instances of the source into disjoint sets called *immediate neighborhoods*: $\{b_1, b_2, b_3\}$, $\{b_4, b_5\}$, and $\{b_6\}$.

Some instances of the source class, called *loners*, contain only one individual in their immediate neighborhood (such as b_6). Others contain many individuals in their immediate neighborhoods (such as the remaining instances of B in the example). Similarly, we may distinguish instances of the destination class by whether they attach to only one instance of the source class (such as c_3) or to many (such as the remaining instances of C in the example).

If we restrict attention to those instances of C that attach to only one instance of B, and the loners of B, the population diagram is the same as a *one-to-one all-to-all* correspondence complex. Each *one-to-many all-to-all* correspondence complex embraces a *one-to-one all-to-all* correspondence complex formed in this way (the latter correspondence complex may, however, have an empty population, if every instance of C happens to attach to many instances of B). We would have expected to find such an embracing by virtue of Theorem 6.1, because the set ∅ that indicates the character *one-to-one all-to-all* is included in the set ">" that indicates the character *many-to-one all-to-all.*

The portion of the population that appears *one-to-one* can be classified by one number, the number of attachments in that portion. The remainder of the population can be classified strictly by listing the number of individuals in each immediate neighborhood. There is no inherent order in the neighborhoods, since there is no inherent order to the individuals (an order, like a sort order, would require another correspondence in addition to *G*). Two correspondence complexes with the same lists of immediate neighborhood sizes (the order of numbers in the lists is not significant) are similar. Since any population of a *many-to-one all-to-all* correspondence complex can be characterized by a list of numbers in this way, all *many-to-one all-to-all* correspondence complexes are similar.

The lists of numbers discussed above are usually too extensive to be useful. A statistical measure can be more valuable. The number of individuals in an immediate neighborhood is called the *width* of the neighborhood. The width of the largest neighborhood is called the *maximum width* of the population, the number such that there are as many larger neighborhoods as smaller ones is called the *median width* of the population, and so on. The choice of a measure depends on the application.

When such a statistical measure is used, the number of instances of *C* must also be specified, so that all populations of *many-to-one all-to-all* correspondences may be described by three numbers, the number of loners of *B*, the number of instances of *C*, and a statistical measure such as the median width of G^*. (We define the width by viewing the attachments spreading out from left to right—here they spread out from right to left, therefore, we are describing the width of the converse G^*.)

4. chr (*G*; *B*, *C*) = "]>"

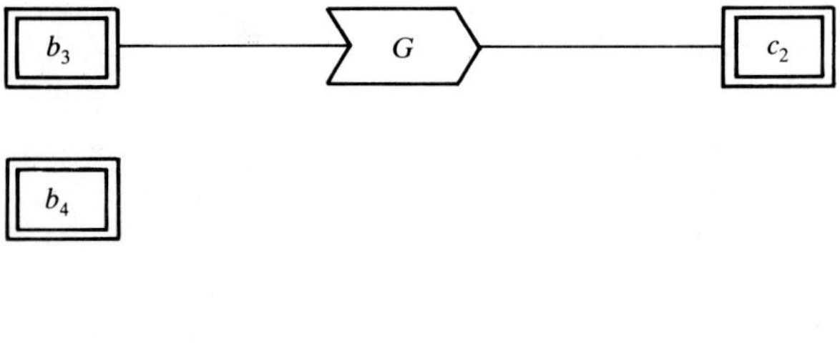

Figure 6.7 Character "]>".

Since "]" ⊂ "]>" and ">" ⊂ "]>", we would expect to see characteristics of both "]" and ">" in a population of "]>". As expected, two varieties of instances of the destination class are found, those that attach to many instances of the source class, such as c_1, and those that attach to one instance of the source class, such as c_2.

Three varieties of instances of the source class are found: the loners such as b_3 in Figure 6.7, those whose immediate neighborhood contains many individuals such as b_1 and b_2, and the orphans such as b_4. The orphans can be considered to be individuals whose immediate neighborhood is empty. The first two varieties of instances of the source class were found in ">", and the third was found in "**]**". Notice that there are no new varieties beyond those determined from the less permissive characters.

Since we had determined that all correspondence complexes of character "**]**" were similar to each other, and that all correspondence complexes of character ">" were similar to each other, and since we have found no new types of individuals beyond those from those two characters, we can conclude that all correspondence complexes of character "**]**>" are similar to each other. A population of a correspondence complex of character "**]**>" can be described by four numbers: the number of orphans of B, the number of loners of B, the number of instances of C, and some statistical measure such as the median width of $\dot{G}^*$.

5. chr (G; B, C) = ">**[**"

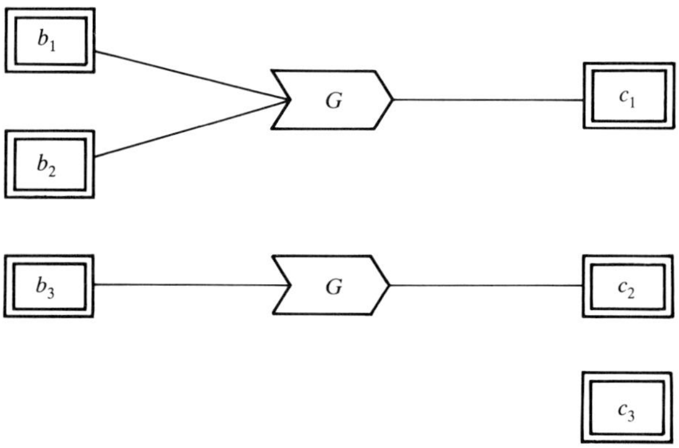

Figure 6.8 Character ">**[**".

Again we find characteristics of the two less permissive characters ">" and "**[**". In this case the orphans are instances of the destination class rather than instances of the source class as in "**]**>". No new varieties appear beyond those in ">" and "**[**" (see its converse "**]**").

We may therefore conclude that all correspondence complexes of character ">**[**" are similar. A population may be described by four numbers: the number of orphans of C, the number of loners of B, the total number of instances of C, and some statistical measure such as the median width of $\dot{G}^*$.

6. chr (G; B, C) = "**][**"

Here we find orphans of both the source class, such as b_3, and the destination class, such as c_3. The correspondence complex is otherwise the same as that of character $\varnothing$.

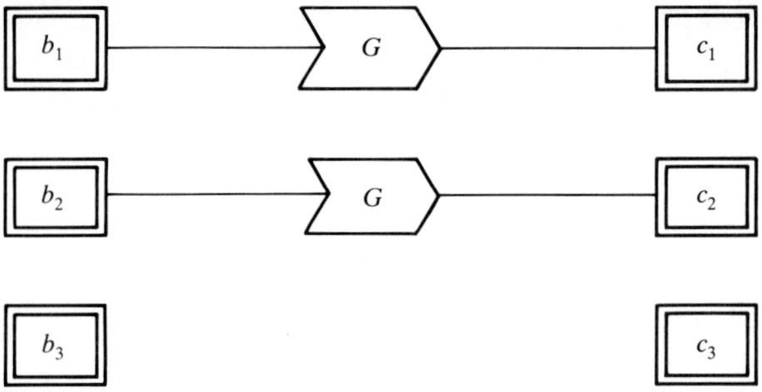

Figure 6.9 Character "**] [**".

All correspondence complexes of character "**] [**" are similar. Their populations are described by three numbers, the number of orphans of B, the number of orphans of C, and the number of attachments of $\dot{G}$.

7. chr (G; B, C) = "**]>[**"

An illustration for this character may be formed by adding orphans of the source class such as b_4 to a population diagram of "**>[**", or equivalently, by adding orphans of the destination class such as c_3 to a population diagram of "**]>**".

All correspondence complexes of character "**]>[**" are similar. Their populations are described by five numbers, the number of orphans of B, the number of loners of B, the number of orphans of C, the number of instances of C, and a statistical measure such as the median width of $\dot{G}$*.

We have shown by systematic examination of all characters, then, that any *one-to-one, one-to-many*, or *many-to-one* correspondence complex is similar to any other correspondence complex with the same character.

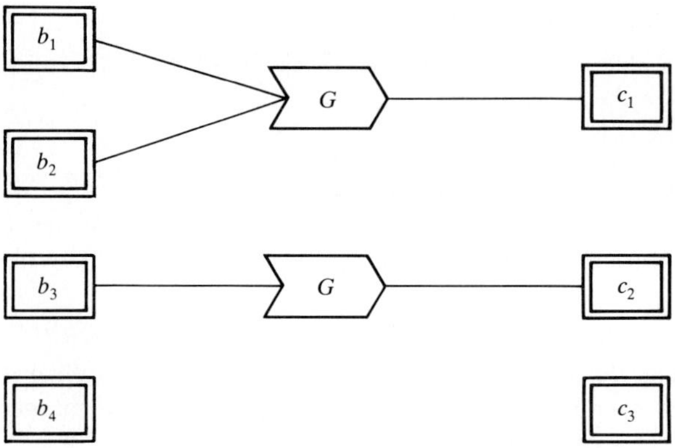

Figure 6.10 Character "**]>[**".

Many-to-Many Correspondence Complexes

Although more restrictive correspondence complexes may be characterized by a few patterns, *many-to-many* correspondence complexes may not. The difficulty comes from the phenomenon of *zigzag*, illustrated in Figure 6.11. This figure shows an attachment path

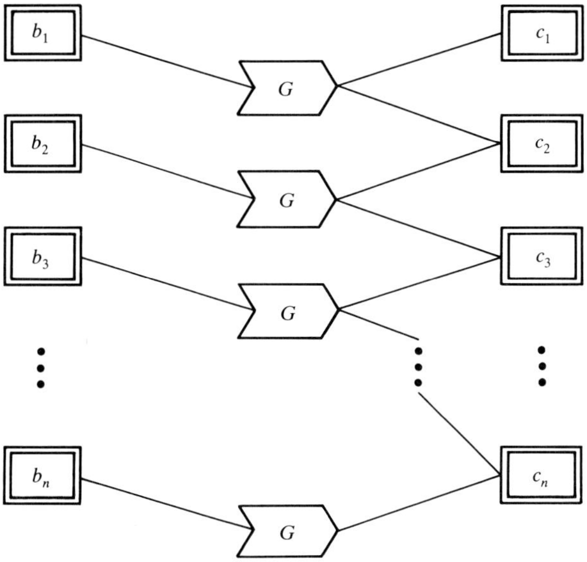

Figure 6.11 Zigzag.

from c_1 to b_1 (via G^*) to c_2 (via G) to b_2, and so on. Such zigzag paths are only possible in *many-to-many* correspondence complexes. In a more restrictive correspondence complex, these paths could contain at most one instance of B, or at most one instance of C. Because of zigzag, all *many-to-many* correspondence complexes are not similar. We will discuss zigzag more thoroughly in Section 6.6.

8. chr (G; B, C) = "<>"

The potential population diagrams of a *many-to-many all-to-all* correspondence complex include nearly all possible ways that instances of B can be attached to instances of C. The only restrictions stem from the *all-to-all* constraints, that is, every instance of B must attach to some instance of C, and every instance of C must attach to some instance of B.

9. chr (G; B, C) = "]<>"

A population diagram is formed by adding orphans of the source class to a diagram of "<>".

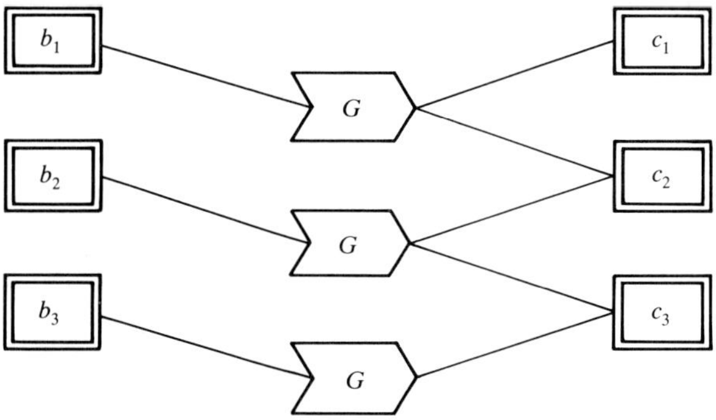

Figure 6.12 Character "<>".

10. chr (G; B, C) = "]<>["

Any population diagram in which instances of B are attached to instances of C shows a potential population of a correspondence complex of character "]<>[".

Conclusion

If a character α is included in a character β, we have shown that any population of a correspondence complex of character α can be transformed into a population of a correspondence complex of character β. We have used this property of characters to classify all *one-to-one, one-to-many*, and *many-to-one* correspondence complexes by *similarity*. *Many-to-many* correspondence complexes can have much more diverse populations, and can not be classified in this way.

6.3 LOOPS

Population Size Inequalities

If a *resolute* correspondence complex (G; B, C) has character "[", "<", or "<[", then the class C must have more instances than the class B, as shown by Figure 6.13. This ability to make predictions from correspondence characters about the number of instances in a resolute population is discussed further in (Jones and Curtice 1988).

Figure 6.13 C has more instances than B.

If unresolved alternation is permitted, the character of G does not relate the number of instances of B and C, as is shown by Figure 6.14. Here, even though G has character "<[", B has more instances than C. This result illustrates the danger of reasoning from population diagrams to determine characteristics of associations. Proofs about associations should always be derived from embracings, which handle unresolved alternations within the framework of data logic.

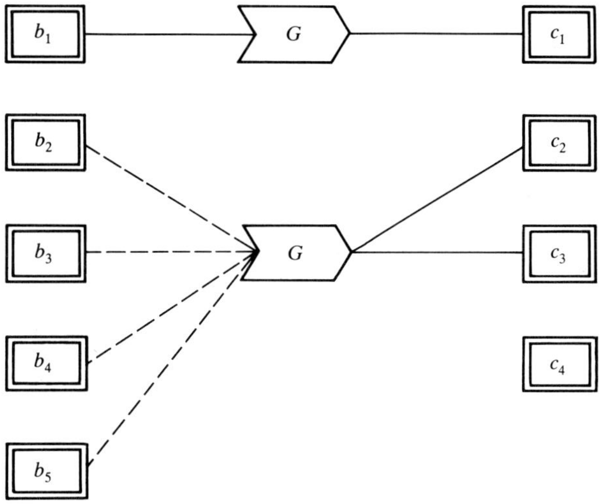

Figure 6.14 *B* has more instances than *C*.

Effect of Unresolved Alternation

We will classify loops by considering the maximal resolute subloops, just as we classified correspondence complexes by considering the maximal resolute subcorrespondences. Several characters can not be attained by *resolute* loops because of population size inequalities, namely "**]**", ">", "**]**>", "**[**", "<", and "<**[**". In a resolute loop, these characters would imply that a class tag could have more instances than itself.

These characters are possible, however, if unresolved alternations are permitted. For example, Figure 6.15 illustrates a potential population of a loop of character "<**[**". In this figure, both b_2 and b_3 participate in an unresolved existential quantification. In the case of b_2, this has the interpretation « there is some instance of « B » that « b_2 » attaches to ». Notice that this expression refers to the *interpretations* of b_2 and of B, so the instance of « B » that « b_2 » attaches to need not be represented in the population. In data logic notation, the population shown in Figure 6.15 would be written

$$\vdash L{:}(b_1, b_2) \;\&\; L{:}(b_1, b_3) \;\&\; (\exists x)\; L{:}|b_2, x| \;\&\; B{:}|x| \;\&\; (\exists y)\; L{:}|b_3, y| \;\&\; B{:}|y|$$

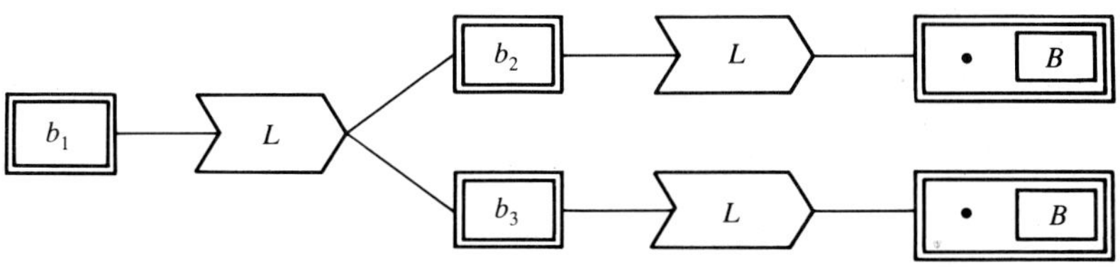

Figure 6.15 The character "<**[**" is attainable in a loop only with unresolved alternation.

Method of Classifying Loops

Population diagrams of loops differ from the population diagrams of pillared correspondence complexes discussed in Section 6.3 because the same instance can attach to itself in a loop: *L*:(*b*, *b*). In a pillared correspondence complex, an individual might be an instance of both class tags, as in the population

$$\vdash B{:}(d)\ \&\ C{:}(d)\ \&\ G{:}(d, d)$$

In the study of similarity, however, this population is treated as an attachment of « *d* as an instance of *B* » to « *d* as an instance of *C* », and so the two *instances* are regarded as different.

In an attachment *L*:(*b*, *b*) controlled by a loop *L*, however, *L* attaches « *b* as an instance of *B* » to « *b* as an instance of *B* ». The instances are the same and the individuals are the same. Thus, we have new population structures to consider when confronted with loops, and it remains to be shown if any populations of loops are similar.

We will examine each of the potential characters of loops in turn. Since we classify loops based on their maximal resolute subloops, we can ignore the characters "**[**", "<", "<**[**", "**]**", ">", and "**]**>". The maximal resolute subloops of loops with these characters must always have character ∅. We can ignore three of the remaining characters because they are formed from converses:

"**]**<" ↔ ">**[**"

"**]**<**[**" ↔ "**]**>**[**"

"**]**<>" ↔ "<>**[**"

1. chr (*L*; *B*, *B*) = ∅

One-to-one all-to-all loops attach individuals in *circles*. A circle may have exactly one element, in which case the individual attaches to itself, as b_1 does in Figure 6.16. A population of a *one-to-one all-to-all* loop can be described by the number of attachments in each circle. This number is called the *circumference* of the circle. A population is therefore described by a list of circumferences, where the order of the numbers in the list is not significant. Thus, Figure 6.16 may be described by either of the lists (1, 4) or (4, 1).

This reasoning shows that all *one-to-one all-to-all* loops are similar, because their differences can be described by a list of quantities. A list of circumferences is usually more precise a description than is needed for a concise description of a population. Some statistical measure such as the *median circumference* can then be used.

2. chr (*L*; *B*, *B*) = "**] [**"

Since the character "**] [**" is more permissive than ∅, patterns found in ∅ may also be found in populations of correspondences of character "**] [**". The new pattern permitted by "**] [**" is individuals attaching in a *chain*, as in a linked list (such as b_4, b_5, and b_6 in Figure 6.17). A chain may have no attachment, and so contain only an individual that is an orphan of both *L* and *L** (such as b_3 in Figure 6.17).

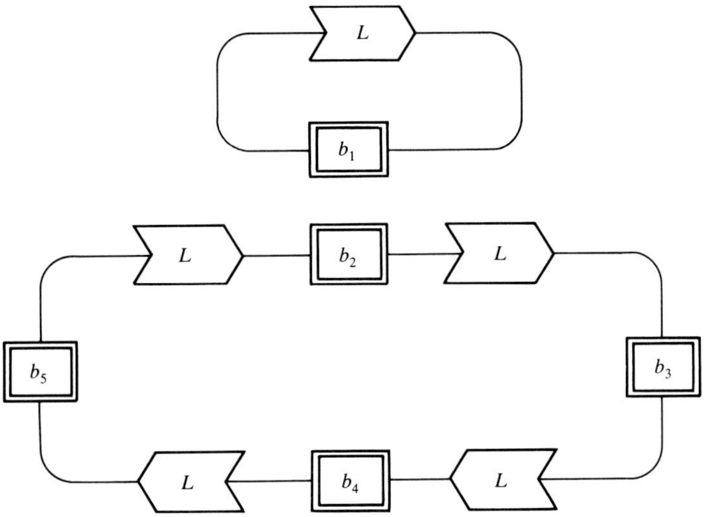

Figure 6.16 Character ∅.

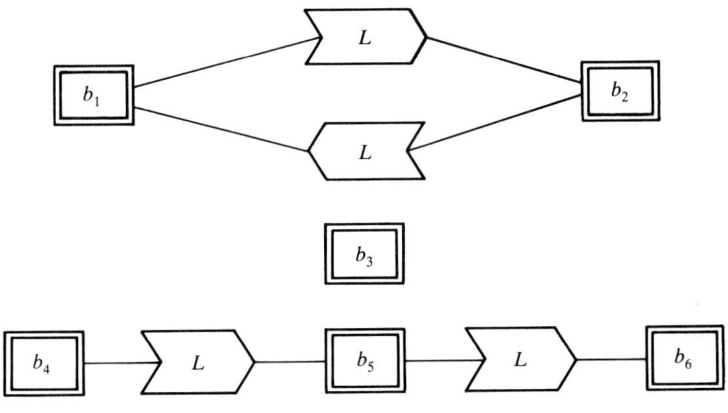

Figure 6.17 Character "] [".

A population of a *one-to-one some-to-some* loop can be described by two lists: a list of circumferences, and a list of *lengths* of attachment chains. Thus, all *one-to-one some-to-some* loops are similar. In Figure 6.17, there is one circle with circumference 2, and two chains of lengths 0 and 2.

A population of a *one-to-one some-to-some* loop can be described by two statistical measures, such as the median circumference and the median chain length. If so, the total number of individuals in attachment circles and the total number of individuals in attachment chains should also be noted.

3. chr (L; B, B) = "**]**<"

The *one-to-many* characters define a hierarchical breakdown of parents and children. The character "**]**<" defines circles of attachments (such as b_1, b_2, and b_3 in Figure 6.18) studded with hierarchical offshoots. This character is rarely seen because it requires that each individual have a parent. Thus, there is no ultimate ancestor as there would be in a more typical tree structure.

A tree can be described by a nested list, formed by counting the number of individuals in each bunch of leaves and indicating the structure above the leaves by nesting. The tree shown by $\{b_1, b_4, b_5\}$ in Figure 6.18 is then represented by (2), and the tree shown by $\{b_2, b_6, b_7, b_8\}$ is represented by ((2)). A circle studded with trees can be represented by a circular list of nested lists (a circular list is a list where the sequence of terms is significant, but the terms may be shifted any number of times and the list is considered to be unchanged). Thus, the sample population in Figure 6.18 would be represented as ((2), ((2)), (0)), or equivalently, as (((2)), (0), (2)). A population of a *one-to-many some-to-all* loop can then be described by a list of these lists of nested lists (because a population of a *one-to-many some-to-all* loop may contain many disjoint diagrams of the form shown in Figure 6.18). Thus, all *one-to-many some-to-all* loops are similar.

4. chr (L; B, B) = "**]**<**[**"

One-to-many some-to-some loops exhibit a more typical parent-child structure. An ultimate ancestor has no parent, and the ultimate descendants have no children. Notice that a population of a loop with character "**]**<**[**" may contain any of the patterns shown so far, because all of the characters discussed have been more restrictive than "**]**<**[**".

Tree structures such as shown in Figure 6.19 can be described by the nested list technique discussed for the character "**]**<". For example, Figure 6.19 would be represented by ((1, (1, (1))), (2)). Thus, all *one-to-many some-to-some* loops are similar. Applying the converse, we have shown that all *one-to-one, one-to-many,* and *many-to-one* loops are similar to all other loops with the same character.

5. chr (L; B, B) = "<>", "**]**<>", or "**]**<>**[**"

The *many-to-many* loops are very free. In a loop L of character "<>", illustrated in Figure 6.20, any instance may attach to any other instance as long as each instance attaches to some other instance (it could attach to itself) by L and by L^*. The conditions are slightly weaker for the character "**]**<>", and for the character "**]**<>**[**" the constraints are lifted altogether. Generally, embracings become far more important than characters when analyzing the populations of *many-to-many* correspondence complexes.

Conclusion

We have classified the potential populations of *one-to-one, one-to-many*, and *many-to-one* loops using similarity. Loops exhibit more intricate populations than pillared correspondence complexes because a loop may operate recursively, establishing attachment circles, chains, and trees. Nevertheless, all but *many-to-many* loops can be described thoroughly.

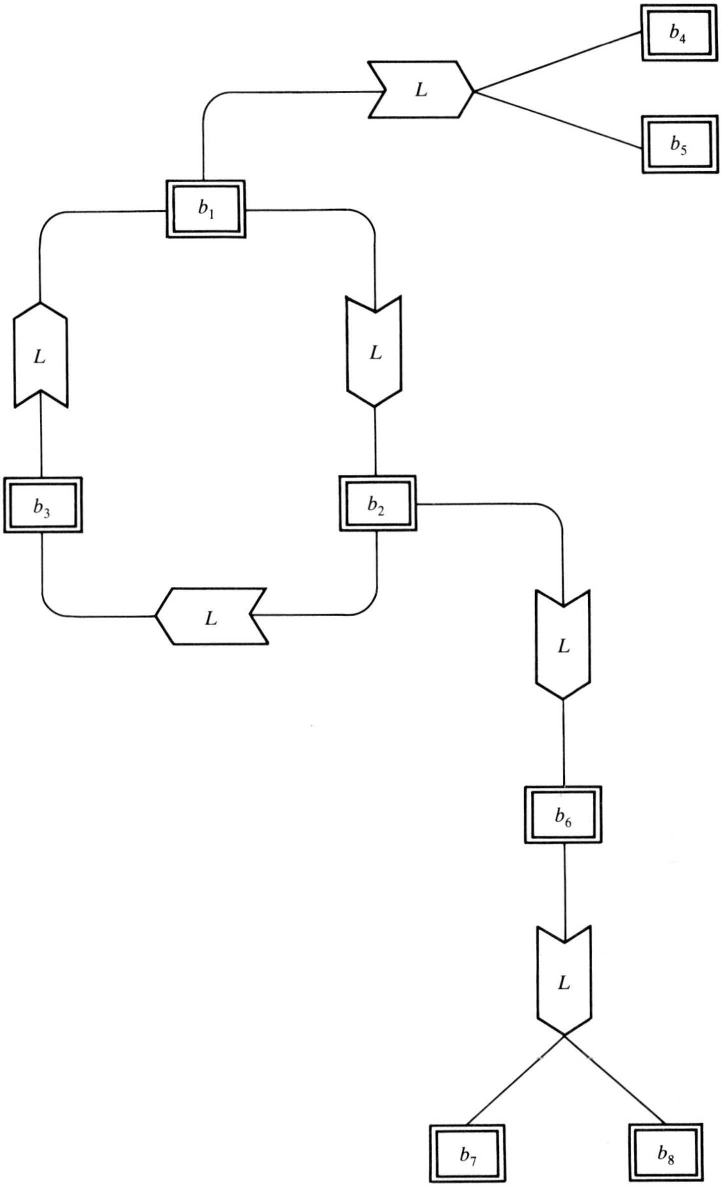

Figure 6.18 Character "ℷ<".

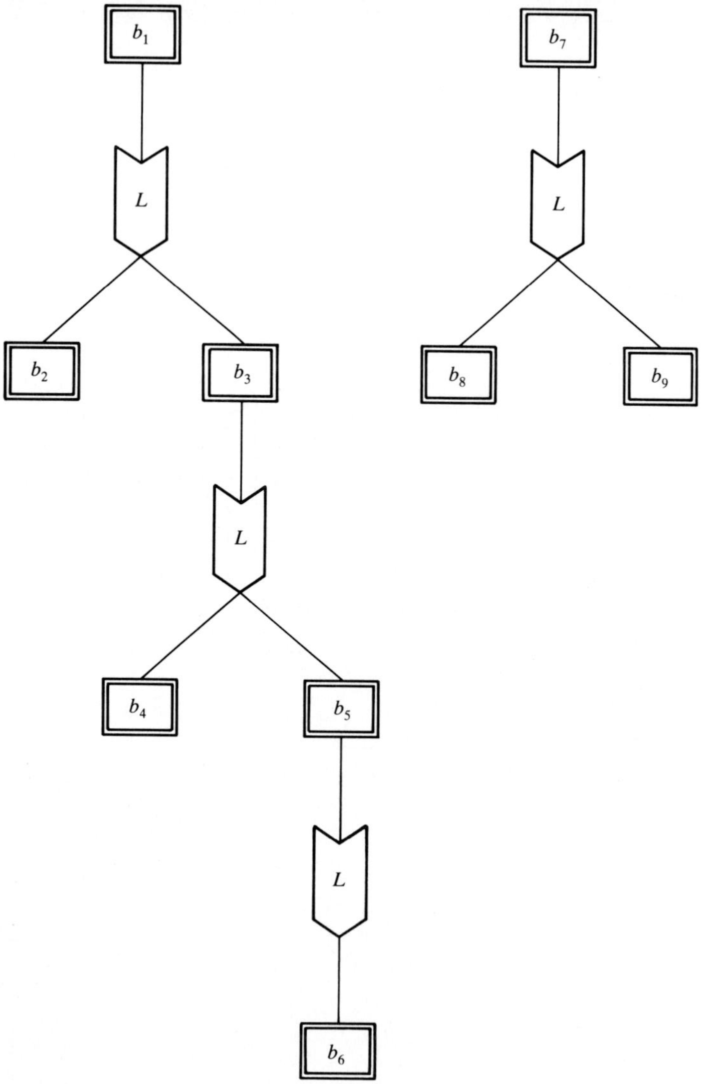

Figure 6.19 Character "]<[".

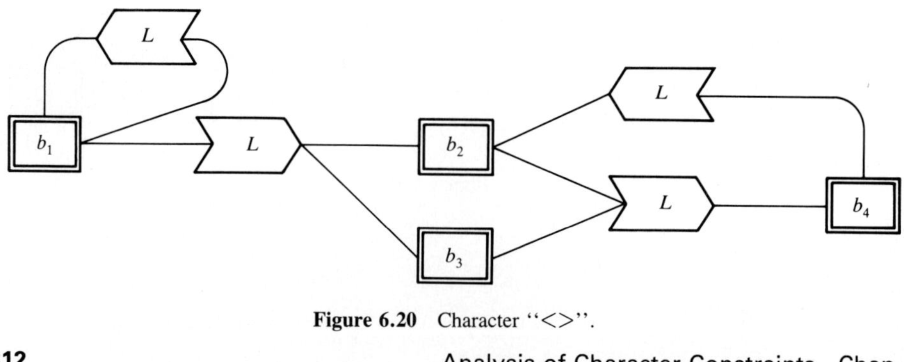

Figure 6.20 Character "<>".

6.4 MULTICORRESPONDENCE DATA STRUCTURES

Data structures can be broken apart into smaller clusters of regular form, each containing many class tags and correspondence tags. We will study two such forms, *paths* and *hubs*. Any data structure comprised only of class tags and correspondence tags (that is, without trio tags or association tags of higher degree) can be described as a union of hubs (some constraints, however, can cross many hubs). This decomposition into hubs is performed automatically by extended associative notation. Paths are the primary means for gathering information from different areas of a data base, and so are used commonly in queries.

Paths

Correspondence complexes may be strung together end to end as shown in Figure 6.21. Such a sequence is called a *path*. Formally, a *path* is a sequence of correspondence complexes $(G_i; B_i, B_{i+1})$ such that the destination class tag of the ith correspondence complex is identical to the source class tag of the i + 1st correspondence complex, for all i. A path may also be shown as the network drawing, Figure 6.22.

A path may be written in the abbreviated notation $(B_1; G_1; B_1; G_2; \ldots; G_n; B_{n+1})$, or if the class tags are understood, as $(G_1, \ldots, G_n)$. The number of constituents of the sequence (n in this case) is called the *length* of the path. The same correspondence tag may appear in more than one position in a path; if so, each appearance is counted in determining the length of the path. The length of a path may also be described using the suffix "-ary," that is, a *binary path* is a path of length two, a *ternary path* is a path of length three, and so on.

The correspondence tags G_i are called the *constituent correspondence tags*, or simply the *constituents*, of the path. The class tags B_i are called similarly the *constituent class tags* of the path. The two class tags B_1 and B_{n+1} are said to be the *ends* of the path. A path $\mathcal{P}$ is said to *traverse* a class tag B if B is a constituent class tag of $\mathcal{P}$. Class tags traversed by a path, other than its ends, are called *intermediate class tags*.

A path $\mathcal{P}$ is said to *include* a path $\mathcal{Q}$, and $\mathcal{Q}$ is said to be a *subpath* of $\mathcal{P}$, if $\mathcal{Q}$ is a path and a subsequence of $\mathcal{P}$. We define the *converse path* of a path $(B_1; G_1; B_2; \ldots; G_n; B_{n+1})$ to be the path $(B_{n+1}; G_n{}^*; \ldots; B_2; G_1{}^*; B_1)$. A path whose first and last class tags are the same is called a *cycle*. A cycle of length three, such as $(A; F; B; G; C; H; A)$, is called a *delta*. Deltas will be particularly important to the study of trio complexes in Chapter 9.

Notice that a path of length one is a correspondence complex and a cycle of length one is a loop. Put another way, a path is a generalization of a correspondence that allows individuals to be attached indirectly rather than directly through a declared correspondence tag, and a cycle is a similar generalization of a loop.

The network form for writing a path must be used cautiously if the path contains cycles. For example, Figure 6.23 could represent $(B; F; C; G; C; H; D; J; C)$, or $(B; F; C; H; D; J; C; G; C)$, or many other similar candidates. In such cases, it is better to list each constituent correspondence tag lexically in sequence than to rely on a network presentation.

The correspondence formed by composing all the reduced correspondences of a path in sequence is called the *composition correspondence* of the path. Thus, the composition correspondence of the path $(B_1; G_1; \ldots; G_n; B_{n+1})$ is

$$\Delta B_1 \circ G_1 \circ \Delta B_2 \circ G_2 \circ \ldots \circ \Delta B_n \circ G_n \circ \Delta B_{n+1}$$

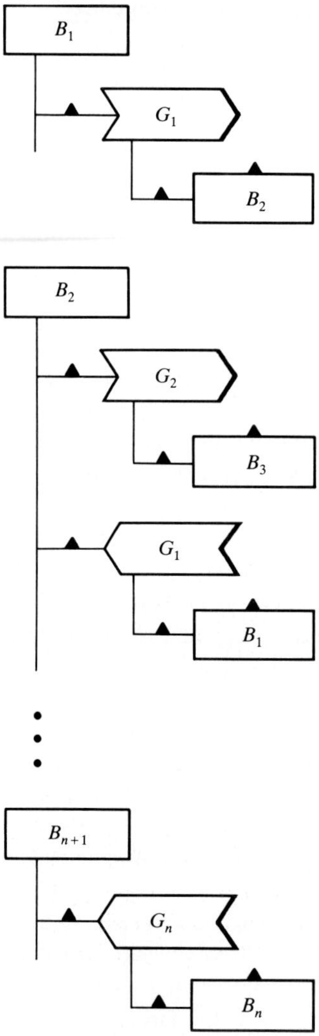

Figure 6.21 A path.

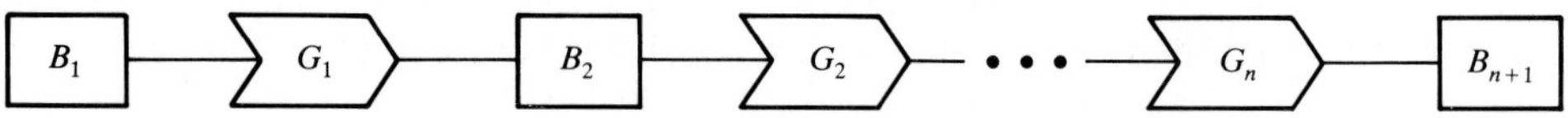

Figure 6.22 A path.

Hubs

A data structure of the form shown in Figure 6.24 is called a *hub*. Formally, a *hub* is a set of correspondence complexes (G_i; B, C_i) such that the source class tags of all the correspondence complexes are identical to some class tag B. The class tag B is called the *center* of the hub.

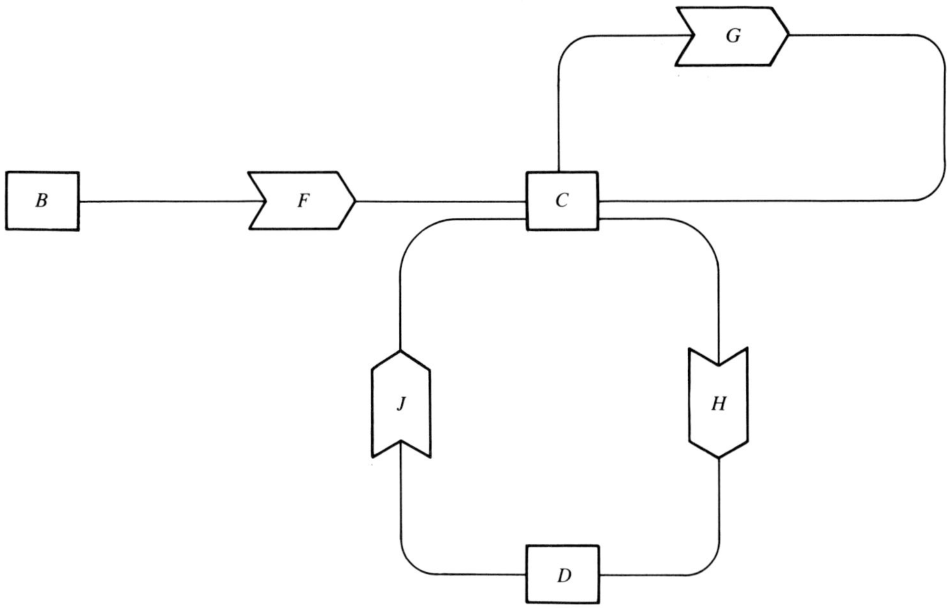

Figure 6.23 A path that includes cycles.

In a network drawing, a hub appears as a set of lines emanating from the center, as shown in Figure 6.25. Each of the correspondence complexes (G_i; B_i, C_i) is called a *spoke* of the hub. The number of spokes is called the *width* of the hub. Notice that the correspondence tags are counted, not the class tags. For example, the hub {(J; B, C), (K; B, C)} has width two. A *binary hub* is a hub of width two, a *ternary hub* is a hub of width three, and so on. Notice that a binary hub is the same as a binary path, making this data structure of particular interest.

Conclusion

We have introduced the two data structures of a *path*, which can be visualized as a line of correspondence complexes arranged end-to-end, and a *hub*, which can be visualized as many correspondence complexes spreading out from a common source.

6.5 ELONGATION FACTORING AND MANTLES

In this section we present a universal method called *elongation* for rewriting a correspondence complex as a path. Elongation explains the sequence of brackets **]**, <, >, **[** that is used to write a character. Partial elongation is also required by some data models: network data models tend to require partial elongation of *many-to-many* correspondence complexes, and relational data models tend to require partial elongation of *from some* and *to some* correspondence complexes.

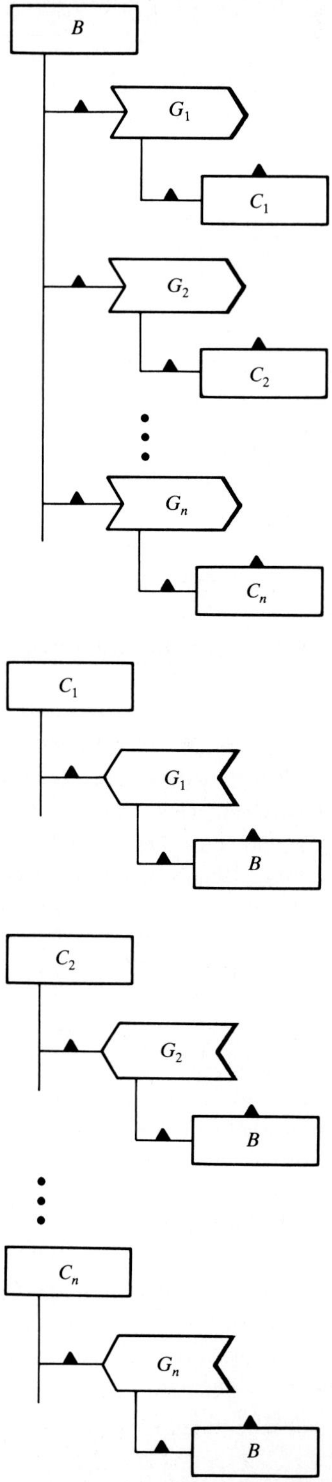

Figure 6.24 A hub.

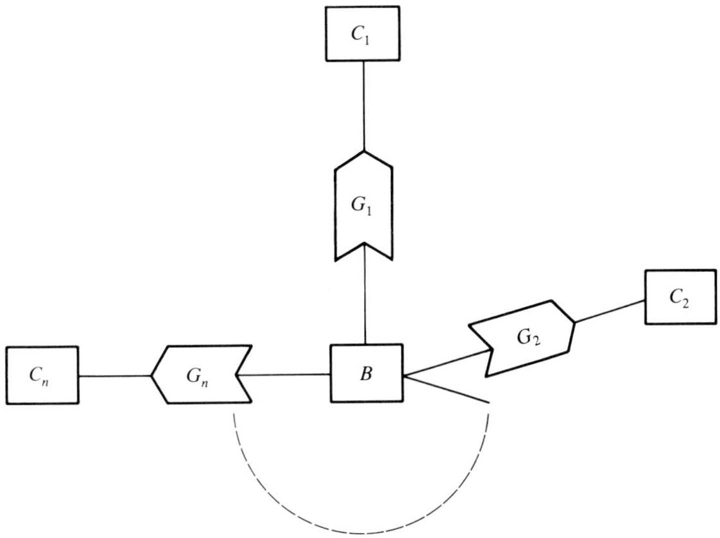

Figure 6.25 A hub.

Factoring of *Optional* Elements

A path $(D_1; H_1; D_2; \ldots ; H_n; D_{n+1})$ is said to be a *factoring* of a correspondence complex $(G; B, C)$ if D_1 is identical to B, D_{n+1} is identical to C, and the reduced correspondence $\Delta B \circ G \circ \Delta C$ is equivalent to (bi-directionally embraced in) the composition correspondence of the path, $\Delta D_1 \circ H_1 \circ \Delta D_2 \circ \ldots \circ H_n \circ \Delta D_{n+1}$.

Any correspondence complex may be factored into a path of length three by leaving the orphans on the ends of the path, and defining the correspondence complex in the middle of the path so that it is *all-to-all*. This factoring is called the *border elongation* of $(G; B, C)$, and is illustrated by Figure 6.26.

The border elongation is defined precisely by the following theorem:

Theorem 6.2. Any correspondence complex $(G; B, C)$ may be factored into the path $(B; \Delta B; \pi^1\dot{G}; \dot{G}; \pi^2\dot{G}; \Delta C; C)$, where $\dot{G}$ indicates $\Delta B \circ G \circ \Delta C$.

Proof. We need to show that the reduced correspondence $\Delta B \circ G \circ \Delta C$ is equivalent to the composition correspondence

$$\Delta B \circ \Delta B \circ \Delta\pi^1\dot{G} \circ \dot{G} \circ \Delta\pi^2\dot{G} \circ \Delta C \circ \Delta C \tag{1}$$

The issue hinges on the definition of the two correspondences $\Delta\pi^1\dot{G}$ and $\Delta\pi^2\dot{G}$. Since $\pi^1\dot{G}$ and $\pi^2\dot{G}$ are not declared classes, there are no declared identity correspondences $\Delta\pi^1\dot{G}$ and $\Delta\pi^2\dot{G}$. We can, however, determine reasonable choices for these correspondences by applying data logic.

Writing $\dot{G}$ out in full yields:

$$\Delta\pi^1\dot{G} \equiv \Delta\pi^1(\Delta B \circ G \circ \Delta C)$$

$$\Delta\pi^2\dot{G} \equiv \Delta\pi^2(\Delta B \circ G \circ \Delta C)$$

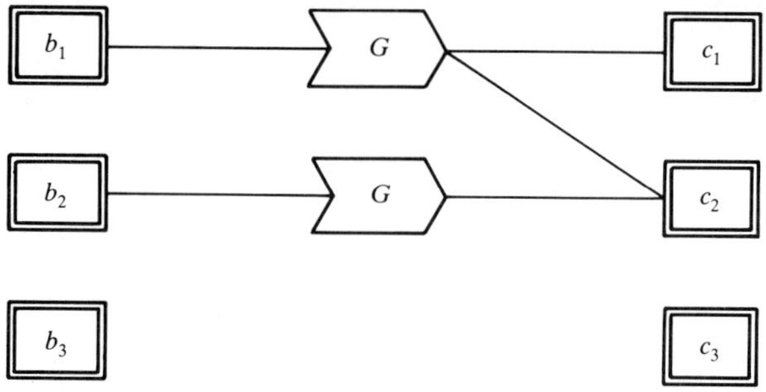

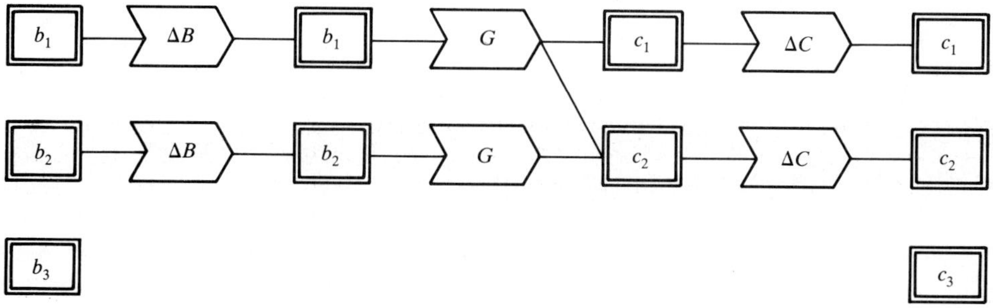

Figure 6.26 A border elongation.

Looking more carefully at $\pi^1\dot{G}$, we have:

$$
\begin{aligned}
(\mathrm{A}x)\ \pi^1\dot{G}{:}|x| &\Leftrightarrow (\exists y)\ \Delta B \circ G \circ \Delta C{:}|x,\ y| \\
&\Leftrightarrow (\exists x')\ (\exists y)\ \Delta B{:}|x,\ x'|\ \&\ G{:}|x',\ y|\ \&\ C{:}|y| \\
&\Leftrightarrow B{:}|x|
\end{aligned}
$$

Thus, $\pi^1\dot{G} \subseteq B$. It is therefore reasonable to carry the identity correspondence of B onto $\pi^1\dot{G}$, that is, to define two images x and y that are each accepted by $\pi^1\dot{G}$ to be the same $\pi^1\dot{G}$ if and only if they are the same B:

$$(\mathrm{A}x)\ (\mathrm{A}y)\ \Delta\pi^1\dot{G}{:}|x,\ y| \Leftrightarrow \pi^1\dot{G}{:}|x|\ \&\ \pi^1\dot{G}{:}|y|\ \&\ \Delta B{:}|x,\ y|$$

The correspondence $\Delta\pi^2\dot{G}$ is defined similarly, except using the identity correspondence of the destination class C:

$$(\mathrm{A}x)\ (\mathrm{A}y)\ \Delta\pi^2\dot{G}{:}|x,\ y| \Leftrightarrow \pi^2\dot{G}{:}|x|\ \&\ \pi^2\dot{G}{:}|y|\ \&\ \Delta C{:}|x,\ y|$$

We may show finally that $\Delta\pi^1\dot{G} \circ \dot{G} \circ \Delta\pi^2\dot{G}$ is equivalent to $\dot{G}$. This will demonstrate the equivalence of Formula (1) with $\dot{G}$, because Formula (1) differs only by the addition of $\Delta B \circ \Delta B$ on the left and $\Delta C \circ \Delta C$ on the right, and these correspondences are defined so that $\Delta B \circ \Delta B \circ \Delta B \equiv \Delta B$ and $\Delta C \circ \Delta C \circ \Delta C \equiv \Delta C$.

$$
\begin{aligned}
(\mathrm{A}x)\ (\mathrm{A}y)\ \Delta\pi^1\dot{G} \circ \dot{G} \circ \Delta\pi^2\dot{G}{:}|x,\ y| \ \Leftrightarrow\ & (\exists x')\ (\exists y')\ \Delta\pi^1\dot{G}{:}|x,\ x'|\ \&\ \dot{G}{:}|x',\ y'| \\
& \&\ \Delta\pi^2\dot{G}{:}|y',\ y| \\
\Leftrightarrow\ & (\exists x')\ (\exists y')\ \pi^1\dot{G}{:}|x|\ \&\ \pi^1\dot{G}{:}|x'|\ \&\ \Delta B{:}|x,\ x'| \\
& \&\ \dot{G}{:}|x',y'|\ \&\ \pi^2\dot{G}{:}|y'|\ \&\ \pi^2\dot{G}{:}|y|\ \&\ \Delta C{:}|y',y| \\
\Leftrightarrow\ & (\exists x')\ (\exists y')\ \pi^1\dot{G}{:}|x|\ \&\ \Delta B{:}|x,\ x'|\ \&\ \dot{G}{:}|x',\ y'| \\
& \&\ \pi^2\dot{G}{:}|y|\ \&\ \Delta C{:}\ |y',\ y| \\
\Leftrightarrow\ & \pi^1\dot{G}{:}|x|\ \&\ \dot{G}{:}|x,\ y|\ \&\ \pi^2\dot{G}{:}|y| \\
\Leftrightarrow\ & \dot{G}{:}|x,\ y|
\end{aligned}
$$

Q.E.D.

Notice that the proof of this theorem relied on the use of the identity correspondences of the classes in the correspondence complex. We could not define a border elongation of a correspondence G alone, because there would then be no means for defining $\Delta\pi^1 G$ and $\Delta\pi^2 G$.

Notice further that since the proof of the theorem was expressed using embracings, the theorem applies to populations that include unresolved alternations. For example, consider the population

$$\vdash B{:}(b)\ \&\ C{:}(c_1)\ \&\ C{:}(c_2)\ \&\ (G{:}(b,\ c_1) \vee G{:}(b,\ c_2))$$

The population of the border elongation would be

$$\vdash B{:}(b)\ \&\ \pi^1\dot{G}{:}(b)\ \&\ ((G{:}(b,\ c_1)\ \&\ \pi^2\dot{G}{:}(c_1)) \vee (G{:}(b,\ c_2)\ \&\ \pi^2\dot{G}{:}(c_2)))$$

The border elongation factoring isolates the *optional* portion of the character of $(G;\ B,\ C)$ at the first and last correspondence complexes, and the *multiple* portion at the center. Recalling that characters may be intersected as sets of brackets, we may write this result as the formulas:

(i) chr $(\Delta B;\ B,\ \pi^1\dot{G})$ = chr $(G;\ B,\ C) \cap$ "**]**"
(ii) chr $(\dot{G};\ \pi^1\dot{G},\ \pi^2\dot{G})$ = chr $(G;\ B,\ C) \cap$ "<>"
(iii) chr $(\Delta C;\ \pi^2\dot{G},\ C)$ = chr $(G;\ B,\ C) \cap$ "**[**"

Thus, the border elongation factoring demonstrates why the *optional* brackets are placed at the ends in the standard sequence of brackets **]**, <, >, **[**.

Factoring of *Multiple* Elements

In the network data model, a *many-to-many* correspondence G from B to C is shown by forming the class BC of "ordered $(b,\ c)$ pairs," and factoring G as a path from B to BC to C. We have seen that this method is imprecise when more than one correspondence may be declared between B and C. Thus, in data logic, we consider the concentration $\mathrm{C}^1\dot{G}$ rather than "ordered $(b,\ c)$ pairs." With this change, *many-to-many* correspondences can be factored through the concentration. The first correspondence complex in the path is then always *from one*, and the second correspondence complex is always *to one*. This factoring is called the *half-elongation* of $(G;\ B,\ C)$, and is illustrated in Figure 6.27.

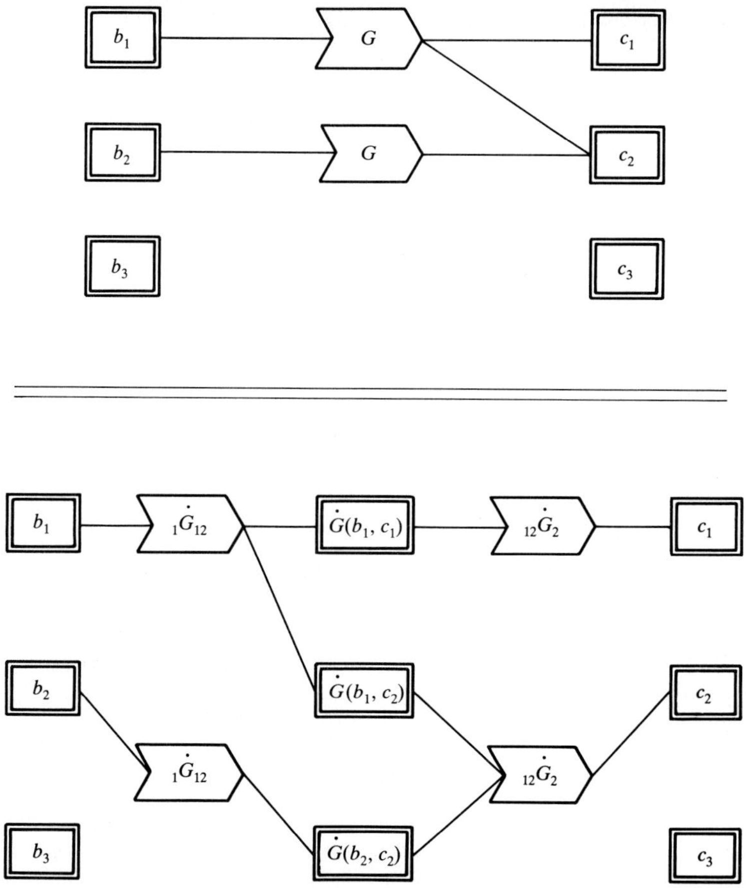

Figure 6.27 A half-elongation.

The half-elongation factoring is defined precisely as follows. For any correspondence complex $(\dot{G}; B, C)$, we may form the concentration $C^1\dot{G}$, the class of attachments of $\dot{G}$. An image accepted by « $C^1\dot{G}$ » is an image of « a B x G+*ing* a C y ». This image is represented by the symbol "$\dot{G}|x, y|$" (the colon that would indicate a proposition is omitted). The concentration is defined by the formula

$$(\mathrm{A}x)\ (\mathrm{A}y)\ C^1\dot{G}{:}|\dot{G}|x, y|| \Leftrightarrow \dot{G}{:}|x, y| \tag{2}$$

We form next the elision correspondence ${}_1\dot{G}_{12}$ that attaches an image x to every assembly accepted by $C^1\dot{G}$ of the form $\dot{G}|x, y|$:

$$(\mathrm{A}x)\ (\mathrm{A}y)\ {}_1\dot{G}_{12}{:}|x, \dot{G}|x, y|| \Leftrightarrow C^1\dot{G}{:}|\dot{G}|x, y|| \tag{3}$$

The correspondence ${}_{12}\dot{G}_2$ attaches every assembly accepted by $C^1\dot{G}$ of the form $\dot{G}|x, y|$ to the image y that appears within it:

$$(\mathrm{A}x)\ (\mathrm{A}z)\ {}_{12}\dot{G}_2{:}|\dot{G}|x, y|, y| \Leftrightarrow C^1\dot{G}{:}|\dot{G}|x, y||$$

The identity correspondence $\Delta C^1\dot{G}$ is defined through the identity correspondences ΔB and ΔC:

$$(Ax)\ (Ax')\ (Ay)\ (Ay')\ \Delta C^1\dot{G}{:}|\dot{G}|x,\ y|,\dot{G}|x',\ y'||\Leftrightarrow \dot{G}{:}|x,\ y|\ \&\ \dot{G}{:}|x',\ y'|\ \&$$
$$\Delta B{:}|x,\ x'|\ \&\ \Delta C{:}|y,\ y'|$$

That is, two assemblies $\dot{G}|x, y|$ and $\dot{G}|x', y'|$ that are each accepted by $C^1\dot{G}$ are the same $C^1\dot{G}$ if x is the same B as x' and y is the same C as y'.

Combining these formulas yields:

$$(Ax)\ (Az)\ \dot{G}{:}|x,\ z|\Leftrightarrow (\exists y)\ (\exists y')\ {}_1\dot{G}_{12}{:}|x,\ y|\ \&\ \Delta C^1\dot{G}{:}|y,\ y'|\ \&\ {}_{12}\dot{G}_2{:}|y',\ z|$$

That is, we have shown that any correspondence complex $(G; B, C)$ may be factored into the path

$$(B;\ {}_1\dot{G}_{12};\ C^1\dot{G};\ {}_{12}\dot{G}_2;\ C)$$

Characters of the Half-Elongation

The correspondence ${}_1\dot{G}_{12}$ is *to one* relative to $(B, C^1\dot{G})$ if and only if G is *to one* relative to (B, C). This result is clear from examining Figure 6.27 so long as $\dot{G}$ is resolute. The more general result is proved by embracings. Thus, $\dot{G}$ is *to one* if and only if

$$(Ax)\ (Ay)\ (Az)\ \dot{G}{:}|x,\ y|\ \&\ \dot{G}{:}|x,\ z|\Rightarrow \Delta C{:}|y,\ z|$$

By the definition of the concentration, Formula (2), this formula is interchangeable with

$$(Ax)\ (Ay)\ (Az)\ C^1\dot{G}{:}|\dot{G}|x,\ y||\ \&\ C^1\dot{G}{:}|\dot{G}|x,\ z||\Rightarrow \Delta C{:}|y,\ z|$$

By the definition of ${}_1\dot{G}_{12}$, Formula (3), this formula is interchangeable with

$$(Ax)\ (Ay)\ (Az)\ {}_1\dot{G}_{12}{:}|x,\ \dot{G}|x,\ y||\ \&\ {}_1\dot{G}_{12}{:}|x,\ \dot{G}|x,\ z||\Rightarrow \Delta C{:}|y,\ z| \qquad (4)$$

The expression on the right side says that y and z are the same C, so $\dot{G}|x, y|$ and $\dot{G}|x, z|$ are the same $C^1\dot{G}$. Formula (4) states, therefore, that ${}_1\dot{G}_{12}$ is *to one*.

We have shown that ${}_1\dot{G}_{12}$ is *to one* if and only if $\dot{G}$ is *to one*. Similarly, ${}_{12}\dot{G}_2$ is *from one* if and only if $\dot{G}$ is *from one*. By construction, ${}_1\dot{G}_{12}$ is *to all* relative to $(B, C^1\dot{G})$ and ${}_{12}\dot{G}_2$ is *from all* relative to $(C^1\dot{G}, C)$. Thus we have shown that:

(i) chr $({}_1\dot{G}_{12}; B, C^1\dot{G})$ = chr $(G; B, C) \cap$ "]<"

(ii) chr $({}_{12}\dot{G}_2; C^1\dot{G}, C)$ = chr $(G; B, C) \cap$ ">["

This factoring is called the *half-elongation* because it splits the character of $(G; B, C)$ into two halves, the first two bracket decisions and the last two.

Elongation Factoring

The *elongation* of $(G; B, C)$ is formed by performing a border elongation followed by a half-elongation of the central correspondence complex. That is, we form the factoring

$$\boxed{(B;\ \Delta B;\ \pi^1\dot{G};\ {}_1\dot{G}_{12};\ C^1\dot{G};\ {}_{12}\dot{G}_2;\ \pi^2\dot{G};\ \Delta C;\ C)}$$

This factoring is illustrated in Figure 6.28.

The characters of the constituents of the path are given by

(i)	$\text{chr}\ (\Delta B;\ B,\ \pi^1\dot{G}) = \text{chr}\ (G;\ B,\ C) \cap$ “**]**”
(ii)	$\text{chr}\ ({}_1\dot{G}_{12};\ \pi^1\dot{G},\ \mathrm{C}^1\dot{G}) = \text{chr}\ (G;\ B,\ C) \cap$ “$<$”
(iii)	$\text{chr}\ ({}_{12}\dot{G}_2;\ \mathrm{C}^1\dot{G},\ \pi^2\dot{G}) = \text{chr}\ (G;\ B,\ C) \cap$ “$>$”
(iv)	$\text{chr}\ (\Delta C;\ \pi^2\dot{G},\ C) = \text{chr}\ (G;\ B,\ C) \cap$ “**[**”

The order of brackets in the characters of the constituents of the elongation factoring is the standard order of brackets within a character: **]**, $<$, $>$, **[**.

Unresolved Alternation

The elongation factoring continues to apply to populations that contain unresolved alternations. For example, consider the population

$$\vdash \dot{G}{:}(b_1,\ c_1) \vee \dot{G}{:}(b_1,\ c_2) \vee \dot{G}{:}(b_2,\ c_2)$$

The population of the concentration of $\dot{G}$ is then

$$\vdash \mathrm{C}^1\dot{G}{:}(\dot{G}(b_1,\ c_1)) \vee \mathrm{C}^1\dot{G}{:}(\dot{G}(b_1,\ c_2)) \vee \mathrm{C}^1\dot{G}{:}(\dot{G}(b_2,\ c_2))$$

The population of ${}_1\dot{G}_{12}$ is

$$\vdash {}_1\dot{G}_{12}{:}(b_1,\ \dot{G}(b_1,\ c_1)) \vee {}_1\dot{G}_{12}{:}(b_1,\ \dot{G}(b_1,\ c_2)) \vee {}_1\dot{G}_{12}{:}(b_2,\ \dot{G}(b_2,\ c_2))$$

and the population of $\pi^1\dot{G}$ is

$$\vdash \pi^1\dot{G}{:}(b_1) \vee \pi^1\dot{G}{:}(b_2)$$

The populations of ${}_2\dot{G}_{12}$ and $\pi^2\dot{G}$ are formed similarly.

Comparison with Network Notations

The order of brackets given by the elongation factoring is the only possible order that will apply to all correspondence complexes. As we will see in Chapter 8, moving either of the *optional* brackets **]** or **[** would make it impossible to convert the elongation factoring back to the original correspondence complex in some cases. Swapping the order of the *multiple* brackets is possible under some restricted conditions, as we will discuss in the next section, but it only applies to a very restricted class of *many-to-many* correspondences.

Brackets can be written alongside lines in network drawings as a means of illustrating data structures. Other network design notations do not follow the proper order of brackets, **]**, $<$, $>$, **[**, as illustrated in Figure 6.29. Bachman suggests an arrow to represent *from many* and *to many*, an unfortunate choice because the arrow suggests motion, and so is continually mistaken for a data flow (Bachman 1983). In addition, the arrow points in the wrong direction: a *one-to-many* correspondence is indicated by the arrow ➛, while it is shown in bracket notation by the bracket $<$.

In “chicken feet” notation, the direction of the *to many* symbol faces in the same way as bracket notation, but the order of decisions is shown improperly as $><$ instead of

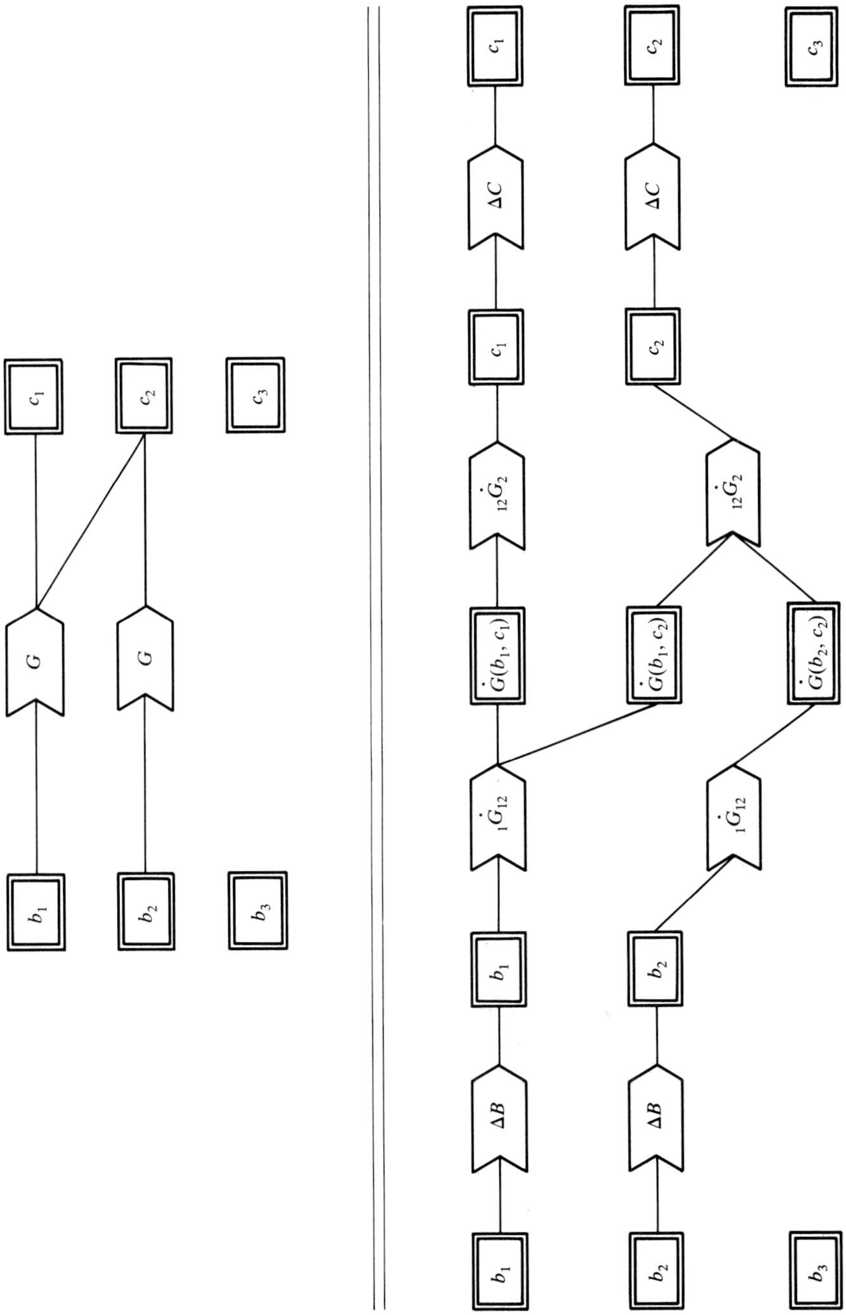

Figure 6.28 An elongation.

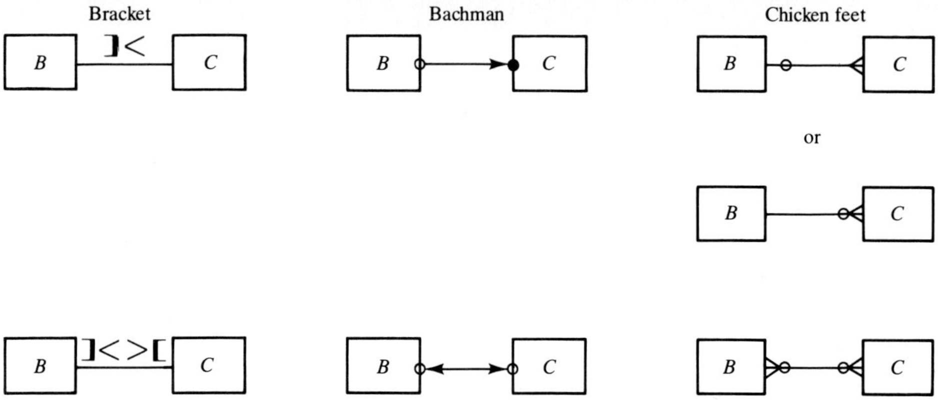

Figure 6.29 Comparison with other notations.

<>. When *optional* decisions are shown, they are often shown inside the *multiple* decisions, resulting in the particularly tortured order >][< or >[]<.

Mantles

It is often useful to assign the concentration an alternative interpretation or *mantle* to clarify the ideas. For example, consider the correspondence complex *Customer Buys Product*, shown in Figure 6.30.

We may want to associate other data with the image of a *Customer Buying* a *Product*, such as *Quantity Purchased* and *Total Dollar Amount Paid*, as shown in Figure 6.31.

We may prefer to create a new class akin to the concentration of *Customer Buys Product*, and relate *Quantity Purchased* and *Total Dollar Amount Paid* to this new class

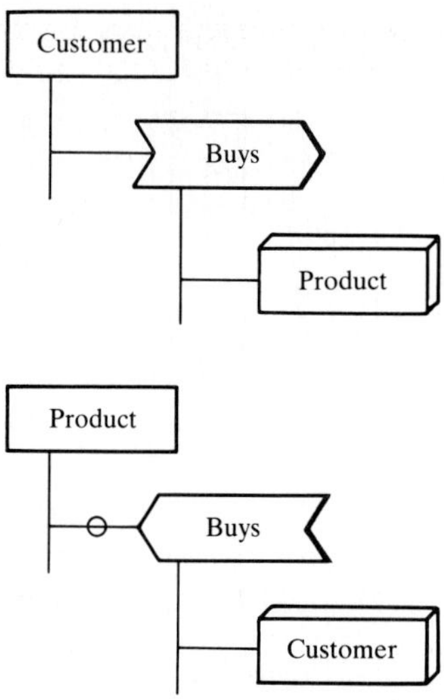

Figure 6.30

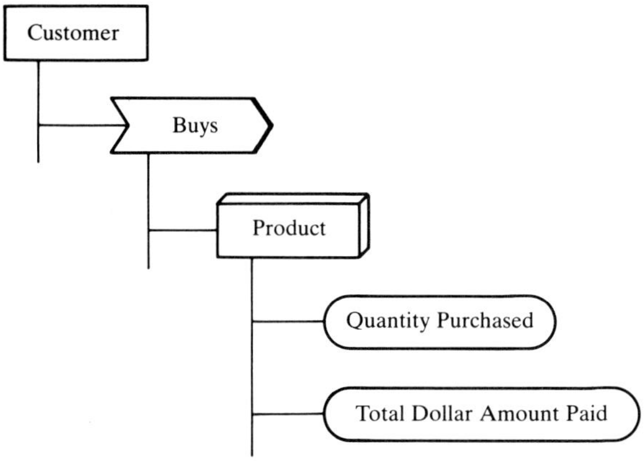

Figure 6.31

directly. Rather than create the concentration, which may cause confusion, a good solution is to form a new class, for example « *Purchase Event* », that stands in the same position as the concentration in a half-elongation. The class « *Purchase Event* » is called a *mantle*. The resulting data structure is illustrated in Figure 6.32.

Notice now that several questions are raised: could a *customer purchase* the same *product* twice? If so, is that two separate *purchase events*? Must money be exchanged each time a *product* is *purchased*? Is an exchange of defective goods a *purchase event*? and so on. These questions are brought to the forefront because the concentration is given a provocative meaning.

Mantles are valuable tools in practical data design, because they bring the abstract idea of a concentration into discussion as an independent idea. Mantles can not be determined by a formal process, but must be created by the designer. Part of the skill of a good data designer is the ability to imagine convincing mantles rapidly.

Designers should be on particular guard against appealing to an existing record keeping document, such as using *Sales Record* as a mantle rather than *Purchase Event* in the example above. While it may appear that this would make matters more familiar, it actually hampers creativity because the use of an existing administrative term such as "sales record" carries with it the implicit assumption that sales will continue to be recorded the same way that they have always been. Data design should always question whether the old procedures are in fact the best way of solving the problem. Thus, it is often most effective to use a mantle that has no preconceived meaning in the organization, and to force the design team to specify what its characteristics should be.

Conclusion

We have shown how any correspondence complex can be redesigned as a path called its *elongation factoring*. This path contains four correspondence complexes, each of which receives one bracket decision from the character of the original correspondence complex. The order of the correspondence complexes in the elongation factoring matches the order of brackets in a character, showing that the order **]**, <, >, **[**, is the proper order for declaring a character.

The middle class in an elongation factoring is the concentration of the reduced correspondence, which is analogous to the ''set of ordered pairs'' in symbolic logic. We have seen how concentrations can be given *mantles*, or new interpretations, and can thereby be declared as class tags.

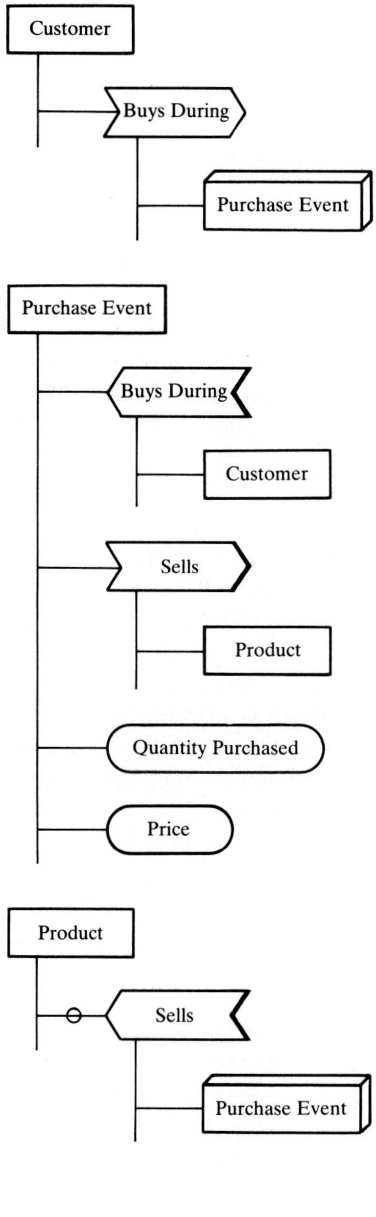

Figure 6.32 Use of a mantle to simplify the trio complex in Figure 6.31.

6.6 ZIGZAG AND BUNDLINGS

Zigzag

Recall that *zigzag* is the property that in a *many-to-many* correspondence complex (G; B, C) permits attachment paths of the form c_1, b_1, c_2, b_2, . . . , as shown in Figure 6.33. We may quantify zigzag in the following way. Given a correspondence complex (G; B, C), form compositions of $\dot{G}$ and $\dot{G}^*$ in alternation, thus:

$$\begin{array}{ll} \dot{G} & \dot{G}^* \\ \dot{G} \circ \dot{G}^* & \dot{G}^* \circ \dot{G} \\ \dot{G} \circ \dot{G}^* \circ \dot{G} & \dot{G}^* \circ \dot{G} \circ \dot{G}^* \\ \cdot & \cdot \\ \cdot & \cdot \\ \cdot & \cdot \end{array}$$

For any correspondence $\dot{G}$, $\dot{G} \subseteq \dot{G} \circ \dot{G}^* \circ \dot{G}$, that is,

$$(\mathrm{A}x)\ (\mathrm{A}y)\ \dot{G}{:}|x,\ y| \Rightarrow (\exists y')\ (\exists x')\ \dot{G}{:}|x,\ y'|\ \&\ \dot{G}^*{:}|y',\ x'|\ \&\ \dot{G}{:}|x',\ y|$$

This is easily seen by taking $x' = x$ and $y' = y$.

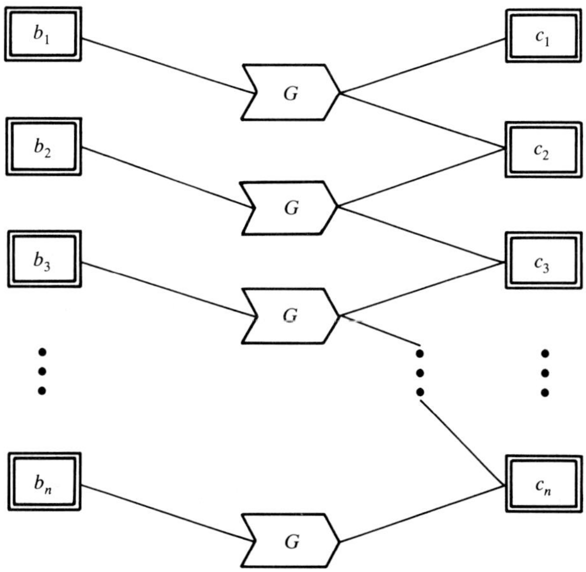

Figure 6.33 Zigzag.

We have, therefore, the chains of embracings:

$$\dot{G} \subseteq \dot{G} \circ \dot{G}^* \circ \dot{G} \subseteq \dot{G} \circ \dot{G}^* \circ \dot{G} \circ \dot{G}^* \circ \dot{G} \subseteq \ldots$$

$$\dot{G}^* \subseteq \dot{G}^* \circ \dot{G} \circ \dot{G}^* \subseteq \dot{G}^* \circ \dot{G} \circ \dot{G}^* \circ \dot{G} \circ \dot{G}^* \subseteq \ldots$$

$$\dot{G} \circ \dot{G}^* \subseteq \dot{G} \circ \dot{G}^* \circ \dot{G} \circ \dot{G}^* \subseteq \ldots$$

$$\dot{G}^* \circ \dot{G} \subseteq \dot{G}^* \circ \dot{G} \circ \dot{G}^* \circ \dot{G} \subseteq \ldots$$

We showed in the proof of Theorem 6.2 that

$$\Delta(\pi^1 \dot{G}) \subseteq \dot{G} \circ \dot{G}^*$$

$$\Delta(\pi^1 \dot{G}^*) \subseteq \dot{G}^* \circ \dot{G}$$

So we may extend the chains to the left to obtain

$$\Delta(\pi^1 \dot{G}) \subseteq \dot{G} \circ \dot{G}^* \subseteq \dot{G} \circ \dot{G}^* \circ \dot{G} \circ \dot{G}^* \subseteq \ldots$$

$$\Delta(\pi^1 \dot{G}^*) \subseteq \dot{G}^* \circ \dot{G} \subseteq \dot{G}^* \circ \dot{G} \circ \dot{G}^* \circ \dot{G} \subseteq \ldots$$

These chains of embracings are called the *zigzag chains* of the correspondence complex $(G; B, C)$. In correspondence complexes where zigzag is controlled, these chains *terminate* and the single directed embracings become bi-directional. The place at which this occurs (called the *termination point* of the chain) is called the *zigzag order* of the correspondence, which is defined to be the maximum number of appearances of $\dot{G}$ in an element of a zigzag chain that represents a distinct correspondence.

Zigzag orders can be established by character decisions. Thus, G is *to one* relative to (B, C) if and only if $\dot{G}$ obeys the embracing

$$\dot{G} \circ \dot{G}^* \subseteq \Delta B$$

If G is *to one*, then any combination from a zigzag chain in which $\dot{G}$ appears more than twice is degenerate, for $\dot{G} \circ \dot{G}^* \circ \dot{G}$ is equivalent to $\dot{G}$ and $\dot{G}^* \circ \dot{G} \circ \dot{G}^*$ is equivalent to $\dot{G}^*$. Thus, if G is *to one* then the zigzag order of $\dot{G}$ is at most two.

Similarly, G is *from one* relative to (B, C) if and only if $\dot{G}$ obeys the embracing

$$\dot{G}^* \circ \dot{G} \subseteq \Delta C$$

So, if G is *from one* then the zigzag order of $\dot{G}$ is at most two.

If G is *one-to-one*, then both $\dot{G} \circ \dot{G}^*$ and $\dot{G}^* \circ \dot{G}$ are degenerate, and so the longest nondegenerate expressions in the zigzag chains are just "$\dot{G}$" and "$\dot{G}^*$". Thus, if G is *one-to-one* then $\dot{G}$ has zigzag order one. Moreover, since the embracings that establish a correspondence to have zigzag order one are precisely the *from one* and *to one* constraints, G is *one-to-one* if and only if $\dot{G}$ has zigzag order one.

Since we showed that the reduced correspondence of a *one-to-many* correspondence complex has zigzag order at most two, and since only *one-to-one* correspondences have zigzag order one, it follows that the reduced correspondence of a *one-to-many* correspondence complex always has zigzag order two. Similarly, the reduced correspondence of a *many-to-one* correspondence complex always has zigzag order two.

It is possible for a correspondence to have zigzag order zero. This occurs if $\dot{G}$ is equivalent to $\Delta(\pi^1 \dot{G})$, that is, if $\dot{G}$ only attaches individuals to themselves. Such a correspondence is called an *anchored loop*.

Bundlings

A correspondence H has zigzag order two if it satisfies the two conditions:

$$H \equiv H \circ H^* \circ H \text{ and } H^* \equiv H^* \circ H \circ H^* \tag{1}$$

These two conditions are interchangeable, for

$$(H \equiv H \circ H^* \circ H) \Leftrightarrow (H^* \equiv (H \circ H^* \circ H)^*)$$
$$\Leftrightarrow (H^* \equiv H^* \circ H \circ H^*)$$

A correspondence that satisfies either of the conditions in Formula (1) is called a *bundling*:

$$\boxed{H \text{ is a bundling} \Leftrightarrow (H \equiv H \circ H^* \circ H)}$$

Bundlings are similar to relations that obey "multivalued dependencies" in the relational model. Any *from one* or *to one* correspondence complex is a bundling. Some *many-to-many* correspondence complexes are also bundlings. Consider, for example, the composition correspondence $\dot{F} \circ \dot{G}$, where F has character ">" and G has character "<". This correspondence is illustrated in Figure 6.34. Notice how the individuals b_1 and b_2 "bundle together" many attachments of the composition correspondence $\dot{F} \circ \dot{G}$.

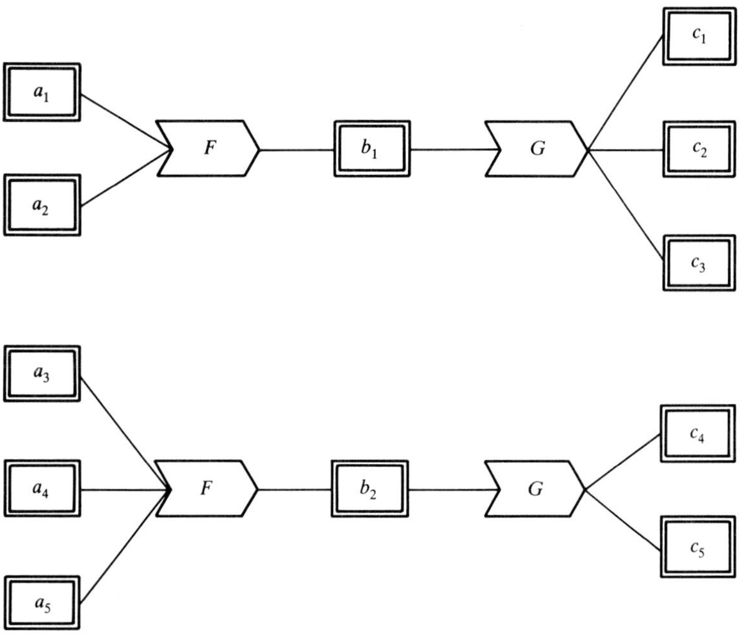

Figure 6.34 A factored bundling.

The following theorem shows that all compositions of the form $\mathring{]}\mathring{>}.\mathring{<}\mathring{[}$ are bundlings.

Theorem 6.3. If F is *to one* and G is *from one* then

$$(\dot{F} \circ \dot{G}) \circ (\dot{F} \circ \dot{G})^* \circ (\dot{F} \circ \dot{G}) \equiv (\dot{F} \circ \dot{G})$$

Proof. Expanding the expression on the left, we obtain

$$\dot{F} \circ (\dot{G} \circ \dot{G}^*) \circ (\dot{F}^* \circ \dot{F}) \circ \dot{G} \tag{2}$$

Since $\dot{G}$ is *from one* and *from all*, $\dot{G} \circ \dot{G}^* \equiv \Delta B$. Since $\dot{F}$ is *to one* and *to all*, $\dot{F}^* \circ \dot{F} \equiv \Delta B$. So the combinations in parentheses in Formula (2) may be deleted, and Formula (2) is equivalent to $\dot{F} \circ \dot{G}$. Therefore $\dot{F} \circ \dot{G}$ is a bundling. Q.E.D.

The following theorem shows that all bundlings can be factored in a similar way.

Theorem 6.4. Any correspondence complex $(H; A, C)$ whose reduced correspondence has zigzag order two can be factored into a path $(A; F; B; G; C)$, where the character of F is included in "$]>$" and the character of G is included in "$<[$".

Proof. We define the instances of the class B to be the immediate neighborhoods in A that are formed by H:

$$(\mathrm{A}X)\ B{:}|\nu X| \Leftrightarrow (\exists z)\ (\mathrm{A}y)\ (X{:}|y| \Leftrightarrow \dot{H}{:}|y,\ z|)\ \&\ (\exists w)\ X{:}|w| \tag{3}$$

The expression $(\exists w)\ X{:}|w|$ prevents B from containing empty classes should $\dot{H}$ be *to some*. Two images are defined to be the same B if the two immediate neighborhoods are equally extensive:

$$(\mathrm{A}X)\ (\mathrm{A}Y)\ \Delta B{:}|\nu X,\ \nu Y| \Leftrightarrow B{:}|\nu X|\ \&\ B{:}|\nu Y|\ \&\ (X \mathrel{\underset{\cdot}{=}} Y)$$

We define F to attach each instance of A to its immediate neighborhood:

$$(\mathrm{A}w)\ (\mathrm{A}X)\ F{:}|w,\ \nu X| \Leftrightarrow B{:}|\nu X|\ \&\ X{:}|w| \tag{4}$$

We show that F is *to all* as follows. From Formula (3) we obtain:

$$(\mathrm{A}X)\ B{:}|\nu X| \Rightarrow (\exists w)\ X{:}|w|$$

Then from Formula (4),

$$(\mathrm{A}X)\ (\mathrm{A}w)\ X{:}|w|\ \&\ B{:}|\nu X| \Rightarrow F{:}|w,\ \nu X|$$

Combining the two yields

$$(\mathrm{A}X)\ B{:}|\nu X| \Rightarrow (\exists w)\ F{:}|w,\ \nu X|$$

We show that F is *to one* as follows:

$$\begin{aligned}(\mathrm{A}w)\ (\mathrm{A}X)\ (\mathrm{A}Y)\ F{:}|w,\ \nu X|\ \&\ F{:}|w,\ \nu Y| &\Rightarrow B{:}|\nu X|\ \&\ B{:}|\nu Y| \\ &\Rightarrow ((\exists z)\ (\mathrm{A}y)\ (X{:}|y| \Leftrightarrow \dot{H}{:}|y,\ z|)) \\ &\quad \&\ ((\exists z')\ (\mathrm{A}y')\ (Y{:}|y'| \Leftrightarrow \dot{H}{:}|y',\ z'|))\end{aligned}$$

From Formula (4) we know that $X{:}|w|$ and $Y{:}|w|$. Thus, $(\exists z)\ \dot{H}{:}|w, z|$ and $(\exists z')\ \dot{H}{:}|w, z'|$. It remains to show, then, that the immediate neighborhood attached to z is equivalent to the immediate neighborhood attached to z'. That is, it remains to show that

$$(\mathrm{A}w)\ (\mathrm{A}w')\ (\exists z)\ \dot{H}{:}|w, z|\ \&\ (\exists z')\ \dot{H}{:}|w, z'|\ \&\ \dot{H}{:}|w', z| \Rightarrow \dot{H}{:}|w', z'|$$

This formula is just the statement that $\dot{H} \circ \dot{H}^* \circ \dot{H} \subseteq \dot{H}$, so F is *to one*.

For each immediate neighborhood X in B, we define G to attach X to each instance of C that a member of X attaches to by $\dot{H}$:

$$(\mathrm{A}X)\ (\mathrm{A}y)\ G{:}|\nu X, y| \Leftrightarrow (\exists z)\ X{:}|z|\ \&\ \dot{H}{:}|z, y| \tag{5}$$

G is *from all* because the immediate neighborhoods were defined by attachments to an instance of C [equate the placetaker y in Formula (5) to the placetaker z in Formula (3)]. To show that G is *from one*, let c be an instance of C and let $\dot{H}$ attach a to c. Then a is in only one immediate neighborhood by $\dot{H}$. Therefore, the immediate neighborhood of a is $c.\dot{H}^*$. Therefore, G^* attaches c to only the one neighborhood $c.\dot{H}^*$, and G is *from one*.

We show finally that $\dot{H} \equiv F \circ G$:

$$
\begin{aligned}
(\mathrm{A}x)\ (\mathrm{A}z)\ F \circ G{:}|x, z| &\Leftrightarrow (\exists Y)\ F{:}|x, \nu Y|\ \&\ G{:}|\nu Y, z| \\
&\Leftrightarrow (\exists Y)\ B{:}|\nu Y|\ \&\ Y{:}|x|\ \&\ (\exists x')\ Y{:}|x'|\ \&\ \dot{H}{:}|x', z| \\
&\Leftrightarrow (\exists z')\ (\exists x')\ \dot{H}{:}|x, z'|\ \&\ \dot{H}{:}|x', z'|\ \&\ \dot{H}{:}|x', z| \\
&\Leftrightarrow \dot{H} \circ \dot{H}^* \circ \dot{H}{:}|x, z| \\
&\Leftrightarrow \dot{H}{:}|x, z|
\end{aligned}
$$

Q.E.D.

Factoring with Unresolved Alternations

Since the proof of Theorem 6.4 was carried out using embracings, it applies even when H contains unresolved alternations. For example, consider the population

$$\vdash (H{:}(a_1, c_1) \vee H{:}(a_2, c_1))\ \&\ (H{:}(a_1, c_2) \vee H{:}(a_2, c_2))$$

Applying Formula (3) yields two instances of B, $b_1 \equiv \nu D_1$ and $b_2 \equiv \nu D_2$ (recall that both D_1 and D_2 are classes), such that

$$\vdash (D_1{:}(a_1) \vee D_1{:}(a_2))\ \&\ (D_2{:}(a_1) \vee D_2{:}(a_2))$$

Formula (4) gives the attachments of F:

$$\vdash (F{:}(a_1, b_1) \vee F{:}(a_2, b_1))\ \&\ (F{:}(a_1, b_2) \vee F{:}(a_2, b_1))$$

Notice, however, that there are no unresolved alternations in the population of G:

$$\vdash G{:}(b_1, c_1)\ \&\ G{:}(b_2, c_2)$$

This asymmetry in F and G shows that the intermediate class B is not defined uniquely when unresolved alternation is allowed. If we had formed B from immediate neighborhoods of H^* in C rather than from immediate neighborhoods of H in A we would have obtained a different factoring, with unresolved alternations in the population of G and none in the population of F. The factoring into F and G is unique, however, if H is resolute. This example shows further how one must reason from embracings rather than from sample populations when considering unresolved alternation.

Bracket Notation for Bundlings

Bundlings occur with such frequency in theoretical work that we introduce a shorthand expression for a bundling in the language of characters. If H is a *many-to-many* bundling, we will write its character as "><" rather than "<>". Thus, if $(H; A, C)$ is *all-to-all*, we would write its character as "><", if it is *some-to-some* we would write its character as "]><[", and so on. Here we depart from thinking of the character as a set and treat it as a string. We call this formulation *positional character notation*. In extended associative notation, a bundling should be declared in its factored form as a path $(A; F; B; G; C)$, and the intermediate class B should be given a descriptive name (a mantle).

Notice that by virtue of the factoring in Theorem 6.4, all bundlings are similar. A population of a bundling can be described as a list of pairs of widths, a width of an immediate neighborhood of F^* together with the width of the immediate neighborhood of G that attaches to the same intermediate instance of B. For example, the population of the bundling in Figure 6.34 can be described by the list ((2, 3), (3, 2)).

Higher Zigzag Orders

Anchored loops, *one-to-one* correspondence complexes, *one-to-many* correspondence complexes, *many-to-one* correspondence complexes, and *many-to-many* bundlings completely exhaust the correspondences with zigzag order less than three. It is possible to extend the concept of zigzag control further to develop new types of *many-to-many* correspondences. For example, we might study correspondences such that

$$H \circ H^* \circ H \circ H^* \subseteq H \circ H^* \qquad (6)$$

Such constraints arise infrequently in practice, most likely because they merely constrain the zigzag to a certain zigzag order, in this case three, but do not allow the zigzag to be factored away as is the case in bundlings. The particular type of population that is permitted by Formula (6) but is prohibited in bundlings is shown in Figure 6.35.

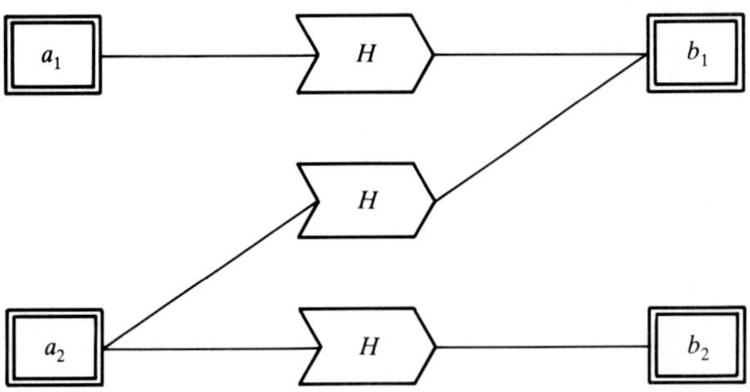

Figure 6.35 An unbundled *many-to-many* correspondence complex.

Conclusion

We have shown how the character constraints of *from one* and *to one* can be viewed as techniques for limiting the *zigzag order* of a correspondence. That is, *one-to-one* correspondences have zigzag order one, and both *one-to-many* and *many-to-one* correspondences have zigzag order two.

Most *many-to-many* correspondences have zigzag orders higher than two, but an important class of *many-to-many* correspondences called *bundlings* have zigzag order two. We have shown how all bundlings may be rewritten as a composition of a correspondence of character no more permissive than "**]**>" with a correspondence of character no more permissive than "<**[**". This result shows how data logic is able to convert between different data structures, in this case a correspondence constrained by an embracing and a binary path.

6.7 CONCLUSION

We have shown how all populations of *one-to-one*, *one-to-many*, and *many-to-one* correspondence complexes may be classified by *similarity*. That is, all such populations fall into recognizable patterns that differ only in relative magnitude. We have extended this analysis to both *pillared* correspondence complexes, in which the two relative class tags are different, and to *loops*, in which the two relative class tags are the same.

We have discussed two methods for converting a correspondence complex into a path. The *elongation factoring* converts a correspondence complex into a path of length four such that the character of each constituent of the path acquires exactly one bracket decision from the original correspondence complex. The elongation factoring may be applied to any correspondence complex, and justifies the standard sequence of brackets **]**, <, >, **[** used to declare a character.

We have also shown how a *bundling*, a particular variety of correspondence complex, can be factored into a binary path. Both the factoring of bundlings and the elongation factoring continue to apply in the presence of unresolved alternation. Other techniques, particularly those that rely on reasoning from sample resolute populations, fail to describe unresolved alternations properly.

A primary application of this chapter will be the facility gained in manipulating characters as sets of brackets. This ability is unique to the extended associative model among major data models. In models that employ network diagrams, for example, we can not isolate an arrow, or a symbol such as "1:M", and prove a theorem about it. Each character incorporates four fairly complex statements of data logic, so the ability to manipulate a character easily gives us a powerful tool for drawing conclusions about data.

7

Embracings of Correspondences

7.1 INTRODUCTION

In this chapter, we consider some effects of explicitly declaring embracings in a data design. We will discuss how logical operations on associations affect embracings, and we will introduce several forms of constraints that are not recognized by the major data models. We also include a case study on the representation of time as an illustration of the use of embracings.

In a data model that does not recognize embracings, most of the data structures that we present in this chapter can not be declared. Such data models typically treat problems that involve embracings as if the embracings were not there. Thus, if a data model does not permit embracings of correspondences, then a problem in which a correspondence H embraces a correspondence G would be modelled so that the correspondence tag "H" does *not* embrace the correspondence tag "G". That is, the data base would allow there to be two individuals that are attached by "G" but not by "H", even though there could be no two images attached by « G » but not by « H ».

Sometimes, such spurious attachments cause no difficulty, and then not declaring the embracing may have no ill effects. However, in other situations, it is important to prohibit these attachments. Suppose, for example, that each attachment is a record of a financial transaction with a large associated dollar value. Spurious attachments could then result in large discrepancies between the recorded dollar amounts and the real dollar amounts.

Data models that do not recognize embracings throw the burden of enforcing the embracing onto the programs that use the data base: the programs must assure that no improper attachments are added or deleted. When many programs use a data base, we argue that constraints such as embracings should be managed as part of the data base, where they are insulated from changes to procedures, and so that all programs that use the data base can take advantage of the constraints that the data obeys.

In Section 7.2, Logic of Embracings, we discuss how the logical operations of data logic affect embracings and characters. For example, if G and H are both *from all* relative to (B, C), then $G \cup H$ is *from all* relative to (B, C) but $G \cap H$ may be *from some*. Thus, in Figure 7.1, $G \cup H$ attaches b_1 to c_1, and b_2 to both c_1 and c_2, so $G \cup H$ appears *from all*. However, $G \cap H$ only attaches b_2 to c_2, so $G \cap H$ is *from some*.

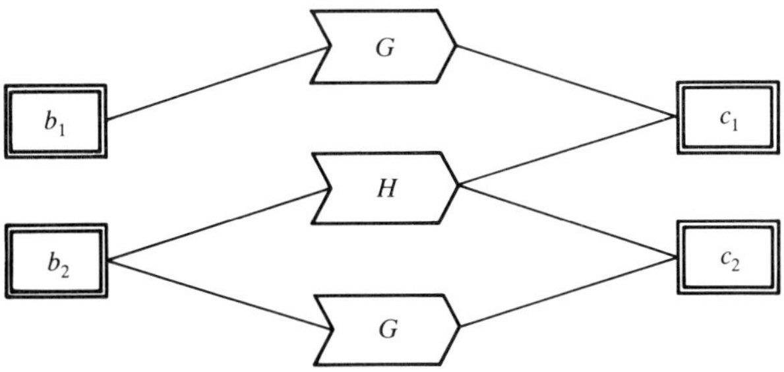

Figure 7.1 $G \cup H$ is *from all* while $G \cap H$ is *from some*.

In Section 7.3, Intercharacter Constraints, we discuss a form of interdependency that can occur between two correspondence complexes with similar character. For example, if both G and H are *from some* relative to (B, C), it may be that any instance of B that attaches to some individual by G must also attach to some individual by H. This embracing is called an *interoptional* embracing, since it is degenerate if either G or H is *from all*. We show further that there is a dual *intermultiple* embracing which interrelates immediate neighborhoods generated by two *from many* correspondences.

In Section 7.4, Orphans-Not-Allowed and Replicates-Not-Allowed, we discuss a similar dual pair of constraints. The *replicates-not-allowed* constraint is familiar in data processing: it refers to a matrix defined so that two individuals may not reside simultaneously in any cell. We show how this constraint can be expressed as an embracing. The replicates-not-allowed constraint has a dual constraint called the *orphans-not-allowed* constraint. This constraint prohibits an individual from attaching by *none* of a given set of correspondence tags. For example, if F and G obey an *orphans-not-allowed* constraint relative to a class tag B, then each instance of B must attach to some individual by F or to some individual by G.

In Section 7.5, Analysis of Cycles, we study cycles by considering embracings obeyed by the composition of their constituents. We consider *anchored cycles*, which are cycles such that navigating around the cycle always results in either an identity or an orphan. We also consider the effects of navigating around a cycle many times, and thereby define the transitive closure of a cycle.

In Section 7.6, we present a case study on the representation of time in data bases. We argue that time should be treated as an image like any other, and so should not be treated by special "temporal logics". We argue that data base applications are concerned primarily with conceptions of time that need not have any physical meaning: times in the future, for example, are critical to forecasting applications, but they are no harder to manage than times in the present or in the past. Data base populations also change with time; by incorporating a time clock of a master engine into embracings, we show how embracings may be applied to disable certain forms of updates.

7.2 LOGIC OF EMBRACINGS

We summarize below some of the basic characteristics of embracings of classes and correspondences. We begin with a recapitulation of some of the characteristics of union and intersection developed in Chapter 2, which we state without proof.

Theorem 7.1. For any associations Q, R, and S of the same degree,

(i) $Q \cap R \subseteq Q$
(ii) $Q \cap R \subseteq R$
(iii) $Q \cap R \equiv R \cap Q$
(iv) $(S \subseteq Q)$ & $(S \subseteq R) \Leftrightarrow (S \subseteq Q \cap R)$

Theorem 7.2. For any associations Q, R, and S of the same degree,

(i) $Q \subseteq Q \cup R$
(ii) $R \subseteq Q \cup R$
(iii) $Q \cup R \equiv R \cup Q$
(iv) $(Q \subseteq S)$ & $(R \subseteq S) \Leftrightarrow ((Q \cup R) \subseteq S)$

Logic of Converses

Theorem 7.3. For any correspondences F and G, $F^* \subseteq G^*$ if and only if $F \subseteq G$.

Proof. The embracing $F \subseteq G$ may be written

$$(\mathrm{A}x)\ (\mathrm{A}y)\ F{:}|x,\ y| \Rightarrow G{:}|x,\ y|$$

By the definition of the converse,

$$(\mathrm{A}x)\ (\mathrm{A}y)\ F^*{:}|y,\ x| \Rightarrow F{:}|x,\ y|$$

$$(\mathrm{A}x)\ (\mathrm{A}y)\ G{:}|x,\ y| \Rightarrow G^*{:}|y,\ x|$$

Combining these expressions, we obtain

$$(\mathrm{A}x)\ (\mathrm{A}y)\ F^*{:}|y,\ x| \Rightarrow G^*{:}|y,\ x|$$

So G^* embraces F^*.

Since $F^{**} \equiv F$, it follows from $F^* \subseteq G^*$ that $F \subseteq G$. Q.E.D.

Theorem 7.4. For any correspondences G and H,

(i) $(G \cap H)^* \equiv G^* \cap H^*$
(ii) $(G \cup H)^* \equiv G^* \cup H^*$

Proof.
(i) $(\mathrm{A}x)\ (\mathrm{A}y)\ (G \cap H)^*{:}|x, y| \Leftrightarrow (G \cap H){:}|y, x|$

$$\Leftrightarrow G{:}|y, x|\ \&\ H{:}|y, x|$$

$$\Leftrightarrow G^*{:}|x, y|\ \&\ H^*{:}|x, y|$$

$$\Leftrightarrow (G^* \cap H^*){:}|x, y|$$

(ii) The proof is similar to the proof of (i). Q.E.D.

Logic of Composition

Theorem 7.5. For any correspondences F and G, $(F \circ G)^* \equiv G^* \circ F^*$

Proof. $(\mathrm{A}x)\ (\mathrm{A}z)\ (F \circ G)^*{:}|x, z| \Leftrightarrow (F \circ G){:}|z, x|$

$$\Leftrightarrow (\exists y)\ F{:}|z, y|\ \&\ G{:}|y, x|$$

$$\Leftrightarrow (\exists y)\ F^*{:}|y, z|\ \&\ G^*{:}|x, y|$$

$$\Leftrightarrow (G^* \circ F^*){:}|x, z|$$

Q.E.D.

Theorem 7.6. For any correspondences F, G, and H,

$$(F \subseteq G) \Rightarrow (F \circ H \subseteq G \circ H)$$

Proof. By the definition of composition,

$$(\mathrm{A}x)\ (\mathrm{A}z)\ F \circ H{:}|x, z| \Leftrightarrow (\exists y)\ F{:}|x, y|\ \&\ H{:}|y, z|$$

If G embraces F, we may substitute G for F on the right side, yielding

$$(\exists y)\ G{:}|x, y|\ \&\ H{:}|y, z|$$

This is the formula for $G \circ H{:}|x, z|$. Q.E.D.

Interaction of Union and Intersection with Composition

Theorem 7.7. For any correspondences F, G, and H,

$$F \circ (G \cup H) \equiv (F \circ G) \cup (F \circ H)$$

Proof. $(\mathrm{A}x)\ (\mathrm{A}z)\ F \circ (G \cup H){:}|x, z| \Leftrightarrow (\exists y)\ F{:}|x, y|\ \&\ (G{:}|y, z| \vee H{:}|y, z|)$

$$\Leftrightarrow (\exists y)\ (F{:}|x, y|\ \&\ G{:}|y, z|) \vee (F{:}|x, y|\ \&\ H{:}|y, z|)$$

$$\Leftrightarrow (\exists y)\ (F{:}|x,\ y|\ \&\ G{:}|y,\ z|) \vee$$
$$(\exists y')\ (F{:}|x,\ y'|\ \&\ H{:}|y',\ z|)$$
$$\Leftrightarrow ((F \circ G) \cup (F \circ H)){:}|x,\ z|$$

Q.E.D.

Theorem 7.7 is illustrated by Figure 7.2. By inspection, the composition $F \circ (G \cup H)$ attaches the same instances of A to instances of C as does the union $(F \circ G) \cup (F \circ H)$.

Unlike union, intersection does not generally distribute with composition:

Theorem 7.8. For any correspondences F, G, and H,

$$F \circ (G \cap H) \subseteq (F \circ G) \cap (F \circ H)$$

Proof. $(\mathrm{A}x)\ (\mathrm{A}z)\ F \circ (G \cap H){:}|x,\ z| \Leftrightarrow (\exists y)\ F{:}|x,\ y|\ \&\ G{:}|y,\ z|\ \&\ H{:}|y,\ z|$

$$\Rightarrow ((\exists y)\ F{:}|x,\ y|\ \&\ G{:}|y,\ z|)\ \&$$
$$((\exists y')\ F{:}|x,\ y'|\ \&\ H{:}|y',\ z|)$$
$$\Rightarrow ((F \circ G) \cap (F \circ H)){:}|x,\ z|$$

Q.E.D.

Notice that the embracing in Theorem 7.8 is directed, while the embracing in Theorem 7.7 is bidirectional. Figure 7.3 shows an example where $F \circ (G \cap H)$ does not embrace $(F \circ G) \cap (F \circ H)$. Here $F \circ (G \cap H)$ leaves a orphan, but $(F \circ G) \cap (F \circ H)$ attaches a to c.

The following theorem gives one case where the embracing is bi-directional.

Theorem 7.9. If F is *to one*, then

$$F \circ (G \cap H) \equiv (F \circ G) \cap (F \circ H)$$

Proof. We need only show that the right side embraces the left. By the definition of intersection,

$$(F \circ G) \cap (F \circ H){:}|x,\ z| \Rightarrow (\exists y)\ F{:}|x,\ y|\ \&\ G{:}|y,\ z|\ \&\ (\exists y')\ F{:}|x,\ y'|\ \&\ H{:}|y',\ z|$$

Since F is *to one*, and x attaches to both y and y', y must be identical to y'. Therefore the right side becomes

$$(\exists y)\ F{:}|x,\ y|\ \&\ G{:}|y,\ z|\ \&\ H{:}|y,\ z|$$

which is the statement $(F \circ (G \cap H)){:}|x,\ z|$. Q.E.D.

Theorem 7.9 is illustrated by Figure 7.4. By inspection, the composition $F \circ (G \cap H)$ attaches the same instances of A to instances of C as the intersection $(F \circ G) \cap (F \circ H)$.

Logic of Characters

The *converse* of a character is formed by changing each bracket that appears in the character to point in the opposite direction. Thus the converse of "**]**" is "**[**", the converse of ">" is "<", and the converse of "**]**<" is ">**[**". One may also form the converse of a

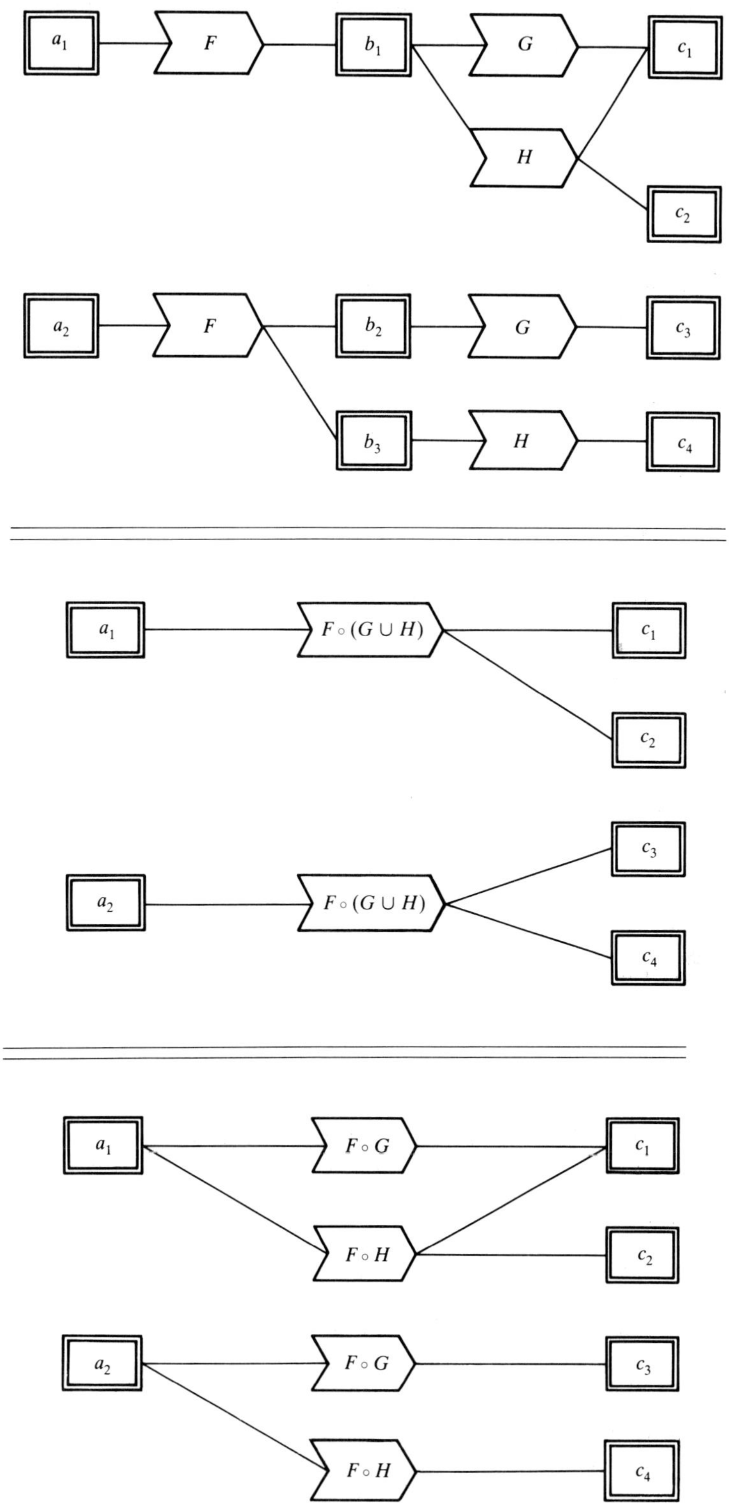

Figure 7.2 Illustration of Theorem 7.7.

character by turning the character upside down. Four characters are their own converses: ∅, "] [", "<>", and "]<>[". The converse of a character α is written "α*". We have then clearly:

Theorem 7.10. The character of (G^*; C, B) is the converse of the character of (G; B, C).

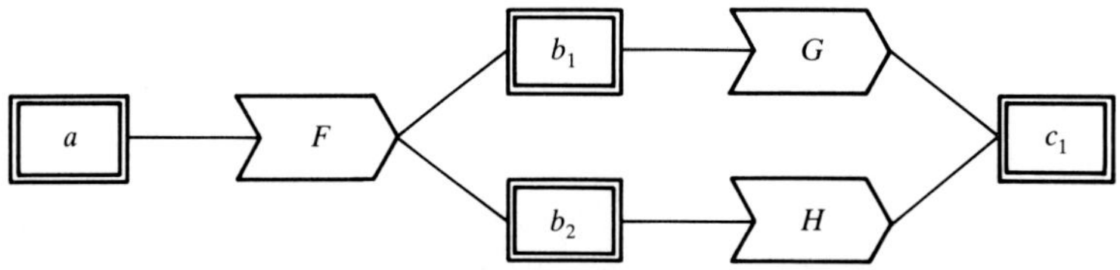

Figure 7.3 Obstacle to strengthening Theorem 7.8.

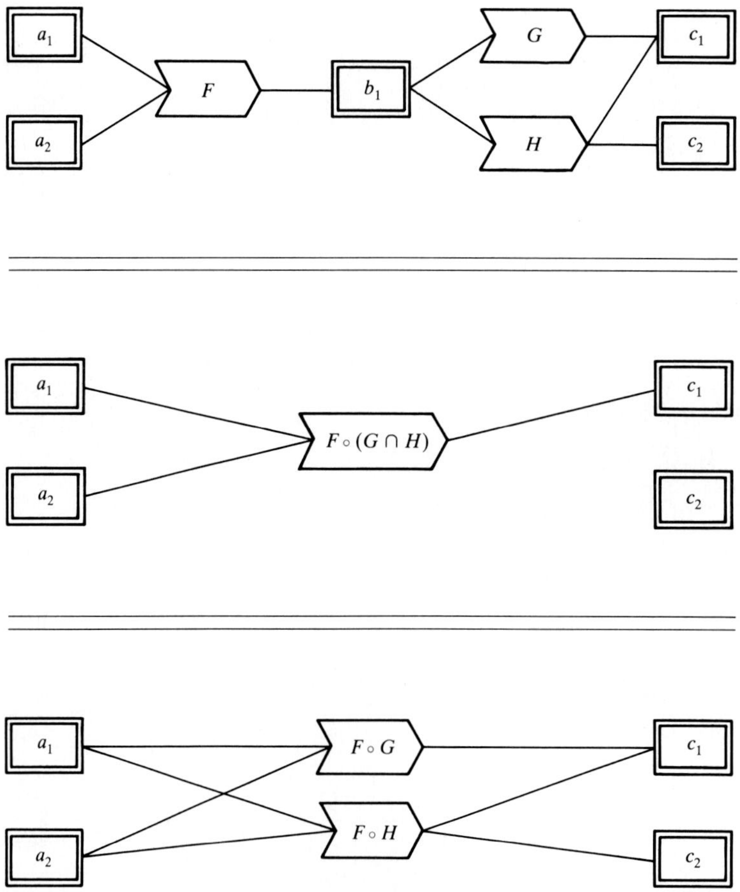

Figure 7.4 Illustration of Theorem 7.9.

Characters interact with embracings in the following ways:

Theorem 7.11. For any correspondences G and H, let $\dot{G}$ be the reduced correspondence of G relative to a pair of classes (B, C), and let $\dot{H}$ be the reduced correspondence of H relative to the same pair of classes (B, C). If $\dot{G} \subseteq \dot{H}$, then

(i) If G is *from all*, then H is *from all*
(ii) If G is *from many*, then H is *from many*
(iii) If G is *to many*, then H is *to many*
(iv) If G is *to all*, then H is *to all*
(v) If H is *from some*, then G is *from some*
(vi) If H is *from one*, then G is *from one*
(vii) If H is *to one*, then G is *to one*
(viii) If H is *to some*, then G is *to some*

Proof. Notice how the *optional* portion and the *multiple* portion of characters behave oppositely in the presence of an embracing. This is because the direction of embracing in the character embracings is opposite. For example, G is *from all* relative to (B, C) if $\dot{G}$ obeys the constraint

$$\Delta B \subseteq \dot{G} \circ \dot{G}^*$$

Since $\dot{G} \subseteq \dot{H}$, we may apply Theorem 7.6 to obtain

$$\Delta B \subseteq \dot{H} \circ \dot{H}^*$$

That is, H is *from all* relative to (B, C). In contrast, H is *from one* relative to (B, C) if

$$\dot{H} \circ \dot{H}^* \subseteq \Delta B$$

Since $\dot{G} \subseteq \dot{H}$, we may conclude that

$$\dot{G} \circ \dot{G}^* \subseteq \Delta B$$

That is, G is *from one* relative to (B, C). Applying the contrapositive law, we may conclude that if G is *from many,* then H is *from many*. The remaining formulas follow by examining the converses G^* and H^*. Q.E.D.

We may deduce the effects of conjunction and alternation on characters using the following rules:

$$G \subseteq G \cup H$$

$$G \cap H \subseteq G$$

Applying these rules to Theorem 7.11 gives the corollary:

Theorem 7.12. For any correspondences G and H, relative to the classes (B, C),

(i) If G is *from all*, then $G \cup H$ is *from all*
(ii) If G is *from many*, then $G \cup H$ is *from many*
(iii) If G is *from some*, then $G \cap H$ is *from some*

(iv) If G is *from one*, then $G \cap H$ is *from one*
(v) If G is *to all*, then $G \cup H$ is *to all*
(vi) If G is *to many*, then $G \cup H$ is *to many*
(vii) If G is *to some*, then $G \cap H$ is *to some*
(viii) If G is *to one*, then $G \cap H$ is *to one*

Conclusion

Embracings can have a direct impact on the characters of correspondences. For example, Theorem 7.11 shows that if G is *from all* relative to (B, C) and $\dot{H}$ embraces $\dot{G}$, then H must be *from all* relative to (B, C). In the presence of embracings, therefore, character decisions for different correspondences may be interrelated: in the case just cited, the designer could not declare H to be *from some* without changing the character of G or removing the embracing $\dot{G} \subseteq \dot{H}$.

We will find many similar *character decision interdependencies* in later sections. We envision that all these interdependencies will be maintained automatically by the design management device. Thus, if the designer were to change H to be *from some* in this example, the design management device would automatically change G to be *from some* at the same time.

7.3 INTERCHARACTER CONSTRAINTS

An Interoptional Constraint Relates Two Correspondence Complexes

We consider two correspondences F and G that obey the following constraint:

If an image i attaches to some image by F^*, then i must attach to some image by G.

This constraint is called an *interoptional constraint*. We will find that the phrasing using the converse F^*, rather than F, will clarify the presentation. An interoptional constraint is illustrated in Figure 7.5. Here b_2 and b_3 must attach to some instances of C by G (in this case, c_2 and c_3), because they attach to instances of A by F. The instances b_1 and b_4 are not affected because they do not attach to instances of A.

An interoptional constraint may be expressed as an embracing as follows. We imagine that the correspondence F is declared relative to (A, B), and that the correspondence G is declared relative to (B, C). Notice that the class B appears in both correspondence complexes, so F^* and G form a binary hub. The interoptional constraint is then

$$(\mathrm{A}y)\ (\exists x)\ F{:}|x, y|\ \&\ A{:}|x|\ \&\ B{:}|y| \Rightarrow (\exists z)\ G{:}|y, z|\ \&\ C{:}|z|$$

Or equivalently,

$$\boxed{\pi^2\dot{F} \subseteq \pi^1\dot{G}} \qquad (1)$$

An interoptional constraint is declared in extended associative notation as shown in Figure 7.6.

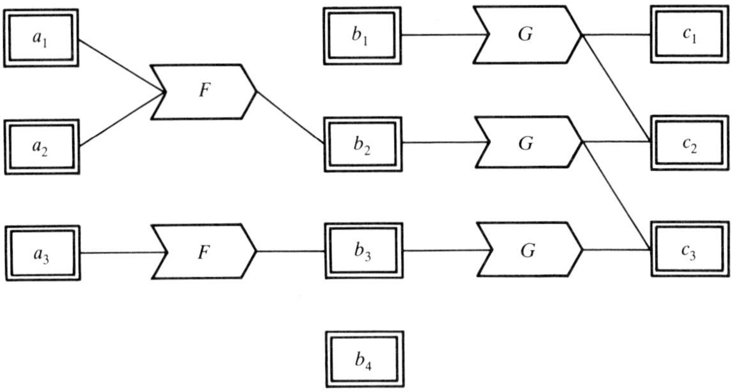

Figure 7.5 Illustration of an interoptional constraint.

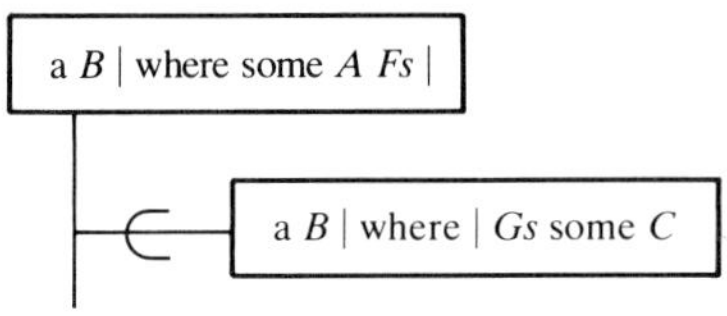

Figure 7.6 Declaration of an interoptional constraint.

An interoptional constraint may operate in both directions, resulting in an equivalence of the form

$$\pi^2\dot{F} \equiv \pi^1\dot{G}$$

In this case, an instance of B must attach to both an instance of A and an instance of C, or to neither.

The interoptional constraint conveys new information only if both F^* and G are *from some*. Thus, if F^* were *from all*, the interoptional constraint would say nothing more than that G was *from all*. Conversely, if G were *from all*, the interoptional constraint would always be obeyed, whichever correspondence F were chosen.

Hubs of width greater than two can exhibit more complex varieties of interoptional constraints. For example, the four correspondence complexes (H_1; B, C_1), (H_2; B, C_2), (H_3; B, C_3), and (H_4; B, C_4) could obey the constraint

$$\pi^2\dot{H}_1 \cap \pi^2\dot{H}_2 \subseteq \pi^1\dot{H}_3 \cup \pi^1\dot{H}_4$$

That is, if an image b accepted by B attaches to both an image accepted by C_1 and an image accepted by C_2 then b attaches to either an image accepted by C_3 or an image accepted by C_4. The designer should use caution when considering declaring interoptional constraints that involve more than two correspondence complexes, because the presence of such constraints may be a clue that the classes are not defined properly. In the example shown, we would be inclined to question whether H_1 and H_2 could not be combined into a single correspondence J, C_1 and C_2 into a single class D, H_3 and H_4 into a single correspondence

K, and C_3 and C_2 into a single class E. We would then be able to write the constraint as an interoptional constraint on a binary hub:

$$\pi^2(\Delta D \circ J \circ \Delta B) \subseteq \pi^1(\Delta B \circ K \circ \Delta E)$$

Effect of an Interoptional Constraint on the Composition Correspondence F ∘ G

An interoptional constraint constrains the scope of a composition correspondence, as the following theorem shows.

Theorem 7.13. For any correspondences F and G,

(i) $\pi^1(F \circ G) \subseteq \pi^1 F$

(ii) If $\pi^2 F \subseteq \pi^1 G$, then $\pi^1(F \circ G) \equiv \pi^1 F$

Proof.

(i) Expanding the hypothesis in data logic notation yields

$$(\mathrm{A}x)\ (\exists z)\ (\exists y)\ F{:}|x,\ y|\ \&\ G{:}|y,\ z| \Rightarrow (\exists y')\ F{:}|x,\ y'|$$

Taking $y' = y$, this is shown easily.

(ii) The embracing $\pi^2 F \subseteq \pi^1 G$ may be written

$$(\mathrm{A}y)\ ((\exists x)\ F{:}|x,\ y|) \Rightarrow (\exists z)\ G{:}|y,\ z|$$

Reordering the quantifiers using data logic yields

$$(\mathrm{A}x)\ ((\exists y)\ F{:}|x,\ y|) \Rightarrow (\exists z)\ G{:}|y,\ z|$$

$$\Rightarrow (\exists z)\ (\exists y)\ F{:}|x,\ y|\ \&\ G{:}|y,\ z|$$

Rewriting, we conclude that $\pi^1 F \subseteq \pi^1(F \circ G)$. The other direction of embracing follows from part (i). Q.E.D.

This theorem is illustrated by Figure 7.7. Thus, in the top portion of the figure, a_1 and a_2 both attach via F, so both a_1 and a_2 are instances of $\pi^1 F$. Yet only a_2 attaches via $F \circ G$, so only a_2 is an instance of $\pi^1(F \circ G)$. In the bottom portion of the figure, all three instances b_1, b_2, and b_3 attach via G, so all three are instances of $\pi^1 G$. Two instances, b_2 and b_3, attach via F^*, so they are instances of $\pi^2 F$. Since $\pi^2 F \subseteq \pi^1 G$, all instances of A (namely, a_1 and a_2) that attach via F also attach via $F \circ G$.

It is possible for $\pi^1(F \circ G)$ to embrace $\pi^1 F$ without $\pi^1 G$ embracing $\pi^2 F$, as shown in Figure 7.8. That is, an interoptional constraint gives a sufficient, but not a necessary, condition that the scope of a composition $F \circ G$ is the same as the scope of the first correspondence F.

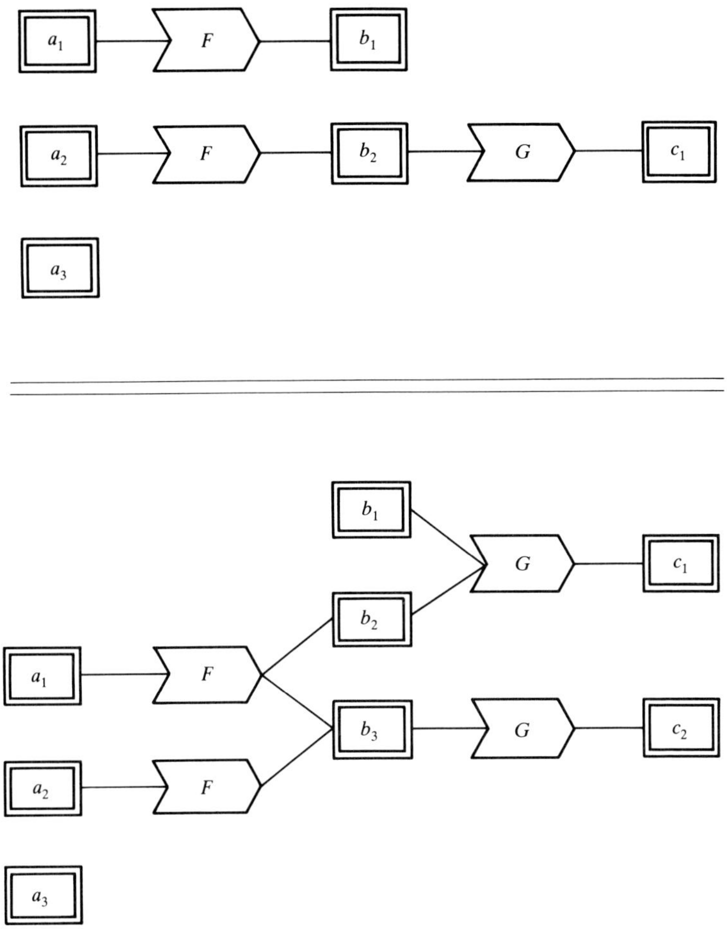

Figure 7.7 Illustration of Theorem 7.13.

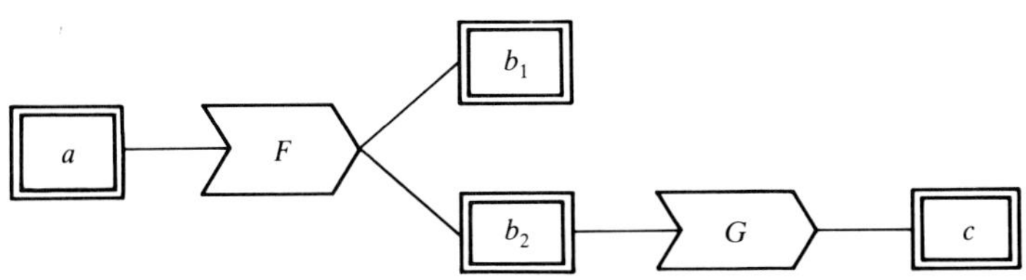

Figure 7.8 Obstacle to strengthening Theorem 7.13.

Intermultiple Constraints

There is a dual constraint to an interoptional constraint that operates only when both F^* and G are *from many*, namely

$$\boxed{\dot{F}^* \circ \dot{F} \subseteq \dot{G} \circ \dot{G}^*} \qquad (2)$$

This constraint is called an *intermultiple constraint*. Interoptional and intermultiple constraints will be referred to generically as *intercharacter constraints*.

An intermultiple constraint is somewhat more difficult to envision than an interoptional constraint. Recall that for any recognizer b and correspondence G, the *immediate neighborhood* of b by G is the class $b.G \circ G^*$. It is the class of all images that attach to images by G that b also attaches to. For example, in Figure 7.9, b_1 is in the immediate neighborhood of b_2 because they both attach to c_1, and b_3 is in the immediate neighborhood of b_2 because they both attach to c_2, but b_3 is not in the immediate neighborhood of b_1. Notice that a recognizer b is in its own immediate neighborhood if and only if it attaches to something via G. An unresolved alternation will suffice, so long as all alternatives have b attaching to some instance by G.

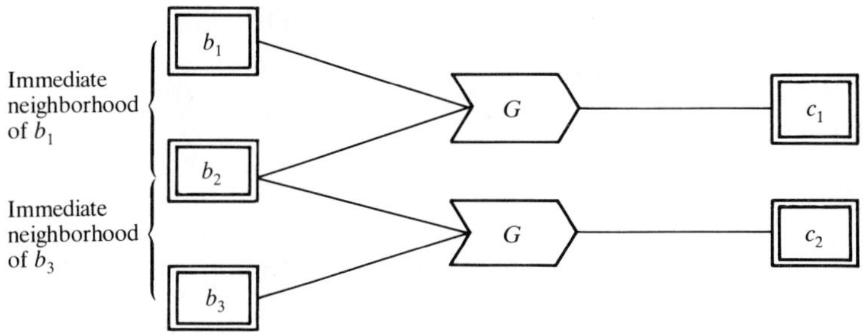

Figure 7.9 Illustration of immediate neighborhoods.

A *from one* constraint says that all immediate neighborhoods have at most one element, or put another way, that all immediate neighborhoods must be included in the immediate neighborhoods by the identity correspondence. That is, the statement that (G; B, C) is *from one* may be viewed as the degenerate intermultiple constraint

$$\dot{G} \circ \dot{G}^* \subseteq \Delta B \circ \Delta B^*$$

The intermultiple constraint, Formula (2), says that the immediate neighborhoods by $\dot{F}^*$ must be included in the immediate neighborhoods by $\dot{G}$. The simplest example is when both $\dot{F}^*$ and $\dot{G}$ are *many-to-one*, in which case the immediate neighborhoods are disjoint. We have then a case such as that shown in Figure 7.10. Here the immediate neighborhood of b_2 by $\dot{F}^*$, for example, is $\{b_2, b_3\}$, and the immediate neighborhood of b_2 by $\dot{G}$ is the larger $\{b_1, b_2, b_3\}$. Similarly, the immediate neighborhood of b_4 by $\dot{F}^*$ is $\{b_4, b_5\}$ and the immediate neighborhood of b_4 by $\dot{G}$ is $\{b_4, b_5, b_6, b_7\}$. All the immediate neighborhoods by $\dot{F}^*$ are included in immediate neighborhoods by $\dot{G}$ in this way, so Figure 7.10 illustrates the intermultiple constraint $\dot{F}^* \circ \dot{F} \subseteq \dot{G} \circ \dot{G}^*$.

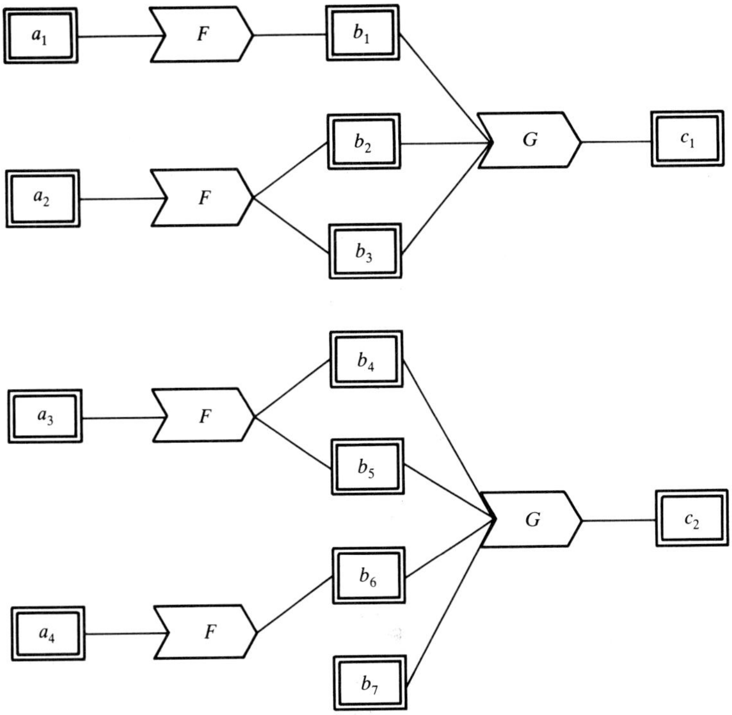

Figure 7.10 Illustration of an intermultiple constraint.

An intermultiple constraint is declared in extended associative notation as shown in Figure 7.11.

A Degenerate Intermultiple Constraint Reduces to an Interoptional Constraint

If F^* were *from one* relative to (B, A), then its neighborhoods would all be of at most one element, so the intermultiple constraint, Formula (2), would reduce to an interoptional constraint. If G is *from one* relative to (B, C), then its neighborhoods are all of at most one element. Since the neighborhoods by F^* would have to be included in the neighborhoods by G, F^* would be *from one* as well, and so the embracing would also reduce to an interoptional constraint. Therefore an intermultiple constraint may be simplified unless both correspondence complexes are *from many*.

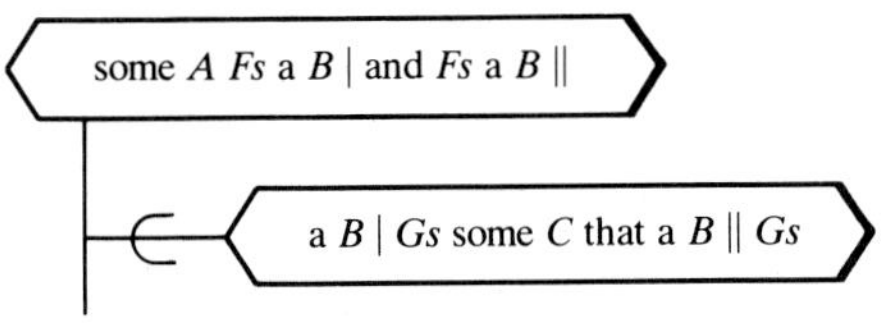

Figure 7.11 Declaration of an intermultiple constraint.

Effect of an Intermultiple Constraint on the Composition $F \circ G$

Theorem 7.14. If $\dot{F}$ is declared relative to (A, B), G is *to one* relative to (B, C), and $\dot{F}^* \circ \dot{F} \subseteq \dot{G} \circ \dot{G}^*$, then $\dot{F} \circ \dot{G}$ is *to one* relative to (A, C).

Proof. G is *to one* when

$$\dot{G} \circ \dot{G}^* \subseteq \Delta B$$

We have then

$$\dot{G}^* \circ (\dot{G} \circ \dot{G}^*) \circ \dot{G} \subseteq \dot{G}^* \circ \Delta B \circ \dot{G} \subseteq \dot{G}^* \circ \dot{G} \subseteq \Delta B$$

By the intermultiple constraint in the hypothesis,

$$\dot{G}^* \circ (\dot{F}^* \circ \dot{F}) \circ \dot{G} \subseteq \dot{G}^* \circ (\dot{G} \circ \dot{G}^*) \circ \dot{G}$$

By Theorem 7.5,

$$(\dot{F} \circ \dot{G})^* \circ (\dot{F} \circ \dot{G}) \equiv \dot{G}^* \circ (\dot{F}^* \circ \dot{F}) \circ \dot{G}$$

Combining these three formulas yields the desired result. Q.E.D.

Theorem 7.14 is illustrated by Figure 7.10 shown earlier. Notice that in Figure 7.10, $F \circ G$ is *to one* even though F is *to many*. Theorem 7.14 shows how an intermultiple constraint can alter the character of a composition correspondence. We will return to this property in Chapter 8.

Interoptional and Intermultiple Constraints Have Different Degrees

The similarity between the interoptional constraint and the intermultiple constraint may be seen as follows. The interoptional constraint is

$$(\mathrm{A}y)\ ((\exists x)\ \dot{F}{:}|x, y|) \Rightarrow (\exists z)\ \dot{G}{:}|y, z|$$

If we add a second universally quantified placetaker, we obtain

$$(\mathrm{A}y_1)\ (\mathrm{A}y_2)\ ((\exists x)\ \dot{F}{:}|x, y_1|\ \&\ \dot{F}{:}|x, y_2|) \Rightarrow (\exists z)\ \dot{G}{:}|y_1, z|\ \&\ \dot{G}{:}|y_2, z|$$

which is an intermultiple constraint. In principle, these embracings could be extended by adding further placetakers, reaching expressions of the form

$$(\mathrm{A}y_1) \ldots (\mathrm{A}y_d)\ (\exists x)\ \dot{F}{:}|x, y_1|\ \&\ \ldots\ \&\ \dot{F}{:}|x, y_d| \Rightarrow$$
$$(\exists z)\ \dot{G}{:}|y_1, z|\ \&\ \ldots\ \&\ \dot{G}{:}|y_d, z|$$

The expressions when $d > 2$ tend to be less important than those where $d = 1$ or $d = 2$. The expressions with $d > 2$ set a threshold number d of instances of a neighborhood, below which they behave exactly the same as expressions of lower degree, and above which they require closer similarity between the two correspondences F^* and G. These higher degree expressions would therefore be most valuable when F^* has a maximum number of elements that may be in any of its immediate neighborhoods, but this is a rare case in practice except for the degenerate case where F^* is *from one*.

Conclusion

We have discussed two forms of constraints, interoptional constraints and intermultiple constraints, that each interrelate the behavior of two correspondence complexes. The ability to declare such constraints and to predict their behavior is a new capability provided by data logic. Most current data base management systems do not permit two different correspondence complexes to be interrelated in this way. These constraints furnish a simple example of the kinds of interactions that can be present in a hub. We have shown that one way to describe these interactions is to form the composition of the two correspondence complexes, using the center of the hub as the intermediate class. The character of the composition correspondence then describes the way in which the two correspondence complexes are related.

7.4 ORPHANS-NOT-ALLOWED AND REPLICATES-NOT-ALLOWED

In this section we investigate two forms of embracings that are generalizations of *from all* and *from one* to hubs. Like intercharacter constraints, they illustrate how embracings can interrelate many correspondence complexes.

Orphans-Not-Allowed

Consider the binary hub $\{(F; A, B), (G; B, C)\}$, and suppose that both F^* and G are *from some*. There may then, in general, be instances of B that attach to no recognizers by either F^* or by G. Such instances are called *orphans* of the hub. An example is b_1 in Figure 7.12.

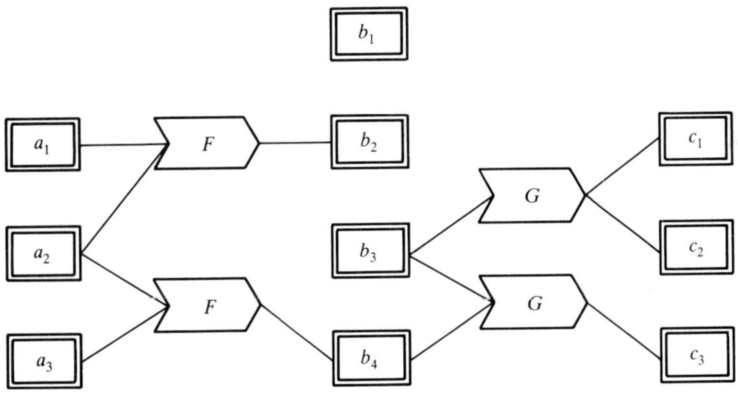

Figure 7.12 The individual b_1 is an orphan.

In the presence of unresolved alternation, an individual is an orphan if each potential alternative leaves it unattached by all correspondences. Thus the tag b in the following is not an orphan:

$$\vdash F{:}(a_1, b) \vee F{:}(a_2, b) \vee G{:}(b, c)$$

Now consider the embracing

$$\boxed{B \subseteq \pi^2\dot{F} \cup \pi^1\dot{G}}$$

That is,

$$(\mathrm{A}y)\ B{:}|y| \Rightarrow ((\exists x)\ F{:}|x, y| \ \&\ A{:}|x|) \lor ((\exists z)\ G{:}|y, z| \ \&\ C{:}|z|) \qquad (1)$$

This embracing says that any image accepted by B must attach to an image accepted by A *or* to an image accepted by C. That is, it says that orphans of the hub $\{F^*, G\}$ are not permitted. The embracing is called an *orphans-not-allowed* constraint, abbreviated ONA $(B; (F^*; A), (G; C))$. An ONA constraint is an example of a useful data structure that requires a union operation on the right side of an embracing (see Section 4.5). Notice that an ONA constraint is satisfied trivially unless F^* and G are both *from some*, since if one correspondence, say F^*, is *from all*, then all instances of B attach to some instance of A, and there are no orphans.

Formal Description of ONA

The orphans-not-allowed constraint may be thought of as a generalization of the *from all* constraint to more than one correspondence. Thus, a correspondence H is said to be *from all* relative to (B, C) if H obeys the constraint

$$(\mathrm{A}x)\ B{:}|x| \Rightarrow (\exists y)\ \dot{H}{:}|x, y|$$

Two correspondence complexes $(H_1; B, C_1)$ and $(H_2; B, C_2)$ obey an orphans-not-allowed constraint if

$$(\mathrm{A}x)\ B{:}|x| \Rightarrow (\exists y_1)\ \dot{H}_1{:}|x, y_1| \lor (\exists y_2)\ \dot{H}_2{:}|x, y_2|$$

And more generally, any hub $\{(H_1; B, C_1), \ldots, (H_n; B, C_n)\}$ obeys an orphans-not-allowed constraint when

$$(\mathrm{A}x)\ B{:}|x| \Rightarrow (\exists y_1)\ \dot{H}_1{:}|x, y_1| \lor \ldots \lor (\exists y_n)\ \dot{H}_n{:}|x, y_n| \qquad (2)$$

This constraint forces each instance of B to have an attachment by at least one of the correspondences $\{\dot{H}_1, \ldots, \dot{H}_n\}$.

The orphans-not-allowed constraint may be declared in extended associative notation using the shorthand shown in Figure 7.13.

Replicates-Not-Allowed

The ONA constraint, which is a generalization of *from some*, has a dual constraint analogous to *from many*. The analogy is found by writing Formula (1) in the expanded form:

$$(\mathrm{A}y_1)\ (\mathrm{A}y_2)\ \Delta B{:}|y_1, y_2| \Rightarrow ((\exists x)\ \dot{F}{:}|x, y_1| \ \&\ \dot{F}{:}|x, y_2|) \lor ((\exists z)\ \dot{G}{:}|y_1, z| \ \&\ \dot{G}{:}|y_2, z|)$$

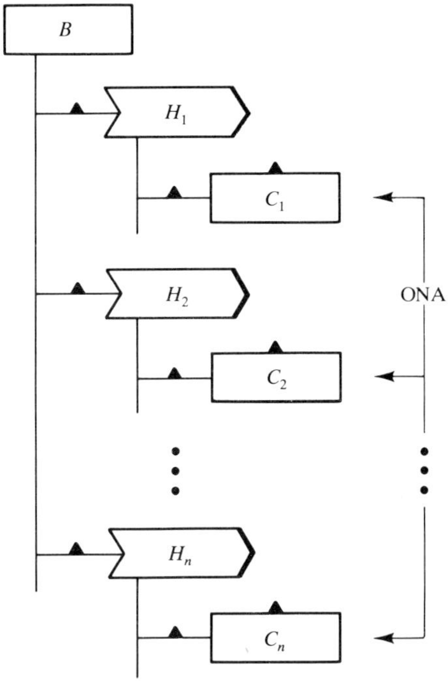

Figure 7.13 Orphans-not-allowed shorthand.

We then reverse the direction of implication and convert the "$\vee$" on the right to "&" to obtain

$$(\mathrm{A}y_1)\ (\mathrm{A}y_2)\ ((\exists x)\ \dot{F}{:}|x, y_1|\ \&\ \dot{F}{:}|x, y_2|)\ \&\ ((\exists z)\ \dot{G}{:}|y_1, z|\ \&\ G{:}|y_2, z|) \Rightarrow \Delta B{:}|y_1, y_2|$$

That is,

$$\boxed{(\dot{F}^* \circ \dot{F}) \cap (\dot{G} \circ \dot{G}^*) \subseteq \Delta B}$$

This embracing says that no two instances of *B* can be attached both to the same instance of *A* and to the same instance of *C*. Notice that it is satisified trivially unless both *F** and *G* are *from many*. It is called a *replicates-not-allowed* constraint, after the similar constraint in the network data model, and is abbreviated "RNA". The terminology stems from picturing the path (*F*, *G*) as a matrix whose rows indicate instances of the class *A*, whose columns indicate instances of the class *C*, and whose cells are filled with all the instances that attach to the instance of *A* in the row and the instance of *C* in the column. For example, the population diagram shown in Figure 7.14 would be shown as the matrix shown in Figure 7.15.

If two or more individuals appear in the same cell of the matrix, each of the individuals in the cell is called a *replicate* relative to the individuals that define the row and the column. Thus b_1 and b_2 are replicates relative to (a_2, c_2), and b_2 and b_3 are replicates relative to (a_3, c_3). The RNA constraint forces there to be no replicates, so that at most one tag appears in any cell. Figure 7.14 therefore does not obey RNA. If b_2 and its attachments are deleted from Figure 7.14, the resulting diagram does obey RNA.

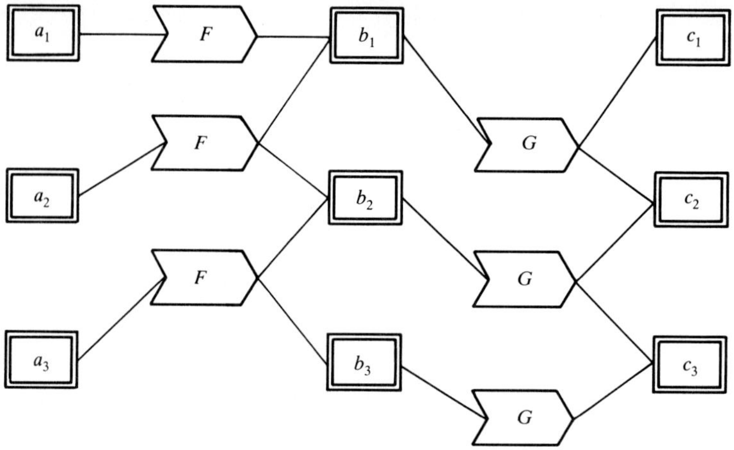

Figure 7.14

	c_1	c_2	c_3
a_1	b_1	b_1	
a_2	b_1	b_1, b_2	b_2
a_3		b_2	b_2, b_3

Figure 7.15 Matrix expression for the population in Figure 7.14.

Notice that because of the unresolved existential quantifier in the definition of composition, an RNA constraint is somewhat stronger than requiring there be at most one tag in any cell. For example, the following population is prohibited by RNA, because either b_1 or b_2 must be a replicate whatever alternative is chosen:

$$\vdash ((F{:}(a_1, b_1) \mathbin{\&} F{:}(a_1, b_2)) \vee (F{:}(a_2, b_1) \mathbin{\&} F{:}(a_2, b_2))) \mathbin{\&} G{:}(b_1, c) \mathbin{\&} G{:}(b_2, c)$$

Yet if no replicates would result from one of the alternatives, the affirmation is permitted. Thus, the following population is permitted by RNA:

$$\vdash ((F{:}(a_1, b_1) \mathbin{\&} F{:}(a_1, b_2)) \vee F{:}(a_2, b_1)) \mathbin{\&} G{:}(b_1, c) \mathbin{\&} G{:}(b_2, c)$$

Formal Description of RNA

Just as the orphans-not-allowed constraint may be considered to be a generalization of a *from all* constraint, so the replicates-not-allowed constraint may be considered to be a generalization of a *from one* constraint. Thus a correspondence H is *from one* relative to (B, C) if it obeys the embracing

$$\dot{H} \circ \dot{H}^* \subseteq \Delta B$$

and two correspondence complexes $(H_1; B, C_1)$ and $(H_2; B, C_2)$ are said to obey a replicates-not-allowed constraint if

$$(\dot{H}_1 \circ \dot{H}_1^*) \cap (\dot{H}_2 \circ \dot{H}_2^*) \subseteq \Delta B$$

More generally, any hub $\{(H_1; B, C_1), \ldots, (H_n; B, C_n)\}$ obeys a replicates-not-allowed constraint if

$$(\dot{H}_1 \circ \dot{H}_1^*) \cap \ldots \cap (\dot{H}_n \circ \dot{H}_n^*) \subseteq \Delta B$$

The RNA constraint may be written in data logic notation using the shorthand

$$\text{RNA } (B; (H_1; C_1), \ldots, (H_n; C_n))$$

or in extended associative notation using the shorthand shown in Figure 7.16.

RNA Constraints Are Used in the Elongation Factoring

RNA constraints occur whenever a concentration is used to elongate or to half-elongate a correspondence complex. Thus, given two recognizers b and c, there is at most one instance $\dot{G}(b, c)$ of the concentration $C^1\dot{G}$ that attaches to *both* b and c. In data logic notation, for any correspondence complex $(G; B, C)$, we have the constraint

$$\text{RNA } (C^1\dot{G}; ({}_{12}\dot{G}_1; B), ({}_{12}\dot{G}_2; C))$$

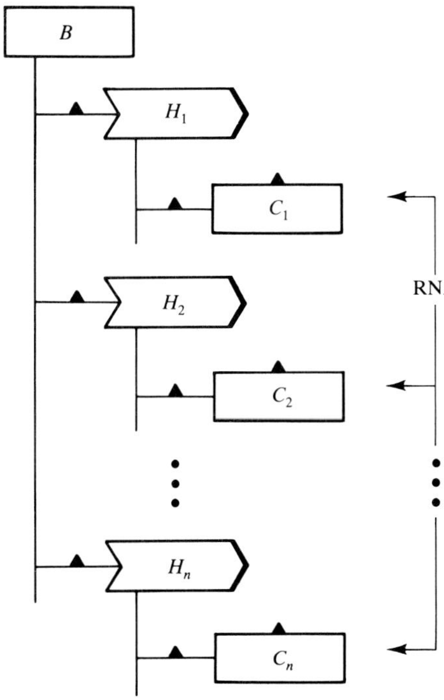

Figure 7.16 Replicates-not-allowed shorthand.

When reinterpreting a concentration using a mantle, designers may choose whether or not to maintain this RNA constraint. Recall, for example, the correspondence *Customer Buys Product* discussed in the last chapter. If a *buying* is reinterpreted as a *Purchase Event*, the question arises whether two *purchase events* can be associated with both the same *customer* and the same *product* (can a *customer* purchase the same *product* more than once?). In many cases, allowing a mantle to have replicates gives a clearer data structure. However, if classes other than B and C correspond to the concentration (as occurs in trios), allowing replicates can change the character of these correspondences.

Conclusion

We have discussed two forms of embracings, *orphans-not-allowed* and *replicates-not-allowed*, that can each relate any number of correspondence complexes gathered into a hub. The replicates-not-allowed constraint is perhaps the more familiar constraint to data base practitioners. Every relation in the relational model, for example, obeys a replicates-not-allowed constraint that forces no two tuples in the relation to be identical.

We have shown that the replicates-not-allowed constraint possesses a dual constraint called *orphans-not-allowed*, which acts on *from some* correspondence complexes gathered into a hub. An *orphans-not-allowed* constraint prohibits an instance from attaching by *none* of a set of correspondences. The orphans-not-allowed constraint is distinctive because it contains alternations on the right side of an embracing. Constraints with alternations on the right side are not recognized by many logical theories of data. We argue, however, that the orphans-not-allowed constraint is a natural generalization of a *mandatory* constraint, and should be accepted as a valid component of data base design.

7.5 ANALYSIS OF CYCLES

Collective Correspondences

A *cycle*, we recall, is a path whose ends are identical. A *loop* is a cycle of length one, that is, a correspondence complex of the form $(L; B, B)$. The composition correspondence of a cycle is a loop.

A correspondence L is said to be *transitive* if $L \circ L \subseteq L$. The simplest example of a transitive correspondence is a correspondence embraced by an identity correspondence. Such a correspondence is called an *anchored loop*. Each attachment of an anchored loop attaches some recognizer to itself. If the composition correspondence of a cycle is embraced in an identity correspondence, we say that the *cycle* is *anchored*.

A correspondence L is *symmetric* if $L^* \equiv L$. A symmetric correspondence has a character that reads the same forwards and backwards, that is, one of the following:

$$\varnothing, \text{“][”}, \text{“><”}, \text{“<>”}, \text{“]><[”}, \text{“]<>[”}$$

A correspondence L is *reflexive* on a class B if $\Delta B \subseteq L$, that is, if L attaches each instance of B to itself.

Correspondences that are reflexive, symmetric, and transitive are called "equivalence relations" in mathematics. All such correspondences are bundlings. We will prefer to call them *collective* correspondences, to avoid confusion with the term *equivalence*, which refers, in data logic, to a bi-directional embracing. Collective correspondences partition a class into disjoint neighborhoods, and attach all recognizers within a neighborhood to each other.

Retroactive Correspondences

A particular variety of symmetric correspondences are *retroactive correspondences*, that is, composition correspondences of the form $G \circ G^*$. A retroactive correspondence is also reflexive on its scope. Thus, consider a reduced correspondence $\Delta B \circ \dot{G} \circ \Delta C \equiv \dot{G}$. If G attaches a recognizer b to some recognizer, then $\dot{G} \circ \dot{G}^*$ attaches b to itself. The class $\pi^1(\dot{G} \circ \dot{G}^*)$ is the class of recognizers that $\dot{G} \circ \dot{G}^*$ attaches some recognizer to. It is embraced by B, so we may define the identity correspondence $\Delta\pi^1(\dot{G} \circ \dot{G}^*)$ by

$$(\mathrm{A}x)\ (\mathrm{A}y)\ \Delta\pi^1(\dot{G} \circ \dot{G}^*){:}|x, y| \Leftrightarrow \Delta B{:}|x, y|\ \&\ (\exists z)\ \dot{G}{:}|x, z|\ \&\ (\exists z')\ \dot{G}{:}|x, z'|$$

Then we have

$$\Delta\pi^1(\dot{G} \circ \dot{G}^*) \subseteq \dot{G} \circ \dot{G}^*$$

The following theorem shows that retroactive correspondences may be treated theoretically without being factored as $G \circ G^*$.

Theorem 7.15. Any reflexive and symmetric loop may be factored as a retroactive correspondence.

Proof. Consider the loop $(L; B, B)$. We assume for simplicity that $L \subseteq B \times B$. Form the half-elongation of L,

$${}_1L_{12} \circ {}_{12}L_2$$

Now consider the loop M on C^1L that attaches any assembly $L(x, y)$ to the assembly $L(y, x)$. Since L is symmetric, M is *all-to-all* and

$${}_{12}L_2 \equiv M \circ {}_{12}L_1$$

So we have

$$L \equiv {}_1L_{12} \circ M \circ {}_{12}L_1$$

We may employ similarly the identity on C^1L (see Section 6.5):

$$L \equiv {}_1L_{12} \circ \Delta(\mathrm{C}^1L) \circ {}_{12}L_1$$

Forming the union of the two expressions,

$$L \equiv {}_1L_{12} \circ (M \cup \Delta(\mathrm{C}^1L)) \circ {}_{12}L_1$$

Now $M \cup \Delta(\mathrm{C}^1L)$ is reflexive because $\Delta\mathrm{C}^1L$ is reflexive. It is symmetric because it is the union of symmetric correspondences. It is also transitive:

$$\begin{aligned}(M \cup \Delta(\mathrm{C}^1L)) \circ (M \cup \Delta(\mathrm{C}^1L))& \\ &\equiv (M \circ M) \cup (M \circ \Delta(\mathrm{C}^1L)) \cup (\Delta(\mathrm{C}^1L) \circ M) \cup (\Delta(\mathrm{C}^1L) \circ \Delta(\mathrm{C}^1L)) \\ &\equiv M \cup \Delta(\mathrm{C}^1L)\end{aligned}$$

Therefore $M \cup \Delta(C^1L)$ is a collective correspondence. It is therefore a bundling, which may be factored as $N \circ N^*$ (see Theorem 6.4). The instances of the intermediate class of the bundling are classes with two instances of the form $L(x, y)$ and $L(y, x)$, or one instance when $\Delta B{:}(x, y)$. Therefore we may write

$$L \equiv ({}_1L_{12} \circ N) \circ (N^* \circ {}_{12}L_1)$$

The right side of this equivalence is a retroactive correspondence. Q.E.D.

Anchored Cycles

Anchored cycles occur frequently in theoretical work. For example, the *from one* constraint $\dot{G} \circ \dot{G}^* \subseteq \Delta B$ is the statement that the cycle $(B; G; C; G^*; B)$ is anchored. We ask more generally what can be said about two correspondences G and H if $G \circ H \subseteq \Delta B$.

Two correspondences I and J that are equivalent relative to $(\pi^1(I \cap J), \pi^2(I \cap J))$ are called *fellows*. Figure 7.17 illustrates two fellow correspondences G and H^*. In this figure, both G and H^* attach b to c_2 and to c_3. G also attaches b to c_1, but since H^* does not attach any individual to c_1, this difference is allowed. Similarly, H^* is allowed to attach b to c_4 because G does not attach any individual to c_4.

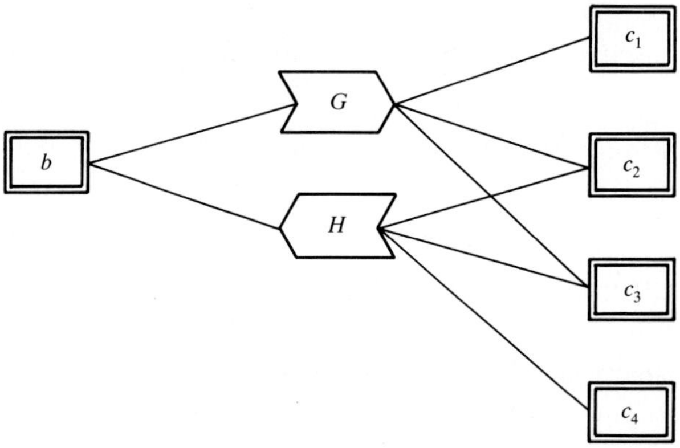

Figure 7.17 G and H^* are fellows.

Theorem 7.16. Let $(\dot{G}; B, C)$ and $(\dot{H}; B, C)$ be two correspondence complexes such that $\dot{G} \circ \dot{H} \subseteq \Delta B$. Then G and H are fellows.

Proof. We have by hypothesis,

$$(\mathrm{A}x)\ (\mathrm{A}z)\ ((\exists y)\ (\exists y')\ B{:}|x|\ \&\ G{:}|x, y|\ \&\ \Delta C{:}|y, y'|\ \&\ H{:}|y', z|\ \&\ B{:}|z|) \Rightarrow \Delta B{:}|x, z|$$

Or equivalently,

$$(\mathrm{A}x)\ (\mathrm{A}y)\ (\mathrm{A}y')\ (\mathrm{A}z)\ B{:}|x|\ \&\ G{:}|x, y|\ \&\ \Delta C{:}|y, y'|\ \&\ H{:}|y', z|\ \&\ B{:}|z| \Rightarrow \Delta B{:}|x, z| \quad (1)$$

Changing $(\mathrm{A}z)$ to $(\exists z)$ and $(\mathrm{A}y)$ to $(\exists y)$, we have

$$(\mathrm{A}x)\ (\mathrm{A}y')\ ((\exists y)\ B{:}|x|\ \&\ G{:}|x, y|\ \&\ \Delta C{:}|y, y'|\ \&\ (\exists z)\ H{:}|y', z|\ \&\ B{:}|z|) \Rightarrow (\exists z')\ \Delta B{:}|x, z'|\ \&\ H{:}|y', z'|\ \&\ C{:}|y'|$$

That is, in embracing notation,

$$\dot{G} \circ \Delta\pi^2\dot{H}^* \subseteq \dot{H}^*$$

Composing with $\Delta\pi^2\dot{G}$ on the right yields

$$\dot{G} \circ \Delta\pi^2\dot{H}^* \circ \Delta\pi^2\dot{G} \subseteq \dot{H}^* \circ \Delta\pi^2\dot{G}$$

It is easily seen that $\Delta\pi^2\dot{H}^* \circ \Delta\pi^2\dot{G} \equiv \Delta\pi^2(\dot{G} \cap \dot{H}^*)$. Further, $\dot{H}^* \equiv \dot{H}^* \circ \Delta\pi^2\dot{H}^*$. We may write, therefore,

$$\dot{G} \circ \Delta\pi^2(\dot{G} \cap \dot{H}^*) \subseteq \dot{H}^* \circ \Delta\pi^2(\dot{G} \cap \dot{H}^*) \tag{2}$$

Changing (Ax) to ($\exists x$) and (Ay') to ($\exists y'$) in Formula (1) yields

$$(\mathrm{A}y)\ (\mathrm{A}z)\ ((\exists y')\ (\exists x)\ B{:}|x|\ \&\ G{:}|x, y|\ \&\ \Delta C{:}|y, y'|\ \&\ H{:}|y', z|\ \&\ B{:}|z|)$$
$$\Rightarrow (\exists x')\ \Delta B{:}|x', z|\ \&\ G{:}|x', y|\ \&\ C{:}|y|$$

That is, in embracing notation,

$$\Delta\pi^2\dot{G} \circ \dot{H} \subseteq \dot{G}^*$$

Forming the converse and composing with $\Delta\pi^2\dot{H}^*$ on the right yields:

$$\dot{H}^* \circ \Delta\pi^2(\dot{G} \cap \dot{H}^*) \subseteq \dot{G} \circ \Delta\pi^2(\dot{G} \cap \dot{H}^*) \tag{3}$$

Combining Formulas (2) and (3) shows that $\dot{G}$ and $\dot{H}^*$ are fellows. Q.E.D.

Powers of Loops

Loops may be composed with themselves to yield new loops. For any loop L, we may form the chain of embracings

$$L \cap \Delta(\pi^1 L) \subseteq L \subseteq (L \circ L) \cup L \subseteq (L \circ L \circ L) \cup (L \circ L) \cup L \subseteq \ldots$$

This is called the *power chain* of L. It may continue arbitrarily far unless constrained by embracings, but in any given finite population it will eventually appear to terminate. Notice that the power chain of a retroactive correspondence $G \circ G^*$ is the zigzag chain of G.

We may define the final correspondence in this chain recursively. It is called the *transitive closure* of L and is written $\uparrow L$:

$$L \subseteq \uparrow L$$

$$L \circ \uparrow L \subseteq \uparrow L$$

$$(\mathrm{A}X)\ ((L \circ X) \subseteq X) \Rightarrow (\uparrow L \subseteq X)$$

Notice that $\uparrow L$ is transitive, but not always symmetric. For example, the transitive closure of the correspondence (x) *Is One Greater Than* (y) relative to the integers attaches a number x to all numbers greater than x, whereas its converse attaches x to all numbers less than x.

The immediate neighborhoods by $\uparrow L$ are disjoint, since $\uparrow L$ is a bundling. They are called the *ultimate neighborhoods* by L (or by G if L is $G \circ G^*$), and attach individuals that may be reached by a path of any length through a population of L.

Conclusion

We have shown how mathematical equivalence relations (collective correspondences) may be defined by embracings. We have discussed how retroactive correspondences, which are present in all character constraints, are allied to more general properties of loops. We have also shown how a transitive closure, which can not be defined in relational algebra, can be defined in data logic.

7.6 CASE STUDY: REPRESENTATION OF TIME

Method of Representing Time

We discuss one way in this section that time can be represented in data bases. We consider in particular concepts of time such as the classes « date of last hire », « time withdrawn from inventory », « effective time of financial transaction », and the like. We argue that all these concepts of time can be viewed as subclasses of a single class *Moment*. This approach allows time management programs to be written using the single class *Moment*, which then (as with object–oriented programming) will automatically apply to all concepts of time in the data base. We refer to concepts of time as *logical time*, which we oppose to the physical phenomena measured by clocks, which we call *physical time*.

We disagree with writers who would assign time a special role in logic, some even altering the axioms to include time (Prior 1967, Freeman and Sellars 1971). Logical time should be represented just as other images are, by symbols that are independent of the images they represent. There is nothing innate about the text ''Friday'' that requires that it represent a day of the week, for example. We call this independence of the tags used to represent time from the images of time the *principle of timeless representation*. By the principle of timeless representation, a program that accesses the class tag *Moment* will continue to function reliably if *Moment* is reinterpreted as representing something other than time, provided, of course, that the constraints on *Moment* are left unchanged.

Physical time affects data bases because they exist in time. In particular, changes to the population (updates, deletions, etc.) take time, which links physical time with the administration of the data base. The effects of physical time on the population are therefore primarily operational, and generally fall within the province of design and operation of data management devices rather than the province of data design. We do not discuss physical time in depth, although we do show how embracings may be applied to disable additions or deletions to populations. For a discussion of the considerable problems raised in understanding physical time, see (Hawking 1988).

Definition of a Moment

We consider first the units of logical time. We can readily conceive of a particular day in the past or the future: « January 28, 1953 » or « January 28, 2053 ». Either of these periods of logical time will be called a *moment*. Notice that we can not consider a *moment* in the future to be part of *physical time*, because it is demonstrably not part of the physical world that we can detect. We would even have some difficulty in concluding that a *moment* in the past was part of physical time, because it too is not directly observable in the present. However, we have no difficulty *conceiving* a *moment* in the past or the future, therefore, such *moments* are part of logical time.

A « *moment* » can be any stretch of time: an hour, a day, a month, but it is a particular stretch of time such as « January 28, 1953 » not a recurring label like « January » that is different every year. We might ask what the smallest duration of a *moment* could be: thus, we can imagine a second, or a tenth of a second, or, using other mnemonic devices, we could even imagine a nanosecond as roughly the time it takes light to travel one foot.

Yet, however small a duration we might imagine, we are not justified in concluding that we can imagine an *infinitesimal* duration of time. The difficulty is the same as we discussed in the foundations of calculus: even if we were to believe that, given a *moment* of duration t, we could imagine a *moment* of duration $t/2$, we can not conclude that we can imagine a moment of infinitesimal duration, because carrying the divisions by two to an infinite extent would require an infinite amount of *physical time*, and we live within the bounds of a finite amount of physical time.

Thus, there are always a finite number of instances of *Moment*, and each *moment* has a nonzero duration. These same comments apply to physical time as well: we can not measure a moment of infinitesimal duration because every measuring instrument contains some nonzero amount of error. No moment that has a smaller duration than our finest measuring instruments can be detected. A physical moment must also always have a *rational* duration by the same reasoning: error must always result after only a small number of decimal places (approximately fifteen decimal places in even the best known physical constants), and so we can never detect an irrational duration.

We would also be on shaky ground were we to insist that a *moment*, even in logical time, be uninterrupted. For example, if « January 28, 1953 » is a valid *moment*, why should « January 28, 1953, except for the times when the power was down » not also be a valid *moment*? We can, of course, break the latter *moment* into smaller disjoint intervals if we wish, but we can not be certain that the constituent *moments* are continuous stretches of time, because we could always imagine that interruptions occur in the *moments* of least duration that we have imagined. Thus, the ''continuity'' of logical time can not be proved, but must be an added supposition. We will prefer not to assume that logical time is continuous, and we will therefore accept *moments* that contain interruptions.

Representation of Time Using Moments

We will represent logical time using a class tag ''*Moment*''. The instances of the class tag ''*Moment*'' are individuals called *moment tags*. A moment tag represents an image of time called a *moment*. We will say that an *event occurs during* a *moment*. Notice that we use the word ''event'' to mean an activity that takes place over a stretch of time, while theories of Physics often assume that an event occurs at an infinitesimal ''point'' in time. Generally, we will represent actions that occur in time by representing the action by some tag that includes the word ''event'', and associating this tag with the class tag ''*Moment*'' through the correspondence tag ''*Occurs During*''.

For example, Figure 7.18 shows the *moment* that an employee is hired using the class *Hiring Event*. This method allows a history of past hires of the employee to be kept along with the most recent hiring (imagine that the employee left the company and later returned). It also allows parameters specific to each hiring event to be kept (for example, whether a personnel service firm was involved, and the amount of commission paid).

An activity of interest could occur many times during a *moment*. For example, the claim « Red the rooster crowed on January 28, 1953 » does not imply that Red crowed only once, merely that Red crowed at least once. It is good discipline to establish a new event tag for each occasion that an activity of interest happens. We could then have several events of Red crowing, all during the same *moment* « January 28, 1953 ».

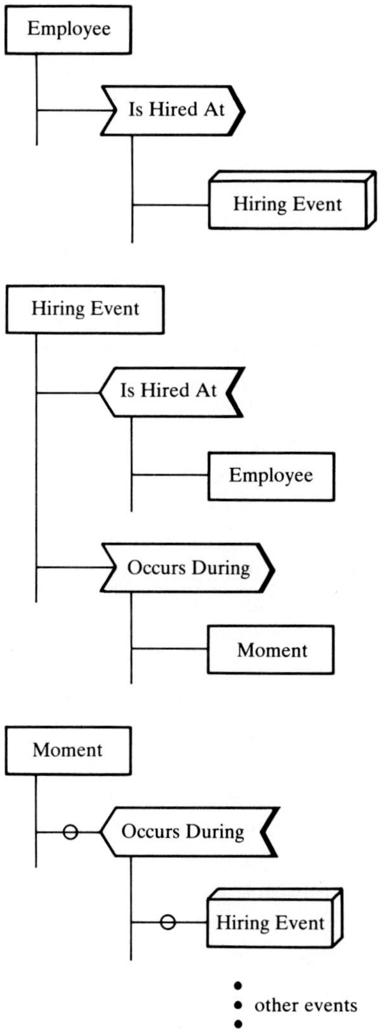

Figure 7.18

Moments Have a Characteristic Structure

Moments may be constructed from other *moments*. For example, we may define a *moment* *u* by saying that all events that occur during the *moment s* or during the *moment t* occur during the *moment u*. For example, *s* could be 9 to 10 AM some particular day, *t* could be 10 to 11 AM the same day, and *u* would then be 9 to 11 AM that day. Of course, there is no requirement that *s* and *t* be contiguous. We model this process using a correspondence *Is The Union Of*, as shown in Figure 7.19.

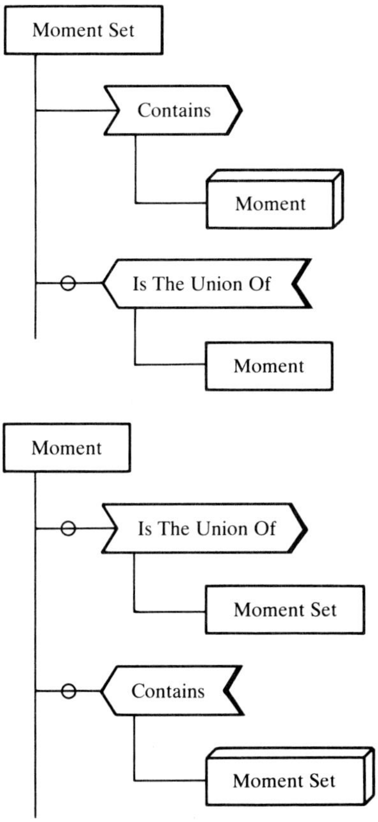

Figure 7.19

Here a « *moment set* » is a set of « *moments* ». If the members of a « *moment set* » change, it is a new « *moment set* ». The destination of *Is The Union Of* is *Moment Set* rather than *Moment* because the proper interpretation of ''*u* is the union of *s* and *t*'' is not « *u* is the union of *s* » and « *u* is the union of *t* », as it would be if we viewed « *Is The Union Of* » as associating *moments* with *moments*. Rather, the proper interpretation is « *u* is the union of {*s*, *t*} ».

The character decisions shown in Figure 7.19 are justified as follows: We have no need in this case study for empty *moment sets*, so *Contains* is *from all*. There may or may not be a *moment* that is the union of all the *moments* in a *moment set* (that is, we accommodate definitions of « *Moment* » that do not incorporate all such unions), so the correspondence *Is The Union Of* is *to some*. Similarly, there may or may not be a *moment set* that each *moment* would be a union of, so *Is The Union Of* is *from some*. Not every *moment* needs to be contained in a *moment set*, so *Contains* is *to some*.

We may define the *intersection* of *moments* similarly. For example, the intersection of the *moments* « 9 to 11 AM January 28, 1953 » and « 10 to 12 AM January 28, 1953 » is the *moment* « 10 to 11 AM January 28, 1953 ». This data structure is shown in Figure 7.20. A given *moment set* is therefore potentially associated with two *moments*: both the union of the *moments* in the set and the intersection of the *moments* in the set.

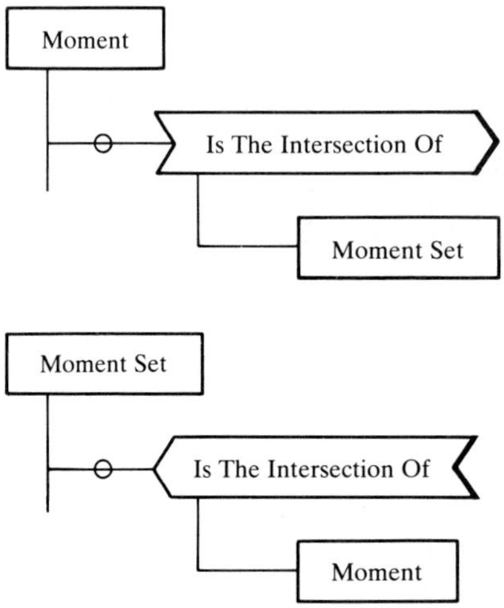

Figure 7.20

If all the logical time occupied by a *moment* « *s* » is also occupied by a *moment* « *t* », we say that *t covers s*. For example,

(1953) *Covers*: (January, 1953)
(January, 1953) *Covers*: (January 28, 1953)

Only a *moment* may *cover* an image, and the only images that may be *covered* are *moments*. These embracings are shown in Figure 7.21.

Each *moment covers* itself, one *moment* may *cover* many *moments*, and many *moments* may *cover* any one *moment*. These embracings are shown in Figure 7.22.

If a *moment t covers* a *moment s* and a *moment u covers t*, then *u covers s*. This embracing is shown in Figure 7.23. This embracing does not say that the attachment (*u*) *Covers*: (*s*) must be physically stored. One would probably implement this correspondence by storing only ⊦ (*t*) *Covers*: (*s*) and ⊦ (*u*) *Covers*: (*t*). The embracing indicates the need to perform a transitive closure operation on the claimed attachments of *Covers* when answering queries.

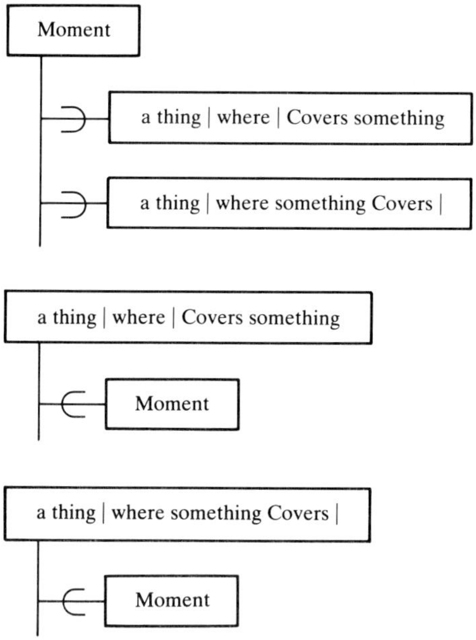

Figure 7.21

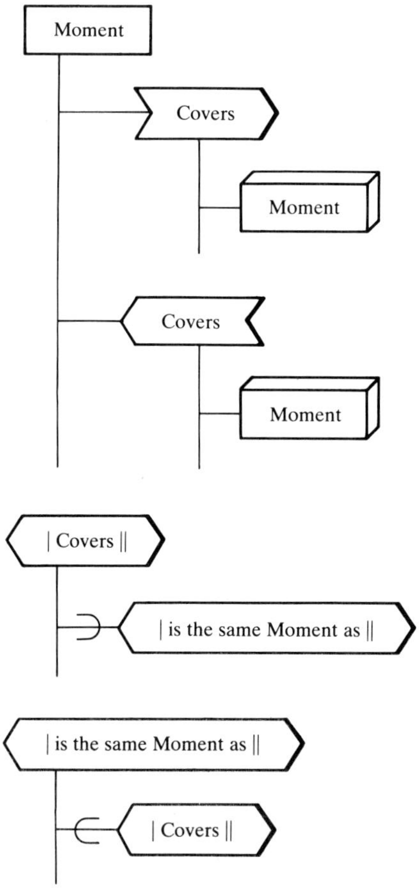

Figure 7.22

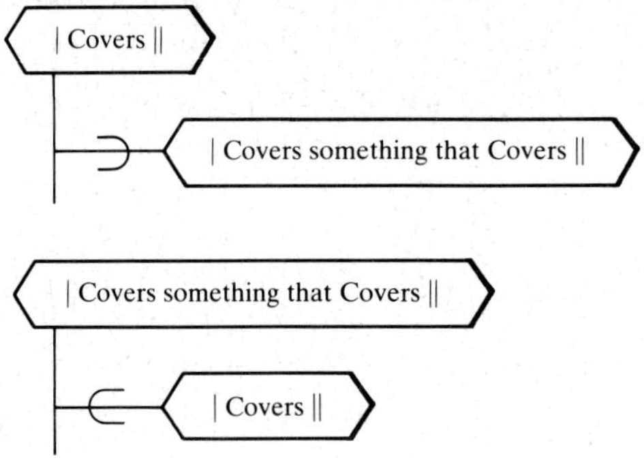

Figure 7.23

Two *moments* may *cover* each other and still be different. For example, « 1:00 PM in New York » and « 10:00 AM in Los Angeles » *cover* each other but are different images. At the first *moment*, for example, the sun is midway up from the horizon, and at the second moment it is overhead. If we were to treat the two *moments* as equivalent, then all images associated with either *moment* would be associated with both, so we would be forced to associate both positions of the sun with both *moments*. There are any number of similar differences between the two *moments*—the numbers 9 and 12, the places New York and Los Angeles, and so on—that serve to distinguish them. Indeed, the only thing similar about the two *moments* is that each *covers* the other.

If *t* is a member of a *moment set s* and *u* is the union of *s*, then *u covers t*. If *t* is a member of a *moment set s* and *v* is the intersection of *s*, then *t covers v*. These embracings are shown in Figure 7.24.

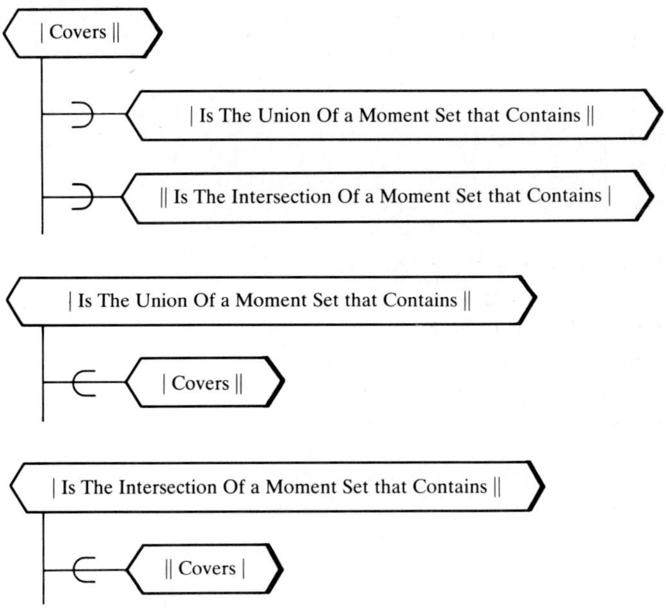

Figure 7.24

The Progression of Time

We say that a *moment s is later than* a *moment t* if all the logical time occupied by *s* is later than all the logical time occupied by *t*. For example, « 1:00 PM to 2:00 PM January 28, 1953 » *is later than* « 10:00 AM to 11:00 AM January 28, 1953 », but neither *moment is later than* « 10:30 AM to 1:30 PM January 28, 1953 ».

Clearly a *moment t* may be *later than* many *moments* and many *moments* may be *later than t*. The latest *moment* on record will have no *moments* that are *later* and the earliest *moment* on record will have no *moments* that it *is later than*. This data structure is shown in Figure 7.25.

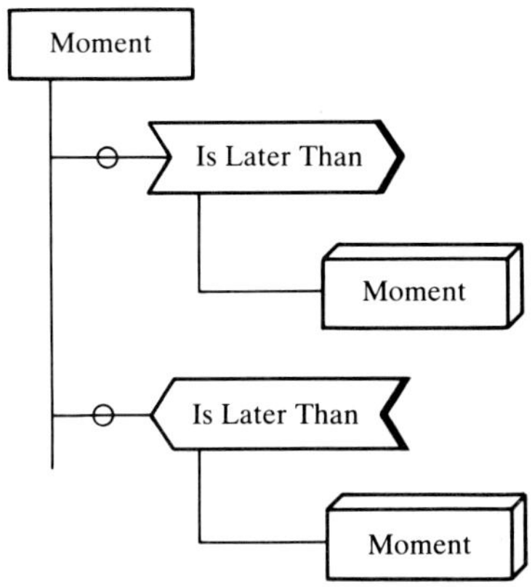

Figure 7.25

Only a *moment* may be *later than* something. If an image *b is later than* a *moment*, then *b* is a *moment*. If a *moment u is later than* a *moment t*, and *t is later than* a *moment s*, then *u is later than s*. If a *moment s covers* a *moment t*, and a *moment u is later than s*, then *u is later than t*. These embracings are shown in Figure 7.26.

Temporal Indices

We have not considered yet the tags normally used to describe *moments*, such as "Monday", "10:00 AM", and the like. The image « Monday » is not a *moment*, because it describes periods of time indefinitely far into the past and into the future. It is better to consider « Monday » to be a *temporal index* that may be associated with moments. We may consider other images that recur periodically, such as « 10:00 », « AM », and « January », to be temporal indices as well. The relationship between *moments* and *temporal indices* is shown in Figure 7.27.

Temporal indices are frequently attached in a circle, as in a clock face, that turns in a specified direction as time progresses. We may indicate these circles by a correspondence *Follows*, as shown in Figure 7.28. For example, "Sunday" *follows* "Saturday", but "Sunday" is not *later than* "Saturday", because Saturday is preceded by the Sunday of a prior week. Clearly, we could develop far more intricate structures for temporal indices, but to do so would take us away from the nature of logical time into the ways we choose to represent it.

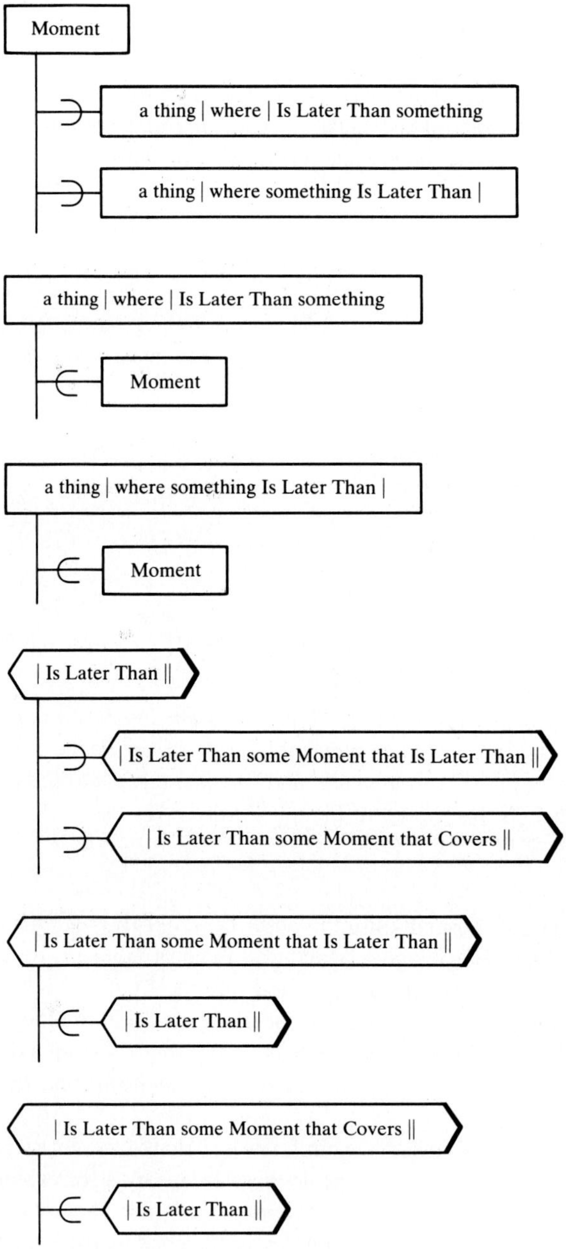
Moment
a thing | where | Is Later Than something
a thing | where something Is Later Than |
a thing | where | Is Later Than something
Moment
a thing | where something Is Later Than |
Moment
Is Later Than	
Is Later Than some Moment that Is Later Than	
Is Later Than some Moment that Covers	
Is Later Than some Moment that Is Later Than	
Is Later Than	
Is Later Than some Moment that Covers	
Is Later Than	

Figure 7.26

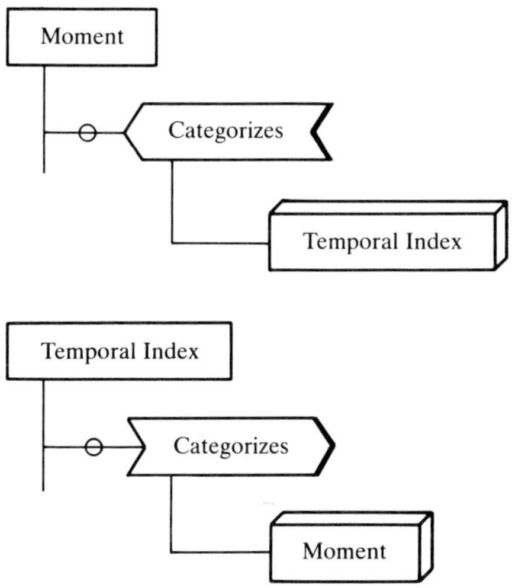

Figure 7.27

It is frequently useful to employ a subclass *Y* of the class *Moment* such that for any instances *s* and *t* of *Y*, either (*s*) *is later than* (*t*), (*t*) *is later than* (*s*), or *s* and *t cover* each other. The class of years is an example. Such a subclass is called a *rectified subclass* of logical time, and obeys the embracings shown in Figure 7.29. Notice the introduction of a new tag *Coincides With* to decompose the embracing into modules.

A class of moments is said to *jointly cover* logical time if its instances, taken together, cover all the moments. Such a class obeys the embracing shown in Figure 7.30.

A rectified subclass need not *jointly cover* logical time. For example, the class of every hour from 8:00 AM to 6:00 PM on every weekday is rectified but might not *jointly cover* logical time, because *moments* from 6:00 PM to 8:00 AM on weekdays and *moments* on the weekend are not *covered*. If *moments* are permitted that occur during the latter periods, then the class does not *jointly cover* logical time. On the other hand, it may be that logical time does not exist for the data base other than during business hours. In that case, the class would *jointly cover* logical time.

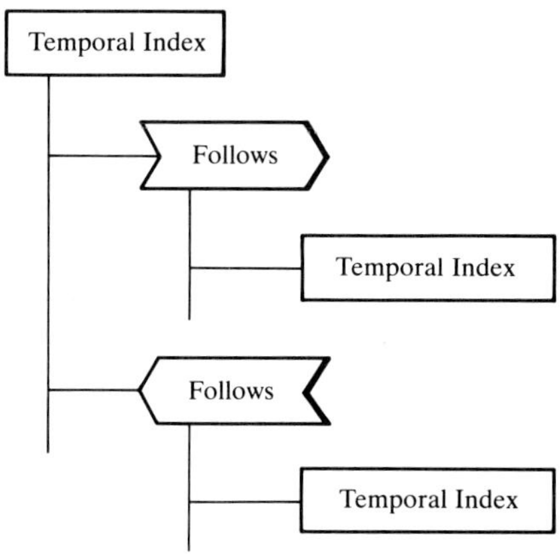

Figure 7.28

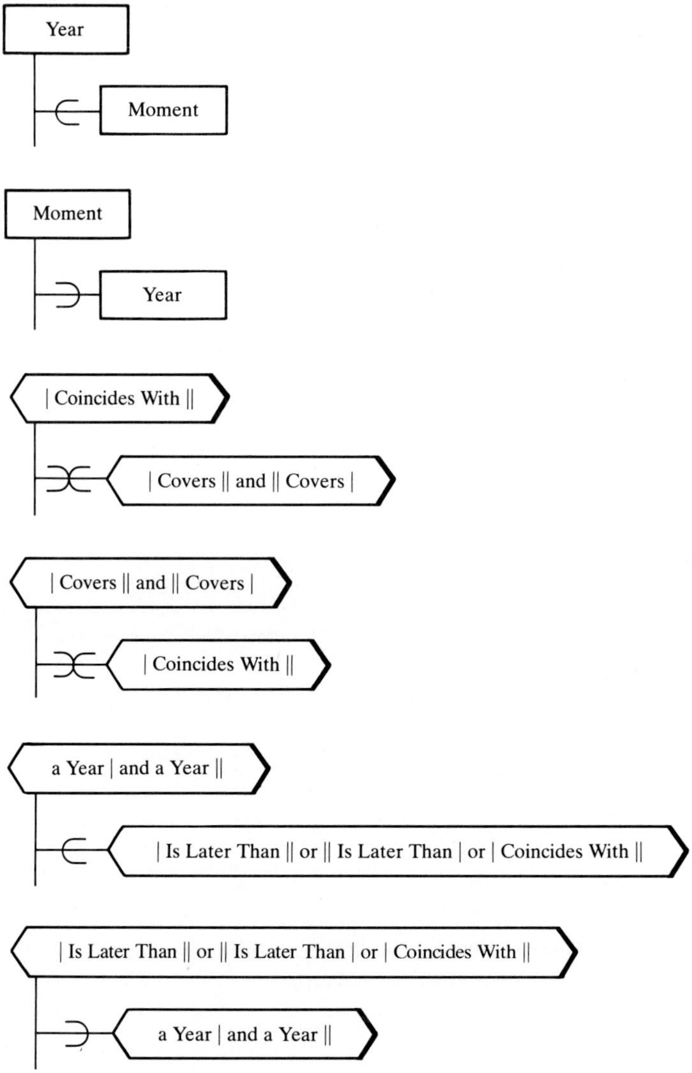

Figure 7.29

Dimensions of Time

Associations of a class with time can involve attaching one instance to several different moment tags within the same association. Consider for example the table of census data shown in Figure 7.31. By way of explanation, a census of the United States is taken every decade. The population is also estimated in certain intervening years. At various times, geographical boundaries of large metropolitan areas are delineated and the areas they enclose are called MSA's or ''metropolitan statistical areas.'' Thus, there is a New York

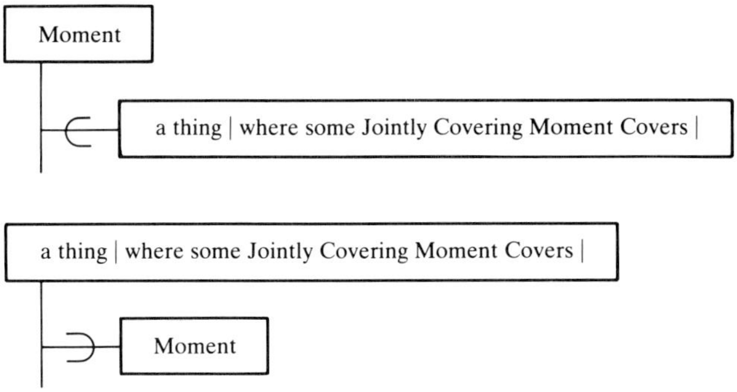

Figure 7.30

MSA, a Los Angeles MSA, and so on. As the distribution of population changes, so do the boundaries of the MSA's. New MSA's may be added as settlements grow to reach metropolitan stature, and old MSA's may be deleted in regions of shrinking population.

In this environment, the deceptively simple question « how has the number of people living in MSA's changed over the years? » is open to several interpretations. One interpretation is « how has the number of people living in the MSA's as defined in 1987 changed? ». The answer to this question is given by the last row of the table, which shows the number of people during the years 1950 to 1986 that were living in the MSA's as defined in 1987, although this includes people during 1950 to 1980 that lived in areas that were not then considered to be metropolitan. A second interpretation is « how did the number of people who lived in MSA's in 1986 change using the different definitions of MSA's during the period 1950 to 1987? » The answer to this question is given by the last column of the table. Notice that the dates when MSA's were defined are different from the dates when the censuses were taken, and are not at ten year intervals.

MSA DEFINITION AS OF—	Number of MSA's	POPULATION				
		1950, Apr. 1	**1960,** Apr. 1	**1970,** Apr. 1	**1980,** Apr. 1	**1986,** July 1
1950 census (Mar. 1952)	169	[1] 84,853,700	106,344,548	122,184,836	128,839,422	135,796,592
1960 census (Nov. 1960)	212	89,316,903	[2] 112,885,139	130,982,661	140,793,427	149,625,595
1964 (Aug. 31) [3]	217	91,644,188	115,876,343	134,700,911	145,503,863	154,902,292
1968 (Jan. 31) [4]	230	93,629,986	118,413,604	137,976,252	149,811,057	159,630,008
1970 census (Feb. 28, 1971)	243	94,579,008	[5] 119,593,498	[6] 139,479,806	151,662,221	161,682,222
1974 (Apr. 30) [7]	265	[8] 100,219,707	[9] 126,613,710	148,198,993	162,753,335	173,621,663
1977 (Dec. 31) [10]	277	101,109,145	127,674,818	149,482,664	164,383,496	175,929,540
1980 census (June 30, 1981)	318	104,172,853	131,318,714	153,693,767	169,430,623	181,188,438
1983 (June 30)	[11] 275	105,214,181	132,633,988	155,410,542	171,776,970	184,020,380
1984 (Oct. 12)	[11] 277	105,269,298	132,707,748	155,519,340	171,955,900	184,265,568
1985 (June 30)	[11] 280	105,411,141	132,886,747	155,700,823	[12] 172,169,456	184,494,926
1986 (June 30)	[11] 281	105,480,924	132,977,193	155,805,452	172,304,016	184,658,470
1987 (June 30)	[11] 281	105,502,622	133,003,058	155,832,688	172,334,547	184,689,318

Figure 7.31 From *Statistical Abstract of the United States,* 1988 ed., p. 873.

With a little imagination, other interpretations can be thought of that involve diagonals of the table, or average values of rows and columns, and so on. Clearly the question, so innocently phrased, is not sufficiently precise to permit a direct answer. The reason is that the underlying data is not a trio

« the population of MSA ① during the year ② is ③ »

but a quartet

« the portion of the population of the United States as counted in the year ① that resides in MSA ② as defined in the year ③ is ④ »

This example shows two things — the dangers of attempting to deduce a data structure by an uncritical examination of potential queries, and the ability for time to appear more than once in an association under different guises.

When moments appear twice in an association, we will say that the association contains multiple *dimensions* of time. We use the word *dimension* because the projection of the association onto moments is usually a Cartesian product. Thus, Figure 7.31 is a matrix with moment tags defining both the rows and the columns and every cell filled.

Sometimes there are embedded rules for the interrelationships between times. For example, the date an item is delivered may need to follow the date the item is requested. Such rules should be viewed very carefully before including them in a design, because omitting them can often provide a more accurate picture of events than including them will. For example, if the rule above is followed, a clerk may be forced to fabricate a request for an unexpected free promotional shipment, and to predate the request simply because of a system constraint.

Master Time

In certain applications, data may be entered into a data base about the physical time when data management actions occur. For example, imagine that a data base management system is structured so that every claim is associated with a time stamp of when it is added to the population. Each such time stamp is said to be a *master clock tick*, and the class of master clock ticks is called *master time*.

Now imagine that a history of alterations to the data base is established, so that each claim is associated with the *master clock tick* at which time it is deleted, as well as the *master clock tick* at which time it is added. Since the data base is assumed not to change unless it is acted on, the data base population changes discretely.

We may model this situation by writing that each claim is attached to all *master clock ticks* during which the claim is established (that is, not just the endpoints but the intervening clock ticks as well). This correspondence is shown in Figure 7.32. Reversing the correspondence, we can see for any *master clock tick* t what the population of the data base was during t.

Two *master clock ticks* s and t can be related so that one is *administratively later* than the other (the word *administratively* is used to indicate that the determination is at the discretion of the master engines). The correspondence *Is Administratively Later Than* is shown in Figure 7.33.

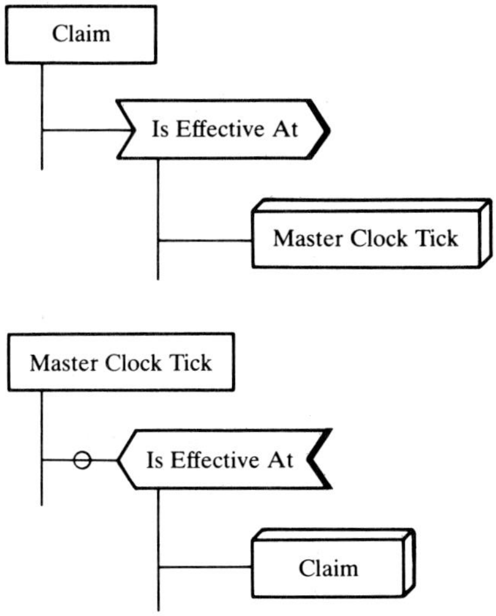

Figure 7.32

Embracings may employ master time to limit updates to associations. For example, let the instances of the special class *Addition Disabled* be handles of classes for which new instances are to be prevented. Let the trio ( ) *Is An Instance Of* ( ) *At* ( ) establish the master clock ticks when an individual is an instance of a class. Now consider the embracing

$$(\mathrm{A}w)\ (\mathrm{A}x)\ (\mathrm{A}z)\ ((\exists y)\ |w|\ \textit{Is An Instance Of}\text{: } |x|\ \textit{At}\ |y|\ \&$$

$$\textit{Addition Disabled}\text{: } |x|\ \&\ |y|\ \textit{Is Administratively Later Than}\text{: } |z|)$$

$$\Rightarrow |w|\ \textit{Is An Instance Of}\text{: } |x|\ \textit{At}\ |z|$$

This embracing says that for any class *B* for which addition is disabled, the population of *B* at any *master clock tick t* must embrace the population of *B* at all *master clock ticks administratively later than t*. That is, it is forbidden to add an instance of *B*.

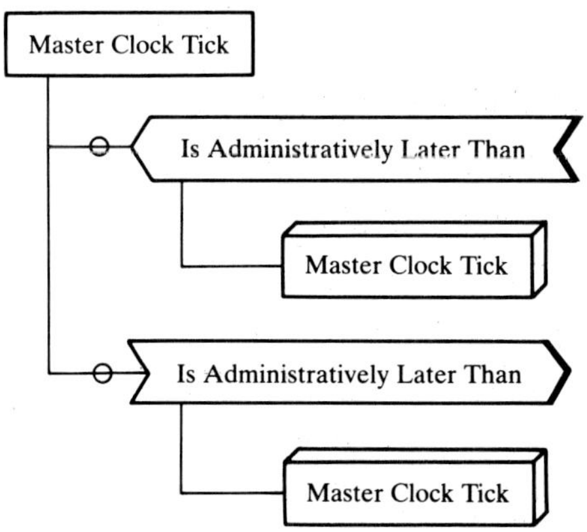

Figure 7.33

The similar embracing

$$(\mathrm{A}w)\ (\mathrm{A}x)\ (\mathrm{A}y)\ ((\exists z)\ |w|\ \textit{Is An Instance Of}{:}\ |x|\ \textit{At}\ |z|\ \&$$

$$\textit{Deletion Disabled}{:}\ |x|\ \&\ |y|\ \textit{Is Administratively Later Than}{:}\ |z|)$$

$$\Rightarrow |w|\ \textit{Is An Instance Of}{:}\ |x|\ \textit{At}\ |y|$$

says that the population of *B* at *t* must embrace the population of *B* at all *master clock ticks* before t. That is, it is forbidden to delete an instance of *B*.

Of course "never add" and "never delete" are implemented more easily by flags that can be read by the master engines to inhibit updates, but our discussion shows that such operations are consistent with, and are even predicted by, the theory of embracings.

The complete extended associative notation for our study of time is presented in Figure 7.34. Embracings of combinations are shown only once (that is, they are not reversed) to conserve space.

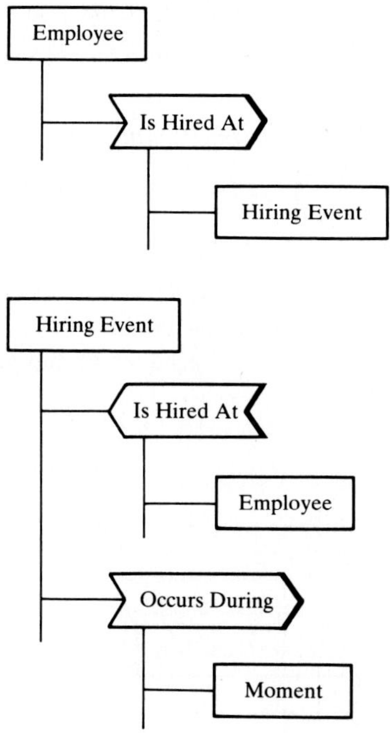

Figure 7.34

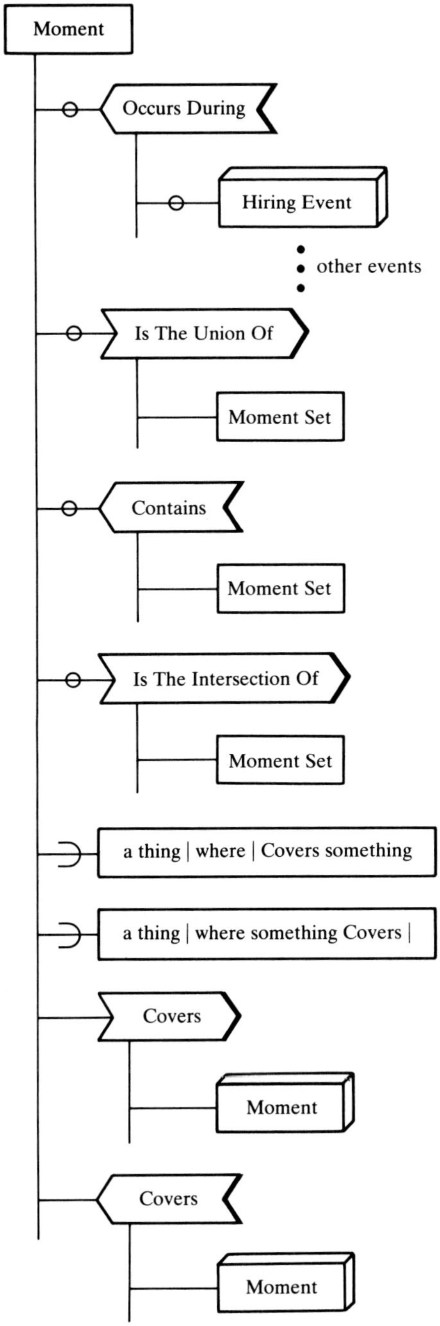

Figure 7.34 *(continued)*

Moment (*continued*)

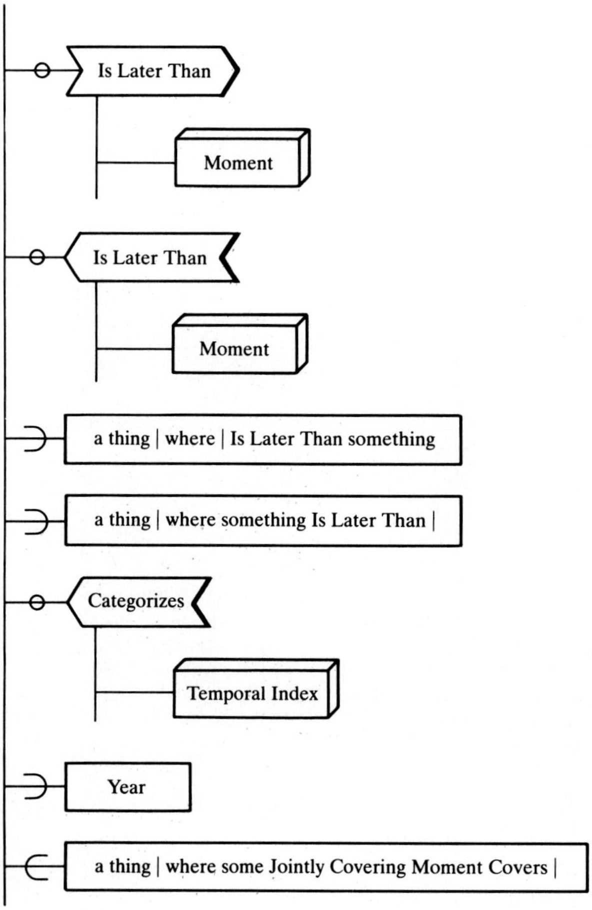

Figure 7.34 (*continued*)

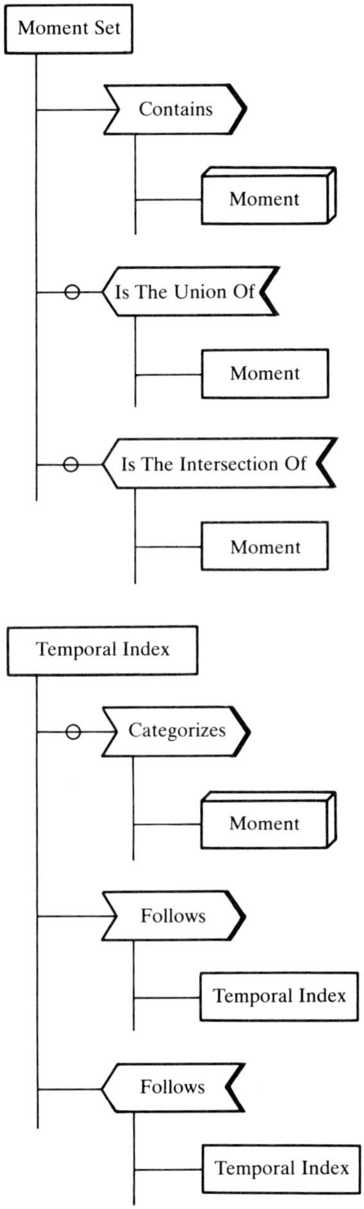

Figure 7.34 *(continued)*

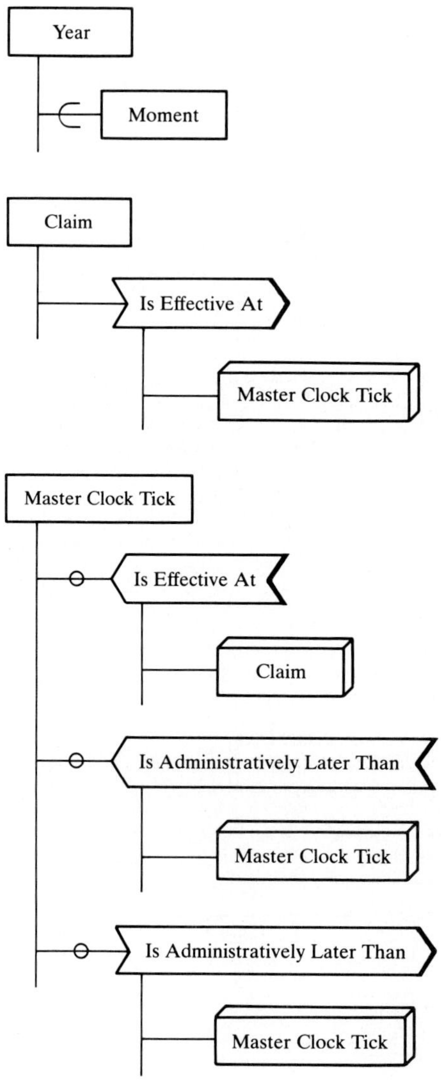

Figure 7.34 *(continued)*

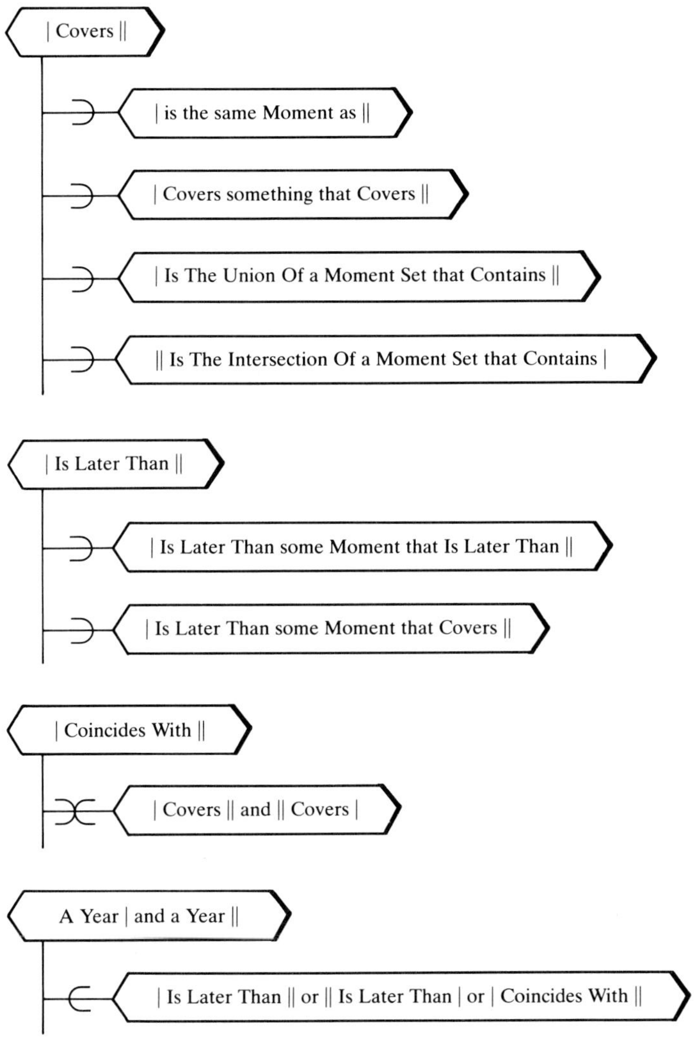

Figure 7.34 *(continued)*

8

Composition Cones

8.1 INTRODUCTION

In this chapter, we investigate binary paths whose composition correspondences are constrained by an embracing. Earlier studies of data have usually supposed that the properties of a composition of two correspondences can be determined from the properties of each correspondence in isolation. Many data models advocate eliminating a correspondence from a data design if it is equivalent to the composition of two correspondences (such a correspondence is said to obey a "transitive dependency"). We show that there are many situations where the composition obeys constraints that can not be predicted from the characters of the constituent correspondences, and so the character of the composition correspondence must be declared separately.

For example, Figure 8.1 illustrates the composition of a *many-to-many all-to-some* correspondence with a *many-to-many some-to-all* correspondence to yield a *one-to-one all-to-all* correspondence. So long as constraints are limited to characters, Figure 8.1 illustrates a temporary coincidence not a new data structure. For example, if F and G are not constrained further, one could attach a_2 to b_4 by F in Figure 8.1, making the composition *many-to-many*. However, with embracings, it is possible to constrain the composition $\dot{F} \circ \dot{G}$ to be *one-to-one all-to-all*. If this constraint is added to the schema, no updates to F will be permitted that would violate the character of $\dot{F} \circ \dot{G}$.

Data structures such as that shown in Figure 8.1 have typically been handled in the past by redesign using different correspondences. The usual method is to declare the composition correspondence $F \circ G$ as a correspondence H, and then to try to deduce F from G and H, or G from F and H. However, these methods will not work for Figure 8.1. Thus, the composition correspondence H has the population shown in Figure 8.2. As can be seen by inspection, F attaches a_1 to both b_1 and b_2, but $H \circ G^*$ attaches a_1 to only b_1. Thus, F is not equivalent to $H \circ G^*$. Further, G leaves b_2 orphan, but $F^* \circ H$ attaches b_2 to c_1. Thus, G is not equivalent to $F^* \circ H$. If all three correspondences F, G, and H are declared, then the constraint $F \circ G \equiv H$ must be declared to force each attachment of H to be reflected properly in attachments of F and G. Thus, the data structure illustrated in Figure 8.1 can only be specified using embracings.

A data base management system that implements embracings would need to check proposed updates both against the character of a constituent correspondence and against the composition character. For example, if a user wanted to add an attachment $F(a, b)$ to the population of F, the data base management system would need to verify that the resulting attachment did not violate the character of $F \circ G$. This would entail, at most, extracting all the attachments of the form $G(b, c_i)$ in the existing population of G and systematically testing whether all the attachments $F \circ G(a, c_i)$ could be added. That is, the system would verify that a remains attached to only one C if $F \circ G$ is *to one*, and that each c_i remains attached only to a if $F \circ G$ is *from one*.

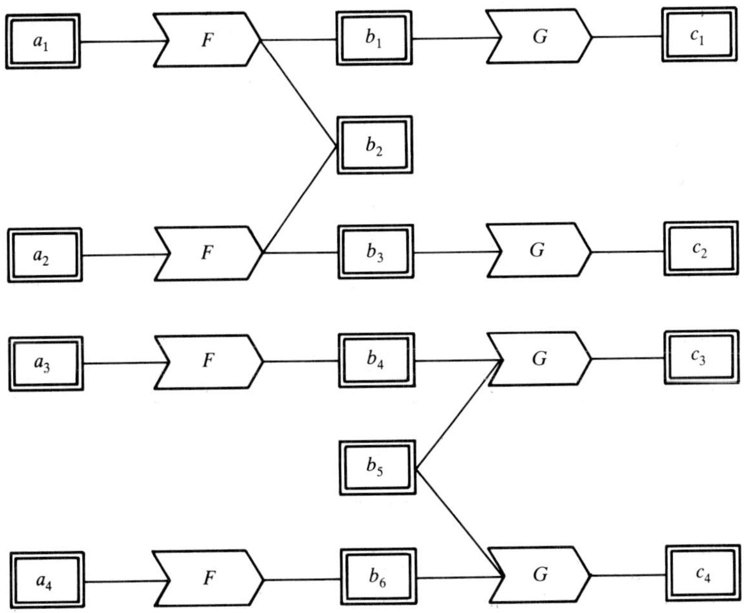

Figure 8.1 “<>[” composes with “]<>” to form ∅.

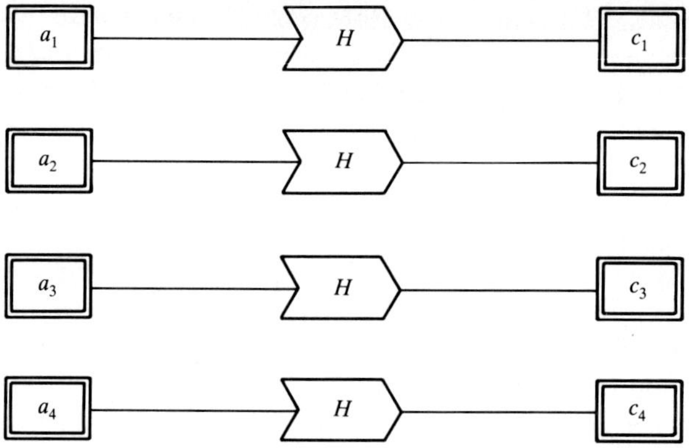

Figure 8.2 The composition of F with G from Figure 8.1.

Deletion is somewhat more complex, because deletions can propagate: if $F(a, b)$ is the only attachment of b and F is *to all*, then deletion of $F(a, b)$ implies that b must be deleted. These propagations occur, however, in data structures that do not constrain composition correspondences, so their management is properly a separate topic. If we assume that F is *to some*, then $F(a, b)$ may be deleted without deleting b. Then the system must verify that a remains attached to some C if $\dot{F} \circ \dot{G}$ is *from all*, and that each of the c_i remain attached to some A if $\dot{F} \circ \dot{G}$ is *to all*. The operations required to manage these additions and deletions are entirely regular operations that are well within the ability of today's computing technology, although they are not available on today's data base management systems.

In Section 8.2, Overview of Composition Irregularities, we present a synopsis of the patterns found in populations of binary paths. We discuss how there is a natural *maximal composition character* for the composition of two correspondences. Additional constraints on the composition correspondence can only make its character more restrictive.

In Section 8.3, Limitations on Composition Characters, we present a variety of basic theorems that affect both the constraints and the relaxations obeyed by composition correspondences. These theorems are used in Section 8.4, Potential Composition Characters, to show that the set of characters that a composition correspondence may exhibit follows a standard pattern called a *composition cone*.

In Section 8.5, Precedence Order, we show that $\dot{F} \circ \dot{G}$ can have only one possible character if the brackets in F and G are arranged in the *precedence order* **]**, >, <, **[**. Notice that precedence order differs from standard order in the arrangement of the *multiple* brackets. Precedence order provides a rapid method of determining when composition irregularities such as shown in Figure 8.1 can not occur.

In Section 8.6, Survey of Composition Cones, we complete the classification of composition correspondences. We compute all the possible characters of composition correspondences $\dot{F} \circ \dot{G}$, and show that many paths, particularly those in which F is *to some* and G is *from some*, present a surprising variety of potential characters.

8.2 OVERVIEW OF COMPOSITION IRREGULARITIES

Composition Correspondences Have a Standard Character Unless Constrained by Embracings

If the constraints in a schema are limited to character constraints (that is, if the schema contains no embracings other than character embracings), then the character of the composition of two correspondences is strictly determined from the characters of its two constituents. This character is called the *maximal composition character*. It is called *maximal* because it is the most permissive character that a composition of two correspondences can exhibit. Further constraints can only make the character less permissive.

The maximal composition character of a composition $\dot{F} \circ \dot{G}$ is written "$\alpha \,\tilde{\cup}\, \beta$", where α indicates the character of F relative to a pair of classes (A, B) and β indicates the character of G relative to a pair of classes (B, C). The maximal composition character is the same as the union of the brackets in the two characters when the brackets of each character are in standard order. That is, any relaxation obeyed by either correspondence may be obeyed by their composition (if F or G is *from some*, for example, then $\dot{F} \circ \dot{G}$ may be *from some*).

When studying composition cones, it is helpful to use *positional* character notation, in which bundlings are written as >< rather than as <> (see Section 6.6). Computation of the maximal composition character for bundlings requires additional rules, which will follow. We define the *optionality* of a character α to contain the first and last brackets of α (the optionality is the intersection $\alpha \cap$ "**][**"). The *multiplicity* of a character is the middle two brackets, either "<", ">", "<>", "><", or, if the correspondence is *one-to-one*, $\varnothing$. The multiplicity of α is also written "mult (α)".

- **(i)** The optionality of $\alpha \,\tilde{\cup}\, \beta$ equals the optionality of $\alpha \cup \beta$.
- **(ii)** If the multiplicity of α is ">" or "><" and the multiplicity of β is "<", then the multiplicity of $\alpha \,\tilde{\cup}\, \beta$ is "><".
- **(iii)** If the multiplicity of α is ">" and the multiplicity of β is "><", then the multiplicity of $\alpha \,\tilde{\cup}\, \beta$ is "><".
- **(iv)** Otherwise, the multiplicity of $\alpha \,\tilde{\cup}\, \beta$ is the union of the *multiple* brackets of α with the *multiple* brackets of β, written in standard order ($\varnothing$, "<", ">", or "<>").

Composition Irregularities

When the character of the composition $\dot{F} \circ \dot{G}$ is less permissive than the maximal composition character, the path $(A; F; B; G; C)$ is said to exhibit a *composition irregularity*. There are five patterns that, in combination, illustrate all composition irregularities:

1. *Coincident diamonding* (<.> becomes *to one* and/or *from one*) illustrated in Figure 8.3. These patterns are established by intermultiple constraints.

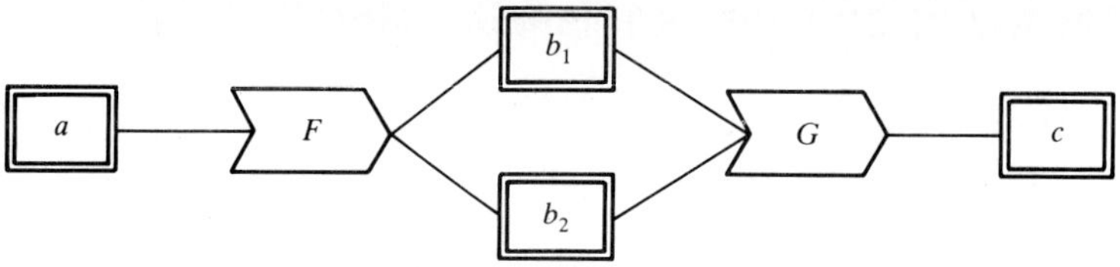

Figure 8.3 "<" composes with ">" to form ∅.

2. *Coincident orphans* (**[**.**]** becomes *from all* and/or *to all*), illustrated in Figure 8.4. These patterns are established by interoptional constraints.

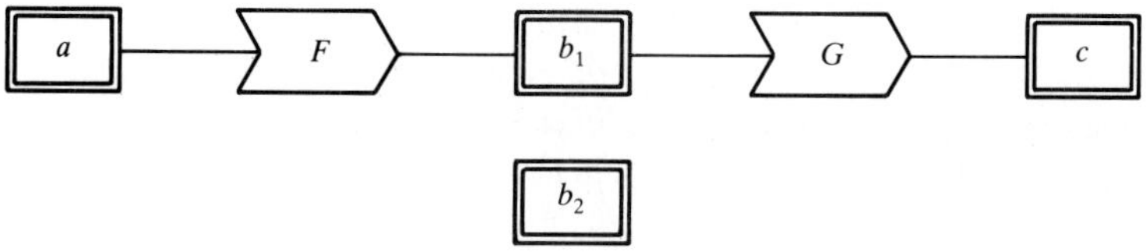

Figure 8.4 "**[**" composes with "**]**" to form ∅.

3. *Division by optional* (>.**]** becomes *from one*), illustrated in Figure 8.5. A similar pattern makes <>.**]** into a *many-to-many* bundling.

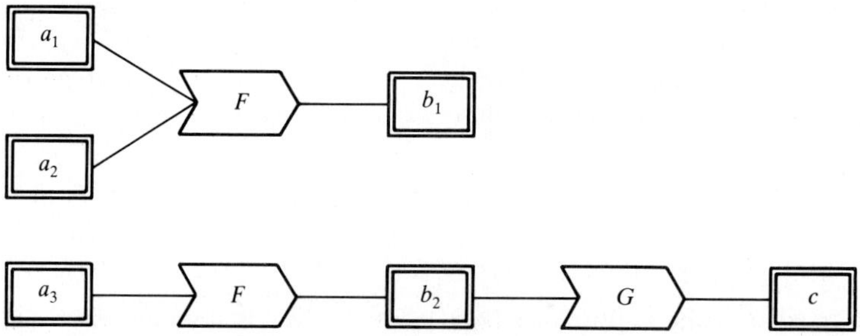

Figure 8.5 ">" composes with "**]**" to form "**]**".

4. *Selection by optional* (<.**]** becomes *to one*), illustrated in Figure 8.6.

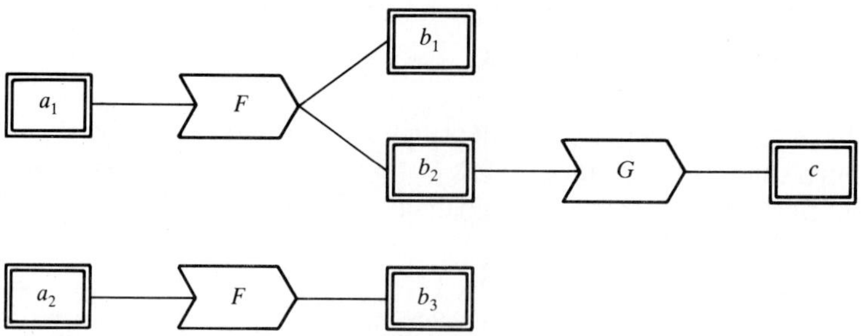

Figure 8.6 "<" composes with "**]**" to form "**]**".

5. *Coverage by multiple* (<.] becomes *from all*), illustrated in Figure 8.7.

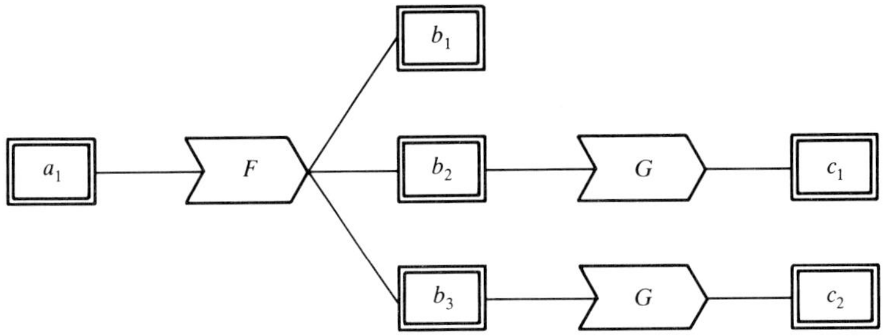

Figure 8.7 "<" composes with "]" to form "<".

A Population May Exhibit Many Irregular Patterns Simultaneously

Composition irregularities may appear in combination. For example, Figure 8.8 exhibits both coverage by *multiple* and selection by *optional*. Figure 8.8 illustrates a data structure where exactly one *item* is extracted from each *production lot* for testing. *Items* from several *production lots* are grouped into a *sample* that is tested as an ensemble. The composition correspondence from *Production Lot* to *Sample* is then *all-to-one*, even though the correspondence from *Production Lot* to *Item* is *to many* and the correspondence from *Item* to *Sample* is *from some*.

The extended associative notation for this data structure is shown in Figure 8.9. The declaration of the character of the composition correspondence is required to form this data structure properly. We could not rewrite the schema showing only the correspondences

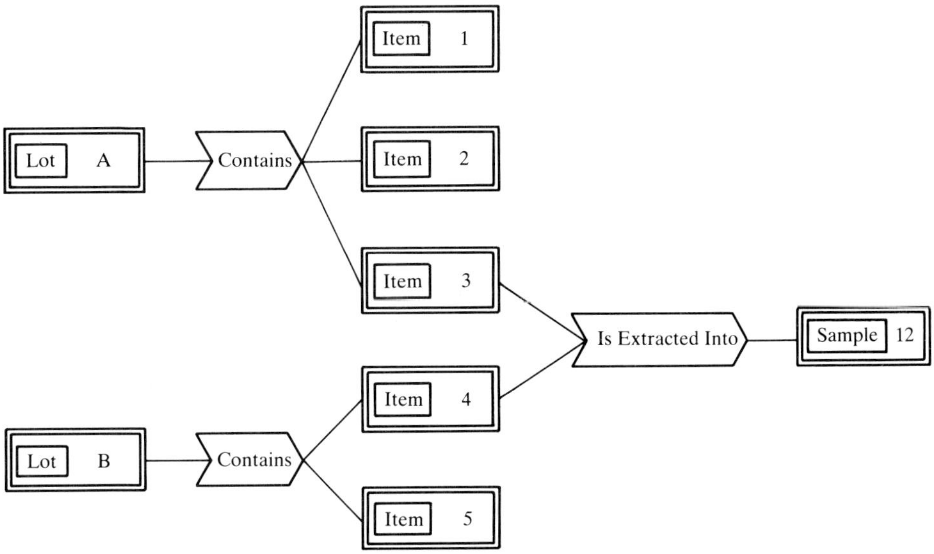

Figure 8.8 "<" composes with "]>" to form ">".

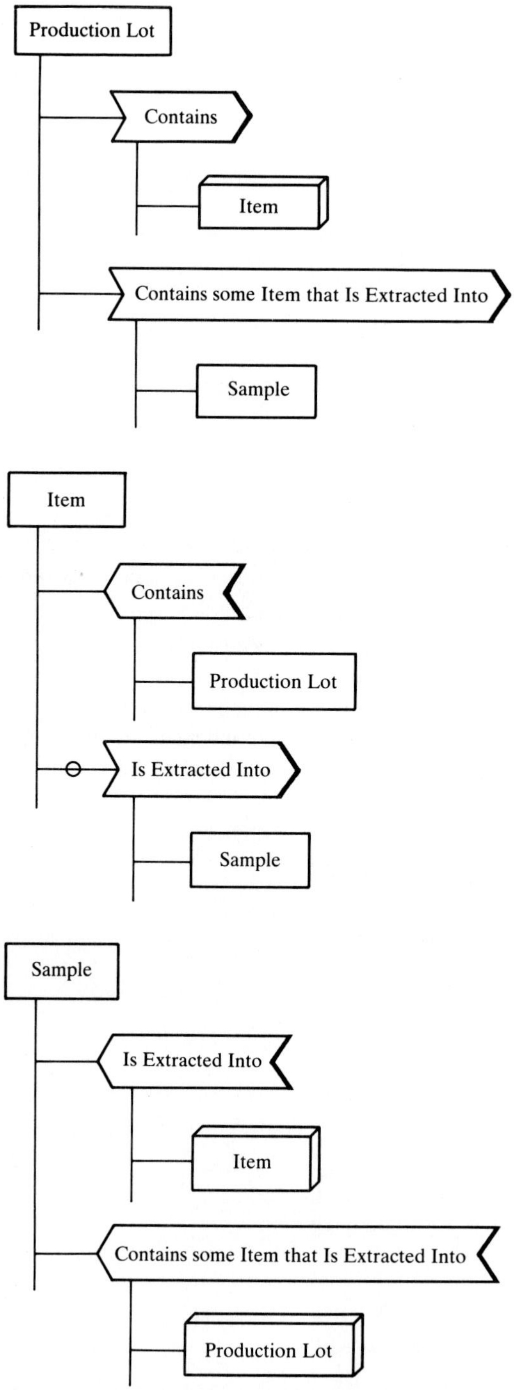

Figure 8.9 Extended associative notation for Figure 8.8.

from *Production Lot* to *Item* and from *Production Lot* to *Sample*, for example, because then we could not identify which *item* was used in a *sample*.

The remainder of this chapter will be devoted to proving that the five irregularities illustrated above are indeed all the possible composition irregularities, to calculating the most restrictive possible characters for $F \circ G$, and to describing the paths that are free from composition irregularities.

8.3 LIMITATIONS ON COMPOSITION CHARACTERS

The Characters of a Composition and Its Constituents Are Related by Logic

The character embracings for two correspondence complexes $(F; (A, B))$ and $(G; B, C))$ logically determine constraints on the composition correspondence $F \circ G$. For example, if F is *from all* and G is *from all*, then $F \circ G$ must be *from all*.

Constraints on the composition correspondence may also affect the constituents. For example, if $F \circ G$ is *from all*, then F must be *from all* (if some instance a attaches through F and then through G to some c, then a must attach through F to some b). Declaring F to be *from some* while it is forced to be *from all* would require needless effort on the part of programs that use the data base, who must allow for orphans of F that will in fact never occur.

Interdependencies among relaxations may be determined by applying the contrapositive law. Thus, if $F \circ G$ is *from some*, then F is *from some* or G is *from some*. In addition, if F is *from some*, then $F \circ G$ must be *from some*. These interdependencies, and other similar interdependencies that we will discuss later, should be programmed into the design management device, and checked automatically.

Method for Determining Logical Relationships

It is typically easier to prove that one *constraint* implies another, but easier to illustrate the contrapositive, that one *relaxation* implies another. For example, we can prove readily that if $F \circ G$ is *from all*, then F must be *from all*. It is easier to illustrate the contrapositive, however: if F is *from some*, then $F \circ G$ must be *from some*, as shown in Figure 8.10. Thus, a_1 is an orphan of both F and $F \circ G$ in Figure 8.10. This figure alone is not a proof, however, because it does not take into account unresolved alternation. For the result to apply to populations that use unresolved alternations, we must use embracings, and embracings are used most clearly when working with constraints rather than with relaxations.

We will therefore find that theorems occur in groups, with one theorem proved using constraints, then a corollary stated using relaxations. Further corollaries may be deduced by applying the converse. For example, if $F \circ G$ is *to all*, then $G^* \circ F^*$ is *from all*, therefore G^* is *from all*, and, applying the converse again, G is *to all*. Thus, if $F \circ G$ is *to all*, then G must be *to all*. By the contrapositive law, if G is *to some*, then $F \circ G$ must be *to some*.

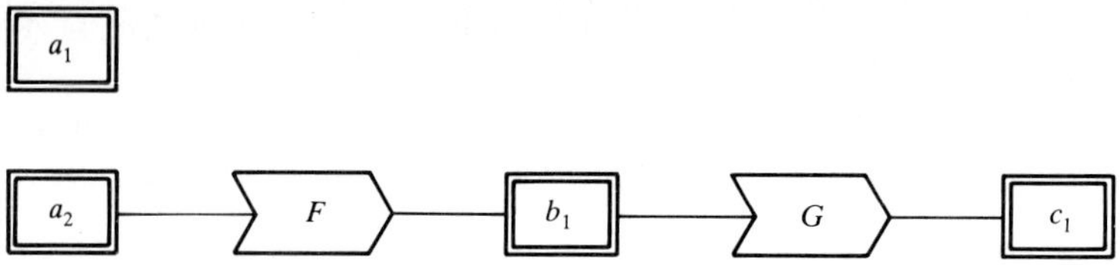

Figure 8.10 If F is *from some,* then $\dot{F} \circ \dot{G}$ is *from some.*

Relationships of Optionality

Theorem 8.1. If $\dot{F} \circ \dot{G}$ is *from all* relative to (A, C), then F is *from all* relative to (A, B).

Proof. We recall Theorem 7.13 from Section 7.3:

For any correspondences F and G,

(i) $\pi^1(F \circ G) \subseteq \pi^1 F$
(ii) If $\pi^2 F \subseteq \pi^1 G$, then $\pi^1(F \circ G) \equiv \pi^1 F$

If $\dot{F} \circ \dot{G}$ is *from all* relative to (A, C), then $\pi^1(\dot{F} \circ \dot{G}) \equiv A$. Part (i) of Theorem 7.13 therefore implies that $A \subseteq \pi^1 F$, so F must be *from all* relative to (A, B). Q.E.D.

Theorem 8.1 implies the corollaries:

Theorem 8.2. If F is *from some* relative to (A, B), then $\dot{F} \circ \dot{G}$ is *from some* relative to (A, C).

Theorem 8.3. If $\dot{F} \circ \dot{G}$ is *to all* relative to (A, C), then G is *to all* relative to (B, C).

Theorem 8.4. If G is *to some* relative to (B, C), then $\dot{F} \circ \dot{G}$ is *to some* relative to (A, C).

Figure 8.10 showed that $\dot{F} \circ \dot{G}$ leaves an orphan instance of A if F leaves an orphan instance of A. As shown in Figure 8.11, $\dot{F} \circ \dot{G}$ can also leave an orphan instance of A if G is *from some.*

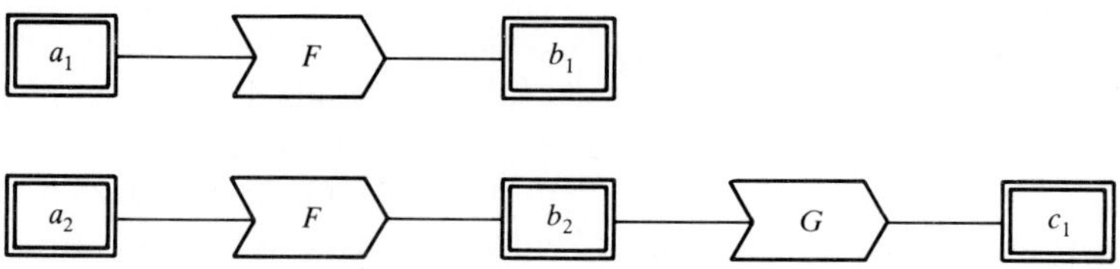

Figure 8.11 F is *from all,* but $\dot{F} \circ \dot{G}$ is *from some.*

Theorem 8.5. If F is *from all* relative to (A, B) and G is *from all* relative to (B, C), then $\dot{F} \circ \dot{G}$ is *from all* relative to (A, C).

Proof. By the second part of Theorem 7.13 (cited in the proof of Theorem 8.1), if $\pi^1 \dot{G} \equiv \Delta B$ and $\pi^1 \dot{F} \equiv \Delta A$, then $\pi^1(\dot{F} \circ \dot{G}) \equiv \Delta A$. Q.E.D.

We have the corollaries:

Theorem 8.6. If $\dot{F} \circ \dot{G}$ is *from some* relative to (A, C) then F is *from some* relative to (A, B) or G is *from some* relative to (B, C).

Theorem 8.7. If F is *to all* relative to (A, B) and G is *to all* relative to (B, C), then $\dot{F} \circ \dot{G}$ is *to all* relative to (A, C).

Theorem 8.8. If $\dot{F} \circ \dot{G}$ is *to some* relative to (A, C) then F is *to some* relative to (A, B) or G is *to some* relative to (B, C).

Relationships of Multiplicity

The theorems about optionality have dual results that relate multiplicities. For example, the dual to Theorem 8.3 states that if $\dot{F} \circ \dot{G}$ is *to one* and F is *to all*, then G must be *to one*. Figure 8.12 illustrates the contrapositive: if G is *to many* and F is *to all*, then $\dot{F} \circ \dot{G}$ must be *to many*.

Notice that if F is *to some*, then $\dot{F} \circ \dot{G}$ might be *to one*. For example, erase the individual a_1 and its attachment by F from Figure 8.12, but leave the individual b_1 and its attachments by G. The resulting diagram appears *one-to-one*, even though G appears *to many*. This is an example of division by *optional*, shown earlier (in a converse form) in Figure 8.5.

Theorem 8.9. If F is *to all* relative to (A, B) and $\dot{F} \circ \dot{G}$ is *to one* relative to (A, C), then G is *to one* relative to (B, C).

Proof. Given that

$$\Delta B \subseteq \dot{F}^* \circ \dot{F}$$

$$\dot{G}^* \circ \dot{F}^* \circ \dot{F} \circ \dot{G} \subseteq \Delta C$$

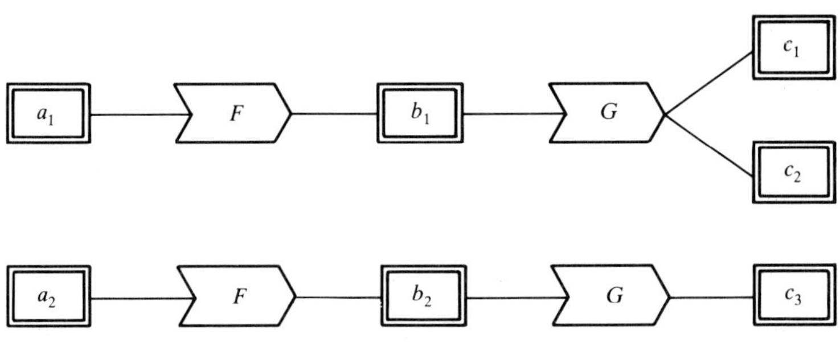

Figure 8.12 If G is *to many* and F is *to all*, then $\dot{F} \circ \dot{G}$ is *to many*.

We can conclude by substitution

$$\dot{G}^* \circ \dot{G} \equiv \dot{G}^* \circ \Delta B \circ \dot{G} \subseteq \dot{G}^* \circ \dot{F}^* \circ \dot{F} \circ \dot{G} \subseteq \Delta C$$

Thus, G is *to one*. Q.E.D.

We have the further corollaries:

Theorem 8.10. If G is *to many* relative to (B, C) and F is *to all* relative to (A, B), then $\dot{F} \circ \dot{G}$ is *to many* relative to (A, C).

Theorem 8.11. If G is *from all* relative to (B, C) and $\dot{F} \circ \dot{G}$ is *from one* relative to (A, C), then F is *from one* relative to (A, B).

Theorem 8.12. If F is *from many* relative to (A, B) and G is *from all* relative to (B, C), then $\dot{F} \circ \dot{G}$ is *from many* relative to (A, C).

The dual result to Theorem 8.5 states that if both F and G are *from one*, then $\dot{F} \circ \dot{G}$ must be *from one*. Figure 8.13 illustrates the contrapositive: if $\dot{F} \circ \dot{G}$ is *from many*, then F is *from many* or G is *from many*. Thus, $\dot{F} \circ \dot{G}$ can become *from many* if F is *from many*, as illustrated by the instances a_1 and a_2, or if G is *from many*, as illustrated by the instances b_2 and b_3.

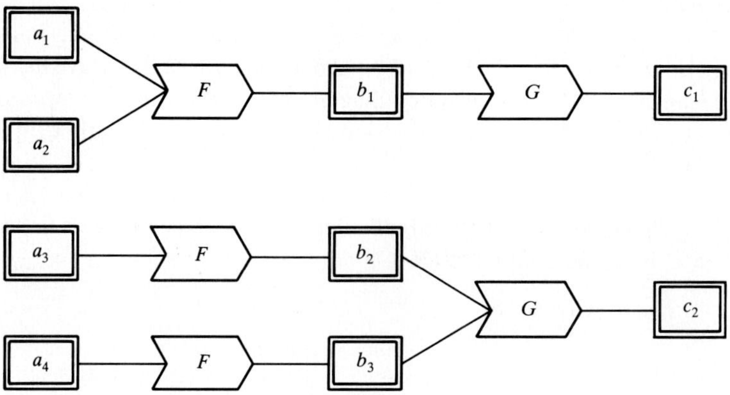

Figure 8.13 If $\dot{F} \circ \dot{G}$ is *from many*, then F is *from many* or G is *from many*.

Theorem 8.13. If F is *from one* relative to (A, B) and G is *from one* relative to (B, C), then $\dot{F} \circ \dot{G}$ is *from one* relative to (A, C).

Proof. The hypothesis is

$$\dot{F} \circ \dot{F}^* \subseteq \Delta A$$

$$\dot{G} \circ \dot{G}^* \subseteq \Delta B$$

Substituting, we obtain

$$\dot{F} \circ \dot{G} \circ \dot{G}^* \circ \dot{F}^* \subseteq \dot{F} \circ \Delta B \circ \dot{F}^*$$
$$\equiv \dot{F} \circ \dot{F}^*$$
$$\subseteq \Delta A$$

Thus $\dot{F} \circ \dot{G}$ is *from one*. Q.E.D.

This theorem has the corollaries:

Theorem 8.14. If $\dot{F} \circ \dot{G}$ is *from many* relative to (A, C), then F is *from many* relative to (A, B) or G is *from many* relative to (B, C).

Theorem 8.15. If F is *to one* relative to (A, B) and G is *to one* relative to (B, C), then $\dot{F} \circ \dot{G}$ is *to one* relative to (A, C).

Theorem 8.16. If $\dot{F} \circ \dot{G}$ is *to many* relative to (A, C), then F is *to many* relative to (A, B) or G is *to many* relative to (B, C).

Conclusion

We have shown that constraints on F and on G force constraints on the composition $\dot{F} \circ \dot{G}$, and that constraints on the composition $\dot{F} \circ \dot{G}$ force constraints on F and on G as well. Applying the contrapositive law, we have shown that relaxations of F or of G are related to relaxations of the composition $\dot{F} \circ \dot{G}$ in a similar way. These interrelationships are entirely regular, in the sense that they are determined by the characters of F and G. We have stated the interrelationships as formal theorems, which will enable them to be programmed into the design management device.

8.4 POTENTIAL COMPOSITION CHARACTERS

Notation for Composition Characters

We will write the character of F relative to (A, B) as "α" and the character of G relative to (B, C) as "β". The set of characters that $\dot{F} \circ \dot{G}$ may exhibit will be written "$\alpha.\beta$". When we write these sets of characters, we will drop the double quotes that we normally use to delimit a character. Thus, if F has character "<>" and G has character "][", we will write the set of possible characters of $\dot{F} \circ \dot{G}$ as

<>.][

When we write a character alone, however, we will retain the double quotes. Thus, in this example, the statement that $\dot{F} \circ \dot{G}$ can have character "]<>[" would be written

"]<>[" ∈ <>.][

Using this notation, the problem of classifying all the possible characters of compositions $\dot{F} \circ \dot{G}$ reduces to asking $20 \times 20 \times 20$ questions of the form

Is γ a member of $\alpha.\beta$?

There are 20 potential characters for α, β, and γ because we will use positional character notation, which includes four bundling characters in addition to the 16 characters written in standard order.

The sets of characters $\alpha.\beta$ have certain regularities that can be exploited. For example, if γ is a member of $\alpha.\beta$, then the converse of γ, γ^*, must be a member of $\beta^*.\alpha^*$:

Theorem 8.17. If $\gamma \in \alpha.\beta$, then $\gamma^* \in \beta^*.\alpha^*$

Proof. If (F, G) is a path such that F has character α, G has character β, and $(F \circ G) \equiv G^* \circ F^*$ has character γ, then (G^*, F^*) has character γ^*, G^* has character β^*, and F^* has character α^*. Q.E.D.

Definition of a Cone

A set of characters S is called a *cone* if any character that is both less permissive than some character in S and more permissive than some (other) character in S is itself in S. That is, S is a cone if it obeys the implication

$$(\alpha \in S)\ \&\ (\beta \in S)\ \&\ (\alpha \subset \gamma)\ \&\ (\gamma \subset \beta) \Rightarrow \gamma \in S$$

In this definition, "<>" is considered to be more permissive than "><". Thus, "<>" is not included in "><[", but it is included in "<>[". "><" is included in all three characters "<>", "><[", and "<>[".

A cone, then, contains all the characters "between" any two characters in the set. The set of all characters is trivially a cone, as are the following sets:

{∅, "]", "[", "]["}

{"]", "]<"}

{"]<", "][", "]<["}

A cone S contains some characters that are the most permissive in S. These characters are called *upper bounds* of S. It also contains some characters that are the least permissive in S. These characters are called *lower bounds* of S. Notice that the elements of a cone are completely determined by its upper and lower bounds. The cones that arise from composition have one upper bound but may have many lower bounds. Each of the examples has one upper bound; the last example has two lower bounds: "]<" and "][".

The Potential Characters of $\dot{F} \circ \dot{G}$ Form a Cone

The remainder of this section will be devoted to proving the following theorem:

Theorem 8.18 (Composition Cone Theorem). For any two characters α and β, the set of all characters that a composition $F \circ G$ may possess when F has character α and G has character β is a cone with upper bound $\alpha \tilde{\cup} \beta$.

We will prove this theorem in three steps. First we prove that any potential character must be included in $\alpha \mathbin{\tilde{\cup}} \beta$. Then we prove that the character $\alpha \mathbin{\tilde{\cup}} \beta$ is attainable for each choice of α and β, establishing that $\alpha \mathbin{\tilde{\cup}} \beta$ is the upper bound. Finally, we prove that the characters of $\dot{F} \circ \dot{G}$ form a cone.

Theorem 8.19. $\text{chr}\ (\dot{F} \circ \dot{G};\ A,\ C) \subset \text{chr}\ (F;\ A,\ B) \cup \text{chr}\ (G;\ B,\ C)$

Proof. Writing the characters explicitly as sets of brackets, the hypothesis is that for any bracket θ,

$$\theta \in \text{chr}\ (\dot{F} \circ \dot{G};\ A,\ C) \Rightarrow \theta \in \text{chr}\ (F;\ A,\ B) \vee \theta \in \text{chr}\ (G;\ B,\ C)$$

The contrapositive of this expression is

$$\theta \notin \text{chr}\ (F;\ A,\ B)\ \&\ \theta \notin \text{chr}\ (G;\ B,\ C) \Rightarrow \theta \notin \text{chr}\ (\dot{F} \circ \dot{G};\ A,\ B)$$

That is, the absence of a bracket in the characters of both F and G must imply the absence of the bracket in $\dot{F} \circ \dot{G}$. Taking each bracket in turn, these are the propositions:

F *from all* and G *from all* $\Rightarrow \dot{F} \circ \dot{G}$ *from all*

F *to one* and G *to one* $\Rightarrow \dot{F} \circ \dot{G}$ *to one*

F *from one* and G *from one* $\Rightarrow \dot{F} \circ \dot{G}$ *from one*

F *to all* and G *to all* $\Rightarrow \dot{F} \circ \dot{G}$ *to all*

These rules were proved in Theorems 8.5, 8.15, 8.13, and 8.7, respectively. Q.E.D.

Theorem 8.19 shows that the character of $\dot{F} \circ \dot{G}$ must be included in the *union* of the two characters α and β. We want to show the more restrictive result that the character of $\dot{F} \circ \dot{G}$ must be included in the maximal composition character $\alpha \mathbin{\tilde{\cup}} \beta$, which differs from the union if F or G are *many-to-many* bundlings.

Theorem 8.20. $\text{chr}\ (\dot{F} \circ \dot{G};\ A,\ C) \subset \text{chr}\ (F;\ A,\ B) \mathbin{\tilde{\cup}} \text{chr}\ (G;\ B,\ C)$

Proof. We need only consider the cases where the maximal composition character differs from the union character. There are three such cases:

(i) mult (α) = ``>''  and mult ($\beta$) = ``<''
(ii) mult (α) = ``><'' and mult ($\beta$) = ``<''
(iii) mult (α) = ``>''  and mult ($\beta$) = ``><''

We know from Section 6.6 that any correspondences that satisfy (i) compose to form a bundling, so they have multiplicity ``><''. For case (ii), if the multiplicity of $\alpha$ is ``><'', then F may be written as $D \circ E$, where mult (chr D) = ``>'' and mult (chr $E$) = ``<'' (see Theorem 6.4). Applying Theorem 8.19 to $E \circ G$, we conclude that mult (chr ($E \circ G$)) = ``<''. Therefore, by (i), the multiplicity of chr ($D \circ (E \circ G)$) is ``><''. Case (iii) follows as the converse of case (ii). Q.E.D.

These theorems demonstrate that no character more permissive than $\alpha \mathbin{\tilde{\cup}} \beta$ may be a member of $\alpha.\beta$, but they do not establish that $\alpha \mathbin{\tilde{\cup}} \beta$ is itself a member of $\alpha.\beta$. We show that $\alpha \mathbin{\tilde{\cup}} \beta$ is indeed a member of $\alpha.\beta$, for any α and β, by describing a procedure that constructs a population of apparent character $\alpha \mathbin{\tilde{\cup}} \beta$. Since this population can only be controlled by a correspondence that is at least as permissive as $\alpha \mathbin{\tilde{\cup}} \beta$, and since we have shown that $\dot{F} \circ \dot{G}$ can not be more permissive than $\alpha \mathbin{\tilde{\cup}} \beta$, this method illustrates a correspondence $\dot{F} \circ \dot{G}$ whose character is exactly $\alpha \mathbin{\tilde{\cup}} \beta$.

Theorem 8.21. For any characters α and β, there are classes A, B, and C, a correspondence F, and a correspondence G such that

(i) $\mathrm{chr}\,(F; A, B) = \alpha$
(ii) $\mathrm{chr}\,(G; B, C) = \beta$
(iii) $\mathrm{chr}\,(\dot{F} \circ \dot{G}; A, C) = \alpha \mathbin{\tilde{\cup}} \beta$

Proof. Take the illustrations of the characters α and β given in Section 6.2. Alter the individuals so that there are two population diagrams, one of apparent character α, the other of apparent character β, so that no individual appears in both diagrams. Extend the diagrams by *one-to-one all-to-all* correspondences as shown in Figure 8.14, always using individuals so that no individual appears in both diagrams. Arrange the diagrams as shown so that each diagram has three columns of individuals. Then erase the imaginary barrier between the two diagrams and consider there to be one diagram. The resulting diagram will have the apparent character $\alpha \mathbin{\tilde{\cup}} \beta$, except that the diagram for a composition such as <.> will illustrate a bundling rather than a correspondence of apparent character "<>". To

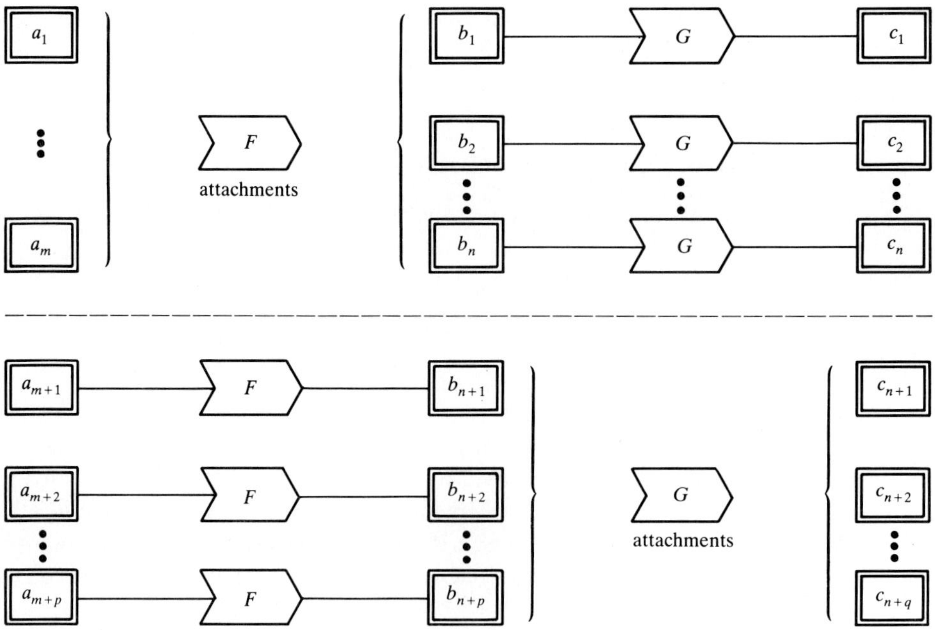

Figure 8.14 Formation of a population diagram for a composition.

illustrate the latter, add an instance of B that attaches to one instance of A from the top diagram and to one instance of C from the bottom diagram. For example, Figure 8.15 shows that "<>[" is a member of <.>[. Q.E.D.

It remains to show that the characters less permissive than the maximal composition character form a cone. We show this by describing a procedure that constructs illustrative populations for every character between a lower bound and the maximal composition character. This shows that $\alpha.\beta$ is a cone, but it does not compute the lower bounds. Lower bounds will be computed in the remaining sections.

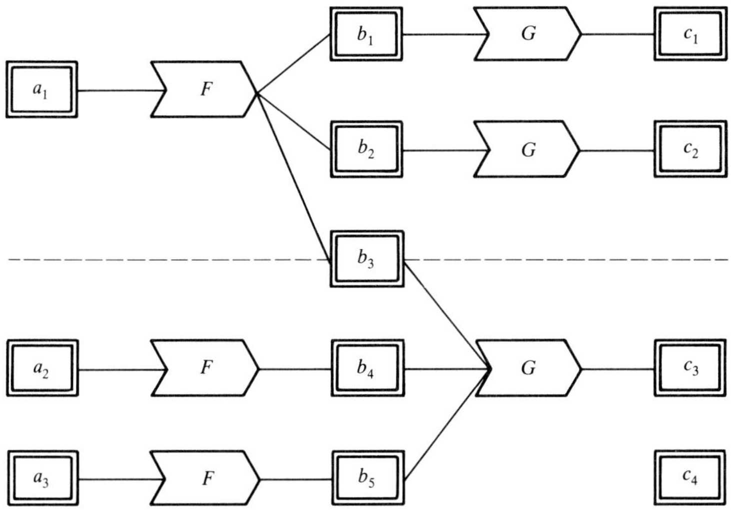

Figure 8.15 Formation of an unbundled *many-to-many* composition.

Theorem 8.22. If there is an example of $\alpha.\beta$ yielding γ, then $\alpha.\beta$ includes the cone with lower bound γ and upper bound $\alpha \,\tilde{\cup}\, \beta$.

Proof. We need to show that given an example population $\hat{P}$ of γ, each of the following is possible:

(i) To make $\hat{P}$ *from some* if α is *from some*
(ii) To make $\hat{P}$ *to many* if α is *to many*
(iii) To make $\hat{P}$ *from many* if α is *from many*
(iv) To make $\hat{P}$ *to some* if α is *to some*

Managing the difference between "><" and "<>" will be considered later in the proof. If we can do all these things, then we can do the same things for β by forming the converse. We must of course be certain that, in changing $\hat{P}$ to accommodate a bracket decision, we do not affect the other possible bracket decisions. For example, in making $\hat{P}$ *from some* we must not also make it *from many* or *to some*.

We deal with each requirement in turn:

(i) Add an orphan instance a_1 of A to $\hat{P}$ to make a population that is *from some*.

(ii) Add claims to $\hat{P}$ of the form shown in Figure 8.16 to make a population that is *from many*.

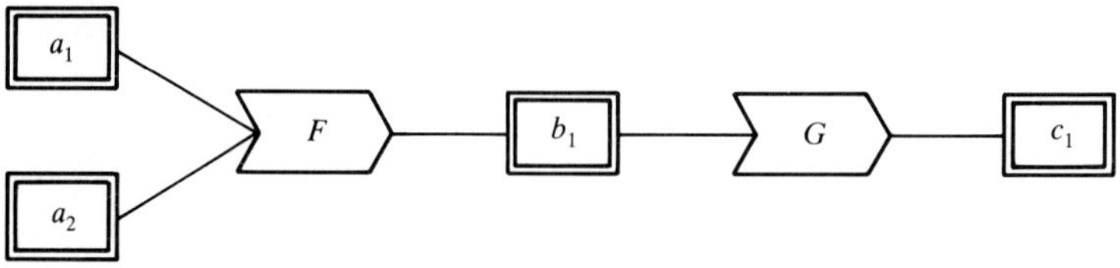

Figure 8.16 Formation of a *from many* composition.

(iii) Add claims to $\hat{P}$ of the form shown in Figure 8.17 to make a population that is *to many*.

(iv) Add an orphan instance c_1 of C to $\hat{P}$ to make a population that is *to some*.

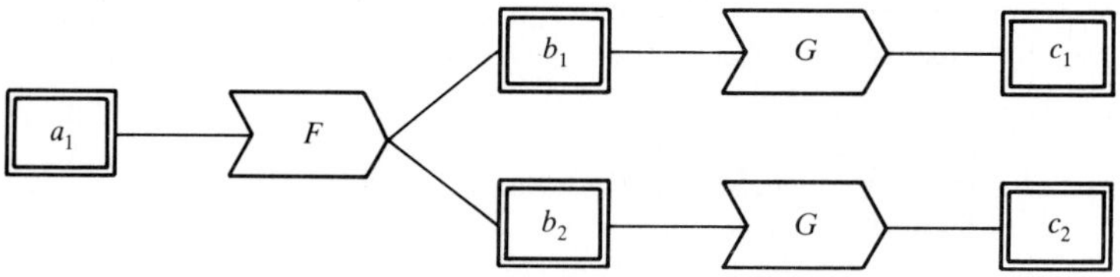

Figure 8.17 Formation of a *to many* composition.

This method of accumulating population diagrams to form an example of a given data structure is called *pasting*.

In the case of ">" and "<", we have only shown that each may be converted into "><". Thus, it is clear from examining (ii) and (iii) that a *many-to-many* population formed from a *many-to-one* correspondence by (iii) or from a *one-to-many* correspondence by (ii) will be bundled. It remains to show that a character of multiplicity "<>" may be formed when the multiplicity of $\alpha \tilde{\cup} \beta$ is "<>". There are three cases to consider:

(i) mult (α) = "<>"

(ii) mult (β) = "<>"

(iii) "<" $\subset \alpha$ and ">" $\subset \beta$

The structures to be added to $\hat{P}$ to make a character of multiplicity "<>" are shown in Figure 8.18. Q.E.D.

This completes the proof of the composition cone theorem (Theorem 8.18).

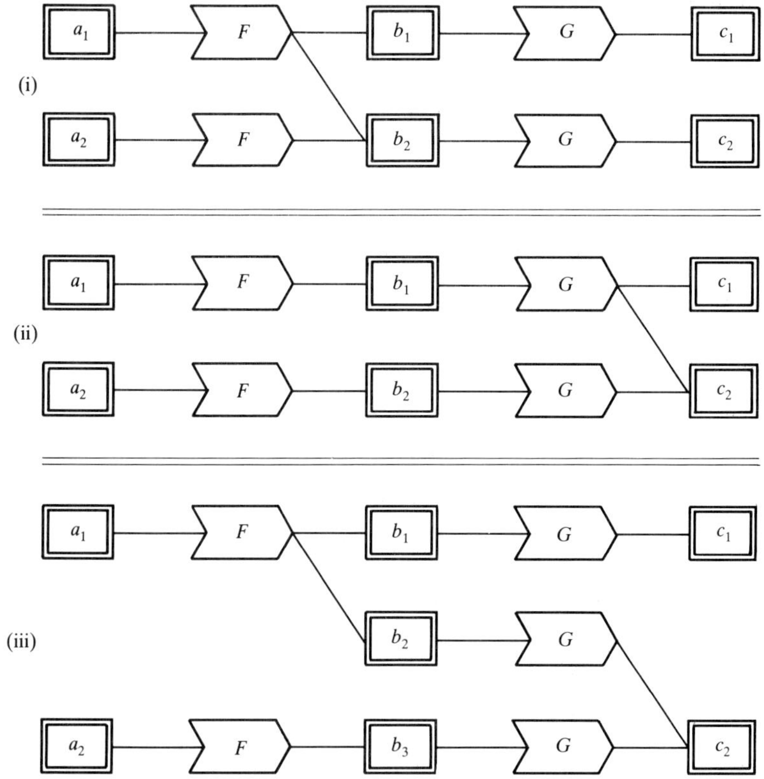

Figure 8.18 Formation of *many-to-many* compositions.

Conclusion

We have shown that the possible characters of a composition $\dot{F} \circ \dot{G}$ form a cone with one upper bound. The upper bound is the character which one would expect $\dot{F} \circ \dot{G}$ to possess: it contains only those constraints common to both F and to G, with a minor wrinkle to accommodate bundlings. In the presence of embracings, some compositions may exhibit more restrictive characters than the upper bound.

8.5 PRECEDENCE ORDER

A Path That Obeys Precedence Exhibits Only One Composition Character

In certain cases, the character of $F \circ G$ must be the maximal composition character, so that no new characters appear in the composition cone. In other words, the lower bound is the same as the upper bound and the composition cone contains only the maximal composition character. When a composition cone contains only one element, we say that the cone is *trivial*. These cases may be determined rapidly by examining the characters of F and G.

Specifically, a path (A; F; B; G; C) is said to *obey precedence* if chr (F; A, B) and chr (G; B, C) are such that when the two characters are strung end-to-end the sequence of brackets follows the *precedence order* **]** → > → < → **[**, allowing repeats. For example, the following character pairs obey precedence:

∅.<
<.∅
<.<
]>.<**[**
]><.<**[**

and the following do not obey precedence:

<.>
[.**]**
<.**]**
>.**]**
><.<>

Notice that any character pair in which two brackets open toward each other does not obey precedence. The character pairs "**[**.<" and ">.**]**" also do not obey precedence, even though the brackets open in the same direction. Notice further that precedence order differs from standard order **]**, <, >, **[** in the placement of the *multiple* brackets. In particular, any factoring that contains an unbundled *many-to-many* correspondence (represented by "<>") does not obey precedence.

We will devote this section to the proof of the following theorem:

Theorem 8.23 (Precedence Theorem). If (α, β) obeys precedence, then $\alpha.\beta$ is trivial.

Properties of Accumulating Correspondences

We will call a correspondence that is *to one* and *to all* an *accumulating correspondence*. Figure 8.19 illustrates an accumulating correspondence. The character of an accumulating correspondence is always included in "**]**>", so its brackets are always in precedence order. The term "accumulating" is inspired by the following example: suppose F is resolute and has character "**]**>", and suppose a number is assigned to each instance of A (such as a "cost" or a "physical weight" for the instance). Then each instance of B may also be assigned a number formed by adding together or *accumulating* all the numbers assigned to the instances of A (that is, a "total cost" or a "total weight" for the instance of B). Accumulating correspondences are found frequently in accounting or assembly applications.

If F is an accumulating correspondence and G is *from some*, then $\dot{F} \circ \dot{G}$ must be *from some*, as illustrated in Figure 8.20. This result is proved by the following theorems:

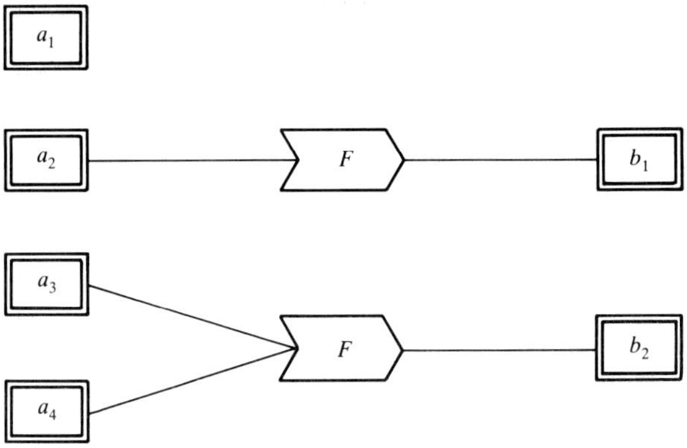

Figure 8.19 An accumulating correspondence.

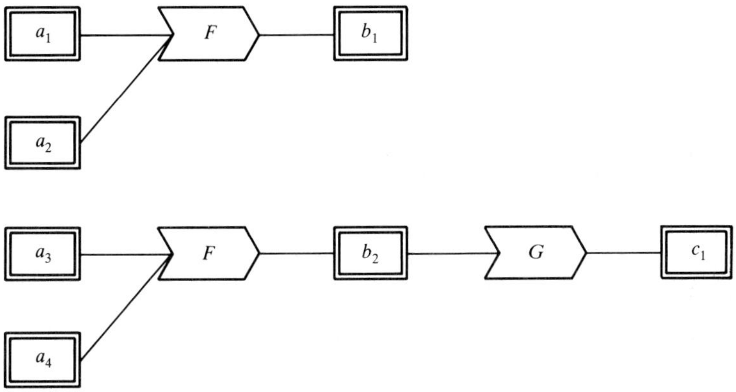

Figure 8.20 If F is an accumulating correspondence and G is *from some*, then $\dot{F} \circ \dot{G}$ is *from some*.

Theorem 8.24. If F is *to one* relative to (A, B) and $\dot{F} \circ \dot{G}$ is *from all* relative to (A, C), then F and G obey the interoptional constraint $\pi^2\dot{F} \subseteq \pi^1\dot{G}$.

Proof. The hypothesis is

$$\dot{F}^* \circ \dot{F} \subseteq \Delta B$$

$$\Delta A \subseteq \dot{F} \circ \dot{G} \circ \dot{G}^* \circ \dot{F}^*$$

Composing with $\dot{F}^*$ on the left and $\dot{F}$ on the right of the latter formula, we obtain

$$\dot{F}^* \circ \dot{F} \equiv \dot{F}^* \circ \Delta A \circ \dot{F} \subseteq \dot{F}^* \circ \dot{F} \circ \dot{G} \circ \dot{G}^* \circ \dot{F}^* \circ \dot{F}$$

$$\subseteq \dot{G} \circ \dot{G}^*$$

Intersecting both sides with ΔB gives

$$\Delta\pi^2\dot{F} \equiv (\dot{F}^* \circ \dot{F}) \cap \Delta B \subseteq (\dot{G} \circ \dot{G}^*) \cap \Delta B \equiv \Delta\pi^1\dot{G}$$

Q.E.D.

If F is *to all*, then $\pi^2\dot{F} \equiv \Delta B$. If the other conditions of Theorem 8.24 are also satisfied, then $\Delta B \subseteq \dot{\pi}^1 G$, so G is *from all*. We have shown then:

Theorem 8.25. If F is *to one* and *to all* relative to (A, B) and $\dot{F} \circ \dot{G}$ is *from all* relative to (A, C), then G is *from all* relative to (B, C).

Applying converse and contrapositive yields:

Theorem 8.26. If F is *to all* and *to one* relative to (A, B) and G is *from some* relative to (B, C), then $\dot{F} \circ \dot{G}$ is *from some* relative to (A, C).

Theorem 8.27. If G is *from all* and *from one* relative to (B, C) and $\dot{F} \circ \dot{G}$ is *to all* relative to (A, C), then F is *to all* relative to (A, B).

Theorem 8.28. If G is *from all* and *from one* relative to (B, C) and F is *to some* relative to (A, B), then $\dot{F} \circ \dot{G}$ is *to some* relative to (A, C).

The dual result to Theorem 8.26 applies if F is an accumulating correspondence and G is *from many*. Then $\dot{F} \circ \dot{G}$ is *from many*, as illustrated in Figure 8.21.

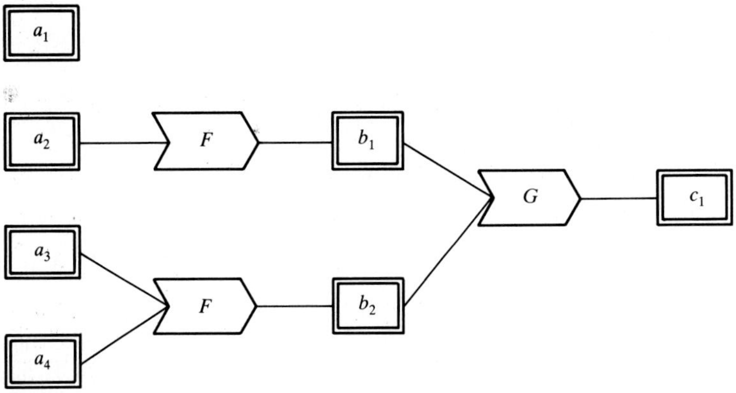

Figure 8.21 If F is an accumulating correspondence and G is *from many*, then $\dot{F} \circ \dot{G}$ is *from many*.

Theorem 8.29. If F is *to one* and *to all* relative to (A, B) and $\dot{F} \circ \dot{G}$ is *from one* relative to (A, C), then G is *from one* relative to (B, C).

Proof. Since F is *to one* and *to all* we have

$$\dot{F}^* \circ \dot{F} \equiv \Delta B$$

Since $\dot{F} \circ \dot{G}$ is *from one* we have

$$\dot{F} \circ \dot{G} \circ \dot{G}^* \circ \dot{F}^* \subseteq \Delta A$$

Composing with $\dot{F}^*$ on the left and $\dot{F}$ on the right gives

$$\dot{F}^* \circ \dot{F} \circ \dot{G} \circ \dot{G}^* \circ \dot{F}^* \circ \dot{F} \subseteq \dot{F}^* \circ \Delta A \circ \dot{F}$$

$$\subseteq \dot{F}^* \circ \dot{F}$$

$$\subseteq \Delta B$$

Since $\dot{F}^* \circ \dot{F} \equiv \Delta B$, we may remove both appearances of the retroactive cycle $\dot{F}^* \circ \dot{F}$ on the left side to obtain

$$\dot{G} \circ \dot{G}^* \subseteq \Delta B$$

So G is *from one*. Q.E.D.

Applying the converse and contrapositive, we have:

Theorem 8.30. If F is *to one* and *to all* relative to (A, B) and G is *from many* relative to (B, C), then $F \circ \dot{G}$ is *from many* relative to (A, C).

Theorem 8.31. If G is *from all* and *from one* relative to (B, C) and $\dot{F} \circ \dot{G}$ is *to one* relative to (A, C), then F is *to one* relative to (A, B).

Theorem 8.32. If G is *from all* and *from one* relative to (B, C) and F is *to many* relative to (A, B), then $\dot{F} \circ G$ is *to many* relative to (A, C).

Proof of the Precedence Theorem

We may now complete the proof of the precedence theorem (Theorem 8.23).

Proof of the Precedence Theorem. We have already shown all the individual results needed to prove the precedence theorem. The precedence theorem is proved by applying the elongation factoring to each pair of brackets in $\alpha.\beta$. We list these pairs with the theorems that demonstrate them alongside.

$\emptyset.\emptyset = \{\emptyset\}$	(8.18)
$\emptyset.] = \{\text{``]''}\}$	(8.26)
$\emptyset.> = \{\text{``>''}\}$	(8.30)
$\emptyset.< = \{\text{``<''}\}$	(8.10)
$\emptyset.[= \{\text{``[''}\}$	(8.4)
$].\emptyset = \{\text{``]''}\}$	(8.2)
$].] = \{\text{``]''}\}$	(8.2)
$].> = \{\text{``]>''}\}$	(8.2, 8.30)
$].< = \{\text{``]<''}\}$	(8.2, 8.10)
$].[= \{\text{``][''}\}$	(8.2, 8.4)
$>.\emptyset = \{\text{``>''}\}$	(8.12)
$>.> = \{\text{``>''}\}$	(8.12)
$>.< = \{\text{``><''}\}$	(8.10, 8.12, 6.3)
$>.[= \{\text{``>[''}\}$	(8.4, 8.12)
$<.\emptyset = \{\text{``<''}\}$	(8.32)
$<.< = \{\text{``<''}\}$	(8.10)
$<.[= \{\text{``<[''}\}$	(8.4, 8.32)
$[.\emptyset = \{\text{``[''}\}$	(8.28)
$[.[= \{\text{``[''}\}$	(8.4)

When two characters α and β have a trivial composition cone, then the set of potential characters of the ternary path (F, G, H) with characters (α, β, γ) is given by the composition cone $(\alpha \tilde{\cup} \beta).\gamma$. The technique of replacing a pair of characters with a single character when the composition cone is trivial is called *coalescence*. We have shown that any pair of characters that each consist of a single bracket may be coalesced. The following formulas show that more complex characters that obey precedence may also be coalesced:

$$
\begin{array}{lll}
\mathbf{]}>.< & = \{\text{``}\mathbf{]}><\text{''}\} & (8.2,\ 8.10,\ 8.12,\ 6.3) \\
\mathbf{]}>.\mathbf{[} & = \{\text{``}\mathbf{]}>\mathbf{[}\text{''}\} & (8.2,\ 8.4,\ 8.12) \\
\mathbf{]}.<\mathbf{[} & = \{\text{``}\mathbf{]}<\mathbf{[}\text{''}\} & (8.2,\ 8.4,\ 8.10) \\
>.<\mathbf{[} & = \{\text{``}><\mathbf{[}\text{''}\} & (8.4,\ 8.10,\ 8.12,\ 6.3) \\
\mathbf{]}>.<\mathbf{[} & = \{\text{``}\mathbf{]}><\mathbf{[}\text{''}\} & (8.2,\ 8.4,\ 8.10,\ 8.12,\ 6.3)
\end{array}
$$

We can now show that any chosen binary path that obeys precedence has a trivial composition cone by elongating both characters and then coalescing them. For example, from $\mathbf{]}><.<\mathbf{[}$ we obtain

$$
\begin{aligned}
\mathbf{]}><.<\mathbf{[} = (\mathbf{]}.>.<).(<.\mathbf{[}) &= (\mathbf{]}.>).(<.<).\mathbf{[} \\
&= \mathbf{]}>.<.\mathbf{[} \\
&= \mathbf{]}>.<\mathbf{[} \\
&= \{\text{``}\mathbf{]}><\mathbf{[}\text{''}\}
\end{aligned}
$$

Q.E.D.

Generalization to Paths of Arbitrary Length

Although we have concentrated on binary paths in this section, the same results apply to paths of any length. Specifically, any sequence of characters $(\alpha_1, \ldots, \alpha_n)$ obeys precedence if it obeys the *coalescence test*, conducted as follows. Test if the first two characters α_1 and α_2 obey precedence. If not, the sequence does not obey precedence and exit. If so, *coalesce* α_1 and α_2 into the maximal composition character $\alpha_1 \tilde{\cup} \alpha_2$. Form a new sequence $(\alpha_1 \tilde{\cup} \alpha_2, \alpha_3, \ldots, \alpha_n)$ and begin again. If the entire sequence may be coalesced in this way, then the sequence obeys precedence and its composition cone is trivial. One may start from either end (α_1 or α_n) and reach equivalent results. Notice that each pair of neighboring correspondences may obey precedence yet the entire sequence may still not obey precedence. For example, $<.\varnothing.>$ does not obey precedence.

Conclusion

We have shown a simple test for determining when composition irregularities do not occur. That is, if the brackets in a path are arranged in the precedence order $\mathbf{]},>,<,\mathbf{[}$ then the character of the composition correspondence is determined from the characters of the correspondences in the path. This test is significant because most pairs of characters do *not* obey precedence, showing that the potential for composition irregularities is widespread.

8.6 SURVEY OF COMPOSITION CONES

In this section, we survey the composition cones $\alpha.\beta$ for all choices of α and β. We list explicitly the lower bounds of 66 composition cones for reference, and we show how all composition cones may be computed from these 66. We show first that we need not consider the cases where α is *from some* or β is *from some*, or the cases where α or β is $\varnothing$. We discuss the remaining characters in stages based on optionality: first the characters when α is *to all* and β is *from all*, then the characters where α is *to all* and β is *from some* (the cases where α is *to some* and β is *from all* may be deduced from the converse), and finally the cases where α is *to some* and β is *from some*.

Constraints on Bundlings

We seek to reduce the number of cases $\alpha.\beta$ that we need to study below the 400 needed if we were to examine every possible composition cone. We must first examine the composition cones that include bundlings more closely. For example, as illustrated in Figure 8.22, if F is an accumulating correspondence and G is not a bundling, then $\dot{F} \circ \dot{G}$ is not a bundling.

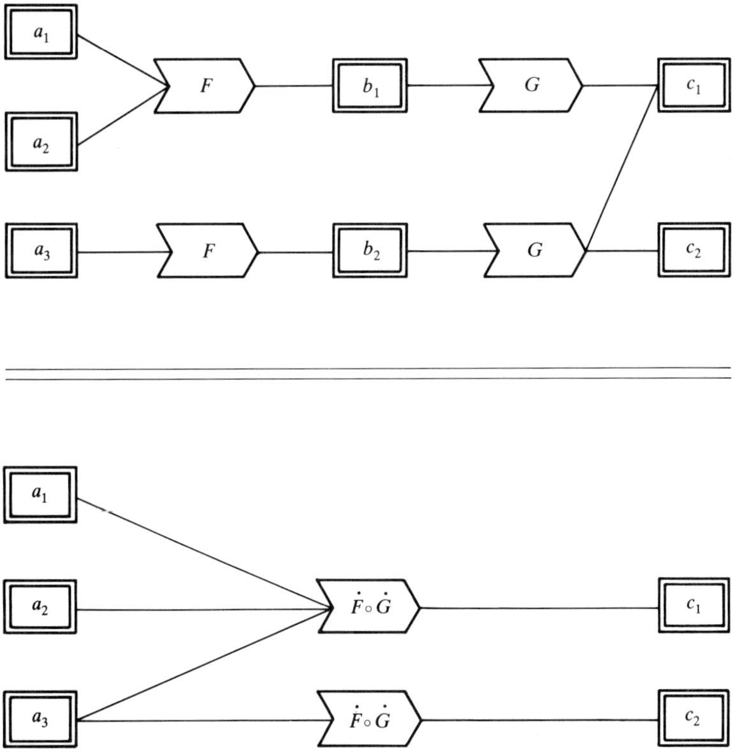

Figure 8.22 If F is an accumulating correspondence and G is unbundled, then $\dot{F} \circ \dot{G}$ is unbundled.

Theorem 8.33. If F is *to one* and *to all* relative to (A, B) and $\dot{F} \circ \dot{G}$ is a bundling, then $\dot{G}$ is a bundling.

Proof. Since F is *to one* and *to all*,

$$\dot{F}^* \circ \dot{F} \equiv \Delta B$$

Since $\dot{F} \circ \dot{G}$ is a bundling,

$$\dot{F} \circ \dot{G} \circ \dot{G}^* \circ \dot{F}^* \circ \dot{F} \circ \dot{G} \subseteq \dot{F} \circ \dot{G}$$

Excising $\dot{F}^* \circ \dot{F}$ and composing on the left with $\dot{F}^*$ gives

$$\dot{F}^* \circ \dot{F} \circ \dot{G} \circ \dot{G}^* \circ \dot{G} \subseteq \dot{F}^* \circ \dot{F} \circ \dot{G}$$

Excising $\dot{F}^* \circ \dot{F}$ on both sides shows that $\dot{G}$ is a bundling. Q.E.D.

Applying the converse and contrapositive yields:

Theorem 8.34. If F is *to one* and *to all* relative to (A, B) and $\dot{G}$ is not a bundling, then $\dot{F} \circ \dot{G}$ is not a bundling.

Theorem 8.35. If G is *from all* and *from one* relative to (B, C) and $\dot{F} \circ \dot{G}$ is a bundling, then $\dot{F}$ is a bundling.

Theorem 8.36. If G is *from all* and *from one* relative to (B, C) and $\dot{F}$ is not a bundling, then $\dot{F} \circ \dot{G}$ is not a bundling.

Elimination of Cones That Incorporate ∅

If α or β is $\varnothing$, then the composition cone $\alpha.\beta$ is trivial:

Theorem 8.37. For any character β, $\varnothing.\beta = \{\beta\}$

Proof. Given that F is *one-to-one all-to-all*, we need to show the five cases:

(i) If G is *from some*, then $\dot{F} \circ \dot{G}$ is *from some*
(ii) If G is *to many*, then $\dot{F} \circ \dot{G}$ is *to many*
(iii) If G is *from many*, then $\dot{F} \circ \dot{G}$ is *from many*
(iv) If G is *to some*, then $\dot{F} \circ \dot{G}$ is *to some*
(v) If G is not a bundling, then $\dot{F} \circ \dot{G}$ is not a bundling

Since F is an accumulating correspondence, case (i) is implied by Theorem 8.26, case (iii) is implied by Theorem 8.30, and case (v) is implied by Theorem 8.34. Case (ii) is implied by Theorem 8.10. Case (iv) is implied by Theorem 8.4. Q.E.D.

Applying the converse we have:

Theorem 8.38. $\alpha.\varnothing = \{\alpha\}$

Elimination of Exterior *Optional* Brackets

If α contains the bracket **]** or β contains the bracket **[**, then the composition cone $\alpha.\beta$ can be computed from the cone $\gamma.\delta$, where γ is α shorn of **]** and δ is β shorn of **[**. The brackets **]** and **[** in these positions are called *exterior brackets* because they appear on the extreme left and right sides of the expression $\alpha.\beta$. The effect of these brackets is to permit orphans which do not participate in the interactions between F and G. Thus, we can study composition cones that possess exterior brackets by imagining that the orphans are removed, studying the interactions without them, and then adding the orphans back.

Theorem 8.39. Let β be a character that does not contain the bracket **[** and let $\gamma = \beta \cup$ "**[**". Then

(i) If $\delta \in \alpha.\gamma$, then there is a character $\zeta \in \alpha.\beta$ such that $\delta = \zeta \cup$ "**[**"
(ii) If $\zeta \in \alpha.\beta$, then $\zeta \cup$ "**[**" $\in \alpha.\gamma$

Proof

(i) We know from Theorem 8.4 that "**[**" $\subset \delta$. Let $\hat{P}$ be a resolute population of $\dot{F} \circ \dot{G}$ with apparent character δ. Delete the instances of C from $\hat{P}$ that are orphans of G^*, making G appear *to all*. Call the resulting population $\hat{Q}$. The only brackets that could be affected by the change from $\hat{P}$ to $\hat{Q}$ are chr $(G; B, C)$ $\cap$ "**[**", which is made $\varnothing$, and chr $(\dot{F} \circ \dot{G}; A, C) \cap$ "**[**", which may or may not be changed. The other brackets are not affected because no attachments are deleted. Thus, the apparent character of G in $\hat{Q}$ is β. Let ζ be the apparent character of $\dot{F} \circ \dot{G}$ in $\hat{Q}$. Then $\delta = \zeta \cup$ "**[**".

(ii) Let $\hat{P}$ be a population with apparent character $\alpha.\beta$ and where $\dot{F} \circ \dot{G}$ has apparent character ζ. Add an instance to C that attaches to no instance of B by G^*. The resulting population has apparent character $\alpha.(\beta \cup$ "**[**"$) = \alpha.\gamma$, and $\dot{F} \circ \dot{G}$ has apparent character $\zeta \cup$ "**[**". Q.E.D.

This theorem shows that the composition cone $\alpha.\gamma$ can be computed from the composition cone $\alpha.\beta$, so that we need not study cones with exterior **[** brackets. Applying the converse eliminates the need to study exterior **]** brackets as well:

Theorem 8.40. Let α be a character that does not contain the bracket **]** and let $\gamma = \alpha \cup$ "**]**". Then

(i) If $\delta \in \gamma.\beta$, then there is a character $\zeta \in \alpha.\beta$ such that $\delta = \alpha \cup$ "**]**"
(ii) If $\zeta \in \alpha.\beta$, then $\zeta \cup$ "**]**" $\in \gamma.\beta$

Survey of Internally *all-to-all* Cones

Just as the brackets $\alpha \cap$ "**]**" and $\beta \cap$ "**[**" are called the *exterior* brackets of $\alpha.\beta$, so the converse brackets $\alpha \cap$ "**[**" and $\beta \cap$ "**]**" are called the *interior* brackets. We will study first the case where both interior brackets are absent, so F is *to all* and G is *from all*. These composition cones may be described completely by the theorems already proved. We list below the lower bound of each cone. The lower bounds shown are the most restrictive characters allowed by the theorems proved earlier. We list the relevant theorems alongside each cone.

Cone	Lower bound	Upper bound	Theorems
>.>	">"	">"	8.23
>.<	"><"	"><"	8.23
>.><	"><"	"><"	8.23
>.<>	"<>"	"<>"	8.34
<.>	∅	"<>"	
<.<	"<"	"<"	8.23
<.><	"<"	"><"	8.10
<.<>	"<"	"<>"	8.10
><.>	">"	"<>"	8.12
><.<	"><"	"><"	8.23
><.><	"><"	"<>"	8.10, 8.12
><.<>	"><"	"<>"	8.10, 8.12
<>.>	">"	"<>"	8.12
<>.<	"<>"	"<>"	8.36
<>.><	"><"	"<>"	8.10, 8.12
<>.<>	"><"	"<>"	8.10, 8.12

The composition of "<" with ">" to yield ∅ is an example of coincident diamonding, illustrated in Figure 8.3. It can be seen by inspection that all cases where the composition cone is not trivial are situations where α contains "<" and β contains ">". Indeed, coincident diamonding is required for the cone not to be trivial, because an RNA constraint on B would force the composition to the maximal composition character. Two of the more bizarre lower bounds are illustrated in Figure 8.23.

Survey of Internally *some-to-all* Cones

We consider next the cones where "**[**" $\not\subset \alpha$ and "**]**" $\subset \beta$. Once these cones are understood, we can also describe the cones where "**[**" $\subset \alpha$ and "**]**" $\not\subset \beta$ by applying the converse.

The cones that contain interior *optional* brackets exhibit the phenomenon of *multiple lower bounds*. This property is derived from the result illustrated in Figure 8.24: if F is *many-to-one*, then $\dot{F} \circ \dot{G}$ can not be both *from all* and *from one*. In the top diagram of the figure, $\dot{F} \circ \dot{G}$ is *from one*, but it is *from some*. Because the immediate neighborhood of a_1 also contains a_2, $\dot{F} \circ \dot{G}$ can not attach to a_1 and remain *from one*. Thus, in the bottom figure, $\dot{F} \circ \dot{G}$ attaches to a_1 and is *from all*, but it is necessarily *from many*.

Theorem 8.41. If F is *to one* relative to (A, B) and $\dot{F} \circ \dot{G}$ is both *from all* and *from one* relative to (A, C), then F is *from one* relative to (A, B).

Proof. Since F is *to one* and *from all*, Theorem 8.24 shows that $\pi^2\dot{F} \subseteq \pi^1\dot{G}$. Since F is *to one*, $\Delta\pi^2\dot{F} \equiv \dot{F}^* \circ \dot{F}$. Thus

$$\dot{F}^* \circ \dot{F} \subseteq \Delta\pi^1\dot{G} \subseteq \dot{G} \circ \dot{G}^*$$

Since $\dot{F} \circ \dot{G}$ is *from one*,

$$\dot{F} \circ \dot{G} \circ \dot{G}^* \circ \dot{F}^* \subseteq \Delta A$$

By the zigzag chain of $\dot{F}$, $\dot{F} \circ \dot{F}^* \subseteq \dot{F} \circ \dot{F}^* \circ \dot{F} \circ \dot{F}^*$. Substituting $\dot{G} \circ \dot{G}^*$ for $\dot{F}^* \circ \dot{F}$, we obtain

$$\dot{F} \circ \dot{F}^* \subseteq \dot{F} \circ \dot{F}^* \circ \dot{F} \circ \dot{F}^* \subseteq \dot{F} \circ \dot{G} \circ \dot{G}^* \circ \dot{F}^* \subseteq \Delta A$$

Thus, F is *from one*. Q.E.D.

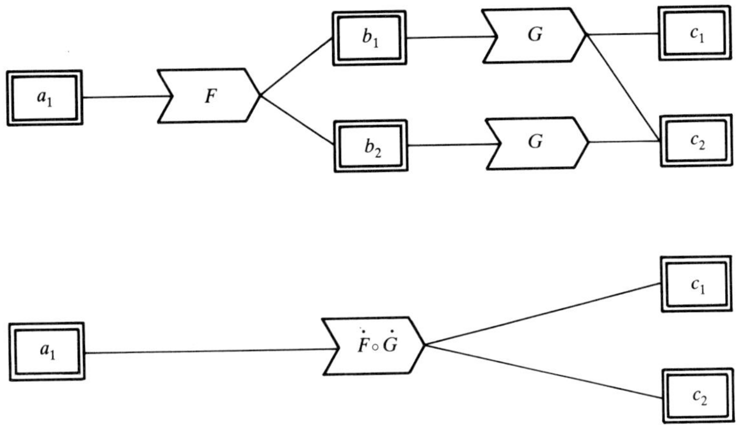

"<" ∈ <.<>

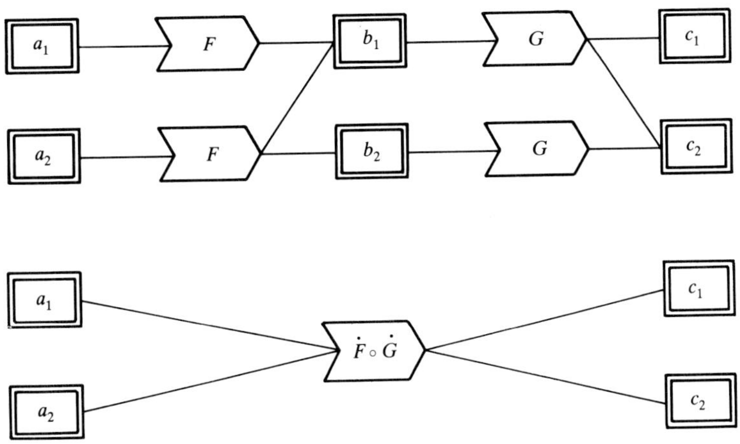

"><" ∈ <>.<>

Figure 8.23 Lower bounds of compositions with *many-to-many*.

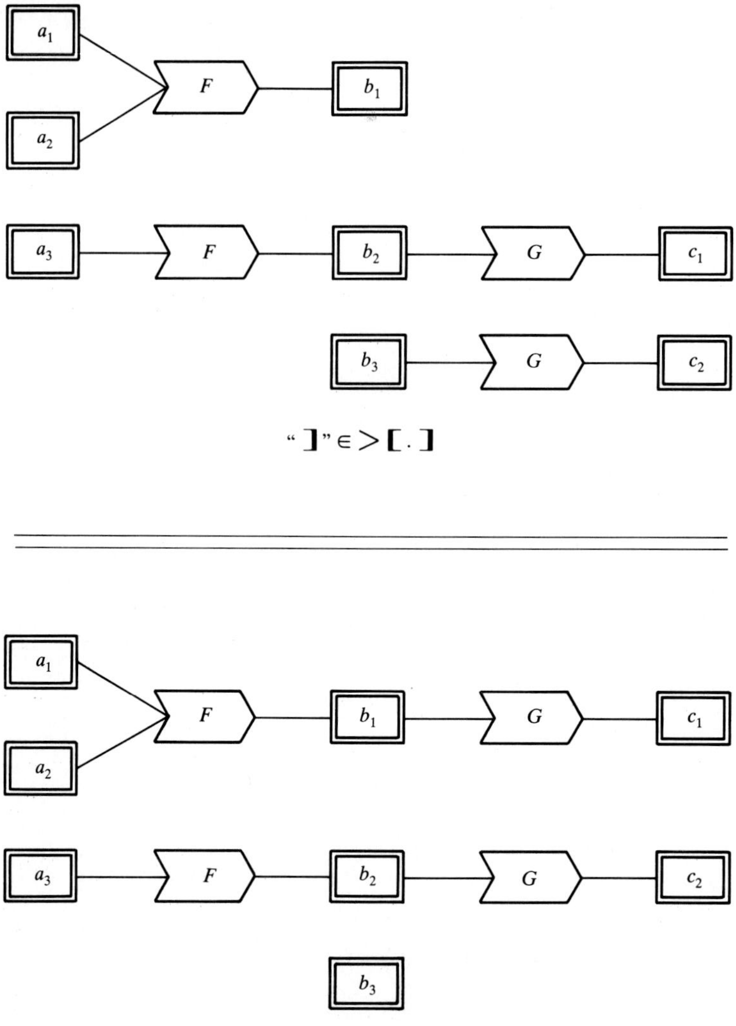

Figure 8.24 ∅ ∉ >[.]

The multiple lower bounds arise because of the two conditions about $\dot{F} \circ \dot{G}$ in the premise of Theorem 8.41. Thus, applying the contrapositive law and rearranging terms yields:

Theorem 8.42. If F is *many-to-one* relative to (A, B), then $\dot{F} \circ \dot{G}$ is *from some* or is *from many* relative to (A, C).

The "or" in the description of $\dot{F} \circ \dot{G}$ gives the multiple lower bounds. It is an unresolved "or", in the sense that the designer could leave it unspecified whether $\dot{F} \circ \dot{G}$ is *from some* or *from many* (or both). Applying the converse yields:

Theorem 8.43. If G is *from one* relative to (B, C) and $\dot{F} \circ \dot{G}$ is both *to one* and *to all* relative to (A, C), then G is *to one* relative to (B, C).

Theorem 8.44. If G is *one-to-many* relative to (B, C), then $\dot{F} \circ \dot{G}$ is *to some* or is *to many* relative to (A, C).

Multiple Lower Bounds with Bundlings

Consider further a case where F is a bundling and G is *from some*. Then $\dot{F} \circ \dot{G}$ can not be both *from one* and *from all*, but it can in certain cases be *one-to-one some-to-all* or *many-to-one all-to-all*, as shown in Figure 8.25. Here, the composition cone ><.] has two lower bounds, ">" and "]". The cone contains every character more restrictive than "]><" except ∅ and "<".

Theorem 8.45. If F is a bundling relative to (A, B) and $\dot{F} \circ \dot{G}$ is both *from all* and *from one* relative to (A, C), then F is *from one* relative to (A, B).

Proof. By Theorem 6.4, we may factor F as $H \circ I$, where H is *to one* and I is *from one*. Then $\dot{F} \circ \dot{G} \equiv (H \circ I) \circ G \equiv H \circ (I \circ \dot{G})$. Applying Theorem 8.41 to the path $(H, I \circ G)$ shows that H is *from one*. Since both H and I are *from one*, F is *from one* by Theorem 8.13. Q.E.D.

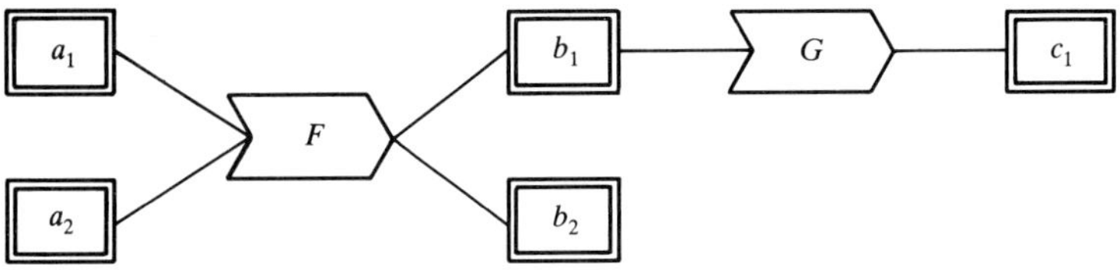

">." ∈ ><.]

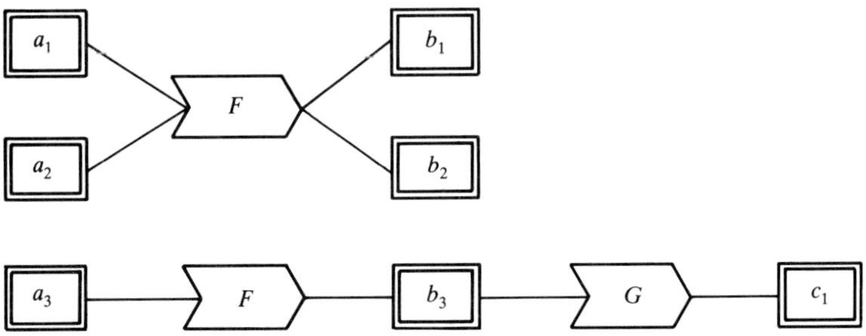

"]" ∈ ><.]

Figure 8.25 ∅ ∉ ><.]

Applying the converse and contrapositive yields:

Theorem 8.46. If F is a *many-to-many* bundling relative to (A, B), then $\dot{F} \circ \dot{G}$ is either *from some* or *from many* relative to (A, C).

Theorem 8.47. If G is a bundling relative to (B, C) and $\dot{F} \circ \dot{G}$ is both *to all* and *to one* relative to (A, C), then G is *to one* relative to (B, C).

Theorem 8.48. If G is a *many-to-many* bundling relative to (B, C), then $\dot{F} \circ \dot{G}$ is either *to many* or *to some* relative to (A, C).

The lower bounds of internally *some-to-all* composition cones are exhibited in the following table:

Cone	Lower bounds	Upper bound	Theorems
>.]	"]"	"]>"	8.26
>.]>	"]>"	"]>"	8.26, 8.30
>.]<	"]<"	"]><"	8.10, 8.26
>.]><	"]><"	"]><"	8.10, 8.26, 8.30
>.]<>	"]<>"	"]<>"	8.26, 8.34
<.]	∅	"]<"	
<.]>	∅	"]<>"	
<.]<	"<"	"]<"	8.10
<.]><	"<"	"]><"	8.10
<.]<>	"<"	"]<>"	8.10
><.]	"]", ">"	"]><"	8.46
><.]>	"]", ">"	"]><"	8.46
><.]<	"]<", "><"	"]><"	8.10, 8.46
><.]><	"]<", "><"	"]><"	8.10, 8.46
><.]<>	"]<", "><"	"]<>"	8.10, 8.46
<>.]	∅	"]<>"	
<>.]>	∅	"]<>"	
<>.]<	"<"	"]<>"	8.10
<>.]><	"<"	"]<>"	8.10
<>.]<>	"<"	"]<>"	8.10

The cones of the form $>.\beta$ are illustrated by division by *optional*, Figure 8.5. The cones of the form $<.\beta$ are illustrated by selection by *optional*, Figure 8.6, and coverage by *multiple*, Figure 8.7. These patterns may also combine with coincident diamonding, Figure 8.3, as shown in Figure 8.26.

A factoring of the form $><.\beta$ is illustrated in Figure 8.27. Factorings of this form are also affected by coincident diamonding.

The factorings of the form $<>.\beta$ show how restrictive a composition with an interior *optional* can be. The only permissive requirement is the persistence of the "<" bracket of β when α is *to all*, as illustrated by Figure 8.28.

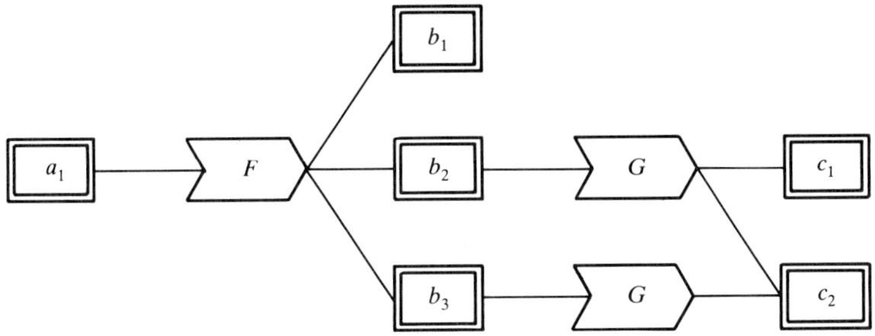

Figure 8.26 "<" ∈ <.]<>

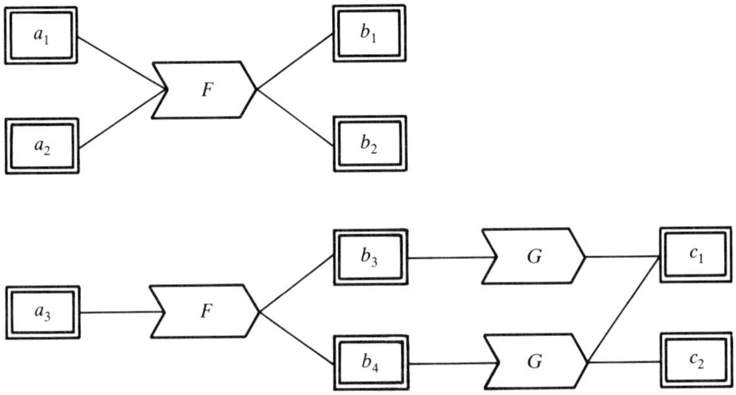

Figure 8.27 "]<" ∈ ><.]<>

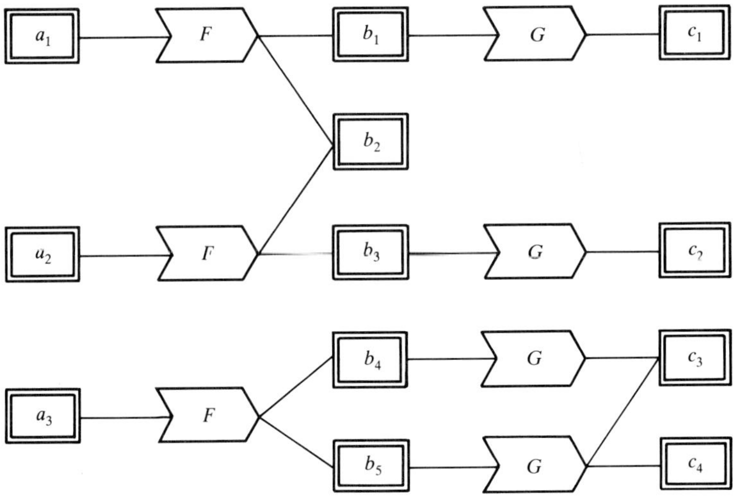

Figure 8.28 "<" ∈ <>.]<>

Survey of Internally *some-to-some* Cones

We consider finally the cones where both “[” ⊂ α and “]” ⊂ β. These cones are fully described by the theorems already proved.

Cone	Lower bounds	Upper bound	Theorems
[.]	∅	“][”	
[.]>	∅	“]>[”	
[.]<	“[”, “<”	“]<[”	8.44
[.]><	“[”, “<”	“]><[”	8.48
[.]<>	∅	“]<>[”	
>[.]	“]”, “>”	“]>[”	8.42
>[.]>	“]”, “>”	“]>[”	8.42
>[.]<	“][”, “>[”, “]<”, “><”	“]><[”	8.42, 8.44
>[.]><	“][”, “>[”, “]<”, “><”	“]><[”	8.42, 8.48
>[.]<>	“]”, “>”	“]<>[”	8.42
<[.]	∅	“]<[”	
<[.]>	∅	“]<>[”	
<[.]<	“[”, “<”	“]<[”	8.44
<[.]><	“[”, “<”	“]<>[”	8.48
<[.]<>	∅	“]<>[”	
><[.]	“]”, “>”	“]><[”	8.46
><[.]>	“]”, “>”	“]<>[”	8.46
><[.]<	“][”, “>[”, “]<”, “><”	“]><[”	8.44, 8.46
><[.]><	“][”, “>[”, “]<”, “><”	“]<>[”	8.46, 8.48
><[.]<>	“]”, “>”	“]<>[”	8.46
<>[.]	∅	“]<>[”	
<>[.]>	∅	“]<>[”	
<>[.]<	“[”, “<”	“]<>[”	8.44
<>[.]><	“[”, “<”	“]<>[”	8.48
<>[.]<>	∅	“]<>[”	

The cones whose lower bounds are not ∅ are illustrated by combining Figures 8.25 to 8.28. The cones whose lower bounds are ∅ are illustrated by variants of Figure 8.1, which shows that ∅ ∈ <>[.]<>.

The cones with *some-to-some* interiors present a staggering diversity of characters. Thus, [.]<>, <[.]>, <[.]<>, <>[.], <>[.]>, and <>[.]<> each contain all 20 possible characters. In these cases, knowing the characters of $\dot{F}$ and $\dot{G}$ says nothing about the character of $F \circ G$!

9

Associations of High Degree

9.1 INTRODUCTION

Real data base designs are not limited to classes and correspondences — nearly every practical data base design includes at least one trio, and many include quartets as well. These higher degree associations — trios, quartets, and so on — have not been clearly described by current data design methods. We show in this chapter how data logic predicts the properties of higher degree associations, and we illustrate these properties by a thorough examination of trio complexes.

Current thinking about trio complexes is limited by problems concerning "null values." These occur when a relationship among three classes A, B, and C may include attachments of instances of two of the classes without there being a triple that includes instances of all three classes. That is, we might have an attached pair (a, b) without there being an instance c such that there is an assembled triple (a, b, c). In the relational data model, such attachments are represented as triples of the form (a, b, NUL), thus inspiring the term "null value." In data logic, this situation is described by saying that the trio complex contains a correspondence F along with a trio T, and that $F{:}(a, b)$ is an attachment controlled by F, but there is no assembly of the form $T{:}(a, b, c)$ controlled by T. Whether or not such attachments of F are permitted is a design decision shown in extended associative notation. There is no prohibition against null values in extended associative notation; on the contrary, null values are viewed as a natural property of trio complexes, and are managed without restraint.

Trio complexes incorporate an essential embracing that is required for them to be specified properly: if (a, b, c) is a triple of the reduced trio $\dot{T}$, then (a, b) must be an attachment of the reduced correspondence $\dot{F}$ (notice that this does not apply, however, to the unreduced trio T). That is, the correspondence $\dot{F}$ includes all the projections of the assemblies controlled by $\dot{T}$ onto the first and second positions, and may, if the design allows the trio complex to contain null values, contain additional attachments as well. In embracing notation, we would write $\pi^{12}\dot{T} \subseteq \dot{F}$. Notice that if $\dot{F}$ does not contain any attachments other than projections of $\dot{T}$, then $\dot{F}$ does not need to be declared, because it may be computed from $\dot{T}$. This is the basis for stable states: correspondences that can be computed by projection are not declared, removing portions of the diagram for a full reversal.

In simple forms of trio complexes (such as the first stable state), the problem of declaring the trio complex can be restructured to remove all the internal embracings. The general case, however, requires embracings. Pineal trio complexes are vivid examples of how embracings are needed to describe trio complexes in the second stable state and in full reversal. In a pineal trio complex, the internal embracings take the form of composition cone constraints, causing structures similar to those illustrated in Chapter 8 within the population of a trio complex. Data models that do not recognize embracings have been unable to describe this full variety of trio complexes.

Trio complexes without null values are described by the relational data model, and so do not require extensive new terminology or techniques. However, extending design methods beyond the relational data model to the full variety of trio complexes has proven to be a perilous undertaking for developers of theory. Easy generalizations about trios are often found to be incorrect when tested rigorously against actual examples. We have, therefore, cast this chapter in a particularly rigorous tone, to make certain that our results apply to all trio complexes. This entails an increase in the amount of mathematics used, but we hope that this is compensated for by the increased certainty of the results.

The design of trio complexes in the general case is a much more intricate activity than is generally assumed. It is apparent that trios can not be designed reliably without automated support from the design management device. There are many character decision interdependencies (making one choice forces another choice elsewhere in the design) that follow completely regular patterns, but that intercombine to such a degree that expecting a designer to proofread each design accurately would be foolish. In the declaration of trios, as in the declaration of embracings, the design management device should take an active part in the specification of the design, becoming a partner instead of solely a draftsman.

In Section 9.2, Convolution and Degenerate Trios, we generalize the concept of a reduced correspondence to form reduced associations of arbitrary degree. We show how the effect of declaring an association relative to other associations can be summarized by the algebraic device of a *convolution* of associations. We show how convolution allows certain trio complexes to be reduced to simpler data structures formed from classes and correspondences. This process is similar to the "normalization" procedures of the relational data model, but the method of convolutions applies more generally to data structures that contain "null values", where normalization is not clearly defined.

In Section 9.3, Comparison with the Relational Data Model, we discuss how the treatment of trio complexes in extended associative notation compares with the treatment of third order relations in the relational data model. We show how the forms of third order relations recognized by the relational data model may be expressed as base state trio complexes in extended associative notation. We comment on how normalization describes some of the characteristics of convolutions of correspondences, and on how management of embracings by foreign keys in the relational data model can have undesirable effects on characters.

In Section 9.4, Character Decision Interdependencies, we discuss how many of the character decisions in the extended associative notation expression of a trio complex are not independent of each other—if one is chosen *from all*, another must be chosen *from all* as well. We give an exhaustive description of these interdependencies, which should be programmed into the design management device. We also show how a trio complex may be expressed as a network diagram, provided that certain embracings are recognized that relate the correspondences in the network to each other.

In Section 9.5, Case Study: List-Position-Word, we present an imaginary case study that illustrates all the decisions in the extended associative notation for a trio complex. This study verifies that trios of the complexity predicted by data logic may be found in practice.

9.2 CONVOLUTION AND DEGENERATE TRIOS

Convolution Describes Correspondence Complexes

Recall that the reduced correspondence $\dot{G}$ of the correspondence complex $(G; B, C)$ is defined by the formula

$$(\mathrm{A}x)\ (\mathrm{A}y)\ \dot{G}{:}|x,\ y| \Leftrightarrow (\exists x')\ (\exists y')\ \Delta B{:}|x,\ x'|\ \&\ G{:}|x',\ y'|\ \&\ \Delta C{:}|y',\ y|$$

We may write this formula in another form as follows. Consider the correspondence H defined by

$$(\mathrm{A}x)\ (\mathrm{A}y)\ H{:}|x,\ y| \Leftrightarrow (\exists x')\ (\exists y')\ \Delta B{:}|x,\ x'|\ \&\ \Delta C{:}|y',\ y|$$

Notice how H is defined by removing the expression "$G{:}|x',\ y'|$" from the definition of $\dot{G}$. As may be seen by inspection, H is independent of the choice of correspondence G. That is, any correspondence declared relative to (B, C) will establish the same correspondence H. The correspondence H is called the *convolution* of (B, C), and is written "$¢(B, C)$". By definition, any reduced correspondence relative to (B, C) is embraced in the convolution $¢(B, C)$. Thus, $\dot{G} \subseteq H$.

We may simplify the definition of $H \equiv ¢(B, C)$ as follows:

$$\begin{aligned}(\mathrm{A}x)\ (\mathrm{A}y)\ H{:}|x,\ y| &\Leftrightarrow (\exists x')\ (\exists y')\ \Delta B{:}|x,\ x'|\ \&\ \Delta C{:}|y',\ y|\\ &\Leftrightarrow B{:}|x|\ \&\ C{:}|y|\\ &\Leftrightarrow B \times C{:}|x,\ y|\end{aligned}$$

Thus, the convolution of a pair of classes is equivalent to their Cartesian product.

A primary use for convolutions is to eliminate the need to declare associations of high degree by showing that they can be formed by convoluting other associations of lower degree. An association that is equivalent to a logical combination of other associations, in particular an association that is equivalent to a convolution, is called *degenerate*. We will see that some "normalization" procedures of the relational data model can be viewed more generally as convolutions. This more general approach applies to associations with null values.

For example, this reasoning shows that a Cartesian product of two classes need not be declared in a data design—it can always be formed from the classes by convoluting them, and therefore it is not an independent idea. Of course, we could have reached this result for correspondences directly from the syntax of embracings, and avoided introducing the convolution. However, we will find that the convolution is a convenient tool to apply to associations of higher degrees.

Relative Complexes

To generalize the convolution, we introduce the idea of a *relative complex*, which may be thought of as a collection of associations that an association could be declared relative to. For example, a pair of classes (B, C) is a relative complex because a correspondence could be declared relative to (B, C). A single class (B) is not a relative complex because a correspondence can not be declared relative to a lone class. A correspondence must be declared relative to a pair of classes, although the same class could appear twice: (B, B).

A relative complex is defined formally as follows. Each association in a relative complex is assigned a string of indices that shows the positions that the association is relative to. These strings will be indicated by lowercase Greek letters: α, β, and so on. Thus, in a correspondence complex $(G; B, C)$, B would be assigned the string $\alpha = (1)$ and C would be assigned the string $\beta = (2)$. We may write the strings α and β as subscripts of a single tag such as "Q". Thus, the relative complex (B, C) would be written $\{Q_\alpha, Q_\beta\}$ or $\{Q_{(1)}, Q_{(2)}\}$.

A relative complex of degree r is defined to be a set of associations $S = \{Q_\alpha, Q_\beta, \ldots\}$ that satisfies the following conditions:

- **(i)** For each member Q_α of S, for each index i in α, $1 \leq i \leq r$.
- **(ii)** No index string α includes all members of $\{1, \ldots, r\}$.
- **(iii)** For each integer i such that $1 \leq i \leq r$, there is an association tag $Q_{(i)}$ in S.
- **(iv)** If Q_α and Q_β are members of S, and β is a permutation of α, then Q_β is a corresponding permutation of Q_α.

The condition (i) determines the degree of the relative complex: r is the smallest integer for which (i) holds. The condition (ii) distinguishes an association complex from a relative complex; an association complex must contain an association whose index string includes all members of $\{1, \ldots, r\}$ while a relative complex must not. The condition (iii) forces there to be a relative class for each position; these classes are needed so that identity will be defined in each position. The condition (iv) assures that a relative complex contains only one association (up to equivalence) for any set of positions.

Consider, for example, a relative complex S of degree two. By condition (iii), S must contain two classes $B \equiv Q_{(1)}$ and $C \equiv Q_{(2)}$. It can have no other members, for by rule (i), only $Q_{(1)}$, $Q_{(2)}$, $Q_{(1,\,2)}$, and $Q_{(2,\,1)}$ are potential members, and by rule (ii), $Q_{(1,\,2)}$ and $Q_{(2,\,1)}$ can not be members. Thus, there is only one form of relative complex of degree two, a pair of classes (B, C).

Relative complexes are more diverse in degrees greater than two. A relative complex of degree r could contain no associations beyond the r classes $Q_{(1)}, \ldots, Q_{(r)}$. This is called a *base* relative complex. Alternatively, a relative complex of degree r may contain an association for each nonempty proper subset of $\{1, \ldots, r\}$, a total of 2^r-2 different associations. This is called a *complete* relative complex. There are other forms of relative complexes between these two extremes. Since $2^r-2 = r$ when $r = 2$, there is only one form of relative complex in degree two. However, the number of associations in a relative complex of degree three may range from 3 to 6, the number in degree four may range from 4 to 14, and so on.

An association tag of degree r in extended associative notation is always declared relative to one or more relative complexes of degree r. The combination of an association of degree r with a relative complex of degree r is called an *association complex* of degree r (also a *correspondence complex,* if $r = 2$, a *trio complex* if $r = 3$, etc.). If an association R is declared relative to a complete relative complex, R is said to be *fully reversed*. If R is declared relative to a relative complex in which some of the possible index strings are omitted, R is said to be declared in an *interim stable state*.

General Definition of Convolution

The convolution of a general relative complex $S = \{Q_\alpha, Q_\beta, \ldots\}$ is formed as follows. Pick an index string α. Let $a, b, c, \ldots$ be the indices that appear in α (for example, if $\alpha = (2, 4, 1)$ then $a = 2$, $b = 4$, and $c = 1$). Then define the association P_α as follows:

$$(\mathrm{A}x_a)\,(\mathrm{A}x_b)\,(\mathrm{A}x_c)\ldots P_\alpha{:}|x_a, x_b, x_c, \ldots| \Leftrightarrow (\exists y_{\alpha,a})\,(\exists y_{\alpha,b})\,(\exists y_{\alpha,c})\ldots \Delta Q_{(a)}{:}|x_a, y_{\alpha,a}| \;\&\; \Delta Q_{(b)}{:}|x_b, y_{\alpha,b}| \;\&\; \Delta Q_{(c)}{:}|x_c, y_{\alpha,c}| \;\&\; \ldots \;\&\; Q_\alpha{:}|y_{\alpha,a}, y_{\alpha,b}, y_{\alpha,c}, \ldots|$$

The association P_α assembles images if each image is the same (according to some identity correspondence) as an image that would be assembled in the same position by Q_α. The complexity of the formula that defines P_α is largely caused by the need to keep indices straight when working with associations of arbitrary degree.

The convolution of $S = \{Q_\alpha, Q_\beta, \ldots\}$ is defined to be the conjunction of P_α, P_β, $\ldots$, conjoining each association on the positions shown in its index string. Thus, let d, e, $f, \ldots$ be the indices that appear in β. Then $\underset{\sim}{¢}S$ is defined by

$$(\mathrm{A}x_1)\ldots(\mathrm{A}x_r)\ \underset{\sim}{¢}S{:}|x_1, \ldots, x_r| \Leftrightarrow P_\alpha{:}|x_a, x_b, x_c, \ldots| \;\&\; P_\beta{:}|x_d, x_e, x_f, \ldots| \;\&\; \ldots$$

The degree of the convolution of a relative complex is always the same as the degree of the relative complex itself. We compute the convolutions of relative complexes of degree three later in this section.

Stable States of Trios

A relative complex of degree three must contain three classes $A \equiv Q_{(1)}$, $B \equiv Q_{(2)}$, and $C \equiv Q_{(3)}$. It may, in addition, contain zero to three of the following correspondences:

$$F \equiv Q_{(1,2)}$$

$$G \equiv Q_{(2,3)}$$

$$H \equiv Q_{(3,1)}$$

We will find it convenient to use the notation A, B, C, F, G, H as above, rather than the more general Q_α notation, when describing trio complexes.

There are therefore eight different trio complexes for T, based on which of the three correspondence tags are chosen:

$$(T;\ A,\ B,\ C) \qquad (T;\ F;\ A,\ B,\ C) \qquad (T;\ F,\ G;\ A,\ B,\ C) \qquad (T;\ F,\ G,\ H;\ A,\ B,\ C)$$

$$(T;\ G;\ A,\ B,\ C) \qquad (T;\ G,\ H;\ A,\ B,\ C)$$

$$(T;\ H;\ A,\ B,\ C) \qquad (T;\ H,\ F;\ A,\ B,\ C)$$

Several of these forms are related by permutations. For example, consider the trio $\pi^{231}T$, defined by

$$(\mathrm{A}x)\ (\mathrm{A}y)\ (\mathrm{A}z)\ \pi^{231}T{:}|x,\ y,\ z| \Leftrightarrow T{:}|z,\ x,\ y|$$

Recalling that $F \equiv Q_{(1,\ 2)}$, declaring T relative to $(F;\ A,\ B,\ C)$ is equivalent to declaring $\pi^{231}T$ relative to $(Q_{(3,1)};\ B,\ C,\ A)$, which has the same form as $(H;\ A,\ B,\ C)$. Once we have investigated any one of the relative complexes that contain one correspondence tag: $(F;\ A,\ B,\ C)$, $(G;\ A,\ B,\ C)$, or $(H;\ A,\ B,\ C)$, we can apply our results to the others by permutation in this way. A similar pattern applies to the relative complexes that contain two correspondence tags: $(F,\ G;\ A,\ B,\ C)$, $(G,\ H;\ A,\ B,\ C)$, and $(H,\ F;\ A,\ B,\ C)$.

Permutation only interrelates two relative complexes if they contain the same number of correspondence tags. Relative complexes that contain different numbers of correspondence tags behave differently, and must be studied separately. Thus, we may divide the study of trio complexes into four patterns based on the number of correspondence tags in the complex: the *base state*, $(T;\ A,\ B,\ C)$; the *first stable state*, $(T;\ F;\ A,\ B,\ C)$, etc.; the *second stable state*, $(T;\ F,\ G;\ A,\ B,\ C)$, etc., and the *fully reversed* trio complex, $(T;\ F,\ G,\ H;\ A,\ B,\ C)$.

Convolution of the Base State

The expression for the reduced trio of a base state trio complex is given by

$$(\mathrm{A}x)\ (\mathrm{A}y)\ (\mathrm{A}z)\ \dot{T}{:}|x,\ y,\ z| \Leftrightarrow (\exists x')\ (\exists y')\ (\exists z')\ \Delta A{:}|x,\ x'|\ \&\ \Delta B{:}|y,\ y'|\ \&\ \Delta C{:}|z,\ z'|\ \&\ T{:}|x',\ y',\ z'|$$

Excising T from the right side gives the formula for the convolution of a base relative complex of degree three:

$$(\mathrm{A}x)\ (\mathrm{A}y)\ (\mathrm{A}z)\ \cent(A,\ B,\ C){:}|x,\ y,\ z| \Leftrightarrow (\exists x')\ (\exists y')\ (\exists z')\ \Delta A{:}|x,\ x'|\ \&\ \Delta B{:}|y,\ y'|\ \&\ \Delta C{:}|z,\ z'|$$

$$\Leftrightarrow A{:}|x|\ \&\ B{:}|y|\ \&\ C{:}|z|$$

That is,

$$\boxed{(\mathrm{A}x)\ (\mathrm{A}y)\ (\mathrm{A}z)\ \cent(A,\ B,\ C){:}|x,\ y,\ z| \Leftrightarrow A \times B \times C{:}|x,\ y,\ z|}$$

Thus, the convolution of a base relative complex of degree three is a Cartesian product. In general, the convolution of a base relative complex of degree r is the Cartesian product of the r classes in the relative complex.

Convolution of the First Stable State

The reduced trio of a first stable state trio complex is given by adding a correspondence F to the formula for a base state trio complex. New placetakers x'' and y'' are used for F, related to x and y by the identity correspondences ΔA and ΔB, respectively:

$$(\mathrm{A}x)\,(\mathrm{A}y)\,(\mathrm{A}z)\ \dot{T}{:}|x,\ y,\ z| \Leftrightarrow (\exists x')\,(\exists y')\,(\exists z')\,(\exists x'')\,(\exists y'')\ \Delta A{:}|x,\ x'|\ \&\ \Delta B{:}|y,\ y'|\ \&\ \Delta C{:}|z,\ z'|\ \&\ T{:}|x',\ y',\ z'|\ \&\ \Delta A{:}|x,\ x''|\ \&\ F{:}|x'',\ y''|\ \&\ \Delta B{:}|y'',\ y|$$

Excising T from the right side and simplifying yields

$$(\mathrm{A}x)\,(\mathrm{A}y)\,(\mathrm{A}z)\ ¢(F;\ A,\ B,\ C){:}|x,\ y,\ z| \Leftrightarrow (\exists x'')\,(\exists y'')\ \Delta A{:}|x,\ x''|\ \&\ F{:}|x'',\ y''|\ \&\ \Delta B{:}|y'',\ y|\ \&\ C{:}|z|$$

Simplifying further, we obtain

$$(\mathrm{A}x)\,(\mathrm{A}y)\,(\mathrm{A}z)\ ¢(F;\ A,\ B,\ C){:}|x,\ y,\ z| \Leftrightarrow \dot{F}{:}|x,\ y|\ \&\ C{:}|z|$$

Thus, the convolution of $(F;\ A,\ B,\ C)$ is the Cartesian product of the reduced correspondence $\dot{F}$ with the class C. That is, $¢(F;\ A,\ B,\ C)$ assembles all the attachments of $\dot{F}$ with all the instances of C, as shown in Figure 9.1.

A trio that is equivalent to the Cartesian product of a correspondence with a class will be called a *barrel trio*. The term is motivated by seeing $\dot{F}$ as the lid of a barrel, and C as the vertical dimension. Once the shape of the lid and the shape of the staves are known, the structure of the barrel is determined. A barrel trio should not be declared in extended

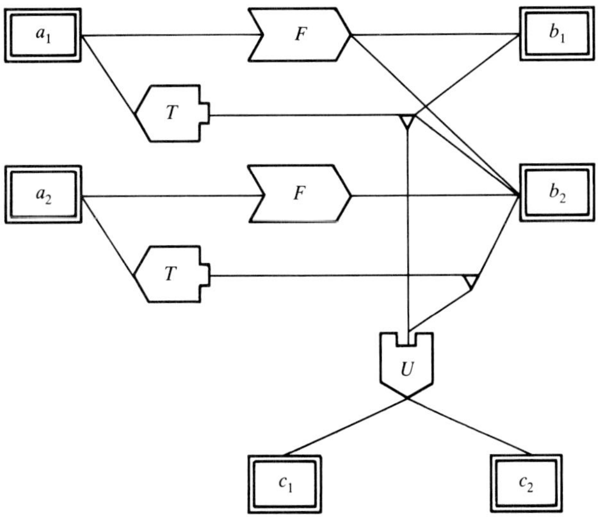

Figure 9.1 A barrel trio.

associative notation. Instead, declare the correspondence complex (F; A, B) and the class C.

Juncture Trios

The convolutions of the remaining stable states may be computed using the reduced correspondence tags $\dot{F}$, $\dot{G}$, and $\dot{H}$. Thus, the convolution in the second stable state is given by

$$\boxed{(\mathrm{A}x)\ (\mathrm{A}y)\ (\mathrm{A}z)\ \cent(F,\ G;\ A,\ B,\ C){:}|x,\ y,\ z| \Leftrightarrow \dot{F}{:}|x,\ y|\ \&\ \dot{G}{:}|y,\ z|}$$

where $\dot{F} \equiv \Delta A \circ F \circ \Delta B$ and $\dot{G} \equiv \Delta B \circ G \circ \Delta C$.

The convolution in the second stable state is the relational ''join'' of the correspondences $\dot{F}$ and $\dot{G}$. We will call a trio that is equivalent to this form of convolution a *juncture trio*. The term ''juncture'' avoids the annoying use of the verb ''to join'' as a noun.

A sample population of a juncture trio T is

$$\vdash T{:}(a_1,\ b_1,\ c_1)$$
$$\vdash T{:}(a_1,\ b_1,\ c_2)$$
$$\vdash T{:}(a_1,\ b_2,\ c_3)$$
$$\vdash T{:}(a_2,\ b_1,\ c_2)$$
$$\vdash T{:}(a_3,\ b_2,\ c_3)$$

This population is the convolution of the two populations:

$$\begin{array}{ll} \vdash F{:}(a_1,\ b_1) & \vdash G{:}(b_1,\ c_1) \\ \vdash F{:}(a_1,\ b_2) & \vdash G{:}(b_1,\ c_2) \\ \vdash F{:}(a_2,\ b_1) & \vdash G{:}(b_2,\ c_3) \\ \vdash F{:}(a_3,\ b_2) & \end{array}$$

Juncture trios are degenerate cases, like null trios and barrel trios, and should not be written as trio complexes in extended associative notation. The test for whether a given trio T is a juncture trio is to ask three questions:

Does $T{:}|x,\ y,\ z|$ if and only if $\pi^{12}T{:}|x,\ y|$ and $\pi^{23}T{:}|y,\ z|$?
Does $T{:}|x,\ y,\ z|$ if and only if $\pi^{23}T{:}|y,\ z|$ and $\pi^{31}T{:}|z,\ x|$?
Does $T{:}|x,\ y,\ z|$ if and only if $\pi^{31}T{:}|z,\ x|$ and $\pi^{12}T{:}|x,\ y|$?

If the answer to any of these questions is yes, then declaring the two correspondences is sufficient, and T should not normally be declared separately.

Normalization Describes Some, but Not All, Juncture Trios

Student-Course-Teacher is a juncture trio that appears frequently in introductory texts. In a typical presentation, the trio

$$(x) \textit{ Is Enrolled In } (y) \textit{ Taught By } (z)$$

is shown to be reducible to two correspondences

$$(x) \textit{ Attends } (y)$$

$$(z) \textit{ Teaches } (y)$$

In the relational data model, the reduction relies on assumptions about the characters of the correspondences. For example, if *Teaches* is *from one*, then the reduction follows the pattern of normalization to third normal form. However, no assumptions about character are necessary in data logic. The degeneracy of the trio is a consequence of its embracings, not its characters. Indeed, both *Attends* and *Teaches* may be *many-to-many some-to-some*. A student might attend no course (if the student is on a leave of absence), or many courses. A course might have no students or many students. A teacher might teach no course or many courses. A course might have no teachers (let study hall be considered a course, for example) or many teachers. The embracing that shows that we are dealing with a juncture trio still holds:

$$|x| \textit{ Is Enrolled In } |y| \textit{ Taught By } |z| \text{ if and only if } |x| \textit{ Attends } |y| \text{ and } |z| \textit{ Teaches } |y|$$

Delta Trios

The convolution in the third stable state is:

$$\boxed{(\mathrm{A}x)\ (\mathrm{A}y)\ (\mathrm{A}z)\ ¢(F, G, H; A, B, C){:}|x, y, z| \Leftrightarrow \dot{F}{:}|x, y| \ \&\ \dot{G}{:}|y, z| \ \&\ \dot{H}{:}|z, x|} \quad (1)$$

Here, $\dot{H} \equiv \Delta C \circ H \circ \Delta A$.

Notice that the convolution is a logical operation that is different from composition and is different from a relational "join." For example, the convolution of the relative complex $S = (F, G, H; A, B, C)$ above is a trio, while the composition is the correspondence (loop):

$$(\mathrm{A}w)\ (\mathrm{A}x)\ \dot{F} \circ \dot{G} \circ \dot{H}{:}|x, w| \Leftrightarrow (\exists y)\ (\exists z)\ \dot{F}{:}|x, y| \ \&\ \dot{G}{:}|y, z| \ \&\ \dot{H}{:}|z, w|$$

and the "join" on B and C is the quartet:

$$\dot{F}{:}|x, y| \ \&\ \dot{G}{:}|y, z| \ \&\ \dot{H}{:}|z, w|$$

A trio equivalent to a convolution of the form shown in Formula (1) will be called a *delta trio*. The name indicates how the three correspondences form a triangle in a network diagram, as shown in Figure 9.2.

An example of a delta trio may be constructed as follows. Imagine a sales planning data base that identifies potential new offerings for a collection of sales outlets. For a sales outlet x, a product y, and a sales territory z, suppose that the data base is a population of the trio

$$(x) \textit{ Could Sell } (y) \textit{ At } (z)$$

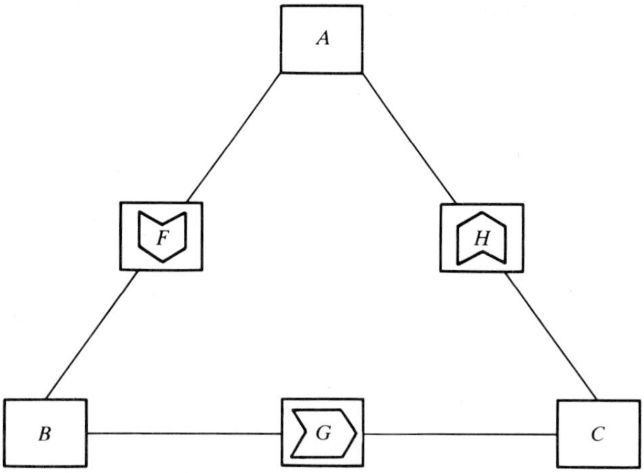

Figure 9.2 A delta.

Suppose that this trio were determined from the three conditions

(i) (x) *Can Receive* (y)—imagine that some items require special handling so not all products can be received at all outlets.

(ii) (x) *Is Located In* (z)—imagine that items are expensive to transport, so that an outlet must be located near the sales point for sales to be economical.

(iii) *There Is A Market For* (y) *At* (z)—imagine that some minimum demand threshold is set above which sales could be economical.

The trio ( ) *Could Sell* ( ) *At* ( ) would be the convolution of these three correspondences if the following embracing is obeyed:

$|x|$ *Could Sell* $|y|$ *At* $|z|$ if and only if $|x|$ *Can Receive* $|y|$, $|x|$ *Is Located In* $|z|$, and *There Is A Market For* $|y|$ *At* $|z|$

If so, ( ) *Could Sell* ( ) *At* ( ) is a delta trio and should not normally be declared in extended associative notation. Instead, declare the three correspondences *Can Receive, Is Located In*, and *There Is A Market For*.

Another common, though somewhat degenerate, example of a delta trio is a juncture trio $F(x, y)$ & $G(y, z)$, where the correspondences F and G are constrained by the composition cone constraint $F \circ G \equiv H$.

General Formula for Reduced Associations

The convolution may be used to simplify the formula for a reduced association. Let an association R of degree r be declared relative to a relative complex S. Then the formula for the reduced association R contains a new set of placetakers for each association in S, related by identity correspondences. The only placetakers that are affected by excising R from this formula when forming the convolution are the placetakers that appear within R;

all the other placetakers are managed within the definition of the convolution. Therefore, the formula for the reduced association $\dot{R}$ may be written as follows:

$$(\mathrm{A}x_1) \ldots (\mathrm{A}x_r)\ \dot{R}{:}|x_1, \ldots, x_r| \Leftrightarrow (\exists y_1) \ldots (\exists y_r)\ \Delta Q_{(1)}{:}|x_1, y_1| \ \& \ldots$$
$$\& \ \Delta Q_{(r)}{:}|x_r, y_r| \ \& \ R{:}|y_1, \ldots, y_r| \ \& \ {¢}S{:}|x_1, \ldots, x_r|$$

Thus, by definition, $\dot{R}$ is embraced in the convolution $¢\{Q_\alpha\}$. In many practical cases, the relative association tags are chosen so that the original association R (not just the reduced association $\dot{R}$) is embraced in the convolution $¢\{Q_\alpha\}$. If so, the association R is said to be *situated within* the relative complex $\{Q_\alpha\}$. If R is situated within $\{Q_\alpha\}$, R and $\dot{R}$ differ only in that $\dot{R}$ incorporates the relative identity correspondences of each of the r relative classes, whereas R need not.

Defaults for Omitted Associations in Stable States

Suppose that an association R is declared relative to a relative complex $S = \{Q_\alpha\}$ in an interim stable state. Then there are some index strings β such that there is no member of S of the form Q_β. Nevertheless, a logically determined *default* association for each such β may be formed from the reduced association $\dot{R}$. Thus, any association complex can in principle be fully reversed, just by adding all the default association tags to the association complex.

The default association Q_β is the projection of the reduced association onto the string β, that is, $Q_\beta \equiv \pi^\beta \dot{R}$. We consider below the defaults for the four stable states of a trio. We will drop the parentheses in the index strings for clarity: thus "Q_{12}" means "$Q_{(1,2)}$".

In the base state, the three correspondences are given by:

$$(\mathrm{A}x)\ (\mathrm{A}y)\ Q_{12}{:}|x, y| \Leftrightarrow (\exists x')\ (\exists y')\ \Delta Q_1{:}|x, x'| \ \& \ \Delta Q_2{:}|y, y'| \ \& \ (\exists z)\ Q_3{:}|z|$$
$$\& \ T{:}|x', y', z|$$

$$(\mathrm{A}y)\ (\mathrm{A}z)\ Q_{23}{:}|y, z| \Leftrightarrow (\exists y')\ (\exists z')\ \Delta Q_2{:}|y, y'| \ \& \ \Delta Q_3{:}|z, z'| \ \& \ (\exists x)\ Q_1{:}|x|$$
$$\& \ T{:}|x, y', z'|$$

$$(\mathrm{A}z)\ (\mathrm{A}x)\ Q_{31}{:}|z, x| \Leftrightarrow (\exists x')\ (\exists z')\ \Delta Q_1{:}|x, x'| \ \& \ \Delta Q_3{:}|z, z'| \ \& \ (\exists y)\ Q_2{:}|y|$$
$$\& \ T{:}|x', y, z'|$$

That is, each is a projection of T, altered by applying the appropriate identity correspondence in each position.

In the first stable state, one correspondence, Q_{12} for illustration, is declared in addition to the three classes. The remaining correspondences are given by:

$$(\mathrm{A}y)\ (\mathrm{A}z)\ Q_{23}{:}|y, z| \Leftrightarrow (\exists z')\ \Delta Q_3{:}|z, z'| \ \& \ (\exists x)\ \dot{Q}_{12}{:}|x, y| \ \& \ T{:}|x, y, z'|$$

$$(\mathrm{A}z)\ (\mathrm{A}x)\ Q_{31}{:}|z, x| \Leftrightarrow (\exists z')\ \Delta Q_3{:}|z, z'| \ \& \ (\exists y)\ \dot{Q}_{12}{:}|x, y| \ \& \ T{:}|x, y, z'|$$

Notice how $\dot{Q}_{12}$ appears in the formulas in addition to T. Thus, even if there is some x such that $T{:}(x, y, z)$, we may not conclude that Q_{23} attaches y to z unless y attaches to x via $\dot{Q}_{12}$* as well.

For example, consider the population:

$$\vdash T{:}(a_1, b_1, c_1) \qquad \vdash Q_{12}{:}(a_1, b_1)$$

$$\vdash T{:}(a_2, b_2, c_2) \qquad \vdash Q_{12}{:}(a_1, b_2)$$

Here, the populations of Q_{23} and Q_{31} are:

$$\vdash Q_{23}{:}(b_1, c_1) \qquad \vdash Q_{31}{:}(c_1, a_1)$$

Q_{23} does not attach b_2 to c_2 because Q_{12} does not attach a_2 to b_2. Q_{31} does not attach c_2 to a_2 for the same reason.

In the second stable state, two correspondences are declared, Q_{12} and Q_{23} for illustration. The remaining correspondence is given by:

$$(\mathrm{A}z)\ (\mathrm{A}x)\ Q_{31}{:}|z, x| \Leftrightarrow (\exists y)\ \dot{Q}_{12}{:}|x, y|\ \&\ \dot{Q}_{23}{:}|y, z|\ \&\ T{:}|x, y, z|$$

So, for z to attach to x via Q_{31}, z must attach to x by the composition $\dot{Q}_{23}{}^* \circ \dot{Q}_{12}{}^*$, and at least one of the instances y that the composition goes through must appear in a triple $T{:}(x, y, z)$.

For example, consider the population:

$$\vdash T{:}(a_1, b_1, c_1) \qquad \vdash Q_{12}{:}(a_1, b_1) \qquad \vdash Q_{23}{:}(b_1, c_2)$$

$$\vdash T{:}(a_2, b_1, c_2) \qquad \vdash Q_{12}{:}(a_1, b_2) \qquad \vdash Q_{23}{:}(b_2, c_1)$$

$$\vdash T{:}(a_2, b_2, c_1) \qquad \vdash Q_{12}{:}(a_2, b_2)$$

The population of Q_{31} is then:

$$\vdash Q_{31}{:}(c_1, a_2)$$

Even though $\dot{Q}_{12} \circ \dot{Q}_{23}$ attaches a_1 to c_1 via b_2, Q_{31} does not attach c_1 to a_1 because T does not assemble (a_1, b_2, c_1).

There are cases where it helps the clarity of presentation to declare relative associations that could, in theory, be defaulted. For example, the formula deriving Q_β from $(R; S)$ may be quite elaborate, so declaring Q_β in extended associative notation could require forming a complicated combination. If Q_β obeys an additional constraint, such as if Q_β embraces some declared association P, or if Q_β is *to one* where theory would permit it to be *to many*, then it may make the design more comprehensible to declare Q_β within the association complex for R than to declare a separate combination.

Conclusion

We have defined the concepts of a relative complex, an association complex, a stable state, and a convolution, for associations of arbitrary degree. We have shown how convolution establishes a family of degenerate trios. These trios need not be declared using the trio complex notation of extended associative notation because they may be computed from correspondences that appear elsewhere in the data structure. The normalization procedures of the relational model can be an aid to identifying degenerate trios, but they do not suffice, as the examples of juncture trios and delta trios show.

In practice it is sometimes valuable to declare a degenerate trio to improve comprehension of the design. For example, a degenerate trio of particular interest to users may be shown explicitly in the design to eliminate the need to reiterate the formula for the trio each time it arises in discussion. Another common reason to write a degenerate trio is to express a character constraint such as *from one* that would be awkward in embracing notation. Either of these uses is a proper application of extended associative notation, whose primary purpose is to render the schema accessible to the widest possible audience. When declaring a degenerate trio in this way, the designer should indicate that the trio is degenerate by declaring it to be equivalent to the appropriate convolution.

9.3 COMPARISON WITH THE RELATIONAL DATA MODEL

To one Correspondences Produce Degenerate Trios

The second and third "normal forms" in the relational data model may be extended using data logic to all trio complexes, as is shown by the following theorem:

Theorem 9.1. The reduced trio of any trio declared relative to a *to one* correspondence is a juncture trio.

Proof. Let a trio T be declared relative to $(A, B, C; F)$ and let F be *to one*. Then

$$(\mathrm{A}x)\ (\mathrm{A}y_1)\ (\mathrm{A}y_2)\ \dot{F}{:}|x, y_1|\ \&\ \dot{F}{:}|x, y_2| \Rightarrow \Delta B{:}|y_1, y_2|$$

Since $\pi^{12}\dot{T} \subseteq \dot{F}$, we have

$$(\mathrm{A}x)\ (\mathrm{A}y_1)\ (\mathrm{A}y_2)\ (\mathrm{A}z_1)\ (\mathrm{A}z_2)\ \dot{T}{:}|x, y_1, z_1|\ \&\ \dot{T}{:}|x, y_2, z_2| \Rightarrow \Delta B{:}|y_1, y_2| \qquad (1)$$

Now consider the projection $\pi^{31}\dot{T}$. By the definition of projection,

$$(\mathrm{A}x)\ (\mathrm{A}y)\ (\mathrm{A}z)\ \pi^{31}\dot{T}{:}|z, x|\ \&\ \pi^{12}\dot{T}{:}|x, y| \Leftrightarrow (\exists y')\ \dot{T}{:}|x, y', z|\ \&\ (\exists z')\ \dot{T}{:}|x, y, z'|$$

By Formula (1), we may conclude from the right side that $\Delta B{:}|y, y'|$. So,

$$(\mathrm{A}x)\ (\mathrm{A}y)\ (\mathrm{A}z)\ \pi^{31}\dot{T}{:}|z, x|\ \&\ \pi^{12}\dot{T}{:}|x, y| \Leftrightarrow \dot{T}{:}|x, y, z|\ \&\ (\exists z')\ \dot{T}{:}|x, y, z'|$$
$$\Leftrightarrow \dot{T}{:}|x, y, z|$$

Therefore $\dot{T}$ is the convolution of $\pi^{31}\dot{T}$ and $\pi^{12}\dot{T}$, so $\dot{T}$ is a juncture trio. Q.E.D.

Thus, if $\pi^{12}\dot{T}$ is *to one*, then do not declare $\dot{T}$ as a trio complex; declare the two correspondences $\pi^{12}\dot{T}$ and $\pi^{31}\dot{T}$ instead. Theorem 9.1 shows that all the correspondences in a nondegenerate trio complex in extended associative notation are *many-to-many*. Theorem 9.1 includes what are called normalizations to the second and third normal forms of third order relations in the relational data model, but Theorem 9.1 may also be applied more generally to relations with "null values."

Trio Forms in the Relational Data Model

Third order relations in the relational data model are similar to base state trio complexes in data logic. A third order relation is often written in the relational data model as $R(A, B, C)$, where A, B, and C are the projections π^1R, π^2R, and π^3R, respectively.

We will assume that A, B, and C are interior class tags. If any of them are exterior class tags, then it may be possible to simplify the declaration of R using oval notation.

The relational data model recognizes three varieties of third order relations:

(i) One domain, say A, is key in R
(ii) A pair of domains, say AB, are key in R
(iii) R is an all-key relation

In case (i), A corresponds *to one* to both B and C. This data structure is a juncture trio by virtue of Theorem 9.1, so it is not shown as a trio complex in extended associative notation. Instead, it is shown as two correspondences, one correspondence F between A and B, and another correspondence G between A and C, as shown in Figure 9.3. The designer must create new verbs F and G to describe these correspondences.

It remains to say whether or not B corresponds *to one* to A, and whether or not C corresponds *to one* to A, that is, whether or not B or C are also key in R. Relational model

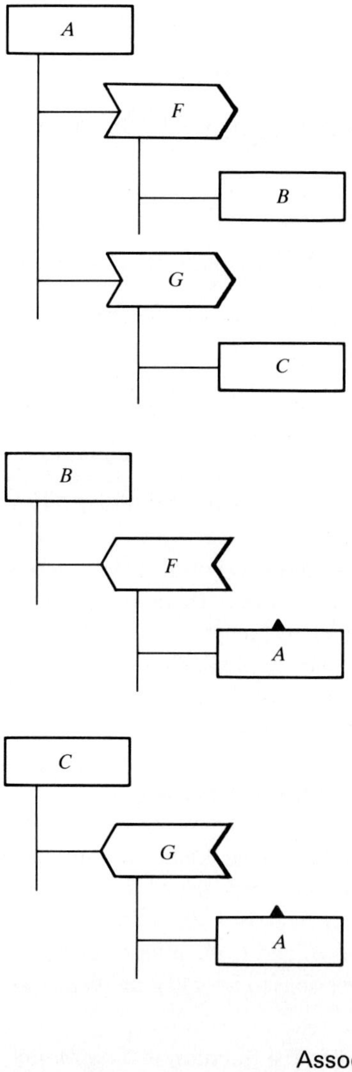

Figure 9.3 The relation $R(A, B, C)$, with A key.

theorists differ on whether such *one-to-one* structures are permitted in the relational data model, but they are allowed in extended associative notation.

Case (ii) may be written as a base state trio complex, as shown in Figure 9.4. There is then an RNA constraint on C^1R, namely, that there is only one instance of C^1R for any pair of instances of A and B. Notice that we show the tag "R" as a verb in extended associative notation, although relational data model designs often use nouns for association tags. These nouns should be converted to verbs when writing in extended associative notation.

It is preferred, however, to write case (ii) in the first stable state, as shown in Figure 9.5. The designer must then create a new verb F to describe the correspondence between A and B.

It is possible, even without null values, for AB, BC, and AC all to correspond *to one* to C^1R, as in the following set of triples:

$$(a_1, b_1, c_1)$$

$$(a_1, b_2, c_2)$$

$$(a_2, b_2, c_1)$$

Such a structure may be written in the base state as shown in Figure 9.6. Or, preferably, it may be written in the fully reversed form as three structures of the form shown in Figure 9.5.

Again, relational model theorists differ as to whether structures such as shown in Figure 9.6, called "alternate keys" or "designated keys," are encompassed by the relational model. Date indicates that only one of the RNA constraints may be enforced at a time: "the *only* [Date's italics] system-guaranteed way of pinpointing some individual tuple is via the combination (R, k), where R is the name of the containing relation and k is the primary key value for the tuple concerned" (Date 1986, p. 250). Maier, on the other hand, allows designated keys other than the primary key (Maier 1983, p. 116).

Case (iii), the all–key relation, is shown in Figure 9.7. It is a base state trio complex with all *mandatory/optional* decisions chosen *mandatory* (*optional* choices might arise if foreign keys are allowed).

Comments on Normalization

The issue of normalization is a methodological rather than a theoretical one. Normalization procedures are usually intended to be equivalent transformations, that is, they are meant to convert between relational data model tables that have the same schema when expressed in data logic. It is not always true that normalization procedures produce equivalent schemas; in particular, *mandatory/optional* decisions may be affected, but the intention is to give as close a similarity as the relational data model permits.

For example, consider a third order relation $R(A, B, C)$ such that A determines B and B determines C (in the language of data logic, R is a trio where $\pi^{12}R$ and $\pi^{23}R$ are both *to one*). Then, according to the rules of normalization, R should be divided into two second order relations:

$$S(\underline{A}, B) \qquad T(\underline{B}, C) \tag{2}$$

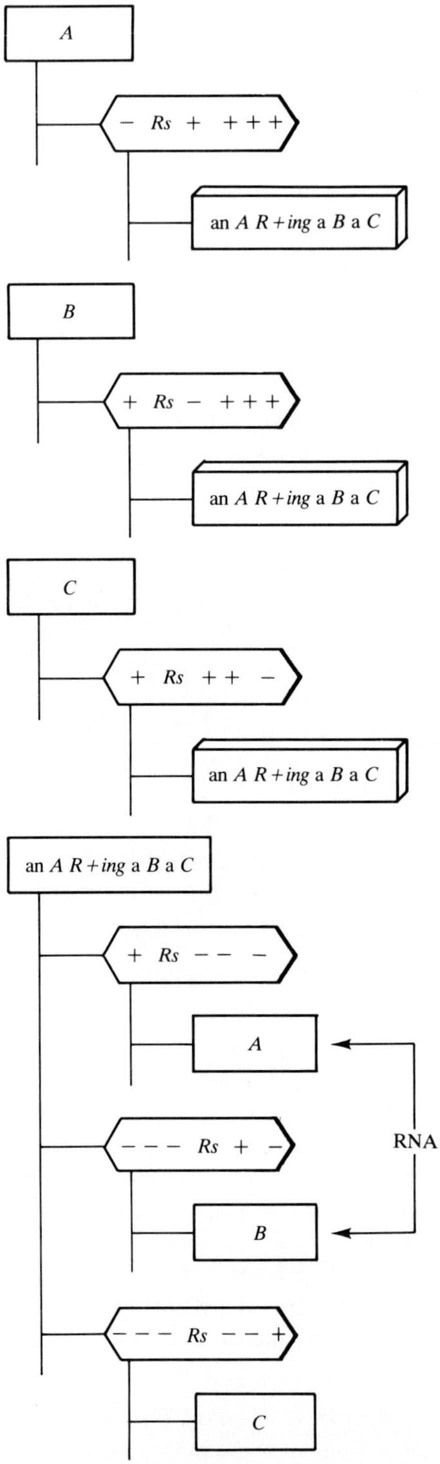

Figure 9.4 *R*(*A*, *B*, *C*) with *AB* key as a base state trio complex.

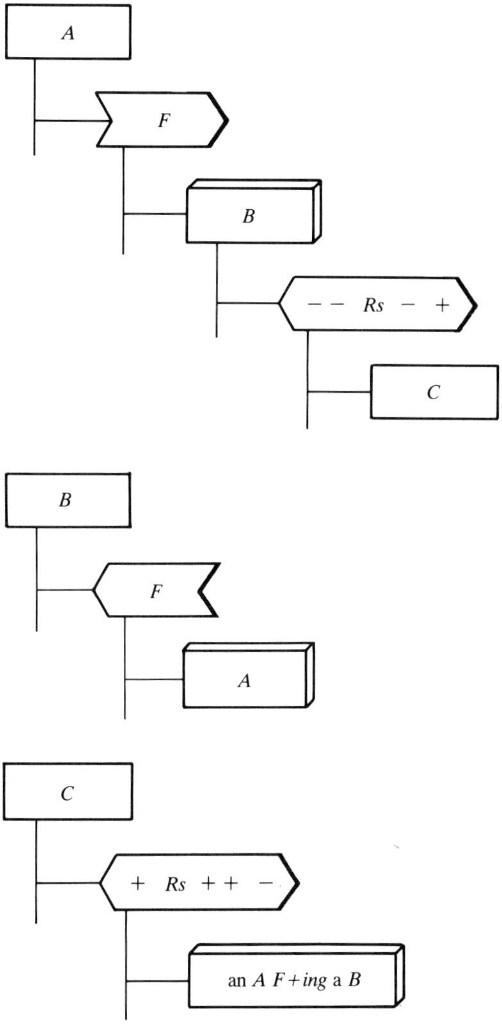

Figure 9.5 *R*(*A*, *B*, *C*) with *AB* key as a first stable state trio complex.

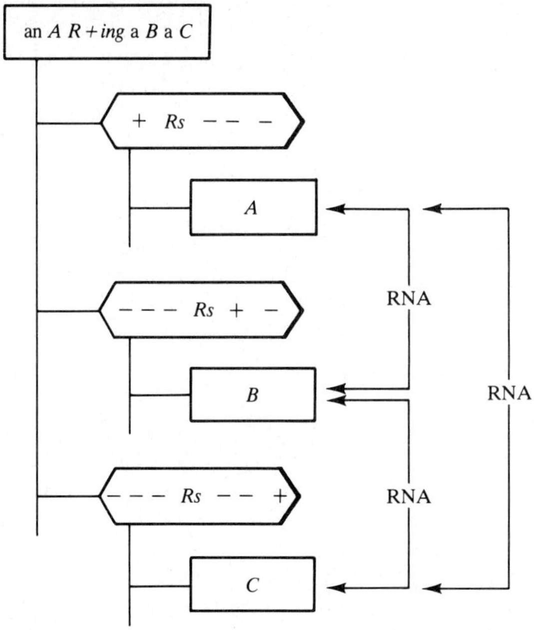

Figure 9.6 $R(A, B, C)$ with AB, AC, and BC key.

In the language of data logic, R is a juncture trio such that $R{:}|x, y, z|$ if and only if $S{:}|x, y|$ and $T{:}|y, z|$. The underlining shows the "key" part of the relations, and indicates that S and T are both *to one*.

If foreign keys are not permitted, the domain "B" in the relation S has no relationship with the domain "B" in the relation T. That is, each can be updated independently. The decomposed form, Formula (2), is thus written more accurately as:

$$S(\underline{A}, B') \qquad T(\underline{B}'', C)$$

If we write $B' \cup B''$ as "B", then S has character ">[" relative to (A, B), and T has character "]>" relative to (B, C). Thus, because of normalization, the composition correspondence $S \circ T$ is *some-to-some*, whereas before normalization, the correspondence $\pi^{13}R$ was *all-to-all*.

Some relational implementations solve this problem by employing "foreign keys." Using foreign keys, one may declare that $B'' \subseteq B'$, or that $B' \subseteq B''$. However, many implementations require that both B' and B'' be key in their respective relations before one may declare that $B' \equiv B''$. In such a case, the designer would be required to declare B' to be key in S, making S *many-to-many*, while before normalization $\pi^{12}R$ was *many-to-one*. Designers should therefore pay particular attention to the effects on characters when normalizing relations.

Methodologically, our view is that associations, when first declared, should be declared in normalized form (we are referring to the second and third normal forms here; extended associative notation does not require that relations be declared in first normal form). That is, for example, one should declare a juncture trio as two correspondences rather than as a trio complex. Other practitioners take the opposite view, that relations should be designed first in unnormalized form, then decomposed to normalized relations.

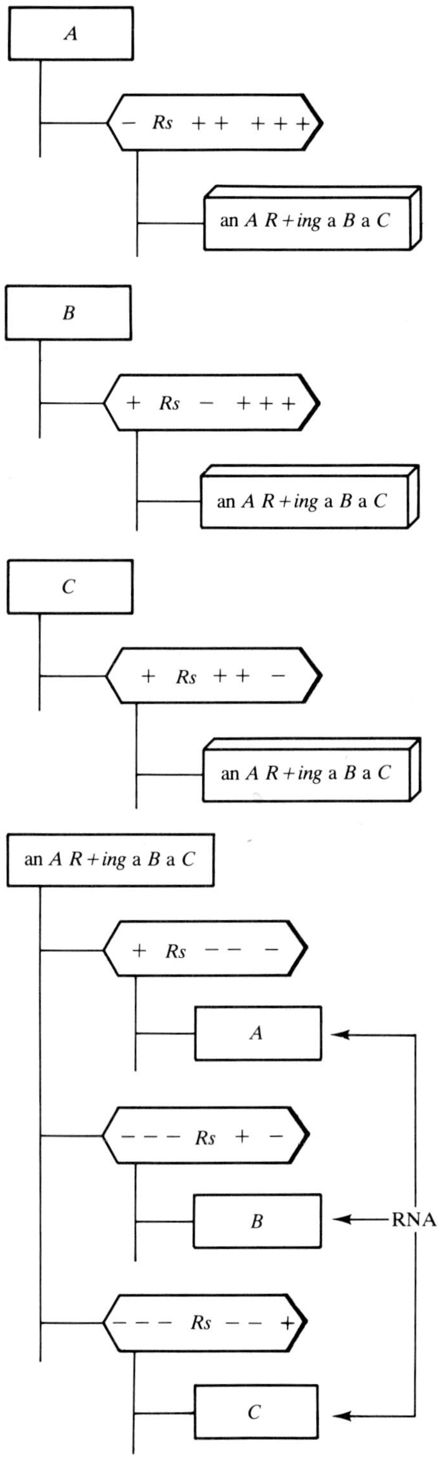

Figure 9.7 $R(A, B, C)$ with ABC key.

Extended associative notation is geared towards declaring a normalized, least permissive, form first, then changing the design if necessary to make it more permissive. Data logic, however, is insensitive to the design method used, and can accommodate either approach.

9.4 CHARACTER DECISION INTERDEPENDENCIES

Trio complexes exhibit many interrelationships among the decisions represented in extended associative notation. Most of the interrelationships are composition cone lower bounds, so may be derived from the techniques developed in Chapter 8. We describe all the decision interrelationships found in trio complexes in this section.

Derivation of the Network Picture of a Trio Complex

A trio complex may be shown as the network diagram, Figure 9.8. The most permissive character possible is shown alongside each correspondence. We will show that Figure 9.8 is a precise description of a trio complex when certain embracings are added. We must first define the elision correspondences shown in Figure 9.8 precisely.

The elision correspondence ${}_{12}\dot{T}_3$ is defined by the formula:

$$(\mathrm{A}x)\ (\mathrm{A}y)\ (\mathrm{A}z)\ {}_{12}\dot{T}_3{:}|\dot{F}|x,\ y|,\ z| \Leftrightarrow \dot{T}{:}|x,\ y,\ z|$$

The concentration of the correspondence ${}_{12}\dot{T}_3$ may be placed in *one-to-one all-to-all* correspondence with the concentration of the trio $\dot{T}$ by rearranging terms:

$$(\mathrm{A}x)\ (\mathrm{A}y)\ (\mathrm{A}z)\ \mathrm{C}^1{}_{12}\dot{T}_3{:}|{}_{12}\dot{T}_3|\dot{F}|x,\ y\ |,\ z|| \Leftrightarrow \mathrm{C}^1\dot{T}{:}|\dot{T}|x,\ y,\ z||$$

Thus, the half-elongation of ${}_{12}\dot{T}_3$ may be viewed as proceeding through the concentration of the trio $\dot{T}$. This result is significant because it applies to any choice of indices in the elision correspondence: the concentrations of ${}_{12}\dot{T}_3$, ${}_{23}\dot{T}_1$, and ${}_{31}\dot{T}_2$ are all in *one-to-one all-to-all* correspondence. The instances of all these concentrations may be viewed as triples $T(x, y, z)$.

We make this reasoning more precise by factoring ${}_{12}\dot{T}_3$ as a correspondence from $\mathrm{C}^1\dot{F}$ to $\mathrm{C}^1\dot{T}$ (written ${}_{12}\dot{T}_{123}$), followed by a correspondence from $\mathrm{C}^1\dot{T}$ to C (written ${}_{123}\dot{T}_3$). The correspondence ${}_{12}\dot{T}_{123}$ is defined by the formula

$$(\mathrm{A}x)\ (\mathrm{A}x')\ (\mathrm{A}y)\ (\mathrm{A}y')\ (\mathrm{A}z)\ {}_{12}\dot{T}_{123}{:}|\dot{F}|\ x,\ y|,\ \dot{T}\ |x',\ y',\ z||$$
$$\Leftrightarrow \Delta A{:}|x,\ x'\ |\ \&\ \Delta B{:}|y,\ y'\ |\ \&\ \dot{T}{:}|x,\ y,\ z|$$

That is, ${}_{12}\dot{T}_{123}$ attaches each assembly $\dot{F}(x, y)$ to all assemblies $\dot{T}(x, y, z)$ where x is the first member and y is the second member. The correspondence ${}_{123}\dot{T}_3$ is defined by

$$(\mathrm{A}x)\ (\mathrm{A}y)\ (\mathrm{A}z)\ (\mathrm{A}z')\ {}_{123}\dot{T}_3{:}|\dot{T}\ |x,\ y,\ z|,\ z'\ | \Leftrightarrow \Delta C{:}|z,\ z'\ |\ \&\ \dot{T}{:}|x,\ y,\ z|$$

That is, ${}_{123}\dot{T}_3$ attaches each assembly $\dot{T}(x, y, z)$ to the instance z in its third position.

The factoring equivalence

$${}_{12}\dot{T}_3 \equiv {}_{12}\dot{T}_{123} \circ {}_{123}\dot{T}_3 \qquad (1)$$

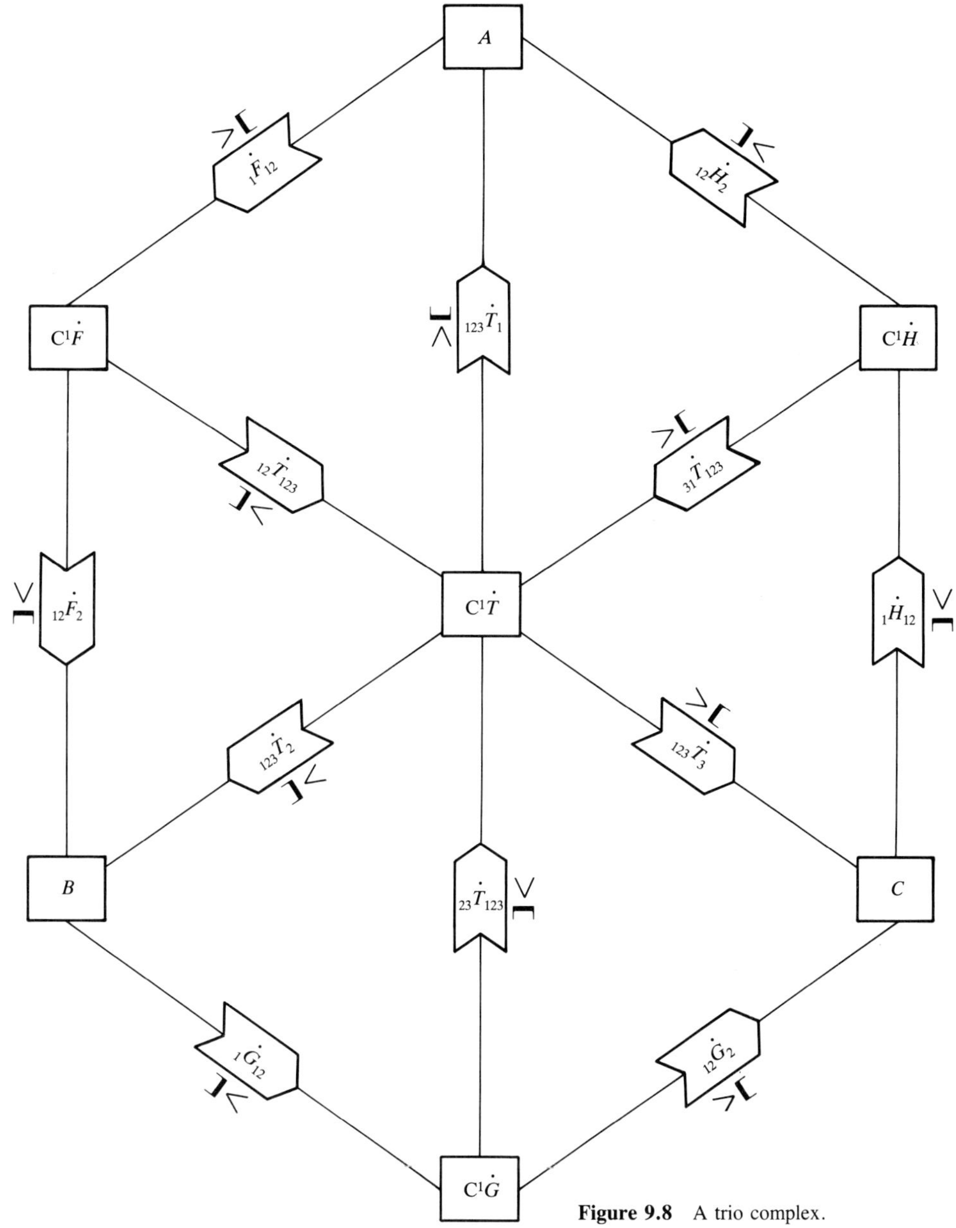

Figure 9.8 A trio complex.

says that an assembly $\dot{F}|x, y|$ attaches to a recognizer z by ${}_{12}\dot{T}_3$ if and only if there is an assembly $\dot{T}|x, y, z|$.

Since $C^1{}_{12}\dot{T}_3$ is in *one-to-one all-to-all* correspondence with $C^1\dot{T}$, the constituents of the factoring, Formula (1), have the same characters as the half-elongation of ${}_{12}\dot{T}_3$. That is,

$$\text{chr}\ ({}_{12}\dot{T}_{123};\ C^1\dot{F},\ C^1\dot{T}) = \text{chr}\ ({}_{12}\dot{T}_3;\ C^1\dot{F},\ C) \cap \text{“]<”}$$

$$\text{chr}\ ({}_{123}\dot{T}_3;\ C^1\dot{T},\ C) = \text{chr}\ ({}_{12}\dot{T}_3;\ C^1\dot{F},\ C) \cap \text{“>[”}$$

This same construction may be carried out for the remaining two elision correspondences ${}_{23}\dot{T}_1$ and ${}_{31}\dot{T}_2$. In all three cases, we have a *one-to-one all-to-all* correspondence between the concentration of the elision correspondence and the concentration of $\dot{T}$. Therefore, all three elision correspondences under consideration may be factored through the same intermediate element $C^1\dot{T}$:

$${}_{12}\dot{T}_3 \equiv {}_{12}\dot{T}_{123} \circ {}_{123}\dot{T}_3$$

$${}_{23}\dot{T}_1 \equiv {}_{23}\dot{T}_{123} \circ {}_{123}\dot{T}_1$$

$${}_{31}\dot{T}_2 \equiv {}_{31}\dot{T}_{123} \circ {}_{123}\dot{T}_2$$

Constraints on the Network Diagram

Figure 9.8 has the appearance of a triangulated hexagon, each triangle containing one of the declared classes *A*, *B*, or *C*, the concentration of a correspondence, and the concentration of the trio. For example, the triangle in the upper left corner is shown in Figure 9.9.

This triangle is a composition cone delta (it is also a cycle anchored at the class *A*). For we have,

$$(\mathrm{A}x)\ (\mathrm{A}y)\ (\mathrm{A}z)\ (\exists y')\ {}_1\dot{F}_{12}{:}|x,\ \dot{F}|x,\ y'||\ \&\ {}_{12}\dot{T}_{123}{:}|\dot{F}|x,\ y'|,\ \dot{T}|x,\ y,\ z||$$

$$\Leftrightarrow \dot{T}{:}|x,\ y,\ z|$$

$$\Leftrightarrow {}_1\dot{T}_{123}{:}|x,\ \dot{T}|x,\ y,\ z||$$

That is,

$$\boxed{{}_1\dot{F}_{12} \circ {}_{12}\dot{T}_{123} \equiv {}_1\dot{T}_{123}} \qquad (2)$$

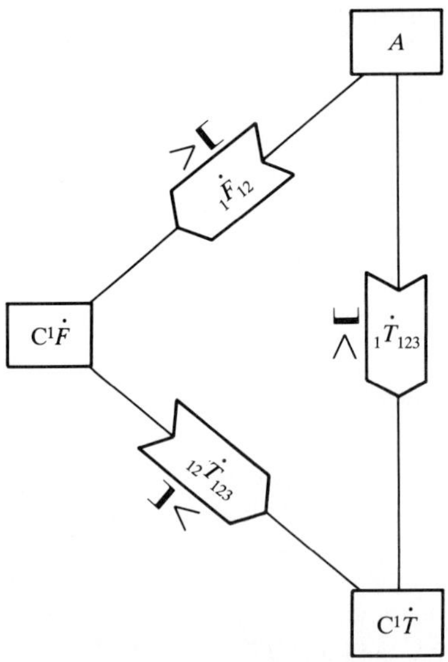

Figure 9.9 A composition cone delta.

Since the triangles inside the hexagon differ only by permutation of indices, a similar composition cone equivalence occurs within every triangle.

The concentrations in Figure 9.8 also obey RNA constraints. Thus, we have trivially:

$$\boxed{\begin{array}{l} \text{RNA } (\mathrm{C}^1\dot{F};\ {}_{12}\dot{F}_1,\ {}_{12}\dot{F}_2) \\ \text{RNA } (\mathrm{C}^1\dot{G};\ {}_{12}\dot{G}_1,\ {}_{12}\dot{G}_2) \\ \text{RNA } (\mathrm{C}^1\dot{H};\ {}_{12}\dot{H}_1,\ {}_{12}\dot{H}_2) \end{array}} \tag{3}$$

An RNA constraint operates on $\mathrm{C}^1\dot{T}$ as well, since it is a concentration of a third degree association:

$$\boxed{\text{RNA } (\mathrm{C}^1\dot{T};\ {}_{123}\dot{T}_1,\ {}_{123}\dot{T}_2,\ {}_{123}\dot{T}_3)} \tag{4}$$

Any Trio Complex Is Interconvertible with a Set of Correspondence Complexes and Embracings

We have shown that any trio complex may be expressed as the collection of elision correspondences shown in Figure 9.8 along with the embracings, Formulas (2), (3), and (4). We may show further that any data structure of similar form may be interpreted as a trio complex, showing that the two representations are interconvertible. This result demonstrates that any network-oriented data model that recognizes all 16 correspondence characters can be extended to recognize all trio complexes by adding the ability to declare positive embracings.

Formally, we say that two schemas $\mathcal{D}$ and $\mathcal{E}$ are *interconvertible* if any population of $\mathcal{D}$ may be converted in a *one-to-one all-to-all* fashion to a population of $\mathcal{E}$ and vice versa, by a purely formal interchange of association tags of $\mathcal{E}$ for association tags of $\mathcal{D}$. We will show that Figure 9.8 is interconvertible with the data structure shown in Figure 9.10, along with the embracings:

$$\begin{array}{llll} I \equiv \Delta A \circ I \circ \Delta W & P \equiv \Delta Z \circ P \circ \Delta A & I \circ Q \equiv P^* & \text{RNA } (W;\ I^*,\ J) \\ J \equiv \Delta W \circ J \circ \Delta B & Q \equiv \Delta W \circ Q \circ \Delta Z & J^* \circ Q \equiv R^* & \text{RNA } (X;\ K^*,\ L) \\ K \equiv \Delta B \circ K \circ \Delta X & R \equiv \Delta Z \circ R \circ \Delta B & K \circ S \equiv R^* & \text{RNA } (Y;\ M^*,\ N) \\ L \equiv \Delta X \circ L \circ \Delta C & S \equiv \Delta X \circ S \circ \Delta Z & L^* \circ S \equiv U^* & \text{RNA } (Z;\ P,\ R,\ U) \\ M \equiv \Delta C \circ M \circ \Delta Y & U \equiv \Delta Z \circ U \circ \Delta C & M \circ V \equiv U^* & \\ N \equiv \Delta Y \circ N \circ \Delta A & V \equiv \Delta Y \circ V \circ \Delta Z & N^* \circ V \equiv P^* & \end{array} \tag{5}$$

Notice that these embracings are essential for the two diagrams to be equivalent. Without them, the network diagram may exhibit populations that can not be populations of a trio complex.

Theorem 9.2 (Trio Decomposition Theorem). For any data structure of the form of Figure 9.10 together with the embracings, Formula (5), we may form correspondences F, G, and H, and a trio T, such that Figure 9.8 is interconvertible with Figure 9.10. That is, any data structure of the form of Figure 9.10 can be considered to represent a trio complex, and any trio complex can be represented by a data structure of the form of Figure 9.10.

Proof. We have already shown that any trio complex can be shown as a data structure of the form of Figure 9.10. The interpretations to be given to each association are

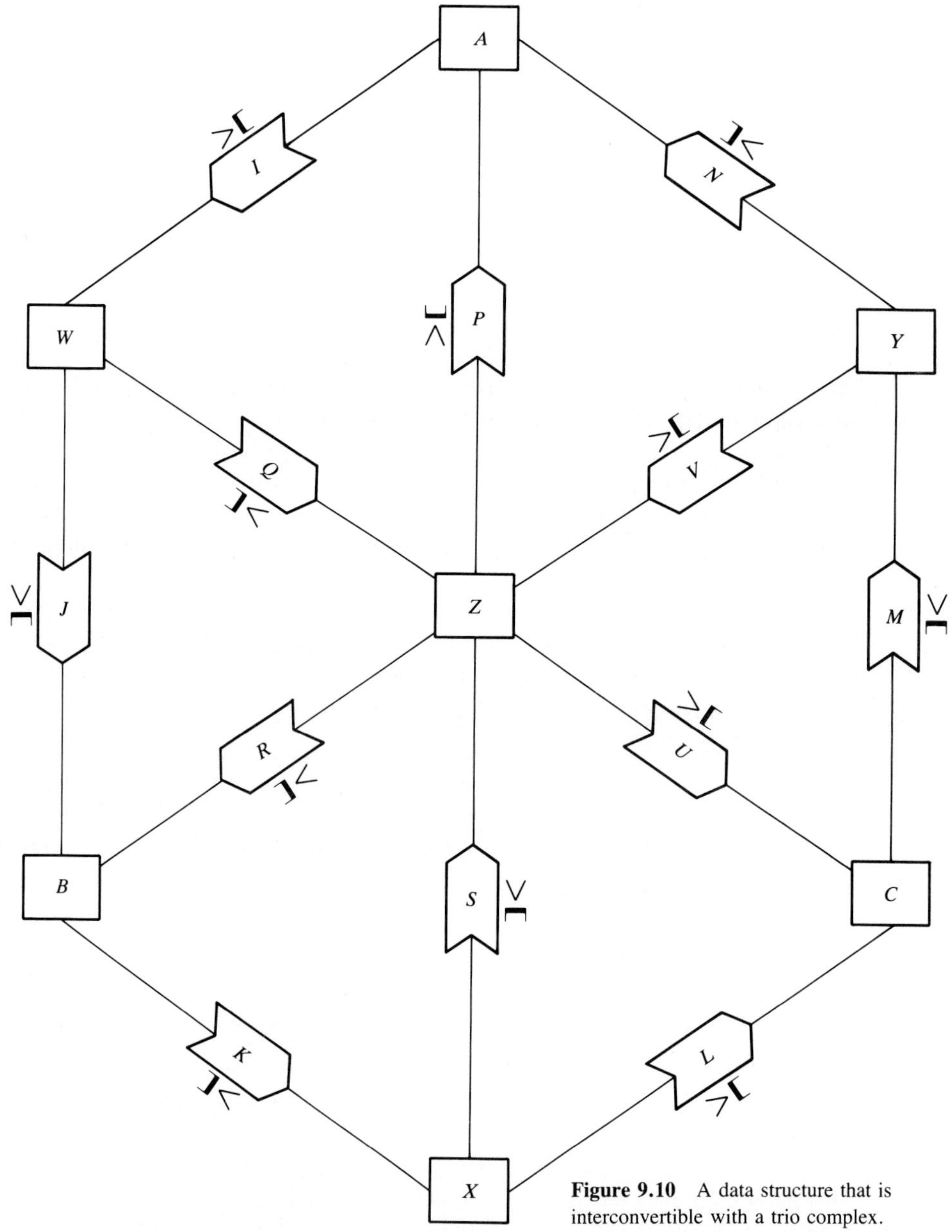

Figure 9.10 A data structure that is interconvertible with a trio complex.

shown in Figure 9.8. It remains to show, given Figure 9.10, that we may form correspondences F, G, and H, and a trio T, that obey the rules of a trio complex.

The correspondences F, G, and H are easily formed. Consider, for example, the correspondences I from A to W and J from W to B. We define the correspondence F to be the composition $I \circ J$. We know from the theory of correspondences that since I^* and J are both *from all* and *to one*, and RNA (W; I^*, J) is obeyed, that W is interconvertible with C^1F. That is, for any instance w of W, the corresponding instance of C^1F is $F{:}(w.I^*, w.J)$. We know further that I is interconvertible with ${}_1F_{12}$ and J is interconvertible with ${}_{12}F_2$.

Given the correspondences I through M, we may therefore form the correspondences F, G, and H as the compositions

$$F \equiv I \circ J$$

$$G \equiv K \circ L$$

$$H \equiv M \circ N$$

We define a trio T by the formula

$$(\mathrm{A}t)\ (\mathrm{A}u)\ (\mathrm{A}v)\ T{:}|t,\ u,\ v| \Leftrightarrow (\exists z)\ P{:}|z,\ t|\ \&\ R{:}|z,\ u|\ \&\ U{:}|z,\ v| \qquad (6)$$

An assembly $T|t,\ u,\ v|$ is therefore associated with at least one image z accepted by Z. Since RNA (Z; P, R, U) is obeyed, there is exactly one such z (that is, all such images z must be the same Z). Since each image accepted by Z attaches to one image accepted by A (by P), one image accepted by B (by R), and one image accepted by C (by U), there is exactly one assembly accepted by C^1T associated with each image accepted by Z. Therefore Z is in *one-to-one all-to-all* correspondence with C^1T, and Z is interconvertible with C^1T.

By examining Formula (6), which defines T from P, R, and U, it is clear that P, R, and U are interconvertible with ${}_{123}T_1$, ${}_{123}T_2$, and ${}_{123}T_3$, respectively. The remaining correspondences, Q, S, and V, may be formed from the correspondences already discussed. For example, consider the correspondence Q. We have

$$(\mathrm{A}w)\ (\mathrm{A}z)\ (I^* \circ P^*){:}|w,\ z|\ \&\ (J \circ R^*){:}|w,\ z| \Leftrightarrow (\exists t)\ I{:}|t,\ w|\ \&\ P{:}|z,\ t|$$
$$\&\ (\exists u)\ J{:}|w,\ u|\ \&\ R{:}|z,\ u|$$

Using the equivalences $P^* \equiv I \circ Q$ and $R^* \equiv J^* \circ Q$, we may write the right side as

$$(\exists t)\ (\exists w')\ I{:}|t,\ w|\ \&\ I{:}|t,\ w'|\ \&\ Q{:}|w',\ z|\ \&\ (\exists u)\ (\exists w'')\ J{:}|w,\ u|$$
$$\&\ J{:}|w'',\ u|\ \&\ Q{:}|w'',\ z|$$

Now, there is at most one instance of W that attaches via Q to z, so $\Delta W{:}|x',\ x''|$. Thus, we may write

$$(\exists t)\ (\exists w')\ I{:}|t,\ w|\ \&\ I{:}|t,\ w'|\ \&\ Q{:}|w',\ z|\ \&\ (\exists u)\ J{:}|w,\ u|\ \&\ J{:}|w',\ u|\ \&\ Q{:}|w',\ z|$$

Since RNA (W; I^*, J) is obeyed, both w and w' can only attach both to t and to u if they are the same W. Thus, we have

$$(\mathrm{A}w)\ (\mathrm{A}z)\ (I^* \circ P^*){:}|w,\ z|\ \&\ (J \circ R^*){:}|w,\ z| \Leftrightarrow (\exists t)\ I{:}|t,\ w|$$
$$\&\ (\exists u)\ J{:}|w,\ u|\ \&\ Q{:}|w,\ z|$$

Since both I^* and J are *from all*, we may reduce this expression to

$$(\mathrm{A}w)\ (\mathrm{A}z)\ (I^* \circ P^*){:}|w, z|\ \&\ (J \circ R^*){:}|w, z| \Leftrightarrow Q{:}|w, z|$$

That is,

$$(I^* \circ P^*) \cap (J \circ R^*) \equiv Q \tag{7}$$

Therefore, Q may be calculated from I, J, P, and R. Similarly, ${}_{12}T_{123}$ may be calculated from ${}_{12}F_1$, ${}_{12}F_2$, ${}_1T_{123}$, and ${}_2T_{123}$:

$$\begin{aligned}(\mathrm{A}x)\ (\mathrm{A}y)\ (\mathrm{A}z)\ {}_{12}F_1{:}|F|x, y|, x|\ \&\ {}_1T_{123}{:}|x, T|x, y, z||\ \&\ {}_{12}F_2{:}|F|x, y|, y|\\ \&\ {}_2T_{123}{:}|y, T|x, y, z|| \Leftrightarrow {}_{12}T_{123}{:}|F|x, y|, T|x, y, z||\end{aligned} \tag{8}$$

Comparing Formulas (7) and (8), we see directly that Q is interconvertible with ${}_{12}T_{123}$. Q.E.D.

Interdependencies Are Determined from Composition Cones

The composition cone constraints on a trio complex may be understood by generalizing from a single delta. We choose the delta in the upper left corner, shown earlier as Figure 9.9. This delta obeys the composition cone embracing

$${}_1\dot{F}_{12} \circ {}_{12}\dot{T}_{123} \equiv {}_1\dot{T}_{123}$$

Five theorems from composition cone theory are relevant:

(T1) If ${}_1\dot{F}_{12}$ is *from all* relative to $(A, \mathrm{C}^1\dot{F})$ and ${}_{12}\dot{T}_{123}$ is *from all* relative to $(\mathrm{C}^1\dot{F}, \mathrm{C}^1\dot{T})$, then ${}_1\dot{T}_{123}$ is *from all* relative to $(A, \mathrm{C}^1\dot{T})$. (Theorem 8.5)

(T2) If ${}_1\dot{F}_{12}$ is *to one* relative to $(A, \mathrm{C}^1\dot{F})$ and ${}_{12}\dot{T}_{123}$ is *to one* relative to $(\mathrm{C}^1\dot{F}, \mathrm{C}^1\dot{T})$, then ${}_1\dot{T}_{123}$ is *to one* relative to $(A, \mathrm{C}^1\dot{T})$. (Theorem 8.15)

(T3) If ${}_1\dot{T}_{123}$ is *from all* relative to $(A, \mathrm{C}^1\dot{T})$, then ${}_1\dot{F}_{12}$ is *from all* relative to $(A, \mathrm{C}^1\dot{F})$. (Theorem 8.1)

(T4) If ${}_1\dot{T}_{123}$ is *to one* relative to $(A, \mathrm{C}^1\dot{T})$ and ${}_{12}\dot{T}_{123}$ is *from all* relative to $(\mathrm{C}^1\dot{F}, \mathrm{C}^1\dot{T})$, then ${}_1\dot{F}_{12}$ is *to one* relative to $(A, \mathrm{C}^1\dot{F})$. (Theorem 8.31)

(T5) If ${}_1\dot{T}_{123}$ is *from all* relative to $(A, \mathrm{C}^1\dot{T})$ and ${}_1\dot{F}_{12}$ is *to one* relative to $(A, \mathrm{C}^1\dot{F})$, then ${}_{12}\dot{T}_{123}$ is *from all* relative to $(\mathrm{C}^1\dot{F}, \mathrm{C}^1\dot{T})$. (Theorem 8.25)

These theorems may all be expressed in a variety of contrapositive forms. Assuming that the character decisions are not contradictory, a unique form for each theorem is given by converting the implications into denials of coincidental decisions:

(T1) !˜((${}_1\dot{F}_{12}$ *from all*) & (${}_{12}\dot{T}_{123}$ *from all*) & (${}_1\dot{T}_{123}$ *from some*))
(T2) !˜((${}_1\dot{F}_{12}$ *to one*) & (${}_{12}\dot{T}_{123}$ *to one*) & (${}_1\dot{T}_{123}$ *to many*))
(T3) !˜((${}_1\dot{T}_{123}$ *from all*) & (${}_1\dot{F}_{12}$ *from some*))
(T4) !˜((${}_1\dot{T}_{123}$ *to one*) & (${}_{12}\dot{T}_{123}$ *from all*) & (${}_1\dot{F}_{12}$ *to many*))
(T5) !˜((${}_1\dot{T}_{123}$ *from all*) & (${}_1\dot{F}_{12}$ *to one*) & (${}_{12}\dot{T}_{123}$ *from some*))

Delta Constraints

The correspondences F, G, and H form a cycle $(A; F; B; G; C; A)$. As we showed in Section 6.3, six cycle characters, "**]**", ">", "**]**>", "**[**", "<", and "<**[**", can not be attained without unresolved alternation. Since the practical aspects of including unresolved alternations remain obscure, we will exclude such deltas from consideration as relative complexes for trios. The additional restrictions are:

(T6) If $\dot{F} \circ \dot{G} \circ \dot{H}$ is *from all* and *from one* relative to (A, A) then $\dot{F} \circ \dot{G} \circ \dot{H}$ is *to all* and *to one* relative to (A, A).

(T7) If $\dot{F} \circ \dot{G} \circ \dot{H}$ is *to all* and *to one* relative to (A, A) then $\dot{F} \circ \dot{G} \circ \dot{H}$ is *from all* and *from one* relative to (A, A).

That is,

(T6) !˜((*F from all*) & (*F from one*) & (*G from all*) & (*G from one*) & (*H from all*) & (*H from one*) & ((*F to some*) $\bigvee$ (*F to many*) $\bigvee$ (*G to some*) $\bigvee$ (*G to many*) $\bigvee$ (*H to some*) $\bigvee$ (*H to many*)))

(T7) !˜((*F to all*) & (*F to one*) & (*G to all*) & (*G to one*) & (*H to all*) & (*H to one*) & ((*F from some*) $\bigvee$ (*F from many*) $\bigvee$ (*G from some*) $\bigvee$ (*G from many*) $\bigvee$ (*H from some*) $\bigvee$ (*H from many*)))

Parallel Singularity

Trios also obey the *parallel singularity theorem*, so called because it affects correspondences whose representative lines are parallel on Figure 9.8. This theorem states that if each A attaches to at most one B, then each AC pair (each instance of $C^1(\dot{H}^*)$) attaches to at most one B.

Theorem 9.3 (Parallel Singularity Theorem). If F is *to one* relative to (A, B), then ${}_{31}\dot{T}_{123}$ is *to one* relative to $(C^1\dot{H}, C^1\dot{T})$.

Proof. Suppose

$$ {}_{31}\dot{T}_{123}{:}|\dot{H}|z, x|, \dot{T}|x, y, z|| \;\&\; {}_{31}\dot{T}_{123}{:}|\dot{H}|z, x|, \dot{T}|x, y_2, z|| $$

By the definition of ${}_{31}\dot{T}_{123}$, this implies

$$ \dot{T}{:}|x, y_1, z| \;\&\; \dot{T}{:}|x, y_2, z| $$

Then, since $\pi^{12}\dot{T} \subseteq \dot{F}$,

$$ \dot{F}{:}|x, y_1| \;\&\; \dot{F}{:}|x, y_2| $$

Since F is *to one* relative to (A, B), $\Delta B{:}|y_1, y_2|$. Q.E.D.

In negative form, the parallel singularity theorem is:

(T8) !˜((${}_1\dot{F}_{12}$ *to one*) & (${}_{31}\dot{T}_{123}$ *to many*))

Survey of Potential Trio Complexes

To verify that there were no further constraints, we programmed a computer to construct representative populations, by pasting, of all trio complexes that satisfied the constraints (T1) to (T8). We included all the analogous constraints formed by choosing different deltas than that shown in Figure 9.9. The program successfully constructed a representative population for each of the trio complexes predicted by the theory. This test shows that no further simplifications of trio complexes are possible. That is, it shows that any theory of trios must incorporate all the varieties discussed in this chapter, or it must explicitly exclude some varieties on other than logical grounds.

This test allowed us further to enumerate the possible varieties of trios. We found that there are a total of 30,660 different character forms of trios. The breakdown by minimal order stable state is as follows:

Base state	360
First stable state	2,850
Second stable state	10,242
Fully reversed	17,208
Total	30,660

Discussion of Interdependencies

The large variety of character interdependencies, (T1) to (T8), becomes less important as the permissiveness of the trio increases. Thus, Theorem 9.1 showed that if any of the relative correspondences were *to one*, then the trio complex could be written as a binary path. Excluding these cases allows us to ignore (T2), (T5), (T6), (T7), and (T8). The remaining interdependencies are:

(T1) $!\tilde{}((_{1}\dot{F}_{12}\ \textit{from all})\ \&\ (_{12}\dot{T}_{123}\ \textit{from all})\ \&\ (_{1}\dot{T}_{123}\ \textit{from some}))$

(T3) $!\tilde{}((_{1}\dot{T}_{123}\ \textit{from all})\ \&\ (_{1}\dot{F}_{12}\ \textit{from some}))$

(T4) $!\tilde{}((_{1}\dot{T}_{123}\ \textit{to one})\ \&\ (_{12}\dot{T}_{123}\ \textit{from all})\ \&\ (_{1}\dot{F}_{12}\ \textit{to many}))$

(T1) and (T3) are straightforward interdependencies among *optional/mandatory* decisions. The last interdependency, (T4), allows data structures of the form shown in Figure 9.11. Here, each instance of A is associated with many instances of B and with many instances of C, yet with exactly one related pair $G(b, c)$. A potential population of this trio complex would be:

$$\vdash F{:}(a_1, b_1) \qquad \vdash H{:}(c_1, a_1) \qquad \vdash T{:}(a_1, b_1, c_1)$$

$$\vdash F{:}(a_1, b_2) \qquad \vdash H{:}(c_2, a_1) \qquad \vdash T{:}(a_2, b_2, c_2)$$

$$\vdash F{:}(a_2, b_2) \qquad \vdash H{:}(c_2, a_2)$$

Trio complexes such as this, where the character of a facial correspondence such as $_{1}\dot{T}_{123}$ differs from both the union character of $(_{1}\dot{F}_{12},\ _{12}\dot{T}_{123})$ and the union character of $(_{2}\dot{H}_{12},\ _{31}\dot{T}_{123})$, are called *pineal*. In trio complexes that are not pineal, the characters of the

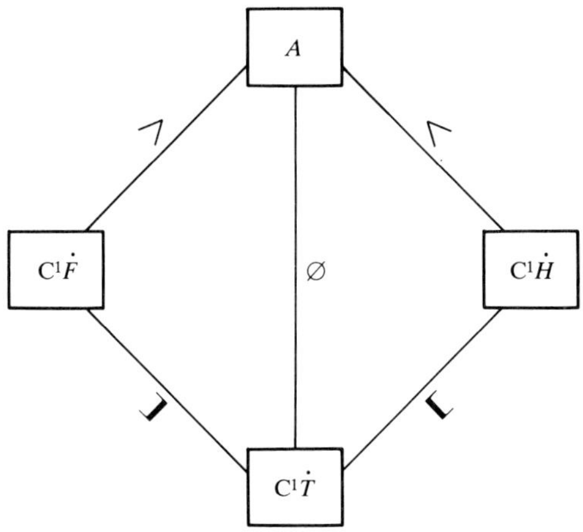

Figure 9.11 A pineal trio complex.

facial correspondences ${}_1\dot{T}_{123}$, ${}_2\dot{T}_{123}$, and ${}_3\dot{T}_{123}$ may be determined from the union characters of other correspondences, and so the facial correspondences do not have to be declared. The existence of pineal trio complexes is responsible for the requirement that the ${}_1\dot{T}_{123}$ correspondence be declared if ${}_{12}\dot{T}_{123}$ and ${}_{13}\dot{T}_{123}$ are both *from some*.

Pineal trio complexes occur only in the second stable state and in full reversal, yet they exhibit a startling variety of forms. We have calculated that 2250 of the second stable state trio forms and 9334 of the fully reversed trio forms are pineal.

Conclusion

We have shown how the interdependencies among character decisions are completely determined by a small set of expressions (T1) to (T8). These interdependencies are easily programmed into the design management device. We have shown that a trio complex is interconvertible with a data structure formed entirely from classes and correspondences along with an indispensable collection of embracings. Thus, embracings are required for the proper declaration of trio complexes in network notations.

9.5 CASE STUDY: LIST-POSITION-WORD

In this case study, we illustrate all the decisions in a fully reversed trio complex. This will show that there are trio complexes that exhibit every possible choice in extended associative notation. Since our examination of the decisions is exhaustive, this case study may also be used as a reference guide for declaring trio complexes. To facilitate comparison among the different data structures, we will use one trio complex throughout, varying its constraints as required.

Only a very generic example can exhibit all possible varieties of trio complexes. We will study the three classes *List, Position,* and *Word*, along with the trio « a *list imposes* a *position on* a *word* ». This example generates a huge number of different kinds of *lists*.

Many of them are familiar: For example, any sentence in a pamphlet can be thought of as a *list*. The sentence is the *list*, and by actually exhibiting the *words* in a given order, the sentence *imposes position* 1 on the first *word* in the sentence, *position* 2 on the second *word*, and so on. Elsewhere in the pamphlet, another sentence—another *list*—could occur with exactly the same *words* in a different order. The second sentence is a different *list*, and it *imposes* different *positions* on the same set of *words*.

The *List-Position-Word* trio complex can be reinterpreted to illustrate any pillared trio complex, that is, any trio complex in which the three relative classes are different. Merely substitute *Project*, *Role*, and *Person* or any other three distinct class tags for *List*, *Position*, and *Word*, and change the verbs to make sense in the new context. There are also trio complexes in which all positions are defined relative to the same class, such as *Part Replaces Part In Usage Part*, and trios defined on two classes, such as *Object Is Resting On Top Of Object During Time Period*. We do not consider the special properties of such trio complexes in this case study, which are related to loops.

Illustrations of Lists

A *word* will be represented by an alphanumeric string, and a *position* will be represented by a positive integer. A *list* will be represented by a numeric string preceded by the letter "L", such as "L99". Examples of *lists* will be shown by exhibiting each *position* associated with the *list*, followed by the set of *words* assigned to each *position*, enclosed in curly brackets "{ }". For example, the following is a *list*:

L1: 1{the} 2{horse} 3{pulled} 4{the} 5{cart}

Notice that the *word* "the" appears twice in this *list*, that is, it *repeats*. Some kinds of lists allow repeats: For example, the same word may reappear many times in an English sentence. Other kinds of lists, such as a list that ranks cities by population size, do not allow repeats.

The *positions* in a *list* need not necessarily be consecutive integers, nor must the first position of a *list* be numbered "1". Thus, the following is a valid *list*:

L2: 5{apple} 8{pear}

Some *lists* have unfilled positions, or *gaps*:

L3: 1{the} 2{horse} 3{pulled} 4{ } 5{cart}

Some *lists* have multiply-filled positions, or *ties*:

L4: 1{the} 2{horse} 3{pulled} 4{our, a, the} 5{cart}

Constraints may apply across *lists*. In the following example, each *word* must be contained in at most one *list*. Once a given *word* is used, it can not be reused except in the same *list*.

L5:	1{a}	2{car}	3{needs}	4{a}	5{driver}
L6:	1{the}	2{cat}	3{ate}	4{the}	5{mouse}

Thus, "a" is not allowed in L6 and "cat" is not allowed in L5.

Verbs

The following verbs will be used consistently throughout the case study. We will say that:

A *list imposes* a *position on* a *word.*
A *list provides* a *position.*
A *position numbers* a *word.*
A *list arranges* a *word.*

Other verbs, such as "contains" and "appears in" will be used informally for illustration. Thus, *lists* may be said to *contain positions* or *words.*

Our treatment of verbs may be unfamiliar to readers acquainted with other data models. We do not make the common assumption that the associations *Provides, Numbers*, and *Arranges* are embraced in Cartesian products of classes. Thus, when we study a correspondence such as *Provides*, we do not assume that *lists* are the only objects that may *provide* things, nor that *positions* are the only things that may be *provided.* We allow a *list* to *provide* a *position* and also to *provide* something else as well. This approach to correspondences and trios is significantly more elaborate than most other theories of data, and is made possible by applying data logic.

Although it is possible to be even more general, and to allow *lists* to *impose positions* that the *list* does not *provide*, we will not be so general here. We will assume that the three relative correspondences embrace the appropriate projections of the trio. That is, we will assume:

If a *list l imposes* a *position p on* a *word w,* then *l provides p*
If a *list l imposes* a *position p on* a *word w*, then *p numbers w*
If a *list l imposes* a *position p on* a *word w*, then *l arranges w*

These three conditions are also described by saying that the trio *Imposes On* is *situated within* the correspondences *Provides, Numbers*, and *Arranges.*

Outline of the Case Study

Because we seek to illustrate all the possible design decisions, we will treat the trio *Imposes On* in its fully reversed form. We recall that this form is always appropriate for a trio: the lower order stable states are shorthands that save effort, but they can be translated to a full reversal by writing the default correspondences explicitly (see Section 9.2).

We will organize the discussion of the design decisions into three sections: *delta decisions,* which affect the three relative correspondences *Provides, Numbers,* and

Arranges; *axial decisions,* which relate the relative correspondences to the trio (and establish the minimum order stable state), and *facial decisions,* which relate the classes to the trio (and establish pineal trios). Each of these groups of decisions appears in a different area of the design notation expression for a trio, and in combination they exhaust all the design decisions.

Delta Decisions

The delta decisions of a trio complex are the design decisions for the relative correspondences *Provides, Numbers,* and *Arranges*. The locations of the delta decisions in extended associative notation are shown in Figure 9.12. We will discuss each decision in turn.

1. Choosing *optional* allows a *list* to *provide* nothing. Such a *list* might still *arrange* one or more *words*, but it could not place the *words* anywhere (they would remain in an "unimposed" holding area). Notice that in decision (1), we have not restricted attention to *providing positions*. For example, a *list* might contain a header as well as a set of *positions*. If (1) is *optional*, a *list* may *provide* no header as well as *providing* no *positions*. If (1) is *mandatory*, a *list* must *provide* something, either a header, a *position*, or something similar. It might still *provide* a header and not a *position*, however.

2. Choosing *optional* allows a *list* to *provide* something other than a *position* (such as a header), and at the same time to *provide* no *position*. Choosing *mandatory* forces a *list* that *provides* something to *provide* at least one *position*. Such a *list* might or might not be able to *provide* a header as well. If both (1) and (2) are *mandatory*, each *list provides* at least one *position*, and we say that *Provides* is *from all*.

Lists that *provide* at least one *position* are called *formatted lists* because they prepare a place or places where *words* can fit. Unformatted *lists* are allowed if either (1) or (2) is *optional*. For example, the empty *list* L7 is an unformatted list:

L7:

There can be no *words* that L7 *imposes positions on* because there are no *positions* in L7. As another example, suppose that the *words* represent applicants for available jobs, and that each available job is represented by a *position*. Then, if no jobs are currently available, a *list* that matches applicants to available jobs would be unformatted.

3. Choosing *single* forces all *lists* to *provide* no more than one *position*. *Lists* that *provide* at most one *position* are called *unsequenced lists* because they cannot induce any ordering on the *words* that are listed. Thus, the following is an unsequenced *list*:

L8: 4{hat, buttercup}

A schema that forces all *lists* to be unsequenced is quite degenerate since the *lists* in such a data base do not arrange *words* in any sequence. Instead, each *list* attaches to a set of *words*, and assigns the set some one *position* number. As was shown in Section 9.3, if (3) is chosen *single*, then the trio complex is a juncture trio, and it suffices to declare the two correspondences *Provides* and *Arranges*. That is, by virtue of the decision to make (3) single, a *list l imposes* a *position p on* a *word w* if and only if *l provides* the *position p* and *l*

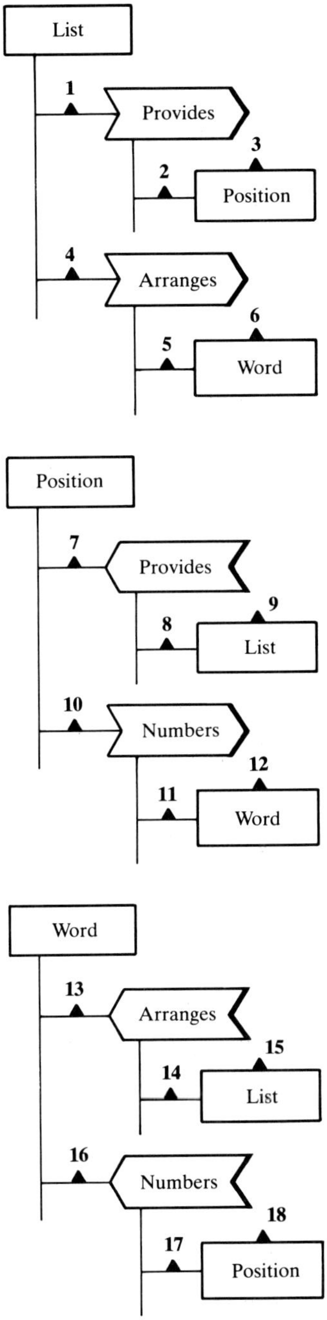

Figure 9.12 Delta decisions.

arranges the *word w*. Thus, the trio *Imposes On* may be calculated from the two correspondences *Provides* and *Arranges*, and so the trio *Imposes On* should not be declared in extended associative notation.

4. Choosing *optional* allows a *list* to *arrange* nothing. That is, the *list* may be assigned a tag before it has any contents. The list may or may not be required to contain *positions* in this case, depending upon the decisions (1) and (2). Choosing (4) *mandatory* forces every *list* to *arrange* something. It is possible for a *list* to *arrange* things other than *words*, icons for example.

5. Choosing *optional* allows a *list* to *arrange* something without *arranging* any *word* (it might *arrange* only icons, for example). If either of the decisions (4) or (5) is *optional*, a *list* may *arrange* no *word*, and *arranges* is said to be *from some*. For example, the following list *arranges* no *word*, even though it does *provide* two *positions*:

L9: 6{ } 8{ }

6. Choosing *multiple* allows a *list* to *arrange* many *words*. This is the normal type of *list*. If this choice is *single*, every *list* must contain at most one *word*, and the trio complex is degenerate.

A *list* that *arranges* at most one *word* is called a *monotonous list*. While monotonous *lists* are degenerate, they still have some interesting properties and varieties. For example, consider a data base restricted to monotonous *lists* that allows repeats [see decision (24)] but does not allow gaps [see decision (20)]. Such *lists* can do nothing more than repeat the same *word* over and over:

L10: 2{aye} 3{aye} 6{aye}

Such *lists* are called *binary lists* because each *list* contains a subset of the set of *positions*.

If a data base also allows gaps, *ternary lists* can be stored. A *ternary list* sprinkles occurrences of the *list's word* over some subset of the *positions*, leaving the other *positions* empty. Thus, the following is a ternary *list*:

L11: 2{yes} 3{yes} 4{ } 6{yes} 9{ }

Monotonous and ternary *lists* can be useful as data structures only programs use.

7. Choosing *optional* allows *positions* that are not *provided* by anything. Imagine, for example, that the *positions* represent honorary awards, and that the *lists* identify people (represented by *words*) who have won them. Notice is given that an award is available by *providing* the *position* that represents the award. It may be possible, then, for an award to be available but for no one to receive it. A *position* is then *provided*, but the *position* is not *imposed on* any *word*. For example, no Nobel Peace Prize was awarded in 1939, although the prize was available.

8. Choosing *mandatory* requires that any *position* that is *provided* by something must be *provided* by a *list*. It is possible for *positions* to be *provided* by things other than *lists*, such as by tables. If both (7) and (8) are *mandatory*, every *position* appears in at least one *list*, and *provides* is said to be *to all*.

Positions that are *provided* by at least one *list* are called *assigned positions* because they are *positions* that have been selected to be used on *lists*—as opposed to those that have not been selected for such use and remain unassigned. The existence or absence of unassigned *positions* is often of little consequence to the trio complex. Deciding the *mandatory/optional* markings at the first and second levels of a trio diagram often has a relatively minor effect on the behavior of the data structure.

9. Choosing *multiple* allows the same *position* to recur on many *lists*. This is the normal type of *position* (many lists may *provide position* 1, for example).

The *positions provided* by a *list* may be viewed as column numbers, and the process of *imposing positions on words* may be viewed as placing *word* sets into a matrix whose rows are *lists* and whose columns are *positions*, as shown in Figure 9.13. If every *position* is *provided* by at most one *list*, then there can be at most one *word* set in any column.

Positions

Lists		1	2	3	4	5
	L1	the		blue	bus	
	L2		radish			
	L3					{ice, snow}

Figure 9.13 The trio population as a matrix.

10. Choosing *optional* allows a *position* to *number* nothing, neither *words* nor any other objects such as icons. A common example would be a *position* that appears on some *list* but happens to be unfilled.

11. Choosing *mandatory* forces any *position* that *numbers* something to *number* some *word*. An example would be a data structure where everything that is both *numbered* and not a *word* (such as a drawing, for example) must have a caption that is a *word* and is *numbered* in the same *position*.

12. Choosing *multiple* allows a *position* to *number* many *words*. The correspondence *numbers* relates *words* to the *positions* that they occupy in each *list* where they appear, so the position 3 *numbers* both the words "cat" and "dog" in the following example:

L12: 1{the} 2{orange} 3{cat}
L13: 1{the} 2{fat} 3{dog}

If the schema mandates that each *position* can *number* at most one *word*, the data base is said to exhibit *reserved positions*. Reserved *positions* allows the contents of each *list* to affect the contents of all other *lists*. For example, consider adding a *list* to the data base with the intention to *impose position* 33 on "apple". If another *list* already *imposes position* 33 on another *word*, the update will be blocked.

13. Choosing *mandatory* requires every *word* to be *arranged* by something. A *word* could be *arranged* by something other than a *list*. For example, a *word* could be *arranged* by a table.

14. Choosing *mandatory* states that any *word* that is *arranged* by something is *arranged* by a *list*. For example, any *word* that appears in a table must also appear in some *list*. If either (13) or (14) is *optional*, there may be a repertoire of *words* on file (orphans of *Arranges**) that have not been used on any *lists*.

15. Making this decision *multiple* indicates that a *word* may be arranged by many *lists*. This is the normal situation, where appearance of a *word* in one *list* does not prevent it from appearing in other *lists* as well.

When no *word* ever appears on two *lists*, all the *lists* have *disjoint vocabularies*. That is, they never have any *words* in common. Disjoint vocabularies are useful when each *list* contains information about different things: one is a list of cities, another a list of sports teams, a third a list of chemical elements, and so on, so that all of the vocabularies are separate.

16. Choosing *optional* allows a *word* to be *numbered* by nothing. For example, suppose that *positions* represent military ranks and *words* represent applicants for military service. An applicant is not assigned military rank until he or she passes a barrage of tests and completes a training program. There are applicants, then, that are not recognized as having military qualifications, and are not *numbered.*

17. Choosing *optional* allows a *word* to be *numbered* by something, yet for the *word* to be associated with no *position*. Continuing the example above, applicants who have completed medical and other tests become ''recruits.'' A recruit has no rank, so a recruit is associated with no *position*. Yet a recruit has status beyond that of an applicant. This situation may be described by saying that the applicant is not *numbered* (decision 16), whereas the recruit is *numbered*, but is not *numbered* by a *position*.

18. Making this decision *single* requires that each *word* be associated with at most one *position*, across all *lists*. For example, suppose that all the *words* in the data base are arranged in a dictionary in alphabetical order, and that all *lists* present each *word* in the *position* that it occupies in the dictionary. Clearly, the trio complex is then degenerate, and it suffices to declare which *words* each *list arranges*, and which *position numbers* each *word*.

Axial Decisions

The axial decisions express relationships between the trio and the relative correspondences. The axial decisions are of considerable theoretical and practical interest because they determine the minimum order stable state of the trio complex. The axial decisions appear in extended associative notation as shown in Figure 9.14. Notice that any of the design structures that show axial decisions could be located in one or both of two alternative places. For example, we could have placed the class tag ''*Position*'' under the cascade *Word-Arranges*-List* instead of under *List-Arranges-Word* as shown.

19. Choosing *optional* allows a *list* to *provide* a *position* that is unoccupied, neither by a *word* nor by some other object such as an icon.

20. Choosing *optional* allows a *list* to *provide* a *position* that might be occupied by something, such as an icon, but is occupied by no *word*. If both decisions (19) and (20) are *mandatory*, then the *positions* that a *list provides* are just the *positions* that the *list imposes on* some *word*. The correspondence *Provides* may therefore be computed from the trio *Imposes On*. This equivalence is what permits the simplifications of stable states.

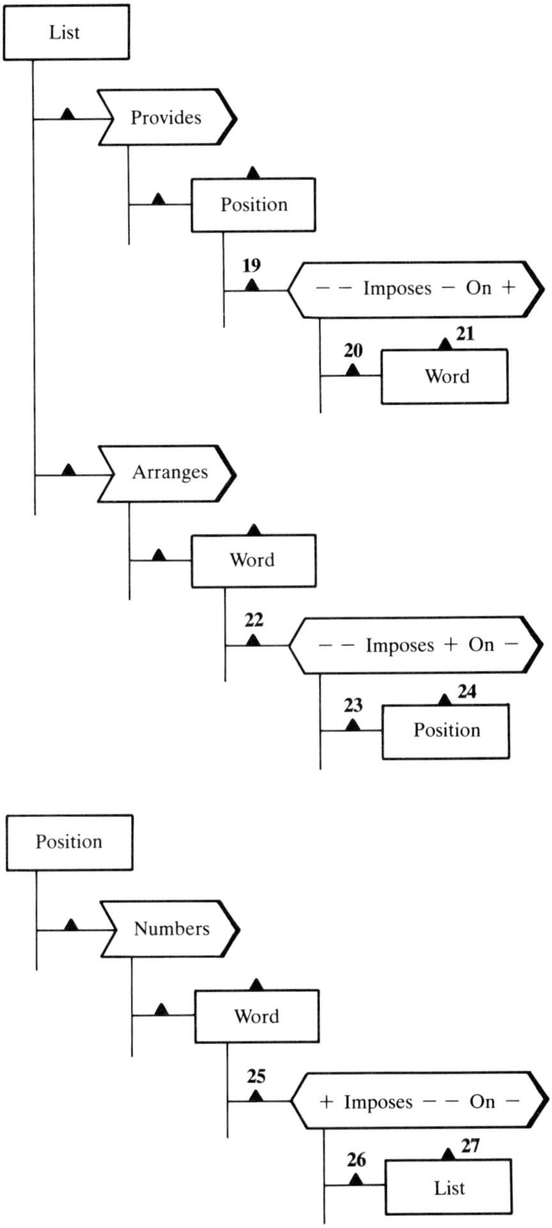

Figure 9.14 Axial decisions.

If either decision (19) or (20) is *optional*, the data base permits a *list* to *provide* a position that contains no *words*. The data base is then said to allow *gaps*. An example of such a *list* is:

L14: 1{A} 2{ } 3{C} 4{D}

Notice that B has been omitted in this case, leaving a gap in *position* 2. Gaps are normal in some kinds of *lists*. For example, a doctor's appointment book (a list of hour long time slots into which patient names are penciled) ought to be able to contain hours when the doctor is available but no patient is scheduled. In other kinds of lists, such as an itinerary (a list of cities to be visited in sequence), gaps may be forbidden. A designer might, however, decide that gaps in an itinerary are useful. For example, a gap might represent « a visit to an unknown city to be selected *en route* ».

A list may also be composed entirely of gaps:

L15: 1{ } 3{ } 6{ }

Gaps, we recall, can occur in conglomerations (see Section 1.7) when a position in a connector is unfilled. Null values can also be seen as gaps in relational "tuples."

Notice that an unformatted *list* which provides no *positions* (see decision 2) is different from the *list* L15 that *provides positions* of which none are filled. *Lists* of the form L15 are also similar to binary *lists* (see decision 6). Each valid *position* is subjected to a binary test in *list* L15: either it is not *provided* (like *position* 2), or it is *provided* but not *imposed* (like *position* 3).

Students of programming may be apprehensive about gaps. Improper treatment of gaps can lead to intransigent programming problems, particularly when one tries to delete a gap. For example, if all gaps are the same, deletion of a gap is a fairly massive operation rippling through the entire data base. But our definition of a gap does not have this problem. A gap is precisely the nonexistent material in some *position i* of some *list j*. What is to be deleted is that particular nonexistent material and no other. Thus deleting a gap does not propagate to any other portion of the data base.

A mechanism for managing gaps may be visualized as follows: There is a set of *positions* that the *list provides*. All these *positions* will be exhibited when the *list* is constructed. Since different *lists* may *provide* a different set of *positions*, it is helpful to visualize the set of pairs of (i) a *list* together with (ii) a *position* that the *list provides*. We will refer to this set as a set of *list-positions*. For each *list-position*, there is an independent set that identifies all the *words* that fit into that *list-position*. Decision (20) controls whether or not that set of *words* is allowed to be empty and hence whether there will be gaps or not.

The layout of these sets makes it clear that there are two ways to delete a gap: one way is to fill it with a *word*; the other is to erase the *position* from the *list*. To fill the gap with a *word*, the mechanism changes the appropriate *word* set belonging to the *list-position* from an empty set to one that contains the chosen *word*. This is simply an act of posting the *word* to a pre-established set that was empty and now is not. On the other hand, to erase the *position* from the *list*, the mechanism erases the *list-position*.

There was no reference to a null value in the foregoing discussion. There is instead a *word* set which, in the last analysis, is the reservation of a region of a program's data space to hold whatever *word* identifiers we wish. Using, for example, the strategy that places a pointer to details about the region in the first bits of the region, information concerning the number of elements currently in the set is available by consulting that pointer. The answer happens to be zero if the *word* set is empty. There is no observable string of bits standing for the "missing" *word* identifier. What is present is some administrative apparatus for managing the reserved region — apparatus that has the same form for all set storage regions whether the sets are filled or empty. There is no null value anywhere.

21. Choosing *multiple* allows a *list* to *impose* the same *position on* many *words*. An example is:

L16: 1{the} 2{horse} 3{pulled} 4{our, a, the} 5{cart}

Here, many words appear in *position* 4. A data base that allows many *words* to occupy the same *position* in a *list* is said to allow *ties*. The words "our", "a", and "the" are *tied* in the *list* L16. Imagine alternatively a *list* that shows the standings of competitors in a sports event. Two competitors with the same standing are tied.

22. Choosing *optional* allows a *list* to *arrange* a *word* that it does not *impose* anything *on*.

23. Choosing *optional* allows a *list* to *impose* something other than a *position* on a *word* that it *arranges*. For example, a *word* might appear in the header of a *list*, and so the list might be considered to *arrange* the *word*, but not *impose* a *position* on it.

If either decision (22) or (23) is *optional*, a *word* may be *arranged* by a *list* without appearing in some *position* in the *list*. Such a *word* is said to be *unsorted*. For example, in an open tennis match, some players will be unknown and therefore unseeded. We may view the player roster as the *list*, the players as the *words* in the *list*, and the seeding as the assignment of *positions* to the players (*words*). The unseeded players then correspond to the unsorted *words*.

Unsorted *words* may be shown as a set that precedes the *words* that *positions* are *imposed on*, as in:

L17: {south, fly} 1{the} 2{cat} 3{ate} 4{the} 5{mouse}

The *words* "south" and "fly" are unsorted in this *list*.

A data base management system may manage unsorteds in the same way as gaps. See decision (20) for a discussion of the programming aspects of such data structures.

24. Choosing *multiple* allows the same *word* to occupy more than one *position* in a *list*. Such a *word* is said to *repeat*, as shown in list L1 at the beginning of this section:

L1: 1{the} 2{horse} 3{pulled} 4{the} 5{cart}

The *word* "the" repeats in the *list* L1. An example of a *list* with gaps, ties, unsorteds, and repeats, that is, an example in which all the axial character decisions discussed so far are made permissively, is:

L18: {car, bus} 1{a} 2{tree, wire} 3{fell} 4{during} 5{a, the} 6{storm} 7{ }

The word "a" repeats because it appears in both *positions* 1 and 5.

25. Choosing *mandatory* requires that something *impose* a *position on* each *word* that the *position numbers*. This need not be a *list*; for example, a table could impose a *position* on the *word*.

26. Choosing *mandatory* requires that whenever something *imposes* a *position p on* a *word w*, there must be a *list* that *imposes* the *position p on* the *word w*. If either (25) or (26) are *optional*, a *position* may *number* a *word* without there being a *list* that *imposes* the *position on* the *word*. Such a data base is said to exhibit *hidden sequencing*.

Hidden sequencing is called *hidden* because it can not be determined by examining *lists*. Suppose, for example, that the *word* "C" is assigned to *position* 100. If there are no *lists* that *provide position* 100, no *lists* will exhibit this assignment. Indeed, if gaps are permitted [decision (20)], a *list* could *provide position* 100 but show a gap in that *position*, again giving no evidence that "C" is *numbered* by 100.

An example of hidden sequencing is given by imagining the *positions* to be open positions in a bureaucracy, and the *words* to be candidates who apply for each *position*. Suppose that each member of a selection committee is asked to provide a *list* of which candidate he or she feels is best for each *position*. Presuming that some candidates are left off each committee member's *list* for any given *position*, the set of candidates (*words*) who apply for a *position* can not be determined by examining the *lists*, so the trio complex exhibits hidden sequencing.

27. Making this decision *single* states that a *word* may not be contained in the same *position* in more than one *list*. While a *word* may continue to be reused freely across *lists* [decision (15)], it can not be reused in the same *position*, as shown by the following *lists*:

L19:	1{the}	2{cat}	3{ate}	4{the}	5{mouse}
L20:	1{but}	2{the}	3{mouse}	4{was}	5{unharmed}

The words "the" and "mouse" appear in both *lists*. Yet these *words* never occupy the same *position* in the different *lists*.

If decision (27) is *multiple*, the data base is said to allow *column duplicates*. As noted in the discussion of decision (9), the data base may be viewed as an array. The data base allows *column duplicates* if it permits a *word* to appear more than once in a column. Imagine the columns (*positions*) as cities, the rows (*lists*) as companies and the *words* as various activities that companies perform for cities, such as street cleaning, facilities management, construction, and so on. In this interpretation, prevention of column duplicates is a powerful rule. It says "every city is required to select at most one company to do a particular activity." All vendors of activities, in other words, get an exclusive franchise with the city.

Facial Decisions

The locations of facial decisions in extended associative notation are shown in Figure 9.15. Facial decisions are completely determined except in pineal trio complexes.

28 and **29.** Choosing (28) *optional* allows a *list* to *impose* some *x* on some *y* without *x* being a *position*, *y* being a *word*, or *x numbering y*. For example, a *list* could *impose* a header reference *on* an icon, and participate in no other way in *imposes on*. If either (28) or (29) is *optional*, there may be *lists* that do not *impose* any *positions* on any *words*. Such a *list* will be called a *benchwarmer list*, because it stays apart from the trio assemblies.

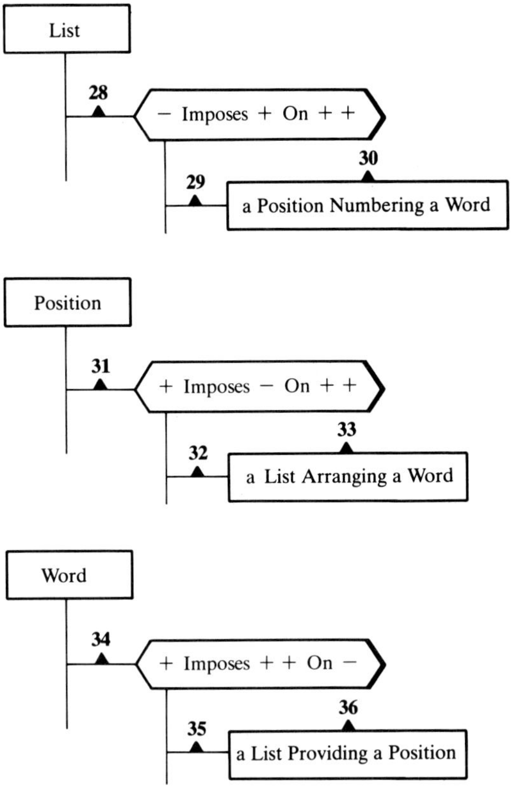

Figure 9.15 Facial decisions.

A benchwarmer *list* may continue to *provide positions* and *arrange words*. For example, consider the *list*:

L21: {pear} 1{ } 2{ }

Here, the *word* "pear" is unsorted [decision (23)], and the two *positions provided* by L21 exhibit gaps [decision (20)]. This *list imposes* no *position on* any *word*, so it is a benchwarmer *list*.

Imagine conversely that there is a rule that every *list* in the data base must *impose* a *position on* some *word*. That is, both (28) and (29) are *mandatory* and benchwarmer *lists* are prohibited. This constraint remains declarable even if the data base permits gaps and unsorteds:

L22: {pear} 1{ } 2{apple}
L23: {apple} 1{grapefruit} 4{ }

The trio complex illustrated by the *lists* L22 and L23 is pineal, because we can not prohibit L21 using decisions (1) through (27) without prohibiting one or both of L22 and L23 as well. This example shows therefore that the decisions (28) and (29) can provide new information about a trio complex.

This example may only be formed if both gaps and unsorteds are permitted. For example, if gaps are not allowed, then any *position* that a *list provides* must be *imposed on* some *word*. With this assumption, a *list* is a benchwarmer *list* if and only if it provides no *position*, and decisions (28) and (29) are *mandatory* if and only if decisions (1) and (2) are *mandatory*. Such interdependencies are responsible for the theoretical result that pineal trio complexes only occur in the second stable state and in full reversal.

30. Choosing *multiple* allows a *list* to *impose* many times. In its most severe form, a *list* might *impose* only one *position* on any given *word* and only show one *word* in any *position*, as in:

L24: 1{the} 2{brown} 3{cow}

The decision (30) here remains *multiple*, since there are three acts of imposing some *position* on some *list*. A *list* that *imposes* many times, the antithesis of a benchwarmer *list*, is called a *utility list*.

An example of a *list* that is neither a utility nor a benchwarmer is a *list* that imposes exactly one *position* on exactly one *word*:

L25: 3{spool}

Such a *list* may also contain gaps and unsorteds:

L26: {tape, recorder} 2{ } 3{spool} 4{ }

The *list* L26 illustrates a further example of a pineal trio complex. If *lists* may *provide* many *positions* and *arrange* many *words*, we would normally expect a *list* to be able to *impose* many times. The *list* L26 shows that this expectation need not be fulfilled. As with L22 and L23 above, a *list* such as L26 may only be formed when the trio complex permits both gaps and unsorteds.

With the illustration of decision (30), we have narrated all the major forms of trio complexes. The remaining decisions, (31) to (36), follow the patterns of decisions (28) to (30). We present therefore only a brief synopsis of decisions (31) to (36).

31. Choosing *mandatory* forces each *position* to be *imposed* by something on something.

32. Choosing *mandatory* forces each *position* that is *imposed* to be *imposed* by a *list* on a *word*. Making both (31) and (32) *mandatory* forces each *position* to be *imposed* by some *list* on some *word*, that is, it prevents benchwarmer *positions*. See decision (28) for further discussion.

33. Choosing *single* forces each *position* to be *imposed on* at most one *word* by at most one *list*. That is, it prevents utility *positions*. See decision (30) for further discussion.

34. Choosing *optional* allows a *word* that nothing *imposes* anything *on*.

35. Choosing *optional* allows a *word* that something *imposes* something *on*, but no *list imposes* a *position on*. If either decision (34) or decision (35) is *optional*, there may be a *word* that no *list imposes* a *position on*, that is, a benchwarmer *word*. See decision (28) for further discussion.

36. Choosing *multiple* allows a *word* to be *imposed on* many times. That is, it permits utility *words*. See decision (30) for further discussion. Readers eager to revisit this case study may note that the elision correspondence to which this decision applies is reversed by the cascade that begins with decision (1).

9.6 CONCLUSION

A trio complex may be described by three forms of decisions: delta decisions, which are decisions about correspondence complexes, and can be handled by the methods of Chapter 6; axial decisions, which determine the stable state of the trio complex; and facial decisions, which describe pineal trio complexes. By describing the properties of each group of decisions, trio complexes are fully described.

We have shown that degenerate trio complexes may be detected by the method of convolution. This method applies to all associations, with or without ''null values,'' and is therefore more general than the normalization procedures of the relational data model.

We have shown how a far greater variety of trio complexes may be described in extended associative notation than in other data models. In particular, extended associative notation allows ''null values'' to be permitted or prohibited in any or all positions of an association complex. In all, extended associative notation allows 30,660 different forms of trio complexes.

This diversity requires embracings. We have shown that trio complexes of the second stable state and full reversal (which include 89 percent of the potential forms) contain internal embracings which must be recognized for the trio to be declared properly. Design methods that do not recognize embracings therefore can not express most varieties of trio complexes.

Data logic furnishes the means for deducing the effects of these internal embracings. Thus, we have calculated, primarily through composition cone theory, all the character decision interdependencies that are present in trio complexes. These interdependencies relate the decisions in the extended associative notation for a trio complex—certain choices logically determine other choices. The interdependencies are entirely regular, however, and do not depend on the particular associations chosen. We have indicated how these interdependencies may be programmed into the design management device, so that obedience to them becomes automatic.

CONCLUSION TO PART 3

Part 3 has emphasized data structures that can not be formed by other data models. Thus, in Chapter 7, we introduced intercharacter embracings, orphans-not-allowed, and anchored cycles. In Chapter 8, we surveyed the vast diversity of composition cones, and in Chapter 9, we surveyed the even vaster diversity of trio complexes.

These different forms of constraints are interrelated. We saw in Chapter 6 that character decisions can be treated as embracings of retroactive cycles. These embracings were then generalized to zigzag chains, which led to the description of bundlings. Bundlings, in turn, were a key aspect of composition cone theory, since they served to distinguish compositions of the form >.< from compositions of the form <.>. Composition cone theory was later applied to give the character decision interdependencies of trio complexes.

In another line of reasoning, generalizing character constraints to hubs yielded intercharacter embracings, orphans-not-allowed, and replicates-not-allowed in Chapter 7. These embracings were applied in Chapter 8 to determine the composition cones of compositions of the form [.] and <.>. Then, in Chapter 9, replicates-not-allowed constraints were seen to describe the behavior of concentrations. This enabled us to show how a trio complex could be converted to a network diagram by adding embracings. It also showed how third order relations in the relational data model could be viewed as base state trio complexes, with associated replicates-not-allowed constraints.

It is particularly significant that so many of the varieties of constraints discussed in earlier chapters find application in the study of trio complexes. We believe that the primary reason that trio complexes have not been fully understood up to now has been the great diversity of patterns that must be comprehended, and the consequential need for a highly powerful analytical method. Embracings furnish this analytical method, because embracings can both describe data base constraints, and can also be combined using data logic to furnish proofs of properties of data structures.

These investigations do not by any means exhaust the new varieties of data structures that may be formed from positive embracings. We have concentrated on simple illustrations of the basic building blocks of positive embracings, that is, on embracings whose formulas have few terms. Thus, orphans-not-allowed is a simple example of the union of correspondences in an embracing. Replicates-not-allowed is a simple example of the intersection of correspondences in an embracing. Composition cones are a simple example of the composition of correspondences in an embracing. Convolution is a simple example of embracings of degree three and higher.

We have no doubt that many other forms of embracings are possible, and that they will provide many new data structures that we have not investigated in this book. Positive embracings are defined open-endedly: any formula, however complex, is a valid positive embracing provided it meets a few syntactic rules. Positive embracings will allow data requirements to be specified far more thoroughly and precisely than has been possible up to now.

Bibliography

ARISTOTLE. 350B.C.a. *Categories*. In Richard McKeon, ed. (1941). *The Basic Works of Aristotle*. New York: Random House. The first systematic study of the classification of ideas — what we now call data structures.

_____ 350B.C.b. *On Interpretation*. In Richard McKeon, ed. (1941). *The Basic Works of Aristotle*. New York: Random House. Discusses the constituents of propositions and their relationship to thought.

_____ 350B.C.c. *Prior Analytics*. Hugh Tredennick, ed. (1938). The Loeb Classical Library, no. 325. Cambridge, Mass.: Harvard University Press. The first systematic study of the laws of reason.

BACHMAN, CHARLES W. 1983. "The Structuring Capabilities of the Molecular Data Model." In Carl G. Davis, et al., eds., *Entity–Relationship Approach to Software Engineering*. Amsterdam: North–Holland. Extends the network data model to incorporate all sixteen correspondence characters.

BOAS, FRANZ. 1911. *Introduction to the Handbook of American Indian Languages*. Preston Holder, ed. (1966). Lincoln, Nebr.: University of Nebraska Press. Provides vivid examples of methods of discourse that are very different from English. Challenges the idea that Western grammatical categories are fundamental to thought.

CANTOR, GEORG. 1895. *Contributions to the Founding of the Theory of Transfinite Numbers*. Philip E. B. Jourdain, ed. (1955). New York: Dover. Introduced the development of arithmetic from set theory. Contains an opposing treatment of mathematical infinities.

CAUCHY, AUGUSTIN LOUIS. 1821. *Cours d'analyse de l'École Royale Polytechnique*. In (1897) *Oeuvres complètes*, series 2, vol. 3. Paris: Gauthier–Villars et fils. Developed the rigorous theory of convergent series.

CHARNIAK, EUGENE, CHRISTOPHER K. RIESBECK, DREW V. MCDERMOTT, and JAMES R. MEEHAN. 1987. *Artificial Intelligence Programming*. Second edition. Hillsdale, N.J.: Lawrence Erlbaum. A survey of practical techniques for developing artificial intelligence applications.

CHELLAS, BRIAN F. 1980. *Modal Logic: an Introduction*. Cambridge, England: Cambridge University Press. A survey of contemporary systems of modal logic. Complements our discussion of definitiveness.

CHEN, PETER PIN–SHAN. 1976. "The entity–relationship model: Toward a unified view of data." *ACM Transactions on Database Systems*. 1(1): 9–36. Introduced a widely used technique for data design.

CHOMSKY, NOAM. 1965. *Aspects of the Theory of Syntax*. Cambridge, Mass.: M.I.T. Press. Discusses the basic principles of generative grammar. Complements our discussion of the representation of ideas in language.

DATE, C. J. 1986. *An Introduction to Database Systems*. 4th ed. 2 vols. Reading, Mass.: Addison–Wesley. Covers the field well, including software and operational topics not discussed in this book. Emphasizes the relational data model. Along with (Maier 1983), one of our principal sources for the relational data model.

DE SAUSSURE, FERDINAND. 1915. *Course in General Linguistics*. Charles Bally, et al., eds. (1959). New York: McGraw–Hill. Places problems of representation in the wider context of the study of language.

DEDEKIND, JULIUS WILHELM RICHARD. 1872. *Continuity and Irrational Numbers*. In Wooster Woodruff Beeman, trans. (1963). *Essays on the Theory of Numbers*. New York: Dover. Presents an opposing definition of the real numbers as subsets of the infinite set of rational numbers.

EUCLID. 300B.C. *The Elements*. Thomas L. Heath, ed. (1956). New York: Dover. 3 vols. Established the principles of reasoning using axioms and postulates.

FAGIN, RONALD. 1982. "Horn Clauses and Database Dependencies." *Journal of the ACM* 29(4): 952–985. Demonstrates the formulation of most data base constraints in terms of a simplified form of positive embracing.

FREEMAN, EUGENE and WILFRID SELLARS, eds. 1971. *Basic Issues in the Philosophy of Time*. LaSalle, Ill.: Open Court. A collection of essays that present alternative viewpoints on the treatment of time.

FREGE, GOTTLOB. 1879. *Begriffschrift*. In Jean van Heijenoort, ed. (1967). *From Frege to Gödel, A Source Book in Mathematical Logic, 1879–1931*. Cambridge, Mass.: Harvard University Press. (English translation) The first complete exposition of the rules of modern logic, later adopted as the core of symbolic logic.

_____ 1884. *The Foundations of Arithmetic*. J. L. Austin, ed. (1980). Evanston, Ill.: Northwestern University Press. Discusses Frege's theory of numbers, along with a careful comparison with theories of other philosophers.

_____ 1892. *On Sense and Reference*. In Peter Geach and Max Black, eds. (1970). *Translations from the Philosophical Writings of Gottlob Frege*. Oxford: Basil Blackwell. Discusses identity and the interpretation of proposition tags.

FROST, RICHARD. 1986. *Introduction to Knowledge Base Systems*. New York: Macmillan. Emphasizes interrelationships among logic, data bases, and knowledge bases. Discusses relevant software and hardware.

GALLAIRE, HERVÉ and JACK MINKER, eds. 1978. *Logic and Data Bases*. New York: Plenum. A collection of articles on the application of logic to data bases.

GAUSS, CARL FRIEDRICH. 1831. *Brief an Schumacher*. In (1900) *Werke*. Göttingen: Königlichen Gesellschaft der Wissenschaften. vol. 8: 215–218. Contains a criticism of the use of infinite numbers in reasoning.

GENESERETH, MICHAEL R. and NILS J. NILSSON. 1987. *Logical Foundations of Artificial Intelligence*. Los Altos, Calif.: Morgan Kaufmann. Systematizes many aspects of modern artificial intelligence research using symbolic logic.

GERGONNE, J. D. 1817. "Essai de dialectique rationelle." *Annales de Mathématiques* 7:189–228. Presents a symbolic notation for Aristotelian logic.

GÖDEL, KURT. 1931. "On formally undecidable propositions of *Principia Mathematica* and related systems I." In Jean van Heijenoort, ed. (1967). *From Frege to Gödel, A Source Book in Mathematical Logic, 1879–1931*. Cambridge, Mass.: Harvard University Press. Contains a proof of the incompleteness of symbolic logic, along with a formal specification of the syntax of symbolic logic.

GOLDBERG, ADELE. 1984. *Smalltalk–80, The Interactive Programming Environment*. Reading, Mass.: Addison–Wesley. An introduction to one of the first object–oriented development environments. Complements our discussion of the impact of embracings on computer systems implementation.

GRANT, JOHN and BARRY E. JACOBS. 1982. "On the Family of Generalized Dependency Constraints." *Journal of the ACM*. 29(4): 986–997. Demonstrates the formulation of most data base constraints in terms of a simplified form of positive embracing.

HAWKING, STEPHEN W. 1988. *A Brief History of Time*. New York: Bantam Books. A nontechnical description of current thinking about the nature of physical time. Complements our study of conceptions of time.

HEYTING, A. 1966. *Intuitionism, an Introduction*. 2nd ed. Amsterdam: North–Holland. An introduction to the methods of intuitionistic logic, which denies that every proposition must be either true or false.

HILBERT, DAVID and WILHELM ACKERMANN. 1938. *Principles of Mathematical Logic*. Robert E. Luce, ed. (1950). New York: Chelsea. Remains one of the finest introductions to symbolic logic.

HOBBES, THOMAS. 1655. *The Elements of Philosophy*. In William Molesworth, ed. (1839). *The English Works of Thomas Hobbes*. Reprinted (1962). Scientia Aalen. One of the first post–medieval works to attempt a thorough redefinition of the foundations of philosophy. Complements our discussion of the representation of ideas by symbols.

HUME, DAVID. 1739. *A Treatise of Human Nature*. Reprinted (1974). Everyman's Library. London: J. M. Dent. 2 vols. Surveys a wide variety of topics, from the nature of ideas to human passions and morality. Complements our discussions of impressions, propositions, affirmation, and time.

JONES, PAUL E. 1964. "Historical Foundations of Research on Statistical Association Techniques for Mechanized Documentation." *Statistical Association Methods For Mechanized Documentation, Symposium Proceedings*. National Bureau of Standards Miscellaneous Publication 269. Discusses the roots of the study of information retrieval in philosophy and psycholinguistics.

_____ 1976. *Data Base Design Methodology: A Logical Framework*. QED Monographs Series, no. 3. Wellesley, Mass.: QED Information Sciences. Introduced the Associative Data Model notation, which forms the core of the extended associative notation presented in this book.

JONES, PAUL E. and ROBERT M. CURTICE. 1988. *Logical Data Base Design*, 2nd ed. Wellesley, Mass.: QED Information Sciences. A discussion of the Associative Data Model with emphasis on its application to practical data design situations. Presents a condensed version of extended associative notation free from embracings and certain design decisions.

JONES, PETER C. and PAUL E. JONES. 1986. "Linguistic Correlates of Data Structures: The THAT Language." *ACM Computer Science Conference Proceedings*. 416. Initial announcement of explanations.

KENT, WILLIAM. 1978. *Data and Reality: Basic Assumptions in Data Processing Reconsidered.* Amsterdam: North–Holland. Emphasizes the need to consider problems of representation when undertaking a data base design.

KLEENE, STEPHEN COLE. 1952. *Introduction to Metamathematics*. Princeton, N.J.: Van Nostrand. An advanced discussion of the foundations of mathematics according to both symbolic and intuitionistic logic.

KNEALE, WILLIAM and MARTHA KNEALE. 1962. *The Development of Logic*. London: Oxford University Press. A history of logic from the ancient Greeks to the twentieth century.

LEIBNIZ, GOTTFRIED WILHELM. 1683. *Of Universal Synthesis and Analysis.*

_____ 1686. *Primary Truths.*

_____ 1714. *Monadology*. Leibniz preferred to write brief dissertations on specific topics, rather than large, integrated works. Broad reading is therefore needed to appreciate Leibniz's thought. The three works cited may be found along with others in G. H. R. Parkinson, ed. (1973). *Leibniz, Philosophical Writings*. London: J. M. Dent. Leibniz opposes our treatment of foundations by advocating indivisible ideas, identity as the foundation of logic, and modality based on possible worlds.

LEWIS, C. I. 1918. *A Survey of Symbolic Logic*. Berkeley, Calif. Presents a formal treatment of modal logic.

LIU, KEN–CHIH and RAJSHEKHAR SUNDERRAMAN. 1990. "Indefinite and Maybe Information in Relational Databases." *ACM Transactions on Database Systems*. 15(1): 1–39. Proposes a method for extending the relational data model to incorporate certain forms of unresolved alternation.

LOCKE, JOHN. 1690. *An Essay Concerning Human Understanding*. Alexander Campbell Fraser, ed. (1959). New York: Dover. 2 vols. An extensive philosophical discussion of the nature of ideas.

LYONS, JOHN. 1977. *Semantics*. Cambridge, England: Cambridge University Press. 2 vols. A comprehensive discussion of the major modern theories of meaning.

MAIER, DAVID. 1983. *The Theory of Relational Databases*. Rockville, Md.: Computer Science Press. A detailed survey of the relational data model. Together with (Date 1986), one of our principal sources for the relational data model.

MARTIN, JAMES. 1976. *Principles of Data–Base Management*. Englewood Cliffs, N.J.: Prentice–Hall. Discusses the purposes and applications of data bases for the nontechnical reader.

PEANO, GIUSEPPE. 1889. *The principles of arithmetic, presented by a new method.* In Jean van Heijenoort, ed. (1967) *From Frege to Gödel, A Source Book in Mathematical Logic, 1879–1931*. Cambridge, Mass.: Harvard University Press. Introduced most of the lexical notation used in symbolic logic.

PLATO. 380B.C.a. *Phaedo*. In Edith Hamilton & Huntington Cairns, eds. (1961). *The Collected Dialogues of Plato*. Princeton, N.J.: Princeton University Press. A wide–ranging discussion of the nature of existence, identity, opposites, and the human soul.

_____ 380B.C.b. *Parmenides*. In Edith Hamilton & Huntington Cairns, eds. (1961). *The Collected Dialogues of Plato*. Princeton, N.J.: Princeton University Press. An extensive discussion of the philosophical problem of the one and the many. Complements our discussion of identity.

POINCARÉ, HENRI. 1908. *Science and Method*. Francis Maitland, trans. (1952). New York: Dover. A critique of the science of the time, including many criticisms of symbolic logic.

PRIOR, ARTHUR N. 1967. *Past, Present and Future*. London: Oxford University Press. Presents an opposing view of modal logic based upon concepts of time.

QUINE, WILLARD VAN ORMAN. 1960. *Word and Object*. Cambridge, Mass.: M.I.T. Press. A provocative discussion of meaning, logic, and language, oriented to problems of philosophy.

_____ 1980. *From a Logical Point of View*. 2nd edition. Cambridge, Mass.: Harvard University Press. A discussion of many topics in the foundations of logic. Contains a critique of modal logic.

RUSSELL, BERTRAND. 1902. *Letter to Frege*. In Jean van Heijenoort, ed. (1967). *From Frege to Gödel, A Source Book in Mathematical Logic, 1879–1931*. Cambridge, Mass.: Harvard University Press. Presented the paradox that bears its author's name.

SAPIR, EDWARD. 1921. *Language*. New York: Harcourt, Brace. A thoughtful discussion of many topics in linguistics. Complements our discussion of the foundations of data theory.

SPIVAK, MICHAEL. 1967. *Calculus*. Menlo Park: Benjamin. An introduction to calculus with particular attention to the mathematical fundamentals.

TSICHRITZIS, DIONYSIOS C. and FREDERICK H. LOCHOVSKY. 1982. *Data Models*. Englewood Cliffs, N.J.: Prentice–Hall. A survey of contemporary techniques for data base design.

TURING, ALAN MATHISON. 1937. "On Computable Numbers, with an Application to the *Entscheidungsproblem*." *Proceedings of the London Mathematical Society*. 42: 230–265. Introduced the concept of a computable number, which is similar to the definition of a real number in data logic.

TURNER, RAYMOND. 1984. *Logics for Artificial Intelligence*. Chichester, England: Ellis Horwood. A survey of alternative systems of logic for computer applications.

VETTER, MAX and R. N. MADDISON. 1981. *Database Design Methodology*. Englewood Cliffs, N. J.: Prentice–Hall. Presents an approach to practical data base design.

WHITEHEAD, ALFRED NORTH and BERTRAND RUSSELL. 1927. *Principia Mathematica*. 2nd ed. Cambridge, England: Cambridge University Press. 3 vols. A thorough treatment of the foundations of mathematics using symbolic logic. Our principal source for symbolic logic.

WITTGENSTEIN, LUDWIG. 1921. *Tractatus Logico–Philosophicus*. C. K. Ogden, trans. (1922). London: Routledge and Kegan Paul. Presents an opposing view of thought in which perception and logic are resolvable into atomic facts.

ZERMELO, ERNST. 1908. *Investigations in the Foundations of Set Theory I*. In Jean van Heijenoort, ed. (1967). *From Frege to Gödel, A Source Book in Mathematical Logic, 1879–1931*. Cambridge, Mass.: Harvard University Press. Presents axioms that remain the foundations of modern set theory.

ZUCKERMAN, MARTIN M. 1974. *Sets and Transfinite Numbers*. New York: Macmillan. A particularly accessible account of the basic principles of set theory.

Glossary

Acceptance

One of two possible outcomes of an examination, the other being rejection.

Accumulating correspondence

A correspondence complex that is both *to one* and *to all*. The character of an accumulating correspondence is thus included in ''$\rceil>$''.

Admissible

A constraint is *admissible* if it satisfies the requirements of practical data base designs. A constraint is admissible according to this book if and only if it is a positive embracing.

Affirmed

(i) A proposition tag p is *affirmed* if p may be deduced from the claims in a population. The statement that p is affirmed is written $\vdash p$. Compare *claim*.

(ii) A proposition « p » is *affirmed* if the symbol ''p'' may be deduced from the claims in a population and ''p'' represents « p ».

Agency choice

The statement that an agency decision is either *mandatory* or *optional*.

Agency decision

A decision of the form « if x is a B, must there be some y such that $x\ Gs\ y$? ». An agency decision is shown on the second or fourth level of a cascade in extended associative notation.

Alien proposition

A proposition that is neither affirmed nor denied.

All-to-all

A correspondence complex is *all-to-all* if it is *from all* and *to all.*

All-to-some

A correspondence complex is *all-to-some* if it is *from all* and *to some.*

Alternation

(i) The *alternation* of two propositions p and q, written "$p \vee q$" and read « p or q », evokes any impression that is evoked by p or by q.
(ii) The *alternation* of two plans r and s is the plan « perform r or perform s ».

Alternative deduction barrier

The principle that the proposition $p \rightarrow q$ is not interchangeable with the proposition $(\tilde{}p) \vee q$ as it is in symbolic logic. The alternative deduction barrier limits the spread of contradictions.

Ambivalence

(i) The *ambivalence* of a class B accepts any image that B both accepts and rejects. Any ambivalence of an omissive class is populable; any ambivalence of a constructive class is unpopulable.
(ii) The *ambivalence* of a recognizer d accepts any impression that d both accepts and rejects.

Ambivalence principle (of associations)

For any omissive association R of degree r, it must be possible to imagine images $b_1, \ldots, b_r$ such that R would both accept and reject $b_1, \ldots, b_r$ if they were presented.

Ambivalence principle (of recognizers)

For any omissive recognizer d, it must be possible to imagine an impression that d would both accept and reject if it were presented.

Ambivalent

(i) A class is *ambivalent* about an image if it both accepts and rejects the image.
(ii) A recognizer is *ambivalent* about an impression if it both accepts and rejects the impression.

Anchored

(i) A correspondence L is *anchored* at a class B if $L \subseteq \Delta B$.
(ii) A cycle is *anchored* if its composition correspondence is anchored.

And

(i) The proposition « p and q » is called the *conjunction* of p and q. It is written "p & q".
(ii) The word "and" indicates an intersection when written inside a shape in extended associative notation.

Any

Indicates definitive quantification, as in "for any x".

Appear

(i) Refers generally to observable properties of symbols. For example, the symbol "b" appears in the conglomeration "*abcd*".
(ii) A population *appears* to obey the definitive proposition $!p$ if the population obeys the incidental proposition p. For example, a class C appears to embrace a class B if C includes B.

Assembly

A conceptual mechanism that accepts assembly manifestations. An assembly is written $R(b_1, \ldots, b_r)$, where R is the association that controls the assembly and $b_1, \ldots, b_r$ are recognizers whose manifestations are accepted by R. An assembly controlled by a correspondence is also called an *attachment*. An assembly is assumed to be a recognizer according to the assembly image principle. See example at *attachment*.

Assembly image principle

The principle that for any association R, the conceptual mechanism that accepts assembly manifestations controlled by R is a recognizer.

Assembly manifestation

A combination of an association of degree r with r images that the association accepts.

Association

An *association* of degree r is a conceptual mechanism that examines r images, accepting or rejecting them. A class is an association of degree one, a correspondence is an association of degree two, a trio is an association of degree three, and a quartet is an association of degree four.

Association complex

An association R together with a set of associations of lower degree which are conjoined with projections of R. Compare *relative complex*.

Association tag

A symbol that represents an association.

Associative Data Model

The data design technique discussed in (Jones and Curtice 1988) and (Jones 1976) on which extended associative notation is based.

Attach

A correspondence G *attaches* a recognizer b to a recognizer c if G accepts a manifestation of b in the first position and a manifestation of c in the second position. For example, the correspondence « Eats » attaches « Joe » to « the cake » if « Joe eats the cake ».

Attachment

(i) A conceptual mechanism that accepts attachment manifestations. For example, a conceptual mechanism that accepts any impression of « Joe eating the cake » (see *attaches*). An attachment is also an assembly controlled by an association of degree two.

(ii) A symbol that represents a conceptual mechanism as defined in (i). A symbolic attachment is often implemented in computerized data bases as a pair of individuals. For example, the record "(*Joe*, *cake #48*)" in the "*Eats*" file represents « Joe eats the cake ». An attachment is written $G(b, c)$, where G is the correspondence that controls the attachment and b and c are recognizers whose manifestations are accepted by G.

Attachment chain

See *chain*.

Attachment circle

See *circle*.

Attachment manifestation

A combination of a correspondence with two images that the correspondence accepts, one in each position. For example, an image of « Joe eating the cake » (see *attaches*).

Attachment path

A set of attachments that may be strung together, as in $\{(a)F(b), (b)G(c), (c)H(d)\}$. An attachment path is used to illustrate a composition correspondence, in this case $F \circ G \circ H$.

Axial

Refers to properties of elision correspondences of the form ${}_{12}T_{123}$ of a trio T. Character decisions of these correspondences are shown on the fourth and fifth levels of extended associative notation.

Axiom

A definitive proposition that supervises any data base.

Barrel trio

A degenerate trio that is equivalent to the Cartesian product of a correspondence complex with a class.

Base relative complex

A string of r classes, used to declare an association of degree r in the base state.

Base state

The stable state of an association that occurs when all *mandatory/optional* decisions below the third level are chosen *mandatory*.

Binary hub

A hub of width two. The same as a binary path.

Binary path

A path of length two. The same as a binary hub.

Binding site

A process by which a thing is accepted, rejected, or not examined. Two different symbols may be accepted by the same binding site (compare *detector*). A binding site is an engine of degree one.

Blank

A string of underscores that indicates a placetaker when representing a class through language, as in « _____ Is A Blender ».

Bootstrap plan

A plan that is inherited biologically. Bootstrap plans are the conjectured source of innate ideas in the mind.

Border elongation

The factoring of a correspondence complex (G; B, C) as the path (B; ΔB; $\pi^1\dot{G}$; $\dot{G}$; $\pi^2\dot{G}$; ΔC; C). The middle correspondence complex of this path is always *all–to–all*.

Bracket

One of the symbols], <, >, or [used to represent a permissive character choice.

Bundling

A correspondence that may be factored into a binary path (A; F; B; G; C) such that F is *to one* relative to (A, B) and G is *from one* relative to (B, C).

Cantor's theorem

The theorem of symbolic logic that the set of all subsets of a set has more members than the set itself.

Cartesian product

The *Cartesian product* of two associations R of degree r and S of degree s is the association $R \times S$ of degree $r + s$ defined by

$$(R \times S){:}|x_1, \ldots, x_r, y_1, \ldots, y_s| \Leftrightarrow R{:}|x_1, \ldots, x_r| \;\&\; S{:}|y_1, \ldots, y_s|$$

Cascade

A string of connected shapes in extended associative notation that proceeds from the extreme left side down and to the right.

Center

The class tag that is identified as common to all correspondence complexes in a hub.

Chain

(i) A sequence of embracings or implications of the form $p_1 \Rightarrow p_2 \Rightarrow \ldots$
(ii) A sequence of attachments of the form $L{:}(b_1, b_2), L{:}(b_2, b_3), \ldots, L{:}(b_{n-1}, b_n)$ such that b_n is an orphan of L and b_1 is an orphan of L^*.

Character

(i) The collection of four character decisions for a correspondence.
(ii) A string formed from a subset of the set of brackets $\{], <, >, [\}$.

Character choice

The outcome of a character decision. See *choice, character decision.*

Character decision

Any of the following decisions for a correspondence complex $(G; B, C)$:

(a) whether G is *from all* or *from some* relative to (B, C)
(b) whether G is *to one* or *to many* relative to (B, C)
(c) whether G is *from one* or *from many* relative to (B, C)
(d) whether G is *to all* or *to some* relative to (B, C)

Character decision interdependency

Refers to interrelationships among the decisions in an association complex of degree three or higher. Certain choices in these association complexes are forced when other choices are made in a particular way.

Character embracing

Any of the embracings that define the restrictive character decisions *from all*, *from one*, *to one*, or *to all*.

Character tag

Refers specifically to a string of brackets used to represent character decisions.

Chevron

A shape used in extended associative notation and population diagrams to indicate a correspondence.

Choice

An outcome of a decision. For example, a designer may make the choice "*to one*" or the choice "*to many*" with respect to a *to one/to many* character decision for a given correspondence complex.

Circle

A sequence of attachments controlled by a loop that may be strung end-to-end so that the destination of the last attachment is the same instance as the source of the first attachment.

Circumference

The number of attachments in an attachment circle.

Claim

(i) A *claim* is a proposition tag that is a member of a data base population. In computer applications, the claims are the proposition tags that are physically resident in the data base. The *affirmed* proposition tags, in contrast, are the proposition tags that may be deduced from the claims by applying logic.
(ii) A proposition tag is *claimed* if it is a member of a data base population.
(iii) A proposition is *claimed* if it is a tag that represents the proposition is a member of a data base population.

Class

A conceptual mechanism by which an image is accepted, rejected, or not examined. If an image that is a manifestation of a recognizer d is accepted by a class C, then d is an instance of C. A class is typically represented in English by a countable noun phrase. A class is an association of degree one.

Class tag

A symbol that represents a class.

Coalescence

The replacement of a trivial composition cone with its sole member, the maximal composition character, when calculating the composition cone of a path.

Coalescence test

The procedure to determine whether or not a path obeys precedence by successive examination of the characters of each pair of adjoining constituent correspondences.

Coincident diamonding

A phenomenon whereby a correspondence that is *to many* may be composed with a correspondence that is *from many* to yield a correspondence that is more restrictive than *many-to-many*.

Coincident orphans

A phenomenon whereby a correspondence that is *to some* may be composed with a correspondence that is *from some* to yield a correspondence that is more restrictive than *some-to-some*.

Collective correspondence

A correspondence that is reflexive, symmetric, and transitive. Similar to an "equivalence relation" in mathematics.

Co-localization

An association formed by placing $[b]$ into a position of an association R from some recognizer b, especially the association $R[b, \ldots]$.

Combination

(i) An expression formed using logical operations, especially a *positive combination*, which is an association formed from declared associations and the operations « and », « or », and « for some image ».
(ii) A textual expression in extended associative notation that is formed from declared association tags and reserved words such as "and", "or", and "some".

Complement

(i) The *complement* of a class « B » is the class « $\overline{B}$ » that accepts any image not accepted by « B » and rejects any image not rejected by « B ».
(ii) The *complement* of a recognizer « d » is the recognizer « $\overline{d}$ » that accepts any impression not accepted by « d » and rejects any impression not rejected by « d ».

Complementary

The performance type « constructive » is *complementary* to the performance type « omissive », and vice versa.

Complete

A system of logic is *complete* if every proposition that is affirmed is provable. Neither data logic nor symbolic logic is complete.

Complete relative complex

A set of associations $\{Q_\alpha\}$ such that α takes on every subset of a set of indices $\{1, \ldots, r\}$ other than the null set and the whole set.

Composition

(i) The *composition* of two correspondences F and G, written $F \circ G$, attaches an image x to an image z if, for some y, F attaches x to y and G attaches y to z.

(ii) More generally, the *composition correspondence* of the path (B_1; G_1; B_2; . . . ; G_n; B_{n+1}) is the composition $\Delta B_1 \circ G_1 \circ \Delta B_2 \circ \ldots \circ G_n \circ \Delta B_{n+1}$.

Composition cone

The cone of possible characters of the composition correspondence of a path, as determined from the characters of its constituents.

Composition cone theorem

The theorem that the set of possible characters of the composition of two correspondences is a cone whose upper bound is the maximal composition character.

Composition irregularity

A path whose composition correspondence has a character that is more restrictive than the maximal composition character.

Compound

An image is a *compound* of an impression with a recognizer that accepts the impression.

Comprehensive proposition

The conjunction of all the claims in a data base population, written "$\dashv$".

Concentration

The *concentration* of an association R, written C^1R, is the class of assemblies controlled by R.

Conceptual factory

A mental faculty that forms associations and recognizers from plans.

Conceptual mechanism

The analog of a physical process, but one that occurs unobservably in the mind and whose essential nature remains mysterious.

Conclusion

The conclusion of an implication $p \Rightarrow q$ is the proposition q.

Cone

A set $\hat{S}$ of characters such that if α and β are in $\hat{S}$, and γ is more permissive than α and less permissive than β, then γ is in $\hat{S}$.

Conformalization

See *proposal method*.

Conformer

A recognizer d is a *conformer* of a class C if and only if d is not an instance of $\overline{C}$.

Conglomeration

A physical combination of a connector with symbols, formed by a connecting engine.

Conjoining engine

An engine that forms the proposition tag "p & q" from two proposition tags p and q.

Conjunction

(i) The *conjunction* of two propositions p and q is the proposition « p and q » that evokes any impression that both p and q evoke. The conjunction of p and q is written p & q.
(ii) The *conjunction* of two plans r and s is the plan « perform r and perform s ».

Connecting engine

An engine that transforms a collection of symbols and a connector into a conglomeration.

Connector

A thing that is used with a connecting engine to form a conglomeration from many things. A connector has many positions to which things in a conglomeration are connected.

Consistent

A set of axioms is *consistent* if the application of the axioms to themselves will not result in any contradictions. Data logic is consistent; symbolic logic can not be proved to be consistent.

Constituent

(i) A symbol bound to the (outermost) connector in a conglomeration (also called an *external constituent*).
(ii) A symbol that is part of a conglomeration and contains no connectors (also called an *ultimate constituent*).
(iii) An association or recognizer used in forming a proposition. For example, « B » and « d » are the constituents of the proposition « B:(d) ».
(iv) A class tag or correspondence tag that appears in a path.

Constraint

A definitive proposition tag that restricts the potential populations of a data base. For example, the statement that a correspondence is *to one* is a constraint. Compare *relaxation*.

Constructive

(i) A *constructive* recognizer does not examine some impressions, and can not both accept and reject an impression in the same performance without contradiction. Compare *omissive*.
(ii) A *constructive* class can not both accept and reject an image in the same performance without contradiction. By the inexhaustibility principle, a constructive class must be able not to examine an image.
(iii) In a *constructive* association, no position can both accept and reject in the same performance without contradiction.
(iv) A *constructive* proposition p evokes any impression that supports p.

Contain

Used to describe a relationship of one object being accepted by or being a constituent of another object, in contrast to *embrace*, which is used to describe a relationship of one classification being broader than another. For example, the class « Person » *contains* the instance « Patricia », but the class « Person » *embraces* the class « Woman ».

Contentual

(i) A class is *contentual* if it examines only the impression within an image, and disregards the recognizer.
(ii) A class B is *contentual* if it embraces the granulation of its melding, $\Gamma\mu B$.

Contradiction

A proposition of the form « p and not p ».

Contrapositive

(i) The *contrapositive* of the embracing « C embraces B » is the embracing « $\overline{B}$ embraces $\overline{C}$ ».
(ii) The *contrapositive* of the implication $p \Rightarrow q$ is the implication $\tilde{}q \Rightarrow \tilde{}p$.

Contrapositive law (of associations)

The law of logic that an association S includes an association R if and only if $\overline{R}$ includes $\overline{S}$. More specifically, S embraces R if and only if $\overline{R}$ embraces $\overline{S}$.

Contrapositive law (of propositions)

The law of logic that a proposition $\tilde{}p$ may be deduced from a proposition $\tilde{}q$ if and only if q may be deduced from p. More specifically, the law that $\tilde{}q$ implies $\tilde{}p$ if and only if p implies q.

Control

(i) An association R *controls* any assembly of the form $R(b_1, \ldots, b_r)$.
(ii) An association R *controls* any localization of R.

Converse character

The converse of a character is formed by transforming **]** to **[**, $<$ to $>$, $>$ to $<$, and **[** to **]**. The converse character of a correspondence G is the character of the converse of G. Also written "*", as in "α*".

Converse correspondence

The *converse* of a correspondence G is the correspondence G^* defined by

$$G^*{:}|x, y| \Leftrightarrow G{:}|y, x|$$

The converse is often represented in language by transforming an active verb to the passive, or vice versa. The converse of G is equivalent to $\pi^{21}G$.

Converse correspondence complex

The *converse* of a correspondence complex $(G; B, C)$ is the correspondence complex $(G^*; C, B)$.

Converse path

The *converse path* of the path $(B_1; G_1; B_2; \ldots ; G_n; B_{n+1})$ is the path $(B_{n+1}; G_n^*; \ldots ; B_2; G_1^*; B_1)$.

Convolution

A particular form of conjunction of associations, used to determine whether an association is degenerate.

Correspondence

A conceptual mechanism that examines two images, accepting both or rejecting both. Two recognizers whose manifestations are accepted are said to be *attached* by the correspondence. A correspondence is typically represented in language by a transitive verb. A correspondence is an association of degree two.

Correspondence complex

A correspondence G together with two classes B and C, written "$(G; B, C)$". The attachments of a correspondence complex are attachments of an image accepted by B with an image accepted by C, controlled by G.

Countable noun phrase

A noun phrase that can be preceded by "a" or "an". Countable noun phrases are used as class tags.

Counterscope

The *counterscope* of a correspondence G is the class of images that G attaches some image to. Written "π^2G". Compare *scope*.

Coverage by multiple

A phenomenon whereby a correspondence that is *to many* may be composed with a correspondence that is *from some* to yield a correspondence that is *from all*.

Cropping

Refers to the ability of a recognizer to focus attention on an aspect of a scene. Topic recognizers do not have this cropping ability.

Cubic proposal method

A proposal method that affects three positions.

Cycle

A path whose ends are identical.

Data

Data is a general term used to describe pieces of data. A *piece of data* is a symbol that represents a proposition and that is an occupant of a *data base*.

Data base

A *data base* consists of three binding sites: *Claim*, *Declared Association*, and *Schema*. The *population* of the data base is the set of occupants of the binding site *Claim*. Each such occupant is a proposition tag, called a *claim*. The two binding sites *Declared Association* and *Schema* form the *data base design*.

Data base design

A data base design supervises the claims in a data base. It consists of the binding site *Declared Association*, which establishes which association tags are supervised, and the binding site *Schema*, which establishes the rules used to supervise the data base.

Data base population

See *population*.

Data logic

The system of logic defined in this book that distinguishes omissive from constructive, distinguishes definitive from incidental, distinguishes deduction from alternation, and recognizes a logic of individuals. Compare *symbolic logic*.

Data management process

A collection of engines that supervise changes to a data base population.

Data structure

A pattern of constraints and relaxations, where the associations are left unspecified or are given no fixed interpretation.

Decision

A determination to be made by a designer whether to affirm or deny a constraint.

Declare

To include an association tag or constraint in a data base design.

Deduce

(i) A proposition q is *deduced* from a proposition p, written $p \rightarrow q$, if each impression evoked by p is also evoked by q. Compare *imply*.
(ii) A plan s is *deduced* from a plan r if each idea accepted by the realization of r is also accepted by the realization of s.

Deductive engine

An engine that forms the proposition tag q from the proposition tags "p" and "$p \rightarrow q$".

Definition

An equivalence between the term that is defined and an expression formed from other terms.

Definitive

A proposition is *definitive* if it expresses characteristics of plans of recognizers or associations and is therefore independent of a choice of population. Compare *incidental*. The proposition that a proposition p is definitive is written $!p$.

Definitive operator

The symbol "!", as in "$!p$", « it must be that p ».

Degenerate

An association is *degenerate* if it can be formed from other associations using logical operations.

Degree

(i) The *degree* of an association is the number of positions it contains.
(ii) The *degree* of an association tag is the number of positions at which the association tag must be conglomerated with individuals to form an assembly.
(iii) The *degree* of an embracing $R \subseteq S$ is the degree of both R and S.
(iv) The *degree* of an engine is the number of binding sites it contains.

Delta

A cycle of length three.

Delta trio

A trio that is equivalent to the convolution of a delta.

Deny

The proposition « b is an instance of B » is *denied* if b is affirmed to be an instance of the opposite of B. This proposition is written "$\blacktriangledown$ B:(b)", or equivalently as "$\vdash$ °B:(b)".

Derived

Refers to symbols that are formed by applying data logic, as opposed to *declared* symbols that appear in a data base design. For example, the class tag "$B \cap C$" is derived from the class tags "B" and "C".

Design management device

A collection of engines that form explanations and enforce the various rules of proper diagramming in extended associative notation.

Destination

(i) The second class in a correspondence complex, that is, the class C in the correspondence complex (G; B, C).
(ii) The second recognizer in an attachment, that is, the recognizer c in the attachment $G(b, c)$.

Detect

A detector *detects* a thing if the detector accepts the thing.

Detection process

Another name for a detector.

Detector

A process that examines a thing, accepting or rejecting it. A detector establishes a symbol: two things that are accepted by the same detector are the same symbol.

Dimension of time

An association may be declared relative to logical time in several positions. Each such position is called a *dimension of time*.

Direct deduction law

The law of logic that $(p \;\&\; (p \rightarrow q)) \Rightarrow q$.

Disjoint

Two associations are *disjoint* if their intersection is unpopulable.

Division by *optional*

A phenomenon whereby a correspondence that is *from many* may be composed with a correspondence that is *from some* to yield a correspondence that is *from one*.

Downstream *optional*

An agency choice or a targeting choice of *optional* below the third level in a declaration of an association complex of degree three or higher.

Duality

The dual embracing to "$B \subseteq C$" is "$C \subseteq B$". In the embracing formulation of characters, *mandatory* and *single* constraints are dual in this way.

Each

Indicates exhaustive quantification, as in "for each x".

Elision correspondence

A correspondence whose attachments are determined from the attachments of another association by employing a concentration.

Elongation

The factoring of a correspondence complex into a path of length four in such a way that the character of each constituent correspondence complex of the path exhibits exactly one of the character decisions of the original correspondence complex, and the order of the constituents of the path follows the standard order of declaring brackets in a character.

Embrace

(i) A binding site C *embraces* a binding site B if any thing that is accepted by B must be accepted by C.
(ii) A class C *embraces* a class B if, for any image d that B accepts, it is predicted that C would accept d.
(iii) A recognizer e *embraces* a recognizer d if any impression that is accepted by d would have been accepted by e if it had been examined by e.
(iv) An engine S *embraces* an engine R of the same degree if any acceptance of symbols by R implies a parallel acceptance of the same symbols by S.
(v) An association S *embraces* an association R of the same degree r if for any images x_1, . . . , x_r such that $R{:}|x_1, \ldots, x_r|$, it is predicted that $S{:}|x_1, \ldots, x_r|$.

Embracing

(i) A proposition tag of the form $\mathcal{F} \subseteq \mathcal{G}$.
(ii) A proposition that an association embraces an association.
(iii) A proposition that a recognizer embraces a recognizer.
(iv) A proposition that a binding site embraces a binding site.

Empty

(i) An *empty class*, incidentally, has no instances. Compare *unpopulable*.
(ii) An *empty recognizer*, incidentally, accepts no impressions. Compare *unpopulable*.

End of a path

Either the source of the first correspondence complex or the destination of the last correspondence complex.

Engine

A procedure that operates upon zero or more things and produces zero or more things. The things that are operated on are bound to input sites, and the things that are produced are bound to output sites.

Equal

(i) Two sets of recognizers are *equal* if each member of each set has an equivalent counterpart in the other set.
(ii) Two sets of symbols are *equal* if each member of each set has an indistinguishable counterpart in the other set.
(iii) Two integers are *equal* if they are equivalent as correspondences.

Equally extensive

Two ideas are *equally extensive* if each includes the other. Two sets are equally extensive if and only if they are equivalent.

Equivalent

Two binding sites, recognizers, sets, classes, associations, or engines are *equivalent* if each embraces the other.

Evoke

A constructive proposition *evokes* an impression if the impression supports the proposition. An omissive proposition *evokes* an impression if the impression does not support the negation of the proposition.

Examination

The activity during a performance of a detector, binding site, engine, recognizer, class, association, interpreting agent, or tagging agent, by which an outcome is determined, either acceptance or rejection.

Exhaustive

(i) Every image is, incidentally, accepted by an *exhaustive* class.
(ii) Every impression is, incidentally, accepted by an *exhaustive* recognizer.

Exhaustive quantification

The formation of ideas from other ideas by adding an exhaustive quantifier, especially the conversion of a deduction to an inclusion.

Exhaustive quantifier

(i) A symbol of the form $(\forall x)$, read « for each x », where x may stand for an association, a recognizer, or an image.
(ii) A symbol of the form $(\forall \iota)$, read « for each impression ι ».

Existential quantification

The formation of ideas from other ideas by adding an existential quantifier, especially the formation of a projection.

Existential quantifier

(i) A symbol of the form $(\exists x)$, read « for some x », where x may stand for an association, a recognizer, or an image.
(ii) A symbol of the form $(\exists \iota)$, read « for some impression ι ».

Explanation

Automatically generated text in extended associative notation that describes the interpretation of a portion of a data design.

Exposed

An exposed individual is reported to the users of a data base; its physical appearance is significant. Compare *hidden*.

Extend

The operation of forming a path in extended associative notation by concatenating cascades.

Extended associative notation

The graphic notation presented in this book that permits declaration of embracings, correspondence complexes, and trio complexes.

Exterior

(i) The population of an *exterior class tag* consists entirely of exposed individuals. An exterior class tag is shown in an oval in population diagrams and in extended associative notation. Compare *interior*.
(ii) The *exterior brackets* of a composition cone $\alpha.\beta$ are the brackets $\alpha \cap$ "**]**" and $\beta \cap$ "**[**". Compare *interior*.

External constituent

A symbol attached to the (outermost) connector in a conglomeration.

Facial decision

Refers to properties of the elision correspondences of the form ${}_1\dot{T}_{123}$ of a trio T. Character decisions of these correspondences are shown at the second and third levels of a cascade, where the third level class tag represents a concentration.

Factoring

A path $\mathcal{P}$ is a *factoring* of the correspondence G if the composition correspondence of $\mathcal{P}$ is equivalent to G.

Fat

A proposition is *fat* if it violates a performance type integrity law. A fat proposition may not be affirmed in data logic.

Fellows

Two correspondences F and G are *fellows* if their reduced correspondences relative to $(\pi^1(F \cap G), \pi^2(F \cap G))$ are equivalent.

Finer

A recognizer d is *finer* than a recognizer e if e embraces d and e is not equivalent to d.

First stable state

The stable state of a trio when at most one downstream *mandatory/optional* decision is chosen *optional*.

Follow

(i) An inclusion $B \subsetneq C$ *follows* performance type integrity if B is constructive or C is omissive. An inclusion need not follow performance type integrity. Compare *obey*.

(ii) A deduction $p \rightarrow q$ *follows* performance type integrity if p is constructive or q is omissive. A deduction need not follow performance type integrity. Compare *obey*.

Formal

Describes processes that operate on symbols, as opposed to conceptual mechanisms that operate on ideas.

Formative

A binding site is *formative* if it is possible to construct or obtain a sufficiently large number of things with ease that will be accepted by the binding site. The concept of formativeness is used to assure that replicas of symbols are freely available.

From all

A correspondence complex $(G; B, C)$ is *from all* if any image accepted by B attaches to some image accepted by C via G. Compare *to all*, *from some*.

From many

A correspondence complex $(G; B, C)$ is *from many* if it is not *from one*, that is, if it is possible for an image accepted by C to attach to images that are different Bs via G^*. Compare *from one*, *to many*.

From one

A correspondence complex $(G; B, C)$ is *from one* if any images y and z that attach via G^* to an image accepted by C must be the same B $(\Delta B{:}| y, z |)$. Compare *to one*, *from many*.

From some

A correspondence complex (G; B, C) is *from some* if it is possible for an image accepted by B to attach to no image accepted by C via G. Compare *to some*, *from all*.

Fully reversed

(i) A trio is *fully reversed* when it is declared relative to a triple of classes and a triple of correspondences.
(ii) An association is *fully reversed* when it is declared relative to a complete relative complex.

Granulation

The class that accepts any image that contains an impression that is accepted by a recognizer d, written "Γd".

Half-elongation

The factoring of a correspondence complex (G; B, C) into the binary path (B; ${}_1\dot{G}_{12}$; $C^1\dot{G}$; ${}_{12}\dot{G}_2$; C). The first correspondence complex in the path is always *from one* and *to all*; the second is always *to one* and *from all*.

Handle

A recognizer that stands for an association (usually a class) in logical formulas. The handle of a class B is written "νB". Handles allow definition of "classes of classes."

Hidden

A *hidden* individual is not reported to users of a data base. Compare *exposed*.

High degree

An assocation of degree greater than two is said to have *high degree*.

Hub

A set of correspondence complexes such that the source of each correspondence complex is the same class tag "B". The class tag "B" is called the *center* of the hub. Compare *path*.

Idea

A general term for concepts of the mind, in contrast with physical objects that can be manipulated. See *impression, image, recognizer, class*, and *association*.

Identical

(i) Two recognizers b and c are *identical* with respect to an identity correspondence ΔB if ΔB attaches b to c.
(ii) Two things are *identical* if they are indistinguishable.

Identity correspondence

A correspondence that determines when two images are the same B, for some class B, usually written "ΔB".

Image

An impression that is accepted by (compounded with) a recognizer.

Image exhaustion principle

The principle that if for each image x, there is the deduction $B{:}|x| \rightarrow C{:}|x|$, then C includes B. The principle is usually applied to definitive propositions, in the form: if for any image x, $B{:}|x|$ implies $C{:}|x|$, then C embraces B.

Immediate neighborhood

The *immediate neighborhood* of a recognizer b by a correspondence G is the class $b.(G \circ G^*)$.

Imply

A proposition p *implies* a proposition q if any impression that p evokes must be evoked by q. The implication $p \Rightarrow q$ is equivalent to the embracing Я$p \subseteq$ Яq.

Impression

A thought, perception, or recollection. An impression that is accepted by a recognizer is an image.

Incidental

A proposition is *incidental* if it is dependent on a choice of populations. Compare *definitive*.

Incidental claim restriction

The rule of practical data bases that each claim does not contain "!" in its expression.

Include

(i) An association S *includes* an association R, written $R \subseteq S$, if each assembly controlled by R is also, incidentally, controlled by S. Compare *embrace*.
(ii) A recognizer e *includes* a recognizer d, written $d \subseteq e$, if each impression accepted by d is also, incidentally, accepted by e.
(iii) A character β *includes* a character α if all the brackets that appear in α also appear in β.
(iv) A path $\mathcal{P}$ *includes* a path $\mathcal{Q}$ if $\mathcal{Q}$ is a subsequence of $\mathcal{P}$.

Indefinite refinement principle

For each populable recognizer d, it is possible to form a populable recognizer e such that d embraces e and e does not embrace d.

Indistinguishable

Two things are *indistinguishable* if they exhibit equal patterns of examination, acceptance, or rejection for all members of a set of binding sites.

Individual

A symbol that represents a recognizer.

Inexhaustibility principle (of associations)

For any constructive association R of degree r, it must be possible to imagine images $b_1, \ldots, b_r$ such that R would neither accept nor reject $b_1, \ldots, b_r$ if they were presented.

Inexhaustibility principle (of recognizers)

For any constructive recognizer d, it must be possible to imagine an impression that d would neither accept nor reject if it were presented.

Inherently definitive

A proposition p is *inherently definitive* if p implies $!p$. Data base constraints are inherently definitive.

Input site

(i) A portion of an engine that accepts a thing for the engine to operate on.
(ii) The portion of a tagging agent that accepts an image.

Insatiable

An association R is *insatiable* if it is impossible for there to be a population of simple propositions controlled by R that is obedient to all the embracings that R participates in. An insatiable association is similar to an "infinite set" in mathematics.

Instance

(i) A recognizer « b » is an *instance* of a class « B » if there is predicted to be an impression ι such that the compound of « b » with ι (an image) would be accepted by « B ».
(ii) An individual "b" is an *instance* of a class tag "B" if "B:(b)" is affirmed.

Instantiation

See *proposal method.*

Instantiation law

The principle that if « B » is a class and « d » is a recognizer, then « B:(d) » is a proposition.

Interchangeable

Two propositions are *interchangeable* when they imply each other.

Intercharacter constraint

Refers generally to interoptional and intermultiple constraints.

Interconvertible

Two schemas $\mathcal{D}$ and $\mathcal{E}$ are *interconvertible* if any population of $\mathcal{D}$ may be converted in a *one-to-one all-to-all* fashion to a population of $\mathcal{E}$, and vice versa, by a purely formal interchange of association tags of $\mathcal{E}$ for association tags of $\mathcal{D}$.

Interim stable state

A form of declaration of a trio or higher degree association that contains fewer relative associations than a full reversal.

Interior

(i) The population of an *interior class tag* consists entirely of hidden individuals. An interior class tag is shown inside a rectangle in population diagrams and in extended associative notation. Compare *exterior*.

(ii) The *interior brackets* of a composition cone $\alpha.\beta$ are the brackets $\alpha \cap$ "**[**" and $\beta \cap$ "**]**". Compare *exterior*.

Intermediate class tag

Any class tag that a path traverses other than the ends of the path.

Intermultiple constraint

An embracing of the form $F^* \circ F \subseteq G \circ G^*$.

Interoptional constraint

An embracing of the form $\pi^2 F \subseteq \pi^1 G$.

Interpretant

An idea whose plan is assigned to a symbol by an interpreting agent.

Interpretation

The set of plans (loosely, the set of realizations of plans) assigned to a symbol in a performance of an interpreting agent.

Interpreting agent

A conceptual mechanism that assigns plans to symbols. The realizations of the plans assigned to a symbol are called *interpretants* of the symbol.

Intersection

(i) The *intersection* of two associations R and S, written $R \cap S$, is the association that accepts whatever both R and S accept.

(ii) The *intersection* of two recognizers is the recognizer that accepts any impression that both recognizers accept.

Juncture trio

A trio formed by conjoining the two correspondence complexes in a binary path.

Jurisdiction

The *jurisdiction* of a class B accepts any images that B accepts or that B rejects. Any jurisdiction of an omissive class is universal; no jurisdiction of a constructive class is universal.

Left side

(i) The *left side* of the embracing $R \subseteq S$ is R.
(ii) The *left side* of the implication $p \Rightarrow q$ is p.

Length

(i) The *length* of a path is the number of constituent correspondence complexes of the path.
(ii) The *length* of an attachment chain is the number of attachments in the chain.

Less extensive

An idea i is *less extensive* than the idea j if j includes i.

Less permissive

A character α is *less permissive* than a different character β if any population that is obedient to α is obedient to β. In characters written in standard order, α is less permissive than β if β includes α and $\alpha \neq \beta$.

Less restrictive

A character α is *less restrictive* than a different character β if any population that is obedient to β is obedient to α. In characters written in standard order, α is less restrictive than β if α includes β and $\alpha \neq \beta$.

Level

Refers to a column of shapes in extended associative notation that are indented an equal distance from the extreme left of the diagram.

Lexical program

A computer program expressed in the symbols of a computer language. A plan is analagous to a lexical program.

Liar paradox

The anomaly of symbolic logic whereby the proposition p defined by $p \Leftrightarrow \neg p$ may neither be affirmed nor denied. The liar paradox is avoided in data logic because the expression "$p \Leftrightarrow \neg p$" violates performance type integrity.

Limited

A class is *limited* if there may be an image that the class does not accept. All constructive classes are limited.

Literal class

A class that examines only the recognizer within an image, and disregards the impression. Compare *contentual class*.

Localization

An association formed by combining an association with recognizers to produce an association of lower degree. For example, $G(b, \ )$ is a class that is a localization of G at b, namely the class of images that G attaches b to.

Logical measure

A technique for measuring the magnitude of some characteristic of data base populations, called *logical* when it is not affected by changing the means of physically storing the population. For example, the number of affirmed instances of a class is a logical measure.

Logical time

(i) Refers generally to concepts of time, in contrast to *physical time*.
(ii) A class of moments.

Loner

An individual whose immediate neighborhood by a correspondence contains only itself.

Loop

A correspondence declared relative to the same class in both positions, as in a correspondence L declared relative to (B, B). Compare *pillared*.

Lower bound

In composition cones, a character γ such that γ is a member of the cone and any other character that γ includes is not a member of the cone. Compare *upper bound*.

Mandatory

(i) Refers generally to the constraints *from all* and *to all*.
(ii) The restrictive choice in an agency decision or a targeting decision.

***Mandatory/Optional* decision**

Refers generally to agency decisions, targeting decisions, *from all/from some* decisions, and *to all/to some* decisions.

Manifestation

(i) A thing is a *manifestation* of a detector if the thing is accepted by the detector.

(ii) If an impression ι is accepted by a recognizer d, then the image of d compounded with ι is a *manifestation* of d.

Mantle

A reinterpretation of a derived association, especially a reinterpretation of a concentration.

Many-to-many

A correspondence complex is *many-to-many* if it is *from many* and *to many*.

Many-to-one

A correspondence complex is *many-to-one* if it is *from many* and *to one*.

Master clock tick

A symbolic representation of an interval of physical time controlled by master engines.

Master engine

An engine that assures that claims are managed in accordance with data logic.

Maximal composition character

The most permissive possible character of the composition of two correspondences, written $\alpha \tilde{\cup} \beta$.

Maximal resolute subcorrespondence

The correspondence $\acute{G}$ whose population is formed from the population of a correspondence G by excluding all unresolved alternations.

Maximum width

The number of individuals in the immediate neighborhood that has the most individuals, for some population of a correspondence.

Median circumference

The number N such that there are as many attachment circles with circumference greater than N as there are attachment circles with circumference less than N, for some population of a loop.

Median width

The number N such that there are as many immediate neighborhoods with more individuals than N as there are immediate neighborhoods with fewer individuals than N, for some population of a correspondence.

Melding

The *melding* μB of a class B is the recognizer that accepts any impression that is incorporated in an image accepted by B.

Member

(i) A conformer of a set of recognizers.
(ii) A constituent of a set of symbols.

Method matrix

A 2×2 binary matrix that shows the performance type and proposal methods of a correspondence in a proposition.

Method tensor

A binary tensor that shows the performance type and proposal methods of an assocation of high degree in a proposition.

Might

Indicates a possible proposition. Thus, ";p" is read « it might be that p ».

Modal

A logic is *modal* if it incorporates concepts such as definitiveness and possibility that qualify assertions. Data logic is modal; symbolic logic is not.

Modal operator

Either of the symbols ";", which indicates possibility, or "!", which indicates definitiveness.

Module

A combination that is formed using one logical operation throughout.

Moment

A conceptual or imaginary period of logical time. A moment need not be a continuous stretch of time.

More extensive

An idea i is *more extensive* than an idea j if i includes j.

More permissive

A character α is *more permissive* than a different character β if any population that is obedient to β is obedient to α. In characters written in standard order, α is more permissive than β if α includes β and $\alpha \neq \beta$.

More restrictive

A character α is *more restrictive* than a different character β if any population that is obedient to α is obedient to β. In characters written in standard order, α is more restrictive than β if β includes α and $\alpha \neq \beta$.

Multiple

(i) Refers generally to the relaxations *from many* and *to many*.
(ii) The permissive choice in a *single/multiple* decision.

Multiplicity

Refers to the portion of a character that contains the *from one/from many* and *to one/to many* character decisions.

Must

Indicates a definitive proposition. Thus, "$!p$" is read « it must be that p ».

Negation

The *negation* of a proposition q, written $\tilde{}q$, evokes any impression that q does not evoke, and does not evoke any impression that q evokes. The negation of the proposition C:(d) is the proposition $\overline{C}$:[d].

Neighborhood

Refers generally to immediate neighborhood or ultimate neighborhood.

Not

(i) Indicates the negation of a proposition.
(ii) Indicates the complement of an association or a recognizer.

Null value

A term used in the relational data model to describe a downstream *optional* choice.

Obey

(i) An embracing $R \subseteq S$ *obeys* performance type integrity if R is constructive or S is omissive. An embracing that does not obey performance type integrity is undescriptive.
(ii) An implication $p \Rightarrow q$ *obeys* performance type integrity if p is constructive or q is omissive. An implication that does not obey performance type integrity is undescriptive.
(iii) A data base population *obeys* a schema if no claim can be derived logically from the population that would contradict a schema element.

Obey precedence

(i) A binary path *obeys precedence* if the brackets in the characters of the two correspondences follow precedence order.
(ii) A path *obeys precedence* if it passes the coalescence test.

Occupant

A detector is an *occupant* of a binding site if a manifestation of the detector is accepted by the binding site.

Occupy

A symbol *occupies* a position in a conglomeration if it is attached to the connector at that position.

Omissive

(i) An *omissive class* accepts or rejects any image presented to it, and may both accept and reject an image without contradiction. Compare *constructive*.
(ii) An *omissive recognizer* accepts or rejects any impression presented to it, and may both accept and reject an impression without contradiction.
(iii) In an *omissive association,* any position may both accept and reject during the same performance.
(iv) An *omissive proposition p* evokes any impression that does not support $\tilde{}p$.

ONA

An abbreviation for orphans-not-allowed. (see *orphans-not-allowed*)

One-to-many

A correspondence is *one-to-many* if it is *from one* and *to many*.

One-to-one

A correspondence is *one-to-one* if it is *from one* and *to one*.

Opposite

(i) The *opposite* of an association *R*, written °*R*, accepts what *R* rejects and rejects what *R* accepts. Compare *complement*.
(ii) The *opposite* of a recognizer *d*, written °*d*, accepts any impression that *d* rejects and rejects any impression that *d* accepts. Compare *complement*.
(iii) The *opposite* of a proposition *p*, written °*p*, evokes any proposition that **Я***p* rejects, and does not evoke any proposition that **Я***p* accepts. Compare *negation*.

Optional

(i) Refers generally to the relaxations *from some* and *to some*.
(ii) The permissive choice in an agency decision or a targeting decision.

Optionality

Refers to the portion of a character that contains the *from all/from some* and *to all/to some* character decisions.

Or

(i) The proposition « *p* or *q* » is called an *alternation* of *p* and *q*. (see *alternation*)
(ii) The word "or" is used to indicate a union of associations in extended associative notation.

Orientation

The order in which position designators appear in an association. For example, « ① Carries ② To ③ » has a different orientation than « ③ Carries ① To ② ».

Orphan

(i) A recognizer b is an *orphan* of a correspondence G if there is no recognizer that G attaches b to.
(ii) An instance b of the center of a hub is an *orphan* of the hub if none of the (reduced) correspondences of the hub attach b to any recognizer.

Orphans-not-allowed

A constraint, abbreviated ''ONA'', that prevents a center of a hub from containing orphan instances relative to some or all of the spokes.

Outcome

The result of an examination, either acceptance or rejection.

Output site

(i) A portion of an engine at which things are produced.
(ii) The portion of an interpreting agent at which images are produced.

Oval

A shape used in population diagrams and in extended associative notation to indicate an exterior class tag.

Oval placement rule

The rule of extended associative notation that an oval never appears at the top of a cascade.

Overlap

Two recognizers *overlap* if their intersection accepts some impression.

Panoramic

The property of topic recognizers that allows any scene accepted by a topic recognizer to be broadened to incorporate additional impressions. Compare *cropping*.

Parallel singularity theorem

A theorem about the interdependency of two *single/multiple* decisions in the declaration of a trio complex.

Pasting

The process of forming a sample population by successive union of standard population diagrams.

Path

A sequence of correspondence complexes such that the destination of each correspondence complex is identical to the source of the next correspondence complex in sequence. Compare *hub*.

Performance

An actual or conceived execution of a detector, binding site, recognizer, engine, association, interpreting agent, or tagging agent. A performance has potentially two steps: a presentation and an examination. A performance must include a presentation, but might include no examination.

Performance type

A *performance type* is one of either ''constructive'' or ''omissive''.

Performance type integrity law (of associations)

If S embraces R and R is omissive, then S is omissive.

Performance type integrity law (of propositions)

If p is omissive and q is constructive, then the proposition $p \Rightarrow q$ is undescriptive.

Performance type integrity law (of recognizers)

If e embraces d and d is omissive, then e is omissive.

Permanent

A binding site is *permanent* if its behavior in performances may be reasonably expected to remain constant.

Permissiveness

Refers to how loosely a data structure limits populations. For example, *one-to-many* is a more permissive character than *one-to-one*. Compare *restrictiveness*.

Permutation

A rearrangement of the order of the positions of an association or of an engine. A permutation of an association is represented by the Greek letter ''π''. For example, $\pi^{231}T$ is the permutation of the trio T defined by $\pi^{231}T{:}|x, y, z| \Leftrightarrow T{:}|z, x, y|$.

Physical time

Refers to the variety of physical events that can be observed using clocks. Compare *logical time*.

Piece of data

A proposition tag that is a member of a data base population, also called a *claim*.

Pillared

A *pillared* correspondence complex $(G; B, C)$ is a correspondence complex where the two relative classes are different. Compare *loop*.

Pineal

A trio complex is *pineal* if it contains a facial constraint that can not be determined from its other constraints.

Placetaker

A position designator that appears in a quantifier, such as "*x*" in "(A*x*)".

Plan

A conceptual procedure that defines what an association or recognizer will accept or reject. The plan of an idea X is often written λX.

Populable

(i) An association is *populable* if it is possible for there to be an assembly that it controls.
(ii) A recognizer is *populable* if it is possible for it to accept an impression.

Populated

(i) A class is *populated* if it accepts some image.
(ii) A recognizer is *populated* if it accepts some impression.

Population

(i) The *population* of a class is the set of all instances of the class (at some given occasion).
(ii) The *population* of a data base is the set of claims that appear in the data base (at some given occasion).
(iii) The *population* of a binding site is the set of all occupants of the binding site (at some given occasion).

Population diagram

An illustration of a data base population.

Position

(i) A place on a connector where things may be connected.
(ii) A mechanism in an association that accepts an image. The number of positions in an association is the degree of the association.
(iii) One of the places enclosed by commas or parentheses in an association tag.
(iv) A portion of a plan at which other plans may be substituted (see *programmatic position*).

Position designator

A symbol such as "①" that represents a position.

Positional character notation

The notation that recognizes the characters "><", "]><", "><[", and "]><[" for *many-to-many* bundlings in addition to the 16 characters written in standard order.

Positive combination

See *combination*.

Positive design restriction

The recommendation followed in this book that admissible constraints be limited to positive embracings.

Positive embracing

An embracing in which all the associations are constructive and the only logical operations used are &, $\bigvee$, and $(\exists x)$. In particular, negation (˜) is not used in a positive embracing. Positive embracings are often written using the operators $\cap$ (in place of &), $\cup$ (in place of $\bigvee$), and π^{α} (in place of $(\exists x)$).

Possibility operator

The symbol ";", as in ";p", « it might be that p ».

Possible

A constructive proposition p is *possible* if there might be an impression that p evokes. The proposition that a proposition p is possible is written ";p".

Postulate

An assumption that a formal process (an engine) may be formed, which will operate on the symbols in a data base population. A postulate establishes a requirement that any candidate data management process must satisfy.

Potential quantifier

(i) A symbol of the form $(\mathrm{E}x)$, read « there might be an x », where x may stand for an association or a recognizer. Equivalent to $;(\exists x)$.
(ii) A symbol of the form $(\mathrm{E}\iota)$, read « there might be an impression ι ». Equivalent to $;(\exists \iota)$.

Power chain

The chain of embracings

$$L \cap \Delta\pi^1 L \subseteq L \subseteq (L \circ L) \cup L \subseteq (L \circ L \circ L) \cup (L \circ L) \cup L \subseteq \ldots$$

Its termination point is the transitive closure of L.

Power class

The class of classes that are included in a given class.

Precedence order

The order of brackets], >, <, [, used to determine whether a composition cone is trivial. Compare *standard order*.

Precedence theorem

The theorem that any path that obeys precedence has a trivial composition cone.

Predict

An occurrence is *predicted* if the occurrence follows from observations according to assumed laws. When considering physical things, these laws include physical laws; when considering ideas, these laws include axioms of logic. See *instance*, *symbol*.

Prefix

A string of placetakers such as (Ax) (Ay) (Az) that appears at the extreme left of a quantified expression. All the quantifiers in the prefix of a positive embracing are universal.

Premise

The *premise* of an implication $p \Rightarrow q$ is the proposition p.

Presentation

(i) An action of testing whether or not a binding site (or, more specifically, a detector) will examine a thing.
(ii) An action of testing whether or not an engine will examine symbols.
(iii) An action of testing whether or not an association will examine images.
(iv) An action of testing whether or not a recognizer will examine an impression.

Primitive association

An association from which elements of data logic are derived. Each primitive association assembles plans.

Primitive operator

An operation of data logic that is not defined from other operators or from primitive associations.

Primitive term

An idea (or its tag) that is not defined from other ideas.

Principle of timeless representation

The principle that any representation of logical time has no requisite connection with the properties of physical time.

Programmatic position

A portion of a plan that enables the plan to be combined with other plans. For example, the plan of the class « ① is a B » is combined with the plan of a recognizer « d » to form the plan of the proposition « d is a B ». The plan of « ① » is then a programmatic position.

Projection

An association formed by existentially quantifying an association, written $\pi^s R$ for some string of indices s. For example, the projection $\pi^1 G$ is the class of images x such that $G{:}|x, y|$ for some y.

Proof

A chain of implications that demonstrates that a proposition is definitively affirmed.

Proposal method

A *proposal method* determines the behavior of the performance type of a proposition with respect to a set of positions within an association. The proposal method *instantiation*, written ( ), indicates that the proposition is constructive if the recognizer in that position is constructive. The proposal method *conformalization*, written [ ], indicates that the proposition is omissive if the recognizer in that position is constructive.

Proposition

An idea that can be believed, that is, a plan whose realization is a populable recognizer. The recognizer is called the *topic recognizer* of the proposition, because it accepts those impressions that the proposition evokes.

Proposition tag

(i) A symbol that represents a proposition (semantic definition).
(ii) A conglomeration of symbols that meets the syntactic criteria of a proposition tag, involving the proper use of logical connectives, association tags, individual tags, and placetakers (syntactic definition).

Quadratic proposal method

A proposal method that affects two positions.

Quantifier

Refers generally to symbols of the form (Ex), ($\exists x$), ($\forall x$) or (Ax).

Quartet

An association of degree four.

Real number

A correspondence that attaches a rational number to each positive integer so that the attachments form a convergent series.

Realization

The *realization* of a plan is the association or recognizer formed by applying the conceptual factory to the plan. The realization of the plan s is written Яs. If p is a proposition, then Яp is the recognizer that accepts the impressions evoked by p, also called the *topic recognizer* of p.

Recognize

A recognizer *recognizes* an impression if it accepts the impression.

Recognizer

A conceptual mechanism that examines an impression, accepting or rejecting it. A recognizer establishes an image: two impressions that are accepted by the same recognizer are the same image. Compare *detector*.

Rectangle

A shape used in extended associative notation and population diagrams to indicate an interior class tag.

Reduced

(i) A *reduced correspondence* is a correspondence formed by composing a correspondence with the identity correspondences of two classes, one class to each position. Thus, the reduced correspondence of the correspondence complex (G; B, C), normally written "$\dot{G}$", is the correspondence $\Delta B \circ G \circ \Delta C$.

(ii) More generally, a *reduced association* is an association formed by conjoining an association with a convolution of associations of lower degree.

Reductio ad absurdum

A chain of implications that leads to a contradiction. In symbolic logic, this is a proof of the negation of the premise, in data logic it is not always so.

Reflexive

A correspondence L is *reflexive* on a class B if $\Delta B \subseteq L$, that is, if L attaches each instance of B to itself.

Rejection

One of two possible outcomes of an examination, the other being acceptance.

Relative

(i) When a correspondence G is declared *relative to* a pair of classes, the character of G expresses aspects of the reduced correspondence $\Delta B \circ G \circ \Delta C$.

(ii) More generally, when an association R is declared *relative to* a relative complex S, the aspects of the association R described in extended associative notation are aspects of a conjunction of R with the convolution of S.

Relative complement

The *relative complement* of an association R in an association S is the association $S \cap \overline{R}$.

Relative complex

A collection of associations relative to which an association may be declared, subject to certain rules of proper formation.

Relative unity principle

The principle of data base design that association tags and individuals should be so defined that for each declared class tag B and for each individual d, if d is an instance of B, then any two manifestations of « d » are the same « B ».

Relaxation

A schema element that is the negation of a definitive proposition tag. For example, the proposition that a correspondence is *to many* is a relaxation, because it is the negation of the constraint *to one*. Compare *constraint*.

Replicate

Two individuals b_1 and b_2 are *replicates* relative to a set of correspondences $\{G_1, \ldots, G_n\}$ if there is some individual c_i that both b_1 and b_2 attach to by G_i, for each i.

Replicates-not-allowed

The constraint, abbreviated ''RNA'', that prevents replicates.

Represent

A symbol *represents* an interpretant if the symbol is assigned the interpretant by an interpreting agent.

Resolute

An association R is *resolute* if unresolved expressions are not allowed in the population of R. For example, a correspondence G is resolute if $(\mathrm{A}x)\ (\mathrm{A}y)\ G{:}(x, y) \Rightarrow\ \vdash G{:}(x, y)$.

Resolved alternation

The alternation $(\vdash p \vee \vdash q)$ is said to be *resolved* because it is affirmed if and only if p is affirmed or q is affirmed. Compare *unresolved alternation*.

Resolved existential quantification

A quantified expression of the form $(\exists x) \vdash \mathcal{F}(x)$ is said to be *resolved* because it implies that there is some symbol s such that $\mathcal{F}(s)$ is affirmed. Compare *unresolved existential quantification*.

Restrictiveness

Refers to how strictly a data structure limits populations. For example, *one-to-one* is more restrictive than *one-to-many*. Compare *permissiveness*.

Retroactive correspondence

A correspondence that is equivalent to $F \circ F^*$, for some correspondence F.

Reversal

The *reversal* of a cascade $B \rightarrow G \rightarrow C$ is the cascade $C \rightarrow G^* \rightarrow B$.

Reversible engine

An engine R is *reversible* if it has an equivalent engine in which input sites and output sites are exchanged.

Right side

(i) The *right side* of the embracing $R \subseteq S$ is S.
(ii) The *right side* of the implication $p \Rightarrow q$ is q.

RNA

An abbreviation for replicates-not-allowed. (see *replicates-not-allowed*)

Russell's paradox

The anomaly of symbolic logic whereby the set R defined by $(\forall x)\ x \notin x \Leftrightarrow x \in R$ may neither contain itself nor not contain itself. In data logic, the class R may not be defined because the definition of R violates performance type integrity.

Same

(i) Two impressions are the *same image* if they are accepted by the same recognizer.
(ii) Two things are the *same symbol* if they are each predicted to be accepted by the same detector.
(iii) Two sets are the *same* if they have the same members. That is, two sets are the same if they are equal.
(iv) Two images are the *same instance* of a class if they are attached to each other by the identity correspondence of the class.

Scene

An impression that incorporates a wide variety of impressions, such as « the French Revolution ».

Schema

A schema determines what proposition tags may appear in a data base population. Specifically, a *schema* is a binding site whose occupants are either constraints (which prohibit certain proposition tags from being claimed) or relaxations (which allow certain proposition tags to be claimed).

Schema element

An occupant of a schema, either a constraint or a relaxation.

Scope

The *scope* of a correspondence G is the class of images that attach to some image via G. Written "$\pi^1 G$". Compare *counterscope*.

Second stable state

The stable state of a trio when at most two downstream *mandatory/optional* decisions are chosen *optional*.

Selection by *optional*

A phenomenon whereby a correspondence that is *to many* may be composed with a correspondence that is *from some* to yield a correspondence that is *to one*.

Semantic definition

A *semantic definition* of a term describes the intended interpretation of the term, but can not be enforced by engines. Compare *syntactic definition*.

Separating engine

An engine that transforms a conglomeration into its constituents. Compare *connecting engine*.

Sequence

A conglomeration of symbols such that each position is occupied.

Set

(i) A *set of recognizers* is a literal class that is defined by its conformers, called *members*.
(ii) A *set of detectors* is an engine where each site acts independently as a detector.
(iii) A *set of symbols* is a collection of material accepted by a set of detectors.

Sheath

(i) The *sheath* of a class C is the class of images that are accepted by both C and $\overline{C}$.
(ii) The *sheath* of a recognizer d is the recognizer that accepts any impression that is accepted by both d and $\overline{d}$.
(iii) The *sheath* of a proposition p is the proposition p & ˜p.

Sheath-free

(i) A class is *sheath-free* if its sheath is unpopulable.
(ii) A recognizer d is *sheath-free* if $d \cap \overline{d}$ is unpopulable.
(iii) A proposition p is *sheath-free* if p & ˜p is undescriptive.

Similar

Two correspondences are *similar* if their maximal resolute subcorrespondences fall into patterns whose differences may be described by sizing parameters alone.

Simple proposition

A proposition of the form « the recognizers $b_1, \ldots, b_r$ are instances of (or are conformers of) the association R », usually written R:($b_1, \ldots, b_r$). Simple propositions may include conformalization proposal methods as well as instantiation proposal methods. Thus, both B:(b) and B:[b] are simple propositions.

Single

(i) Refers generally to the constraints *from one* and *to one*.
(ii) The restrictive choice in a *single/multiple* decision.

***Single/Multiple* decision**

(i) The decision whether or not a correspondence is *to one* or *to many* relative to a pair of classes.

(ii) The decision whether or not a correspondence is *from one* or *from many* relative to a pair of classes.

Some

Indicates existential quantification, as in ''for some x''.

Some-to-all

A correspondence complex is *some-to-all* if it is *from some* and *to all.*

Some-to-some

A correspondence complex is *some-to-some* if it is *from some* and *to some.*

Something

The word ''something'' is used in explanations to indicate existential quantification over images.

Source

(i) The first class in a correspondence complex, that is, the class B in the correspondence complex $(G; B, C)$.
(ii) The first recognizer in an attachment, that is, the recognizer b in the attachment $G(b, c)$.

Spoke

A correspondence complex that is a member of a hub.

Stable state

A valid form for declaring a trio or higher degree association in extended associative notation.

Standard order

The order of brackets **]**, <, >, **[**, used to declare a character. Compare *precedence order*.

Stationing

The process of determining and declaring the parameters that render the interpretation of a proposition tag unambiguous.

Subclass

A class B is a *subclass* of a class C if C includes B.

Subpath

A path $\mathcal{Q}$ is a *subpath* of a path $\mathcal{P}$ if $\mathcal{Q}$ is a subsequence of $\mathcal{P}$.

Substitute

(i) To replace a placetaker by a symbol, as in the replacement of ''x'' with ''d'' in forming ''B:[d]'' from ''(Ax) B:[x]''.

(ii) To replace a programmatic position by the plan of an idea, as in the replacement of « x » with « d » in forming « B:[d] » from « (Ax) B:[x] ».

(iii) To replace one idea with another idea, leaving the remainder of an expression unchanged. For example, to conclude from $B \subseteq C$ and B:(d) that C:(d), substituting C for B.

Substituting engine

An engine that substitutes symbols for placetakers, according to the rules of syntax for proposition tags.

Supervise

A data base is generally assumed to incorporate a schema that *supervises* the data base. The claims in the data base population are assumed to *obey*, that is, not to contradict, the supervising schema.

Support

An impression *supports* a proposition if the impression illustrates the contention of the proposition. For example, an impression of a blue sky supports the proposition « the sky is blue ». Compare *evoke*.

Symbol

A thing that is predicted to be accepted by (detected by) a detector. Two things that are accepted by the same detector are the same symbol.

Symbolic logic

The system of logic developed by Frege, Whitehead, Russell, and Hilbert, which does not distinguish omissive from constructive, does not distinguish definitive propositions from incidental propositions, treats deduction as a form of alternation, and does not recognize logical operations upon individuals. Compare *data logic*.

Symmetric

A correspondence is *symmetric* if it is equivalent to its converse.

Symphonic view

The *symphonic view* of a performance of an engine comprises all the symbols examined by each input and output site, and the outcome at each site, but it does not include the sequence of operations during the performance.

Synonym

An association tag used in extended associative notation as a shorthand for a combination.

Syntactic definition

A *syntactic definition* of a term establishes observable conventions that reflect the intended interpretation of the term given by the semantic definition. The syntactic definition can be enforced by engines, but can not guarantee that the term is interpreted as intended.

Tag

A symbol is a *tag* of an interpretant if the symbol is assigned the interpretant by an interpreting agent. Symbols are often described by the type of idea that they represent. Thus a *class tag* represents a class, a *proposition tag* represents a proposition, and so on.

Tagging agent

A conceptual mechanism that assigns symbols to plans of ideas. Compare *interpreting agent.*

Targeting choice

The statement that a targeting decision is either *mandatory* or *optional.*

Targeting decision

A decision of the form « if a *B Gs* something, must the *B G* some *C*? ». A targeting decision is shown on the third or fifth level of a cascade in extended associative notation.

Template

The entire portion of an extended associative notation diagram that is attached to the vertical line drawn below an association tag, when the association tag appears at the upper left.

Temporal index

An image, such as « Monday », that describes moments that recur repeatedly.

Terminate

A chain of embracings $R_0 \subseteq R_1 \subseteq \ldots$ *terminates* if for some value n, for any $i > n$, $R_i \equiv R_n$. The smallest such value n is the *termination point* of the chain.

Termination point

See *terminate.*

Ternary hub

A hub of width three.

Ternary path

A path of length three.

Thing

A tangible object, animate or inanimate. A physical object is called a *thing* before it is detected by some detector. A detected thing is called a *symbol.*

Tile

The hexagonal shape used in extended associative notation to indicate an association of degree three or higher.

Tile-relative notation

Refers to the use of the symbols "+" and "−" within a tile in extended associative notation to express positional relationships within a cascade.

To all

A correspondence complex (G; B, C) is *to all* if any image accepted by C is attached to some image accepted by B via G^*. Compare *from all*, *to some*.

To many

A correspondence complex (G; B, C) is *to many* if it is not *to one*, that is, if it is possible for an image accepted by B to attach via G to images that are different Cs. Compare *from many*, *to one*.

To one

A correspondence complex (G; B, C) is *to one* if any images y and z that attach via G^* to an image accepted by B must be the same C ($\Delta C{:}|\, y, z\,|$). Compare *from one*, *to many*.

To some

A correspondence complex is *to some* if it is not *to all*. That is, the correspondence complex (G; B, C) is *to some* if it is possible for an image accepted by C to attach to no image accepted by B via G^*. Compare *from some*, *to all*.

Topic recognizer

The *topic recognizer* of a proposition p, written Яp, accepts any impression that p evokes. The topic recognizer of a proposition is also the realization of the proposition.

Transitive

A correspondence L is *transitive* if $L \circ L \subseteq L$.

Transitive closure

The correspondence, written $\uparrow L$, that attaches two individuals x and y if there is a path of attachments controlled by L of arbitrary length from x to y.

Traverse

A path *traverses* a class tag when the class tag is a constituent of the path.

Trio

An association of degree three.

Trio complex

A trio together with a triple of classes and up to three correspondences that the trio is declared relative to.

Trio decomposition theorem

The theorem that shows that a trio complex is equivalent to a data structure that contains only classes, correspondences, and embracings. This theorem establishes the link between network data models and associations of higher degree, and establishes the need for embracings for declaring associations of degree greater than two.

Trio tag

A symbol that represents a trio.

Trivial composition cone

A composition cone that contains only one member, the maximal composition character.

Ultimate constituent

A symbol that is part of a conglomeration and contains no connectors.

Ultimate neighborhood

An immediate neighborhood of the transitive closure of a correspondence.

Uncertainty principle of impressions

The principle that any recognizer that accepts an impression may accept many impressions. Consequently, an unquantified proposition may not contain two independent statements about the same impression.

Undescriptive

A proposition is *undescriptive* if it must evoke no impression.

Undetermined

A character decision is *undetermined* if neither choice is declared (for example, if it is not said whether the correspondence complex is *from all* or *from some*).

Unequal

Two numbers m and n are *unequal* if any class that is sheath-free according to an identity correspondence ΔC and that has m instances according to ΔC must not have n instances according to ΔC.

Union

(i) The *union* of two associations R and S, written $R \cup S$, is the association that accepts any image that either R or S accepts.
(ii) The *union* of two recognizers is the recognizer that accepts any impression that either recognizer accepts.

Union character

The *union character* of a path is the union of all the characters of the constituent correspondence complexes of the path.

Universal

(i) A *universal association* of degree r, written $\square^r$, must accept any r images.
(ii) A *universal class*, written $\square$, must accept any image.
(iii) A *universal recognizer*, written $\mu\square$, must accept any impression.

Universal quantifier

(i) A symbol of the form (Ax), read « for any x », where x may stand for an association, a recognizer, or an image. Equivalent to $!(\forall x)$.
(ii) A symbol of the form (Aι), read « for any impression ι ». Equivalent to $!(\forall\iota)$.

Unpopulable

(i) An *unpopulable association* must control no assemblies. An unpopulable association is written $\varnothing^r$, where r is the degree of the association.
(ii) An *unpopulable class* must not accept any images, and is written $\varnothing$.
(iii) An *unpopulable recognizer* must not accept any impressions, and is written $\mu\varnothing$.

Unresolved alternation

The alternation $(p \vee q)$ is said to be *unresolved* because it may be affirmed without p being affirmed or q being affirmed. Compare *resolved alternation.*

Unresolved existential quantification

The quantified expression $(\exists x)\ \mathcal{F}(x)$ is said to be *unresolved* because it may be affirmed even if there is no symbol s such that $\mathcal{F}(s)$ is affirmed. Compare *resolved existential quantification.*

Upper bound

In composition cones, the character that includes every member of the cone. Compare *lower bound.*

Vacant

A *vacant* symbol is a symbol with no interpretation, that is, a symbol that is not accepted by the input site of an interpreting agent.

Width

(i) The number of correspondence complexes in a hub.
(ii) The number of individuals in an immediate neighborhood. See also *maximum width, median width.*

Zigzag

The pattern of attachments $G(a, b)$, $G^*(b, c)$, $G(c, d)$, $G^*(d, e)$, . . .

Zigzag chain

One of the following two chains:

$$H \subseteq H \circ H^* \circ H \subseteq H \circ H^* \circ H \circ H^* \circ H \subseteq \ldots$$

$$\Delta(\pi^1 H) \subseteq H \circ H^* \subseteq H \circ H^* \circ H \circ H^* \subseteq \ldots$$

Zigzag order

The termination point of a zigzag chain.

Special Alphanumeric Expressions

C^1

$C^1 R$ represents the concentration of the association R.

chr

Indicates a character, as in chr $(G; B, C)$ for the character of the correspondence complex $(G; B, C)$.

Claim

A binding site tag used to define a data base. The occupants of *Claim* are pieces of data.

$Claim_i$

The subscript is used when comparing different data bases: $Claim_1$ is a different data base from $Claim_2$.

Declared Association

A binding site whose occupants are declared association tags of a data base design.

mult (α)

Indicates the arrangement of the *multiple* brackets in the character α, either $\varnothing$, "<", ">", "<>", or "><".

$\mathbb{N}$

Represents the class of positive integers.

ONA

Stands for orphans-not-allowed.

$\mathcal{P}B$

Represents the power class of B.

$\mathbb{Q}$

Represents the class of rational numbers.

$\mathbb{R}$

Represents the class of real numbers.

RNA

Stands for replicates-not-allowed.

Schema

A binding site whose occupants are schema elements.

$\mathbb{Z}$

Represents the class of integers.

0

The number zero. The omissive correspondence that attaches the handle of a class B to the handle of an identity correspondence ΔC if all constructive instances of B are not identical to themselves according to ΔC.

1

The number one. The constructive correspondence that attaches the handle of a class B to the handle of an identity correspondence ΔC if there is exactly one constructive instance of B according to ΔC.

2

The number two. The constructive correspondence that attaches the handle of a class B to the handle of an identity correspondence ΔC if there are exactly two constructive instances of B according to ΔC.

Greek Letters

Γ

Γd represents the granulation of the recognizer d.

Δ

ΔB represents the identity correspondence « ① is the same B as ② ».

λ

λX represents the plan of the idea X.

μ

μB represents the melding of the class B.

$\mu\varnothing$

$\mu\varnothing$ represents an unpopulable recognizer.

$\mu\Box$

$\mu\Box$ represents a universal recognizer.

ν

νX represents the handle of the association X.

π^s

A projection onto a string s formed from the set of indices used to declare the association that is projected. For example, $\pi^{12}R(,)$ is defined as $(\exists x_3)\ (\exists x_4)\ R(x_1, x_2, x_3, x_4)$. If each possible index appears in s, $\pi^s R$ indicates a permutation of R.

Expressions with Parentheses and Similar Delimiters

$B(\ )$

Represents a class.

$B(b)$

Represents the assembly « b in the role of a B »

$B{:}(b)$

Represents the proposition « b is an instance of B ».

$B[b]$

Represents the topic recognizer of the proposition $B{:}[b]$.

$B{:}[b]$

Represents the proposition « b is a conformer of B ».

$B{:}|x|$

Represents « B accepts the image x », used only in quantified expressions such as $(\exists x)\ B{:}|x|$.

$G(,)$

Represents a correspondence. The places between the comma and the parentheses are filled to form an attachment, such as $G(b, c)$.

$(\ )G(\ )$

Represents a correspondence. The places inside the parentheses are filled to form an attachment, as in $(b)G(c)$. This attachment is equivalent to $G(b, c)$.

$G(b,)$

Represents the localization of G at b, that is, the class of images that G attaches b to.

$G(b, c)$, $(b)G(c)$

Both represent the attachment « b $G{+}ing$ c ».

$G{:}(b, c)$, $(b)G{:}(c)$

Both represent the proposition « b Gs c ».

$G{:}([b], (c))$

Represents a proposition whose quadratic proposal method is instantiation, whose proposal method in the first position is conformalization, and whose proposal method in the second position is instantiation.

$G{:}|x, y|$

Represents « G accepts the image x in position ① and the image y in position ② ». Used only in quantified expressions such as $(\exists x)$ $(\exists y)$ $G{:}|x, y|$.

$G|x, y|$

Represents an attachment manifestation (an image) formed by assembling the images x and y with the correspondence G.

$(G; B, C)$

Indicates the correspondence complex formed from the correspondence G and the classes B and C.

$(A; F; B; G; C)$

Represents the binary path formed from the two correspondence complexes $(F; A, B)$ and $(G; B, C)$.

$T(\ ,\ ,\ )$

Represents a trio. Each place enclosed by commas or parentheses is filled to form an assembly, as in $T(a, b, c)$.

$(\ )T(\ )U(\ )$

Represents a trio. Each place within parentheses is filled to form an assembly, as in $(a)T(b)U(c)$. This assembly is equivalent to $TU(a, b, c)$.

$(a)T(b)U(c)$

Represents the assembly « *a T+ing b U c* ».

$(a)T{:}(b)U(c)$

Represents the proposition « *a Ts b U c* ».

Punctuation Marks

.

(i) Indicates localization. "$b.G$" is equivalent to "$G(b,\ )$".
(ii) Indicates a composition cone, as in $\alpha.\beta$, or $<>.\mathbf{]}\,\mathbf{[}$.
(iii) Indicates a compound of a recognizer with an impression, as in $d.\iota$. Used only when ι is a placetaker in a quantified expression.

!

Indicates that a proposition is definitive, as in $!p$. Equivalent to ˜;˜.

;

Indicates that a proposition is possible, as in $;p$. Equivalent to ˜!˜.

:

Indicates a proposition, as in $B{:}(d)$, « d is an instance of B », in contrast to $B(d)$, « d in the role of a B ». When used with impressions, the parentheses are omitted, as in $(\exists\iota)\ d{:}\iota$, « some impression is accepted by d ».

“ ”

Indicates a symbol, as in “x” for the letter x. Compare « ».

« »

Indicates an idea, as in « house » for the conceptual mechanism that defines a house. Compare “ ”.

Brackets

]

Indicates *from some*.

<

Indicates *to many*.

>

Indicates *from many*.

[

Indicates *to some*.

<>

Indicates *many-to-many*.

><

Indicates a *many-to-many* bundling.

$\overset{\circ}{]}$

The circle indicates an undetermined bracket decision.

Superscripts and Diacritical Marks

*

Indicates the converse, as in G^* for the converse of the correspondence G, or α^* for the converse of the character α.

$\acute{G}$

Indicates the maximal resolute subcorrespondence of the correspondence G.

$\dot{G}$, $\dot{T}$

Indicates a reduced association, properly used only when the association complex is understood from context. For example, the reduced correspondence $\dot{G}$ for the correspondence complex $(G; B, C)$ is the correspondence $\Delta B \circ G \circ \Delta C$.

$\hat{C}$

Indicates the set of instances of a class C.

$\overline{B}$, $\overline{d}$

Indicates a complement.

$°B$, $°d$

Indicates an opposite.

Quantifiers

$(\mathrm{A}x)$

A universal quantifier, read « for any x », where x may stand for a recognizer, an image, or an association.

$(\mathrm{A}\iota)$

A universal quantifier, read « for any impression ι ».

$(\forall x)$

An exhaustive quantifier, read « for each x », where x may stand for a recognizer, an image, or an association.

$(\forall \iota)$

An exhaustive quantifier, read « for each impression ι ».

$(\mathrm{E}x)$

A potential quantifier, read « there might be an x », where x may stand for a recognizer, an image, or an association.

$(\mathrm{E}\iota)$

A potential quantifier, read « there might be an impression ι ».

$(\exists x)$

An (unresolved) existential quantifier, read « for some x », where x may stand for a recognizer, an image, or an association.

$(\exists \iota)$

An (unresolved) existential quantifier, read « for each impression ι ».

Logical Operators

$\vdash$

Indicates affirmation, for example ''$\vdash p$'' represents « it is affirmed that p ».

$\vdash_2$

The subscript is used to distinguish different data bases. Thus, $\vdash_2 p$ indicates that p is affirmed in the data base ''2''.

$\dashv$

Represents a comprehensive proposition. ($\vdash p$) is equivalent to ($\dashv \rightarrow p$).

$\blacktriangledown$

Indicates denial, for example $\blacktriangledown p$ represents « it is denied that p ». Equivalent to $\vdash {}^{\circ}$.

~

Indicates negation, as in $\tilde{}p$.

&

Indicates conjunction, as in p & q, read « p and q ».

$\bigvee$

Indicates (unresolved) alternation, as in $p \bigvee q$, read « p or q ».

$\acute{\bigvee}$

Indicates resolved alternation, as in $p \acute{\bigvee} q$.

$\cup$

Indicates a union, as in $B \cup C$.

$\tilde{\cup}$

Indicates maximal composition character, as in $\alpha \tilde{\cup} \beta$.

$\cap$

Indicates an intersection, as in $B \cap C$.

$\varnothing$

(i) Represents an unpopulable class.
(ii) Represents the character of a *one-to-one all-to-all* correspondence complex.

$\varnothing^r$

Represents an unpopulable association of degree r.

$\square$

Represents a universal class.

$\square^r$

Represents a universal association of degree r.

$\times$

Indicates Cartesian product, as in $R \times S$.

$\circ$

Indicates composition, as in $F \circ G$ for the composition of F and G.

$\subset$

Indicates inclusion of sets.

$\not\subset$

$S \not\subset T$ indicates that the set T does not include the set S.

$\underset{\cdot}{\subset}$

Indicates an inclusion of associations or an inclusion of recognizers, as in $B \underset{\cdot}{\subset} C$.

$\subseteq$

Indicates an embracing, as in $B \subseteq C$.

$\supseteq$

The embracing $B \subseteq C$ is written equivalently as $C \supseteq B$.

$\rightarrow$

(i) Indicates a deduction, as in $p \rightarrow q$.
(ii) Indicates the procession down and to the right of the association tags in a cascade, as in $B \rightarrow G \rightarrow C$.

$\leftrightarrow$

$p \leftrightarrow q$ is equivalent to $(p \rightarrow q)$ & $(q \rightarrow p)$.

$\Rightarrow$

Indicates an implication, as in $p \Rightarrow q$.

$\Leftarrow$

The implication $p \Rightarrow q$ is written equivalently as $q \Leftarrow p$.

$\Leftrightarrow$

Indicates an interchangeability. $p \Leftrightarrow q$ is equivalent to $(p \Rightarrow q)$ & $(q \Rightarrow p)$.

$\uparrow$

Indicates a transitive closure, as in $\uparrow L$.

$=$

(i) Indicates equality of numbers.
(ii) Indicates equality of sets.
(iii) Indicates that the same idea is substituted for two placetakers.

$\doteqdot$

Indicates a bi-directional inclusion, as in $B \doteqdot C$.

$\neq$

Indicates unequality of numbers.

$\equiv$

Indicates equivalence, that is, a bi-directional embracing, as in $B \equiv C$.

$\in$

Indicates membership in a set, as in $t \in S$.

$\notin$

Indicates that an individual is not a member of a set, as in $t \notin S$.

①

A position designator, representing the first position in an association.

②

A position designator, representing the second position in an association.

______

A blank, as in « _____ Is A Plumber ».

$+$

Indicates addition of numbers, as in $m + n$.

¢

Indicates convolution, as in ¢S for the convolution of the relative complex S.

${}_1G_{12}$

Represents the elision correspondence between the scope of G and the concentration of G that attaches an instance b to all attachments of the form $G(b, c)$.

${}_1T_{23}$

Represents the elision correspondence that attaches an individual a to all the assemblies $G(b, c)$ such that $T{:}(a, b, c)$.

Я

Яs represents the realization of the plan s. If s represents a proposition, then Яs represents its topic recognizer.

Index

B

C

D

E

F

G

H

I

J

K

L

M

N

O

P

Q

R

S

T

V

W

Z